Advanced

Physics for You

Keith JOHNSON **Simmone HEWETT** **Sue HOLT** **John MILLER**

With the active support of: Martin Gregory, Tim Akrill,
Patrick Organ, Andy Raw, Ian Jackson, George Snape,
Nicola Thomas, Stuart Devereux, Michael Johnson,
John Bailey, Janet Oswell, John Hepburn, Jason Howell,
Jane Cope, Kerry Parker, Averil Macdonald, Tricia New,
Ann Johnson, Paul Deehan, Marilyn Miller, Pat McNeil

Stanley Thornes (Publishers) Ltd

First published in 2000 by
Stanley Thornes (Publishers) Ltd
Delta Place, 27 Bath Road, Cheltenham GL53 7TH
United Kingdom

00 01 02 03 04 05 / 10 9 8 7 6 5 4 3 2 1

A catalogue record of this book is available from the British Library.

ISBN 0 7487 5296 X

Typeset by TechSet Ltd, Gateshead, Tyne & Wear
Printed and bound in Italy by G. Canale & C.S.p.A., Borgaro T.se, Turin

Also in this series:
Advanced Chemistry for You, by Lawrie Ryan   ISBN 0 7487 5297 8
Advanced Biology for You, by Gareth Williams   ISBN 0 7487 5298 6

Everything should be made as simple as possible, but not simpler.

Albert Einstein

There is no higher or lower knowledge, but one only, flowing out of
experimentation.

Leonardo da Vinci

I do not know what I may appear to the world, but to myself
I seem to have been only a boy playing on the seashore, and
diverting myself in now and then finding a smoother pebble or
a prettier shell than ordinary, while the great ocean of truth
lay all undiscovered before me.

Sir Isaac Newton

Introduction

Advanced Physics for You is designed to help and support you during your advanced Physics course.
It will help you whether you are following an Advanced Subsidiary (AS) course or a full Advanced level (A2) course.

The book is carefully laid out so that each new idea is introduced and developed on a single page or on two facing pages. Words have been kept to a minimum and as straightforward as possible, with clear diagrams, and a cartoon character called 'Phiz'.
Pages with a red triangle in the top corner are the more difficult pages and can be left at first.

Each important fact or new formula is clearly printed in **heavy type** or is in a coloured box.
There is a summary of important facts at the end of each chapter, to help you with revision.

Worked examples are a very useful way of seeing how to tackle problems in Physics. In this book there are over 200 worked examples to help you to learn how to tackle each kind of problem.

Throughout the book there are 'Physics at Work' pages. These show you how the ideas that you learn in Physics are used in a wide range of interesting applications.

At the back of the book there are extra sections giving you valuable advice on key skills, study skills, practical work, revision and examination techniques, as well as help with mathematics.

There is also a useful analysis of how the book covers the different examination syllabuses, with further details on the web-site at www.nelsonthornes.com/ap4u.htm

At the end of each chapter there are a number of questions for you to practise your Physics and so gain in confidence. They range from simple fill-in-a-missing-word sentences (useful for doing quick revision) to more difficult questions that will need more thought.

At the end of each main topic you will find a section of further questions which are taken from actual advanced level examination papers.
For all the questions, a 'Hints and Answers' section at the back of the book gives you helpful hints if you need them, as well as the answers.

We hope that reading this book will make Physics more interesting for you and easier to understand. Above all, we hope that it will help you to make good progress in your studies, and that you will enjoy using **Advanced Physics for You**.

Keith Johnson
Simmone Hewett
Sue Holt
John Miller

Contents

Chapters marked * are usually not in AS level, only in A2.
For more details see page 428 and the web-site at
www.nelsonthornes.com/ap4u.htm

Electricity and Magnetism

Matter and Molecules

Nuclear Physics

Extra Sections

1 Basic Ideas

How fast does light travel? How much do you weigh?
What is the radius of the Earth?
What temperature does ice melt at?

We can find the answers to all of these questions by measurement.
Speed, mass, length and temperature are all examples of *physical quantities.*
Measurement of physical quantities is an essential part of Physics.

In this chapter you will learn:
- the difference between 'base' and 'derived' units,
- how you can use units to check equations,
- how to use 'significant figures',
- how to deal with vectors.

Measuring temperature …

… and time …

Stating measurements

All measurement requires a system of units.
For example: How far is a distance of 12?

Without a unit this is a meaningless question. You must always
give a measurement as *a number multiplied by a unit.*

For example:

12 m   means   12 multiplied by the length of one metre.
9 kg   means   9 multiplied by the mass of one kilogram.

But what do we mean by one metre and one kilogram?
Metres and kilograms are two of the seven internationally agreed
base units.

… and weight

Base quantities and units

The Système International (SI) is a system of
measurement that has been agreed internationally.
It defines 7 base quantities and units, but
you only need six of them at A-level.

The 7 base quantities and their units are listed
in the table:

Their definitions are based on specific physical
measurements that can be reproduced, very
accurately, in laboratories around the world.

The only exception is the kilogram. This is the
mass of a particular metal cylinder, known as the
prototype kilogram, which is kept in Paris.

Base quantity		Base unit	
Name	Symbol	Name	Symbol
time	t	second	s
length	l	metre	m
mass	m	kilogram	kg
temperature	T, θ	kelvin	K
electric current	I	ampere	A
amount of substance	n	mole	mol
luminous intensity *(Not used at A-level)*		candela	cd

Derived units

Of course, we use far more physical quantities in Physics than just the 7 base ones. All other physical quantities are known as **derived quantities.** Both the quantity and its unit are derived from a combination of base units, using a defining equation:

Example 1
Velocity is defined by the equation:

$$\text{velocity} = \frac{\text{distance travelled in a given direction (m)}}{\text{time taken (s)}}$$

Both distance (ie. length) and time are base quantities. The unit of distance is the metre and the unit of time is the second. So from the defining equation, the derived unit of velocity is **metres per second**, written **m/s** or **m s^{-1}**.

Example 2
Acceleration is defined by the equation:

$$\text{acceleration} = \frac{\text{change in velocity (m s}^{-1})}{\text{time taken (s)}}$$

Again combining the units in the defining equation gives us the derived unit of acceleration. This is **metres per second per second** or **metres per second squared**, written **m/s^2** or **m s^{-2}**.

What other units have you come across in addition to these base units and base unit combinations?
Newtons, watts, joules, volts and ohms are just a few that you may remember.
These are special names that are given to particular combinations of base units.

(But what about newtons, joules, volts, ohms...?)

Example 3
Force is defined by the equation:

force = mass (kg) $\times$ acceleration (m s^{-2})   (see page 47)

The derived unit of force is therefore:
kilogram metres per second squared or **kg m s^{-2}**.
This is given a special name: the **newton** (symbol **N**).

The table below lists some common derived quantities and units for you to refer to.

Some of the combinations are quite complicated. You can see why we give them special names!

Physical quantity	Defined as	Unit	Special name
density	mass (kg) $\div$ volume (m^3)	kg m^{-3}	
momentum	mass (kg) $\times$ velocity (m s^{-1})	kg m s^{-1}	
force	mass (kg) $\times$ acceleration (m s^{-2})	kg m s^{-2}	newton (N)
pressure	force (kg m s^{-2} or N) $\div$ area (m^2)	kg m^{-1} s^{-2} (N m^{-2})	pascal (Pa)
work (energy)	force (kg m s^{-2} or N) $\times$ distance (m)	kg m^2 s^{-2} (N m)	joule (J)
power	work (kg m^2 s^{-2} or J) $\div$ time (s)	kg m^2 s^{-3} (J s^{-1})	watt (W)
electrical charge	current (A) $\times$ time (s)	A s	coulomb (C)
potential difference	energy (kg m^2 s^{-2} or J) $\div$ charge (A s or C)	kg m^2 A^{-1} s^{-3} (J C^{-1})	volt (V)
resistance	potential difference (kg m^2 A^{-1} s^{-3} or V) $\div$ current (A)	kg m^2 A^{-2} s^{-3} (V A^{-1})	ohm (Ω)

▶ Homogeneity of equations

We have seen that all units are derived from base units using equations. This means that in any correct equation the base units of each part must be the **same**. When this is true, the equation is said to be homogeneous. Homogeneous means 'composed of identical parts'.

Example 4

Show that the following equation is homogeneous: kinetic energy $= \frac{1}{2} \times$ mass $\times$ velocity^2

From the table on page 7:

Unit of kinetic energy = joule = $kg\ m^2\ s^{-2}$

Unit of $\frac{1}{2} \times$ mass $\times$ velocity^2 = kg $\times$ $(m\ s^{-1})^2$ = $kg\ m^2\ s^{-2}$ (Note: $\frac{1}{2}$ is a pure number and so has no unit.)

The units on each side are the same and so the equation is homogeneous.

This is a useful way of checking an equation. It can be particularly useful after you have rearranged an equation:

Example 5

Phiz is trying to calculate the power P, of a resistor when he is given its resistance R, and the current I, flowing through it. He cannot remember if the formula is: $P = I^2 \times R$ or $P = I^2 \div R$. By checking for homogeneity, we can work out which equation is correct:

Using the table on page 7:   Units of P = watts (W) = $kg\ m^2\ s^{-3}$

Units of I^2 = A^2

Units of R = ohms (Ω) = $kg\ m^2\ A^{-2}\ s^{-3}$

Multiplying together the units of I^2 and R would give us the units of power. So the first equation is correct.

One word of warning. This method shows that an equation could be correct – but it doesn't prove that it is correct!

Can you see why not? Example 4 above is a good illustration. The equation for kinetic energy would still be homogeneous even if we had accidentally omitted the $\frac{1}{2}$.

▶ Prefixes

For very large or very small numbers, we can use standard prefixes with the base units.
The main prefixes that you need to know are shown in the table:

Prefix	Symbol	Multiplier
giga	G	10^9
mega	M	10^6
kilo	k	10^3
milli	m	10^{-3}
micro	μ	10^{-6}
nano	n	10^{-9}
pico	p	10^{-12}
femto	f	10^{-15}

Example 6

a) Energy stored in a chocolate bar = 1 000 000 J

    = 1×10^6 J
    = 1 megajoule
    = 1 MJ

b) Wavelength of an X-ray = 0.000 000 001 m
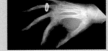
    = 1×10^{-9} m
    = 1 nanometre
    = 1 nm

▷ The importance of significant figures

What is the difference between lengths of 5 m, 5.0 m and 5.00 m?

Writing 5.00 m implies that we have measured the length more precisely than if we write 5 m.

Writing 5.00 m tells us that the length is accurate to the nearest centimetre.
A figure of 5 m may have been rounded to the nearest metre.
The actual length could be anywhere between $4\frac{1}{2}$ m and $5\frac{1}{2}$ m.

The number 5.00 is given to three **significant figures** (or 3 **s.f.**).

To find the number of significant figures you must *count up the total number of digits, starting at the first non-zero digit, reading from left to right.*
The table gives you some examples:

It shows you how a number in the first column (where it is given to 3 s.f.) would be rounded to 2 significant figures or 1 significant figure.

In the last example in the table, why did we change the number to 'standard form'?
Writing 1.7×10^2 instead of 170 makes it clear that we are giving the number to two significant figures not three.
(If you need more help on standard form look at the **Check Your Maths** section on page 400.)

3 s.f.	2 s.f.	1 s.f.
4.62	4.6	5
0.00501	0.0050	0.005
3.40×10^8	3.4×10^8	3×10^8
169	1.7×10^2	2×10^2

Significant figures and calculations

How many significant figures should you give in your answers to calculations?
This depends on the precision of the numbers you use in the calculation. Your answer cannot be any more precise than the data you use. This means that you should round your answer to the same number of significant figures as those used in the calculation.

If some of the figures are given less precisely than others, then round up to the **lowest** number of significant figures.
Example 7 explains this.

Make sure you get into the habit of rounding all your answers to the correct number of significant figures. You may lose marks in an examination if you don't!

Example 7
The swimmer in the photograph covers a distance of 100.0 m in 68 s.
Calculate her average speed.

$$\text{speed} = \frac{\text{distance travelled}}{\text{time taken}} = \frac{100.0 \text{ m}}{68 \text{ s}} = 1.4705882 \text{ m s}^{-1}$$

This is the answer according to your calculator.
How many significant figures should we round to?

The distance was given to 4 significant figures. But the time was given to only 2 significant figures. Our answer cannot be any more precise than this, so we need to round to 2 significant figures.

Our answer should be stated as: 1.5 m s^{-1} (2 s.f.)

Vectors and scalars

Throwing the javelin requires a force. If you want to throw it a long distance, what two things are important about the force you use?

The javelin's path will depend on both the **size** and the **direction** of the force you apply.

Force is an example of a *vector* quantity.
Vectors have both size (magnitude) and direction.
Other examples of vectors include: velocity, acceleration and momentum. They each have a size and a direction.

Quantities that have size (magnitude) but *no* direction are called **scalars**. Examples of scalars include: temperature, mass, time, work and energy.

The table shows some of the more common vectors and scalars that you will use in your A-level Physics course:

Scalars	Vectors
distance	displacement
speed	velocity
mass	weight
pressure	force
energy	momentum
temperature	acceleration
volume	electric current
density	torque

Look back at the table of base quantities on page 6.
Are these vectors or scalars? Most of the base quantities are scalars.
Can you spot the odd one out?

Representing vectors

Vectors can be represented in diagrams by arrows.

- **The length of the arrow represents the magnitude of the vector.**

- **The direction of the arrow represents the direction of the vector.**

Here are some examples:

Force vectors
A horizontal force of 20 N:

A vertical force of 10 N:

Using the same scale, how would you draw the vector for a force of 15 N at 20° to the horizontal?

Velocity vectors
A velocity of 30 m s^{-1} in a NE direction:

A velocity of 20 m s^{-1} due west:

45°

Using the same scale, how would you draw the vector for a velocity of 15 m s^{-1} in a NW direction?

▶ Vector addition

What is 4 kg plus 4 kg? Adding two masses of 4 kg **always** gives the answer 8 kg. Mass is a scalar. You combine scalars using simple arithmetic.

What about 4 N plus 4 N? Adding two forces of 4 N can give any answer between 8 N and 0 N.
Why do you think this is?
It's because force is a vector. When we combine vectors we also need to take account of their **direction**.

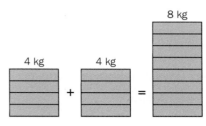

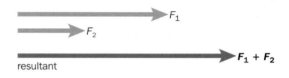

Scalars are simply added together

Often in Physics we will come across situations where two or more vectors are acting together. The overall effect of these vectors is called the **resultant**. This is the single vector that would have the same effect.
To find the resultant we must use the directions of the 2 vectors:

Vectors acting along the same straight line

Two vectors acting in the **same** direction can simply be added together:

$$\text{Resultant} = F_1 + F_2$$

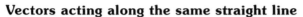

If the vectors act in **opposite** directions, we need to take one direction as positive, and the other as negative, before adding them:

$$\text{Resultant} = F_1 + (-F_2) = F_1 - F_2$$

Example 8
Phiz is standing on a moving walkway in an airport.
The walkway is moving at a steady velocity of 1.50 m s^{-1}.
a)   Phiz starts to walk forwards along the walkway at 2.00 m s^{-1}.
     What is his resultant velocity?

     Both velocity vectors are acting in the same direction.
     Resultant velocity = 1.50 m s^{-1} + 2.00 m s^{-1}
                          = 3.50 m s^{-1} in the direction of the walkway.

b)   Phiz then decides he is going the wrong way. He turns round and starts to run at 3.40 m s^{-1} in the opposite direction to the motion of the walkway. What is his new resultant velocity?

     The velocity vectors now act in opposite directions.
     Taking motion in the direction of the walkway to be positive:
     Resultant velocity = +1.50 m s^{-1} − 3.40 m s^{-1}
                          = −1.90 m s^{-1} (3 s.f.)

     As this is negative, the resultant velocity acts in the opposite direction to the motion of the walkway. He moves to the left.

▶ Perpendicular vectors

To find the resultant of two vectors (X, Y) acting at 90° to each other, we draw the vectors as adjacent sides of a rectangle:

The resultant is the **diagonal** of the rectangle, as shown here:

There are 2 ways to find the resultant.

1. By calculation

The **magnitude** (size) of the resultant vector R can be found using Pythagoras' theorem:

$$R^2 = X^2 + Y^2$$

The **direction** of the resultant is given by the angle θ:

$$\tan \theta = \frac{\text{opposite}}{\text{adjacent}} = \frac{Y}{X} \qquad \therefore \ \theta = \tan^{-1}\left(\frac{Y}{X}\right)$$

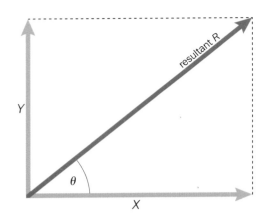

2. By scale drawing

You can also find the magnitude and direction of the resultant by using an accurate scale drawing.

Example 9

Two tugs are pulling a ship into harbour. One tug pulls in a SE direction. The other pulls in a SW direction. Each tug pulls with a force of 8.0×10^4 N. What is the resultant force on the ship?

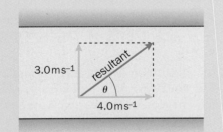

The two forces act at 90° to each other. Using Pythagoras' theorem:

Magnitude of resultant $= \sqrt{(8.0 \times 10^4 \text{ N})^2 + (8.0 \times 10^4 \text{ N})^2}$

$\qquad = \sqrt{1.28 \times 10^{10}} \text{ N}$

$\qquad = \underline{1.1 \times 10^5 \text{ N}} \quad$ (2 s.f.)

Since both tugs pull with the same force, the vectors form adjacent sides of a square.
The resultant is the diagonal of the square. So it acts at 45° to each vector.
The resultant force must therefore act <u>due south</u>.

Example 10

A man tries to row directly across a river.
He rows at a velocity of 3.0 m s^{-1}.
The river has a current of velocity 4.0 m s^{-1} parallel to the banks.
Calculate the resultant velocity of the boat.

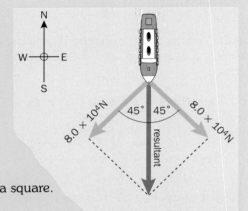

The diagram shows the two velocity vectors.

We can find their resultant using Pythagoras' theorem:

Size of resultant $= \sqrt{(3.0 \text{ m s}^{-1})^2 + (4.0 \text{ m s}^{-1})^2} = \sqrt{25} \text{ m s}^{-1} = 5.0 \text{ m s}^{-1}$

Direction of resultant: $\tan \theta = \dfrac{\text{opposite}}{\text{adjacent}} = \dfrac{3.0}{4.0} \qquad \therefore \ \theta = \tan^{-1}\left(\dfrac{3.0}{4.0}\right) = 37°$

So the resultant velocity is <u>5.0 m s^{-1} at 37° to the bank.</u>

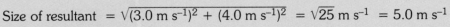

▷ Vector subtraction

The diagram shows the speed and direction of
a trampolinist at two points during a bounce:

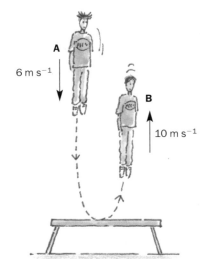

What is the trampolinist's change in **speed**
from A to B?

Change in speed   = new speed – old speed
              = 10 m s⁻¹ – 6 m s⁻¹
              = 4 m s⁻¹

What about his change in **velocity**?
To find the change in a vector quantity
we use vector subtraction:

Change in velocity = new velocity – old velocity
              = 10 m s⁻¹ *up* – 6 m s⁻¹ *down*

Remember, with vectors we must take account of the direction.
In this example let us take the upward direction to be positive,
and the downward direction to be negative.

We can then rewrite our equation as:

Change in velocity = +10 m s⁻¹ – (– 6 m s⁻¹)
              = +10 m s⁻¹ + 6 m s⁻¹
              = +16 m s⁻¹

So the change in velocity is 16 m s⁻¹ in an *up*ward direction.

Can you see that subtracting 6 m s⁻¹ downwards is the same as
adding 6 m s⁻¹ acting upwards?
***Vector subtraction is the same as the addition of a vector of
the same size acting in the opposite direction.***

*Two negatives
make a
positive.*

Example 11
A boy kicks a ball against a wall with a horizontal velocity of 4.5 m s⁻¹.
The ball rebounds horizontally at the same speed.
What is the ball's change in velocity?

Although the speed is the same, the velocity has changed. Why?
Velocity is a vector, so a change in direction means a change in
velocity.

Let us take motion towards the wall as positive,
and motion away from the wall as negative.

Change in velocity = new velocity – old velocity
              = (– 4.5 m s⁻¹) – (+ 4.5 m s⁻¹)
              = – 4.5 m s⁻¹ – 4.5 m s⁻¹
              = – 9.0 m s⁻¹ (2 s.f.)

So the change in velocity is 9.0 m s⁻¹ in a direction away from the wall.

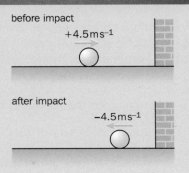

before impact
+4.5ms⁻¹

after impact
–4.5ms⁻¹

▷ Resolving vectors

We have seen how to combine two vectors that are acting at 90°, to give a single resultant. Now let's look at the reverse process.

We can **resolve** a vector into two **components** acting at right angles to each other. The component of a vector tells you the effect of the vector in that direction.

So how do we calculate the 2 components?
Look at the vector V in this diagram:

We can resolve this vector into two components, V_1 and V_2, at right angles to each other:

    V_1 acts at an angle θ_1 to the original vector.
    V_2 acts at an angle θ_2 to the original vector.

$(\theta_1 + \theta_2 = 90°)$

To find the size of V_1 and V_2 we need to use trigonometry:

$$\cos\theta_1 = \frac{adjacent}{hypotenuse} = \frac{V_1}{V} \qquad \text{Rearranging this gives: } \boldsymbol{V_1 = V\cos\theta_1}$$

$$\cos\theta_2 = \frac{adjacent}{hypotenuse} = \frac{V_2}{V} \qquad \text{Rearranging this gives: } \boldsymbol{V_2 = V\cos\theta_2}$$

So to find the component of a vector in any direction you need to *multiply by the cosine of the angle between the vector and the component direction.*

Example 12
A tennis player hits a ball at 10 m s⁻¹ at an angle of 30° to the ground.
What are the initial horizontal and vertical components of velocity of the ball?

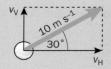

Horizontal component: $v_H = 10\cos 30° = \underline{8.7 \text{ m s}^{-1}}$ (2 s.f.)

The angles in a right angle add up to 90°.
So the angle between the ball's path and the *vertical* = 90° − 30° = 60°

Vertical component: $v_V = 10\cos 60° = \underline{5.0 \text{ m s}^{-1}}$ (2 s.f.)

Example 13
A water-skier is pulled up a ramp by the tension in the tow-rope. This is a force of 300 N acting horizontally. The ramp is angled at 20.0° to the horizontal.

What are the components of the force from the rope acting (a) parallel to, and (b) perpendicular to the slope?

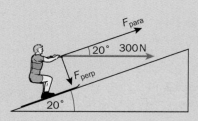

Angle between the rope and the parallel slope direction = 20°
So, angle between the rope and the perpendicular direction = 90° − 20° = 70°

a) Component of force **parallel** to ramp $F_{para} = 300 \text{ N} \times \cos 20° = \underline{282 \text{ N}}$ (3 s.f.)

b) Component of force **perpendicular** to ramp $F_{perp} = 300 \text{ N} \times \cos 70° = \underline{103 \text{ N}}$ (3 s.f.)

Summary

There are 6 base quantities that you need for A-level (time, length, mass, temperature, electric current, and amount of substance).
All other quantities are derived from these.

For an equation to be correct it must be homogeneous. This means that all the terms have the same units.
But remember, a homogeneous equation may not be entirely right!

You should always give your numerical answers to the correct number of significant figures.

Scalars have size (magnitude) only.

Vectors have size (magnitude) and direction.
Vectors can be represented by arrows.

When vectors are added together to find the resultant, we must take account of their direction.

For vectors acting along the same straight line we take one direction as positive and the other as negative.

To add two perpendicular vectors you can use Pythagoras' theorem: $R^2 = X^2 + Y^2$

A single vector can be resolved to find its effect in two perpendicular directions.
The component of a vector in any direction is found by multiplying the vector by the *cosine* of the angle between the vector and the required direction.

Subtracting a vector is the same as adding a vector of the same size, acting in the opposite direction.

▷ **Questions**

1. Can you complete the following sentences?
   a) Measurements must be given as a number multiplied by a ....
   b) Seconds, metres and kilograms are all .... units. Units made up of combinations of base units are known as .... units.
   c) Vector quantities have both .... and .... Scalars have only ....
   d) The single vector that has the same effect as two vectors acting together is called the ....
   e) The effect of a vector in a given direction is called the .... in that direction.
   f) The .... of a vector in any direction is found by mutiplying the .... by the .... of the angle between the vector and the required direction.

2. a) What is the unit of force expressed in base units? What special name is given to this combination of base units?
   b) What is the unit of pressure expressed in base units? What special name is given to this combination of base units?

3. The drag force F, on a moving vehicle depends on its cross-sectional area A, its velocity v, and the density of the air ρ.
   a) What are the base units for each of these four variables?
   b) By checking for homogeneity, work out which of these equations correctly links the variables:
   i) $F = k\ A^2\ \rho\ v$
   ii) $F = k\ A\ \rho^2\ v$
   iii) $F = k\ A\ \rho\ v^2$
   (The constant k has no units.)

4. Rewrite each of the following quantities using a suitable prefix:
   a) 2 000 000 000 J
   b) 5900 g
   c) 0.005 s
   d) 345 000 N
   e) 0.000 02 m

5. In a tug-of-war one team pulls to the left with a force of 600 N. The other team pulls to the right with a force of 475 N.
   a) Draw a vector diagram to show these forces.
   b) What is the magnitude and direction of the resultant force?

6. Two ropes are tied to a large boulder. One rope is pulled with a force of 400 N due east. The other rope is pulled with a force of 300 N due south.
   a) Draw a vector diagram to show these forces.
   b) What is the magnitude and direction of the resultant force on the boulder?

7. A javelin is thrown at 20 m s^{-1} at an angle of 45° to the horizontal.
   a) What is the vertical component of this velocity?
   b) What is the horizontal component of this velocity?

8. A ball is kicked with a force of 120 N at 25° to the horizontal.
   a) Calculate the horizontal component of the force.
   b) Calculate the vertical component of the force.

Further questions on page 104.

2 Looking at Forces

We use forces all the time, often without even noticing.
What forces are you using right now?
As you sit reading this book, forces keep you in the chair,
hold your chair together and allow you to turn the pages.

Forces are involved whenever objects interact. This is true
for objects as big as planets, or as small as atoms.

In this chapter you will learn:
- about the different types of forces that exist,
- what causes these forces,
- how to draw the forces acting on an object.

There are three basic types of force that exist in our universe.

Surfers need to balance the forces carefully

▷ 1. Gravitational force

All objects with mass attract each other with a gravitational force.
So why don't you feel yourself being pulled towards other objects
all the time? We only really notice gravitational forces caused by
extremely massive objects such as the Earth.
It is the gravitational pull of the Earth that keeps your feet on the
ground and gives you weight. We will look at gravitational forces
in more detail in Chapter 8.

In conversation people often use the word 'weight' when they
really mean mass. So what is the difference? What do these
words actually mean?

Your mass is the amount of matter you contain.
Mass is measured in **kilograms (kg)**.

Your weight is the force of gravity pulling you down.
Weight, like all forces, is measured in **newtons (N)**.

Isaac Newton is said to have 'discovered' gravity when an apple fell on his head!

Weight and mass are linked by this equation:

Weight = mass × g
(in N) (kg) (N kg^{-1})

In symbols:

$$W = mg$$

g is known as the **gravitational field strength** or
the **acceleration due to gravity**.
On Earth $g = 9.81$ N kg^{-1} (or 9.81 m s^{-2}).
So every 1 kg has a weight of 9.81 N.
(In calculations it is often rounded up to 10 N kg^{-1}.)

Example 1
A man has a mass of 70.0 kg. What is his weight (a) on Earth, where $g = 9.81$ N kg^{-1},
(b) on the Moon, where $g = 1.60$ N kg^{-1} and (c) on Jupiter, where $g = 26.0$ N kg^{-1}?

a) On Earth: weight $W = mg$ = 70.0 kg × 9.81 N kg^{-1} = <u>687 N</u> (3 s.f.)

b) On the Moon: weight $W = mg$ = 70.0 kg × 1.60 N kg^{-1} = <u>112 N</u> (3 s.f.)

c) On Jupiter: weight $W = mg$ = 70.0 kg × 26.0 N kg^{-1} = <u>1820 N</u> (3 s.f.)

▷ 2. Electromagnetic force

Electromagnetic forces cause attraction and repulsion between positive and negative electric charges.
They also cause magnetic poles to attract and repel.

Opposite charges attract: | Opposite poles attract:

Like charges repel: | Like poles repel:

Hair-raising repulsion between electric charges!

Electromagnetic forces play a vital part in holding our world together. Our world is made of atoms. But what holds atoms together?

Electromagnetic attraction holds negatively charged electrons to the positive nucleus. Electromagnetic forces hold molecules together, and control all chemical reactions.

You may have already come across the links between electricity and magnetism if you studied the electric motor and generator at GCSE. We will look at electromagnetic effects in more detail in Chapter 18.

▷ 3. Nuclear forces

You might not have met this last group of forces. They are only experienced by sub-atomic particles. There are two types:

1. **Weak nuclear force**

    These are the forces involved in the radioactive decay of atoms. We will look at this in more detail in Chapter 29.

2. **Strong nuclear force**

    We have said that electromagnetic forces hold electrons to the nucleus, but what holds the nucleus together? Why does the repulsion between positive protons in the nucleus not force the nucleus apart? The answer is that they are held together by the strong nuclear force.

    Is this stronger or weaker than electromagnetic force? The fact that the nucleus stays together tells us that this is the strongest force of all, though it only acts over a very short range.

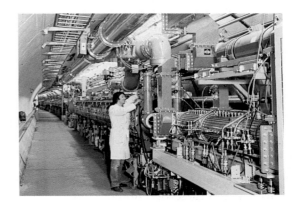

The CERN research facility in Geneva. Scientists at CERN are carrying out experiments to find out more about weak and strong nuclear force.

But what about simple pushing and pulling forces?
Where do they fit in? At first glance it is hard to see how the forces you use when pushing a trolley or pulling a rope can be one of these three types. Can you work out which type they are?

All the forces involved when objects are in direct contact are **electromagnetic** forces.
For example, your pushing force is due to repulsion between the electrons of the atoms in your hand and those in the object!

We will look in more detail at these everyday contact forces on the next few pages.

▶ Friction forces between solid surfaces

Friction tries to prevent motion between two surfaces in contact.
Friction can cause surfaces to heat up and eventually wear away.

But is friction always a bad thing? What would our world be like
without it?
Think about how hard it is to walk over a surface such as ice
where the friction is reduced. With no friction between you and
the ground you could not walk forwards at all. How many objects
around you right now would collapse without friction to hold
screws and nails in place? Even your clothes would unravel
without friction to hold the fibres together! And without friction
you could not even pick anything up to hide your embarrassment!
So perhaps friction is not such a bad thing after all.

Loss of friction would be a problem!

Look at the many ways you either use or try to reduce friction
when you ride a bicycle:

*You can reduce your friction with the air by
crouching low, wearing a streamlined helmet and
tight clothing, and even by shaving your legs!*

*Friction keeps your hands on
the handlebars*

*The brakes operate by applying
friction between the wheel rim
and the brake blocks*

*Oil is used to reduce the friction
in the gears and chain*

*Friction between the tyres
and the road allows you to
move forwards*

Friction keeps your feet on the pedals

What causes friction?

You may think that some surfaces are perfectly smooth, but take a
look at this magnified photograph:

On a microscopic scale, the surfaces are very uneven. They are
only actually in contact at a few points. This means that the
forces pushing the surfaces together act on a very small area.

This creates huge pressures that can weld the surfaces together.
To make the surfaces slide over each other we have to break
these welds. This is what creates the frictional force.

Magnified photo of the surface of paper

What does the size of the frictional force depend on?
There are two key factors:
a) the type of surfaces in contact, and
b) how hard the surfaces are pressed together.

In which direction does the force of friction act?
As it is trying to stop things moving, friction always
acts parallel to the surfaces in contact, and in the
opposite direction to the motion.

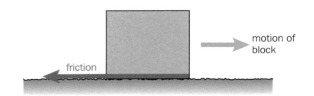

Motive force

We call a force that drives something forwards a 'motive force'. Motive forces are created by friction.

We have already seen that you need friction to enable you to walk. Let's now look at this in more detail.

Imagine that you are standing on a friction-free surface. (A sheet of ice is a good approximation.) To take a step forwards you need to lift one foot off the ground and push off with the other foot. If there was no friction, what would happen as you push off? Your foot on the ground would slip backwards.

Friction is what stops your foot slipping. In which direction does this force of friction act? Remember that friction always acts in the *opposite* direction to the motion it is trying to prevent. To stop your foot slipping backwards the friction force must act in a forward direction. It is this friction force that drives you forwards at each step.

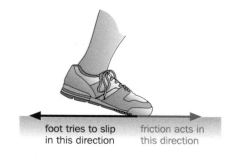

foot tries to slip in this direction   friction acts in this direction

The motive force needed to drive a car forwards is produced in a similar way. But doesn't the engine drive a car forwards? No, not directly. The engine power turns the car's wheels. Without friction the wheels would just spin on the spot.

The diagram shows you the front wheel of a car on a road:

As the wheel turns, friction is created at the point of contact between the wheel and the road. At this point the wheel is moving backwards. To prevent this motion the friction force must act in the *opposite* direction. So friction provides the forwards force that drives the car.

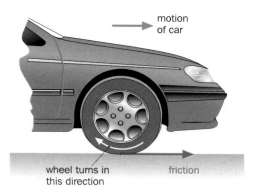

motion of car

wheel turns in this direction   friction

▶ Fluid resistance (drag)

Liquids and gases are *fluids* – they both flow. When you push an object through a fluid, you can feel a resistance to the movement. This is another form of friction. Friction in fluids is often called 'drag'. Drag forces try to prevent motion between objects and fluids.

The faster an object moves through a fluid, the greater the drag produced. Can you think why? The faster the relative motion, the more molecules that need to slip past each other each second.

Drag also depends on the **viscosity** of the fluid. The viscosity of a fluid is a measure of how easily it will flow. Thick, sticky liquids such as treacle are very viscous. An object moving through treacle would suffer a lot of drag. Even air has some viscosity. Air resistance is a common example of a drag force. This can be a useful force if you need to slow down quickly.

So what causes drag when an object moves through a fluid? To move through it you need to push the fluid out of the way. Friction is created by contact between the molecules of the fluid and those of the solid surface. There is also friction between the molecules in the different layers of fluid.

How can you reduce drag? This is a common problem faced by car and aircraft designers. The answer is to use streamlined shapes. The air then flows past the object smoothly, reducing the drag.

The streamlined shape of a dolphin helps it to move easily through water

▷ More pushes and pulls

'Normal' contact forces

The force of gravity pulls you towards the centre of the Earth. But what stops you sinking into the ground? The answer is the 'normal' contact force, sometimes called the 'normal' reaction. This is a force that exists wherever two solid surfaces are in contact. The word 'normal' means **at 90°** to the surfaces.

What causes this force? Remember that there are only a few basic types of force (see page 16). Contact forces are due to the electromagnetic forces acting between the atoms and molecules of the two surfaces in contact.

The diagram shows you the direction of the normal contact force for two surfaces in contact:
The 2 forces in the diagram are equal but opposite.

contact force of
ground on box

contact force of
box on ground

Tension

When we stretch a wire or string we say that it is in a state of tension. The stretched wire or string will exert a tension force that pulls on the object it is connected to. The tension force acts *along* the wire.

What creates the tension?
When a material is stretched its molecules move further apart. An attractive electromagnetic force between the molecules acts to pull them back together again, creating tension.

Compressive forces are produced by the opposite effect. When a solid is squashed its molecules move closer together. A repulsive electromagnetic force tries to push them further apart.

We will look at tension and compression in solids in more detail in Chapter 23.

Golden Gate suspension bridge near San Francisco. The roadway is supported by cables under tension.

Pressure

People sometimes confuse pressure and force. Pressure tells us how concentrated a force is. It is the *force per unit area:*

$$\text{pressure} = \frac{\text{force (in N)}}{\text{area (in m}^2)} \quad \text{or} \quad p = \frac{F}{A}$$

The SI unit of pressure is the **pascal (Pa)**. $1\ \text{Pa} = 1\ \text{N m}^{-2}$.
In the formula F must be the 'normal' force, at 90° to the surface.

Why do camels have large flat feet? By spreading their weight over a large area they reduce the pressure that they exert on the ground. This means they are less likely to sink into the sand.

Sharpened knives cut more easily, for the opposite reason. A sharp edge has a smaller area. This creates a greater pressure when you press down, making it easier to cut through things.

Is pressure a scalar or a vector? Although its calculation involves force, which you know is a vector, pressure is a *scalar* quantity.

Why is it easier to walk over soft snow in skis rather than boots? Skis increase your area of contact. This reduces the pressure on the snow.

Example 2
A man can lie safely on a bed of nails by spreading his weight over 750 nails. He weighs 600 N and the area of each nail is 8.0×10^{-6} m². Calculate the average pressure on each nail.

Average weight acting on each nail $= \dfrac{600 \text{ N}}{750 \text{ nails}} = 0.8$ N per nail

Average pressure on each nail, $p = \dfrac{F}{A} = \dfrac{0.8 \text{ N}}{8.0 \times 10^{-6} \text{ m}^2}$

$\qquad\qquad\qquad = 1 \times 10^5 \text{ N m}^{-2}$

$\qquad\qquad\qquad = 1 \times 10^5 \text{ Pa}$

Lift

Try this quick experiment. Hold a strip of paper just below your lips and blow across its **top** surface. What happens?

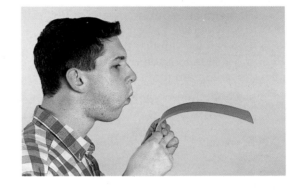

You might expect the paper to be forced downwards, but in fact it lifts up!
The **fast** moving air creates a region of **low** pressure.
So the pressure above the paper is lower than the pressure below it.

The pressure difference creates a net upward force, known as **lift**.
Example 3 shows how the force can be calculated.

Lift forces are essential for flight. The wings of birds and aircraft have a special shape called an **aerofoil**:
This causes air to move faster over its upper surface than its lower surface.
The resulting pressure difference creates the lift force.

Why do aeroplanes need to move at high speed for take-off?

The faster the flow of air over the wings, the greater the lift created. To climb into the sky the lift forces must be greater than the weight of the plane.
Once the plane is at the correct altitude the two forces must be balanced. The lift force must balance the weight.

What other forces are balanced if the speed is steady?
The drag or air resistance on the plane must balance the forward thrust from the engine.

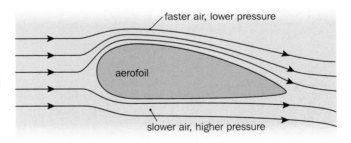

faster air, lower pressure

aerofoil

slower air, higher pressure

Example 3
An aeroplane's wings have a total surface area of 480 m².
The pressure difference between the upper and lower surfaces of each wing is 6500 Pa. Calculate the lift created.

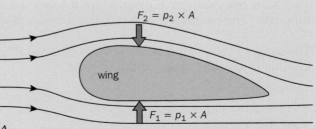

$F_2 = p_2 \times A$

wing

$F_1 = p_1 \times A$

$p = \dfrac{F}{A}$ and so: $F = p \times A$

$\therefore$ Lift force $= F_1 - F_2 = (p_1 \times A) - (p_2 \times A) = (p_1 - p_2) \times A$

$\therefore$ Lift force $=$ pressure difference $\times$ area $= 6500 \text{ Pa} \times 480 \text{ m}^2$

$\qquad\qquad\qquad = \underline{3.12 \times 10^6 \text{ N}}$ (3 s.f.)

▶ Free-body force diagrams

We have seen that forces are caused by the interaction of two objects.
Can you remember how we represent forces in diagrams?
Forces are vector quantities, so they are drawn as vector arrows (*see* Chapter 1).
This can be straightforward, but in a single physics problem you may have to deal with several interacting objects and many different forces.

Even a simple example such as a man standing on the Earth involves four forces. Can you work out what these are?

1. The Earth exerts a gravitational force of attraction on the man (his weight).
2. The man exerts a gravitational force of attraction on the Earth.

3. The Earth exerts a normal contact force on the man.
4. The man exerts a normal contact force on the Earth.
   (Remember: 'normal' means at 90°.)

So how can we simplify this?
For most situations we only need to draw a **free-body force diagram**.
This is a diagram that shows all the forces acting on *just one object.*

Here are the free-body force diagrams for the man, and for the Earth:

Free-body force diagram for the man

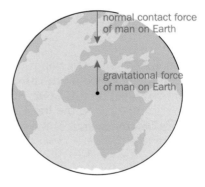

Free-body force diagram for the Earth

Here are some examples of the free-body force diagrams that you will need to draw to solve mechanics problems:

1. Balanced beams

This is the free-body force diagram for a beam resting on two supports. The diagram shows only the forces *acting on the beam:*

The weight of a uniform beam is taken to act at its centre (see Chapter 3 for more about *centre of mass*).

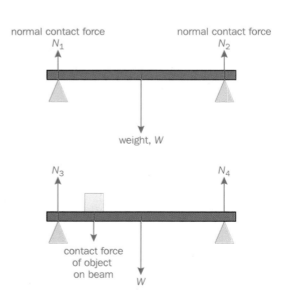

If an object is placed on the beam, it will exert a normal contact force on the beam. This force is numerically equal to the object's weight.

2. Suspended objects

Here is the free-body force diagram for a
bungee jumper at the bottom of a jump:

It shows the two forces **acting on the person**
at that instant.

Which of these two forces is larger at this point?
Why does the person bounce back up?

3. Objects resting against rough and smooth surfaces

The words 'rough' and 'smooth' have a particular meaning in Physics.
If a surface is described as 'rough' we need to take account of friction.
If a surface is described as 'smooth' we can treat it as friction-free.
This is often done to make a problem easier.

So how does this affect our free-body force diagrams?
As an example take a look at this free-body force diagram for a ladder
resting against a wall. It shows only the forces **on the ladder:**

In this example the ground is a 'rough' surface but the wall is 'smooth'.
At the point of contact with the smooth wall there is only a normal
contact force.
At the rough ground though we need to show two forces acting.
These are the normal contact force and the friction force.

The normal contact forces act at 90° to each surface.
How do we decide the direction of the friction force? Think about
which way the ladder would move if it started to slip. The bottom of
the ladder would slip away from the base of the wall. We draw the
friction force in the opposite direction to oppose this motion.

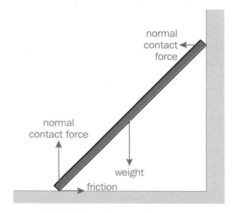

A ladder leaning against a wall

4. Moving objects

Here you also need to remember to include any drag forces.

a) Free-body force diagram for a car on a level road:

Where on the car do the contact forces and friction
with the road actually act? Notice that even though
the car is in contact with the road at each of the
four wheels, we can simplify this to show a single
overall contact force and a single motive force.

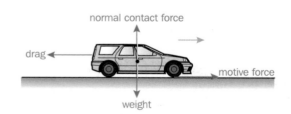

b) Free-body force diagram for a car on a slope:

Check that you are happy with the direction of these
forces. Weight acts vertically downwards.
The normal contact force acts at 90° to the road.
The motive force acts along the slope in the direction
that the car is moving. The drag force acts parallel
to the road and in the opposite direction to the motion.

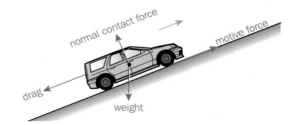

23

▷ Physics at work: Friction and car braking

Hydraulic braking

Brakes operate by creating high friction between the brake pads and the turning wheels.
The brake pads are pressed together using hydraulic power. Hydraulic systems use liquids to transmit pressure from where it is applied (at the brake pedal) to where it is needed (at the wheels).

Friction causes the brakes to heat up. Overheating can cause brakes to lose their effectiveness. For safety, brakes need to be designed to prevent this happening.

Cars use two main types of brakes:

Disc brakes

Each wheel has a steel disc which rotates with the wheel.
When you apply the brakes, the hydraulic pressure
forces the friction pads against each side of the disc:

Disc brakes are less prone to over-heating, because they
cool quickly in the open air-stream.

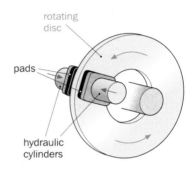

Drum brakes

These use steel drums at each wheel.
Hydraulic pressure forces two friction strips, called shoes,
against the inside of each brake drum:

As drum brakes are more enclosed, cooling fins on the
drums may be needed to prevent overheating.

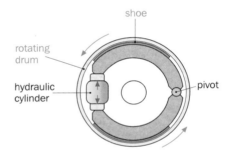

Antilock braking systems (ABS)

Skidding is caused by the wheels locking if you brake too hard.
ABS uses sensors to monitor the rotation of the wheel while you are braking.
If the sensors detect a sudden fall in wheel rotation, the brakes are momentarily released.
The system repeatedly releases and applies pressure so that the wheels can continue to turn.
This enables you to stop safely in a shorter distance without skidding.

Tyre treads

Racing cars use smooth tyres called 'slicks'. These maximise the
area of contact between the tyre and the road. This produces high
friction to grip the road, increasing the motive force or traction.

So why do conventional tyres have grooves cut into them?

Racing slicks are only safe to use in dry road conditions. If water
comes between the tyre and the road, the friction is reduced.
The tyres lose their grip and the car can 'hydroplane' - the driver
loses control of the car as it glides over a film of water.

Grooves are cut into a tyre to help prevent this. The grooves take
the water out from under the tyre, improving its grip on the road.

*The tread pattern is designed
to disperse water efficiently*

Summary

The three basic types of forces are gravitational, electromagnetic and nuclear (strong and weak).
Contact forces are caused by the electromagnetic forces between the atoms and molecules of each object.

Weight and mass are linked by the equation: **Weight** (N) = **mass** (kg) $\times$ $\boldsymbol{g}$ (N kg^{-1})

Friction is a force that tries to stop things moving.
Friction acts parallel to the surfaces in contact.
Friction in fluids is called drag.

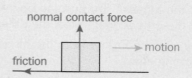

A normal contact force acts at 90° to the two surfaces in contact.

A free-body force diagram shows all of the forces acting on just **one** object.
You need to know how to draw these for a range of mechanics problems.

You need to understand the link between force and pressure: $p = \dfrac{F}{A}$
The units of pressure: 1 N m^{-2} = 1 Pa (1 pascal)

▷ Questions

(Take g = 9.81 N kg^{-1})

1. Can you complete these sentences?
    a) The .... of an object is the amount of matter it contains. It is measured in ....
    b) Weight is the force of .... pulling down on an object. Weight is measured in ....
    c) The formula that connects mass and weight is ....
    d) .... tries to prevent motion between two surfaces in contact. Friction always acts in a direction .... to the motion.
    e) Surfaces that are friction-free are described as .... Surfaces where friction acts are described as ....
    f) Pressure is defined as .... divided by .... It is measured in .... or ....

2. What is the weight of a 65.0 kg woman:
    a) on Earth where g = 9.81 N kg^{-1}?
    b) on Pluto where g = 2.31 N kg^{-1}?

3. Which weighs more, a 100 kg mass on Earth (g = 9.81 N kg^{-1}) or a 120 kg mass on Venus (g = 8.87 N kg^{-1})?

4. A spaceship weighs 10 800 N on a planet where g = 7.20 N kg^{-1}. What would it weigh on a smaller planet where g = 4.30 N kg^{-1}?

5. A brick has mass 3.00 kg, dimensions 30 cm $\times$ 10 cm $\times$ 7.0 cm. Calculate the force and the pressure exerted by the brick on the table when it rests on:
    a) the smallest face,
    b) the largest face.

6. Explain the following:
    a) Camels have large flat feet.
    b) Drawing pins have pointed ends.
    c) A ladder would be useful if you had to rescue someone who had fallen through thin ice.
    d) Tractors have large tyres.

7. A 1 cm steel cube of mass 8 g rests on a steel surface. Although the surfaces appear smooth, they are only in contact over 0.01% of the total area.
    a) Calculate the weight of the steel cube.
    b) Calculate the actual contact area.
    c) Calculate the pressure exerted at the contact points.

8. Draw a free-body force diagram for:
    a) a woman standing on the ground;
    b) a ladder resting at an angle between a rough wall and rough ground;
    c) the same ladder as in (b) but this time with a man standing $\frac{1}{4}$ of the way up from the bottom;
    d) a picture hanging symmetrically from a nail by a cord. The cord is at an angle of 30° to the top edge of the picture on each side.

9. An aeroplane has a mass of 3.5 $\times$ 10^5 kg and wings of total surface area 450 m^2. Calculate:
    a) the weight of the plane,
    b) the lift force if the plane's altitude is constant,
    c) the pressure difference between the upper and lower surfaces of the wings for this lift.

Further questions on page 104.

3 Turning Effects of Forces

Why are door handles usually on the opposite edge of the door to the hinges? Try pushing open a door near the hinge, and then at the other edge, to feel the difference for yourself.

By pushing further from the hinge you produce a much larger turning effect.

When you need to undo a tight nut, a spanner with a long handle is more effective than a short one, for the same reason.

By applying the force further from the pivot you create a greater turning effect.

In this chapter you will learn:
- how to calculate the turning effect of a force,
- the conditions needed for an object to be balanced or 'in equilibrium',
- the meaning and significance of centre of gravity.

Conditions for equilibrium

If an object is stationary all the forces acting on the object must cancel out. We say that the object is **in equilibrium**.

But is the reverse true? If there is no overall force acting on an object, does this mean it is in equilibrium?

To answer this question for yourself, look at these two diagrams:

In both cases, the force up equals the force down, and so they cancel out.

In the first diagram, the rod would remain stationary.
It is in equilibrium.

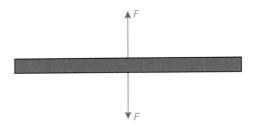

But what happens to the second rod when we apply these forces?
Although the forces cancel out they don't act along the same line.
The two forces will create a turning effect or **torque**.
The rod will start to rotate clockwise, so it is not in equilibrium.

From this example you should be able to see that if an object is in equilibrium, **two** things must be true:

1. there is no net force acting in any direction, *and*

2. there is no net turning effect about any point.

The size of the turning effect produced by a force is called the **moment of the force**.

▷ Calculating moments

Try this simple experiment. Hold a ruler horizontally and hang
a weight on the ruler near your hand. Try to keep the ruler
horizontal as you move the weight further from your hand.
How does the turning effect change?

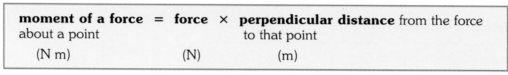

Now try it with a heavier weight.
You can feel that the turning effect or moment depends on the
size of the force (the weight) **and** the distance from your hand.

We calculate the moment of a force using this equation:

moment of a force =	**force** ×	**perpendicular distance** from the force
about a point		to that point
(N m)	(N)	(m)

Moments are measured in **newton-metres**, written **N m**.

Example 1
Calculate the moment of the pushing force on the pedal in
the diagram:

Moment = force × *perpendicular* distance to pivot

= 15 N × 0.20 m

= 3.0 N m

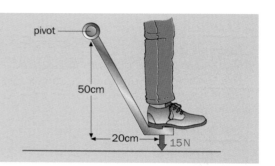

Couples

When two forces are acting that are equal in size and opposite in
direction but not along the same straight line, we say they form
a **couple**. A couple has no resultant force. It only produces a
turning effect.
Your hands on a steering wheel can provide a couple to turn the
wheel:

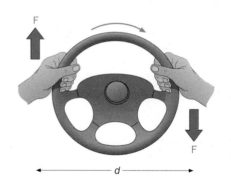

We calculate the moment of a couple using this equation:

couple =	**magnitude of one force** ×	**perpendicular distance** between
		the two forces forming the couple
(N m)	(N)	(m)

or   **couple = $F × d$**

Example 2
Calculate the couple produced by the forces acting on
the metre rule in the diagram:

Couple = $F × d$ = 12 N × 1 m = 12 N m

Compare this with the answer you get by calculating
the *total moment* about *any* point on the metre rule.
(To do this, find the moment of each force separately and them add them together.)
What do you notice? Do you always get the *same* answer?

▷ Principle of moments

Moments can be clockwise or anti-clockwise.
Look at the photograph of the children on the seesaw:

The weight of the child on the left produces a moment that tries to turn the seesaw anti-clockwise.
The weight of the child on the right produces a clockwise moment.

If the seesaw is balanced what does this tell us about these two moments? For an object to be in equilibrium (balanced) there must be no overall turning effect about any point.
The clockwise and anti-clockwise moments must cancel out.

This is summed up by **the principle of moments:**

> When an object is in equilibrium:
> **sum of the clockwise moments = sum of the anti-clockwise moments**
> about any point   about the same point

Example 3
The seesaw in the diagram is balanced.
Use the principle of moments to calculate
the weight, W.

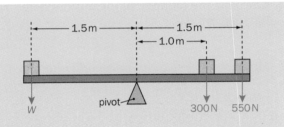

Taking moments about the pivot:

$$\text{sum of anti-clockwise moments} = \text{sum of clockwise moments}$$
$$W \times 1.5 \text{ m} = (300 \text{ N} \times 1.0 \text{ m}) + (550 \text{ N} \times 1.5 \text{ m})$$
$$W \times 1.5 \text{ m} = 300 \text{ N m} + 825 \text{ N m}$$
$$W \times 1.5 \text{ m} = 1125 \text{ N m}$$
$$\therefore W = \frac{1125 \text{ N m}}{1.5 \text{ m}} = \underline{750 \text{ N}} \quad (2 \text{ s.f.})$$

Example 4
The diagram shows the forces acting on your forearm when you hold a weight with your arm horizontal. Your elbow joint acts as a pivot:

The clockwise moments produced by the weight of your arm and the weight in your hand must be balanced by an anti-clockwise moment from your biceps muscle.
Use the principle of moments to calculate the force exerted by your biceps, F_B.

Taking moments about the elbow:

$$\text{sum of clockwise moments} = \text{sum of anti-clockwise moments}$$
$$(20 \text{ N} \times 0.16 \text{ m}) + (60 \text{ N} \times 0.32 \text{ m}) = (F_B \times 0.040 \text{ m})$$
$$22.4 \text{ N m} = F_B \times 0.040 \text{ m}$$
$$\therefore F_B = \frac{22.4 \text{ N m}}{0.040 \text{ m}} = \underline{560 \text{ N}} \quad (2 \text{ s.f.})$$

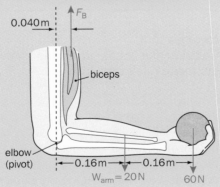

Note that any reaction force at the pivot would have **no** moment about this point, as the perpendicular distance is zero.

▶ Centre of gravity (centre of mass)

Imagine you are carrying a heavy ladder on your shoulder.
How would you position it so that it balanced?
You would rest the **centre** of the ladder on your shoulder.
This point is called its **centre of gravity**.
Although gravity is pulling down on every part of the ladder, the whole weight of the ladder can be treated **as if it acts at this point**.
You can certainly feel the whole weight on your shoulder!

What is the difference between centre of gravity and centre of mass?
The **centre of gravity** of an object is the point at which we can take its entire **weight** to act.
The **centre of mass** of an object is the point at which we can take its entire **mass** to be concentrated.

(In places where the gravitational field strength is uniform, the centre of gravity and the centre of mass are at the same point.
This is true for all objects near the surface of the Earth.)

Locating centres of gravity (centres of mass)

For uniform, symmetrical objects the centre of gravity is at the geometric centre.
The diagrams show you the position of the centre of gravity G, for some common shapes:

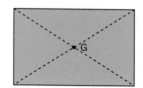

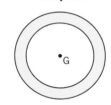
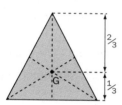

An object will always balance if you support it at its centre of gravity.
Check this for yourself with something simple like a ruler or a book.

Why does a plumb-line always hang vertically?
If you hang an object up, so that it can swing, it will always come to rest with its centre of gravity directly below the point of support.
Why is this?
If the line of the weight does not go through the pivot, then there is a moment to make the object turn. It turns until there is no moment.

For irregular shapes you can use this idea to find their centre of gravity:

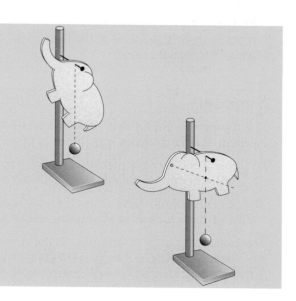

Example 5   Finding the centre of gravity of an irregular lamina
A lamina is a thin, flat shape. In this example our irregular lamina is an elephant shape cut from flat card.

Hang the card freely from a pin, so that it can swing freely:
When it comes to rest, use a plumb-line to draw a vertical line on the card from this support.
The centre of gravity must be somewhere on this line.

Now hang the card from a different point. Use the plumb-line again to draw a second vertical line. The centre of gravity must be on this line as well. So the centre of gravity is where the lines cross.

How can you check this? You can either draw a third line, which should cross at the same place, or try to balance the card at this point.

▷ Solving equilibrium problems

You can find one or more unknown forces acting on an object in equilibrium by following these 3 steps:

1. Draw a free-body force diagram for the object. Remember to show the weight of the object acting at its centre of gravity.

2. Calculate moments about one or more points. Read the tip:

3. Resolve the forces to find the total force acting in a convenient direction (eg. vertically, or horizontally). This must be zero.

By rearranging the equations that these steps produce, you will be able to find the unknown forces.

> *Tip: If there are two unknown forces, take moments about a point through which one of the unknown forces acts.*
>
> *As this unknown force has no moment about this point, it will not appear in your equation.*
>
> *This is used in Example 6.*

Example 6
A diver weighing 650 N stands at the end of a uniform 2.0 m long diving board of weight 200 N. What are the reaction forces at the supports A and B, if the board is balanced as shown in the diagram?

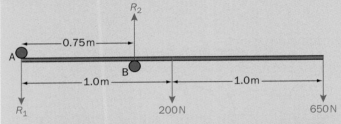

Take moments about **A**:   clockwise moments = anti-clockwise moments

$$(200\text{ N} \times 1\text{ m}) + (650\text{ N} \times 2\text{ m}) = R_2 \times 0.75\text{ m}$$
$$200\text{ N m} + 1300\text{ N m} = R_2 \times 0.75\text{ m}$$
$$1500\text{ N m} = R_2 \times 0.75\text{ m}$$
$$\therefore R_2 = \frac{1500\text{ N m}}{0.75\text{ m}} = \underline{2000\text{ N}}$$

To find R_1 you have a choice:

Method 1. Resolve vertically:

$$R_2 = R_1 + 650\text{ N} + 200\text{ N}$$
$$2000\text{ N} = R_1 + 850\text{ N}$$
$$\therefore R_1 = 2000\text{ N} - 850\text{ N} = 1150\text{ N}$$
$$= \underline{1200\text{ N}} \text{ (2 s.f.)}$$

Method 1 is usually easier.

Method 2. Take moments about **B**:
anti-clockwise moments = clockwise moments
$$R_1 \times 0.75\text{ m} = (200\text{ N} \times 0.25\text{ m}) + (650\text{ N} \times 1.25\text{ m})$$
$$R_1 \times 0.75\text{ m} = 862.5\text{ N m}$$
$$\therefore R_1 = \frac{862.5\text{ N m}}{0.75\text{ m}} = \underline{1200\text{ N}} \text{ (2 s.f.)}$$

Summary

The moment is the turning effect produced by a force:
Moment of a force about a point (in N m) = force (N) × perpendicular distance from the force to the point (m)

A couple is the turning effect due to two equal forces acting in the opposite direction:
Couple (in N m) = magnitude of one force (N) × perpendicular distance between the two forces in the couple (m)

The principle of moments states that, for an object in equilibrium:
sum of the clockwise moments about any point = sum of the anti-clockwise moments about that point

The centre of gravity of an object is the point at which its entire weight appears to act.
An object will balance if supported at its centre of gravity.
A freely suspended object will always come to rest with its centre of gravity directly below the point of suspension.

▶ Questions

1. Can you complete these sentences?
a) The moment of a force about a point is equal to the force multiplied by the .... distance from the .... to that point.
b) Moments are measured in ....
c) The principle of moments states that, if an object is in ...., the total .... moments are .... to the total .... moments.
d) The centre of gravity is the point through which the whole .... of the object seems to act.
e) A couple consists of two forces of equal .... acting in .... directions. A couple has no resultant force. It produces only a .... effect.

2. a) A mechanic applies a force of 200 N at the end of a spanner of length 20 cm. What moment is applied to the nut?
b) Would it be easier to undo the nut with a longer or shorter spanner? Explain your answer.

3. The diagrams show rulers balanced at their centres of gravity.
What are the missing values X, Y and Z?

a)
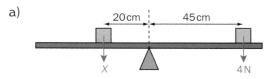

b)
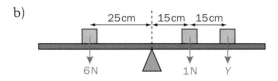

c)
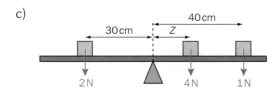

4. Explain the following:
a) A Bunsen burner has a wide heavy base.
b) Racing cars are low, with wheels wide apart.
c) A boxer stands with his legs well apart.
d) A wine glass containing wine is less stable.
e) Lorries are less stable if carrying a load.

Further questions on page 105.

5. Calculate the size of these couples:

a)
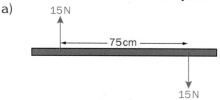

b)
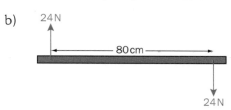

6. The uniform rulers in the diagrams are balanced. The rulers are 1.0 m long and weigh 1.0 N. Find the missing values X and Y.

a)
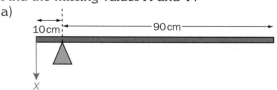

b)
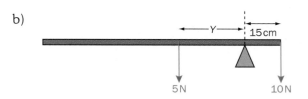

7. Two men are carrying a uniform ladder of length 12 m and weight 250 N. One man holds the ladder 2.0 m from the front end and the other man is 1.0 m from the back of the ladder.
a) Draw a free-body force diagram for the ladder.
b) Calculate the upward contact forces that each man exerts on the ladder.

8. The diagram shows a woman using a lever to lift a heavy object. The lever consists of a uniform plank of wood pivoted as shown. The plank is 3.0 m long and weighs 200 N. The object weighs 1200 N.

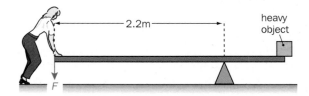

a) Draw a free-body force diagram showing all the forces acting **on the plank**.
b) Calculate the downward force F she needs to apply to keep the plank balanced.
c) What is the reaction force at the pivot?

4 Describing Motion

We live in a world full of movement. Humans, animals and the many forms of transport we use are obvious examples of objects designed for movement. This chapter is about the Physics of motion.

In this chapter you will learn:
- how to describe motion in terms of distance, displacement, speed, velocity, acceleration and time,
- how to use equations that link these quantities,
- how to draw and interpret graphs representing motion.

▷ Distance and displacement

Distance and displacement are both ways of measuring how far an object has moved. So what is the difference?

Distance is a scalar. Displacement is a **vector** quantity (see page 10). Displacement is the distance moved in a particular direction.

The snail in the picture moves from A to B along an irregular path: The **distance** travelled is the total length of the dotted line.

But what is the snail's **displacement**?
The magnitude of the displacement is the length of the straight line AB. The direction of the displacement is along this line.

▷ Speed and velocity

The speed of an object tells you the distance moved per second, or the '**rate of change of**' distance:

$$\text{average speed} = \frac{\text{distance travelled (m)}}{\text{time taken (s)}}$$

Speed is a scalar quantity, but velocity is a vector.
Velocity measures the rate of change of **displacement**:

$$\text{average velocity} = \frac{\text{total displacement (m)}}{\text{time taken (s)}}$$

Both speed and velocity are measured in **metres per second**, written **m/s** or **m s^{-1}**. With velocity you also need to state the direction.

Using these equations you can find the **average** speed and the **average** velocity for a car journey.
A speedometer shows the actual or **instantaneous** speed of the car. This varies throughout the journey as you accelerate and decelerate.

So how can we find the instantaneous speed or velocity at any point? The answer is to find the distance moved, or the displacement, over a very small time interval. The smaller the time interval, the closer we get to an instantaneous value (see also page 34).

Military jet
450 m s^{-1}

Racing car
60 m s^{-1}

Cheetah
27 m s^{-1}

Sprinter
10 m s^{-1}

Tortoise
0.060 m s^{-1}

Example 1
The boat in the diagram sails 150 m due south and then 150 m due east.
This takes a total time of 45 s.
Calculate (a) the boat's average speed, and (b) the boat's average velocity.

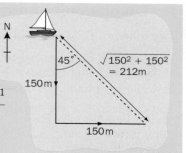

a) average speed $= \dfrac{\text{distance travelled}}{\text{time taken}} = \dfrac{150 \text{ m} + 150 \text{ m}}{45 \text{ s}} = \dfrac{300 \text{ m}}{45 \text{ s}} = \underline{6.7 \text{ m s}^{-1}}$

b) average velocity $= \dfrac{\text{displacement}}{\text{time taken}} = \dfrac{212 \text{ m}}{45 \text{ s}} = \underline{4.7 \text{ m s}^{-1}}$ in a $\underline{\text{SE direction}}$

▷ Acceleration

Acceleration is the rate of change of velocity:

$$\text{acceleration} = \frac{\textbf{change in velocity (m s}^{-1}\textbf{)}}{\textbf{time taken (s)}}$$

Acceleration is measured in metres per second per second, or metres per second squared, written $\textbf{m/s}^2$ or $\textbf{m s}^{-2}$.
It is a vector quantity, acting in a particular direction.

The change in velocity may be a change in *speed*, or *direction* or both.
If an object is slowing down, its change in velocity is negative.
This gives a negative acceleration or 'deceleration'.

▷ Indicating direction

It is important to state the direction of vectors such as displacement, velocity and acceleration. In most motion problems you will be dealing with motion in a straight line (*linear motion*).
In this case you can use + and – signs to indicate direction.
For example, with horizontal motion if you take motion to the **right** as *positive* then:

- 3 m means a displacement of 3 m to the left
+ 8 m s^{-1} means a velocity of 8 m s^{-1} to the right
- 4 m s^{-2} means an acceleration of 4 m s^{-2} to the left
    (*or* a deceleration of an object moving towards the right)

The sign convention you choose is entirely up to you.
In one question it may be easier to take *up* as positive whereas in another you might use *down* as positive. It doesn't matter as long as you keep to the *same* convention for the entire calculation.

The runner is going round the curve at a constant speed.
So how can she also be accelerating?
Because her direction is changing,
and so her velocity is changing.

Example 2
A ball hits a wall horizontally at 6.0 m s^{-1}. It rebounds horizontally at 4.4 m s^{-1}.
The ball is in contact with the wall for 0.040 s. What is the acceleration of the ball?

before impact
$+6.0 \text{ m s}^{-1}$

Taking motion *towards* the wall as positive:

change in velocity $=$ new velocity $-$ old velocity
$= (-4.4 \text{ m s}^{-1}) - (+6.0 \text{ m s}^{-1})$
$= -10.4 \text{ m s}^{-1}$

after impact
-4.4 m s^{-1}

acceleration $= \dfrac{\text{change in velocity}}{\text{time taken}} = \dfrac{-10.4 \text{ m s}^{-1}}{0.040 \text{ s}} = \underline{-260 \text{ m s}^{-2}}$ Negative, therefore in a direction *away from* the wall.

▷ Displacement–time graphs

The diagram shows a graph of displacement against time, for a car:

What type of motion does this straight line represent?
The displacement increases by equal amounts in equal times. So the object is moving at **constant velocity**.

You can calculate the velocity from the graph:

$$\text{Velocity from O to A} = \frac{\text{displacement}}{\text{time taken}}$$

$$= \text{gradient of line OA}$$

The steeper the gradient, the greater the velocity.

Velocity is a vector so the graph also needs to indicate its direction. Positive gradients (sloping upwards) indicate velocity in one direction. Negative gradients (sloping downwards) indicate velocity in the opposite direction.

How would you draw a displacement–time graph for a stationary object? If the velocity is zero, the gradient of the graph must also be zero. So your graph would be a horizontal line.

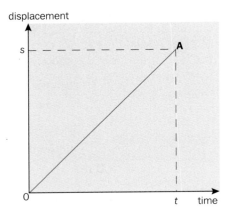

The gradient of a displacement-time graph gives us the velocity

This second graph is a curve. How is the velocity changing here? The gradient of the graph is gradually increasing. This shows that the velocity is increasing. So the object is **accelerating**.

We could find the *average* velocity for this motion by dividing the total displacement s, by the time taken t $(= s / t)$.

But how do we find the actual (instantaneous) velocity at any point? The instantaneous velocity is given by the gradient at that point. This is found by drawing a tangent to the curve and calculating its gradient $(= \Delta s / \Delta t$, see the labels on the graph, see page 404).

What would the gradient of a *distance*–time graph represent? In this case the gradient would give the scalar quantity, *speed*.

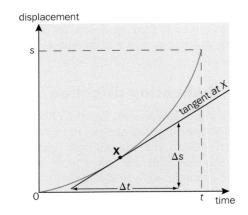

▷ Velocity–time graphs

This graph shows the motion of a car travelling in a straight line:

It starts at rest, speeds up from O to A, travels at constant velocity (from A to B), and then slows down to a stop (B to C).
What does the gradient tell us this time?

$$\text{Gradient of line OA} = \frac{\text{change in velocity}}{\text{time taken}} = \text{acceleration}$$

The steeper the line, the greater the acceleration.

A positive gradient indicates acceleration. A negative gradient (eg. BC) indicates a negative acceleration (deceleration).

Straight lines indicate that the acceleration is constant or uniform.

If the graph is curved, the acceleration at any point is given by the gradient of the tangent at that point.

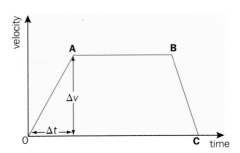

The gradient of a velocity-time graph gives us the acceleration

The **area** under a velocity–time graph also gives us information. First let's calculate the displacement of the car during its motion.

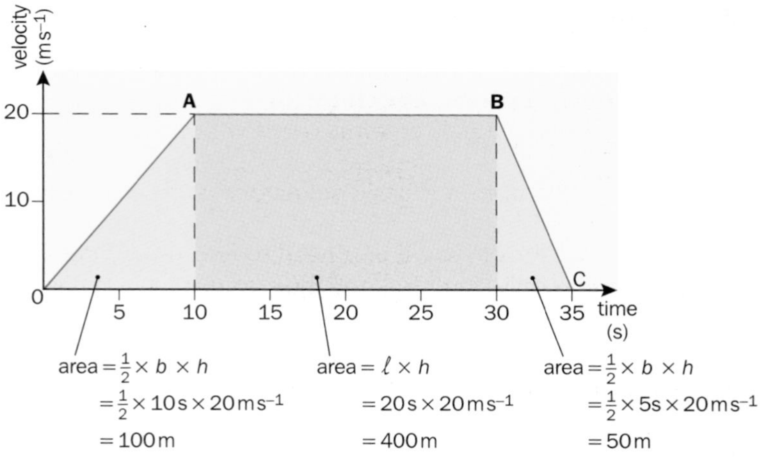

velocity (ms⁻¹)
20
10
0
A
B
C
5
10
15
20
25
30
35
time (s)
area = ½ × b × h
= ½ × 10s × 20ms⁻¹
= 100m
area = ℓ × h
= 20s × 20ms⁻¹
= 400m
area = ½ × b × h
= ½ × 5s × 20ms⁻¹
= 50m

From O to A:
displacement $= \text{average velocity} \times \text{time taken}$
$= (\frac{1}{2} \times 20 \text{ m s}^{-1}) \times 10 \text{ s}$
$= 100 \text{ m}$

From A to B:
displacement $= \text{average velocity} \times \text{time taken}$
$= 20 \text{ m s}^{-1} \times 20 \text{ s}$
$= 400 \text{ m}$

From B to C:
displacement $= \text{average velocity} \times \text{time taken}$
$= (\frac{1}{2} \times 20 \text{ m s}^{-1}) \times 5 \text{ s}$
$= 50 \text{ m}$

Compare these values with the areas under the velocity–time graph. (They are marked on the diagram.) What do you notice?
In each case ***the area under the graph gives the displacement***.

This also works for non-linear velocity–time graphs:

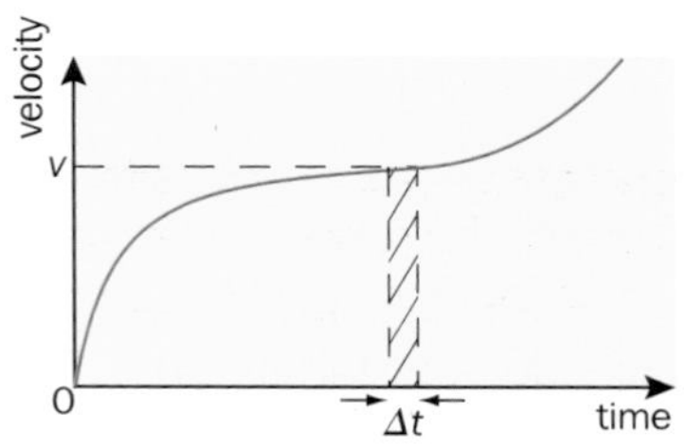

velocity
v
0
Δt
time

Area of shaded strip $= v \times \Delta t$ = average velocity × time interval
= displacement in this interval

Adding up the total area under the curve would give us the total displacement during the motion.

What does the area under a *speed*–time graph represent?
This gives us the *distance* moved.

Example 3
The velocity–time graph represents the motion of a stockcar starting a race, crashing into another car and then reversing.

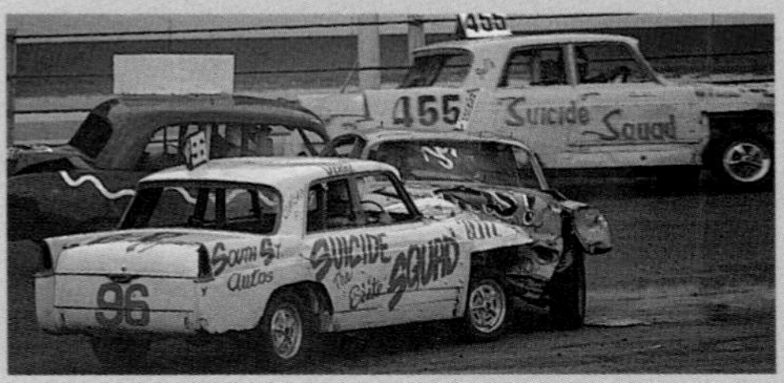

a) Describe the motion of the car during each labelled section.
b) What is the maximum velocity of the car?
c) At which point does the car crash?
d) Does the car reverse all the way back to the start point?

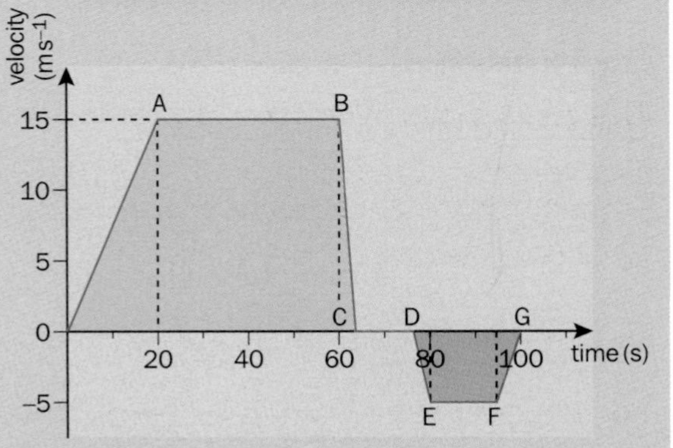

velocity (ms⁻¹)
15
10
5
0
−5
A
B
C
D
E
F
G
20
40
60
80
100
time (s)

a) 0 to A: The car accelerates.
A to B: Moving at constant velocity.
B to C: The car rapidly decelerates to a standstill.
C to D: The car is not moving.
D to E: The velocity is increasing again but the values are negative. Why? The car is starting to reverse.
E to F: The car is now reversing at constant velocity.
F to G: The car decelerates and stops.

b) From the graph, maximum velocity = $\underline{15 \text{ m s}^{-1}}$.

c) The car crashes at point B. This causes the rapid deceleration.

d) The area under the positive part of the velocity–time graph (shaded blue) gives the forward displacement of the car.
The negative area (shaded red) gives the distance that the car reversed.
As the red area is smaller than the blue area, we can see that the car did not reverse all the way back to the start point.

▶ Equations of motion

These are 4 equations that you can use whenever an object moves with **constant, uniform acceleration** in a straight line.
The equations are written in terms of the 5 symbols in the box:

They are derived from our basic definitions of acceleration and velocity.
Check your syllabus to see if you need to learn these derivations, or whether you only need to know how to use the equations to solve problems.

s = displacement (m)
u = initial velocity (m s^{-1})
v = final velocity (m s^{-1})
a = constant acceleration (m s^{-2})
t = time interval (s)

Derivations

From page 33, $$\text{acceleration} = \frac{\text{change in velocity}}{\text{time taken}} = \frac{\text{final velocity} - \text{initial velocity}}{\text{time taken}}$$

Writing this in symbols: $a = \dfrac{v - u}{t}$

So $at = v - u$ which we can rearrange to give $\boxed{v = u + at}$ . . . . . (1)

From page 32, $$\text{average velocity} = \frac{\text{displacement}}{\text{time taken}}$$

If the acceleration is constant, the average velocity during the motion will be half way between u and v. This is equal to $\frac{1}{2}(u + v)$.
Writing our equation for velocity in symbols:

$\frac{1}{2}(u + v) = \dfrac{s}{t}$ which we can rearrange to give $\boxed{s = \frac{1}{2}(u + v)\,t}$ . . . . . (2)

Using equation (1) to replace v in equation (2):

$s = \frac{1}{2}(u + u + at)\,t$

$\therefore\ s = \frac{1}{2}(2u + at)\,t$ which we can multiply out to give $\boxed{s = ut + \frac{1}{2}at^2}$ . . . . . (3)

From equation (1), $t = \dfrac{v - u}{a}$

Using this to replace t in equation (2):

$s = \frac{1}{2}(u + v)\,\dfrac{(v - u)}{a}$

$\therefore\ 2as = (u + v)(v - u)$

$\therefore\ 2as = v^2 - u^2$ which we can rearrange to give $\boxed{v^2 = u^2 + 2as}$ . . . . . (4)

Note:

- You can use these equations only if the acceleration is **constant**.

- Notice that each equation contains only 4 of our five '$s\ u\ v\ a\ t$' variables.
  So if we know any 3 of the variables we can use these equations to find the other two.

Example 4
A cheetah starts from rest and accelerates at 2.0 m s⁻² due east for 10 s.
Calculate   a) the cheetah's final velocity,
                   b) the distance the cheetah covers in this 10 s.

First, list what you know: s = ?
                                        u = 0 (= 'from rest')
                                        v = ?
                                        a = 2.0 m s⁻²
                                        t = 10 s

a) Using equation (1): $v = u + at$

     $v = 0 + (2.0 \text{ m s}^{-2} \times 10 \text{ s}) = \underline{20 \text{ m s}^{-1}}$ due east

b) Using equation (2): $s = \frac{1}{2}(u + v)t$

     $s = \frac{1}{2}(0 + 20 \text{ m s}^{-1}) \times 10 \text{ s} = \underline{100 \text{ m}}$ due east

Or you could find the displacement by plotting a velocity–time graph
for this motion. The magnitude of the displacement is equal to
the area under the graph. Check this for yourself.

Example 5
An athlete accelerates out of her blocks at 5.0 m s⁻².
a) How long does it take her to run the first 10 m?
b) What is her velocity at this point?

First, list what you know: s = 10 m
                                        u = 0
                                        v = ?
                                        a = 5.0 m s⁻²
                                        t = ?

a) Using equation (3): $s = ut + \frac{1}{2}at^2$

     ∴ 10 m = $0 + (\frac{1}{2} \times 5.0 \text{ m s}^{-2} \times t^2)$ So $t^2 = \dfrac{10 \text{ m}}{2.5 \text{ m s}^{-2}} = 4.0 \text{ s}^2$ ∴ $\underline{t = 2.0 \text{ s}}$

b) Using equation (1): $v = u + at$

     $v = 0 + (5.0 \text{ m s}^{-2} \times 2.0 \text{ s}) = \underline{10 \text{ m s}^{-1}}$ (2 s.f.)

Example 6
A bicycle's brakes can produce a deceleration of 2.5 m s⁻².
How far will the bicycle travel before stopping, if it is moving
at 10 m s⁻¹ when the brakes are applied?

First, list what you know: s = ?
                                        u = 10 m s⁻¹
                                        v = 0
                                        a = − 2.5 m s⁻² (negative, because *decelerating*)

Using equation (4): $v^2 = u^2 + 2as$

     $0 = (10 \text{ m s}^{-1})^2 + (2 \times -2.5 \text{ m s}^{-2} \times s)$

     $0 = 100 \text{ m}^2 \text{ s}^{-2} - (5.0 \text{ m s}^{-2} \times s)$ So $s = \dfrac{100 \text{ m}^2 \text{ s}^{-2}}{5.0 \text{ m s}^{-2}} = \underline{20 \text{ m}}$ (2 s.f.)

▷ Newton's Third Law

In Chapter 2 we looked at forces acting between two objects. Newton realised that forces cannot exist in isolation. **Forces always act in pairs.**
This is Newton's third law of motion:

> **If an object A exerts a force on an object B, then B exerts an equal but opposite force on A.**

This is sometimes written as:

> **To every action force there is an equal but opposite reaction.**

The term *opposite* in these definitions means in the *opposite direction*.

You exert a force on the trolley but the trolley exerts an equal force back on you

So why don't these forces just cancel out, with no effect?

This is the most common misconception about Newton's third law forces. The most important thing to remember is that the two forces act on **different** objects.

The motion of an object is determined solely by the forces acting on it. This is why the free-body force diagrams that you learned about on page 22 are so useful when solving problems.
Remember those diagrams show all the forces acting on just **one** object.

You can test Newton's third law for yourself in some simple experiments:

Example 3
Two people on roller-blades stand facing each other:

If Adam pushes Ben away from him, Ben will move off backwards. But what happens to Adam? Does he remain stationary?

No. He also moves backwards because, during the push, Ben will exert an equal but opposite force on him.

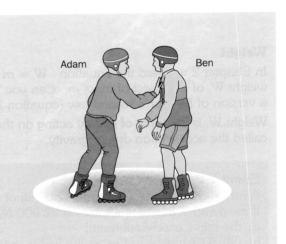

The force of Adam = The force of Ben
     on Ben   on Adam
   (to the right)   (to the left)

Can you see that **changing round the words** on the left-hand side tells you what the words should be on the right-hand side?

Example 4
Set up two force-meters as shown in the diagram:

One measures the force that you exert on the table when you pull.
The other force-meter measures the force that the table exerts on you.

As you pull, what do you notice about the two readings?
The readings on both meters are identical.

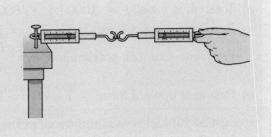

Identifying Newton's third law pairs

Spotting a Newton's third law pair of forces is not always easy. The diagram shows the 2 forces acting on a person standing on Earth:

The forces are equal in size and opposite in direction but they are **not** a Newton pair. Why not?

Remember that the two forces in a Newton pair always act on **different** objects.
But here the upward force is the contact force of the Earth *on the person*, and the weight is the force of gravity *on the person*.
So both of these forces act on the **same** object, the person.

normal contact force

weight

The diagram is a free-body force diagram for the person (as on page 22). The Newton's third law pairs for the two forces are not shown here. What would these be?
The matching forces are (a) the contact force of the person *on the Earth* and (b) the gravitational pull of the person *on the Earth* (see Example 5). These forces are irrelevant if we are only concerned with the motion of the person.

To help you identify Newton pairs you can use the following checklist. Each force in a Newton's third law pair:

- has the same magnitude (size),
- acts along the same line but in opposite directions,
- acts for the same time,
- acts on a **different** object,
- is of the same type (eg. two contact forces, or two gravitational forces)
- can be identified by changing round the words as in Example 3.

Example 5
The diagrams show the forces acting when a gymnast balances on a beam. They have been drawn as free-body force diagrams, showing all the forces acting on (a) the gymnast, (b) the beam, (c) the Earth.

Can you identify each of the 4 Newton pairs? Remember that each force in a pair will be acting on a **different** object.

The matching pairs are numbered and colour coded to help you:

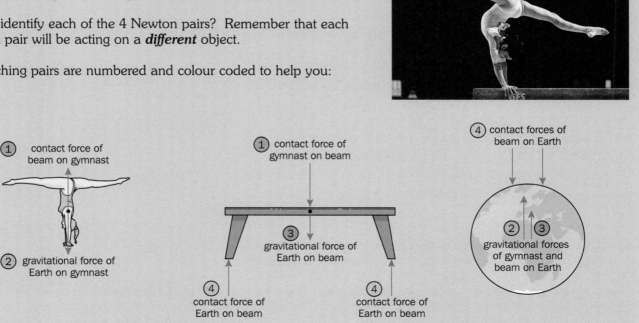

① contact force of beam on gymnast

② gravitational force of Earth on gymnast

① contact force of gymnast on beam

③ gravitational force of Earth on beam

④ contact force of Earth on beam

④ contact force of Earth on beam

④ contact forces of beam on Earth

② ③ gravitational forces of gymnast and beam on Earth

▶ Newton's Laws: more worked examples

Example 6

A glider weighing 8000 N is being towed horizontally through the air at a steady speed. The diagram shows the forces acting on the glider. If the drag force D is 600 N, calculate:
a) the tension T, in the tow-line
b) the lift force L, on the glider.

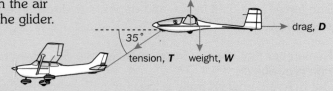

a) Steady horizontal speed means no horizontal acceleration.
So resultant horizontal force = 0
∴ total force acting to the left = total force acting to the right
$$T \cos 35° = D = 600 \text{ N}$$
$$\therefore T = \frac{600 \text{ N}}{\cos 35°} = 732.5 \text{ N} = \underline{730 \text{ N}} \text{ (2 s.f.)}$$

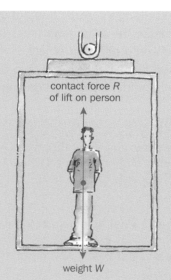

components of T

b) Travelling horizontally so there is no vertical acceleration
So resultant vertical force = 0
∴ total force acting upwards = total force acting downwards
$$L = W + T \cos 55°$$
$$= 8000 \text{ N} + (730 \text{ N} \times \cos 55°) = 8420 \text{ N} = \underline{8400 \text{ N}} \text{ (2 s.f.)}$$

Example 7

The diagram shows the forces acting on a person in a lift. The person has a mass of 70 kg. Taking $g = 10 \text{ N kg}^{-1}$, calculate the contact force R when:
a) the lift is at rest
b) the lift is accelerating upwards at 1.0 m s^{-2}
c) the lift is accelerating downwards at 2.0 m s^{-2}
d) the lift is ascending at a steady speed.

contact force R
of lift on person

weight W

a) As the person is not moving, the resultant force on him is zero.
∴ contact force R acting upwards = weight W acting downwards
$$= \text{mass} \times g$$
$$= 70 \text{ kg} \times 10 \text{ N kg}^{-1} = \underline{700 \text{ N}}$$

b) Accelerating **up**wards. Applying Newton's second law:
resultant **up**wards force $(R - W)$ = mass $\times$ acceleration
$$R - 700 \text{ N} = (70 \text{ kg} \times 1.0 \text{ m s}^{-2})$$
$$\therefore R = 70 \text{ N} + 700 \text{ N} = \underline{770 \text{ N}}$$

c) Acceleration **down**wards. Applying Newton's second law:
resultant **down**wards force $(W - R)$ = mass $\times$ acceleration
$$700 \text{ N} - R = (70 \text{ kg} \times 2.0 \text{ m s}^{-2})$$
$$\therefore R = 700 \text{ N} - 140 \text{ N} = \underline{560 \text{ N}}$$

d) Constant speed implies no acceleration, so resultant force = 0
∴ contact force acting upwards = weight acting downwards = mass $\times$ g = 70 kg $\times$ 10 N kg^{-1} = $\underline{700 \text{ N}}$

Can you see why you feel heavier as a lift accelerates upwards, and lighter as it accelerates downwards? Normally you feel a contact force from the floor equal to your weight. As the lift accelerates upwards, you experience a greater contact force, and so you feel heavier. The opposite is true for downward acceleration.

Example 8

A car of mass 1200 kg tows a caravan of mass 1800 kg
along a level road. They are linked by a rigid tow-bar.
The car accelerates at 1.80 m s⁻² pushed by a motive force
of 5600 N. The resistive force on the car due to friction and
air resistance is 65.0 N. Calculate:
a) the resistive force F on the caravan,
b) the tension T in the tow-bar.

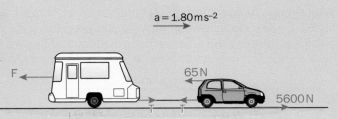

a) The tension in the tow-bar pulls equally on the car and on the
   caravan. If we start by looking at the car and caravan together
   we can ignore tension, as the tension forces balance out.
   The car and the caravan must have the same acceleration as
   they are linked by a rigid bar.

   Applying Newton's second law ($F = ma$) to the car and the caravan together:

$$\textbf{Force} \; = \; \textbf{mass} \; \times \; \textbf{acceleration}$$
$$(5600 \text{ N} - 65 \text{ N} - F) \; = \; (1200 \text{ kg} + 1800 \text{ kg}) \times 1.80 \text{ m s}^{-2}$$
$$5535 \text{ N} - F \; = \; 3000 \text{ kg} \times 1.80 \text{ m s}^{-2}$$
$$5535 \text{ N} - F \; = \; 5400 \text{ kg m s}^{-2} \; = 5400 \text{ N}$$
$$\therefore \; F \; = \; 5535 \text{ N} - 5400 \text{ N} \; = \underline{135 \text{ N}} \quad (3 \text{ s.f.})$$

b) We can find the tension in the tow-bar by applying Newton's
   second law to either the car or the caravan. We will do both here.
   Always start by drawing free-body force diagrams for each one:

   Method 1: Forces on **car** (apply $F = ma$)
$$5600 \text{ N} - 65 \text{ N} - T \; = \; 1200 \text{ kg} \times 1.80 \text{ m s}^{-2}$$
$$5535 \text{ N} - T \; = \; 2160 \text{ kg m s}^{-2} \; = 2160 \text{ N}$$
$$\therefore \; T \; = \; 5535 \text{ N} - 2160 \text{ N} \; = 3375 \text{ N} \; = \underline{3380 \text{ N}} \quad (3 \text{ s.f.})$$

   Method 2: Forces on **caravan** (apply $F = ma$)
$$T - 135 \text{ N} \; = \; 1800 \text{ kg} \times 1.80 \text{ m s}^{-2}$$
$$T - 135 \text{ N} \; = \; 3240 \text{ kg m s}^{-2} \; = 3240 \text{ N}$$
$$\therefore \; T \; = \; 3240 \text{ N} + 135 \text{ N} \; = 3375 \text{ N} \; = \underline{3380 \text{ N}} \quad (3 \text{ s.f.})$$

Example 9

A battery powered wheelchair can provide a motive force of 170 N.
The person and wheelchair have a combined weight of 1000 N
and the total resistive force acting is 20 N.
What is the maximum angle θ of the ramp that will allow the
wheelchair to travel up it at a steady speed?

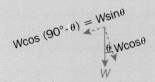

Steady speed means no acceleration, and so
no resultant force along the slope.

So: total force $\;=\;$ total force
    up slope $\qquad$ down slope
$$F \; = \; R \; + \; W \sin \theta$$
$$170 \text{ N} \; = \; 20 \text{ N} + (1000 \text{ N} \times \sin \theta)$$
$$\therefore \; \sin \theta \; = \; \frac{170 \text{ N} - 20 \text{ N}}{1000 \text{ N}} \; = 0.15$$
$$\therefore \; \theta \; = \; \sin^{-1} 0.15 \; = \underline{8.6°} \quad (2 \text{ s.f.})$$

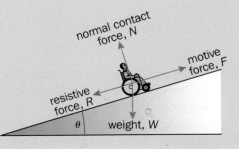

▷ Impulse

Why do you 'follow through' in sports such as tennis that involve hitting a ball? By following through you keep the force acting on the ball for a **longer time**. To see the advantage of this we need to refer back to our first version of Newton's second law, as given on page 46:

$$\text{resultant force} = \frac{\text{change in momentum, } \Delta(mv)}{\text{time taken, } \Delta t}$$

Rearranging this gives:

Force × **time** =	**change in momentum**	
(N) (s)	(kg m s^{-1})	

This tells us that the greater the force on an object and the longer it acts for, the greater the change in the object's momentum.

By following through when you hit a tennis ball you increase the time that the force acts for. This produces a greater change in the ball's momentum.
Similarly, by drawing your hands backwards when you catch a ball you can reduce the sting. Can you see why? The momentum of the ball is reduced over a longer time, reducing the force on your hands.

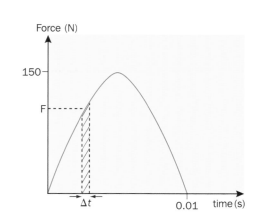

The quantity 'force × time' is known as **impulse**. Impulse measures the *effect* of a force. Impulse is measured in newton seconds (N s). These are equivalent to the units of momentum (kg m s^{-1}):

$$\mathbf{1\ N\ s\ =\ 1\ kg\ m\ s^{-1}}$$

Example 10
a) What is the impulse produced by a force of 4 N acting for 3 s?
   Impulse = F × t   = 4 N × 3 s   = <u>12 N s</u>

b) What *effect* will this impulse have on the velocity of (i) a 2 kg mass and (ii) a 3 kg mass?

   (i) An impulse of 12 N s will produce a change in momentum p, of 12 kg m s^{-1}.
   Momentum $\boldsymbol{p}$ $\boldsymbol{=mv}$
   So, if the mass m is 2 kg, the change in velocity v must be <u>6 m s^{-1} in the direction of the force</u>.

   (ii) If the mass m is 3 kg, the change in velocity v must be <u>4 m s^{-1} in the direction of the force</u>.

Force–time graphs

The graph shows how the force applied to a golf ball by a club varies with time:

What does the area under the curve tell us?

Area of the shaded strip   = F × Δt

   = impulse produced during the small time interval Δt

Force (N)

150

F

Δt 0.01   time (s)

We could divide the whole area under the curve into tiny strips and find the impulse produced in each interval. Adding together the area of each strip would then give us the total impulse. So:

Area under a force–time curve = total impulse acting = total change in momentum produced

Example 11

The graph shows the force acting on a tennis ball of mass 60 g during a return shot.
a) What is the impulse on the ball?
b) If the ball reaches the player with velocity of 22 m s^{-1} moving to the left, what is the velocity of the return shot to the right?

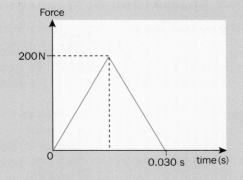

a) Impulse = area under curve = area of triangle
$= \frac{1}{2} \times$ base $\times$ height $= \frac{1}{2} \times 0.030$ s $\times 200$ N $= \underline{3.0 \text{ N s}}$

b) An impulse of 3.0 N s gives a change in momentum of 3.0 kg m s^{-1} in the direction of the force, ie. to the right.
Initial momentum of ball = mv = 0.060 kg $\times$ 22 m s^{-1} = 1.3 kg m s^{-1} to the left.

Remembering that momentum is a vector quantity, and taking motion to the right as positive:
Change in momentum = new momentum − old momentum
+ 3.0 kg m s^{-1} = new momentum − (− 1.3 kg m s^{-1})
∴ new momentum, p = 3.0 kg m s^{-1} − 1.3 kg m s^{-1} = 1.7 kg m s^{-1}

∴ new velocity $= \dfrac{p}{m} = \dfrac{1.7 \text{ kg m s}^{-1}}{0.060 \text{ kg}} = \underline{28 \text{ m s}^{-1}}$

Example 12

A helicopter hovers by forcing a column of air downwards. The force down on the air produces an equal force up on the helicopter (Newton's third law) which must balance its weight.

What is the maximum weight of the helicopter if the rotors force 1000 kg of air downward at 15 m s^{-1} each second?

Change in momentum of air in 1 s = mv = 1000 kg $\times$ 15 m s^{-1} = 15 000 kg m s^{-1}

Force acting on air $= \dfrac{\text{change in momentum}}{\text{time taken}} = \dfrac{15\,000 \text{ kg m s}^{-1}}{1 \text{ s}} = 15\,000 \text{ kg m s}^{-2} = 15\,000 \text{ N}$

∴ Upward force on helicopter = maximum weight = $\underline{15\,000 \text{ N}}$ (2 s.f.)

Example 13

Water leaves a hose pipe of cross-sectional area 3.2×10^{-4} m^2 with a horizontal velocity of 3.0 m s^{-1}. It strikes a vertical wall and runs down it without rebounding. What is the force exerted on the wall?
(Density of water, ρ_W = 1000 kg m^{-3})

The water travels at 3 m s^{-1}, so in 1 s a 3 m jet of water leaves the pipe.

Volume of water hitting the wall in 1 s = length $\times$ area of jet
= 3 m $\times$ 3.2 $\times 10^{-4}$ m^2 = 9.6 $\times 10^{-4}$ m^3

∴ Mass of water hitting the wall in 1 s = volume $\times$ density
= 9.6 $\times 10^{-4}$ m^3 $\times$ 1000 kg m^{-3} = 0.96 kg

Horizontal momentum before hitting wall = mv = 0.96 kg $\times$ 3.0 m s^{-1} = 2.88 kg m s^{-1} each second
Horizontal momentum after hitting wall = 0

Force of wall on water $= \dfrac{\text{change in momentum}}{\text{time taken}} = \dfrac{0 - 2.88 \text{ kg m s}^{-1}}{1 \text{ s}} = -2.88 \text{ kg m s}^{-2} = -2.88 \text{ N}$

∴ By Newton's third law, force of water on wall = 2.88 N = $\underline{2.9 \text{ N}}$ (2 s.f.)

▷ Conservation of Momentum

Suppose you can just reach the bank from a boat:

Why are you likely to get wet if you try to step out? What happens to the boat as you step forward? We can explain why the boat moves away from the bank using Newton's laws.

As you step from the boat, the boat exerts a contact force on you to propel you forwards. This must be equal but opposite to the force exerted by you on the boat (Newton's third law). Both of these forces act for the same time.

Now apply Newton's second law ($F = \Delta(mv)\,/\,\Delta t$) to both you and the boat. Since the force and the time are the same, both you and the boat have the same change in momentum, but in **opposite** directions. So as you gain momentum towards the bank, the boat gains equal momentum away from the bank.

But what is the overall change in momentum here?
Remember that momentum is a vector quantity.
Equal changes in opposite directions cancel out.
Consequently, the overall change in momentum is always zero.
This is known as the **principle of conservation of momentum:**

> Whenever objects interact, their **total momentum** in any direction remains **constant**, provided that no external force acts on the objects in that direction.

Investigating conservation of momentum

You can investigate the principle of conservation of momentum using a linear air track:

The air track helps to eliminate the external force of friction. Using light gates to measure the speed of the gliders, you can set up simple experiments to find their total momentum before and after collisions. You can use magnets or springs to repel the gliders away from each other.

glider $m_1 = 0.3$ kg   glider $m_2 = 0.2$ kg

Some typical results are given in this table:
Here motion to the right is taken as positive, and motion to the left as negative.

	Before the interaction				After the interaction			
	Velocity of glider 1 u_1 (m s^{-1})	Velocity of glider 2 u_2 (m s^{-1})	$m_1 u_1$ (kg m s^{-1})	$m_2 u_2$ (kg m s^{-1})	Velocity of glider 1 v_1 (m s^{-1})	Velocity of glider 2 v_2 (m s^{-1})	$m_1 v_1$ (kg m s^{-1})	$m_2 v_2$ (kg m s^{-1})
1	0.50	0	0.15	0	0.30	0.30	0.09	0.06
2	0.50	−0.50	0.15	−0.10	−0.30	0.70	−0.09	0.14
3	0	0	0	0	−0.40	0.60	−0.12	0.12
4	0.40	0.20	0.12	0.04	0.30	0.35	0.09	0.07

How do these results support the principle of conservation of momentum?
If you look carefully you can see that in each case:

$$m_1 u_1 \;+\; m_2 u_2 \;=\; m_1 v_1 \;+\; m_2 v_2$$

So:

> **Total momentum before the interaction = Total momentum after the interaction**

We use this equation in problems involving collisions or explosions.

We often use the principle of
conservation of momentum,
to solve problems where objects
collide or explode apart.

Here are some examples:

*Snooker players use the conservation of
momentum instinctively with every shot*

*The downward momentum of the hot gases
equals the upward momentum of the rocket*

Example 14 **Collisions**

a) A car of mass 1000 kg moving at 20 m s⁻¹ collides with a car
of mass 1200 kg moving at 5.0 m s⁻¹ in the same direction.
If the second car is shunted forwards at 15 m s⁻¹ by the impact,
what is the velocity v, of the first car immediately after the crash?

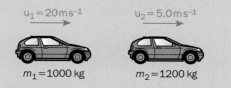

$u_1 = 20 \text{ms}^{-1}$ $u_2 = 5.0 \text{ms}^{-1}$

$m_1 = 1000$ kg $m_2 = 1200$ kg

Taking motion to the right as positive:

$$\textbf{Momentum before collision} = \textbf{Momentum after collision}$$

$$(1000 \text{ kg} \times 20 \text{ m s}^{-1}) + (1200 \text{ kg} \times 5 \text{ m s}^{-1}) = (1000 \text{ kg} \times v) + (1200 \text{ kg} \times 15 \text{ m s}^{-1})$$

$$20\,000 \text{ kg m s}^{-1} + 6000 \text{ kg m s}^{-1} = (1000 \text{ kg} \times v) + 18\,000 \text{ kg m s}^{-1}$$

$$\therefore 8000 \text{ kg m s}^{-1} = 1000 \text{ kg} \times v$$

$$\therefore \quad v = \underline{8.0 \text{ m s}^{-1}} \text{ (to the right, since the answer is positive)}$$

b) If the cars collide head-on at the same speeds as in (a),
what would their combined velocity v, be after the collision if
they stick together on impact?

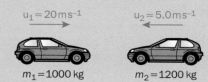

$u_1 = 20 \text{ms}^{-1}$ $u_2 = 5.0 \text{ms}^{-1}$

$m_1 = 1000$ kg $m_2 = 1200$ kg

Taking motion to the right as positive:

$$\textbf{Momentum before collision} = \textbf{Momentum after collision}$$

$$(1000 \text{ kg} \times 20 \text{ m s}^{-1}) - (1200 \text{ kg} \times 5 \text{ m s}^{-1}) = (1000 \text{ kg} + 1200 \text{ kg}) \times v$$

$$20\,000 \text{ kg m s}^{-1} - 6000 \text{ kg m s}^{-1} = 2200 \text{ kg} \times v$$

$$\therefore 14\,000 \text{ kg m s}^{-1} = 2200 \text{ kg} \times v$$

$$\therefore \quad v = \underline{6.4 \text{ m s}^{-1}} \text{ (to the right, since the answer is positive)}$$

Example 15 **Explosions**

a) A bullet of mass 10 g is fired at 400 m s⁻¹ from a rifle of mass 4.0 kg.
What is the recoil velocity v, of the rifle?

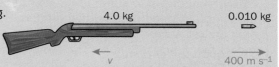

4.0 kg   0.010 kg

v 400 m s⁻¹

Before the gun is fired there is no momentum. The gun and the
bullet are not moving. Taking motion to the right as positive:

$$\textbf{Momentum before explosion} = \textbf{Momentum after explosion}$$

$$0 = (0.010 \text{ kg} \times 400 \text{ m s}^{-1}) + (4.0 \text{ kg} \times v)$$

$$0 = 4.0 \text{ kg m s}^{-1} + (4.0 \text{ kg} \times v)$$

$$\therefore \quad v = \underline{-1.0 \text{ m s}^{-1}} \text{ (to the left, since the answer is negative)}$$

b) The bullet is fired into a block of wood of mass 390 g resting on
a smooth surface. If the bullet remains embedded in the wood,
calculate the velocity v, that the block moves off at.

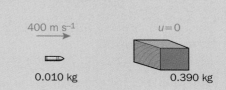

400 m s⁻¹ $u = 0$

0.010 kg   0.390 kg

$$\textbf{Momentum before collision} = \textbf{Momentum after collision}$$

$$(0.010 \text{ kg} \times 400 \text{ m s}^{-1}) + 0 = (0.010 \text{ kg} + 0.390 \text{ kg}) \times v$$

$$4.0 \text{ kg m s}^{-1} = 0.400 \text{ kg} \times v$$

$$\therefore \quad v = \underline{10 \text{ m s}^{-1}} \text{ (to the right, since the answer is positive)}$$

▷ Physics at work: Car safety

Seat belts

Seat belts save lives!
In a collision with a stationary object, the front of your car stops almost instantly. But what about the passengers?

Unfortunately they will obey Newton's first law, and continue moving forwards at constant velocity until a force changes their motion.
If you are not restrained, this force will be provided by an impact with the steering wheel or windscreen.
This can cause you serious injury, even at low speeds.

A seat belt helps you to decelerate in a more controlled way, reducing the forces on your body. So how does this work?

Look at the graph. It compares the forces acting on a driver involved in a collision with, and without, a seat belt:

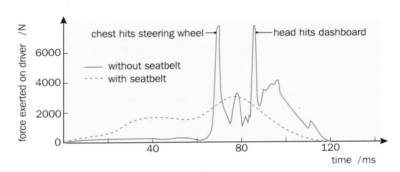

A seat belt does not hold you rigidly in position.
In an accident it is designed to stretch about 25 cm. This allows the restraining force to act over a **longer** time.

Newton's second law ($F = \Delta(mv) / \Delta t$) tells us that the longer the time Δt, the **smaller** the force F, needed to reduce the passenger's momentum, $\Delta(mv)$.

Crumple zones

Modern cars seem to suffer far greater damage in a collision than old-fashioned solid-bodied models. Does this mean they are less safe?
In fact the opposite is true. The more your car crumples, the more likely you are to walk away from an accident!

By crumpling, the car takes a longer time to come to rest. This means a lower rate of change of momentum. And Newton's second law tells us that this means smaller forces acting on the passengers.

This is why crumple zones are deliberately built into bonnets, boots and bumpers.

Other parts of the car, such as the passenger cell, are designed as rigid cages to maximise passenger protection. Forces from a side impact are transmitted away around the roof and floor of the car.

▷ Physics at work: Car safety

Air-bags

Air-bags are designed to provide a cushion between your face and the steering wheel or dashboard. This can reduce the pressure on your face by more than 80% in a collision.

Without an air-bag, your head would hit the steering wheel about 80 milliseconds (80 ms) after an impact.
To be of any use, the crash must be detected **and** the air-bag must be inflated in less than 50 ms!

So the bag is inflated explosively. This could be dangerous if it inflated accidentally under normal driving conditions.
What triggers the air-bag? Why does it only inflate during a collision and not whenever you brake hard?
We can calculate this:

Detecting the crash, inflating the air-bag (and deflating it again so the driver can see) must all take place in less time than it takes you to blink!

In a collision you are brought to rest very rapidly, say 100 ms (0.10 s).
Even at low speeds this produces high deceleration. For example, at just 20 mph (9 m s⁻¹):

$$\text{acceleration} = \frac{v - u}{t} = \frac{0 - 9\ \text{m s}^{-1}}{0.10\ \text{s}} = \underline{-90\ \text{m s}^{-2}} = -9.2\ g \quad \text{(where } g = \text{acceleration due to gravity)}$$

(This means that your seat belt must be able to exert a force of 9 times your body weight without snapping!)

Now compare this with the deceleration during an emergency stop, even at high speed.
The Highway Code gives the shortest stopping distance for a car travelling at 70 mph (31 m s⁻¹) as 96 m.
However this is made up of a thinking distance of 21 m and a braking distance of 75 m. (The thinking distance is the distance travelled before the driver reacts and starts to brake.) The braking distance is the distance travelled while decelerating. We can find this deceleration using one of our equations of motion (from page 36):

$$v^2 = u^2 + 2as$$
$$0 = (31\ \text{m s}^{-1})^2 + (2 \times a \times 75\ \text{m}) \quad \text{So} \quad a = -\frac{(31\ \text{m s}^{-1})^2}{(2 \times 75\ \text{m})} = \underline{-6.4\ \text{m s}^{-2}} = -0.65\ g$$

This is 14 times smaller than the deceleration in even a low speed collision. An acceleration sensor can easily detect the difference between the two, and so only activate the air-bag in a collision.

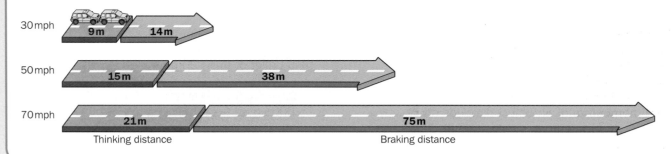

30 mph — 9 m — 14 m

50 mph — 15 m — 38 m

70 mph — 21 m — 75 m

Thinking distance — Braking distance

Head restraints

Head restraints are designed to reduce neck injury. They are particularly effective in rear-impact accidents.

As the car is shunted forwards, the back of your seat pushes your body forwards.
If you do not have a head restraint, the inertia of your head means that it stays behind, while your body moves forward.
This can cause 'whiplash' injuries.

Summary

Newton's First Law:
If there is no resultant force acting on an object,
- if it is at rest, it will stay at rest,
- if it is moving, it keeps on moving at a constant velocity (at constant speed in a straight line).

Newton's Second Law:
The rate of change of momentum of an object is directly proportional to the resultant force acting on it:
$$F = \frac{\Delta(mv)}{\Delta t}$$
The change of momentum takes place in the direction of that force.
If the mass is constant, then **Force = mass × acceleration** or $F = ma$

Newton's Third Law:
If an object A exerts a force on an object B, then B exerts an **equal** but **opposite** force on A.

The inertia of an object is its reluctance to change velocity. Inertia increases with increasing mass.

The **momentum**, p, of an object depends on its mass m, and velocity v: $p = mv$
The principle of conservation of momentum states that, whenever objects interact, their total momentum remains constant, provided that no external force acts on the objects, so:
     Total momentum before the interaction = Total momentum after the interaction

Impulse measures the effect of a force:
Impulse (N s) = **force × time = change in momentum produced** (kg m s^{-1})
The area under a force–time curve gives the total impulse acting, which equals the total change in momentum produced.

The unit of force is the **newton**. The newton can be defined in two ways:
- 1 newton is the resultant force needed to cause a rate of change of momentum of 1 kg m s^{-1} each second, or
- 1 newton is the resultant force needed to give a mass of 1 kg an acceleration of 1 m s^{-2}.

▶ Questions

(Take $g = 10$ m s^{-2})

1. Can you complete these sentences?
   a) A .... is needed to change the motion of an object.
      Forces can .... or decelerate an object, to change the object's .... (ie. speed or direction).
   b) The momentum of an object depends on its .... and .... Momentum is measured in ....
   c) The equation $F = ma$ is only valid in situations where .... is constant.
   d) One newton is the resultant force needed to give a mass of .... an acceleration of ....
   e) Forces in a Newton's third law pair have equal .... but act in opposite ....
   f) Impulse depends on .... and .... It is measured in ....
      The impulse of a force equals the change in .... produced. Total impulse can be found from the area under a .... – .... graph.
   g) In collisions and explosions, the total .... remains constant, provided that no external .... acts.

2. Calculate the momentum of:
   a) an elephant of mass 2000 kg moving at 3 m s^{-1}
   b) a bullet of mass 20 g moving at 300 m s^{-1}.

3. What is the force needed to give a train of mass 25 000 kg an acceleration of 4 m s^{-2} ?

4. A car of mass 1500 kg accelerates away from traffic lights. The car produces a constant motive force of 9000 N. The initial drag force opposing the motion is 1500 N.
   a) What is the initial acceleration?
   b) Why does this acceleration gradually decrease even though the force from the engine is unchanged?

5. A grasshopper of mass 2.4×10^{-3} kg jumps upwards from rest. By pushing with its legs for 1.2 ms it achieves a take-off speed of 0.65 m s^{-1}. Calculate:
   a) its upward momentum,
   b) the force exerted by its legs.

6. Explain, with examples, how to identify a Newton's third law pair of forces.

7. A man is standing on a chair resting on the ground.
   a) Draw 3 free-body force diagrams, for
      i) the man,
      ii) the chair, and
      iii) the Earth,
      showing all the forces acting on each object.
   b) Show clearly which of these forces are Newton pairs of equal but opposite forces.

8.

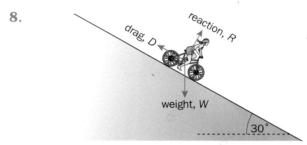

The diagram shows the forces acting on a cyclist freewheeling down a hill. Her total mass, including the bicycle is 79 kg. She accelerates from rest to 6.0 m s^{-1} in 3.0 s.
   a) What is her acceleration?
   b) Calculate the weight, W.
   c) By applying Newton's second law along the slope, find the drag force, D.
   d) After a few seconds she reaches a steady speed down the slope. What is the drag force now? Why has it changed?

9. An empty lift has a mass of 1200 kg. It is supported by a steel cable attached to the roof. Draw a diagram showing the two forces acting on the lift.

   Find the tension in the lift cable when the lift is:
   a) ascending at a steady speed,
   b) accelerating upwards at 1.5 m s^{-2},
   c) accelerating downwards at 2.0 m s^{-2}.

10. During a serve, a tennis racket is in contact with the ball for 25 ms. The 60 g ball leaves the racket with a horizontal velocity of 31 m s^{-1}. If its initial horizontal velocity was zero, calculate:
    a) the change in momentum of the ball,
    b) the impulse from the racket,
    c) the average force exerted on the ball.

11. A car moving at 25 m s^{-1} collides with a wall. The driver of mass 65 kg is brought to rest by his seat belt in 0.20 s. Calculate:
    a) the driver's change in momentum,
    b) the average force exerted by the seat belt on the driver.
    c) How many times greater is this force than the driver's own weight?

12.

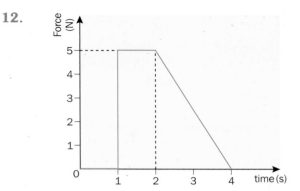

The graph shows the force acting on a 3.0 kg mass over a period of 4.0 s.
    a) Use the graph to calculate the total impulse.
    b) What change in momentum does this impulse produce?
    c) If the mass was initially at rest, what is its velocity after the 4 s?

13. During a hailstorm 0.54 kg of hail-stones fall on to a flat roof in 6.0 s without rebounding. The hail hits the roof at 12 m s^{-1}. Calculate:
    a) the change of momentum each second,
    b) the force exerted on the roof.

14. A glider of mass 200 g is moving at 0.60 m s^{-1} along an air-track. It collides with a second stationary glider of mass 250 g.
    If the gliders stick together on impact, calculate their new combined speed.

15. A car of mass 1500 kg travelling at 12 m s^{-1} collides head-on with a lorry moving at 20 m s^{-1}. The lorry has a mass of 9000 kg. If the collision reduces the speed of the lorry to 15 m s^{-1}, what is the car's velocity after the impact?
    In which direction is this?

16. A snooker ball moving at 2.0 m s^{-1} collides head-on with an identical but stationary ball. After the collision the second ball moves off at 1.5 m s^{-1}. What is the new velocity of the first ball?

17. A rocket of total mass 3500 kg is moving at 250 m s^{-1} through space. When the booster rockets are fired 1200 kg of burnt fuel is ejected from the back of the rocket at 20 m s^{-1}. What is the new speed of the rocket?

18. A cannon fires a cannonball of mass 55 kg at 35 m s^{-1}. The cannon recoils at 2.5 m s^{-1}.
    a) What is the mass of the cannon?
    b) If the cannonball becomes embedded in a target of mass 600 kg, at what speed does the target move immediately after impact?

Further questions on page 107.

6 Work, Energy and Power

Holding a heavy set of weights above your head may feel like hard work, but in a Physics sense you are doing no work at all!
You are doing work only when you move the weights up.
In Physics, work is done only **when a force moves.**

In this chapter you will learn:
- how to calculate work and power,
- the equations for kinetic and potential energy,
- how to use the principle of conservation of energy to solve problems.

Work and energy

We can calculate the work done when a force moves using this equation:

Work done, W = force, F × displacement, s
in the direction of the force
(joules)   (newtons)   (metres)

Note that although force and displacement are vectors, work is a **scalar** quantity.

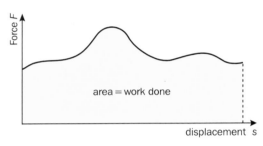

If the force, F, varies with displacement, s, the work done can be found from the area under a F–s graph

What if the force and displacement are not in the same direction, as in the diagram?   In this case you need to resolve the force to find the component acting in the direction of the displacement:

$$\text{Work done, } W = F\cos\theta_1 \times \text{displacement, } s$$

What about the vertical component of the force, $F\cos\theta_2$?
This does no work, because there is no movement in the vertical direction.

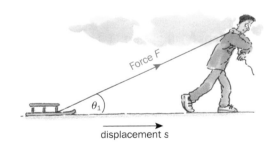

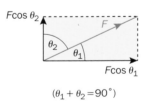

$(\theta_1 + \theta_2 = 90°)$

Doing work requires energy. Energy is often defined as the ability to do work. Energy is also a scalar quantity.

Doing work involves a transfer of energy from one form to another. For example, when you use your muscles to move an object some of the stored energy in your body is transferred to kinetic (movement) energy.
The amount of work done tells you how much energy has been transferred from one form to another:

Work done = Energy transferred

Both work and energy have the same unit, the joule (J):

1 joule is the work done (or energy transferred) when a force of 1N moves through a distance of 1m (in the direction of the force).

A joule is a small unit of energy.

▷ Power

If two cars of the same weight drive up the same hill, they do the same amount of work. But what if one car is more powerful than the other?

Although the total energy transferred in reaching the top is the same for both cars, the more powerful car will get there **faster**.
Power is a measure of how fast work is done, or energy is transferred:

$$\text{Power, } P = \frac{\text{work done, } \Delta W}{\text{time taken, } \Delta t} = \frac{\text{energy transferred, } \Delta E}{\text{time taken, } \Delta t}$$

If the work rate is not steady, these equations give the **average** power.

The unit of power is the watt, W.
1 watt = 1 joule per second

In her muscles, stored energy is transferred to kinetic energy. The more powerful the athlete, the faster she reaches her top speed.

Combining the equations for power and work done gives us another equation for calculating power:

$$\text{Power} = \frac{\text{work done}}{\text{time taken}} = \frac{\text{force} \times \text{displacement}}{\text{time taken}}$$

$$= \text{force} \times \text{average velocity (in the direction of the force)}$$

Or in symbols:

$$P = F \times v$$
$$(\text{W}) \quad (\text{N}) \quad (\text{m s}^{-1})$$

Example 1
A man weighing 650 N runs up the hill in the diagram:
It takes him 15 s to reach the top.
Calculate:
a) the work he has done,
b) the power output of his legs.

a) The force is the man's weight. This acts vertically so the displacement needed is the **vertical** height climbed.

Work done = force × displacement in direction of force
$$= 650 \text{ N} \times 12 \text{ m}$$
$$= 7800 \text{ J}$$

b) **Power** $= \dfrac{\text{work done, } \Delta W}{\text{time taken, } \Delta t} = \dfrac{7800 \text{ J}}{15 \text{ s}} = 520 \text{ J s}^{-1} = \underline{520 \text{ W}}$

Example 2
A speed boat is travelling at a steady speed of 15 m s^{-1}.
The resistance to its motion as it moves through the water is 1800 N.
Calculate:
a) the force F, exerted by the boat's propeller on the water,
b) the power output of the engine.

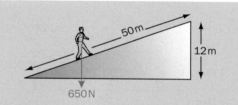

a) By Newton's third law, the force F, exerted **by the boat on the water** = force exerted **by the water on the boat**.
The boat is not accelerating so this force must be balanced by the resistance to motion. So $F = \underline{1800 \text{ N}}$

b) Power, $P = F \times v = 1800 \text{ N} \times 15 \text{ m s}^{-1} = \underline{27\,000 \text{ W}}$

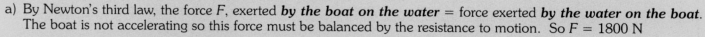

▶ Types of energy

How many different types of energy can you think of? Heat energy, light energy, chemical energy, kinetic energy, sound energy and electrical energy are just some of the labels you may have come across. In fact there are only two basic types of energy: kinetic energy and potential energy.

Kinetic energy (KE or E_k)

Kinetic energy is the energy an object has because of its **motion**.
We can calculate the kinetic energy an object has, using this equation:

Phiz using elastic PE on his Physics homework. What other energy types can you spot?

Kinetic energy	=	$\frac{1}{2}$ ×	mass ×	speed^2
(joules)			(kg)	(m s^{-1})^2

or $E_k = \frac{1}{2} m v^2$

Potential energy (PE or E_p)

'Potential' means 'stored'. Potential energy is the energy **stored** in an object due to its position, state or shape. Potential energy exists in various forms. Some examples are given in the table:

In mechanics we are usually concerned with **gravitational potential energy** (GPE). This is the energy gained by an object when it is lifted up against the force of gravity.
We can calculate the amount of gravitational potential energy that an object gains, using this equation:

Type of potential energy	Examples of where stored
Gravitational PE	Water held behind a dam
Chemical PE	Food and fuels
Elastic PE	Stretched spring
Electrical PE	Electric field
Nuclear PE	Particles in an atomic nucleus

Change in gravitational potential energy	=	mass ×	gravitational field strength ×	change in height
(joules)		(kg)	(N kg^{-1} *or* m s^{-2})	(m)

Or in symbols: $\Delta E_p = m\, g\, \Delta h$

Notice that this equation gives you the **change** in potential energy, not an absolute value. You can choose to take potential energy to be zero at any convenient point, usually ground level.

Where do we get these equations from?

KE equation

The diagram shows a force F acting on an object so that it accelerates from rest to a velocity v over a distance s.

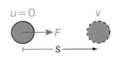

Using one of the motion equations (page 36):

$$v^2 = u^2 + 2as = 0 + 2as \qquad \therefore a = \frac{v^2}{2s}$$

$$
\begin{aligned}
\text{KE gained} = \text{work done} &= F \times s \\
&= ma \times s \quad \text{(since } F = ma\text{)} \\
&= m\frac{v^2}{2s} \times s \\
&= \tfrac{1}{2} m v^2
\end{aligned}
$$

PE equation

The diagram shows an object of mass m lifted vertically through a height Δh.

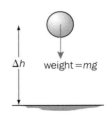

The force acting vertically is the object's weight (mg).

$$
\begin{aligned}
\text{PE gained} = \text{work done against gravity} \\
= \text{force} \times \text{distance} \\
= mg \times \Delta h
\end{aligned}
$$

▷ Interchange between KE and PE

Why do roller-coasters always start by lifting the cars to the highest point on the track? Is it just to build up your anticipation?

At the top of the track the cars have their maximum gravitational potential energy. A motor is needed to lift the cars up, but from then on they can freewheel along the track. As the cars accelerate downwards the stored potential energy is transferred to kinetic energy.

What happens to the speed of the cars as they climb up again? The cars slow down as some of the KE is transferred back to PE. There is a continual interchange between PE and KE during the ride.

You can test this for yourself using a heavy ball on a smooth curved track. Release the ball and its PE is transferred to KE as it accelerates. The ball continues to roll until all the KE is transferred back to PE again.

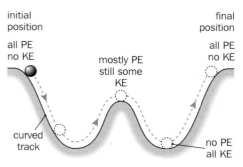

If there is no friction, how far would the ball travel along the track before it first stops moving?
When it stops it has no KE. All the energy must have been transferred back to PE. As this must be the same PE it started with, the ball would roll until it reaches a point on the track which has the same height as the release height (if there is no friction).

With no friction, the ball will roll until it reaches its initial height, regardless of the shape of the track

The interchange between PE and KE forms the basis of many examination questions. Here are two typical examples:

Example 3
A tennis ball is dropped from a height of 2.0 m.
Ignoring air resistance, at what speed does it hit the ground?
(Take $g = 10$ m s^{-2})

As the ball falls, its PE is transferred to KE:

$$\textbf{PE lost} = \textbf{KE gained}$$
$$m\ g\ \Delta h = \tfrac{1}{2}\ m\ v^2$$
$$\not{m} \times 10 \text{ m s}^{-2} \times 2.0 \text{ m} = \tfrac{1}{2} \times \not{m} \times v^2$$
$$\therefore\ v^2 = 40 \text{ m}^2 \text{ s}^{-2} \qquad \text{So}\quad v = \sqrt{40 \text{ m}^2 \text{ s}^{-2}} = \underline{6.3 \text{ m s}^{-1}}\ (2 \text{ s.f.})$$

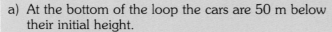

Notice that you do **not** need to know the mass of the ball as the mass m, cancels out on each side of the equation.

Example 4
In the roller-coaster in the diagram the cars are released from rest at a height of 50 m.
Ignoring friction, what is the speed of the cars at
(a) the bottom and (b) the top of the loop?
(Take $g = 10$ m s^{-2})

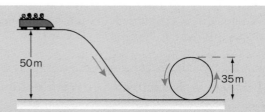

a) At the bottom of the loop the cars are 50 m below their initial height.

$$\textbf{PE lost} = \textbf{KE gained}$$
$$m\ g\ \Delta h = \tfrac{1}{2}\ m\ v^2$$
$$\not{m} \times 10 \text{ m s}^{-2} \times 50 \text{ m} = \tfrac{1}{2} \times \not{m} \times v^2$$
$$\therefore\ v^2 = 1000 \text{ m}^2 \text{ s}^{-2}$$
$$\text{So}\quad v = \sqrt{1000 \text{ m}^2 \text{ s}^{-2}} = \underline{32 \text{ m s}^{-1}}\ (2 \text{ s.f.})$$

b) At the top of the loop the cars are just 15 m below their initial height.

$$\textbf{PE lost} = \textbf{KE gained}$$
$$m\ g\ \Delta h = \tfrac{1}{2}\ m\ v^2$$
$$\not{m} \times 10 \text{ m s}^{-2} \times 15 \text{ m} = \tfrac{1}{2} \times \not{m} \times v^2$$
$$\therefore\ v^2 = 300 \text{ m}^2 \text{ s}^{-2}$$
$$\text{So}\quad v = \sqrt{300 \text{ m}^2 \text{ s}^{-2}} = \underline{17 \text{ m s}^{-1}}\ (2 \text{ s.f.})$$

Conservation of energy

On the previous page we looked at the interchange between kinetic energy and potential energy. But often kinetic energy is lost without any obvious increase in potential energy.

For example, what happens to the kinetic energy when a parachutist lands or a car crashes? Where does your kinetic energy go when a bicycle slows down when you stop pedalling?

In all of these cases the energy is transferred to the surroundings which become warmer. We say that the energy is **dissipated**.

In the case of the bicycle this is a gradual process through friction. In a car crash there is a sudden transfer that causes heating of the crumpled metal and the surrounding air:

The surroundings are often said to gain 'heat energy'. The correct term for this is **internal energy**. Internal energy is the name given to the total KE and PE of all the atoms or molecules of a substance. We will look at this in more detail in Chapter 24.

The main point here is that the energy does not just disappear. Energy cannot be used up. It is always transferred to other, often less obvious, forms. The **principle of conservation of energy** is one of the most fundamental rules in Physics:

> **Energy can be transferred from one form to another, but it cannot be created or destroyed.**
> **The total amount of energy always stays the same.**

You can solve many problems in mechanics by applying the principle of conservation of energy.
Always remember to include any work done or energy transferred to internal energy in overcoming frictional forces.
Friction is the most likely reason for apparent energy 'loss' from a system.

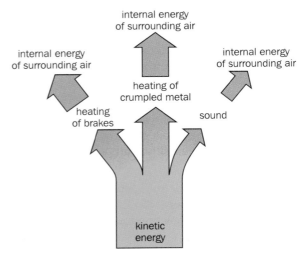

energy transfers in a car crash

An Energy Transfer Diagram, or 'Sankey' diagram of the energy transfers in a car crash

---

Example 5
A skier of mass 75 kg accelerates from rest down the slope in the diagram. At the bottom of the slope he is travelling at 40 m s^{-1}. What is the average frictional force opposing his motion down the slope? (Take $g = 10$ m s^{-2})

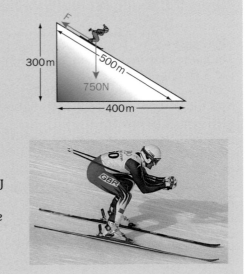

In travelling down the slope, the energy is conserved, so:
PE lost = KE gained + Work done against friction

PE lost $= m g \Delta h = 75$ kg $\times 10$ m s$^{-2} \times 300$ m $= 225\,000$ J
KE gained $= \frac{1}{2} m v^2 = \frac{1}{2} \times 75$ kg $\times (40$ m s$^{-1})^2 = 60\,000$ J
$\therefore$ Work done against friction $= 225\,000$ J $- 60\,000$ J $= 165\,000$ J

Work done against friction $=$ frictional force $\times$ distance in direction of force
$\qquad 165\,000$ J $= F \times 500$ m
$\qquad \therefore F = \dfrac{165\,000 \text{ J}}{500 \text{ m}} = \underline{330 \text{ N}}$ (2 s.f.)

▷ Energy crisis

We often hear about the global energy crisis. But if energy is always conserved, how can it be running out?
The problem is that as we 'use' energy in our everyday lives it is all eventually transferred to internal energy in our surroundings. It is then almost impossible to transfer back to any useful form.

For example, our cars are powered by the chemical potential energy stored in petrol. The engine transfers some of this to kinetic energy but the rest is 'wasted' as heat. As the car comes to a stop, its kinetic energy is also transferred to heat due to friction at the brakes and between the tyres and the road. The heat generated is all eventually transferred to the surrounding air.

So energy is not being used up, but it is being dissipated in the environment. This is why we need to conserve our limited supplies of fossil and nuclear fuels. The energy stored in these can be converted into a wide range of useful forms.
As these high grade energy sources run out, we will need to make more use of 'renewable' sources such as biomass, solar, geothermal, wind, wave, tidal and hydro-electric power (see page 250).

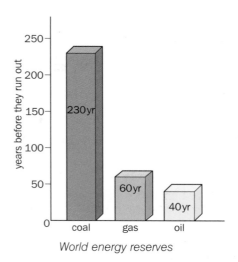

World energy reserves

▷ Efficiency

A machine is any device that transfers energy from one form to another. Cars, electric motors and our bodies are all examples of machines.
Unfortunately when energy is transferred, not all of it is transferred in a useful way. So what happens to the rest of the transferred energy? Usually some energy is 'wasted' as internal (heat) energy.

The proportion of energy that is **usefully** transferred is called the **efficiency** of the machine:

$$\text{efficiency} = \frac{\text{useful energy output}}{\text{total energy input}} = \frac{\text{useful power output}}{\text{total power input}}$$

Efficiency is a ratio. It has no units. Efficiency can also be expressed as a percentage, by multiplying by 100%.

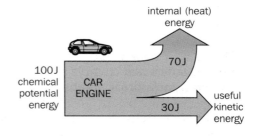

For every 100 J of energy in the fuel, only 30 joules are transferred usefully. The engine's efficiency is 0.30 or 30%.

Example 6
A water wheel is powered by 3600 kg of water falling through a height of 5.0 m each minute.
If the power output is 1200 W, what is the efficiency of the wheel?
(Take $g = 10$ m s^{-2})

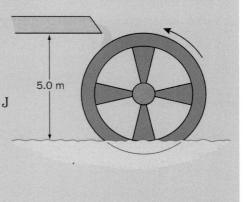

PE lost by falling water = Energy gained by the wheel

PE lost in 1 minute $= m\,g\,\Delta h = 3600$ kg $\times 10$ m s$^{-2} \times 5.0$ m $= 180\,000$ J

$\therefore$ Power provided $= \dfrac{\text{energy transferred, } \Delta E}{\text{time taken, } \Delta t} = \dfrac{180\,000 \text{ J}}{60 \text{ s}} = 3000$ W

Efficiency $= \dfrac{\text{power output}}{\text{power input}} = \dfrac{1200 \text{ W}}{3000 \text{ W}} = \underline{0.40}$ (or $\underline{40\%}$)

▷ Elastic and inelastic collisions

In Chapter 5 we saw that when objects collide, the total *momentum* is always conserved (if there is no external resultant force), so:

Total momentum before = Total momentum after

When we consider energy, the result may be different.
The *total* energy is also always conserved, but the kinetic energy may not be.
It depends on whether the collision is **elastic** or **inelastic**.

Elastic collisions

These are collisions in which kinetic energy is conserved:

Total KE before collision = Total KE after collision

In a gas, the collisions between the molecules are elastic.
What would happen if they weren't elastic? Repeated collisions would slow the gas molecules down, so they would then eventually settle at the bottom rather than filling their container!

Collisions between snooker balls are very nearly elastic.

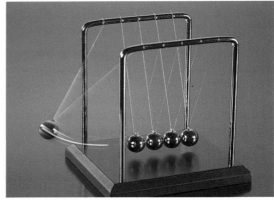

In this Newton's cradle the moving ball collides elastically with a stationary one of the same mass. The total KE and momentum are transferred from ball to ball.

Inelastic collisions

Most collisions are inelastic.
Some of the initial kinetic energy is apparently 'lost'.
It is transferred to other forms, usually internal (heat) energy.

For inelastic collisions:

Total KE before collision > Total KE after collision

Crash barriers and crumple zones of cars are specifically designed to collide *in*elastically, to absorb the kinetic energy in a crash.

In an inelastic collision, KE is 'lost'

Example 7
A gas molecule of mass 2.0×10^{-26} kg moving at 600 m s^{-1} collides with a stationary molecule of mass 10×10^{-26} kg.
The first molecule rebounds at 400 m s^{-1}.
Is this collision elastic or inelastic?

Taking motion to the right as positive:

Total momentum before collision = Total momentum after collision

$$(2.0 \times 10^{-26} \text{ kg} \times 600 \text{ m s}^{-1}) = (2.0 \times 10^{-26} \text{ kg} \times -400 \text{ m s}^{-1}) + (10 \times 10^{-26} \text{ kg} \times v)$$

$$\therefore \quad 1200 \text{ kg m s}^{-1} = -800 \text{ kg m s}^{-1} + (10 \text{ kg} \times v)$$

$$\therefore \quad 1200 \text{ kg m s}^{-1} + 800 \text{ kg m s}^{-1} = 10 \text{ kg} \times v$$

$$\therefore \quad v = \frac{2000 \text{ kg m s}^{-1}}{10 \text{ kg}} = 200 \text{ m s}^{-1}$$

Total KE *before* collision $= \frac{1}{2} m v^2 = \frac{1}{2} \times 2.0 \times 10^{-26}$ kg $\times (600$ m s$^{-1})^2 = 3.6 \times 10^{-21}$ J

Total KE *after* collision $= [\frac{1}{2} \times 2.0 \times 10^{-26}$ kg $\times (400$ m s$^{-1})^2] + [\frac{1}{2} \times 10 \times 10^{-26}$ kg $\times (200$ m s$^{-1})^2] = 3.6 \times 10^{-21}$ J

Since the total KE is the same before and after the collision, the collision is elastic.

Summary

Work done, W = force, F × displacement in the direction of the force, s
If the force acts at an angle θ to the displacement: $W = F \cos \theta \times s$

Energy is the ability to do work. Work and energy are measured in joules (J). Work done = Energy transferred.

Power is the rate of doing work. Power, $P = \dfrac{\text{work done}, \Delta W}{\text{time taken}, \Delta t} = \dfrac{\text{energy transferred}, \Delta E}{\text{time taken}, \Delta t}$ or $P = Fv$
1 Watt = $1\ \mathrm{J\ s^{-1}}$

The two types of mechanical energy are kinetic energy ($E_\mathrm{k} = \frac{1}{2} m v^2$) and potential energy ($\Delta E_\mathrm{p} = m g \Delta h$).
Energy is always conserved, though it is not always transferred in useful forms.

Efficiency $= \dfrac{\text{useful energy output}}{\text{total energy input}} = \dfrac{\text{useful power output}}{\text{total power input}}$ (× 100%)

If kinetic energy is conserved in a collision, the collision is elastic.
In inelastic collisions some of the initial kinetic energy is transferred to other forms.
Momentum is always conserved, if no resultant external force is acting.

▷ Questions

(Take $g = 10\ \mathrm{m\ s^{-2}}$)

1. Can you complete these sentences?
   a) .... is the ability to do work. Both work and energy are measured in ....
   b) 1 J is the work done when a force of .... moves through a distance of .... in the direction of the force.
   c) Power is a measure of the .... of energy transfer. It is measured in ....
      1 watt = 1 .... per ....
   d) The two main types of energy are .... energy and .... energy.
   e) The total KE and PE of the molecules of a substance is called its .... energy.
   f) In an elastic collision .... energy is conserved. If some energy is transferred to other forms a collision is described as ....

2. A cyclist is travelling along a level road at $8.0\ \mathrm{m\ s^{-1}}$. Her legs provide a forward force of 150 N. How much work does she do in 10 s?

3. A car with a 54 kW engine has a top speed of $30\ \mathrm{m\ s^{-1}}$ on a horizontal road. Calculate:
   a) the force driving the car forward at the top speed,
   b) the resistance to the car's motion at this speed.
      (Hint: When moving at its top speed the car has zero acceleration.)

4. A lift and passengers weigh 15 000 N. Ignoring friction, what is the power of the motor needed to move the lift up at a steady speed of $3.0\ \mathrm{m\ s^{-1}}$?

5. A cyclist of mass 100 kg is freewheeling down a hill inclined at 10° to the horizontal.
   He keeps his brakes on so that he travels at a steady speed of $6.0\ \mathrm{m\ s^{-1}}$. The brakes provide the only force opposing the motion.
   Draw a diagram showing the forces acting on the cyclist. Calculate:
   a) the component of his weight acting down the hill,
   b) the braking force,
   c) the work done by the brakes in 3 s.

6. A pump lifts 200 kg of water per minute through a vertical height of 15 m. Calculate the output power. Calculate the input power rating of the pump if it is
   a) 100% efficient,   b) 65% efficient.

7. A tennis ball of mass 60 g is dropped from a height of 1.5 m. It rebounds but loses 25% of its kinetic energy in the bounce.
   Ignoring any air resistance, calculate:
   a) the velocity at which the ball hits the ground,
   b) the velocity at which it leaves the ground,
   c) the height reached on the rebound.

8. A 10 kg child slides down a 3.0 m long slide inclined at 30° to the horizontal. A friction force of 35 N acts along the slide. Calculate:
   a) the potential energy lost in reaching the bottom,
   b) the work done against friction on the slide,
   c) the child's kinetic energy at the bottom of the slide,
   d) the child's velocity at the bottom of the slide.

Further questions on page 108.

7 Circular Motion

What do CD players, satellites, spin-dryers, fairground rides and the hammer thrower in the photograph have in common? They all use circular motion.

In this chapter you will learn:
- why an object moving in a circle must be accelerating,
- the equations we use to describe circular motion,
- how to use these equations with horizontal and with vertical circles.

What makes an object move in a circle?

Do you remember Newton's first law (see page 45)?
This says that an object continues to move in a **straight** line unless a resultant force acts on it.
So to make something move in a circle we need a force.

For example, the hammer thrower in the photograph makes the hammer move in a circle using the pull of the wire.

In which direction does the force act?

Your own experiences of circular motion may lead you to the wrong answer here.

Imagine yourself on the 'chairoplane' ride in the photograph:

What force do you feel as you swing round in a circle?
It *feels* as if you are being pushed outwards.
People often talk, *wrongly,* about an outwards or 'centrifugal' force.

In fact, the force on you is *in*wards!
Your body is trying to obey Newton's first law, and so your body tries to keep moving in a straight line.
What stops you going in a straight line is the chair pushing you *in*, *towards the centre of the circle.*

To make an object move in a circle you always need a resultant force towards the centre of the circle.

This is called a **centripetal force**.

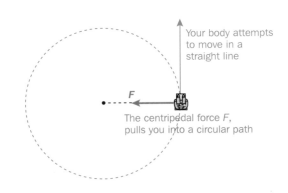

Your body attempts to move in a straight line

F

The centripedal force *F*, pulls you into a circular path

Although a centripetal force is needed to keep an object moving in a circle, it does **no** work on the object. Can you see why not?

At any point the object is moving in a direction along a tangent to the circle. The force is always at 90° to this, towards the centre of the circle.
So there is no movement in the direction of the force, and so no work is done.

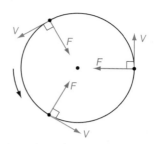

Force and velocity are always at right angles

What if the centripetal force stops?

Think about the hammer thrower again.
The centripetal force comes from the pull of the wire.
When the wire is released, the centripetal force suddenly stops.
What happens to the hammer?

Newton's first law gives us the answer. Without a force to keep changing its direction, an object will carry on moving in a straight line. This will be along a tangent to the circle.

So the hammer flies off in a straight line in the direction it was heading when it was released. You can see the importance of timing your release carefully!

Where does the centripetal force come from?

The centripetal force is not some new force acting on the object. Centripetal force is just the name we give to the resultant force acting on the object in a direction towards the centre of the circle. Here are some examples:

The Earth in orbit
The Earth orbits the Sun along an almost circular path.
What provides the centripetal force here?

The Sun's gravitational pull on the Earth provides the centripetal force that keeps us in orbit.
In a similar way, the Moon is kept in orbit by the gravitational pull of the Earth.

An electron orbiting the nucleus
An electron needs a centripetal force to keep it in orbit around the nucleus. What provides the centripetal force here?

The force towards the centre of the circle comes from the attraction between the positively-charged nucleus and the negatively-charged electron.

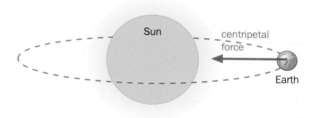

A car on a banked track
The diagram shows the forces acting on the fast moving car:
Which two of these forces contribute towards the centripetal force?

The normal reaction and the force of friction both have a component towards the centre of the circle.
These combine together to give the resultant centripetal force that is needed to make the car go round the curve.

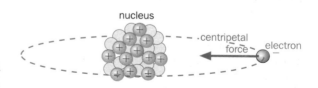
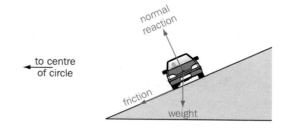

▶ Measuring rotation

Measuring angles

You will be used to measuring angles in degrees,
but angles can also be measured in another unit – the **radian**.
This is the unit we use for circular motion.

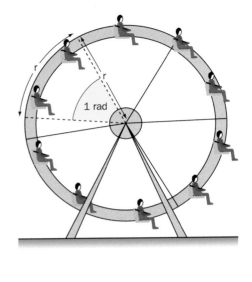

The diagram shows a Ferris wheel with 1 radian marked on it:
To turn through one radian you need to move a distance round
the circle equal to its radius, r.
Using the diagram, roughly how many radians are there in a circle?

We can calculate this number exactly using the definition
of the radian:

$$\text{angle } \theta \text{ in radians} = \frac{\text{length of arc, } s}{\text{radius, } r} \quad \text{or} \quad \theta = \frac{s}{r}$$

For a full circle (360°), the arc length is the circumference ($2\pi r$).

$\therefore$ Angle in radians $\theta = \dfrac{s}{r} = \dfrac{2\pi r}{r} = 2\pi \quad (\approx 6.28 \text{ rad})$

So:

$$360° = 2\pi \text{ radians}$$

Angles in radians (rad) are often written as multiples of π.

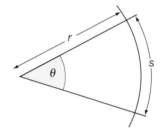

Look back at the Ferris wheel diagram.
We can now calculate how many degrees there are in 1 radian:

$1 \text{ radian} = \dfrac{360°}{2\pi} \approx \mathbf{57°}$

Example 1
A toy train moves round a circular track of radius 0.50 m.
a) How many radians has the train turned through in moving
    1.4 m along the track?
b) What is this angle in degrees?

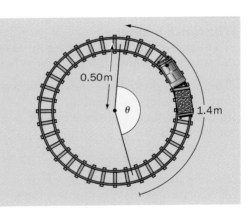

a) Angle in radians $= \dfrac{s}{r} = \dfrac{1.4 \text{ m}}{0.50 \text{ m}} = \underline{2.8 \text{ rad}} \quad$ (2 s.f.)

b) Angle in degrees $= 2.8 \text{ rad} \times \dfrac{360°}{2\pi \text{ rad}} = \underline{160°} \quad$ (2 s.f.)

Time period and frequency

For circular motion, the **time period T** is the time for
one complete rotation. Time period is measured in seconds.

The **frequency f** is the number of rotations per second:

$$\text{frequency, } f = \frac{\text{number of rotations}}{\text{time taken}}$$

$$T = \frac{1}{f} \quad \text{and} \quad f = \frac{1}{T}$$

Frequency is measured in units of per second (s^{-1}).
This unit is also given the special name **hertz (Hz)**.
One rotation per second = 1 Hz.

Measuring angular speed

The photo shows a girl on a roundabout:

How can we describe how fast she is moving?
There are two ways:

1. We can calculate her **linear speed, v** at any instant.
   This is the speed she would move off at, along a tangent
   to the circle, if there was no centripetal force.

2. We can also calculate the angle θ she turns through
   in a given time.
   This is called her **angular speed, ω**:

$$\text{angular speed, } \omega = \frac{\text{angle turned through, } \theta \text{ (rad)}}{\text{time taken, } t \text{ (s)}} \quad \text{or} \quad \omega = \frac{\theta}{t}$$

Angular speed is measured in radians per second (rad s^{-1}).
ω is sometimes called the 'angular velocity'.
It is also called the 'angular frequency'.

We can also calculate the angular speed if we know
the time period T or the frequency f of the motion.
One revolution is 2π radians. This takes T seconds.

So $\omega = \dfrac{\theta}{t} = \dfrac{2\pi}{T} = 2\pi f$ (since $1/T = f$), so: $\quad \boxed{\omega = \dfrac{2\pi}{T}} \quad$ and $\quad \boxed{\omega = 2\pi f}$

Linking v and ω

The skaters in the picture all turn through an angle of 360° (2π rad)
together. They all have the same **angular** speed, ω.
But which skater has the fastest **linear** speed v?

The skater on the outside covers the greatest distance.
She must move at a higher speed than those near the centre, to
keep up. For one revolution:

$$\text{speed, } v = \frac{\text{distance}}{\text{time}} = \frac{\text{circumference}}{\text{time period}} = \frac{2\pi r}{T}$$

But $\dfrac{2\pi}{T} = \omega$, so: $\quad \boxed{v = r\omega}$

So linear speed v increases with the radius r of the circle.

Example 2
The minute hand on a watch is 6.40 mm long. Calculate: (a) its frequency,
(b) its angular speed and (c) the speed of its free end.

a) Time period T for 1 revolution = 1 hour = 60×60 s = 3600 s.
   So $f = \dfrac{1}{T} = \dfrac{1}{3600 \text{ s}} = \underline{2.78 \times 10^{-4} \text{ Hz}}$ (3 s.f.)

b) Angular speed $\omega = 2\pi f = 2\pi \times 2.78 \times 10^{-4} \text{ Hz} = \underline{1.75 \times 10^{-3} \text{ rad s}^{-1}}$

c) Linear speed $v = r\omega = 6.40 \times 10^{-3} \text{ m} \times 1.75 \times 10^{-3} \text{ rad s}^{-1} = \underline{1.12 \times 10^{-5} \text{ m s}^{-1}}$

▷ Centripetal acceleration

How can you accelerate yet keep moving at constant speed?
The answer is to move in a circle!
Because your direction keeps changing, your *velocity* must also
be changing. This means that you are accelerating.
This is known as **centripetal acceleration**.

The fighter pilot in the photograph experiences very high
accelerations during a turn. This can reduce the blood flow
to the brain. The acceleration is sometimes measured in g's
where $1\,g$ is $9.8\ \text{m s}^{-2}$. Accelerations above $4\,g$ can lead to
tunnel vision and unconsciousness.

The faster the plane and the tighter the turn, the greater the
acceleration. In fact:

> **centripetal acceleration, a** $= \dfrac{\textbf{speed}^2}{\textbf{radius}}$ or $a = \dfrac{v^2}{r}$

Since $v = r\omega$,
we can also write $a = \dfrac{v^2}{r} = \dfrac{r\omega \times r\omega}{r} = r\omega^2$ so: $a = r\,\omega^2$

Remember that acceleration is a vector quantity.
Which direction is it in?
The acceleration is in the same direction as the centripetal force
that causes it. This is *towards the centre of the circle.*

Example 3
A car moves at $10\ \text{m s}^{-1}$ around a bend of radius 50 m.
What is its centripetal acceleration?

$$a = \frac{v^2}{r} = \frac{(10\ \text{m s}^{-1})^2}{50\ \text{m}} = \frac{100\ \text{m}^2\ \text{s}^{-2}}{50\ \text{m}} = \underline{2.0\ \text{m s}^{-2}}$$

▷ Centripetal force

Newton's second law tells us that: force = mass × acceleration

We have two equations for centripetal acceleration.
Multiplying them by the mass m of the object moving in a circle
gives us two equations for the resultant centripetal force:

$F = \dfrac{m\,v^2}{r}$ and $F = m\,r\,\omega^2$

Example 4
Helen Sharman was the first Briton in space. She orbited Earth
once every 91.8 minutes in the Mir space station.
Mir had a mass of 21 100 kg and an orbit radius of 6750 km.
Calculate a) Helen's angular speed in orbit,
          b) the centripetal force on Mir (provided by the pull of gravity).

a) Angular speed $\omega = \dfrac{\theta}{t} = \dfrac{2\pi}{T} = \dfrac{2\pi\ \text{rad}}{91.8 \times 60\ \text{s}} = \underline{1.14 \times 10^{-3}\ \text{rad s}^{-1}}$ *Helen Sharman with Russian astronauts*

b) Centripetal force $F = m\,r\,\omega^2 = 21100\ \text{kg} \times 6750 \times 10^3\ \text{m} \times (1.14 \times 10^{-3}\ \text{rad s}^{-1})^2 = \underline{1.85 \times 10^5\ \text{N}}$

▷ Moving in horizontal circles

The car in the photograph is skidding out of control as it tries
to turn a corner. Why?
There is not enough centripetal force to keep it moving in a circle.

The diagram shows the forces acting on a car cornering
on a level road. What provides the centripetal force?

The only force with a component towards the centre of the circle
is the frictional force between the tyres and the road.
So friction provides the centripetal force.

The higher the speed and the tighter the bend, the greater
the centripetal force needed.
We can use the equations on the opposite page to calculate
the frictional force needed to corner safely:

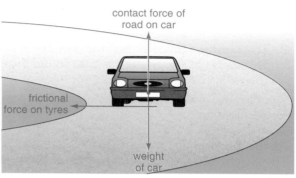

contact force of
road on car

frictional
force on tyres

weight
of car

Example 5
What is the centripetal force needed for a car of mass 1000 kg
to follow a curve of radius 50.0 m at 18.0 m s⁻¹ (≈ 40 mph)?

$$F = \frac{m\,v^2}{r} = \frac{1000 \text{ kg} \times (18.0 \text{ m s}^{-1})^2}{50.0 \text{ m}} = \underline{6480 \text{ N}}$$

Worn tyres and wet or icy road conditions will reduce the friction
available. How could you take the corner safely with less friction?
Slow down!

Circling at an angle

The diagram shows the forces acting on a person on a
'chairoplane' ride.
What provides the resultant centripetal force here?
It comes from the tension T in the chain. Although the tension is
not horizontal, it has a component towards the centre of the circle.
The component towards the centre is $T \cos \theta$.
So:

$$\text{Centripetal force} = T \cos \theta = \frac{m\,v^2}{r}$$

What about the vertical component of the tension?
This component balances the weight of the chair and rider.

What happens as the ride speeds up?
The chairs swing out further. Can you see why?

The faster the ride, the greater the centripetal force needed.
Swinging further out increases the component of tension acting
towards the centre of the circle.
The tension force must also increase to balance the weight.

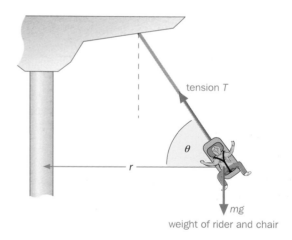

tension T

θ

r

mg
weight of rider and chair

Similar forces are needed for aircraft banking.
Why must the pilot tilt the plane to turn it in a circle?

The lift force on the plane always acts at 90° to the wings.
Tilting the plane gives a component of lift towards the centre of
the circle.
This is the resultant centripetal force needed to turn the plane.

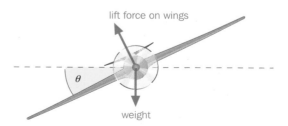

lift force on wings

θ

weight

▷ Moving in vertical circles

Have you ever looped the loop on a roller-coaster ride?
What stops you falling out? As long as the speed is high enough
you will stay in contact with your seat.
To understand why, we need to look at the resultant centripetal
force on the riders.

To keep you moving in a circle there must be a resultant
centripetal force ($= mv^2/r$) acting towards the centre of the circle.

What provides this force?
Only two forces act on a rider moving round the loop:

1. The rider's **weight mg**. This does not change.

2. The **contact force R** that the seat exerts on the rider.
   This varies in size as the car goes round the circle.

The diagram shows these forces at different positions
round the loop:

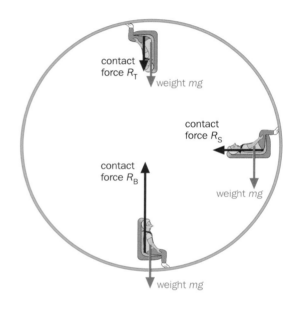

contact force R_T
weight mg

contact force R_S

contact force R_B

weight mg

weight mg

At the bottom
The weight and the contact force R_B are in opposite directions.
Which is the larger force? We need a resultant force towards the
centre, to provide the centripetal force. So the contact force must
be bigger than the weight.
At the bottom:
$$R_B - mg = \frac{m v^2}{r}$$

At the top
Both the weight and the contact force R_T act downwards towards
the centre of the circle. Together they provide the centripetal force:
$$R_T + mg = \frac{m v^2}{r}$$

At the side
The contact force R_S alone provides the centripetal force.
Can you see why? The weight acts vertically downwards
so it has no component towards the centre of the circle.
At the side:
$$R_S = \frac{m v^2}{r}$$

Can you see that the contact force is much larger at the bottom
than at the top of the loop? At the bottom of the loop the seat
pushes up on you with a large force. This is why you feel yourself
being pushed into your seat more at the bottom.

Failing to loop the loop!

As long as the ride is fast enough, it is impossible for you to fall out.
But what happens if the ride slows down?
If you are moving more slowly, the centripetal force needed is smaller.
This means that the contact force from the seat will be smaller.

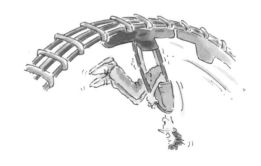

If the contact force at the top drops to zero, you will **just** make the loop.
Any slower than this and your weight will be larger than the
required centripetal force. If this happens you will fall out of your seat!

Example 6
A roller coaster has a vertical loop of radius 12 m.
The cars hurtle round the loop at 14 m s^{-1}. Calculate:
a) the centripetal force needed on a passenger of mass 60 kg,
b) the contact forces on the passenger at the top and bottom of the loop.
c) At which point in the loop does the passenger feel heaviest?

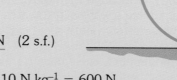

a) Centripetal force, $F = \dfrac{m\,v^2}{r} = \dfrac{60 \text{ kg} \times (14 \text{ m s}^{-1})^2}{12 \text{ m}} = \underline{980 \text{ N}}$ (2 s.f.)

b) Taking $g = 10$ N kg^{-1}, the passenger's weight $= mg = 60$ kg $\times$ 10 N kg^{-1} = 600 N
Using the notation on the opposite page,

At the top: $R_T + mg = \dfrac{m\,v^2}{r}$

$R_T + 600 \text{ N} = 980 \text{ N}$

$\therefore \ R_T = 980 \text{ N} - 600 \text{ N} = \underline{380 \text{ N}}$

At the bottom: $R_B - mg = \dfrac{m\,v^2}{r}$

$R_B - 600 \text{ N} = 980 \text{ N}$

$\therefore \ R_B = 980 \text{ N} + 600 \text{ N} = \underline{1580 \text{ N}}$

c) We judge our weight from the size of the contact force on us.
The passenger feels heaviest when the contact force is largest. This is at the bottom of the loop.

Example 7
What is the minimum speed for a roller coaster with a vertical
loop of radius 12 m?

At the top of the loop: $R_T + mg = \dfrac{m\,v^2}{r}$

When $R_T = 0$, $mg = \dfrac{m\,v^2}{r}$

Rearranging this gives: $v^2 = r\,g = 12 \text{ m} \times 10 \text{ m s}^{-2}$

$\therefore \ v = \sqrt{120 \text{ m}^2 \text{ s}^{-2}} = \underline{11 \text{ m s}^{-1}}$ (2 s.f.)

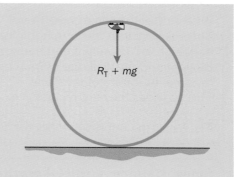

$R_T + mg$

▷ **Weightlessness**

To be truly 'weightless' you must be at a place where there is no
gravitational field at all.
So why do astronauts in orbit around the Earth appear to be
weightless?

We sense our weight from the size of the contact force pushing
against us.
Imagine standing in a stationary lift. The upward contact force
that you feel on your feet equals your weight downwards.

But what if the cable snaps? Both you and the lift fall freely with
the same acceleration due to gravity. You feel weightless as you
no longer feel the floor pushing up on you.

An astronaut in orbit is like a person in a free-falling lift.
The astronaut feels weightless because there is no contact force
between her and the spacecraft.
The spacecraft and the astronaut are both falling freely around the
Earth (see page 82) with the same centripetal acceleration.

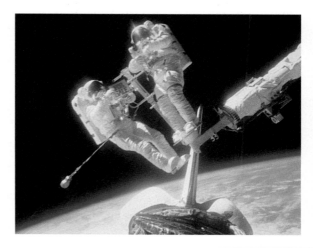

▷ Physics at work: Circular motion

Spin-dryer

A spin-dryer removes excess water from clothing by rotating a perforated drum at high speed.
The water is thrown out through the holes.
But if the centripetal force always acts towards the centre of the circle, why is the water thrown out?

The clothes keep moving in a circle because the contact force of the drum provides the centripetal force.
But the water droplets can pass through the holes in the drum.
The drum then exerts no force on them.
So the water droplets obey Newton's first law.
They carry on moving in a straight line.

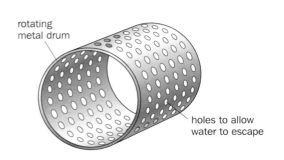

rotating metal drum

holes to allow water to escape

Bobsleigh bends

Why does a bobsleigh move up the wall of the run when it goes round a corner?
There must be a resultant centripetal force on the bobsleigh for it to follow a circular path.

Where does this force come from?
There is very little friction on the ice so the main forces on the bobsleigh are its weight and the normal contact force.
By going up the wall, the normal contact force has a component towards the centre of the circle.
This provides the centripetal force.

The faster the bobsleigh takes the bend, the higher it goes.

normal contact force

weight

Space stations: artificial gravity!

Being weightless in space looks like fun but how does it affect the human body?
Our bodies are designed to work under the force of gravity.
Astronauts' muscles get smaller and their bones get weaker when they are not used to support body weight.
Body fluids are affected too. Astronauts often complain of blocked sinuses and congestion. Spending too long in a weightless environment can damage your health!

Astronauts are spending longer periods living and working in space. So how can we overcome the health risks?

One way is to create 'artificial gravity' on a space station.
How does this work?
Artificial gravity can be produced by having a doughnut-shaped space station spinning about its central axis.
An astronaut on the space station feels the centripetal force exerted on him by the rim.
An astronaut in the position shown feels a force 'upwards' from the 'floor'. This gives him the impression of weight.

The faster the station spins and the larger its diameter the greater the artificial gravity produced.

Summary

To move an object in a circle there must be a resultant force on it, towards the centre of the circle.

This is called the centripetal force: $F = \dfrac{m v^2}{r}$ or $F = m r \omega^2$

An object moving at steady speed in a circle is accelerating because its direction keeps changing.

This centripetal acceleration, a, is towards the centre of the circle $a = \dfrac{v^2}{r}$ or $a = r \omega^2$

Angles in circular motion are measured in radians (2π radians $= 360°$; 1 radian $\approx 57°$).

Angular speed ω is the angle turned through per second: $\omega = \dfrac{\theta}{t}$

Angular speed ω and linear speed v are linked by the equation: $v = r \omega$

Frequency f is the number of rotations per second (in Hz). Time period T is the time taken for one rotation.

$$\omega = 2\pi f \qquad \omega = \dfrac{2\pi}{T} \qquad T = \dfrac{1}{f} \qquad f = \dfrac{1}{T}$$

▶ Questions

1. Can you complete these sentences?
   a) An object cannot move in a circle unless there is a resultant force acting .... the centre of the circle. This is called a .... force.
   If this force is removed, the object will continue moving in a .... line, because of Newton's .... law.
   b) The centripetal force causes a centripetal .... The bigger the linear .... (in m s⁻¹) and the smaller the .... of the circle, the bigger the acceleration.
   c) The number of rotations in one second is known as the .... This is measured in ....
   The time for one rotation is called the ....
   d) One revolution is 360° or .... radians.

2. Convert these angles into radians:
   360°, 180°, 90°, 45°, 30°, 1°.

3. Convert these angles into degrees:
   2π rad, $\pi/2$ rad, $\pi/3$ rad, 1 rad.

4. A car wheel turns through 6 radians in 0.2 seconds. What is its angular speed?

5. A spin dryer whirls clothes at an angular speed of 85 rad s⁻¹. The drum has a radius of 0.20 m. Calculate the speed of the clothes.

6. Complete this table:

Period (s)	Frequency (Hz)	Angular speed (rad s⁻¹)
	25	
4.2		
		12

7. When a CD rotates at an angular speed of 10.5 rad s⁻¹, how long does one revolution take?

8. A car of mass 800 kg moves in a circle of radius 30 m at a speed of 8.0 m s⁻¹. Calculate:
   a) its centripetal acceleration,
   b) the centripetal force acting.

9.

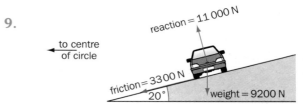

The diagram shows the forces on a car on a banked track. What is the resultant centripetal force?

10. The Earth takes one year to orbit the Sun along a path of radius 1.5×10^{11} m. Calculate:
    a) the frequency of the Earth's orbit,
    b) the Earth's angular speed.
    c) At what linear speed is the Earth moving?

11. A pilot has a weight of 800 N. He flies his plane at 60 m s⁻¹ in a vertical circle of radius 100 m.
    a) Calculate the centripetal force on the pilot.
    b) Draw a diagram to show the two forces on the pilot at (i) the top and (ii) the bottom of the loop.
    c) What is the contact force of the seat on the pilot at (i) the top and (ii) the bottom of the loop?
    d) Express your answers to (c) as multiples of the pilot's weight.

Further questions on page 109.

8 Gravitational Forces and Fields

Gravity is something we take for granted. It seems obvious to us that a dropped object will fall. But why? What is gravity? How do we explain it?
Isaac Newton is credited with 'discovering' gravity when an apple fell on his head. He suggested that the apple fell due to a force of attraction between the apple and the Earth.

One of Newton's greatest achievements was to extend this idea to *all* objects that have mass. He realised that *all masses attract each other with a gravitational force.*

You know that gravity is pulling you towards the Earth as you read this. But did you realise that there is also a small force of attraction between you and this book (and *every* other object with mass in the Universe for that matter!)?

In this chapter you will learn:
* how to calculate the gravitational force,
* what we mean by gravitational field,
* about the motion of satellites in orbit.

▷ Gravitational force

All objects with mass attract each other with a gravitational force. The size of the force between any two objects depends on their masses and how far apart they are.
We can calculate the force F, between two objects of mass m_1 and m_2, using Newton's law of gravitation:

$$F = \frac{G\, m_1\, m_2}{r^2}$$

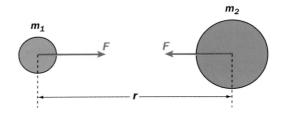

Newton wrote this equation for point masses. However we can use the law with real objects if we assume that the mass of each object is concentrated at its centre of mass (see page 29).
The distance r is measured between the centres of mass.

G is a constant of proportionality known as the **gravitational constant**. G has a value of 6.67×10^{-11} **N m^2 kg^{-2}**.

This is a very small number. What does this tell us about the size of gravitational forces?
Gravitational forces are very weak unless we are looking at objects with enormous mass such as stars and planets.

gravitational force of the Earth on Phiz

gravitational force of Phiz on the Earth

Remember that gravitational force is a mutual attraction. You attract the Earth with the same force that the Earth attracts you! However this force has more effect on you, because you are much lighter than the Earth.
Which of Newton's laws of motion is about this idea of equal but opposite forces? (See page 48.)

An inverse square relationship

Newton's law of gravitation is an example of an **inverse square law**.
Inverse means that as the separation of the masses **increases**,
the gravitational force **decreases**.
In this case the force decreases in proportion to the **square** of the
distance.

So: $2 \times$ distance   gives $\frac{1}{4} \times$ gravitational force

   $3 \times$ distance   gives $\frac{1}{9} \times$ gravitational force

   $10 \times$ distance   gives $\frac{1}{100} \times$ gravitational force

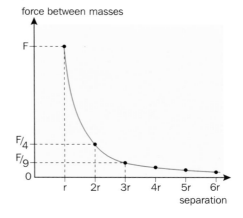

force between masses

Example 1
The gravitational force of attraction between two marbles placed with
their centres 1.0 m apart is 8.00×10^{-14} N.
What would be the force of attraction if they were placed 4.0 m apart?

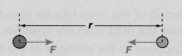

The separation is 4 times as great so the force must fall to $\frac{1}{(4)^2}$ or $\frac{1}{16}$th of the original force.

$\therefore$ New force of attraction $= \frac{1}{16} \times 8.00 \times 10^{-14}$ N $= \underline{5.0 \times 10^{-15}$ N} (2 s.f.)

Example 2
The Moon orbits the Earth along a path of radius 3.84×10^8 m.
The mass of the Moon, M_M, is 7.35×10^{22} kg.
The Earth's mass, M_E, is 6.00×10^{24} kg.
$G = 6.67 \times 10^{-11}$ N m^2 kg^{-2}

a) The gravitational force of attraction between the Earth and the
   Moon keeps the Moon in orbit. Calculate the size of this force.

b) A rocket of mass 42 000 kg is fired from Earth to the Moon.
   What is the net gravitational force on the rocket when it is
   3.00×10^8 m from the centre of the Earth?

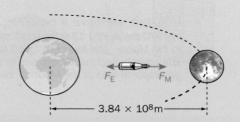

a) $F = \dfrac{G\,M_E\,M_M}{r^2} = \dfrac{6.67 \times 10^{-11} \times 6.00 \times 10^{24} \text{ kg} \times 7.35 \times 10^{22} \text{ kg}}{(3.84 \times 10^8 \text{ m})^2} = 1.99 \times 10^{20}$ N   (3 s.f.)

b) Gravitational force between rocket and Earth,

$F_E = \dfrac{G\,M_E\,m}{r^2} = \dfrac{6.67 \times 10^{-11} \times 6.00 \times 10^{24} \text{ kg} \times 42\,000 \text{ kg}}{(3.00 \times 10^8 \text{ m})^2} = 187$ N

Gravitational force between rocket and Moon,

$F_M = \dfrac{G\,M_M\,m}{r^2} = \dfrac{6.67 \times 10^{-11} \times 7.35 \times 10^{22} \text{ kg} \times 42\,000 \text{ kg}}{(3.84 \times 10^8 \text{ m} - 3.00 \times 10^8 \text{ m})^2} = 29.2$ N

The net force on the rocket is the vector sum of these two forces,

$\therefore$ Net force $= 187$ N $- 29.2$ N $= \underline{158 \text{ N towards the Earth}}$ (3 s.f.)

At some point on its journey the net force on the rocket will be zero. At this point $F_E = F_M$.
Is this point closer or further from the Moon?

In fact, the forces balance at 3.45×10^8 m from Earth. Try working this out for yourself.

▷ Satellites

Have you ever had the feeling that you were being watched?
Well you'd be right! Several thousand **artificial satellites** circle
the Earth. These 'eyes in the sky' are continually watching over us.

Can you name our oldest satellite?
The original Earth satellite is the Moon. This is a **natural satellite**.
A satellite is any object held in orbit around a larger one by
gravitational attraction. The Earth itself is a satellite of the Sun.

Artificial satellites have many uses.
Observation satellites monitor the weather, map changes in land
use and vegetation, track pollution and watch over military targets.
Satellites are also used for space observation.
Orbiting telescopes can probe deep into space without interference
from the Earth's atmosphere.

We also increasingly rely on satellites for navigation and global
communications. Satellites are big business.

View from a weather satellite (in 'false colour')

Into orbit: falling through space

Why do satellites stay in orbit rather than fall back to Earth?
In fact, satellites are **continually falling**.
A rocket engine carries a satellite to the correct height and into a
path parallel to the Earth's surface. The engines are then stopped.
The only force then acting is the Earth's gravitational pull, so the
satellite goes into free fall.

As it was initially moving parallel to the Earth's surface, the satellite
falls along a curved path, like a projectile (see page 40).
As the Earth curves away beneath it, the satellite never hits the
ground, but continues round its orbit.
The satellite must move at exactly the right velocity for its orbit.

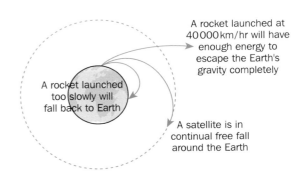

A rocket launched at 40 000 km/hr will have enough energy to escape the Earth's gravity completely

A rocket launched too slowly will fall back to Earth

A satellite is in continual free fall around the Earth

Types of orbit

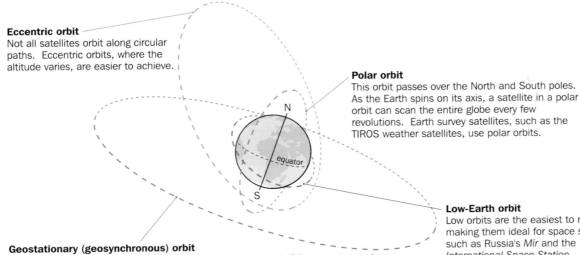

Eccentric orbit
Not all satellites orbit along circular
paths. Eccentric orbits, where the
altitude varies, are easier to achieve.

Polar orbit
This orbit passes over the North and South poles.
As the Earth spins on its axis, a satellite in a polar
orbit can scan the entire globe every few
revolutions. Earth survey satellites, such as the
TIROS weather satellites, use polar orbits.

Low-Earth orbit
Low orbits are the easiest to reach,
making them ideal for space stations
such as Russia's *Mir* and the
International Space Station.

Geostationary (geosynchronous) orbit
A satellite 35 900 km above the Earth's equator takes exactly 24 hours to complete
one orbit. As the Earth spins, the satellite appears to stay fixed in the sky.
Geostationary orbits are used for communications satellites such as the INTELSAT
network. The METEOSAT weather satellites are also placed in geostationary orbit
to continuously monitor large areas of the globe.

Satellite calculations

Can you remember the equations for circular motion?
If not, look back at the previous chapter now (page 72).
For calculations on the motion of satellites you will need to combine
the equations for gravitation with those for circular motion.

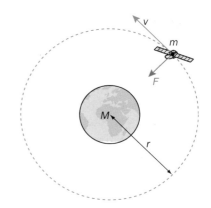

A centripetal force is needed to keep a satellite moving along a
circular path. Where does this force come from?
The only force acting on the satellite is Earth's gravity. The centripetal
force is provided by this gravitational attraction. For a satellite of
mass m in an orbit of radius r and velocity v about a planet of mass M:

Gravitational force of attraction = mass × centripetal acceleration

$$\frac{GMm}{r^2} = m \times \frac{v^2}{r}$$

Substituting $g = \dfrac{GM}{r^2}$ (from page 81) gives:

$$\not{m}g = \not{m}\frac{v^2}{r} \qquad \therefore \qquad \boxed{g = \frac{v^2}{r}}$$

You will find these equations very useful for solving satellite problems.

Example 5
A spaceship orbits the Moon travelling at 1460 m s^{-1}. How high is it
above the Moon's surface? The Moon has a mass of 7.35×10^{22} kg
and a radius of 1.74×10^6 m. ($G = 6.67 \times 10^{-11}$ N m^2 kg^{-2})

Gravitational force of attraction = mass × centripetal acceleration

$$\frac{GM\not{m}}{\not{r^2}} = \not{m} \times \frac{v^2}{\not{r}}$$

Cancelling, and rearranging gives: $\quad r = \dfrac{GM}{v^2} = \dfrac{6.67 \times 10^{-11} \times 7.35 \times 10^{22} \text{ kg}}{(1460 \text{ m s}^{-1})^2} = 2.30 \times 10^6$ m

Remember r is measured from the centre of mass,
$\therefore$ height above the surface $= 2.30 \times 10^6$ m $- 1.74 \times 10^6$ m $= \underline{5.60 \times 10^5 \text{ m}}$ (3 s.f.)

Example 6
A geostationary satellite must orbit the Earth along a path of
radius 4.23×10^7 m. Use this information to calculate:
a) the speed of the satellite,
b) the gravitational field strength at this height, and
c) the mass of the Earth.
($G = 6.67 \times 10^{-11}$ N m^2 kg^{-2})

a) For a geostationary orbit the period of rotation, $T = 24$ hours $= 24 \times 60 \times 60$ s $= 86\,400$ s
Circumference of orbit $= 2\pi r$

$$\textbf{Speed} = \frac{\textbf{distance}}{\textbf{time}} = \frac{2\pi r}{T} = \frac{2\pi \times 4.23 \times 10^7 \text{ m}}{86\,400 \text{ s}} = \underline{3080 \text{ m s}^{-1}} \text{ (3 s.f.)} \text{ (about 6000 mph)}$$

b) Gravitational field strength, $\boldsymbol{g} = \dfrac{v^2}{r} = \dfrac{(3080 \text{ m s}^{-1})^2}{4.23 \times 10^7 \text{ m}} = \underline{0.224 \text{ N kg}^{-1}} \text{ (3 s.f.)}$

c) $\boldsymbol{g} = \dfrac{GM}{r^2}$ and so: $\quad M = \dfrac{gr^2}{G} = \dfrac{0.224 \text{ N kg}^{-1} \times (4.23 \times 10^7 \text{ m})^2}{6.67 \times 10^{-11}} = \underline{6.01 \times 10^{24} \text{ kg}} \text{ (3 s.f.)}$

▷ Physics at work: Satellites

Hubble Space Telescope (HST)

The Hubble telescope was launched into low-Earth orbit in 1990.
At its altitude of 600 km it orbits the Earth once every 97 min.
Power is provided by an array of solar panels.
A system of gyroscopes allows astronomers to point the telescope in the right direction.

Its main mirror is just 2.4 m across and yet it produces images with far better resolution than much larger ground-based telescopes.
How is this possible?
In its position in space it receives light from the faintest stars without the absorption or distortion caused by the Earth's atmosphere.

HST images are helping scientists to improve estimates of the age of the Universe (see page 158).
Observations of distant galaxies are providing evidence for the existence of black holes.
Its wide-field planetary camera is also providing high quality images of planets and other objects in our solar system.

Shuttle astronauts successfully repairing the Hubble telescope's flawed main mirror in 1993

Laboratories in space

Construction of the International Space Station (ISS) started in 1998. 16 countries are working in partnership to create the largest spacecraft ever built. ISS is a multi-module design. It is being assembled in orbit, 400 km above the Earth.
Each module is launched separately using the US Space Shuttle, and Russian Proton and Soyuz rockets.

Once completed the space station will house a permanent crew of 7 working in six laboratories.
They will perform long-duration experiments in areas including materials and life sciences and medical research.
But why not carry out this research in ground-based laboratories?
Scientists hope that the 'free fall' environment will allow them to produce materials and pharmaceuticals with far greater purity than is possible on Earth.

Astronauts gaining operational experience aboard Russia's Mir space station. Mir was the world's first permanent space station

Global Positioning System (GPS)

Some cars now have navigation systems. How do these work?

A network of 24 satellites orbiting 17 500 km above Earth is continuously transmitting radio time signals.
A computer in the car or in a hand-set picks up these time signals.
The computer calculates the time taken for a satellite signal to reach it. By taking readings from four satellites the computer can quickly calculate its own position on the Earth.

Ships, aircraft and even hikers can use GPS for navigation.
Civilian hand-sets are accurate to within 100 m anywhere on Earth.
The system provides the US military with information accurate to within an amazing 1.5 m!

One of 24 NAVSTAR satellites in the GPS network

▷ Physics at work: Gravitational pull

Reaching Saturn

The diagram shows the flight path for Cassini, a probe launched in 1997 on a mission to study Saturn. Why does it take such a circuitous route?

Probes use the gravitational pull of other planets to swing themselves towards their target:

At each planetary fly-by, a 'slingshot' effect increases the probe's speed.

Fly-bys of Venus, Earth and Jupiter are needed to gain enough speed to overcome the enormous gravitational pull of the Sun and eventually reach Saturn.

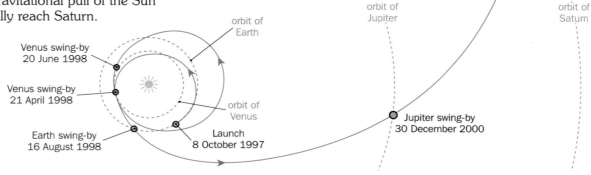

Saturn arrival
1 July 2004

orbit of Jupiter

orbit of Saturn

orbit of Earth

Venus swing-by
20 June 1998

Venus swing-by
21 April 1998

orbit of Venus

Earth swing-by
16 August 1998

Launch
8 October 1997

Jupiter swing-by
30 December 2000

The Big Crunch?

The Universe is thought to have been created in the 'Big Bang' around 15 000 million years ago. It has been expanding ever since (see page 158). But will this expansion go on forever?

To answer this question we need to know the amount of mass in the Universe.

Scientists have shown that there is not enough visible matter in the Universe to create enough gravitational attraction to stop the expansion. The result would be an '**open universe**' – one that expands forever.

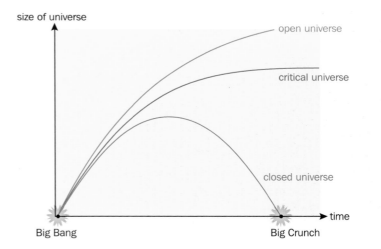

size of universe

open universe

critical universe

closed universe

Big Bang

Big Crunch

time

But is there more mass out there than we can see? Many scientists believe that the Universe contains lots of invisible *'dark matter'*.

Evidence for its existence comes from the gravitational effect of its mass on visible galaxies. With just enough of this dark matter we would have a '**critical universe**' – one that eventually stops expanding at infinite time.

A universe with more mass than this would create enough gravitational pull to eventually stop the expansion and then put it into reverse. The universe would contract back in on itself. This is the '**closed universe**' model. This would eventually lead to the Big Crunch!

What would happen then? One theory is that another Big Bang would start the cycle off again.

▷ Gravitational potential, V

You have come across the word 'potential' before when we calculated changes in gravitational potential energy (ΔE_P) in Chapter 6.
Do you remember the equation for this? (See page 62.)
Close to the Earth's surface $\Delta E_P = m g \Delta h$.
For this we assumed that g is a constant (= 9.81 N kg^{-1}).

However, when you calculate energy changes over large distances in space you cannot use this equation. Can you see why?
In space, the value of g changes as the distance from Earth changes.

So instead we use a quantity called **gravitational potential** (given the symbol V). The gravitational potential at any point tells us the potential energy *of each kilogram of mass* at that point.

The potential energy depends on the mass M which causes the gravitational field, and the distance r from the centre of mass:

$$V = -\frac{GM}{r}$$

G is the gravitational constant.
V is measured in **joules per kilogram** (J kg^{-1}). Like energy, gravitational potential is a scalar quantity. It has magnitude only.

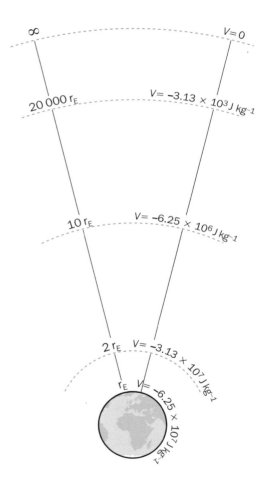

Why is V negative?

In Chapter 6 we said that you can choose the point at which potential energy is zero. This is usually ground level.

But what if we are comparing the potentials of a person standing on Earth and a person on Mars? What common point could we take as the zero here?
Gravitational potential is defined so that $V = 0$ **at an infinite distance away.**
But potential energy increases the higher we lift an object, ie. the further we are from Earth. So how can V keep increasing and eventually reach zero? The answer is that V must have negative values.

Gravitational potential, V, at a point is defined as
the work done against gravity when a 1 kg mass is brought from infinity to that point.
This must be negative as gravity pulls the masses together. We only do work *against* gravity if the 1 kg mass is moved further away.

You can see from the diagram that V has its most negative value at the planet's surface. It becomes less negative as we move higher.
You can check these values using the equation for V.

Example 7
Calculate the gravitational potential V, at 4.50×10^{20} m from the centre of a star of mass 8.45×10^{40} kg.
($G = 6.67 \times 10^{-11}$ N m^2 kg^{-2})

$$V = -\frac{GM}{r} = -\frac{6.67 \times 10^{-11} \text{ N m}^2 \text{ kg}^{-2} \times 8.45 \times 10^{40} \text{ kg}}{4.50 \times 10^{20} \text{ m}} = \underline{-1.25 \times 10^{10} \text{ J kg}^{-1}} \quad \text{(3 s.f.)}$$

• $V = ?$

←————→
4.50×10^{20} m

Equipotentials

All points at the same height above the Earth must have the same gravitational potential. A line joining all the points with the same potential is called an **equipotential**.
This is like a contour line on a map.

The diagram shows the equipotential surfaces around the Earth:

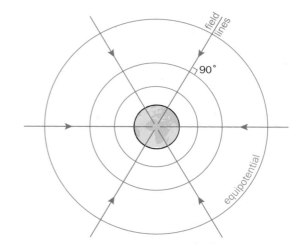

For a radial field like this the equipotentials are concentric spheres. The gravitational field lines cross the equipotential surfaces at right angles. This means that the gravitational force acts at 90° to the equipotentials.
If an object such as a satellite moves along an equipotential its potential energy does not change. As there is no movement in the direction of the force, no work is done.

Energy changes

So how do we calculate the work done, or energy change, when an object moves from one point in a field to another?
First we need to find the change in gravitational potential.
This gives us the change in energy *per kilogram*. So to find the total energy change we need to multiply by the mass of the object:

> **Energy change** (J) = **change in gravitational potential** (J kg^{-1}) × **mass** (kg)

Example 8
Calculate the energy change when a rocket of mass 50 000 kg moves from the surface to a height of 3.50×10^6 m above the Earth.
The Earth has a mass of 6.00×10^{24} kg and a radius of 6.40×10^6 m.
($G = 6.67 \times 10^{-11}$ N m^2 kg^{-2})

Remembering that the distance r is measured from the centre of mass:

V at the surface $= -\dfrac{GM}{r} = -\dfrac{6.67 \times 10^{-11}\text{ N m}^2\text{ kg}^{-2} \times 6.00 \times 10^{24}\text{ kg}}{6.40 \times 10^6\text{ m}} = -6.25 \times 10^7$ J kg^{-1}

V at 3.50×10^6 m $= -\dfrac{GM}{r} = -\dfrac{6.67 \times 10^{-11}\text{ N m}^2\text{ kg}^{-2} \times 6.00 \times 10^{24}\text{ kg}}{(6.40 \times 10^6 + 3.50 \times 10^6)\text{ m}} = -4.04 \times 10^7$ J kg^{-1}

∴ Change in potential, $\Delta V = (-4.04 \times 10^7$ J kg$^{-1}) - (-6.25 \times 10^7$ J kg$^{-1}) = 2.21 \times 10^7$ J kg^{-1}

∴ Total energy change $= \Delta V \times$ mass of rocket $= 2.21 \times 10^7$ J kg$^{-1} \times 50\,000$ kg $= \underline{1.11 \times 10^{12}\text{ J}}$ (3 s.f.)
The energy change is positive. Work must be done against gravity to move the rocket away from Earth.

Linking V and g

The graph shows the relationship between gravitational potential V, and distance, x, from the centre of the Earth:
Notice how the gradient gradually decreases.
The value of the gradient at any point gives the value of g, the gravitational field strength, at that distance:

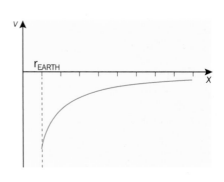

> $g = -\dfrac{\Delta V}{\Delta x}$ = potential gradient

We will look at potential again when we study electric fields in Chapter 21.

Summary

All masses attract each other with a gravitational force. Force $F = \dfrac{G\,m_1\,m_2}{r^2}$

The universal constant of gravitation, $G = 6.67 \times 10^{-11}$ N m^2 kg^{-2}

The **gravitational field strength g**,
gives the force acting on each kilogram of mass in a gravitational field: $g = \dfrac{F}{m}$ or $F = mg$
g is a vector quantity. It is measured in N kg^{-1}.

In a radial field: $g = \dfrac{GM}{r^2}$

The **gravitational potential V**,
gives the potential energy of each kilogram of mass in a gravitational field.
V is a scalar quantity. It is measured in J kg^{-1}.

In a radial field: $V = -\dfrac{GM}{r}$

V is taken to be zero at infinity. Change in energy $=$ change in gravitational potential $\times$ mass

▶ Questions

You will need the following data:

$G = 6.67 \times 10^{-11}$ N m^2 kg^{-2}
$g = 9.81$ N kg^{-1} at the Earth's surface
Mass of the Earth $= 6.00 \times 10^{24}$ kg
Radius of the Earth $= 6.4 \times 10^{6}$ m
Mass of the Sun $= 2.00 \times 10^{30}$ kg

1. Can you complete these sentences?
   a) The gravitational force between two objects depends on their .... and their ....
   b) Newton's law of gravitation is an example of an inverse .... relationship.
   If the separation doubles, the force ....
   c) A gravitational .... is a region in which a mass feels a gravitational force.
   Field lines can indicate the .... and the .... of a field.
   Round the Earth, the shape of the gravitational field is ....
   d) The gravitational field strength, g (in N kg^{-1}) has the same value as the .... due to gravity (in m s^{-2}) at that point.
   The value of g on the surface of the Earth is .... N kg^{-1}.
   e) A satellite that takes *exactly* 24 hours to complete one orbit of the Earth is described as ....
   f) A line joining all points with the same potential is called an ....
   g) To find the energy change when an object moves from one point in a field to another we multiply the change in .... by the .... of the object.

2. a) Using $W = mg$ calculate the weight of a 2.0 kg mass on Earth.
   b) Using Newton's law of gravitation calculate the gravitational force on a 2.0 kg mass on the Earth's surface.
   c) What do you notice about your answers to parts (a) and (b)?

3. Calculate the gravitational force between
   a) two protons of mass 1.67×10^{-27} kg separated by 1.40×10^{-14} m,
   b) a dog of mass 35 kg in the UK and a 60 kg kangaroo on the other side of the world in Australia,

   c) two stars of mass 4.00×10^{33} kg and 6.00×10^{30} kg separated by 3.65×10^{20} m.

4. The Earth orbits the Sun along a path of radius 1.50×10^{11} m.
   a) Find the gravitational force exerted by the Earth on the Sun.
   b) Saturn has a mass 95 times the Earth's and an orbit radius 9.5 times the Earth's.
   Compared to Earth, does it exert a larger or smaller force on the Sun?

5. Two stars of mass 6.2×10^{32} kg and M kg are 1.4×10^{16} m apart. The net gravitational force is zero at P, 1.5×10^{15} m from M along the line between the two stars. What is the value of M?

6. a) Find g at 200 000 m above the Earth's surface.
   b) An astronaut has a mass of 70 kg.
      What is her weight (i) on Earth and (ii) at 200 000 m?

7. a) Calculate the value of g at points R, $2R$, $3R$, $4R$ and $5R$ from the centre of the Earth, where R is the Earth's radius.
   b) Use your values from part (a) to plot a graph of g against distance from the Earth, starting at the Earth's surface:

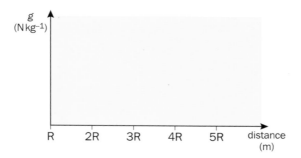

8. How far above the Earth's surface is g
   a) one quarter of its value at the surface,
   b) one ninth of its value at the surface?

9. Find the radius of Mars given that the gravitational field strength, g, at its surface is 3.73 N kg^{-1} and its mass is 6.42×10^{23} kg.

10. Find the mass of Jupiter given that the gravitational field strength, g, at its surface is 25.9 N kg^{-1} and its radius is 7.15×10^7 m.

11. A mass of 5.00 kg feels a force of 16.6 N at a point 200 km above the surface of Mars.
    a) Calculate the value of g at this point.
    b) The radius of Mars is 3390 km. Calculate its mass.

12. A geostationary satellite orbits the Earth travelling at 3080 m s^{-1}.
    a) What is its period of rotation?
    b) Calculate its height above the Earth's surface.

13. Calculate the velocity of Venus in its orbit around the Sun. The radius of its orbit is 1.08×10^{11} m.

14. A satellite orbits the Earth 8 times each day. It travels at 6150 m s^{-1}. Calculate:
    a) its period of rotation,
    b) its centripetal acceleration.

15. a) Calculate the gravitational potential at the Earth's surface.
    b) At what height above the Earth does the potential fall to half this value?

16.

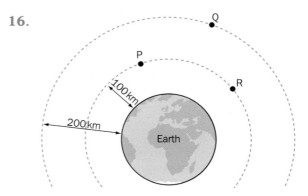

   a) Calculate the gravitational potential at the points P and Q shown in the diagram.
   b) How much energy is needed to move a rocket of mass 33 000 kg from P to Q?
   c) Explain why no work is done as the rocket moves from P to R.

17. The gravitational potential 4.5×10^7 m from the centre of a planet is -1.3×10^8 J kg^{-1}.
    a) Calculate the mass of the planet.
    b) Why is the potential negative?

18. The Moon has a mass of 7.35×10^{22} kg and a radius of 1740 km.
    a) Calculate the gravitational potential at its surface.
    b) A probe of mass 100 kg is dropped from a height of 1 km onto the Moon's surface. Calculate its change in potential energy.
    c) If all the potential energy lost is converted to kinetic energy, calculate the speed at which the probe hits the surface.

19. A satellite of mass 19 500 kg orbits the Earth along a path of radius 6.9×10^6 m. Calculate:
    a) the speed of the satellite,
    b) the kinetic energy of the satellite,
    c) the gravitational potential at this altitude,
    d) the change in potential energy in moving the satellite from the Earth's surface to its orbit,
    e) the minimum energy needed to place the satellite in this orbit. (Ignore friction with the atmosphere.)

Further questions on page 109.

9 Simple Harmonic Motion

We have already looked at one type of periodic motion, circular motion in Chapter 7.
We now look at a second type, where an object repeatedly moves backwards and forwards, or up and down, in a regular way.

In the photograph the baby bouncer is attached to a doorway by a large spring. The bouncing baby moves up and down about a central point. This is an example of a periodic motion called **simple harmonic motion** (**SHM**).

In this chapter you will learn:
- how to describe SHM using graphs and equations,
- about the energy transfers involved in SHM,
- the effects of damping and resonance.

SHM is child's play

Keeping time

Why do some old clocks use a pendulum?
A pendulum oscillates backwards and forwards with a regular beat.
Even as the oscillation dies away, its **time period** (the time for one complete oscillation) stays the same.

Why? Because the amplitude of the swing also decreases.
The pendulum moves a smaller distance at a slower speed, and the time stays the same.

This effect was first noticed by Galileo in 1581. He watched the lamps in Pisa's cathedral swinging backwards and forwards. The time for each swing stayed almost the same even as the swinging died down. Galileo realised that this regular motion could be used for time keeping.

All clocks rely on some type of periodic motion.
Oscillating pendulums are still used in many mechanical clocks.
Modern quartz watches use the regular vibrations of quartz crystals and atomic clocks rely on the natural vibrations of atoms such as caesium.

When an object oscillates with constant time period even if the amplitude varies, we say it is moving with simple harmonic motion (SHM).

The regular oscillations of a pendulum through a small angle are approximately simple harmonic.

SHM is a common type of motion.
The pistons in a car engine, a cork bobbing up and down on water and a vibrating guitar string all move with SHM.

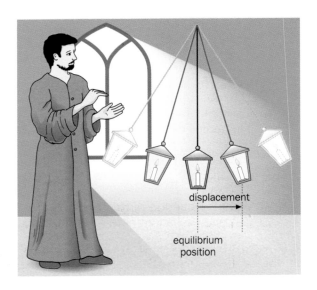

displacement

equilibrium position

Let's look in more detail at what happens during SHM.
Imagine yourself on the swing in the photograph:
We'll assume you swing through only a small angle (moving almost horizontally) so then your motion will be simple harmonic.

First think about your velocity

How does your **velocity** change as you move backwards and forwards?
At each end of the oscillation you are stationary for a moment. The swing speeds up as you move back towards the centre. Once you go past this point you start to slow down again.

Remember that velocity is a vector so we also need to consider its direction. We can take forward motion as positive and backward motion as negative.

Now let's think about your acceleration

In which direction are you **accelerating** during each swing?
Starting at A in the diagram you speed up towards the centre. You are accelerating towards B, the centre.

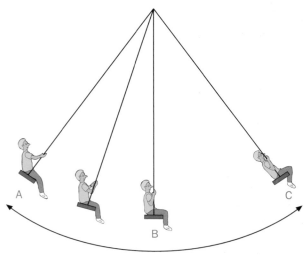

Once past the middle you slow down until you stop again at C.
But deceleration is the same as negative acceleration, so decelerating away from B is the same as accelerating towards B. So you are still accelerating *towards the centre!*

From point C you accelerate back towards the centre again. From B to A you decelerate to a stop. But again you are really accelerating towards B.

Can you see that throughout the motion your acceleration is *always* directed towards the central point, B?
B is called the **equilibrium position**.
It is where you come to rest when you stop moving.

How does the size of the acceleration change?

This is perhaps easier to see with another common example of SHM – a mass with a spring. The mass in the diagram is tethered between 2 identical springs. When you pull the mass to one side and let go, it oscillates backwards and forwards.

What pulls the mass back to the centre each time?
When the mass is displaced to the left, T_1 decreases and T_2 increases so the resultant pull of the springs is to the right. Similarly, when the mass is displaced to the right, the resultant pull is to the left, to the centre. The more you displace the mass, the greater the resultant force that pulls it back.

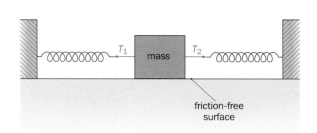

How does this affect the acceleration?
Newton's second law tells us that the greater the force, the greater the acceleration. So the greater the displacement away from the centre, the greater the acceleration.

In summary, for an object moving with simple harmonic motion:

- **the acceleration is always directed towards the equilibrium position at the centre of the motion,**

- **the acceleration is directly proportional to the distance from the equilibrium position.**

▶ Graphs of SHM

One way to represent the simple harmonic motion of an object is to draw graphs of its displacement, its velocity and its acceleration against time.

What would a **displacement–time graph** look like for a simple pendulum? We can produce this graph directly using a pendulum pen like the one in the diagram:

As the pen swings back and forth it draws over and over the same line on the paper underneath.
But what if we pull the paper along steadily beneath the pen?
The pen would draw a regular wave. This is the shape of the displacement–time graph for SHM. The graph is *sinusoidal*. It is the shape of a sine or cosine curve.

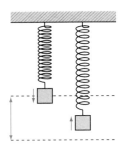

paper moving at steady speed

Remember that displacement is a *vector* quantity.
Displacements in one direction are taken as positive and those in the opposite direction are negative.

One complete oscillation means a movement from one extreme to the other and back again. The time this takes is called the **time period T.** The number of oscillations in one second is called the **frequency f.** Frequency is measured in hertz (Hz).

You have met these quantities before in the chapter on circular motion (page 70). Remember that:

$$f = \frac{1}{T}$$ and $$T = \frac{1}{f}$$

The **amplitude A** of the motion is the maximum displacement. Note that this is measured from the **centre** of the oscillation.

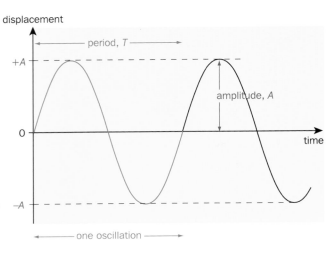

Comparing oscillations

Imagine two masses on springs bouncing up and down side by side. How can these oscillations differ?
They could have different periods and amplitudes.

Even if these are the same, how else can they differ?
The oscillations could be out of step. To describe how far out of step two oscillations are we use the idea of **phase.**
Phase measures how far through a cycle the movement is.

By analogy with circular motion, one complete oscillation has a phase of **2 π radians** (see page 70). The phase difference between two oscillations is usually given in radians:

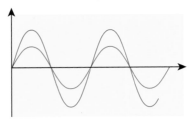

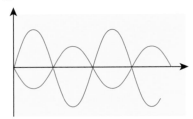

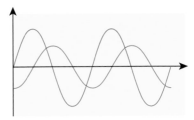

These oscillations are in step. They are **in phase**. The phase difference is zero.

These oscillations are a $\frac{1}{2}$-cycle out of step. They are in **anti-phase**. The phase difference is π rad (180°).

These oscillations are a $\frac{1}{4}$-cycle out of step. The phase difference is π/**2** rad (90°).

Linking displacement, velocity and acceleration

The picture shows a boy on a swing:

For small angles the swing moves with simple harmonic motion.

What will graphs of the boy's displacement, velocity and acceleration against time look like?

We already know that the graph of **displacement** against time is sinusoidal. This is the first graph:

At which point during the motion have we started timing?
At $t = 0$ the displacement is zero. So timing must have started as the swing passed through the equilibrium position, B.

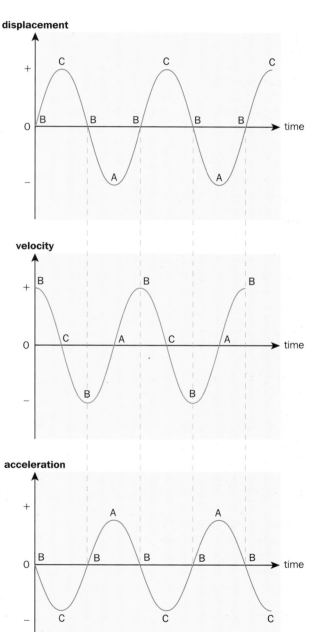

Remember that **velocity** is the rate of change of displacement. So the velocity at any point is equal to the *gradient* of the displacement–time graph (see page 34).

Look at this displacement–time graph again.
Where is the gradient at its maximum? The gradient is steepest when the displacement is zero. The gradient falls to zero as the swing reaches its maximum amplitude.

This tells us that the velocity is greatest at the centre of the motion, falling to zero at each extreme (as you already know).

The second graph shows the **velocity–time graph** for the motion:
The forward motion of the swing is taken as positive.
The backward motion is taken as negative.

How can we use this velocity–time graph to work out the swing's **acceleration**? Acceleration is the rate of change of velocity. So the acceleration is the *gradient* of the velocity–time graph.

Look at this velocity–time graph again.
The gradient is steepest when the velocity is zero.
This is at the maximum amplitude. The acceleration increases as the displacement increases. This was discussed on page 91.

This last graph shows the **acceleration–time graph** for the swing:
Acceleration to the right is positive and to the left is negative.

Notice that when the displacement is positive, the acceleration is negative. Can you see why?
As the swing moves forwards from B to C and back again, the displacement is positive. The acceleration towards the centre is to the left. This is the negative direction.
As the swing moves from B to A and back again the displacement is now negative. The acceleration towards the centre is now to the right and so the acceleration is positive.

Look at these 3 graphs carefully.
Think about the motion of the swing and make sure you understand how the three graphs are related.
And you thought swings were child's play!

▶ Equations for SHM

Linking acceleration *a* and displacement *x*

The most important equation for SHM links the acceleration *a*
of an object with its displacement *x* from the centre of the oscillation.

The acceleration is **directly proportional** to the displacement, or:

$$a \propto x$$

We can write this as an equation by inserting a constant of
proportionality:

$$\boxed{a = -(2\pi f)^2 x}$$

The *f* in the constant is the frequency of the oscillation.
This is the number of oscillations per second measured in hertz (Hz).

Why is there a minus sign in the acceleration equation?
This is because the acceleration is always back towards the centre.
So the acceleration is always in the opposite direction to
the displacement, as discussed on page 93.

The maximum displacement is called the amplitude, *A*. Do not
confuse this with the acceleration *a*.

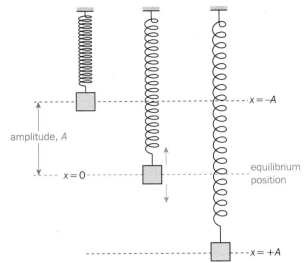

Example 1
The pendulum of a grandfather clock oscillates once every 2.0 s.
Calculate : a) its frequency,
           b) its acceleration when it is 50 mm from the midpoint.

a) frequency $f = \dfrac{1}{T} = \dfrac{1}{2.0\ \text{s}} = \underline{0.50\ \text{Hz}}$ (2 s.f.)

b) acceleration $a = -(2\pi f)^2 x$
$= -(2\pi \times 0.50\ \text{Hz})^2 \times 0.05\ \text{m}$
$= \underline{-0.49\ \text{m s}^{-2}}$ (towards the centre)

A pendulum clock

Linking displacement *x* and time *t*

The equation for acceleration can be solved mathematically to
give two equations for the displacement, *x*.
The solutions depend on the point at which timing starts.

You have already seen that the displacement–time graph for SHM
is sinusoidal. So the equations for this shape of graph must be
sines or cosines. In fact:

> If timing starts at the **centre** of the oscillation: $\ x = A \sin 2\pi f t$
>
> If timing starts at the maximum displacement: $\ x = A \cos 2\pi f t$

These equations give the displacement *x* after a time *t*.
A is the amplitude of the oscillation and *f* is the frequency.

The angles are in **radians** so you must have your calculator in
radian mode when calculating the value of the sine or cosine.

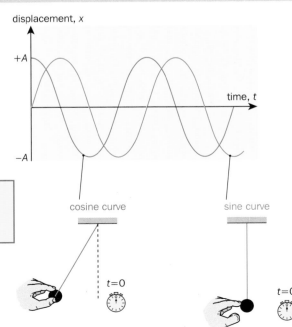

Example 2
A plucked guitar string vibrates at 260 Hz with an amplitude of 2.0 mm.
The vibration is timed from when the string moves through the centre
of its oscillation.
Assuming the motion is SHM, find the displacement of the string after 0.50 s.

Since timing starts at the centre,

$$x = A \sin 2\pi f t$$
$$\therefore \quad x = (2.0 \times 10^{-3} \text{ m}) \times \sin (2\pi \times 260 \text{ Hz} \times 0.50 \text{ s}) \quad \text{[Calculator in radian mode!]}$$
$$= (2.0 \times 10^{-3} \text{ m}) \times 0.894$$
$$= 1.8 \times 10^{-3} \text{ m} \quad (2 \text{ s.f.})$$

Linking velocity v and displacement x

If an object is moving with SHM, its velocity at any point can be
found using this equation:

$$v = \pm 2\pi f \sqrt{A^2 - x^2}$$

f is the frequency, A is the amplitude and x is the displacement
from the equilibrium position. Notice that the velocity can be
positive or negative depending on its direction.

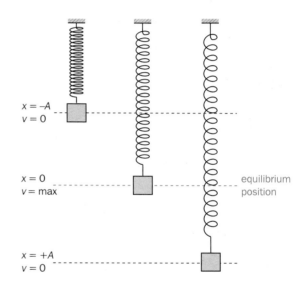

How does this equation tie in with what you already know about
the velocity during SHM?

Look at the equation. What happens to v as x gets smaller?
The value of v increases. So an object moving with SHM speeds
up as it moves towards the centre.

What value for v does the equation give us at the maximum
displacement? At the maximum displacement x equals the
amplitude A. So the velocity here must be zero.

We can use this equation to find the **maximum** velocity during
simple harmonic motion.
What is the value of x when the object is moving fastest?
The maximum velocity is at the equilibrium position where the
displacement is zero. So the equation becomes:

$$v_{max} = \pm 2\pi f \sqrt{A^2 - 0^2}$$

$$v_{max} = \pm 2\pi f A$$

Example 3
A baby in a bouncer bounces up and down with a time period of 1.2 s and
an amplitude of 90 mm. The motion can be assumed to be simple harmonic.
Calculate (a) the frequency of the bounces and (b) the baby's maximum velocity.

a) frequency $f = \dfrac{1}{T} = \dfrac{1}{1.2 \text{ s}} = 0.83 \text{ Hz}$ (2.s.f.)

b) maximum velocity $v_{max} = \pm 2\pi f A$
$$= \pm 2\pi \times 0.83 \text{ Hz} \times 0.090 \text{ m} = \pm 0.47 \text{ m s}^{-1}$$

▷ The simple pendulum

A pendulum oscillates with SHM provided the amplitude is small.
Try timing small oscillations for a simple pendulum.

What does the time period depend on?
There are two things you can vary: the mass of the bob and
the length of the string. Try changing the mass.
What effect does this have? Surprisingly, the mass has **no** effect
on the time period of a pendulum.
What effect does changing the **length** have? As the string gets
longer you should find that the time period increases.

In fact, the time period T of a pendulum can be found from:

$$T = 2\pi\sqrt{\frac{l}{g}}$$

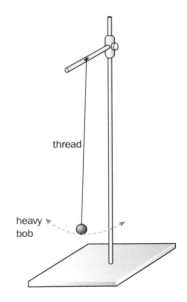

l is the length of the pendulum (in metres). This is measured
to the **centre** of mass of the bob.
g is the acceleration due to gravity (in m s^{-2}, see page 38).
Notice that you do not need to know the mass of the bob.

Example 4
Calculate the time period of a pendulum of length 0.75 m.
Take $g = 9.8$ m s^{-2}.

$$T = 2\pi\sqrt{\frac{l}{g}} = 2\pi\sqrt{\frac{0.75 \text{ m}}{9.8 \text{ m s}^{-2}}} = 2\pi\sqrt{0.076 \text{ s}^2} = \underline{1.7 \text{ s}}$$

Measuring the acceleration due to gravity, *g*

We generally treat the acceleration due to gravity on Earth as a
constant. In fact g varies with your latitude (north–south) and
your height above sea-level. Metal ore deposits in the Earth's crust
can also affect the value.
The actual values for g range from about 9.78 m s^{-2} at the equator
to 9.83 m s^{-2} at the North Pole.

How can you use a simple pendulum to measure g accurately?
Look back at the equation for the period of a pendulum.
You can measure the time period T with a stopwatch.
If you know the length of the pendulum then you can rearrange
the equation to calculate g.

To get a reliable figure you should measure the time period for
several lengths of the pendulum. See also page 396.
You can then find g by plotting a graph. What should you plot?

Compare the equation for the period of a pendulum with the
equation for a straight line: $y = mx + c$ (see page 405):

Can you see that plotting T on the y-axis against $\sqrt{l}$ on the
x-axis should give a straight line, through the origin?

The gradient of this graph would equal $2\pi/\sqrt{g}$

By finding the gradient (page 404) you can work out a value for g.

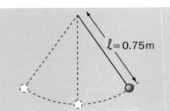

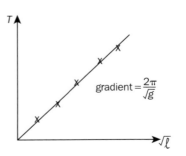

▷ A mass on a spring

Hang a mass on a spring, pull it down a small way and let go.
What happens?
The mass bounces up and down about its equilibrium position.
It oscillates with simple harmonic motion.

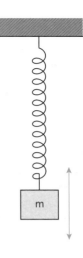

What affects the time period of this oscillation?
This time the **mass** does have an effect.
The greater the mass the slower it accelerates. This will increase
the time for each oscillation.

What else affects the period?
The other variable is the **stiffness** of the spring. A stiffer spring will
pull the mass back to its equilibrium position with more force.
This produces greater acceleration. If the mass moves faster
the time period will decrease.

In fact, the time period T for a mass m oscillating on a spring is
given by this equation:

$$T = 2\pi\sqrt{\frac{m}{k}}$$

The stiffness of the spring is represented by the **spring constant k**
(see page 282). This is a constant for a particular spring.
The spring constant is measured in newtons per metre (N m⁻¹).

The open coil spring in this diagram can make a mass oscillate
horizontally over a friction-free surface. When compressed the
spring pushes to the right. When extended it pulls to the left.

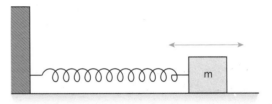

Can we use the same equation to find the time period here?
The mass m and spring constant k are the same whether the
motion is horizontal or vertical. Since these are the only things
that the period depends on, we can use the same equation.

Example 5
At the bottom of a bungee jump the woman in the photograph
bounces up and down on the end of the bungee rope through
an amplitude of 2.0 m.
The woman's mass is 66 kg.
The rope has a spring constant of 240 N m⁻¹.

Assuming the bouncing is SHM, calculate:
a) the period of the oscillations,
b) the frequency of the bounces,
c) the maximum acceleration during a bounce.

a) period $T = 2\pi\sqrt{\dfrac{m}{k}} = 2\pi\sqrt{\dfrac{66 \text{ kg}}{240 \text{ N m}^{-1}}} = \underline{3.3 \text{ s}}$

b) frequency $f = \dfrac{1}{T} = \dfrac{1}{3.3 \text{ s}} = \underline{0.30 \text{ Hz}}$

c) The acceleration is greatest at the maximum displacement
from the centre, i.e at $x = 2.0$ m
acceleration $a = -(2\pi f)^2 x = -(2\pi \times 0.30 \text{ Hz})^2 \times 2.0 \text{ m} = \underline{-7.1 \text{ m s}^{-2}}$ (towards the equilibrium position)

▷ Energy in SHM

Imagine yourself back on the swing. At which points do you have your maximum and minimum kinetic energy?

At the maximum amplitude of your swing, you are stationary for a moment. At these two points your kinetic energy is zero. Your kinetic energy reaches its maximum at the centre as you speed up towards this point.

Remember that energy is always **conserved**. So where does the increase in kinetic energy come from?
Think about how your potential energy changes.

Your gravitational potential energy has its maximum value at the extremes and its lowest value at the centre. So in moving from A to B in the diagram, your potential energy is transferred to kinetic energy. As you slow down from B to C, your kinetic energy is transferred back to potential energy again.

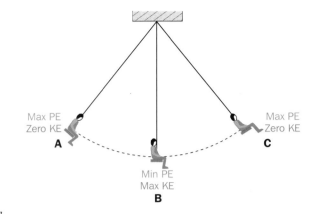

All simple harmonic motion involves this continual transfer between kinetic energy and potential energy.
The **total** amount of energy in the system remains constant.

To keep things simple we usually choose to take the potential energy to be zero at the equilibrium position.

The graph shows how the potential energy and kinetic energy vary with displacement for an object moving with SHM:

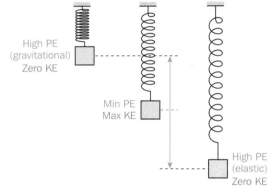

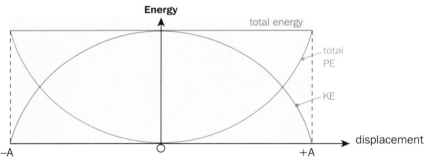

Energy and amplitude

The more energy you put into a system, the bigger the oscillations will be. Think about a mass on a spring. The more you pull it down, the more it oscillates. But is the relationship linear?
Does putting in twice the energy give you twice the amplitude?

To work this out let's look at the energy of an object moving with SHM as it moves through its equilibrium position.
At this point the object is moving at its maximum velocity and the total energy is all kinetic energy:

Total energy $= KE = \frac{1}{2}\,m\,v_{\text{max}}^2 = \frac{1}{2}\,m\,(2\pi f A)^2 = \frac{1}{2}\,m\,(4\pi^2 f^2)\,A^2$

> **Total energy** $\propto$ **A^2**

So to make the system oscillate with **twice** the amplitude you need to give it **four** times the energy.

Energetic oscillations

▷ Damping

So far we have assumed that no energy is lost from an
oscillating system and that it continues to oscillate indefinitely.
What actually happens in practice?
If you leave a pendulum or a mass on a spring oscillating
it eventually slows down and stops. The time period stays
the same as the amplitude gets smaller and smaller.

Why does this happen? Air resistance slows the object down.
Energy is lost from the system in overcoming this friction.
This effect is called **damping**.
In this case, air resistance provides **light damping**.
The oscillations take a long time to die away.

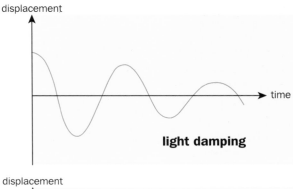

displacement

time

light damping

Now imagine a pendulum moving through water.
Once released it would take longer to return to its equilibrium
position and it would hardly oscillate at all.
Water would provide **heavier damping**:

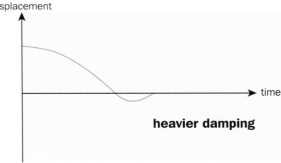

displacement

time

heavier damping

Damping is often applied to oscillating systems deliberately.
In car suspension systems, for example, 'shock absorbers' or
dampers are fitted to the suspension springs.
These quickly damp the vibrations when a car goes over a bump.
Driving would be very uncomfortable without them!
The level of damping used in a car's suspension needs to stop the
oscillations as quickly as possible. Damping that allows an object
to move back to its equilibrium position in the *quickest* possible
time without oscillating is called **critical damping**:

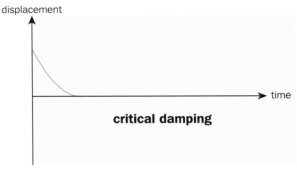

displacement

time

critical damping

What happens if you increase the damping above this critical level?
If a system is **overdamped** it does not oscillate.
It takes a long time to return to its equilibrium position:
A pendulum moving through thick treacle would be overdamped.

Overdamping is useful where rapid fluctuations need to be ignored.
An example of this is a car fuel gauge. Overdamping stops
the pointer oscillating as the fuel sloshes about in the tank.

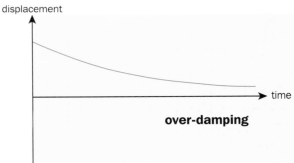

displacement

time

over-damping

*Drums are lightly damped by
the surrounding air*

Car suspensions use critical damping

Fuel gauges are overdamped

▷ Resonance

If you want to make a child's swing go higher, how do you time your pushes? You push in time with the swing's movement. You need to match the frequency of your pushing force with the **natural frequency** or 'resonant' frequency of the swing.

You can *force* objects to vibrate at any frequency, but all oscillating systems have their own natural frequency.
And if the driving frequency is the same as the natural frequency the amplitude builds up and up. Energy is transferred from the driver to the vibrating object. This effect is called **resonance**.

The graph shows how the amplitude of oscillation varies with the frequency of the driving force:

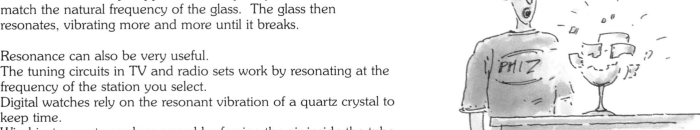

Have you ever sat on a bus and felt it judder or rattle at a certain speed? If so you have experienced resonance first hand.
Resonance also causes the violent vibrations of a washing machine at some spin speeds.

Resonance can be destructive.
The vibrations can build up to dangerous levels. Cartoons sometimes show glasses smashing when someone hits a high note. This can really happen. The frequency of the sound must match the natural frequency of the glass. The glass then resonates, vibrating more and more until it breaks.

Resonance can also be very useful.
The tuning circuits in TV and radio sets work by resonating at the frequency of the station you select.
Digital watches rely on the resonant vibration of a quartz crystal to keep time.
Wind instruments produce sound by forcing the air inside the tube to resonate.
There are more examples of resonance on the opposite page.

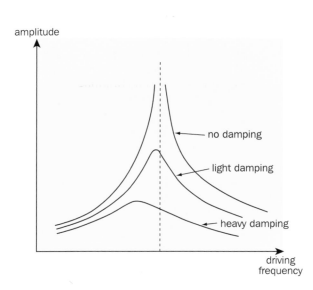

Resonance and damping

Damping absorbs energy. This reduces the effect of resonance.
The graph shows the effect of different levels of damping on the resonance peak.

You can see that as the damping increases:

- the amplitude of the resonance peak decreases,

- the resonance peak gets broader,

- the 'resonant frequency' gets slightly lower,
  so the peak moves to the left on the graph.

Damping is used where resonance could be a problem.

A good example is the damping of buildings in earthquake zones. The foundations are designed to absorb energy.
This stops the amplitude of the building's oscillations reaching dangerous levels when an earthquake wave arrives (page 121).

100

▷ Physics at work: Resonance

The Tacoma Narrows bridge

In 1940 in Washington state, USA, the Tacoma Narrows suspension bridge collapsed just three months after opening. A steady crosswind caused swirling air, which set the bridge vibrating. By chance, these vibrations matched a natural frequency of the bridge.

The bridge resonated and started to oscillate with increasing violence. Eventually the amplitude of the oscillations was too great for the structure to stand and it collapsed:

Resonance has caused other bridge disasters. In 1850, over 200 French soldiers died when the bridge they were marching over resonated with their steps and collapsed. This is why soldiers always break step when they march over a bridge.

Magnetic Resonance Imaging (MRI)

This picture showing the insides of the body was produced using magnetic resonance imaging (MRI). How does this work? Our bodies contain a lot of hydrogen, mostly in water. The proton in a hydrogen nucleus spins. A spinning charged particle has a magnetic field, so the protons act like small magnets. These are normally aligned in random directions. Placing a patient in a strong magnetic field keeps these mini magnets almost in line. Their field axis just rotates, a bit like a spinning top. This is called **precessing**.

Radio waves with the same frequency as this precessing can make the nuclei *resonate*. The protons gain energy and their magnetic axes flip through 180°. When the radio pulse finishes, the protons flip back again or 'relax'. As they relax they give out radio signals that can be detected outside the body. The strength of the signal depends on the amount of water in the body tissue. This is different for different types of tissue. A computer builds up an image from the strength and duration of the signals.

So what is it used for? MRI can detect cancerous tissue. The active cells need high blood flow. Blood is mainly water, so cancerous tissue produces a strong signal. MRI also gives excellent images of the brain because of the high blood flow to your grey matter. Unfortunately, the cost of producing the large magnetic fields needed to cover the body make this one of the most expensive imaging techniques.

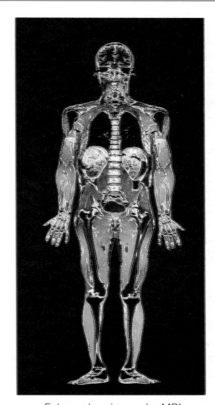

False colour image by MRI

How do microwaves cook food?

Microwave ovens use resonance. The frequency of the microwaves almost equals the natural frequency of vibration of a water molecule. This makes the water molecules in food resonate. This means they take in energy from the microwaves and so they get hotter. This heat conducts and cooks the food.

The slight mismatch of frequencies is deliberate. It prevents all the energy being absorbed at the surface and allows the microwaves to penetrate deeper into the food. See also page 177.

Summary

When an object moves with simple harmonic motion (SHM),
- the time period is constant,
- the acceleration is always directed towards the same point. This is the equilibrium position.
- the acceleration is directly proportional to the displacement from the equilibrium position.

You need to know how to use these equations:

$$a = -(2\pi f)^2 x$$

$$x = A \sin 2\pi f t \quad \text{(if timing starts at the centre)}$$

$$\text{or} \quad x = A \cos 2\pi f t \quad \text{(if timing starts at the maximum amplitude)}$$

$$v = \pm 2\pi f \sqrt{A^2 - x^2} \quad \text{so that:} \quad v_{max} = \pm 2\pi f A$$

A simple pendulum and a mass on a spring move with SHM: $\qquad T = 2\pi \sqrt{\dfrac{l}{g}} \qquad T = 2\pi \sqrt{\dfrac{m}{k}}$

During SHM energy is repeatedly transferred from kinetic to potential and back again.
The total energy remains constant. The total energy is proportional to the **square** of the amplitude.
Energy can be lost from an oscillating system through damping.

If the driving frequency = the natural frequency, the object gains energy and the amplitude increases.
This is called resonance. Damping reduces the effect of resonance.

▷ Questions

1. Can you complete these sentences?
   a) The time for one oscillation is called the time .... This stays the same, even if the size, or ...., of the swing decreases.
   b) The mid-point of the oscillation is called the .... position. The distance away from this point is called the ....
   c) During SHM the .... of the object is always directed towards the equilibrium position.
   d) The acceleration is directly proportional to the ....
   e) The velocity is greatest at the .... At the maximum displacement the velocity is ....

2. A pendulum has a time period of 3.0 s and an amplitude of 0.10 m.
   Calculate:
   a) its frequency,
   b) its maximum acceleration.

3. The displacement of a girl on a swing is given by the equation $x = A \sin 2\pi f t$.
   a) Sketch a graph of displacement against time.
   b) Sketch a velocity–time graph for the girl on the same axes.
   c) What is the phase difference between the two graphs?

4. A mass on a spring bounces up and down at 1.4 Hz. The motion is SHM with an amplitude of 50 mm.
   Calculate:
   a) the acceleration at displacements of $\pm$ 1 cm, $\pm$ 2 cm, $\pm$ 3 cm, $\pm$ 4 cm and $\pm$ 5 cm.
   b) Use these values to plot a graph of acceleration against displacement.

5.

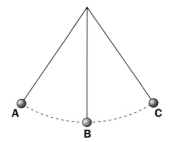

   The diagram shows a pendulum oscillating to and fro.
   Copy the diagram and add labels showing all the positions where:
   a) the acceleration is maximum,
   b) the acceleration is zero,
   c) the velocity is maximum,
   d) the velocity is zero,
   e) the kinetic energy is maximum,
   f) the potential energy is maximum.

6. A mass of 10 kg bounces up and down on a spring. The spring constant is 250 N m^{-1}.
   Calculate:
   a) the time period of the oscillation,
   b) the frequency of the bounce.

7. Calculate the time period for a pendulum of length 2.0 m. Take $g = 9.81$ m s^{-2}.

8. Find the length of a pendulum with a time period of 2.00 s. Take $g = 9.81$ m s^{-2}.

9. A baby of mass 9.0 kg bounces with a period of 1.2 s in a baby bouncer.
   What is the spring constant for the bouncer?

10. The time periods are measured for a simple pendulum and a mass on a spring on Earth. The measurements are then repeated with exactly the same apparatus on the Moon. One of the time periods is now different. Which one is it? Explain your answer.

11. The graph shows the motion of a bungee jumper at the end of a jump. You can assume that the motion is simple harmonic.

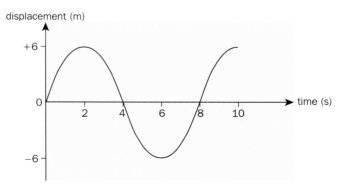

displacement (m)

a) What is the amplitude of the motion?
b) What is the time period?
c) Calculate the frequency of the bounces.
d) Use your values to work out the maximum acceleration during this motion.

12. The diagram shows a mass tethered between two springs. It is displaced 10 cm then released. The mass oscillates with SHM with a frequency of 0.55 Hz.

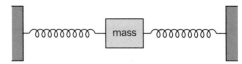

   Calculate:
   a) the maximum velocity of the mass,
   b) the velocity when the mass is 8.0 cm from the equilibrium position.

13. A sewing machine needle moves up and down through a total vertical distance of 2.0 cm. The frequency of the oscillation is 2.4 Hz. Assuming the motion is SHM, calculate:
   a) the amplitude of the motion,
   b) the maximum acceleration of the needle.

14. The table gives values for the time period T against length l for a simple pendulum.

T (s)	0.90	1.25	1.80	2.53	3.59
l (m)	0.20	0.40	0.80	1.60	3.20
$\sqrt{l}$					

   a) Copy out the table and fill in the values for $\sqrt{l}$.
   b) Use these values to plot a graph with T on the y-axis and $\sqrt{l}$ on the x-axis.
   c) Calculate the gradient of your graph.
   d) Use the value of the gradient to find the acceleration due to gravity g. (Hint: see page 96)

15. The graph shows how the kinetic energy of a mass on a spring varies with displacement.

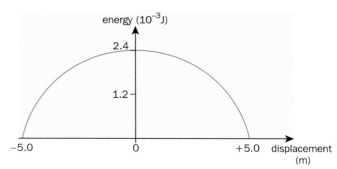

   a) What is the amplitude of the motion?
   b) Calculate the frequency of the oscillations given that the time period is 2.0 s.
   c) Calculate the maximum velocity of the mass.
   d) Calculate the maximum acceleration of the mass.
   e) Sketch a curve of total potential energy against displacement for the mass on the spring.

16. A punchbag of mass 0.60 kg is struck so that it oscillates with SHM. The oscillation has a frequency of 2.6 Hz and an amplitude of 0.45 m.
   Calculate:
   a) the maximum velocity of the bag,
   b) the maximum kinetic energy of the bag.
   c) What happens to this energy as the oscillations die away?

17. At a certain engine speed a car's rear view mirror starts to vibrate strongly. Explain why this happens.

Further questions on page 110.

▷ Basic ideas and vectors

1. For each of the four concepts listed in the left hand column select the correct example. [4] (Edex)
   A base quantity: mole   length   kilogram
   A base unit: volt   ampere   coulomb
   A scalar quantity: torque   velocity   energy
   A vector quantity: mass   weight   density

2. A student measures the length of an object with a metre rule having 1 mm divisions. Explain which of the following could be a correct measurement of the length. 0.4 m, 0.39 m, 0.392 m, 0.3917 m.

3. Name four different base quantities, stating the unit of each and, by reference to density and force, explain how derived units may be expressed in terms of these base units. [7] (OCR)

4. Explain, using the equation:
   pressure $+ \frac{1}{2} \times$ density $\times$ speed^2 = constant
   how base units may be used to test the homogeneity of physical equations. [7] (OCR)

5. When a body moves with speed v through a liquid of density ρ, it experiences a force F known as the drag force. Under certain circumstances, this force is related to ρ and v by the expression: $F = k\rho v^2$ where k is a constant. Determine the unit of the constant k in terms of base SI units. [4] (OCR)

6. The diagram shows a picture supported by two wires. The wires exert forces at A and B as shown:

   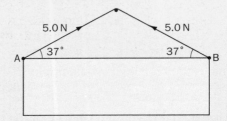

   a) Resolve the force acting at B to calculate its vertical and horizontal components. [3]
   b) Calculate the weight of the picture assuming it hangs freely. [1] (AQA)

7. a) Find the resultant of the forces shown below: [2]

   b) Why are perpendicular directions chosen when resolving vectors? [2] (W)

8. Water flows from a nozzle with an initial velocity of 5.8 m s^{-1} at an angle of 45° to the horizontal. Show that the horizontal component of the velocity is 4.1 m s^{-1}. [2] (OCR)

▷ Forces

9. The free-body force diagram shows the two principal forces acting on a parachutist at the instant of first contact with the ground.

   What does the force A represent? [1]
   What does the force B represent? [1]
   Why are these forces not equal? [2] (Edex)

10. The diagram shows the Moon in its orbit about the Earth. Draw and label two free-body force diagrams, one for the Earth and one for the Moon. Ignore the effects of any other bodies. [2] (Edex)

11. Two tugs A and B pull a ship along the direction XO. Tug A exerts a force on the ship of 3.0×10^4 N at an angle of 15° to XO. Tug B pulls with a force of 1.8×10^4 N at an angle θ to XO.

    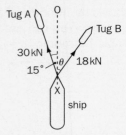

    a) Find the angle θ for the resultant force on the boat to be along XO. [3]
    b) Find the value of the resultant force. [3] (OCR)

12. An athlete with a broken leg is in traction while the bone is healing. The diagram shows a system of pulleys for providing the traction force. All the pulleys are frictionless so that the tension in the rope is the same everywhere. $g = 9.8$ N kg^{-1}

    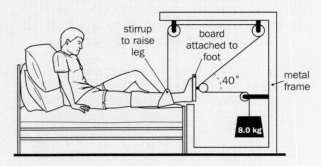

    a) Find the magnitude of the total horizontal force exerted on the leg by the system. [2]
    b) Find the total upward force exerted on the leg by the system. [1]
    c) Explain why the force found in (a) does not move the patient to the bottom of the bed. [2] (AQA)

▷ Forces and Moments

13. A car moves forward along a straight level road at constant speed. State the direction and origins of
a) two forces opposing forward motion of the car,
b) the driving force maintaining the motion of the car against the forces opposing motion,
c) two vertical forces acting on the car. [6] (OCR)

14. An aircraft of weight 1.8×10^6 N flies at a constant height. The pressure difference between the top and bottom of the wings is 1.5×10^4 Pa. Assuming that the lift is produced only by the wings, calculate the effective area of the wings. [3] (OCR)

15. State the principle of moments. [2]
The diagram shows a lorry on a light bridge.

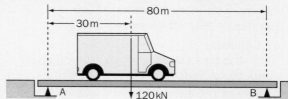

a) Calculate the downwards force on each of the bridge supports A and B. [4]
b) Sketch a graph to show how the force on support A changes as the centre of gravity of the lorry moves from A to B.
Mark scales on your axes. [3] (Edex)

16. A crane has a jib (AC) of mass 2500 kg pivoted at A. The jib is supported by a horizontal cable BC. The centre of mass of the jib is at D.

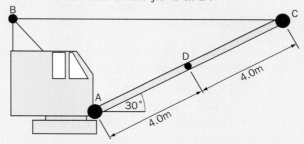

a) On a copy of the diagram draw three arrows to represent the three forces acting on the jib. [3]
b) Calculate the tension in the cable BC. [2] (OCR)

17. A beam of length *l* and weight *W* is supported horizontally from two spring balances A and B. The reading on balance A is twice that on B.

a) Find the position of the centre of gravity of the beam. [2]
b) Explain whether you consider the beam to be uniform. [2] (W)

18. Figure 1 shows a gardener pulling a roller of mass 85 kg over a step. The roller has a radius of 0.25 m. The handle is attached to an axle through the centre of the roller.

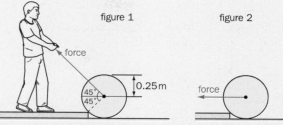

a) Determine the magnitude of the force that will just move the roller when the force is applied as shown in figure 1. [2]
b) Determine the force which would be required if the handle were pulled horizontally (figure 2). [2]
c) Without further calculation, draw a sketch graph showing how the magnitude of the force varies with the angle that the handle makes with the horizontal, between 0 and 90°. [2] (AQA)

19. The head may be considered as supported on a lever in which the atlas vertebra at the top of the spine acts as a pivot.

a) When the head is upright the pull of the muscles at the back of the neck supports the weight of the head. Sketch, then draw arrows on your diagram to represent these two forces. Mark the position of the pivot on the diagram. [2]
b) The weight of the head is 75 N and its line of action is 0.040 m in front of the atlas vertebra. Calculate the force exerted by the neck muscles which act vertically 0.055 m behind. [2] (OCR)

20. The diagram shows a child's mobile which is supported from the ceiling by a thread of negligible weight. AB is a uniform horizontal rod.

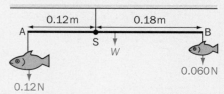

a) By taking moments about point S, show that the weight *W* of the rod is 0.12 N. [3]
b) A third fish of weight 0.30 N is suspended from the middle of the rod. The thread supporting the mobile is moved along the rod so that the rod remains horizontal. On which side of the centre of the rod is the thread now attached? Explain how you arrived at your answer. [2] (AQA)

Further questions on mechanics

▷ **Motion**

21. A car of mass 800 kg travels along a straight level road. The graph shows its speed against time.

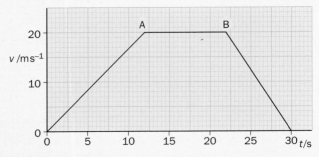

Use the graph to find:
a) the initial acceleration   [1]
b) the total distance travelled   [2]
c) the average speed for the journey.   [1] (OCR)

22. A car drives off from rest and travels in a straight line. The speedometer readings taken at a succession of times throughout the journey are given in the table.

t/s	0	10	20	30	40	50	60	70	80	90	95
v/m s^{-1}	0.0	2.1	6.9	17.8	22.6	24.4	22.9	16.7	10.0	3.3	0.0

a) Plot a velocity-time graph for the whole journey.[7]
b) Find i) the approximate time at which the acceleration is a maximum, and the value of the maximum acceleration,
   ii) the time at which the acceleration is zero.   [4]
c) Estimate i) the distance travelled before the acceleration becomes zero, ii) the average velocity up to this point. Explain your method.   [7]

23. A sky-diver jumps from an aircraft and initially falls without using a parachute. The graph shows how the speed of the sky-diver varies during this part of the drop.

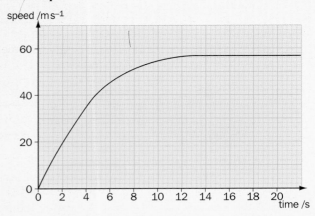

a) Determine the terminal speed.   [1]
b) The terminal speed is reached 13 s after leaving the aircraft. Estimate the distance fallen before reaching the terminal speed.   [2]
c) Say why the speed becomes constant. [2] (AQA)

24. A stone is projected horizontally from the top of a vertical sea cliff 49 m high, with a speed of 20 m s^{-1}. Neglecting air resistance, calculate:
a) the time that it takes for the stone to reach the sea,   [1]
b) the distance of the point of impact with the sea from the base of the cliff,   [1]
c) the velocity of the stone as it hits the sea. [4]
d) If air resistance had been taken into account, explain whether
   i) the time of flight,
   ii) the final velocity
   would increase, decrease or stay the same. [3](W)

25. An aircraft is at rest at one end of a runway which is 2.2 km long. The aircraft accelerates along the runway with an acceleration of 2.5 m s^{-2} until it reaches its take-off speed of 75 m s^{-1}.

a) Calculate:
   i) the time taken to reach take-off speed,
   ii) the distance travelled in this time.   [4]
b) Just as the aircraft reaches take-off speed, a warning light comes on in the cockpit. The maximum possible deceleration of the aircraft is 4.0 m s^{-2} and 2.5 s elapses before the pilot takes any action, during which time the aircraft continues at its take-off speed. Determine whether or not the aircraft can be brought to rest in the remaining length of runway. [4] (AQA)

26. A spacecraft which is landing on the Moon, uses its engines to keep its speed of descent constant at 5.0 m s^{-1} from the time when the craft is 14 m above the Moon's surface until it is 4.0 m above the surface. The engines are then switched off and the spacecraft falls freely to the Moon's surface. The acceleration of free fall on the Moon's surface is 1.6 m s^{-2}.

Calculate, for the spacecraft,

a) the speed of impact,
b) the time taken to travel the last 4.0 m,
c) the time taken to fall the full 14 m. [5] (AQA)

27. A ball is released from rest at a height of 0.9 m above a horizontal surface.

a) Find its speed as it reaches the surface. [2]

b) The effect of the bounce is to reduce the speed of the ball to two-thirds of the value in part (a). Find:
   i) the change in speed in the impact,
   ii) the change in velocity in the impact. [3]

c) Plot a graph of the velocity of the ball from the moment of its release until it reaches the maximum height after its first bounce.
   The ball takes 0.43 s to reach the surface.
   Assume that the bounce takes a negligible time.
   Show all your calculations.   [5] (OCR)

▷ Newton's laws of motion and momentum

28. State Newton's second law of motion. [2]
You are asked to test the relation between force and acceleration by experiment.
a) Draw and label a diagram of the apparatus you would use.
State clearly how you would use the apparatus and what measurements you would make. [6]
b) Explain how you would use your measurements to test the relationship between force and acceleration. [3] (Edex)

29. The diagram shows a view from above of two air-track gliders, A, of mass 0.30 kg, and B, of mass 0.20 kg, travelling towards each other at the speeds shown. After they collide and separate A travels with a speed of 0.20 m s⁻¹ from right to left.

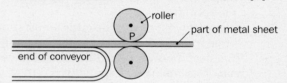

a) Apply the principle of conservation of momentum to this collision, and hence find the velocity of B after the collision.
b) What general condition must be satisfied for momentum to be conserved in a collision? [5]
c) Explain the difference between a perfectly elastic collision and an inelastic collision. Show that the collision described above is inelastic. [2] (AQA)

30. a) Explain how it is possible for a rocket motor to provide a propulsive force even when the rocket is in outer space. [4]
b) A space probe has a total mass (structure + fuel) of 2.0×10^3 kg of which 1.2×10^3 kg is fuel. It is fitted with a rocket motor which exerts a constant force of 400 N in outer space.
Calculate the acceleration of the rocket
i) when full of fuel,
ii) when the fuel is nearly used up. [4]
c) Rocket motors work most efficiently in a vacuum. Suggest why they might produce a smaller propulsive force when operating inside the atmosphere. [3] (OCR)

31. The Saturn V rockets which launched the Apollo space missions had the following specifications:
mass at lift-off 3.0×10^6 kg
velocity of exhaust gases 1.1×10^4 m s⁻¹
initial rate of fuel consumption 3.0×10^3 kg s⁻¹
a) Calculate the thrust produced at lift-off, and
b) resultant force on the rocket at lift-off. [4] (AQA)

32. A parachutist lands with a vertical velocity of 7.0 m s⁻¹ and no horizontal velocity. The parachutist, of mass 85 kg, lands in one single movement, taking 0.25 s to come to rest.
a) Calculate the average retarding force on the parachutist during the landing. [4]
b) Explain how the parachutist's loss of momentum on landing is consistent with the principle of conservation of momentum. [2] (AQA)

33. A person is standing on the floor of a lift which is accelerating uniformly upwards.
a) Draw a free-body diagram showing all the forces acting upon the person. [2]
b) What are the Newton's Third Law reactions to each of these and on what does each act? [4]
c) Which, if any, of the forces in (a) changes as the acceleration changes? Give brief reasons. [2] (W)

34. This question is about the motion of a sheet of steel passing through a rolling mill.
a) A sheet of hot steel of mass 400 kg is carried along a conveyor at 0.80 m s⁻¹.
Calculate the momentum of the sheet. [2]

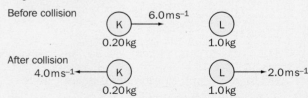

b) At the end of the conveyor, the sheet is inserted at 0.80 m s⁻¹ between two rollers which reduce the thickness of the sheet from 0.018 m to 0.012 m. The width of the sheet is unchanged.
i) Show that the increase in speed of the sheet as it passes through the rollers is 0.40 m s⁻¹.
ii) On a copy of the diagram, draw an arrow to show the direction of the resultant force on the sheet at P as it passes between the rollers. [3]
c) The original length of the sheet is 2.4 m.
i) How long does it take for the sheet to pass between the rollers?
ii) Find the magnitude of the resultant force on the sheet during the rolling process. [3](OCR)

35. The diagram shows a body K of mass 0.20 kg and moving at a speed of 6.0 m s⁻¹, colliding with a stationary body L of mass 1.0 kg. K rebounds with a speed of 4.0 m s⁻¹ and L is driven forwards with a speed of 2.0 m s⁻¹.

Before collision

K → 6.0ms⁻¹   L
0.20kg   1.0kg

After collision

4.0ms⁻¹ ← K   L → 2.0ms⁻¹
0.20kg   1.0kg

a) Show that the collision is elastic. [4]
b) Calculate the impulse applied to L by K. [2](Edex)

Further questions on mechanics

▷ Work, energy and power

36. A person raises and lowers a dumb-bell of mass 2.5 kg through a vertical distance of 0.40 m, 50 times in 60 s.
   a) Show that the useful work performed by the arm muscles during this activity is 490 J.　　[2]
   b) Estimate the rate of conversion of energy in the muscles for the person during this activity. Assume that the muscles convert energy into useful work with an efficiency of 20%. [3] (OCR)

37. Power can be calculated from the product of force applied and velocity.
   a) Justify this expression, starting from the definition of power.　　[2]
   b) A cyclist pedalling along a horizontal road provides 200 W of useful power reaching a steady speed of 5.0 m s⁻¹. What is the value of the drag force against which the cyclist is working? [2]
   c) The drag force is proportional to the speed of the bicycle.
      i) Show that the useful power the cyclist must produce at speed v along the flat is proportional to v^2.
      ii) Predict what power the cyclist must produce to reach a speed of 6.0 m s⁻¹ along the flat. [4]
   d) What useful power would the cyclist have to develop to maintain a speed of 5.0 m s⁻¹ when climbing a hill of 1 in 30? Take the mass of the cyclist plus bicycle to be 100 kg.　　[4] (OCR)

38. A car of mass 1500 kg is moving at a uniform speed of 12 m s⁻¹ down a slope with the engine switched off and its brakes applied.
   The slope makes an angle of 10° with the horizontal.
   a) If the only force opposing the motion is due to the brakes, calculate the magnitude of this force.
   b) Calculate the work done in 2.0 s by the brakes.
   　　[5] (AQA)

39. A catapult fires an 80 g stone horizontally. The graph shows how the force on the stone varies with distance through which the stone is being accelerated horizontally from rest.

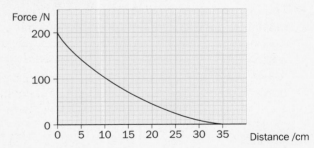

   a) Use the graph to estimate the work done on the stone by the catapult.　　[4]
   b) Calculate the speed with which the stone leaves the catapult.　　[2] (Edex)

40. The graph shows how the height above the ground of the top of a soft bouncing ball varies with time.　　[6] (Edex)

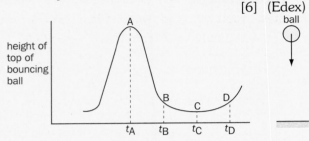

Describe the principal energy changes which occur between the times t_A and t_B, t_B and t_C, t_C and t_D.

41. The water-wheel of a restored water-mill provides the torque necessary to drive machinery in the mill. The wheel is driven by the weight of water held in buckets at its rim, which are filled with water from the mill-pond above the wheel, and empty below.

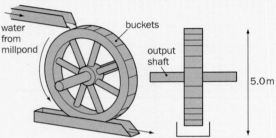

The maximum flow rate without excessive spillage is 18 m³ of water per minute, which falls a vertical distance of 5.0 m from mill-pond to exit channel. The wheel turns at 7.0 rev min⁻¹ and produces a torque of 7.5 kN m at its output shaft.
   a) Calculate the available power input to the wheel provided by the falling water, explaining your reasoning. (Density of water = 1000 kg m⁻³)
   b) Calculate the output power (torque × angular velocity) of the wheel.
   c) Hence show that the efficiency of this water wheel as an energy converter is 0.37. [7] (AQA)

42. A typical take-off speed for a flea of mass 4.5 × 10⁻⁷ kg, jumping vertically, is 0.80 m s⁻¹. It takes such a flea 1.2 ms to accelerate to this speed.
   a) Show that the average acceleration is 670 m s⁻².
   b) Calculate the force required to produce this acceleration.
   c) Calculate the average power produced during the acceleration.　　[5] (AQA)

43. The engine of a car of mass 1200 kg works at a constant rate of 18 kW at the wheels. The top speed of the car is 30 m s⁻¹.
   a) Find the resistance to its motion at its top speed.
   b) Assuming that the resistance to motion is proportional to the speed of the car, calculate the acceleration of the car at the instant when its speed is 10 m s⁻¹.　　[7] (W)

▷ **Circular motion**

44. A stone of mass 0.50 kg is attached to an inextensible string and whirled in a vertical circle of radius 0.98 m at a constant speed of 7.0 m s^{-1}.
a) Calculate i) the angular speed of the stone,
ii) the centripetal acceleration of the stone,
iii) the least tension in the string.
b) At which point in the motion is the tension in the string least?   [7] (W)

45. A model plane, of mass 0.15 kg, flies so that its centre of mass travels in a horizontal circular path of radius 10.0 m.
a) The plane completes two circuits in 21 s. Calculate the angular velocity of the plane. [2]

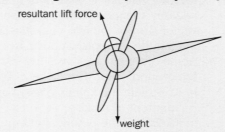
resultant lift force
weight

b) The diagram shows a simple frontal view of the plane showing the forces during flight. It assumes the rudder does not produce any sideways force. Calculate: [3] (W)
i) the total vertical component of the lift force,
ii) the total horizontal component of the lift force.

46. A boy ties a string to a rubber bung and then whirls it so that it moves in a horizontal circle at constant speed.

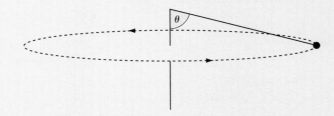
θ

a) i) Copy the diagram. Draw and label arrows representing the forces acting on the bung. Assume that air resistance is negligible.
ii) Hence explain why the string is not horizontal.
iii) Give the direction of the resultant force on the bung. State the effect it has on the motion of the bung.   [4]
b) The mass of the bung is 0.060 kg, the length of the string from the boy's hand to the bung is 0.40 m and θ is 75°.
i) Show that the tension in the string is 2.3 N.
ii) Calculate the resultant force on the bung.
iii) Find the speed of the bung.   [4] (OCR)

▷ **Gravitation**

47. The 'engine' of a hang-glider is the gravitational field of the Earth. Hang-gliders drop slowly through the air during their flight. The weight of a hang-glider, including the pilot, is 900 N. When in forward flight, the sinking speed is approximately 1.2 m s^{-1}.
a) Calculate the decrease in gravitational potential energy per second. Explain what happens to this potential energy.   [4]
b) The maximum steady power output of a fit racing cyclist is about 400 W. Explain why sustained man-powered flight is hard to achieve. [2] (Edex)

48. Tides vary in height with the relative positions of the Earth, the Sun and the Moon, which change as the Earth and the Moon move in their orbits. Two possible configurations are shown below.

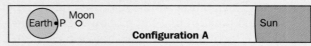
Configuration A

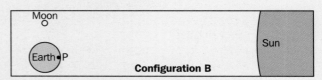
Configuration B

Consider a 1 kg mass of sea water at position P. This mass experiences forces F_E, F_M and F_S due to its position in the gravitational fields of the Earth, the Moon and the Sun respectively.
a) Draw labelled arrows on copies of both diagrams to indicate the three forces experienced by the mass of sea water at P.   [3]
b) State and explain which configuration of the Sun, the Moon and the Earth will produce the higher tide at position P.   [2] (AQA)

49. a) The diagram shows a series of equipotentials around the planet showing values of the gravitational potential.

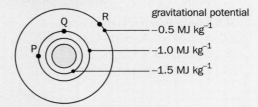
gravitational potential
−0.5 MJ kg^{-1}
−1.0 MJ kg^{-1}
−1.5 MJ kg^{-1}

A spacecraft of mass 3000 kg orbits the planet. Calculate, showing your reasoning, the changes in the gravitational potential energy of the spacecraft when it moves from
i) P to Q,   ii) Q to R.   [4]
b) With reference to the diagram explain why
i) the potentials all have a negative sign,
ii) the equipotential surfaces are spheres centred on the centre of the planet.   [2] (OCR)

Further questions on mechanics

▷ Simple Harmonic Motion

50. The first graph shows one cycle of the displacement–time graphs for two mass-spring systems X and Y that are performing SHM.

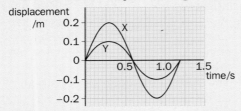

a) i) Determine the frequency of the oscillations. [2]
   ii) The springs used in oscillators X and Y have the same spring constant. Using information from the graph, show that the mass used in oscillator Y is equal to that used in oscillator X.
   iii) Explain how you would use one of the graphs to confirm that the motion is SHM. [4]

b) The second graph shows how the potential energy of oscillator X varies with displacement.

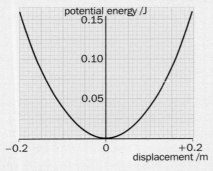

   i) Sketch a copy of the the second graph and draw a line to show how the kinetic energy of the mass used in oscillator X varies with its displacement. Label this A. [1]
   ii) Draw a line on your graph to show how the kinetic energy of the mass used in oscillator Y varies with its displacement. Label this B. [2]

c) Use data from the graphs to determine the spring constant of the springs used. [3] (AQA)

51. A friend has a toy which consists of a wooden bird suspended on a long spring, as in the diagram.

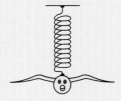

a) Describe what measurements you would make to find out whether the vertical oscillations of the bird on the spring approximate to SHM. [6]

b) In an accident, the wings are broken off the bird, reducing its mass and air resistance. The body alone still oscillates in a vertical line. State and explain three changes that would occur in the oscillations when compared with those before the accident. [6] (OCR)

▷ Synoptic questions on Mechanics

52. The shot-putter shown in the diagram throws the shot forwards with a velocity of 12 m s⁻¹ with respect to his hand, in a direction 54° to the horizontal. At the same time the shot-putter's body is moving forward horizontally with a velocity of 3.0 m s⁻¹.

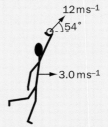

a) Draw a vector diagram to show the addition of the two velocities of the shot at the moment of release. Hence, or otherwise, show that the vector sum of the two velocities has a magnitude of approximately 14 m s⁻¹. [2]

b) At the moment of release, the shot is 2.3 m above the ground. The shot has a mass of 7.3 kg.
   i) Calculate the kinetic energy of the shot at the moment of release. [2]
   ii) Calculate the potential energy, relative to the ground, of the shot immediately on release. [2]
   iii) Use the law of conservation of energy to calculate the speed of the shot as it hits the ground. (Neglect air resistance) [2]
   iv) Sketch the variation of the shot's speed with time, up to the moment when it touches the ground. [2] (AQA)

53. The diagram shows a smooth wooden board 30 cm long. One end is raised 15 cm above the other. A 100 g mass is placed on the board. The two forces acting on the 100 g mass are shown on the free-body force diagram.

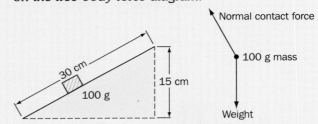

a) Explain why the resultant force on the 100 g mass acts parallel to the board and downwards. [2]

b) Calculate the magnitude of this resultant force. [2]

c) Calculate the kinetic energy gained by the 100 g mass as it slides 20 cm down the slope. [2]

d) The smooth board is replaced by a similar rough board which exerts a frictional force of 0.19 N on the 100 g mass. Calculate the new value for the kinetic energy gained by the 100 g mass as it slides 20 cm down the slope. [2]

e) Explain why the final kinetic energy of the 100 g mass is greater when the board is smooth. [2] (Edex)

54. A car of mass 1200 kg makes the journey shown in the speed against time graph shown.

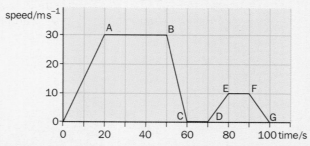

a) Calculate the total distance travelled during the journey of duration 100 s. [3]
b) During the section OA the road is horizontal. For the section OA, calculate
   i) the acceleration,
   ii) the force required to accelerate the car,
   iii) the work done in accelerating the car. [5]
c) When the car is moving at 30 m s⁻¹ there is a drag force of 500 N.
   i) Calculate the power required during the section AB to maintain a constant speed on a level road.
   ii) For part of section AB the car travels up hill, rising 1.0 m in every 20 m along the road. Calculate the extra power required when going up hill at a constant speed of 30 m s⁻¹.
d) At B the driver applies the brakes and slows down to stop at C. Describe the energy transfers which occur over the section BC. [2]
e) During section EF of the journey the car travels round a corner of radius 15 m at a constant speed of 10 m s⁻¹.
   i) Calculate the extra force exerted on the car.
   ii) Explain whether this changes the power required to propel the car. [4] (OCR)

55. This question is about safety design of cars.
In a test rig, a car travelling at 25 m s⁻¹ collides with a barrier. The car is brought to rest in 1.0 s. Without detailed calculations, use your knowledge of Physics to answer the following questions.
a) Explain whether, and in what ways, conservation of energy and linear momentum apply in this collision. [4]
b) Show that the average force on the car can be found by considering changes in momentum. Discuss the factors which determine the magnitude of the force. [4]
c) The dummy in the driver's seat is wearing a seat belt which restrains it. Explain why wearing a seat belt may reduce injuries in a real collision. [3]
d) In a similar test, an airbag inflates within 0.05 s of the impact, filling the space between the dummy and the steering wheel. Discuss ways in which the inflation and subsequent slower deflation of the airbag reduce the risk of serious injury. [3] (OCR)

56. In a fairground side-show a prize (a can of drink) is won by knocking it off a shelf by firing a wooden ball from a spring-loaded gun. The can is made to slide along the shelf by the impact of the ball. The dimensions of the prize and the shelf are shown in the diagram. The can has a mass of 0.40 kg and the ball a mass of 0.020 kg. $g = 9.8$ m s⁻².

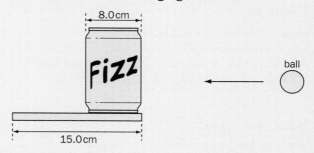

a) When the speed of the can immediately after the collision is 0.90 m s⁻¹, the can just falls off the rear of the shelf. Calculate the kinetic energy of the can immediately after the collision and the average frictional force between the can and the shelf. [3]
b) If the collision were perfectly elastic, the can would just fall off the shelf when the impact is "head-on" and the speed of the ball is 9.5 m s⁻¹. Determine the velocity of the ball immediately after impact for an elastic collision. [3]
c) The stall holder thinks that there would be less chance of the prize being won if a way could be found of making the ball, travelling at 9.5 m s⁻¹, stick to the can.
Suggest whether this idea is worth following up and briefly justify your answer. [3] (AQA)

57. The speed of a bullet can be estimated by firing it horizontally into a block of wood suspended from a long string, so that the bullet becomes embedded in the centre of the block. The block swings so that the centre of mass rises a vertical distance of 0.15 m. The mass of the bullet is 10 g and the mass of the block is 1.99 kg.
a) Assuming that air resistance can be neglected, calculate the speed of the block + bullet immediately after the impact. [3]
b) Calculate the speed of the bullet before the impact. [2] (AQA)

58. An empty railway truck of mass 10 000 kg is travelling horizontally at a speed of 0.50 m s⁻¹.
a) For this truck calculate the momentum and the kinetic energy. [2]
b) Sand falls vertically into the truck at a constant rate of 100 kg s⁻¹.
Calculate the additional horizontal force which must be applied to the truck, if it is to maintain a steady speed of 0.50 m s⁻¹. [2] (AQA)

10 Wave Motion

During an earthquake, the energy that waves carry is terrifying:

In this chapter you will learn:
- about wavelength, period, and amplitude of a wave,
- the difference between transverse and longitudinal waves,
- about phase difference, and polarisation.

What is a wave?

Look at the 5 diagrams down this page:

Phiz is holding one end of a long multi-coloured rope that is fastened to a wall at the other end.
The diagrams are **snapshots**. Each snapshot shows what Phiz and the rope look like at one instant of time.
Each diagram is like one 'frame' in a cinema film.

In **snapshot 1**, the rope is straight because Phiz has not begun to move his hand.

1

In **snapshot 2**, Phiz has moved his hand quickly upwards.
Look at the red section of the rope in this snapshot:

Can you see that the part held in his hand has moved most, while the part further away is lagging behind?

The sudden pull on the rope has stretched the part near his hand, and this tension is pulling the rope upwards.
The far end of the red part of the rope has not yet moved, so the green section has not yet been pulled upwards.

2

In **snapshot 3**, he has moved his hand quickly back down to the place it started from. The green section of the rope is being pulled upwards, while his hand is pulling the red section back down.

Compare the green section of the rope in snapshot 3 with the red section in snapshot 2. Can you see that it looks *exactly* the same?

3

Now look at what has happened in **snapshots 4 and 5**:
Although Phiz has not moved his hand, the up-and-down movement of the rope has continued.
First the green section of rope pulled the blue section upwards, and then the blue section pulled the next one up in its turn.

4

Look at the **shape** that is moving along the rope in these five snapshots. This is a **wave pulse**.
The *energy* put into the rope by Phiz is moving along the rope, being passed on from one section to the next.

Although the wave shape and the energy moves right along the rope, each part of the rope is *only moving up and down.*

5

▷ Wavelength λ

On the opposite page you saw how Phiz sent a wave pulse along a rope by moving his hand up and down once.

What if he were to carry on moving his hand up and down in a regular way, oscillating about the central point? The picture shows Phiz doing this with a slinky spring: (A slinky spring is often used to observe waves, because they travel much slower than along a rope.)

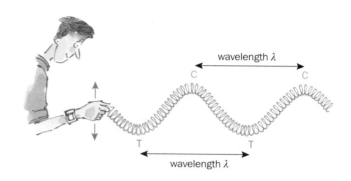

This diagram shows a **continuous wave**, not a pulse. This wave has equally spaced crests (**C**) and troughs (**T**). The wave-shape you see here is called a **sine wave**.

The distance between any point on a wave and the next *identical* point on that wave is called the **wavelength**. The symbol for wavelength is λ (the Greek letter lambda).

Wavefronts

You have probably studied waves with a **ripple tank**:

An electric motor is used to vibrate a straight bar or a small dipper which is touching the surface of the water.

When a small dipper is used to make the waves, you get a regular pattern of concentric circles. (You can use a stroboscope to 'freeze' the motion of the waves, which makes them easier to observe.)

Look at this snapshot of the circular pattern that is produced:

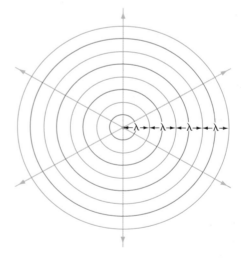

The central blue dot shows the place where the dipper is moving up and down, and the blue circles mark the **crests** of the waves that are produced. These blue circles are equally spaced, because the distance between each wave-crest and the next, is one wavelength.

Each blue circle is a **wavefront**. A wavefront is a line joining points at the same position along a wave.

The red circles are the **troughs** of the waves, which are exactly half-way between the wave crests. These red circles are also wavefronts.

Diagrams of wavefronts are useful when you want to see the direction in which waves are moving. The waves move **at right-angles** to the wavefronts, as shown by the green arrows in the diagram.

Example 1
In the scale diagram above, showing circular wavefronts, the diameter of the outermost circle is actually 32 cm. What is the wavelength of the waves?

From the diagram, this distance from one side of the diagram to the other side is 8 wavelengths,

so: $\lambda = \dfrac{32 \text{ cm}}{8} = \underline{4.0 \text{ cm}}$ (2 s.f.)

▷ Period

Look at these snapshots of a wave going along a rope:

The 5 snapshots are equally spaced in time.

The time it took Phiz's hand to go from the centre of the oscillation to the top, between snapshots 1 and 2, is equal to the time for the return trip between snapshots 2 and 3.

In the same way, moving from the centre of the motion to the lowest point, between snapshots 3 and 4, took the same time as the return trip, between snapshots 4 and 5.

You can measure this regularity in two different ways, using the periodic time or using the frequency.

The *time* it takes an oscillation or a wave to repeat is called the **periodic time** or the **period**. Its symbol is *T*.

This exact repeat of a wave or oscillation is **one cycle**.

After one cycle, every particle along the wave has returned to the same position, and is moving in the same direction as it was at the beginning of that cycle.

Example 2

In the snapshots above, the time between each diagram and the next is 0.20 s. What is the period of the wave?

The rope and his hand are in exactly the same position in snapshots 1 and 5. The time between these two snapshots is four intervals of 0.20 s.

∴ The time period *T* of the wave is $4 \times 0.20 \text{ s} = \underline{0.80 \text{ s}}$ (2 s.f.)

▷ Frequency

tuning fork

For fast oscillations, the period is too small to measure easily. So instead of counting the number of seconds for 1 oscillation, we count the **number of oscillations (or cycles) in one second.**

This is the **frequency**. It is measured in **hertz** (symbol **Hz**).

The frequency and period are related by this equation:

$$\text{frequency, } f \atop \text{(Hz)} = \frac{1}{\text{period, } T \text{ (s)}} \quad \text{or} \quad f = \frac{1}{T}$$

See also page 70.

Some oscillations are fast

Example 3

In example 2, the period of the wave was 0.80 seconds. What is its frequency?

$$f = \frac{1}{T} = \frac{1}{0.80 \text{ s}} = 1.25 \text{ Hz} = \underline{1.3 \text{ Hz}} \quad (2 \text{ s.f.})$$

For the waves we meet in Physics, the periods are often very small, so the frequency is high.
In these cases, the frequency is measured not in hertz but in kilohertz (kHz), megahertz (MHz) or even gigahertz (GHz).

$$1 \text{ kHz} = 1000 \text{ Hz} = 10^3 \text{ Hz}$$
$$1 \text{ MHz} = 10^6 \text{ Hz}$$
$$1 \text{ GHz} = 10^9 \text{ Hz}$$

▷ The wave equation

Look at the snapshots 1 and 5 on the opposite page.

The repeat between snapshots 1 and 5 is exactly one cycle.
During this time, the wave has moved one wavelength.
The wave frequency is the number of cycles in one second.

What do you get if you multiply:
(number of waves in 1 second, f) × (length of 1 wave, λ)?

This is the distance moved in one second – so it is the **speed**.

This shows that we can write this equation:

Measuring wave speed

speed, c = **frequency, f** × **wavelength, λ**
(m s⁻¹)$\qquad$(Hz)$\qquad\qquad$(m)

or $\quad$ $c = f\lambda$

The usual symbol for wave speed is c, but sometimes v is used.
So you may see: $\quad v = f\lambda$

Example 4
Station Radio 4 on 'Long Wave' radio has a frequency of 198 kHz.
What is the wavelength of the waves that arrive at your radio?
The speed of radio waves (electromagnetic radiation) is 3.00×10^8 m s⁻¹.

In the equation, the frequency must always be in hertz, not kilohertz.
198 kHz = 198×10^3 Hz

$$c = f\lambda$$
$$3.00 \times 10^8 \text{ m s}^{-1} = 198 \times 10^3 \text{ Hz} \times \lambda$$
$$\therefore \quad \lambda = \frac{3.00 \times 10^8 \text{ m s}^{-1}}{198 \times 10^3 \text{ Hz}} = \underline{1520 \text{ m}} \quad \text{(3 s.f.)} \quad \text{(That's nearly a mile!)}$$

Can you see why this answer has 3 significant figures?

It is because the precision of your answer should always be the
same as the precision of the data you are given (see page 9).
The frequency and the speed were both quoted to 3 s.f.

Is the wave speed constant?

The speed of electromagnetic waves was given in Example 4
as 3.00×10^8 m s⁻¹, but this is strictly true only in a vacuum.
The waves slow down in a dense medium like water or glass.

Sometimes when a wave travels through a medium,
different wavelengths travel at different speeds.

This called **dispersion**, because the waves separate out.

A storm out at sea generates water waves with many different
wavelengths. Hours later, long-wavelength waves arrive at the
shore, with short-wavelength waves following later.
This is because, in deep water, waves with long wavelengths
travel faster than short wavelength waves.

Surfers know that longer waves arrive first

▷ Transverse and longitudinal

Look at the snapshots of waves on a rope on page 114.

Each part of the rope oscillated up and down, while
the wave went from left to right in each diagram.
That was an example of a **transverse wave.**
The displacements were always *perpendicular* to the wave
velocity. The movement of each part of the rope was at
right angles to the direction in which the wave moved.

That is not the only possibility.
Look at these snapshots showing Phiz pushing the end of a
slinky spring **in** and **out** again:
The blue arrows show how Phiz's hand is moving.

Look at the compressed region of the spring.
Can you see the compression moving steadily to the right?
This is a **compression** wave going along the spring.
As the wave moves along, a **rarefaction** moves along
behind it, where the coils of the spring are pulled apart.

Look carefully at the two coils marked 'x' in each snapshot:

The separation of these coils decreases and then increases,
as a compression and then a rarefaction passes through
them. These coils are oscillating to and fro along the
direction in which the slinky spring is lying.

This is an example of a **longitudinal wave.**
The separate displacements of each oscillating part of the
spring are **in the same direction** as the wave velocity.

Examples of longitudinal and transverse waves

Compression waves in matter are longitudinal waves.
Sound waves are longitudinal waves of a frequency that
can be heard; higher frequencies are called *ultrasound*.

Electromagnetic waves, such as radio, are transverse.
Although there is no actual side-to-side movement here,
the electric and magnetic fields in the wave are both vectors
at right angles to the velocity of the wave.

Other types of waves can be more complicated.

There are several sorts of **earthquake waves**: some pass
through the Earth and others move along the surface.
The earthquake waves that pass through the Earth are
- the faster primary waves, which are longitudinal, and
- the slower secondary waves, which are transverse.

Water waves are also more complicated than they appear.
They look transverse, but this is not quite true.
Just watch a cork bobbing about on water while waves
pass. It does move up and down, but it also moves forward
and back.
Water waves are both transverse and longitudinal.

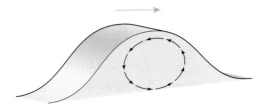

radio waves

Radio waves are transverse, but
sound waves are longitudinal

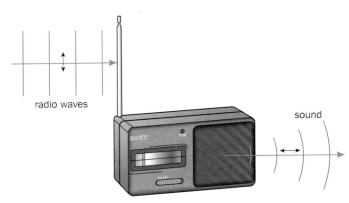

Water waves are more complicated

▷ Polarisation

Look at the photograph of television aerials:

Each aerial is pointing towards the television transmitter, and it is important that all the aerial rods are set the same way, either all vertically or all horizontally. Why is this necessary?

This is because the radio waves carrying television signals are **polarised**. Some transmitters transmit vertically polarised waves, and some transmit horizontally polarised waves. The aerial rods have to be parallel to the plane of polarisation of the transmitter.

This means that two different transmitters using the same frequency can be used. They cannot interfere with each other if they have different polarisation. This is only possible because electromagnetic waves, like radio, are *transverse*.

How are transverse waves polarised?

The oscillations in a transverse wave are at right angles to the direction in which the wave is travelling.
But in which direction are the displacements of these oscillations?

Are they vertical, like wave A? Or horizontal, like wave B?
Or are the oscillations in some other direction?

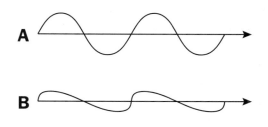

Plane-polarised waves have the oscillations in one plane only, such as wave A by itself, or wave B by itself.
The light coming through Polaroid sunglasses is like this.

Unpolarised waves are a mixture of all possible planes of oscillation. The light from your lamp is like this.

Now imagine you are *facing* the oncoming waves A and B.
The diagram here shows:
- polarised wave A, where the plane of oscillation is vertical,
- polarised wave B, where the plane of oscillation is horizontal,
- an *un*polarised mixture of waves with different planes.

Plane polarised   Unpolarised

Using Polaroid to reduce reflected glare

Most sources of light give off unpolarised light. The light can be polarised by *absorbing* all the planes of polarisation *except one*.

Polaroid plastic is used in some sunglasses. It contains many tiny crystals, all lined up together. These absorb all the planes of oscillation except the vertical one, like wave A in the diagram above.

Light can also be polarised **by reflection**.
Some of the light reflected from water is polarised with the plane of polarisation horizontal, like wave B above.

If you wear sunglasses made from Polaroid plastic, reflection off the water surface is absorbed, because its plane of polarisation is perpendicular to the plane of polarisation of the Polaroid.
This means you are not dazzled by the reflected glare from the water.

If two pieces of Polaroid are 'crossed' so that their transmission planes are at right-angles, no light will get through.
Liquid crystal displays (LCDs) on watches, calculators and portable computers use polarised light to show dark and light areas.

Polaroid sunglasses help anglers to see the fish

▷ Waves spreading through space

If your desk light is too dim for reading, you move it closer to the book. You need the book closer to the source of the waves, because the energy that waves carry gets spread more thinly as the waves spread out.
If you go twice as far from the light, will it be half as bright?
No – look at this example, which uses aerosol paint to represent the energy in waves.

Move the lamp closer to increase the brightness

Phiz and his aerosol paint spray

Phiz is holding an aerosol paint spray at 50 cm from a wall:

He squirts the aerosol for one second, and it makes a circular patch of paint, of radius 10 cm, on the wall.
The area of this patch is $\pi R^2 = \pi \times (10 \text{ cm})^2 = 314 \text{ cm}^2$

Now he moves along the wall, and stands **twice** as far from the wall – 100 cm away.
He gives this part of the wall a one-second spray, too.
How big is this patch of paint?

Because he is standing twice as far from the wall, the radius of the patch is doubled, to 20 cm.
The area of this patch is $\pi R^2 = \pi \times (20 \text{ cm})^2 = 1256 \text{ cm}^2$
This area is **four times** as big as the area of first patch.

At double the distance, a quarter the thickness

How does the thickness of paint compare in these patches?
The same amount of paint was sprayed on each – a burst lasting one second. But the second patch had **four** times the area, so the paint on it must be **four** times thinner.

The inverse square law

The paint thickness and the distance from this spray follow an **inverse square** relationship, a very common relationship in Physics.

The same relationship is true for the **intensity** of a wave.
(The paint thickness represents the intensity of a wave.)

Intensity is the **energy per second per square metre** of surface.
Intensity is measured in W m⁻².

At a distance R from a source, all the energy is spread out over a sphere of radius R, so the intensity is:

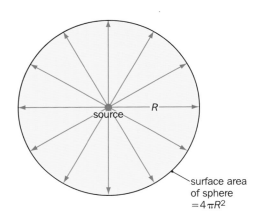

surface area
of sphere
$= 4\pi R^2$

$$\text{Intensity } I = \frac{\text{energy/second of the source}}{\text{surface area of a sphere, radius } R} = \frac{\text{Power of source, } P \text{ (W)}}{4\pi R^2 \text{ (m}^2)} \quad \text{or} \quad I = \frac{P}{4\pi R^2}$$

Example 7
The intensity of light at 1.3 m from a lamp is 1.0 W m⁻².
Calculate: (a) the output power of the lamp, (b) the intensity at 0.7 m from the lamp.

a) $I = \dfrac{P}{4\pi R^2}$ so: $1.0 \text{ W m}^{-2} = \dfrac{P}{4\pi \times (1.3 \text{ m})^2}$ $\therefore P = 1.0 \text{ W m}^{-2} \times 4\pi \times 1.69 \text{ m}^2 = \underline{21 \text{ W}}$ (2 s.f.)

b) $\therefore I = \dfrac{P}{4\pi R^2} = \dfrac{21 \text{ W}}{4\pi \times (0.7 \text{ m})^2} = \dfrac{21 \text{ W}}{4\pi \times 0.49 \text{ m}^2} = \underline{3.4 \text{ W m}^{-2}}$ (2 s.f.)

▷ Physics at work: Waves

Earthquake detection

The crust of the Earth is made from a number of **tectonic plates**, rather like the tiles on a bathroom floor. These plates push against one another, driven by convection currents in the mantle underneath. From time to time, the plates suddenly slip under these pushing forces, and there is an earthquake.

At a distant earthquake detection station, earthquake waves disturb a delicately-balanced **seismometer**, which oscillates with the tiny vibrations received from the earthquake. A trace of the oscillations is produced on a roll of paper marked with the time the vibrations occurred.

The centre, or **focus**, of the earthquake, is deep underground. Four sorts of earthquake waves spread out from the focus. Two of these, called **primary (p)** and **secondary (s)** waves, travel through the Earth, and two others travel along the surface of the crust.
The p-waves and s-waves do not travel together: the p-waves are longitudinal compression waves, and they travel faster than the transverse s-waves.

The seismograph trace will show the time delay between the arrival of p-waves and the arrival of s-waves. By knowing the speeds of p-waves and s-waves, geologists can use this time delay to calculate the distance between the earthquake focus and the seismograph. By working with other seismograph stations, they can pinpoint the focus of the earthquake exactly.

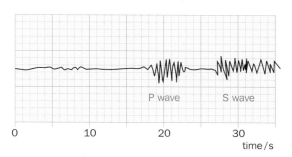

A seismometer recording

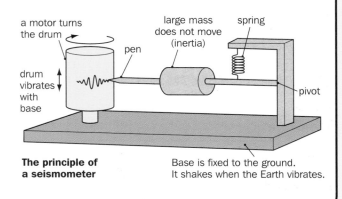

The principle of a seismometer

Base is fixed to the ground. It shakes when the Earth vibrates.

Measuring sound intensity in decibels

Everyone has heard of the **decibel (dB)**. But what is a decibel?

The decibel scale is used to compare *two* different amounts of *power*. One of these is the power of the sound being measured, but what is the other?
The reference point that was chosen is the threshold of hearing – the power of the quietest sound it is possible to hear.

The decibel is not a simple linear scale, because your nervous system does not respond in a simple linear way.
A **logarithmic (log) scale** is used. In this logarithmic scale, an increase of 10 decibels (=1 bel) means the sound has 10 times more power; but an increase of 20 decibels means it has 100 times more power; and 30 decibels has 1000 times more power.

The log scale makes the numbers manageable. The noise power from a jet aircraft 20 m away is 100 000 000 000 000 ($=10^{14}$) times bigger than the power of a sound at the threshold of hearing, but the log scale brings this factor down to 140 dB.

The diagram shows some values on the decibel scale for sounds often classified as noise. You may not consider a disco as noise, but there's no doubt that the sound is powerful enough to cause pain and even permanent damage to your ears.

Decibels

Decibels		
140	Hearing damage	Jet aircraft at 20 m
130		
120	Pain Threshold	Disco
110	London Airport limit (daytime)	
100		Pneumatic drill
90	Current limit for lorries	Heavy urban traffic
80		
70		
60		Normal conversation
50		
40		
30		Whisper
20		
10		
0	Hearing Threshold	

The decibel scale of sounds (a log scale)

Tsunami!

In many coastal regions in the Pacific Ocean, an earthquake brings a fresh danger in its wake - a **tsunami**, or tidal wave.

The photograph shows damage caused on Hawaii after a 10-metre tsunami struck in 1960. Hawaiians are well aware of the danger, and a 'Big Wave' warning sends everyone hurrying inland to higher ground.

If you lift one end of a tray of water a small distance and then drop it, a wave will be generated which passes along the water surface. This is a small-scale tsunami.
In the Pacific Ocean, tsunamis are created in this way by sudden movements of the ocean floor during an earthquake or volcanic eruption. The 1960 tsunami, which took lives and damaged property throughout the Pacific, was caused by an earthquake in Chile, 10 000 km away.

At sea, tsunamis do not look impressive, being only about a metre high, with a huge wavelength of about 100 km, but they travel at speeds of about 200 m s^{-1} (over 400 m.p.h.!) As they reach shallow water they slow down, and the tsunami 'tail' catches up with its 'head', giving a dramatic increase in height. The tremendous amounts of energy in a tsunami can strip coastal areas of sand, vegetation and houses.

The 1960 tsunami caused great damage

The supernova explosion that produced the Crab nebula should have made gravitational waves

Gravitational waves

When you think of 'waves', what comes to your mind? Water waves, perhaps, or sound, or electromagnetic radiation, or earthquakes. But gravity waves?

We are used to gravity as a constant field, but in some circumstances there could be rapid gravity changes. This is only likely in some great, cataclysmic astronomical event, such as a supernova, or two black holes colliding. The theory of relativity predicts that the sudden change in gravity field should send gravitational waves through the Universe.

But how can gravitational waves be detected? The problem is that gravity is a very weak long-range force which is hard to measure.

Experiments have been set up with large solid metal cylinders about 2 metres long, delicately mounted. If a gravitational wave hits one of these cylinders, the squashing and relaxing as the wave passes will change the dimensions of the cylinder very slightly – by less than the size of an atom!
Gravitational waves have not yet been observed directly, but astronomers are confident that greater refinement of detecting techniques will reveal them.

It is hoped that this could open up a whole new field of astronomical observations, just as neutrino, X-ray and gamma-ray astronomy have done in recent years.

Summary

Oscillations can produce waves, which carry energy.
The energy carried by a wave depends on its amplitude. In fact: energy $\propto$ (amplitude)^2

The frequency f of a wave is related to its period T by: $f = \dfrac{1}{T}$

The wavelength λ, frequency f, and speed v, of a wave are related by the equation: $v = f \lambda$

Phase difference, measured in degrees or radians, gives the difference between similar points on two waves.

In *transverse* waves, oscillations are at right angles to the direction in which the wave is moving.
In *longitudinal* waves, oscillations are in the same direction in which the wave is moving.

Transverse waves can be polarised by removing all components except those in one particular plane of oscillation, but longitudinal waves cannot be polarised.

As a wave spreads out, the intensity I of the wave gets less by the inverse-square law: $I = \dfrac{P}{4\pi R^2}$

▷ Questions

1. Can you complete these sentences?
   a) Oscillations often make waves which carry .... away from the place where the waves started.
   b) The time it takes any of the oscillating parts of the wave to repeat is called the ...., while the distance over which it repeats is called the ....
   c) The energy contained in a wave is directly proportional to the square of the ...., which is measured from the .... of oscillations to the highest or lowest value.
   d) .... are lines joining points along the wave with the same phase, and are useful in describing the movement of waves.
   e) When waves do not exactly coincide, they have a phase ...., which is measured in .... or radians.
   f) Waves such as sound, where the oscillations are in the wave direction, are .... waves.
      Waves such as light, where the oscillations are at 90° to the wave direction, are .... waves.
   g) Only .... waves can be polarised.

2. Copy and complete this table:

period T	frequency f
2.0 s	
20 ms	
	440 Hz
	91.5 MHz

3. A ripple tank dipper makes 8 water waves in a time of 2 s. When it is just about to make the 9th wave, the first wave has travelled 48 cm from the dipper.
   a) Calculate the frequency of the waves.
   b) What is the wavelength of the waves?
   c) Use $v = f \lambda$ to find the wave speed.
   d) Check your answer to (c) using the equation speed = distance / time

4. Primary (longitudinal) earthquake waves travel at 7500 m s^{-1}, while secondary (transverse) waves travel at 4500 m s^{-1}. Calculate the time delay between the two types arriving at a seismographic research station 800 km from the centre of the earthquake.

5. The speed of deep water waves is given by:
   $$v = \sqrt{\frac{\lambda g}{2\pi}} \quad \text{where} \quad g = 9.8 \text{ m s}^{-2}$$
   a) How does this equation show that water waves undergo dispersion?
   b) Use the equation to calculate the speed of water waves of wavelength (i) 50 m (ii) 100 m.
   c) Calculate the time delay between 100 m and 50 m waves arriving at a point 20 km away.

6. A water wave has an amplitude of 50 cm. A 100 m wavefront of this wave carries 250 kJ of energy. What would be the energy carried by 100 m of a wave with the same wavelength but an amplitude of 150 cm?

7. Sketch diagrams to show two waves with a phase difference of (a) 180°, (b) $\pi/2$ radians, Label the phase difference in each case.

8. Radio aerial rods must be in the correct plane, either vertical or horizontal, depending on the transmitter. If you mount the aerial the wrong way, the signal received is weak. Use the terms 'transverse' and 'plane-polarised' to explain these observations.

9. A high-efficiency lamp gives an intensity of 0.4 W m^{-2} on a newspaper 2 m away.
   a) What is the output power of the lamp?
   b) What is the intensity 4 m away from the lamp?

Further questions on page 160.

123

▷ Physics at work: Digital signals

Why digital?

When you connect a microphone to an oscilloscope, what you see is an **analogue signal**. It shows how the amplitude of the sound wave changes with time: When an analogue signal is transmitted by radio, electrical interference can add 'noise' to it and distort it.

A digital signal consists of a stream of pulses at regular times set by a 'clock' chip.
The signal is coded into a series of pulses and spaces, representing the binary digits 1 and 0:

Noise just changes the shape of the pulses, but not the pattern of pulses and spaces.
It is this pattern that carries the information, so digital signals do not get distorted by noise.
When the signal is received, it can be stored as digital data, or used to produce a display on a computer monitor, or converted back into analogue form to drive a loudspeaker.

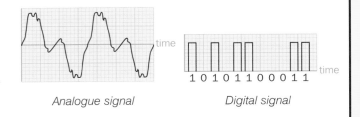

Analogue signal   *Digital signal*

Digital sampling

How can you turn an analogue signal into a digital one?
The signal is *sampled* regularly, as this diagram shows:
The red lines show the sampled digital data – it is the value nearest but below the signal. The size of each sample is converted to a *binary* number, shown in red.
In this example, there are eight possible levels between 0 and 7, so each value can be stored in 3 *bits* (**bi**nary dig**its**).
This means that each sample will be sent as a group of 3 bits.

Audio CDs have 16-bit samples recorded at 44 kHz.
16 bits give you $2^{16} = 65\ 536$ possible levels, and the signal is sampled 44 000 times each second (that's every 22.7 μs).

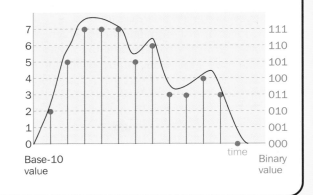

Base-10 value   Binary value

Bandwidth

The bandwidth of a signal tells you the range of frequencies in it.

The human ear can detect sound waves from about 20 Hz to about 20 kHz, but a telephone system has a narrow bandwidth of only 4 kHz.

This means that the 'phone makes your voice sound flat and woolly, because any frequencies in your voice greater than 4 kHz are not transmitted.

FM radio channels have a much wider bandwidth, 250 kHz, which you need for high-quality music.

Television channels broadcast video as well as sound, so they need a larger bandwidth, about 8 MHz. These bandwidths can be a large fraction of the available frequencies for radio and TV, but they are only a tiny fraction of the frequency of light. This is a good reason for sending signals along optical fibres.

Sending signals together

When digital pulses can be sent at high speed, several signals can be sent together.
This is called **multiplexing**, and the diagram shows how it is done:

In this example, the value (1 or 0) is taken from each of the three signals *in turn* to produce a combined chain of pulses.

When this combined signal is received, it is *de-multiplexed* into the separate signals.

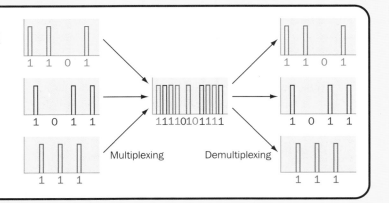

▷ Physics at work: Communication systems

Communication systems are often drawn in a block diagram like this one:

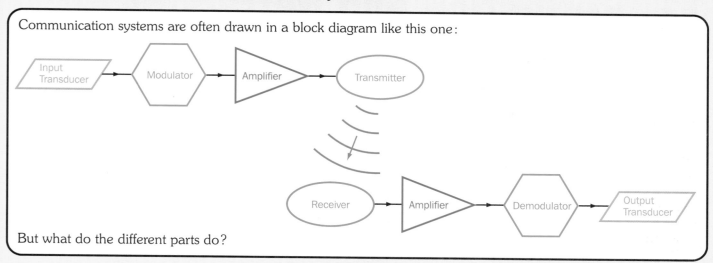

But what do the different parts do?

Input and output transducers

In any communication system, you need something measurable to communicate. This might be your voice, video pictures in a news programme, an ultrasound scan of an unborn baby, or infra-red satellite images of weather patterns.

The input transducer turns the sound, light, ultrasound or infra-red into electrical signals that can be processed further.

At the end of the process, the output transducer turns the electrical signals into a form that you can see, or hear, or store on your computer.

Modulation and demodulation

The transducers produce electrical variations, but these cannot be transmitted as they are. The modulator uses the input signal (from the transducer) to *modify* a **carrier wave**, which is then transmitted (see also page 176).

In a radio transmitter, the electrical signal from a microphone is used to change the amplitude (or the frequency) of a radio-frequency signal (about 1 MHz). In optical fibre systems, a flashing LED (light-emitting diode, see page 248) transmits the digital signals in light of much higher frequency, about 4×10^{14} Hz.

When the transmitted signal has been received and amplified, the demodulator converts this into a signal that can be used by the output transducer. In a slightly different way, computers communicate along telephone lines by modulating and demodulating a signal, using a **mo**dulator-**dem**odulator. This is usually called a **modem**.

Amplifiers

As the signals pass along any system, they get weaker. In electrical circuits, this is because energy is lost in heating the wires. In optical fibres, the glass absorbs some of the light. In radio transmission, energy spreads out, and does not all reach the receiver. To compensate for these losses, the signal must be made larger or *amplified*.

This is done before the signal is transmitted, and again after it is received.

Transmitter and receiver

Many different methods are used to send the signals from the transmitter to the receiver. Radio signals can be sent through space, or as electrical signals along cables, although they travel slower along cables.

One popular method is to send light signals along optical fibres, as optical fibres are less likely to pick up unwanted signals, or 'noise', which can affect radio.
The *signal to noise ratio* is an important measure.
If the amplitude of the signal is 100 times as big as the amplitude of the noise, the signal to noise ratio is 100.
Just try listening to Medium Wave radio at night – the signal to noise ratio is poor.

11 Reflection and Refraction

From ultrasound scans to the Hubble space telescope, from mirages to optical fibres: there is a huge range of uses of reflection and refraction.

In this chapter you will learn:
- how waves are reflected and refracted,
- about critical angle and total internal reflection,
- how images are formed by lenses.

Reflection of waves

How is light reflected? The Dutch scientist Christian Huygens was the first to argue that light is a *wave*. (Other scientists at the time, like Newton, argued that light travelled like a bullet.)
Huygens suggested an idea, (now called Huygens' construction), to help us explain how waves move.
He said each part of a wavefront is like a point source of tiny circular waves. These 'wavelets' add up to give another wavefront, one wavelength away.

Look at the incident (red) waves in this diagram:

The first wavefront produces sets of circular wavelets that add together to make the next wavefront. This wavefront then does the same thing to make the next wavefront, and so on.

This continues until the waves meet the reflector. Wavelets (coloured blue) are produced at the reflector and add up to make wavefronts (blue) coming back as shown.

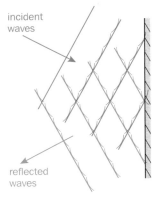

How waves reflect

It is far easier to follow a **ray diagram** than a wave diagram.
A *ray* is a very narrow band of waves and is drawn as a straight line in the direction of movement of the waves.

Look at this ray diagram of the *same* reflection:

This diagram illustrates the 2 laws of reflection:

1. When light is reflected, the incident ray, the reflected ray and the normal all lie in the same plane.
2. The angle *i* between the incident ray and the normal is the same as the angle *r* between the reflected ray and the normal.

'Normal' means a line drawn at right-angles (90°) to the reflector.

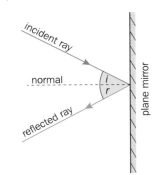

Ray diagrams are helpful in complex cases such as the reflection of light by a concave mirror, shown here:

Imagine how difficult it would be to draw this using Huygens' construction! With rays, it is much easier.

The dotted lines, which go to the centre C, of the curved mirror, are the normals. So we can easily use the laws of reflection to predict where the rays will be reflected to.

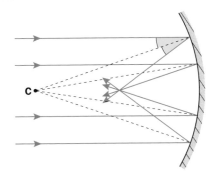

Reflection by a curved mirror

▷ Refraction and a change in speed

Is the pencil in this photograph really bent?

No, it is the light passing from water to air that is bent. The light is **refracted**. But your brain knows from experience that light normally travels in straight lines, so the pencil looks bent.

Why does refraction occur when light moves from water to air, or from air to water?

Look at this diagram showing wavefronts moving from air into water:

Can you see that the wavefronts are closer together in the water?

This is because **light travels slower in water**.
When a wavefront moves into water it slows down, and the one behind catches up with it, until that second wavefront also moves into the water.
It is this slowing down that makes the waves change direction.

This is because the end of the wavefront labelled B has only just entered the water, and so it has had a chance to overtake the end labelled A, which has been travelling slower since it entered the water a short time earlier.

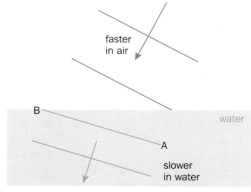

How waves refract

▷ Snell's Law

The ray diagram shows the refraction more clearly:

The angle of incidence *i*, is the angle between the incident ray and the normal. It is larger than the angle of refraction *r*, when light moves into a substance where it travels **slower**.

A substance in which light travels slower is said to be **optically denser**. Water is optically more dense than air.

The young Dutch astronomer Willebrord Snell discovered a mathematical relationship in 1621. It is called Snell's Law:

$$\frac{\textbf{sin (angle of incidence, } i)}{\textbf{sin (angle of refraction, } r)} = \textbf{constant} \quad \text{or} \quad \frac{\textbf{sin } i}{\textbf{sin } r} = \textbf{\textit{n}}$$

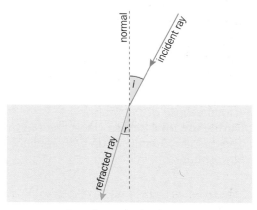

Ray diagram of refraction

The constant, **n** is called the **refractive index**.

In its full form, **n** has two suffixes to show the two substances between which the light is moving. So the refractive index for light going from air into water is written: $_{air}\textbf{\textit{n}}_{water}$

As the refractive index is a ratio, it has no units.

Example 1
The diagrams above show light refracting as it travels from air into water.
The angle of incidence $i = 27.0°$, and the angle of refraction $r = 20.0°$.
Calculate the refractive index $_{air}n_{water}$

$$_{air}\textbf{\textit{n}}_{water} = \frac{\textbf{sin } i}{\textbf{sin } r} = \frac{\sin(27.0°)}{\sin(20.0°)} = \frac{0.454}{0.342} = \underline{1.33} \quad (3 \text{ s.f.})$$

▷ Refractive index and the speed of light

Light is refracted because it slows down or speeds up, as we saw on the previous page.
Because of this, the refractive index n, can also be written as a ratio of two speeds:

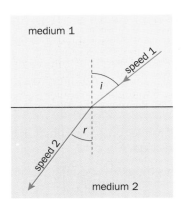

medium 1

speed 1

i

speed 2

r

medium 2

$$\text{medium 1}\,\boldsymbol{n}\,\text{medium 2} = \frac{\textbf{speed of light in medium 1}}{\textbf{speed of light in medium 2}}$$

where the word **medium** means the substance that the light is travelling through.

Example 2
The refractive index for light moving from a vacuum into air is 1.0003, and the speed of light in a vacuum, $c = 2.9979 \times 10^8$ m s^{-1}.
What is the speed of light in air?

$$\text{vacuum}\,\boldsymbol{n}\,\text{air} = \frac{\textbf{speed of light in vacuum}}{\textbf{speed of light in air}}$$

$$\therefore\ 1.0003 = \frac{2.9979 \times 10^8 \text{ m s}^{-1}}{\text{speed of light in air}}$$

$$\therefore\ \text{speed of light in air} = \frac{2.9979 \times 10^8 \text{ m s}^{-1}}{1.0003} = \underline{2.9970 \times 10^8 \text{ m s}^{-1}}\quad \text{(5 s.f.)}$$

Air and vacuum

Look at the speed of light in air in Example 2.
It is so *very* close to the speed in a vacuum that you need to calculate to 5 significant figures to show the difference.

The very slight refraction when light goes from the vacuum of space into our atmosphere is normally not noticed, except during a total eclipse of the Moon.
During the total eclipse stage, the Moon is not invisible, but appears very faintly, lit up with sunlight refracted by the Earth's atmosphere:

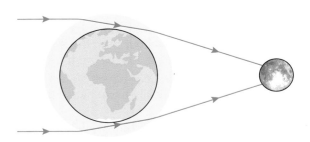

Refraction by the Earth's atmosphere (exaggerated)

Absolute refractive index

When light is going from one medium to another, the refractive index is called the **relative** refractive index, and has two suffixes.
For example, for light travelling from glass into water it is written as: $_{\text{glass}}n_{\text{water}}$

When light is going from a **vacuum** to another medium, the value of the refractive index is called the **absolute** refractive index.
This has only one suffix.
For example, for light travelling from a vacuum into glass it is written as: n_{glass}

Because the speed of light in air is so very close to that in a vacuum that you can usually treat air as if it were a vacuum.
In Example 1, you could have written the answer as:

$$n_{\text{water}} = 1.33 \quad \text{instead of} \quad _{\text{air}}n_{\text{water}} = 1.33$$

Optically, air is almost the same as a vacuum, but in other ways it is very different

128

Relative and absolute refractive indexes

The relationship between relative and absolute refractive indexes can be seen in this worked example:

Example 3
Light travels at speeds of 2.34×10^8 m s^{-1} in oil, at 2.00×10^8 m s^{-1} in glass and at 3.00×10^8 m s^{-1} in a vacuum.
Calculate:
a) the absolute refractive index of oil,
b) the absolute refractive index of glass, and
c) the relative refractive index for light going from oil into glass.

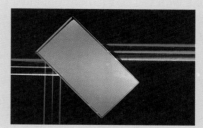

a) $\quad n_{\text{oil}} = \dfrac{\text{speed of light in vacuum}}{\text{speed of light in oil}} = \dfrac{3.00 \times 10^8 \text{ m s}^{-1}}{2.34 \times 10^8 \text{ m s}^{-1}} = \underline{1.28}$

b) $\quad n_{\text{glass}} = \dfrac{\text{speed of light in vacuum}}{\text{speed of light in glass}} = \dfrac{3.00 \times 10^8 \text{ m s}^{-1}}{2.00 \times 10^8 \text{ m s}^{-1}} = \underline{1.50}$

c) $\quad _{\text{oil}} n_{\text{glass}} = \dfrac{\text{speed of light in oil}}{\text{speed of light in glass}} = \dfrac{2.34 \times 10^8 \text{ m s}^{-1}}{2.00 \times 10^8 \text{ m s}^{-1}} = \underline{1.17}$

Look at the answers to Example 3.

If you check the arithmetic, you will find that the following relationship holds true:

> **Relative refractive index from medium 1 to medium 2** $=$ $\dfrac{\textbf{absolute refractive index of medium 2}}{\textbf{absolute refractive index of medium 1}}$

or $\quad \boxed{ _1\boldsymbol{n}_2 = \dfrac{\boldsymbol{n}_2}{\boldsymbol{n}_1} }$

For example: $\quad _{\text{oil}} n_{\text{glass}} = \dfrac{n_{\text{glass}}}{n_{\text{oil}}}$

Passing into a less dense medium

In Example 3, you saw that the relative refractive index of light going from glass into oil, which is optically less dense, is less than 1. What does this mean?
A refractive index less than 1 means that the light is speeding up, so it is refracting **away from** the normal.

Look at the diagram:

This is identical to the diagram on the opposite page, except that the ray is going the other way, from medium 2 to medium 1, so that the relative refractive index is:

$$_{\text{medium 2}}\boldsymbol{n}_{\text{medium 1}} = \dfrac{\text{speed of light in medium 2}}{\text{speed of light in medium 1}}$$

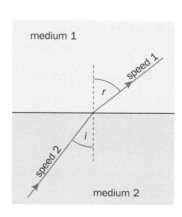

Compare this with the equation at the top of the opposite page.
Can you see that the following equation is true?

$$\boxed{ _{\text{medium 2}}\boldsymbol{n}_{\text{medium 1}} = \dfrac{1}{_{\text{medium 1}}\boldsymbol{n}_{\text{medium 2}}} }$$

▷ Critical angle and refractive index

Look at the diagram, which shows 3 rays of light passing from water into air:

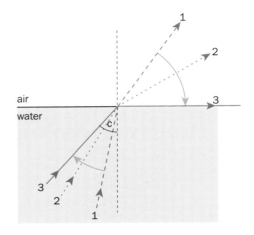

The rays 1, 2, 3 meet the surface at different angles of incidence, and so have different angles of refraction.
As the angle between the incident ray and the normal increases, the refracted ray gets closer and closer to the water surface.
Finally, with ray 3, the light only just escapes from the water.

The angle between ray 3 and the normal in water is called the **critical angle, c**. This is the largest angle at which refraction out of a denser medium is just possible.

How can we calculate the critical angle?
We can apply Snell's Law for light going from air into water along this same path. Air is optically very much the same as a vacuum, so we can use the absolute refractive index.

$$n_{water} = \frac{\sin i}{\sin r} = \frac{\sin (90°)}{\sin c} \qquad \text{but } \sin (90°) = 1$$

so $$\boxed{n_{water} = \frac{1}{\sin c}}$$

Example 4
The (absolute) refractive index of crown glass is 1.5. What is its critical angle?

$$n_{glass} = \frac{1}{\sin c}$$

$$\therefore \quad 1.5 = \frac{1}{\sin c}$$

$$\therefore \quad \sin c = \frac{1}{1.5} = 0.67 \qquad \therefore \quad \underline{c = 42°}$$

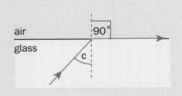

▷ Total Internal Reflection

The diagrams above show refraction, but they don't show any reflection. However, every time that a ray meets a boundary between two mediums, some light is reflected.
Even though glass is transparent, you can see a reflection in a window. Just look at the photograph on page 126.

Now look at the dashed ray in this diagram:

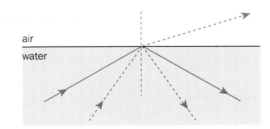

The angle of incidence as it meets the surface is *less* than the critical angle, so this ray is refracted out of the water, but *some* of the light is reflected back into the water.
This is *partial* internal reflection.

Now look at the continuous ray in the diagram:

The angle of incidence here is *greater* than the critical angle, so *no* light is refracted out of the water.
All of the light is reflected back into the water.
This is **total internal reflection**.

It is a very useful phenomenon, as explained on the next page.

▷ Optical fibres

Look at this diagram of an optical fibre:

The angle at which the ray meets the normal at the surface is always much more than the critical angle, so the ray continues down the fibre, with total internal reflection.
At the other end, Phiz can see the light after many total internal reflections.
The thickness of the fibre is greatly exaggerated here, so the angle of incidence in a real fibre is a much bigger angle than in this diagram.

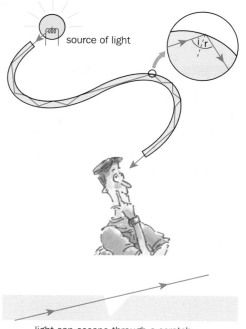

source of light

Optical fibres in communication

Fibre-optic cables are now widely used in communication for carrying telephone and TV signals.
However, there are two problems to be overcome.

If there are any scratches on the fibre, the light can escape, because a ray can meet the surface of the scratch with an angle of incidence less than the critical angle.

This is easily cured by coating the fibre with a tougher outside layer, made of plastic or glass with a *lower* absolute refractive index. See the diagram below.

Any scratch will then occur on the *outside* of the coating layer, and the boundary with the core stays smooth.

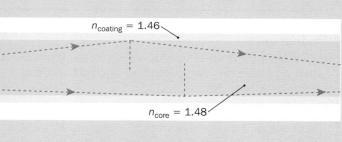

light can escape through a scratch

Example 5
The diagram shows an optical fibre with a core of refractive index 1.48 and a coating of refractive index 1.46. What is the critical angle for this fibre?

$$_{coating}\boldsymbol{n}_{core} = \frac{\boldsymbol{n}_{core}}{\boldsymbol{n}_{coating}} = \frac{1.48}{1.46} = 1.01$$

but:
$$\boldsymbol{n} = \frac{1}{\sin c}$$

$$\therefore \ 1.01 = \frac{1}{\sin c}$$

$$\therefore \ \sin c = \frac{1}{1.01} = 0.990 \qquad \therefore \ c = 81.9° \quad \text{(3 s.f.)}$$

$n_{coating} = 1.46$

$n_{core} = 1.48$

There is another problem which is more serious. Look at the diagram above.
Can you see that the upper ray is taking a longer path than the lower one, so it takes longer to travel down the fibre?

Modern telecommunications involves digital pulses travelling in quick succession along optical fibres, and it is important that they travel together. If one pulse followed the longer path, it could arrive later than a pulse that started after it, giving a faulty signal.

This is solved by trapping the light in the very narrow core region in the middle of a *monomode* optical fibre. The core of a monomode fibre is a hundred times thinner than a human hair.

Light travels down the centre of a monomode fibre

▷ Physics at work: Using refraction and reflection

Using refraction to check the quality of liquids

It is important in many industries to check the quality of liquids. It is important to know whether oil has the right density, or whether the 'wort' used to make beer has the right amount of sugar.
You can test this by measuring its refractive index, because changes in density or concentration will change the refractive index.

One device that is often used is a **deflection refractometer**. This can be run continuously, without any need to remove samples for testing.
The testing cell has two triangular boxes, as shown.

One part holds a reference liquid with the correct refractive index, coloured yellow in the diagram.
A sample of the liquid to be tested, coloured green in the diagram, runs continuously through the other half.

If the two liquids have the same refractive index, then light follows the path shown by the solid red ray.
If the reference liquid bends the light downwards as it leaves the yellow box, the sample liquid immediately bends it upwards by an identical amount.

However, if the refractive index of the sample is too large, or too small, the two deviations are not equal. The light is moved to one side or the other, as shown by the dotted ray, where it falls on a photo-detector, which can sound an alarm.

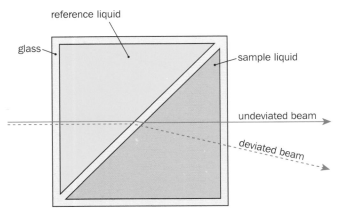

reference liquid

glass

sample liquid

undeviated beam

deviated beam

Endoscopes

An endoscope is often used to examine the digestive tract when a patient develops vomiting or diarrhoea that continues longer than expected.

It is a flexible tube that allows the doctor to look directly at the inside of the digestive tract to make a diagnosis, and possibly even to treat the problem with tiny surgical tools that can be manipulated through the endoscope.

In order to see inside the patient, light has to be taken down the endoscope to light up the region of interest. This is done with a bundle of optical fibres (see page 131).

The doctor has to be able to view the region inside the patient, and so a second fibre-optic bundle carries an image back up the endoscope to the doctor's eye.
This image can viewed directly by the doctor or shown on a television screen.

For 'keyhole' surgery, a rigid endoscope called a laparoscope is used. This often has a third bundle of optical fibres, to carry laser light which can be used to cut and seal the tissue.

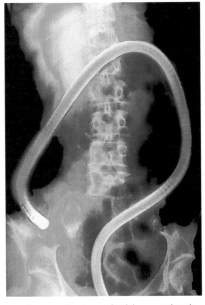

An X-ray of an endoscope inside a patient's colon

132

▷ Lenses

On page 126 we saw how a curved mirror can change the direction of rays of light. The rays started out parallel, and they ended up **converging** to a point.
This is exactly how big optical and radio telescopes bring the signals from distant objects to a focus.

Another way to converge light rays is to use a **convex lens**:

The diagram shows some parallel rays passing through a thin glass lens. Each ray is refracted when it meets each surface, following Snell's Law (page 127).
But because the two surfaces are curved, the rays are converged.

Can you see that these **parallel** rays are converged so that they all pass through one point?
This point is called the **principal focus** **F** of the lens.

It lies on the **principal axis**, the line passing through the centre of the lens and which is perpendicular to the lens.

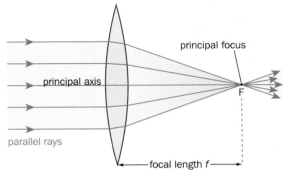

A converging (convex) lens

Focal length and Power

The **focal length** f of a lens is the distance from its middle to the principal focus F. The focal length depends on the curvature of the glass surface, and on the type of glass that is used.

A more powerful lens is one that bends the light more, and has a **shorter** focal length.
You can use this equation to calculate the power of a lens:

$$\textbf{Power} = \frac{1}{\textbf{focal length (m)}}$$ or $$P = \frac{1}{f}$$

Thick lenses are more powerful

Power is measured in **dioptres (D)**; the focal length must be in metres.

Example 6
The optician's prescription for a converging spectacle lens is marked $+0.2$ D.
What is the focal length of this lens?

$$P = \frac{1}{f}$$

$$\therefore\ 0.2\ D = \frac{1}{f} \qquad \therefore\ f = \frac{1}{0.2\ D} = \underline{5\ m} \quad (1\ \text{s.f.})$$

The lens shown above is a converging or convex lens.
This diagram shows a **concave** or **diverging** lens:

The diverging lens makes parallel light rays spread out or diverge. They diverge as if they were coming from the one point.
This point is called a **virtual principal focus**, because the rays do not pass through it, but diverge as if they had come from it.

Spectacles or contact lenses that are used to correct short sight use diverging lenses (see page 137).

A diverging lens has a negative power. eg. -0.2 D.

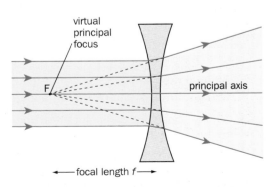

A diverging (concave) lens

▷ Forming images with lenses

What is happening as you are reading these words?

The light reflected from the paper reaches the curved cornea at the front of your eye, and then the lens inside your eye, and together these make the light converge to produce an **image** on the retina of your eye.

Because the rays of light from the object actually travel to the image, we say a **real** image is produced.
The light energy leaving the object is concentrated on one point of your retina, stimulating the cells there.

Ray diagrams

Look at this diagram. It shows 3 rays:

Ray **A**, which is travelling parallel to the principal axis, is refracted to go through the principal focus F on the far side of the lens (as in the diagram on page 133).

Ray **B** going through the centre of the lens, and ray **C** along the principal axis, are undeviated.
This is because the centre of the lens is parallel-sided, like window-glass. Any refraction that happens at one surface is cancelled by opposite refraction at the other surface.

Example 7 shows how these 3 rays can be used to find where an image is, in 6 steps:

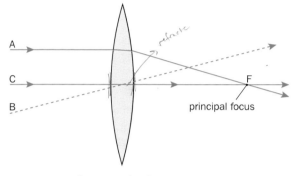

A converging lens

Example 7
An object 2 cm tall is placed 40 cm from a convex lens of focal length 15 cm. Find the position and size of the image.

1. Set out x- and y-axes on graph paper, like this:
   The y-axis of the graph will represent the lens, which is drawn in dotted outline on top of it.

2. Choose vertical and horizontal scales to fit the values given. These scales can be different from each other. Look at the scales on the diagram.

3. Draw the object, to scale, and in position.
   Here it's shown as a pencil stub.

4. Draw a ray (**A**) from the top of the object parallel to the principal axis up to the vertical line representing the lens. Now continue this ray to pass through the principal focus F on the other side of the lens.

5. Draw a ray (**B**) from the top of the object passing straight through the centre of the lens.

6. Where these two rays meet must be the top of the image. The image fits between this point and the principal axis, as shown in the diagram.

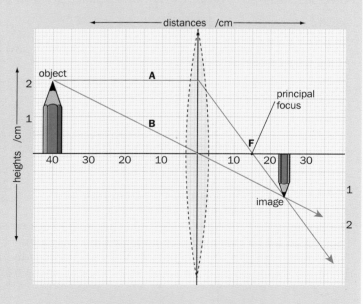

You can see that the image is <u>24 cm</u> from the lens.
It is <u>1.2 cm tall</u>, and it is ***inverted*** (upside-down).

Virtual images in diverging lenses

When light leaves an object, it spreads out (diverges).
A **concave** lens makes the light diverge even more, so the rays will not meet. It will produce a *virtual image* behind the lens.

A ray diagram can find the position and the size of the virtual image produced by a diverging lens, as shown here:

It is drawn in the same way as for a converging lens, except that the ray of light parallel to the principal axis bends *out*wards along a line drawn from the principal focus on the incident side of the lens. This line is shown here in blue.

The top of the virtual image is found where the two rays of light seem to come from, by tracing backwards.
You can see that the image would appear to be the right way up, and is smaller than the object.

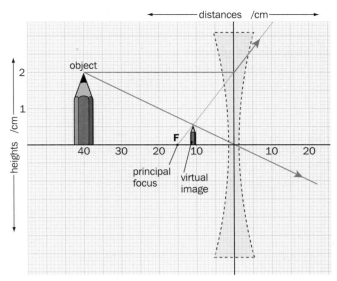

The lens equation

To calculate the distance of an image from the lens, we use the lens equation.

$$\frac{1}{\text{object distance, } u} + \frac{1}{\text{image distance, } v} = \frac{1}{\text{focal length, } f} \qquad \text{or} \qquad \frac{1}{u} + \frac{1}{v} = \frac{1}{f}$$

This equation uses a system called *'real is positive'*, meaning:

- Distances to real objects and real images are positive.
- Distances to virtual images are negative.
- The focal length of a converging lens is positive, because it has a real principal focus; but that of a diverging lens is negative.

Object and image distances are measured from the centre of the lens.
Hint: you will find the 1/x key of your calculator useful here!

Magnification

Whenever a lens forms an image, the ratio of distances is the same as the ratio of the sizes. This is the magnification.

$$\text{Magnification} = \frac{\text{image size}}{\text{object size}} = \frac{\text{image distance, } v}{\text{object distance, } u}$$

Observing a real image

Example 8
An 2.0 cm object is placed 40 cm from a diverging lens of focal length 15 cm.
Find the position and the size of the image.

The lens is diverging (concave), so it has a *virtual* focus. So we write $f = -15$ cm

$$\frac{1}{u} + \frac{1}{v} = \frac{1}{f} \qquad \therefore \quad \frac{1}{40 \text{ cm}} + \frac{1}{v} = \frac{1}{-15 \text{ cm}} \qquad \therefore \quad 0.025 + \frac{1}{v} = -0.066$$

$$\therefore \quad \frac{1}{v} = -0.066 - 0.025 = -0.092 \qquad \therefore \quad v = \frac{1}{-0.092} = \underline{-11 \text{ cm}} \quad \text{(2 s.f.)}$$

The answer is negative, so the image is *virtual*, 11 cm from the lens – exactly as shown in the ray diagram above.

$$\text{Magnification} = \frac{v}{u} = \frac{11 \text{ cm}}{40 \text{ cm}} = 0.28 \qquad \therefore \quad \text{Size of image} = 0.28 \times 2.0 \text{ cm tall} = \underline{0.56 \text{ cm tall}} \quad \text{(2 s.f.)}$$

▷ Physics at work: Using mirrors and lenses

Magnifying glasses

A converging lens can be used to focus parallel light to a point, and can give a real image of an object that is not too close. This is what happens in a camera.

But what happens if the object is very close?

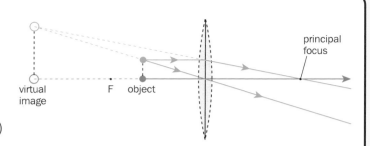

The diagram shows what happens:

Different colours show rays coming from the top (blue) and the bottom (red) of an object.

The rays diverge too sharply to make a real image. So an *eye* receiving the light coming from the lens has the impression that the rays have come from the places where the dotted lines come from.
This is because the *eye* and brain together 'know' that light always travels in straight lines.
This gives a *virtual* image.

The virtual image is not only further from the lens: it is *larger* than the object. This is a **magnifying glass**.

Magnifying glasses are used very widely – they're not just used by stamp collectors and Sherlock Holmes. Whenever an optical instrument (such as a microscope or a pair of binoculars) has an eyepiece, it usually has a magnifying lens in it.

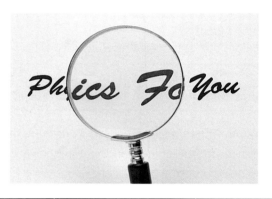

The Hubble Space Telescope being launched

The Hubble Space Telescope

Modern astronomical telescopes are not very different from the original one that Isaac Newton used to look at the sky.
They are usually just large converging mirrors, with photographic detectors mounted at the focus.
They are not really 'telescopes' in the ordinary sense at all – they are giant cameras!

One problem with these giant mirrors is that the exact shape of the curve should be *parabolic*, which is not quite the same as the surface of a sphere.
This is so that all the rays of light, from all parts of a wide mirror, are focussed to exactly the same place. Great care is needed to mould the mirror, and then polish it, to exactly the right shape.

The 2.4 metre mirror of the Hubble space telescope was launched by the Space Shuttle in 1990.
It was moulded and polished to such great accuracy that no part of the surface was out of place by more than a tiny fraction of a wavelength.

Unfortunately, due to human error, this mirror was very accurately polished to the *wrong* curvature! So a 'rescue' shuttle mission was necessary to fit it with correcting optics, like a pair of glasses.

▷ Physics at work: the human eye

The eye and accommodation

As light enters the curved cornea of your eye, it is refracted, and then refracted again as it goes into the liquid in front of the lens, then into the lens, and then into the liquid behind the lens.

Most of the bending takes place at the cornea: this is where there is the biggest relative refractive index.

The cornea is convex, so it makes light rays converge towards the retina.
The lens is optically denser than the fluids in the eye, and so it makes the rays from the cornea converge slightly more.
Your eye adjusts the power of the lens until there is a sharp image on the cornea – this action is called **accommodation**.

The lens is elastic, and in its natural state is fat, with greater power. The ciliary muscle is a ring of muscle round the eye, and the lens is attached to it by lots of ligaments.
When the ciliary muscle is relaxed, the lens is pulled thinner by the ligaments and becomes less powerful, so that the eye is focused at distant objects.
When the ciliary muscle is contracted, the ligaments become slack and the lens moves back into its natural fat shape.

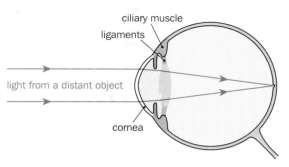

ciliary muscles relaxed and lens pulled thin

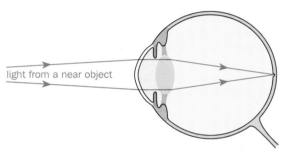

ciliary muscles contracted and so lens relaxes, gets fatter

Short sight

In some eyes, the cornea is too sharply curved, and the rays of light converge too much.
Even with the lens at its thinnest, the light converges to a point in front of the retina, except for very close objects. Because the light does not converge on to the retina, the image is blurred.

If you are **short sighted**, this is the probable cause.

The defect is easily corrected by wearing **concave** (diverging) spectacles or contact lenses.
These make the light diverge slightly, compensating for the converging power of the cornea.

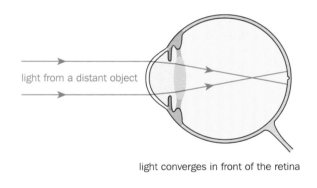

light converges in front of the retina

Long sight

If the cornea of your eye is not sharply curved enough, the rays of light do not meet at all.
Even with the lens at its fattest, the light converges to a point behind the retina, except for very distant objects.

This is **long sight**. It is corrected with a **convex** lens that makes the light converge, enhancing the converging power of the cornea.

Older people often become long-sighted for a different reason – the eye lens loses its elasticity with age, and cannot change back fully into its fattest shape.

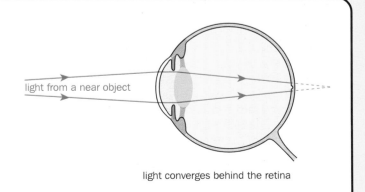

light converges behind the retina

137

Summary

The laws of reflection: 1. the angle of incidence i = the angle of reflection r

2. the incident ray, the reflected ray and the normal all lie in the same plane.

Snell's Law for refraction: $\dfrac{\sin i}{\sin r} = n$, the refractive index

The absolute refractive index of a medium is $n_{medium} = \dfrac{\text{speed of light in vacuum (or air)}}{\text{speed of light in the medium}}$

The relative refractive index when light moves from medium 1 into medium 2 is

$$_1n_2 = \dfrac{\text{speed of light in medium 1}}{\text{speed of light in medium 2}} = \dfrac{n_2}{n_1}$$

The critical angle c for a medium is related to the refractive index n by: $\quad n = \dfrac{1}{\sin c}$

If the angle of incidence, in the optically more-dense medium, is greater than the critical angle, then total internal reflection takes place.
Optical fibres carry light signals by total internal reflection.

Converging lenses can form real or virtual images, but diverging lenses form only virtual images.
Ray diagrams can predict the position and size of images in lenses.

The lens equation is: $\quad \dfrac{1}{\text{object distance}} + \dfrac{1}{\text{image distance}} = \dfrac{1}{\text{focal length}} \quad$ or $\quad \dfrac{1}{u} + \dfrac{1}{v} = \dfrac{1}{f}$

where negative values of v refer to virtual images, and negative values of f refer to diverging lenses.

▷ Questions

1. Can you complete these sentences?
   a) When light is reflected, the angles of incidence and reflection are ....
   b) In refraction, the relationship between the angle of incidence and the angle of refraction is given by ....'s Law.
   c) The absolute .... index of a substance is the factor by which the speed of light is slowed down in the substance, compared with the speed in a ....

   When light passes from one medium to another, you need to use the .... refractive index.
   d) Light going from a dense medium to a less dense medium speeds up, and the rays bend .... from the normal.
   If the angle with the normal is more than the .... angle, the light cannot escape, and it is totally internally ....
   e) Lenses refract light to form images: a .... lens can form both real and virtual images, but a diverging lens forms only .... images.
   f) The .... length of a lens is the distance from the lens to the .... focus.
   g) The reciprocal of the focal length in metres gives you the .... of the lens, which is measured in .... For converging lenses, the power is positive, while for diverging lenses, the power is ....

2. The diagram shows refraction of a ray of light as it passes from medium 1 to medium 2.

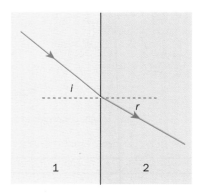

   a) Is the light slowing down or speeding up?
   b) Measure the angles of incidence and refraction on the diagram, and
   c) Use them to calculate the refractive index $_1n_2$.

3. Copy and complete this table for refraction of light from air into water, refractive index 1.33.

i /°	30			70
r /°			40	

4. On page 127, refraction of waves is shown. The wavelength in the faster medium, before refraction, is $1.6 \times$ bigger than the wavelength in the slower medium, after refraction.
   a) As the frequency is the same, how many times faster is the wave travelling before refraction compared with after refraction?
   b) What is the refractive index for this refraction?

5. The speed of light in vacuum and in two different glasses is given in this table.

Medium	Speed of light /m s^{-1}
Vacuum	3.00×10^8
Flint glass	1.86×10^8
Crown glass	1.97×10^8

   a) Calculate the absolute refractive indexes of flint glass and crown glass.
   b) Calculate the relative refractive index for light going from crown glass to flint glass.
   c) Calculate the critical angle for light going from flint glass to crown glass.

6. A spear-fisherman is about to catch a fish:

   a) On a copy of the diagram, draw a ray of light going from the fish to the fisherman's eye.
   b) Use the diagram to explain why the fisherman knows that he must not aim directly at where he sees the fish if he is to catch it. Should he aim high or low?

7. A stepped-index optical fibre is made of two different glasses. The glass in the central core has an absolute refractive index of 1.53, while that in the outer cladding has an absolute refractive index of 1.49. Calculate the critical angle for light travelling along the core.

8. Copy and complete this table relating the powers of lenses to their focal lengths.

Type of lens	Focal length	Power
Converging	0.5 m	
Diverging	25 cm	
		+ 0.2 D
		− 0.50 D

9. If you have thin lenses close together, you get the power of the combination by adding the powers of the different lenses together. A combination lens for a camera contains two converging lenses of focal lengths 20 cm and 40 cm, and a diverging lens of focal length 50 cm. Find the power and the focal length of the combination.

10. The optical prescription for a pair of spectacles is: Right eye, −3.50 D   Left eye, −4.00 D.
    a) Are these lenses thinner at the middle or at the edges?
    b) Which lens has the greatest curvature?
    c) Which is the weaker eye?

11. Use ray diagrams to find the position and size of the virtual image formed when a pound coin, 2.2 cm in diameter, is placed 20 cm from:
    a) a diverging lens of focal length 40 cm,
    b) a converging lens of focal length 40 cm.

12. Use the lens equation to complete this table. A negative focal length means that the lens is a diverging lens.

u /cm	30	45		20	40
v /cm	30		60		
f /cm		15	20	50	−40

13. The lens in a camera has a focal length that must be the same as the smallest possible distance between the lens and the film.
    a) Draw a diagram to show why the focal length must be equal to this distance if the camera is to take a photograph of a very distant object.

    The lens in this camera is 5.0 cm from the film when adjusted for a distant object, and 5.5 cm away from the film when adjusted for the closest possible object.
    b) What is the focal length of the lens?
    c) What is the image distance when the lens is at its furthest from the film?
    d) Use the lens equation with the answers to parts (b) and (c) to find the distance to the closest possible object that the camera can photograph.

14. The velocity of sound in air is 340 m s^{-1}. In water, the velocity of sound is 1500 m s^{-1}.
    a) What is the relative refractive index?
    b) Explain in detail what happens if a sound wave from a submerged submarine meets the surface at an angle of 70°.
    c) Under what circumstance could you get total internal reflection?

Further questions on page 161.

12 Interference and Diffraction

Isaac Newton did not believe that light could be a wave, but later a physicist called Thomas Young showed that light travels in waves. In fact, the interference and diffraction of light cannot be explained any other way.

In this chapter you will learn:
- what happens when two waves meet and 'superpose',
- how waves diffract through a gap,
- how waves from two or more sources can 'interfere'.

The Principle of Superposition

What happens when 2 waves are *superposed* – are in the same place at the same time.
This principle tells you how to find the result:

> The resultant displacement at any point is found by adding the displacements of each separate wave.

This adding-together of waves is called **interference**.

Look at the diagram. It shows two identical waves (coloured red and blue) which are adding together to give a resultant:

There is no phase difference, so they are *in phase* (see page 117).
The resultant wave is shown in black:

At *point A*, each wave is in the middle of its oscillation, so there is no displacement, and the resultant is zero as well.

At *point B*, the red and blue waves are at their lowest points, at the bottom of a trough. So the resultant has a displacement downwards, of the red amplitude *plus* the blue amplitude.

Point C, like point A, has a zero resultant.
Point D is the same as point B, but the displacements are upwards.

These 2 waves have added together to give a bigger wave.
This is called **constructive interference.**

This second diagram shows 2 waves that are *in anti-phase:*

Look at points W, X, Y and Z.

At each one, the red wave has an equal and *opposite* displacement to the blue wave.
The resultant at *every* point is therefore zero, and so the waves always cancel each other everywhere, as shown by the black line:

These two waves have cancelled out.
If the 2 waves were sound waves, there would be silence.
If the 2 waves were light waves, there would be darkness.
This is called **destructive interference.**

Thomas Young, who showed that waves can bend round corners and add up to give nothing!

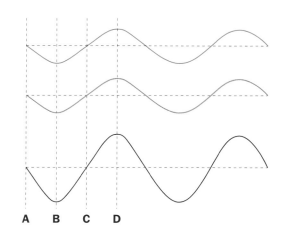

A   B   C D

Adding 2 waves that are in phase

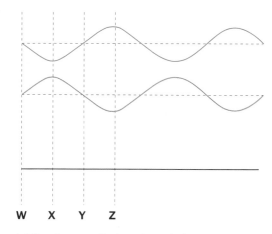

W   X   Y   Z

Adding 2 waves that are in anti-phase

Interference with reflected waves

Have you noticed how the signal on a portable radio, tuned to an FM station, changes when you walk about near it?

This is due to interference – 2 sets of radio waves are getting to the radio, one directly from the transmitter, and one reflected off you.

To see how radio waves interfere like this, you can use microwaves. A school microwave transmitter emits electromagnetic waves with a wavelength of about 3 cm (see page 175).

Metal sheets reflect microwaves, just as they reflect the waves inside a microwave oven. They act as a mirror.

Some microwave equipment and a vertical metal sheet are shown in the photograph:

The receiver will receive *two* waves: one directly from the transmitter, and one after it is reflected from the mirror.

By adjusting the position of the sheet, you can get a maximum signal at the detector.
If you move the metal sheet a few millimetres, the signal drops to a minimum.
If you move the sheet a bit more, the signal rises to a maximum again.

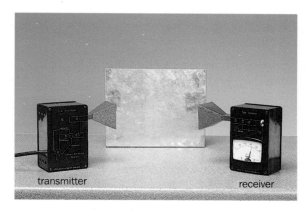

3 cm microwave apparatus

Phase difference and Path difference

Look at diagram 1, which shows the position of the reflector when the signal at the receiver B is a maximum:

It is a maximum because the wave coming directly from A, and the wave reflected at X, are adding together constructively at B.

Now look at diagram 2, where the reflector has been moved outwards from X. As it moved out, the signal became weaker, and then became a maximum again when the mirror is at Y.

It is a maximum because the waves at B are again adding together constructively. This means that the reflected waves must now be travelling an extra whole wavelength.
It means the **path difference** between path AXB and path AYB is one wavelength (1 λ).

Each extra wavelength in the path difference gives a **phase difference** of 360°. (See page 117.)

Path difference of 1λ = phase difference of 360° (2π rads)

A path difference of a whole number of wavelengths gives constructive interference (a maximum).
If the path difference has a extra half-wavelength it gives destructive interference (a minimum).

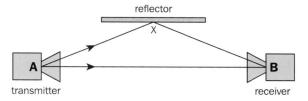

Diagram 1.   The waves at B are in phase

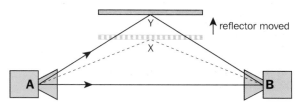

Diagram 2.   The waves at B are in phase again

Example 1
In the experiment shown above, when the distance AXB is 72.0 cm, the signal at B is very strong (a maximum).
The metal sheet is moved away slowly.
The signal at B weakens and then becomes a maximum again when AYB is 75.1 cm.
Calculate the wavelength of the microwaves.

AYB is exactly one wavelength more than AXB.   ∴ Wavelength λ = 75.1 cm − 72.0 cm   = 3.1 cm

141

▷ Stationary or Standing Waves

Waves involve movement and changes, such as the movement of air molecules. How can they be stationary?

Sometimes waves can be trapped in a space, such as the 'twang' going up and down a guitar string. This is due to superposition.

Adding reflected waves

To understand how waves can be trapped, look at this series of 5 snapshots:

They show a wave, coloured red, moving from left to right. It meets an identical wave, coloured blue, moving in the **opposite** direction at the same speed.
The 2 waves superpose to give a resultant wave, shown in black:

Vertical dashed lines in orange and green have been drawn to show the movement of the waves more clearly.
Each dashed line is a quarter of a wavelength from its neighbour.

Each snapshot is a quarter of a period after the one before, and so the pattern repeats after 4 snapshots.

For snapshots **1**, **3** and **5**, the resultant is zero everywhere. This is because the two waves that are combining are **in anti-phase**. They interfere destructively and cancel out.

For snapshots **2** and **4**, the resultant is large, because the two waves are **in phase**. They interfere constructively.

Now look at the waves where they cross the green and orange dashed lines.
Where the resultant crosses the green dashed lines, the value is zero for all 5 snapshots. At these points, the two combining waves always cancel.
These points are called **nodes**. There is no oscillation at a node.

Where the resultant crosses the orange dashed lines, the resultant wave oscillates with large amplitude. It goes zero, very large positive, zero, very large negative, zero ... and so on.
These are called **anti-nodes**, points of maximum oscillation.

Look at any red or blue wave on these diagrams:
Can you see that the distance from a green line to the next green one is always half a wavelength? And that the same is true for the orange lines? This means that:

Distance between nodes = distance between antinodes = $\frac{1}{2}\lambda$.

Trapping waves on a string

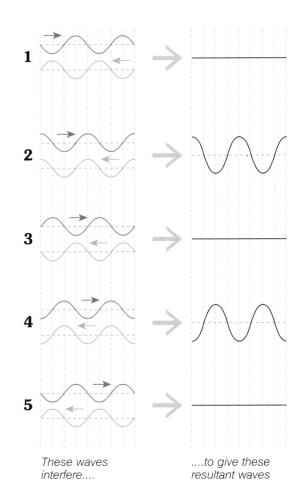

These waves interfere....

....to give these resultant waves

Example 2
Two loudspeakers emit sound waves of the same wavelength. When a microphone is moved between them, quiet places are observed 20 cm apart. What is the wavelength of the sound waves?

The quiet places are nodes, where the sound waves cancel each other, by destructive interference (see the green lines above).
Distance between nodes = $\frac{1}{2}\lambda$ = 20 cm.   So the wavelength of the sound waves is 2 × 20 cm = <u>40 cm</u>

Standing waves and Resonance

In the lab, you can trap waves on a string by attaching a vibration generator to a long rubber cord, fastened firmly at the other end:

The vibrator sends waves along the string. The waves reflect back from the far end, and meet waves on their way from the vibration generator.
So we have 2 identical waves, travelling in opposite directions, just like the red and blue waves in the opposite page.

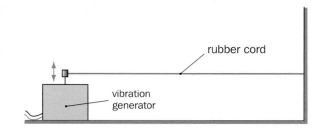

At certain frequencies, the rubber cord vibrates with a large amplitude. These are **resonant** frequencies of the system.
Resonance occurs when the frequency that is driving the system – from the vibration generator – matches a natural frequency of the system (see also page 100).

Nodes and Antinodes

This diagram shows what the string is doing:
At the nodes (N), the string does not move at all, and you can see the string quite distinctly.

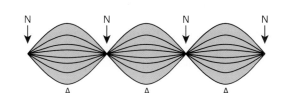

At the antinodes (A), the string oscillates with maximum amplitude, and so it appears as a blur.

Between the nodes and the antinodes, the string would oscillate, but with less amplitude than at the antinodes.
The appearance is of a set of blurry loops.
These are called **stationary waves**, or **standing waves**, because the pattern does not move along the string.

The resonant frequencies of a stretched string

If you increase the frequency of the vibration generator, you find that only certain frequencies produce a standing wave.

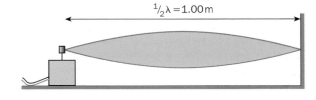

This is because you must have a whole number of stationary wave 'loops' fitting into the length of the string.
The length of each loop is exactly half of the wavelength of the waves sent from the vibration generator.

This first pattern has only one loop. The distance between nodes, $\frac{1}{2}\lambda$, is 1.0 m, so the wavelength, $\lambda = 2.0$ m.

In this example, the frequency $f = 10$ Hz so the speed of the waves travelling along this string is 20 m s^{-1} (you can check this by using $v = f\lambda$ from page 115).

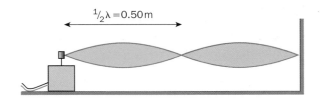

The second pattern has two loops. The distance between nodes, $\frac{1}{2}\lambda$, is now 0.50 m, so the wavelength $\lambda = 1.0$ m.
The wavelength has halved, because the frequency has doubled to 20 Hz.

Can you predict the rest of the pattern of resonances for this string?

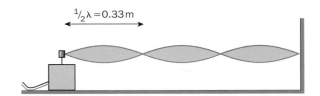

Frequency, f /Hz	10	20	30	40	50	60	etc.
Wavelength, λ /m	2.0	1.0	0.66	0.5	0.4	0.33	etc.
Number of loops	1	2	3	4	5	6	etc.

▷ Diffraction

Look at this photograph of water waves entering a harbour:

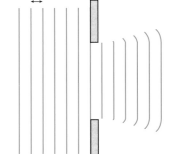

The wavefronts out at sea are straight, but when they pass through the gap, they curve round into regions you would not expect them to reach.

This bending of waves when they pass through a gap, or curve round edges, is called **diffraction**.

Diffraction and wavelength

How much do waves diffract when they go through a gap? It depends on the *wavelength* of the waves, and the *size of the gap* they are passing through.

Look at this first diagram of straight waves in a ripple tank. The waves are passing through a gap between two barriers:

Can you see that the gap is much bigger than the wavelength? When waves pass through a gap much bigger than the wavelength, the wavefronts bend just a little at the edges. There is not much diffraction. There is a clear shadow behind the barrier.

Now look at the second diagram:
Can you see that the gap is about the same size as the wavelength? This time, the wavefronts bend round in circular arcs.

> **When waves pass through a gap that is similar in size to their wavelength, there is a lot of diffraction.**

For light waves: the wavelength of light is much, much smaller than the size of a window. That's why sunlight makes sharp shadows in the room, and does not bend round the corners.

Light is seen to be diffracted only if it passes through a very narrow gap (see the opposite page). This shows us that light is a wave motion with a very small wavelength.

For sound waves: the wavelength of sound is similar in size to a doorway. Sound waves passing through a doorway are diffracted as in the second diagram. That's why someone outside can hear you talking, even when they can't see you!

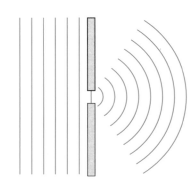

Example 3
Radio 4 transmits on FM at a frequency of 92.5 MHz.
Calculate the wavelength, and use it to explain why listeners in deep valleys cannot pick up Radio 4 FM.
(Speed of radio waves $c = 3.00 \times 10^8$ m s^{-1})

$$c = f\lambda$$

$$\therefore 3.00 \times 10^8 \text{ m s}^{-1} = 92.5 \times 10^6 \text{ Hz} \times \lambda \qquad \therefore \lambda = \frac{3.00 \times 10^8 \text{ m s}^{-1}}{92.5 \times 10^6 \text{ Hz}} = \underline{3.24 \text{ m}}$$

Because the FM wavelength is small compared with the size of mountains and valleys, it does not diffract much, so it does not bend down into the valleys.

Long wave radio may have a wavelength of 1500 m, so it does diffract round hills and into valleys.

144

Measuring diffraction

Light has a very short wavelength, so to see its diffraction you need a very small pin-hole.
This diagram shows what you see on a screen when you pass red laser light through a tiny hole:

In the centre is a red circle of light, called the **central maximum.**

Can you see that there is fainter ring around it?
This ring is called a **subsidiary maximum**.
It is where light from some parts of the hole is interfering *constructively* with light from other parts of the hole.

Between the central maximum and the subsidiary maximum there is a region with **no** light. This is where light from some parts of the hole is interfering destructively with light from other parts of the hole, so it cancels out. This is a **minimum**.

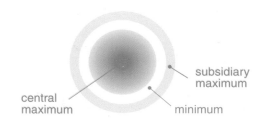

If you use a ripple tank to investigate the diffraction through a gap, you will see a pattern like this:

The blue arrow lies along a region with no waves, between the central maximum and a subsidiary maximum.

If we want to describe the amount of diffraction, we measure the **angle** between the central maximum and this first minimum.
It is labelled θ (theta) on the diagram.

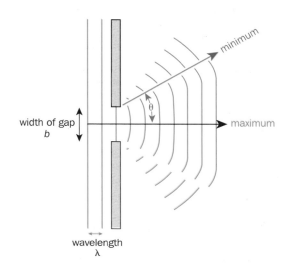

If you look very carefully at diffraction through a hole, you will see that there are several minima and subsidiary maxima. These get fainter and fainter as you go out from the centre.

Calculating diffraction angles

Look at either one of the two diffraction diagrams above.

If you plot **intensity** against **angle** from the centre, you get a graph like this:

It shows the intensity is greatest in the centre of the pattern.
θ is the angle of the first minimum.

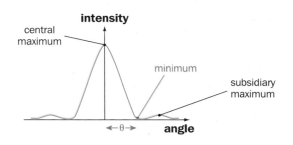

You can calculate θ, the angle of the first minimum, by:

| Sine of the angle of the first minimum $= \dfrac{\text{wavelength of the waves, } \lambda}{\text{width of the gap, } b}$ | or | $\sin \theta = \dfrac{\lambda}{b}$ |

It does not matter what units you use for the wavelength and for the gap width, but they must be the same units.

Example 4
Microwaves of wavelength 3.0 cm pass through a gap of width 5.0 cm.
What is the angle of the first minimum of the diffraction pattern?

$$\sin \theta = \frac{\lambda}{b} = \frac{3.0 \text{ cm}}{5.0 \text{ cm}} = 0.60$$

By using the 'inverse sine' function on the calculator, you will find that $\theta = \sin^{-1}(0.60) = \underline{37°}$

▷ Resolution

Imagine using a telescope to look at two stars that are very close together. It is important to be able to separate or **resolve** the two stars into separate images.

However, diffraction can make waves from different objects overlap and blur. In a telescope, the gap through which the waves are being diffracted is the objective lens. This makes the images of stars into little discs surrounded by the 'haloes' of subsidiary maxima (see page 145).

The diagrams on the right show two red stars seen in this way:

In the first diagram, the images of the two stars can be separated. Although the diffraction patterns overlap, it is easy to see that there are two different images. We say that the images **can be resolved.**

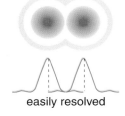

easily resolved

The second diagram shows the images of two stars closer together. It is **just** possible here to make out that there are two images very close together. The images here are **just resolved.**

just resolved

The third diagram has the two images even closer together. The two images blur into one here, and you could not tell that there are two different stars. You would think it was one bright star. The images here are **not resolved.**

What test can we apply to see if two images will be resolved?

A simple practical test is called **Rayleigh's criterion.**
Look at the graphs underneath the images of the two stars:

not resolved

The critical case is shown in the middle diagram, where the stars are **just** resolved. It shows **the centre of one image overlaps the first minimum of the second image.**

Rayleigh's criterion uses the diffraction equation on page 145 to give the smallest angular separation of two sources that **can** be resolved:

Sine of the angular separation of two sources $\geqslant \dfrac{\text{wavelength of the waves, } \lambda}{\text{width of the gap, } b}$	or $\quad \sin \theta \geqslant \dfrac{\lambda}{b}$

Example 5
A car's headlights are 1.5 m apart, and give out light of average wavelength 500 nm.
You are 5.0 km away, and the diameter of the pupil of your eye is 3.0 mm.
Would you see two separate headlights, or just a patch of light?

When the angles are small like this, we can say:
$\tan \theta \approx \sin \theta \approx \theta$ in radians.

This small angle approximation lets us write:

$\sin \theta \approx \theta \approx \dfrac{1.5 \text{ m}}{5.0 \text{ km}} = \dfrac{1.5 \text{ m}}{5000 \text{ m}} = 0.00030$ radians

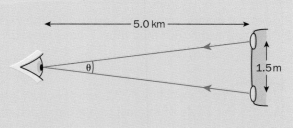

Also, $\dfrac{\lambda}{b} = \dfrac{500 \text{ nm}}{3.0 \text{ mm}} = \dfrac{500 \times 10^{-9} \text{ m}}{3.0 \times 10^{-3} \text{ m}} = 0.00017$

Since $\sin \theta$ is bigger than $\dfrac{\lambda}{b}$ then the sources **will** be resolved by your eye.

You should see two separate headlights (assuming you are not short-sighted).

▷ Physics at work: Radio astronomy

Radio Astronomy – the Big Dish

The famous 76 m diameter radio telescope at Jodrell Bank, near Manchester, was designed by Sir Bernard Lovell. It is used to investigate radio signals from space. These radio signals give information that you cannot get from optical telescopes.

The Lovell telescope was the first of the huge reflectors built for radio astronomy, and it is still one of the biggest.

The wavelength of these signals is about 0.21 m.
A large telescope is needed to resolve radio sources, because the wavelength is large. It is the ratio of wavelength λ to gap width b that determines resolution (see opposite page).

But what is the gap width in this case? It is the diameter of the reflecting dish itself. The smallest angle that the Lovell telescope can resolve, using the equation on the opposite page, is 0.16°.

The Lovell telescope is movable and can be pointed at any part of the sky. But it is a huge dish, and it is not feasible to make a movable dish very much bigger.

One ingenious solution was found in Puerto Rico in the Caribbean: a valley of roughly the right shape was turned into a huge radio telescope 305 m across, four times as big as the Lovell telescope.

Because it is four times bigger, it can resolve an angle that is four times smaller, and because it has 16 times the area, it can detect signals that are 16 times weaker.

The Lovell telescope at Jodrell Bank

The Arecibo telescope in Puerto Rico

The MERLIN network

Very Long Baseline Interferometry

As the example above shows, even a telescope the size of an entire valley cannot resolve angles smaller than 0.04°.
At optical wavelengths, the unaided human eye is 200 times better than this, while the 10m Keck optical telescope in Hawaii is 800 000 times better.
How can the resolution of radio telescopes be improved?

As if by magic, MERLIN provided the answer.
MERLIN is the **M**ulti-**E**lement **R**adio-**L**inked **I**nterferometer **N**etwork, an array of radio telescopes distributed around Great Britain. The telescopes are up to 217 km apart.

By combining the radio signals electronically at Jodrell Bank, the entire network acts as a single huge telescope, 217 000 m across. To combine these signals, you need to know the time at which the signals arrive with great accuracy, and modern atomic clocks provide this precision.

It is not surprising that the United States, with a huge area on which to put radio telescope dishes, has improved on MERLIN.
The Very Long Baseline Array is run by the US National Radio Astronomy Observatory.
It has ten identical radio telescopes ranging from Hawaii, in the middle of the Pacific Ocean, to the US Virgin Islands in the Caribbean – over 9000 km.
Certainly a very long baseline!

How much bigger can a baseline become?
Well, the US National Radio Astronomy Observatory and NASA have plans to put a radio telescope in orbit!

▷ Physics at work: Interference

Sounding brass

Stationary waves on a string give patterns of frequencies that are mathematically very simple: if the lowest resonant frequency is 100 Hz, then as you increase the frequency, you get resonance at 200 Hz, 300 Hz, 400 Hz, 500 Hz and so on.
Play these signals on a loudspeaker to a musician, and he or she will recognise them as part of a musical scale – the harmonic series.
In fact, these are the very notes that could be played on early trumpets like the one in the photograph:

The lowest notes – 100 Hz, 200 Hz, and 300 Hz – are rather widely spaced, and it is hard to play tunes with so many frequencies missing. As you go higher, the notes sound closer together, allowing the trumpeter to play tunes.

The high notes of the natural trumpets used in early music are so difficult to play that only a few very talented players like Crispian Steele-Perkins (above) use them.
In a modern trumpet, valves add extra lengths of tubing when you press keys. If you have a greater length of vibrating air, a new set of lower frequencies is available. These fill in the gaps between the easier low notes, so tunes can be played in the easier low register.

So trumpet playing has now become easy? Not a bit of it!
Modern virtuosi like Wynton Marsalis (right) are so skilled that composers just write music that is even more difficult.

Oil films and Soap bubbles

Superposition in Young's experiment and the diffraction grating happens because the wavefront was divided into different parts that travelled on different routes, and then met and interfered.
But there are other interference effects that work in quite a different way.

Thin-film interference happens when you have a thin layer of transparent material, such as oil on water, or the thin film of soapy water in a bubble.
Some waves (ABC in the diagram) reflect off the top of the layer, while some (ABDEF in the diagram) pass through it and reflect off the bottom.
When these 2 waves meet again (at CF), there is a path difference between them, and so they interfere.
Depending on the thickness of the film, they will interfere constructively or destructively.

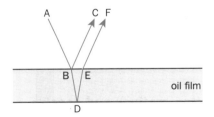

Colours in a thin soap film

Why are thin films coloured, as in this photo?

The path difference in the diagram may be a whole number of wavelengths for red light, but not for blue. This will give an interference maximum that looks reddish.

At other places the film is slightly thinner or thicker, and light of a different colour will interfere constructively.

The iridescent colours on the wings of a fly are also due to thin-film interference.

▷ Physics at work: Diffraction

Satellite television

Geostationary communications satellites, which rotate with the Earth, and so appear to stay in the same part of the sky, are widely used in communications (see page 82).
They were first suggested by science fiction writer Arthur C Clarke back in 1956, but even he could not have guessed how much use those satellites would get, with telephone, the Internet, and, above all, television channels.

But how does a satellite send television signals to all of Western Europe, for example?

The signal is sent, as a microwave beam, from a dish on Earth to a geostationary satellite over the equator, to the south of Europe.

Because of diffraction at its edges, the transmitting dish must be quite large, to make sure that enough power reaches the satellite.

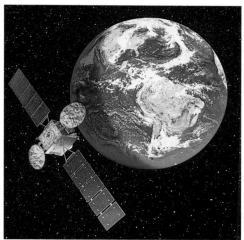

When the satellite re-transmits the TV signal, diffraction is no longer a nuisance, but a help.
The ratio of wavelength to dish size is carefully calculated to ensure that the beam spreads just enough.
Too much spread, and the signal becomes too weak to detect with the satellite dish on your house.
Too little spread, and the beam will not cover the target area (the whole of Western Europe).

Investigating the extreme ultraviolet

Until satellites and space probes became available, astronomy was restricted to light and to radio – because the atmosphere absorbs the other regions of the electromagnetic spectrum. Now, there are telescopes in space looking at all regions of the spectrum, from radio waves down to gamma rays. In most cases, the telescope is a reflecting dish, just like the Lovell radio telescope (page 147) or the Hubble telescope's reflecting mirror (page 136).

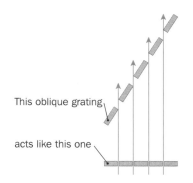

This oblique grating

acts like this one

Astronomers need to measure the wavelengths of the radiation received. For visible wavelengths, diffraction gratings are used.

These are made from glass, which has lines (slits) scratched into it with a sharp point moving in a straight line. The scratching apparatus is pushed along about 1 μm by a screw to make the next scratch. Although this needs precision, it is not difficult.

But the wavelength of the extreme ultraviolet is 100 times smaller than this, and so this method is not possible.

The method that is used is to cut a very fine grating, and then to tilt it obliquely, as the diagram shows.
The oncoming radiation 'sees' the grating almost edge on, which makes the slits appear closer.

The Orbiting and Retrievable Far and Extreme Ultraviolet Spectrograph (ORFEUS) used these oblique gratings to allow astronomers to analyse wavelengths as small as 40 nm.

This map of the Universe shows details of the high-energy ultraviolet radiation emitted by different stars, as detected by ORFEUS:

The data has helped astronomers work out what may be going on inside these stars.

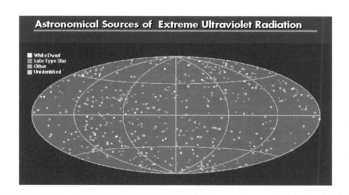

Astronomical Sources of Extreme Ultraviolet Radiation

White Dwarf
Late-Type Star
Other
Unidentified

▷ Physics at work: Age of the Universe

Hubble's Law and the Age of the Universe

The first realistic estimates of the distances to many galaxies were made by Edwin Hubble in the 1920s.

This followed ground-breaking work by the astronomers Henrietta Leavitt and Vesto Slipher in the previous decade.

Hubble found that galaxies were much more distant than anyone thought: the Universe suddenly became a much larger place than people had suspected.

Hubble also measured the Doppler shifts of these galaxies, and showed that the **more distant** galaxies had bigger redshifts, so were moving away **faster**.

He analysed these results to produce Hubble's Law:
the velocity v with which a galaxy is moving away from us is directly proportional to its distance d from us,

so: $v = H\,d$ where H is the Hubble constant.

From this equation you can work out how long it would take a galaxy, moving at its speed v, to travel the distance d. This is an estimate of the **time** since all matter was created at one place in the Big Bang.

Recent observations with the Hubble space telescope have given values of H which suggest that the Universe is between 10 and 15 billion years old.

Edwin Hubble …

… and the space telescope named in his honour

Speed traps

Busy stretches of road are dangerous for pedestrians, and this danger is increased when motorists *exceed* the speed limit.

The police monitor the speeds at accident black-spots with radar guns, which can detect the speed of oncoming traffic up to 100 metres away.
But how do they work?

The radar gun sends microwaves towards the car, which acts as a moving mirror.
The waves reflected back to the gun have a shorter wavelength (higher frequency) because of the Doppler effect.

In fact there is a double effect here. The image in a moving mirror travels at **twice** the speed of the mirror, so the formula in this case is $\dfrac{\Delta f}{f} = \dfrac{2\,v}{c}$ (compare this with page 156).

The microwave receiver in the radar gun detects the difference in frequency Δf between the emitted signal and the received signal.
The speed of the car is calculated from this, and displayed automatically on a screen.

A speed trap in action

▷ Physics at work: Blood flow

Measuring blood flow

It's difficult to measure blood flow without cutting into the patient – and that's the last thing you want to do to someone suffering from burns.
The laser Doppler technique can be used to measure blood flow. It uses the same principle as the radar speed trap, with laser light instead of microwaves, and red blood cells instead of cars.

As the blood flows along the capillaries near the surface of the skin, the red laser light is reflected by the red cells carried along in the fluid.
Blood approaching the detector raises the frequency of the light, while that moving away reduces it.
This broadens the single frequency given out by the laser into a range of frequencies in the reflected light.

The amount of frequency broadening, and the amplitude of the reflected signal, are processed to display on a screen the concentration of moving blood cells.

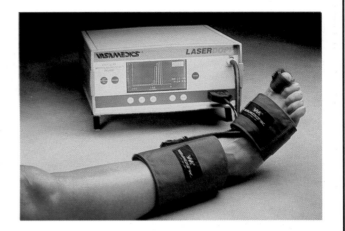

Summary

Waves change in wavelength and in frequency when given out by a moving object.
The Doppler equation gives a change in wavelength $\Delta\lambda$ and a change in frequency Δf by:

$$\frac{\Delta\lambda}{\lambda} = \frac{v}{c} \qquad \text{and} \qquad \frac{\Delta f}{f} = \frac{v}{c}$$

The light given out by moving stars or galaxies is Doppler-shifted.
It is red-shifted for retreating objects, and blue-shifted for approaching objects.
Distant galaxies are red-shifted due to the expansion of the Universe.

The ratio $\dfrac{\Delta\lambda}{\lambda}$ is called the red-shift parameter z, of a galaxy.

▷ Questions

1. Can you complete these sentences?
   a) When a source of waves moves towards you, the wavelength of the waves becomes ...., caused by the .... effect.
   This also makes the frequency become ....
   b) Stars or galaxies moving away from the Earth appear to have their spectral lines shifted towards .... wavelengths. This is called ....
   A galaxy moving towards us would have a ....-shift.

2. When the light reaching us from the *edges* of the Sun is analysed with a high precision spectrometer, it is found that the light from one side is red-shifted slightly, while the light from the opposite side has a blue-shift of the same size.
   What does this show you about the Sun?

3. The siren of an ambulance emits sound at a frequency of 1000 Hz.
   a) Calculate the wavelength of the sound. (The speed of sound, $c = 340$ m s⁻¹)
   b) The ambulance is moving away from you at a speed of 25 m s⁻¹. Calculate the wavelength of the sound waves reaching your ear.
   c) Calculate the frequency that you hear.

4. The spectrum of a galaxy shows a line in its spectrum with a wavelength of 398.5 nm. When the wavelength of the same spectral line is measured in the laboratory, it is 396.8 nm.
   a) Calculate the redshift parameter z for this galaxy.
   b) Calculate the speed with which the galaxy is moving away from us. (Speed of light, $c = 3.00 \times 10^8$ m s⁻¹)

▷ Waves

1. In a ripple tank a wooden bar touching the surface vibrates with SHM at 8 Hz. The transverse water wave produced is represented below.

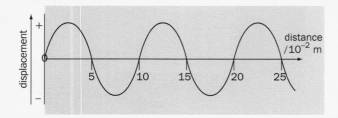

a) Define displacement and wavelength. [2]
b) Derive the equation for the speed c of the wave, $c = f\lambda$, where f is the frequency and λ the wavelength. [2]
c) Calculate the speed of the wave shown in the diagram. [1] (W)

2. The graph shows the displacement of particles in a transverse progressive wave against distance from the source at a particular instant with points labelled A, B, C, D and E.

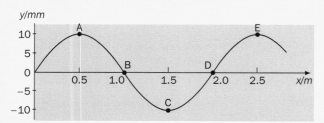

a) Write down the letters of
   i) all the points at which the speed of the particle is a maximum,
   ii) all the points at which the magnitude of the acceleration of the particle is a maximum,
   iii) two points which are in phase,
   iv) two points which are 90° out of phase. [4]
b) State the amplitude and wavelength of the wave. [2] (AQA)

3. Write an essay on the topic of waves and wave motion.
a) Describe the motions of the particles in transverse and longitudinal waves, and explain why polarisation is a phenomenon associated with transverse waves. [6]
b) Explain the terms *frequency, wavelength, speed, period, displacement and amplitude,* and show how these quantities may be obtained from graphical representations of both transverse and longitudinal waves. [10]
c) Describe an experiment to determine the frequency of a sound wave in air. [5] (OCR)

4. The diagram shows the variation with time t of the displacement x of the cones of two identical loudspeakers A and B placed in air.

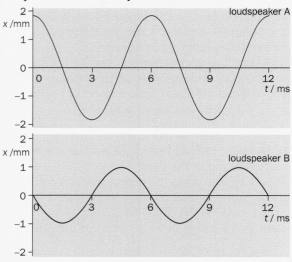

a) Calculate the frequency of vibration of the loudspeaker cones. [3]
b) Deduce the phase angle by which the vibrations of cone B lead those of cone A. [2]
c) State the type of wave produced in the air in front of each loudspeaker. [1]
d) Suggest, with a reason, which loudspeaker is likely to be producing the louder sound. [2]
e) The speed of sound waves in air is 340 m s^{-1}. Calculate the wavelength of the waves. [2] (OCR)

5. The speed v of ocean waves in deep water is given by the relationship
$$v = \sqrt{\frac{g\lambda}{2\pi}}$$
where g is the gravitational field strength and λ is the wavelength of the waves.
a) Derive an expression for the period T of the waves in terms of g and λ. [3]
b) Calculate the value of T when the wavelength of the waves is 8.0 m. [1] (AQA)

6. a) Explain what is meant by *unpolarised* light, and by *plane polarised* light. [2]

*

b) A light source appears bright when viewed through two pieces of polaroid, as shown in the diagram. Describe what is seen when B is rotated slowly through 180° in its own plane. [2]
c) State, giving your reasoning, which of the following types of waves can be polarised: *radio, ultrasonic, microwaves, ultraviolet.* [2] (AQA)

▷ **Reflection and Refraction**

7. The diagram shows a ray of light incident on the face of a cube made of glass of refractive index 1.50.

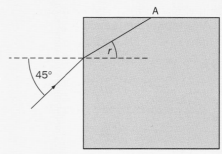

a) Calculate
   i) the angle r,
   ii) the critical angle for the glass–air interface. [3]
b) Use your answer to determine the path of the ray of light through the glass cube.
   Mark the path on a copy of the diagram and show the appropriate angles at the surfaces. [2]
c) When a drop of liquid of refractive index 1.40 is placed on the upper surface of the cube so as to cover point A, light emerges from the block at A. Explain, without calculation, how this occurs.
   [2] (AQA)

8. A postage stamp is examined through a converging lens held close to the observer's eye.
A virtual magnified image of the stamp is produced with the image being the same way up as the object.
a) Draw a ray diagram showing the situation above. Label the object and image and mark the focal points of the lens. [4]
b) The object is 0.09 m from the lens and the image is formed 0.36 m from the lens.
   Determine the magnification (size of image/size of object) of the stamp produced. [2] (AQA)

9. a) State the laws of reflection of light.
   Draw a diagram to show how a plane mirror can be used to turn a ray of light through 90°. [3]

b) State Snell's law for the refraction of light.
   The right-angled prism shown, made of glass of refractive index 1.53 may also be used to turn a ray of light through 90° using *total internal reflection*. Calculate the critical angle for the glass of the prism. Draw the path of a ray of light which is turned through 90° by the prism. [4]
c) Discuss the relative merits of the plane mirror and the right-angled prism as devices to turn a ray of light through 90°. [2] (OCR)

10. The graph shows the variation of refractive index n with wavelength λ for light travelling in water.
The diagram shows a mixture of red and violet light incident on an air/water surface.

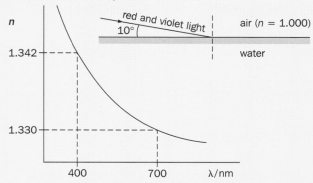

a) Calculate the angles of refraction for red and violet light. Mark them on a copy of the diagram. [4]
b) If the refractive index were independent of the wavelength, what changes would you need to make to your diagram? [2] (Edex)

11. The diagram (not to scale) shows a ray of monochromatic light entering a multimode optical fibre at such an angle that it just undergoes total internal reflection at the boundary between the core and the cladding.

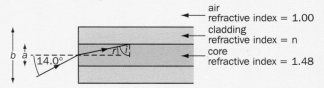

a) Suggest appropriate magnitudes for the diameters labelled a and b. [2]
b) Calculate the angles r and i. [3]
c) Hence estimate the refractive index n of the cladding. [2]
d) On a copy of the diagram, show what would happen to the ray of light if it were incident at an angle slightly greater than 14°. [3] (Edex)

12. The graph shows how refractive index varies across the diameter of a step index multimode optical fibre.

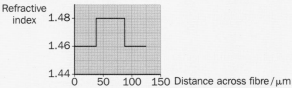

a) Calculate the critical angle for light travelling between the core and the cladding of the fibre. [2]
b) On a copy of the graph, show the variation of refractive index for a step index monomode optical fibre made from materials of refractive index 1.45 and 1.47. [2]
c) Calculate the time taken for a light pulse to travel 5.00 km along this monomode fibre. [3] (Edex)

Further questions on waves

▷ Interference and Diffraction

13. The diagram shows an arrangement to produce fringes by Young's two slits method.

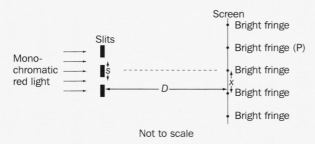

Not to scale

  a) State suitable values for *s* and *D* if clearly observable fringes are to be produced. [2]

  b) Explain how the bright fringe labelled P is formed. [2]

  c) What would be the effect on the fringe width *x* of
    i) increasing the slit separation *s*, and
    ii) illuminating the slits with blue light. [2]

  d) To obtain an interference pattern the light from the two slits must be coherent.
    What is meant by the term *coherent*? [1] (Edex)

14. For Young's two slit interference experiment, describe and explain the effect on the appearance of the fringes of

  a) reducing the separation of the slits but keeping the width of each slit constant,

  b) making each of the two slits wider but keeping the slit separation constant. [4] (AQA)

15. The diagram shows a loudspeaker which sends a note of constant frequency towards a vertical metal sheet. As the microphone is moved between the loudspeaker and the metal sheet the amplitude of the vertical trace on the oscilloscope continually changes several times between maximum and minimum values. This shows that a stationary wave has been set up in the space between the loudspeaker and the metal sheet.

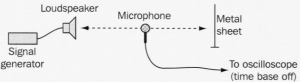

  a) How has the stationary wave been produced? [2]

  b) State how the stationary wave pattern changes when the frequency of the signal generator is doubled. Explain your answer. [2]

  c) What measurements would you take, and how would you use them, to calculate the speed of sound in air? [4]

  d) Suggest why the minima detected near to the metal sheet are much smaller than those detected near the loudspeaker. [2] (Edex)

16. The apparatus shown was used to demonstrate a transverse standing wave on a string. Both the weight and the distance between the pin and the pulley were kept constant. At 480 Hz there was a standing wave pattern and each loop was 10 cm long. At a higher frequency there were two more loops than at 480 Hz and each loop was 8 cm long.

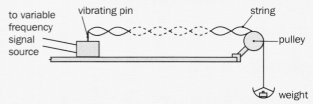

  a) Explain why standing waves occur at particular frequencies only. [2]

  b) Calculate the speed of the waves in the string. [3]

  c) Show that, at 480 Hz, eight loops would be created. [2] (W)

17. Parallel light is incident normally on a diffraction grating.

  a) Light of wavelength 5.9×10^{-7} m gives a first order image at 20.0° to the normal. Determine the number of lines per m on the grating. [2]

  b) Light of another wavelength gives a second order image at 48.9° to the normal. Calculate this wavelength. [2]

  c) What is the highest order in which both these wavelengths will be visible? Justify your answer. [2] (AQA)

18. The diagram shows water waves, produced by two sources A and B, in a ripple tank. The circles represent adjacent crests at a particular instant. The waves are moving with a speed of 80 mm s⁻¹.

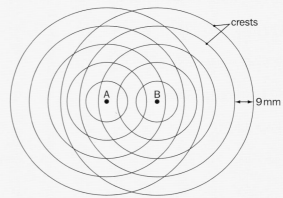

  a) From the diagram find the wavelength and frequency of the waves. [4]

  b) On a sketch of the diagram draw two lines
    i) joining successive points at which maximum constructive interference occurs, (Mark this line C)
    ii) joining successive points at which the adjacent destructive interference takes place. (Mark this line D) [4] (OCR)

▷ **Synoptic questions on waves**

19. The diagram shows a woman with long sight looking in a plane mirror. She cannot focus clearly on the image of the end of her nose when it is less than 225 mm from the mirror.

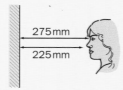

a) Calculate her least distance of distinct vision (near point distance). [2]
b) State what type of lens is needed to correct her near point distance to 250 mm.
 Explain how the lens corrects the vision and calculate the power of the lens. [5] (AQA)

20. a) What is meant by the superposition of waves? [2]

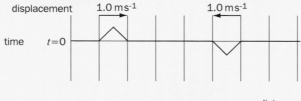

b) The diagram shows two wave pulses moving at 1.0 m s^{-1} in opposite directions along a string. They are drawn at time $t = 0$.
 On a copy of the diagram, draw the profile of the string at times $t = 1$ s, 2 s, 3 s.
 The vertical lines are 1.0 m apart. [5] (OCR)

21. This question is about a radar speed trap.
 A microwave transmitter T, emitting radiation of wavelength 0.030 m, is placed adjacent to a receiver R as in the diagram.
 Some of the output of T is fed directly to R and some is reflected from the metal sheet M.

a) The position of M is adjusted until the signal detected by R is a maximum. M is then moved slowly towards T and R. It is observed that the signal drops, reaching a minimum when M has been moved 0.0075 m. Explain why the signal has decreased from a maximum and why the minimum signal is not zero. [4]
b) The sheet M is removed and the device pointed at a car which is moving straight towards it at constant speed. The signal detected at R is observed to fluctuate in amplitude at a frequency of 1.2 kHz. Calculate the speed of the car. [3] (OCR)

22. Here is a section of a step index glass fibre.

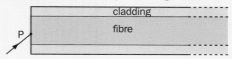

a) On a copy of the diagram, continue the path of the ray which enters at P and is contained within the fibre. [2]
b) Explain the condition under which the maximum angle of incidence is achieved for a ray which is contained within the fibre. [2]
c) What is the function of the cladding? [1]
d) State the necessary condition for the refractive index of the cladding. [1] (OCR)

23. Sound travels by means of longitudinal waves in air and solids. A progressive sound wave of wavelength λ and frequency f passes through a solid from left to right. The diagram X represents the equilibrium positions of a line of atoms in the solid.
 Diagram Y represents the positions of the same atoms at time $t = t_0$.

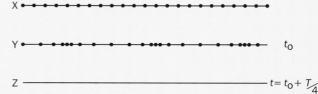

a) Explain why the wave is longitudinal. [1]
b) On a copy of the diagram Y label:
 two compressions (C), two rarefactions (R) and the wavelength of the wave. [3]
c) Along the line Z mark the positions of the two compressions and the two rarefactions at a time t given by $t = t_0 + T/4$. (T = period). [2] (Edex)

24. The left diagram shows an arrangement for investigating interference using microwaves. Two vertical slits S_1 and S_2 are at equal distances from the transmitter. A receiver is moved along the line AB. The right graph shows how the amplitude of the received signal varies with position along AB.

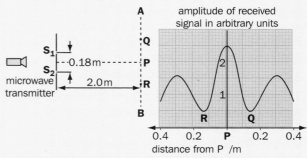

a) Explain why there is a maximum signal at P and a minimum signal at Q. [4]
b) The centres of the slits are 0.18 m apart and P is 2.0 m from the slits. Determine the wavelength and frequency of the microwaves. [4] (AQA)

14 Photons and Electrons

Just over a hundred years ago, everyone thought that Physics was nearly finished. They thought everything important had been discovered, and nothing was left except to tidy up some loose ends, and make some more accurate measurements.

How wrong that was! Within a few years, everyone's understanding of Physics had to be radically changed.

In this chapter you will learn:
- how metals can emit electrons,
- about photons – particles of light,
- how electrons can behave as waves.

Photons and electrons at work

The discovery of the electron

In the 19th century, physicists tried to see if gases would conduct by connecting two metal electrodes in a sealed tube.
They *do* conduct – you can see this in neon lights – but very high voltages are needed.

When experiments were done with gases that were at low pressures, unusual things were observed. The **cathode** (the negative electrode) gave off strange invisible 'rays', and these were called '**cathode rays**'.

J J Thomson measured the bending of these 'rays' in electric and magnetic fields. In 1897 he showed that they were streams of tiny negative particles, about a thousand times smaller than a hydrogen atom – he called them **electrons**. Soon everyone accepted that all matter contained these tiny negative particles.

Neon signs use electrons and photons

Heating metals to drive off electrons

Electrons can be pulled out of metals by very high voltages, but an easier method is used in television sets, and in the cathode ray oscilloscope (or CRO, see page 244).

If a metal cathode (a negative electrode) is **heated**, electrons leave the surface without needing a high voltage.
This is called **thermionic emission**.

This heating is done with a hot wire like an electric lamp filament, and sometimes the hot wire itself is used as the cathode.

If a positive electrode (an 'anode') is nearby, then the electric field between the cathode and the anode exerts a force on each free electron, as shown in the diagram:

The negative electrons are attracted to the positive anode.
The force makes the electrons accelerate towards the anode, and they gain kinetic energy.

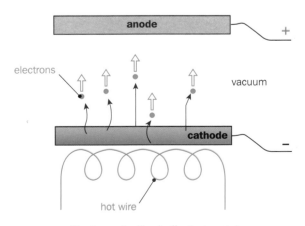

Electrons 'boiling' off a hot metal

Electron streams

Electron streams – 'cathode rays' – can be easily observed in the laboratory. A typical electron tube is shown in the diagram:

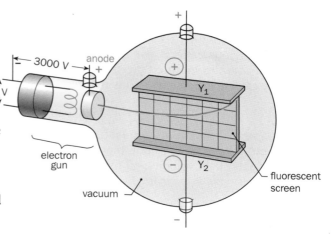

The tube is evacuated (the air is removed) so that air molecules do not get in the way of electrons.
Electrons are emitted from the hot metal wire or cathode (−). They are attracted to the cylindrical anode (+). They accelerate across the gap, to a high speed. Electrons that pass through a hole in the end of the cylinder then carry on at a steady speed. This is an **electron gun** (see also page 260).

You can deflect this stream of electrons with magnetic or electric fields, just as J J Thomson did. The diagram shows them deflected by two charged plates labelled Y_1 and Y_2. The direction in which the beam bends shows that electrons are *negatively* charged, and the large deflections show that the mass of the electron is tiny.

Electron kinetic energy and the electron–volt

The kinetic energy E_k gained when a charge accelerates across a potential difference is given by:

Energy transferred, E_k	**=**	**charge, Q**	**×**	**p.d., V**
(joules)		(coulombs)		(volts)

or $E_k = Q V$

(See also page 194, but note that here we are using E, not W, as the symbol for energy.)

For electrons (and other sub-atomic particles), a smaller unit called the **electron-volt**, symbol **eV**, is often used:

Energy transferred, E_k	**=**	**charge**	**×**	**p.d., V**
(electron-volts)		(electrons)		(volts)

The charge on the electron, $e = 1.6 \times 10^{-19}$ C. It follows that: **1 eV = 1.6×10^{-19} J**

Example 1
An electron is accelerated by a p.d. of 500 V. The electronic charge, $e = 1.6 \times 10^{-19}$ C.
Calculate the gain in kinetic energy a) in joules, b) in electron-volts.

a) $E_k = Q V = 1.6 \times 10^{-19}$ C $\times 500$ V $= \underline{8.0 \times 10^{-17}}$ J (2 s.f.)

b) E_k = number of electrons × p.d., $V = 1 \times 500$ V $= \underline{500 \text{ eV}}$

Using light to free electrons

One way to drive out electrons is by heating, as we've seen.
This diagram shows another way to emit free electrons:

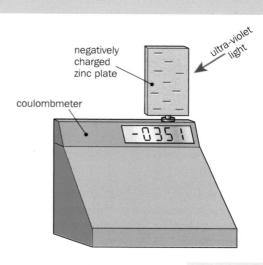

A negatively-charged, clean zinc plate will keep its charge in dry air for a long time.
However, if you shine ultra-violet light on it, it loses its charge very rapidly. The ultra-violet light gives the electrons the energy that they need to escape the metal.
The coulombmeter shows the negative charge decreasing.

This is the **photo-electric effect**.
Electrons given off in this way are often called *photo-electrons*.

There are more details on the next page.

▶ The Photoelectric effect

When you heat the metal cathode in an electron tube, like the one on the previous page, it gives off electrons. If you heat the metal more, it liberates more electrons, because the increased internal energy excites the free electrons more.

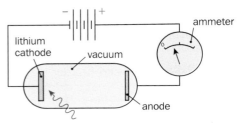

Dim blue light

So what happens when you shine light on a metal?

In Chapter 10 on Waves you learnt that waves with bigger amplitude carry more energy. For light, bigger amplitude means brighter light, so a brighter light will give off more photo-electrons. Is this right? No, surprisingly, it is **wrong!**

Look at these diagrams, which show what happens when light shines on a clean surface of the metal lithium:

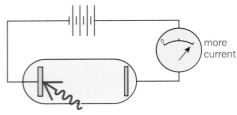

Bright blue light

- A dim blue light will make the lithium give off a few electrons, so there will be a small, measurable current.

- A brighter blue light will give a bigger photoelectric current, because there are more photo-electrons.

  This seems exactly what you would expect . . . **BUT**

- A red light, just as bright as the bright blue light, gives off **no** electrons at all, and the current is zero!

This is impossible to explain – **if** light is a wave.

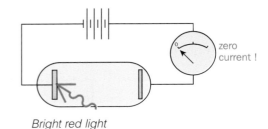

Bright red light

Light : particles and not waves?

The German physicist Max Planck suggested that electromagnetic **energy comes only in 'lumps',** called **quanta.**
Although he suggested this to solve a quite different problem (in thermodynamics), Albert Einstein used the idea to explain this photoelectric effect.

Einstein suggested that **each** lump, or **quantum**, of light energy can provide the energy for **one** electron to escape the metal.
If the quantum is too small, the electron cannot escape from the metal surface.

Dim blue light

If light is made of tiny particles like this, then it makes sense to give them a particle name. Modern particle names usually end in '–on,' so a light particle is called a **photon**.

Now we can explain the 3 results listed above:

- The photons of blue light contain enough energy to eject electrons from lithium. A dim blue light has few photons, so few electrons are liberated. This gives a small photo-electric current.

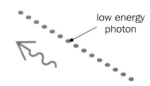

Bright blue light (more photons)

- A bright blue light has more of these high-energy photons; so more electrons are liberated, giving a larger photo-electric current.

- But red light consists of photons that do **not** have enough energy to emit electrons from lithium.
Even though a bright red light has very many of these photons, not one of them has enough energy to eject an electron.

*Bright red light
(photons have less energy)*

166

▷ Planck's equation and photon energy

In his work on thermodynamics, Planck produced this equation:

Energy of a photon, E	=	the Planck constant, h	×	frequency, f
(joules)		(joule-second)		(hertz)

or

$$E = h f$$

The Planck constant $= 6.6 \times 10^{-34}$ J s.

This is an astonishing equation!
On the left hand side, you have the energy of a **particle**.
On the right hand side, you have the frequency of a **wave**.
For light, you need to use **both** particle and wave ideas.

Example 2
Blue light has a frequency of 7.7×10^{14} Hz, while red light has a frequency of 4.3×10^{14} Hz.
Calculate the energy of a photon of each. The Planck constant, $h = 6.6 \times 10^{-34}$ J s.

Blue light: $E = h f = 6.6 \times 10^{-34}$ J s $\times 7.7 \times 10^{14}$ Hz $= \underline{5.1 \times 10^{-19}\text{ J}}$ (2 s.f.)

Red light: $E = h f = 6.6 \times 10^{-34}$ J s $\times 4.3 \times 10^{14}$ Hz $= \underline{2.8 \times 10^{-19}\text{ J}}$ (2 s.f.)

These figures agree with the observations on the opposite page.
The energy of a photon of blue light is much more than the energy
of a photon of red light.

The energies in Example 2 seem incredibly small.

It is often clearer to write energies in electron-volts,
and Example 1 on page 165 shows that there is a
'scaling factor' of 1.6×10^{-19} J per eV:

Energy in joules = energy in eV $\times 1.6 \times 10^{-19}$ J eV^{-1}

Lower energy photons   *Higher energy photons*

Example 3
Convert the energy of the blue photon in Example 2 from J into eV.

Energy of photon $= 5.1 \times 10^{-19}$ J $= \dfrac{5.1 \times 10^{-19}\text{ J}}{1.6 \times 10^{-19}\text{ J eV}^{-1}} = \underline{3.2\ eV}$ (2 s.f.)

2 eV

The energy of a typical visible photon

Photons and the Electromagnetic Spectrum

Photons of visible light have energies between 1.7 eV and 3.2 eV.
But what about the invisible parts of the electromagnetic spectrum?

Infra-red radiation has a smaller frequency than red light, so its
photons have **less** energy. Microwaves and radio waves have
photons with even less energy.

Going along the electromagnetic spectrum in the other direction,
ultra-violet radiation has higher frequency than blue light, so its
photons are **more** energetic. That explains why UV light is
hazardous.

X-rays and gamma-rays have even higher frequency, and so their
photons have even more energy (and so are even more dangerous).

Ultra-violet photons are dangerous

▷ Escaping from a metal – the work function

We've seen that all photons carry energy, but red light cannot liberate electrons from lithium metal, even though blue light can.

Look at the graph shown here:

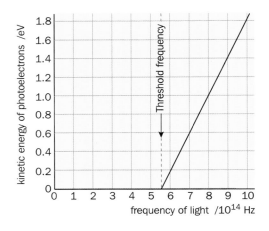

It shows the *energy* of the photo-electrons that are emitted from lithium metal for different *frequencies* of light.
Light of frequency less than 5.6×10^{14} Hz does not give any photo-electrons. This is called the cut-off or **threshold frequency**, f_0.

The graph goes up as a straight line – as the frequency of light goes up, the energy of the emitted electrons goes up as well.

The gradient of this line is the Planck constant, h.
This is true for any metal, not just lithium.

Using Planck's equation $E = hf$ we can convert the frequency of the incident light to energy of the photons.
We then get a clearer picture if we plot the *energy* of the emitted electrons against the *energy* of the incident photons of light.

This is shown on the second graph:

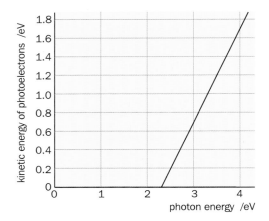

When the photon energy is 3 eV, the energy of an emitted photo-electron is 0.7 eV – that's 2.3 eV less.
Because the graph is a straight line, this difference of 2.3 eV is true for all photo-electrons emitted from lithium.
If you look at the place where the graph cuts the photon energy axis, you will see that's 2.3 eV as well.

This 2.3 eV is the smallest quantity of energy that is needed for an electron to be given off from lithium. It is called the **work function** of this metal and has the symbol ϕ (the Greek letter phi).
These graphs show us that for lithium metal, $\phi = 2.3$ eV.

At the cut-off point, all the energy of the photon goes to removing the electron from the metal, so the **work function** $\phi = hf_0$.

The work function is larger for less reactive metals, like zinc. It is harder to remove electrons from these metals, and so ultra-violet light is needed.

In calculations, you may be given the **cut-off wavelength** λ_0, the longest wavelength of light that emits photo-electrons. You can use this to find the threshold frequency f_0 as in this example.

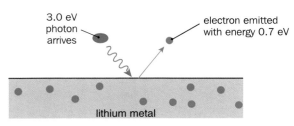

A photon must have more than 2.3 eV to overcome the work function of lithium metal

---

Example 4
The cut-off wavelength, λ_0, for potassium is 550 nm. Calculate the work function ϕ in joules.
The speed of light $c = 3.0 \times 10^8$ m s^{-1} and the Planck constant $h = 6.6 \times 10^{-34}$ J s.

First find the threshold frequency f_0, and then use Planck's equation.

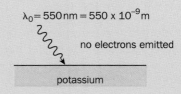

From page 115: $c = f_0 \lambda_0$

$\therefore$ $3.0 \times 10^8 \text{ m s}^{-1} = f_0 \times 550 \times 10^{-9} \text{ m}$

$\therefore$ $f_0 = \dfrac{3.0 \times 10^8 \text{ m s}^{-1}}{550 \times 10^{-9} \text{ m}} = \underline{5.5 \times 10^{14} \text{ Hz}}$ (2 s.f.)

$\phi = hf_0 = 6.6 \times 10^{-34} \text{ J s} \times 5.5 \times 10^{14} \text{ Hz} = \underline{3.6 \times 10^{-19} \text{ J}}$ (2 s.f.)

▶ Einstein's photoelectric equation

When a photo-electron has absorbed a photon and escaped
from the metal, it has only kinetic energy.
Conservation of energy shows us that:

Kinetic energy of the electron = energy of photon – energy needed to escape from the metal

The minimum energy needed to escape from the metal is the
work function, ϕ. This gives us **Einstein's equation**:

> **Maximum kinetic energy of electron, E_k = the Planck constant, h × frequency, f – work function, ϕ**

So : $\boxed{E_k = h\,f - \phi}$ or $\boxed{\tfrac{1}{2}\,m\,v^2 = h\,f - \phi}$

You can use the last form of the equation if you need to calculate
the speed of the electrons.

Example 5
Light of frequency 6.70×10^{14} Hz shines on to clean caesium metal.
What is the maximum kinetic energy of the electrons emitted?

The work function of caesium is 3.43×10^{-19} J and
the Planck constant, $h = 6.63 \times 10^{-34}$ J s.

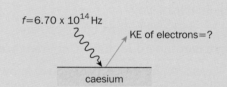

$E_k = h\,f - \phi$

$\quad = 6.63 \times 10^{-34}\text{ J s} \times 6.70 \times 10^{14}\text{ Hz}\ -\ 3.43 \times 10^{-19}\text{ J}$

$\quad = 4.44 \times 10^{-19}\text{ J}\ -\ 3.43 \times 10^{-19}\text{ J}$

$\quad = \underline{1.01 \times 10^{-19}\text{ J}}\quad (3\text{ s.f.})$

Measuring the work function

Photo-electrons are given out when light shines on to the surface of
a reactive metal, but the surface must be clean and shiny. This is
only possible with a reactive metal if there is no air, so the metal
must be kept in a vacuum.

Compare this circuit diagram with the photocell circuit on page 166.
This circuit has the power supply facing in the opposite direction.
Instead of helping the electrons round the circuit, it is trying to
push them back into the reactive metal caesium.

To find the work function of caesium, you increase the p.d. of the
power supply gradually until the ammeter shows there is no current.
When this happens, the maximum kinetic energy of the photo-
electrons is equal to the potential energy provided by the power
supply.
The voltmeter reading gives you the kinetic energy, in electron-volts,
gained by the photo-electrons for those particular photons (at that
particular frequency of light).

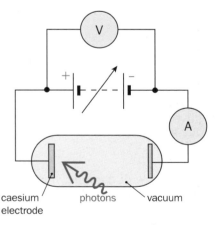

Measuring the work function ϕ

You can repeat this experiment with different frequencies of light
and plot a graph like the one at the top of the opposite page.
The point where the graph cuts the horizontal axis gives the
threshold frequency f_0, which you can use to calculate the work
function as in Example 4.

▷ Electrons as waves

Electron beams produce a very strange effect if they strike thin layers of graphite carbon, as this diagram shows:

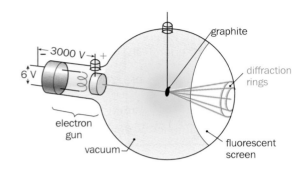

Most of the electrons pass straight through the very thin graphite, but others pass through at certain angles only, giving rings on the fluorescent screen.

These rings are like the interference maxima you get when light waves pass through diffraction gratings (see page 150).

But where is the diffraction grating in this case?
And what are the waves that are diffracting?

De Broglie's idea

In 1924, nearly 20 years after Einstein explained the photoelectric effect, a young French student named Louis de Broglie (pronounced *Broy*) made a bold suggestion.

We thought that light was a wave, he said. And now we see it can be a particle as well. Is it possible that electrons, which we thought were particles, can also be waves?

In Chapter 12, you saw the two key facts that convinced physicists that light was a wave:
- light can be diffracted by a gap, and
- light can superpose to give interference patterns.

The electron tube experiment above shows exactly that! Electrons are diffracted by the gaps between atoms, and give maxima on the fluorescent screen where they are in phase.

Waves or particles?   Wavicles?

De Broglie's theory suggested that the wavelength of electron waves was very small, about the size of an atom. So the separation of the slits in a diffraction grating for electrons would have to be small too – about the size of an atom.

Look at the diagram of electrons striking atoms in graphite:

The atoms are in regular columns, shown by the green lines. The gaps between these columns of atoms are regularly spaced, just like a diffraction grating. There are interference maxima on each side of the central maximum, just as in an ordinary diffraction grating exposed to light (see page 150).

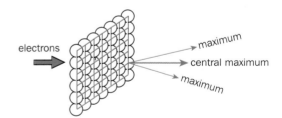

Graphite atoms diffracting electrons

The atoms are also in regular rows, shown by the red lines. These give interference maxima above and below the central maximum, but they are not shown on the diagram.

In a real sample of graphite, there are many layers of atoms:

These are not parallel but jumbled, rather like a pile of loose papers on a desk.
The diffraction maxima from these different layers are all at the same angle to the central maximum, but in all possible directions. These add together to give the rings seen on the fluorescent screen.

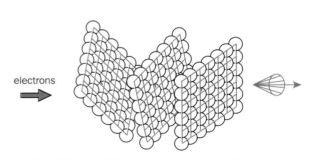

Graphite has different layers arranged at random

▷ De Broglie's equation

Planck's equation for the energy of a photon is $E = h f$.

De Broglie suggested a similar equation for the electron.
In his equation, the left hand side is not energy, but another
important measure of a moving particle – its momentum.

(Momentum is mass multiplied by velocity, $m v$, see page 46.)

In a similar way, the right hand side has the other important
measure of a wave – its wavelength.
De Broglie's equation is:

Momentum = mass × velocity

Momentum of the particle, $m v$ $= \dfrac{\text{the Planck constant, } h \ (\text{J s})}{\text{wavelength of the wave, } \lambda \ (\text{m})}$ (kg m s^{-1})	or	$m v = \dfrac{h}{\lambda}$	so	$\lambda = \dfrac{h}{m v}$

Remember:

- For photons, always use Planck's equation. $E = h f$

- For the wave behaviour of sub-atomic 'particles'
  like electrons, always use de Broglie's equation. $\lambda = \dfrac{h}{m v}$

Example 6
Electrons are travelling at a speed 2.0×10^6 m s^{-1}.
Calculate the de Broglie wavelength of the electrons.

The mass of the electron is 9.1×10^{-31} kg.
The Planck constant $h = 6.6 \times 10^{-34}$ J s.

Momentum = mass × velocity $= 9.1 \times 10^{-31}$ kg $\times$ 2.0×10^6 m s^{-1} $= 1.8 \times 10^{-24}$ kg m s^{-1}

$\lambda = \dfrac{h}{m v} = \dfrac{6.6 \times 10^{-34} \text{ J s}}{1.8 \times 10^{-24} \text{ kg m s}^{-1}} = \underline{3.6 \times 10^{-10} \text{ m}}$ (2 s.f.)

Electron waves and the Atom

Are electrons waves? Electron diffraction shows this is true, but
there is other evidence as well.

The model of the atom that you studied at GCSE was first suggested
by Ernest Rutherford (see page 329).
It has electrons orbiting a central positive nucleus, like the planets
around the Sun.

It was quickly realised that this model is physically impossible.
If the electrons, which are negatively charged, moved in circles,
electromagnetic theory shows they would radiate energy.
But this would make them slow down and spiral into the nucleus.
Luckily, this does not happen, or matter could not exist!

But what keeps electrons in their orbits?

The answer comes from the fact that electrons behave as waves.
Electrons are trapped within the atom in the same way as stationary
waves are trapped on a rope (see page 143). The diagram shows a
very simplified view of an electron trapped in this way:

Theory based on stationary wave ideas can predict the spectra of
atoms accurately.

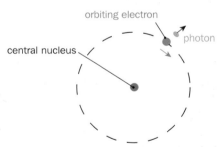

Rutherford's atom

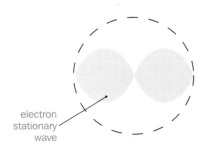

Electron-wave atom

▶ Physics at work: Photons and electrons

Photocells and energy production

The photoelectric effect was first studied with reactive metals such as caesium. Nowadays there is far more interest in semiconductors, because some of these can also convert photon energy into electrical energy.
That is, they convert light energy directly into electrical energy. These **photovoltaic** photocells, made from silicon, have been used for over forty years.

Early uses were in places where other electric sources were inconvenient. The orbiting satellite Vanguard 1 was fitted with photovoltaic solar panels as long ago as 1958.
Devices with low current demands, such as pocket calculators, often use photovoltaic cells.

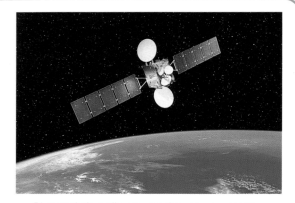
Photovoltaic cells are used to power satellites

The first photovoltaic power station on Earth was built in California in 1982, rated at 1 MW. Although this is small by power station standards, there has been much progress since then, with photovoltaic efficiencies continually improving, and costs coming down.

Photovoltaics are not yet economical for many countries, but their use is bound to increase because of the increasing cost, pollution and scarcity of fossil fuels, as well as the problems experienced by the nuclear industry. See also page 250.

Electron microscopes

A problem with ordinary 'light' microscopes occurs at high magnifications.
When the objects you are looking at are about the size of a wavelength of light – for example, the chromosomes in a cell nucleus – then a lot of diffraction occurs (see page 144). People using early microscopes at high magnifications often saw stripy 'structures' inside the cell (due to interference of light) which were not actually present at all!

The way to get better resolution is to use smaller wavelengths, such as X-rays. Unfortunately, you cannot focus X-rays, as they go straight though any 'lens' that you make.

A solution is to use **electron beams**.
The wave nature of electrons means that they can be reflected from microscopic objects just like light waves.

Example 6 on page 171 shows that electrons travelling at 2×10^6 m s^{-1} have a wavelength very like that of X-rays. The 'lenses' used to focus the electron beam consist of magnetic fields which exert forces on the moving electrons.

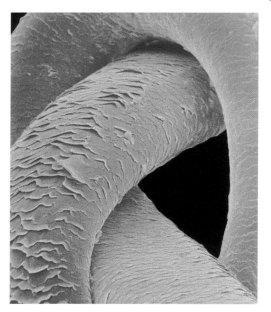
An electron-micrograph of a knot in a human hair

Electron microscopes use a wonderful combination of particle and wave properties.
The electrons are accelerated to a high speed by a high voltage – this is a particle effect.
They then reflect off the object on the microscope stage – this is a wave effect.
They are then brought to a focus with magnetic fields and detected – these are particle effects once more.

By accelerating with high enough voltages, the wavelength of the electrons is small enough to give the detail shown in this electron-micrograph.

Summary

Electrons can be driven out of metals by heating (thermionic emission), or by shining light upon them (photoelectric effect).
Electron energies are often measured in electronvolts (eV) where $1\ eV = 1.6 \times 10^{-19}$ J.
The photoelectric effect shows that light can be thought of as particles, called photons.

Planck's equation: The energy of a photon, $E = hf$. A packet of energy is called a quantum (plural: quanta)

To remove electrons from a metal requires a minimum amount of energy called the work function ϕ.
Einstein's photoelectric equation: Maximum kinetic energy of a photo-electron, $E_k = hf - \phi$.
The work function $\phi = hf_0$ where f_0 is the threshold frequency.

Beams of electrons can be diffracted and interfere, showing that electrons can act like waves.

De Broglie's equation for 'particle' waves: momentum, $mv = \dfrac{h}{\lambda}$ or $\lambda = \dfrac{h}{mv}$

▶ Questions

1. Can you complete these sentences?
   a) Negative particles called .... were first discovered by J J Thomson.
   These can be driven out of a metal by heating, (called .... emission) or by shining .... on it (called the .... effect).
   b) A convenient, small unit of energy for use in atomic calculations is the ....
   The conversion factor between energy in joules and energy in electron-volts is: $1\ eV = $ .... J
   c) When light of high enough frequency shines on a metal, photo-electrons are ....
   The lowest frequency is called the .... frequency.
   Blue light has a .... frequency than red light.
   d) The energy arrives in quanta or 'lumps' whose size depends on the .... of the light.
   A particle of light is called a ....
   To drive out a photo-electron, the photon must have more energy than the .... function of the metal.
   e) Light can behave as a .... as well as a wave.
   Electrons are normally thought of as particles, but they can also behave as ....

2. Calculate the energy (i) in joules and (ii) in electron-volts when an electron is accelerated through a p.d. of
   a) 10 V,
   b) 10 kV.
   (Charge on electron, $e = 1.6 \times 10^{-19}$ C)

3. Calculate the energy (i) in joules and (ii) in electron-volts of a photon of:
   a) radio waves of frequency 100 MHz,
   b) microwaves of wavelength 10 cm,
   c) infra-red of wavelength 1 mm,
   d) ultra-violet light of wavelength 100 nm,
   e) X-rays of wavelength 10 nm.
   (Speed of light, $c = 3.0 \times 10^8$ m s^{-1})
   (The Planck constant, $h = 6.6 \times 10^{-34}$ J s)

4. The table gives the kinetic energy of photo-electrons emitted from a metal surface for different frequencies of light.

Electron energy /10^{-19} J	Frequency /10^{14} Hz
0.22	5.00
0.88	6.00
1.54	7.00
2.20	8.00
2.87	9.00

   a) Plot a graph of electron energy (vertically) against frequency (horizontally).
   b) Use the graph to find the work function of the metal.
   c) Find the gradient of the graph. Can you recognise what this is?

5. A photocell cathode is made of a metal with a work function 2.8 eV.
   a) Light of wavelength 400 nm shines on the cathode. Will photoelectrons be emitted?
   b) The cathode is now illuminated with ultra-violet radiation, and electrons are emitted with energy 1.4 eV. Calculate the wavelength of the ultra-violet radiation.
   (Speed of light, $c = 3.0 \times 10^8$ m s^{-1})
   (Charge of electron, $e = 1.6 \times 10^{-19}$ C)
   (The Planck constant, $h = 6.6 \times 10^{-34}$ J s)

6. Electrons are accelerated to a kinetic energy of 500 eV. Calculate their
   a) velocity,
   b) momentum,
   c) de Broglie wavelength.
   (Mass of electron, $m = 9.1 \times 10^{-31}$ kg)
   (Values of e and h as in question 5.)

Further questions on page 188.

15 Spectra and Energy Levels

From the time that our ancestors first gazed at rainbows, spectra have been a source of both wonder and new understanding.

From gamma rays to radio waves, spectra have given us new understanding, ranging from the structure of atoms to the nature of distant quasars.

In this chapter you will learn:
- about the electromagnetic spectrum,
- about absorption and emission spectra,
- how spectra depend upon energy jumps.

Natural spectral analysis

The electromagnetic spectrum

The diagram shows the entire electromagnetic spectrum:

What do you notice about the numbers on the scales?

The scales are both *logarithmic* – they do not go up in equal steps, but in equal *ratios*. Every number is ten times bigger than the adjacent smaller one.

Why is it not possible to have a regular linear scale?

The smallest division here is about 10^{-12} m. If you try to draw this diagram using a linear scale with just one millimetre of scale representing 10^{-12} m, the diagram would have to be very big to show the longest radio wavelength – it would stretch out beyond the planet Pluto!
Logarithmic scales have their uses!

Don't forget, when reading these scales, that $10^0 = 1$, and that you must key 10^8 (for example) into a calculator as 1×10^8 by pressing 1 EXP 8 (see also page 401).

Photon energies and the electromagnetic spectrum

In Chapter 14, you calculated the energy of photons, both in joules and in a useful smaller unit – electron-volts (eV).
The diagram shows the regions of the electromagnetic spectrum described by *wavelength* and by *photon energy* (in eV):

- Wavelength is used when you need to consider the *wave properties* of the radiation.
  You needed to do this when we looked at diffraction and interference (in Chapter 12).

- Photon energy is used when you need to consider the *particle properties* of the radiation.
  You needed to do this for the photoelectric effect, and you will need it in this chapter too.

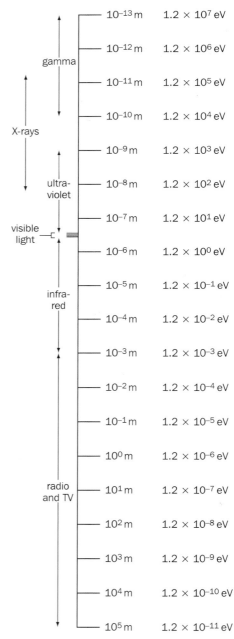

10^{-13} m	1.2×10^7 eV
10^{-12} m	1.2×10^6 eV
10^{-11} m	1.2×10^5 eV
10^{-10} m	1.2×10^4 eV
10^{-9} m	1.2×10^3 eV
10^{-8} m	1.2×10^2 eV
10^{-7} m	1.2×10^1 eV
10^{-6} m	1.2×10^0 eV
10^{-5} m	1.2×10^{-1} eV
10^{-4} m	1.2×10^{-2} eV
10^{-3} m	1.2×10^{-3} eV
10^{-2} m	1.2×10^{-4} eV
10^{-1} m	1.2×10^{-5} eV
10^0 m	1.2×10^{-6} eV
10^1 m	1.2×10^{-7} eV
10^2 m	1.2×10^{-8} eV
10^3 m	1.2×10^{-9} eV
10^4 m	1.2×10^{-10} eV
10^5 m	1.2×10^{-11} eV

gamma, X-rays, ultra-violet, visible light, infra-red, radio and TV

Electromagnetic wavelengths and energies

▷ The regions of the electromagnetic spectrum

The diagram on the opposite page shows the usual way in which the spectrum is divided up, but there are no sudden boundaries between the different regions.

Gamma radiation and X-rays

Radioactive nuclei emit gamma rays, which are mostly in the energy range from 10^4 eV to 5×10^6 eV.

X-rays are produced when high-speed electrons decelerate quickly. High-energy X-rays have shorter wavelengths than low-energy gamma rays, so it is impossible to tell them apart by observation. They are given different names only because of the way they are produced.

How do we classify unknown 'cosmic' photons coming from space? 10 keV (10^4 eV) is usually chosen as the boundary. For example, the Chandra X-ray Observatory satellite is sensitive to photons up to 10 keV, while the Compton Gamma Ray Observatory satellite detects photons from 10 keV to beyond 10 MeV.

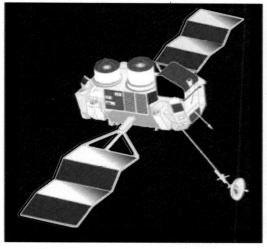

The Compton gamma-ray observatory

Example 1

Calculate the wavelength of a high-energy 'cosmic' photon with energy of a GeV ($= 10^9$ eV).

The electronic charge, $e = 1.6 \times 10^{-19}$ C, the speed of light, $c = 3.0 \times 10^8$ m s^{-1}, and the Planck constant, $h = 6.6 \times 10^{-34}$ J s.

1 eV $= 1.6 \times 10^{-19}$ J (from page 165) so: 10^9 eV $= 10^9 \times 1.6 \times 10^{-19}$ J $= 1.6 \times 10^{-10}$ J

$E = hf$ (from page 167) so: 1.6×10^{-10} J $= 6.6 \times 10^{-34}$ J s $\times f$ $\therefore$ $f = \dfrac{1.6 \times 10^{-10} \text{ J}}{6.6 \times 10^{-34} \text{ J s}} = 2.4 \times 10^{23}$ Hz

$c = f\lambda$ (from page 115) so: 3.0×10^8 m s^{-1} $= 2.4 \times 10^{23}$ Hz $\times \lambda$

$$\therefore \lambda = \frac{3.0 \times 10^8 \text{ m s}^{-1}}{2.4 \times 10^{23} \text{ Hz}} = 1.2 \times 10^{-15} \text{ m} \approx 10^{-15} \text{ m}$$

This is written as a power of ten (as just an order of magnitude) because that is the accuracy of the data (10^9 eV).

Ultra-violet (UV) This energetic, ionising radiation is given off by electrical discharges, such as sparks and lightning.
It is also given out by stars such as our Sun. The ozone layer in our atmosphere absorbs UV with a wavelength less than 300 nm (3×10^{-7} m) but its recent thinning increases the risk of skin cancers.

Visible light Whether electromagnetic radiation is visible or not seems very clear – you can either see it or you can't! The range is clear enough for humans, 400 nm to 700 nm, but other animals have eyes sensitive to different ranges. Eg. bees can see ultra-violet.

Infra-red (IR) is produced by all hot bodies.
This was the first invisible part of the electromagnetic spectrum to be discovered (by the astronomer William Herschel in 1800).
A common application of IR, produced by 'light' emitting diodes (or LEDs, see page 248), is found in remote controls for televisions:

Radio wavelengths range from millimetres, as used in radar and in microwave ovens, up to tens of kilometres used for submarine communications. Their photon energy is small.

Infra-red, but not produced by a hot object

▷ Physics at work: Electromagnetic waves

Synchrotron radiation

In the past, X-rays were always produced by high-speed electrons colliding with a heavy metal anode. Now researchers can use a different source – a synchrotron.

Synchrotrons were invented as 'atom smashers'. These are particle accelerators that create high-energy beams of protons or electrons to use as bullets to fire into matter (see page 366).
The particles are speeded up with electric fields, while magnetic fields keep them moving in circles (see page 227).

Synchrotrons had one big disadvantage: when charged particles accelerate, they lose energy by radiation. Anything which moves in a circular path is accelerating all the time, so the charged particles moving in circles lose energy (as electromagnetic radiation) all the time. Depending on the kinetic energy of the charged particles, this radiation can have different wavelengths, from infra-red to gamma-rays.

The disadvantage is now turned into an advantage: at certain energies the synchrotron radiation turns out to give a beautiful beam of X-rays. Physicists use synchrotron radiation to study many aspects of the structure of matter at the atomic and molecular scale, from semiconductors to protein molecules.

Synchrotron radiation

Radio frequency bands

In the electromagnetic spectrum, 'Radio' covers a huge range of wavelengths, from 1 mm to 100 km!
They are divided into several frequency bands, as shown in this diagram:

The very short wavelengths of **microwaves** mean that they spread out less by diffraction than longer waves.

This makes them ideal for radar and for line-of-sight communications such a satellite broadcasts and mobile phones.

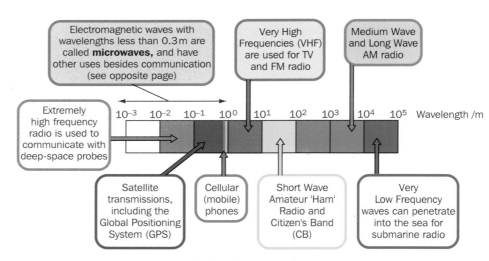

High quality radio broadcasts use very high frequencies (VHF).

They carry signals by Frequency Modulation (FM), where the *frequency* of the radio wave becomes bigger or smaller to match the amplitude of the sound wave it is carrying.

Long wavelength radio waves diffract around hills and over the horizon, so they have a very large range.

They carry signals by Amplitude Modulation (AM), where the *amplitude* of the radio wave becomes bigger or smaller to match the amplitude of the sound wave it is carrying.

▷ Physics at work: Electromagnetic waves

Colour vision

If you use a magnifying glass to look at a television screen, you will see that it consists of tiny dots or stripes of red, green and blue. How can these three dots combine to give the entire range of colours you see on a TV screen?

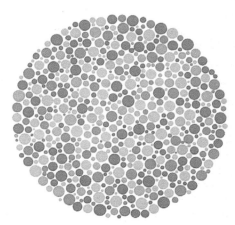

The reason that only three colours are needed is due to the way in which the human *eye* works. The retina of the *eye* has two different types of light-sensitive cells: *rods* and *cones*.

The *rod* cells are more sensitive, and allow you to see at low levels of light. These are the cells you use when it's very dark. However they are not sensitive to colour. Have you noticed that you can't see colours in dim light?

The *cone* cells are less sensitive to light, but they do detect different colours. There are three sorts of cone cells, each sensitive to a different region of the visible spectrum: red, green and blue.

If you can see '45', then you are not red-green colour-blind

Yellow light, midway between red and green in the spectrum, excites both sorts of cone cells. The brain combines these signals, and interprets them as yellow.

However, the brain is complex, and sometimes insists that a colour is present despite what the cone cells tell it: a photograph of grass with no green in it whatsoever can still 'look' green!

One visual deficiency is common. Red/green colour-blindness occurs in about one man in twenty, although it is rare in women. A deficiency in either the red or the green cones means that green, red and their combinations can be confused. This deficiency is named *daltonism* after John Dalton, the scientist who first investigated it. He was red/green colour-blind himself, and he created a sensation when he turned up at a Quaker meeting in a bright red coat: he thought it was brown.

Microwave ovens

If you calculate the energy of microwave photons (by $E = h f$), you find it is quite small. How can a microwave oven heat food with such weak photons?
It is because the microwave frequency – about 2.5 GHz – matches the frequency at which molecules of water in the food vibrate. So resonance occurs (see page 100).
This causes the amplitude of oscillation of the water molecules to get greater and greater.
This increases the internal energy of the water and the food gets hotter.

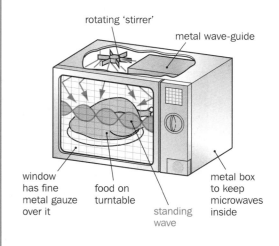

rotating 'stirrer'

metal wave-guide

window has fine metal gauze over it

food on turntable

standing wave

metal box to keep microwaves inside

People often say that 'microwaves heat the food from the middle'. This is not true, for the microwaves penetrate only a few millimetres, but that is still better than an ordinary oven, where the food is just heated by hot air around the outside.

Inside the oven, there are many examples of wave behaviour:

A rotating 'stirrer' at the top reflects the microwaves to different parts of the oven, and the metal walls of the oven reflect the microwaves back into the food.

The door is covered with metal gauze which 'looks' solid to the microwaves – the holes are much smaller than a wavelength.

Inside the oven, the reflected waves set up standing wave patterns, so there are areas of destructive interference, where the microwaves cancel out. Food at those points won't cook, so the turntable rotates to move the food between the microwave nodes and anti-nodes.

▷ Coloured spectra

Look at the two kinds of yellow lights in the photographs:

They both look yellow, because they both stimulate the same cells in the retina of your eye. The only real difference that you can see is that a street light is more powerful, so it seems brighter.

However, if you examine their spectra, you get a quite different picture.

Continuous and Line spectra

Look at these three diagrams of spectra. They show the wavelengths present in visible light from 3 different sources.

The *first* spectrum is from an ordinary light bulb like the one inside the car's indicator. This is a **continuous spectrum**.
All visible wavelengths are present in the light, and the eye sees the light as white.

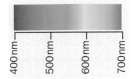

Continuous spectrum : white light

The *second* spectrum is from white light filtered by the yellow plastic of the car's indicator. The blue end of the spectrum, and part of the red end, have been *absorbed* by the yellow plastic.
The brain sees the remaining range of wavelengths as yellow.
This is also a continuous spectrum, but over a limited range.

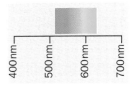

Filtered spectrum : yellow light

The *third* spectrum is from the sodium street-light. It is not a continuous spectrum at all – it is a **line spectrum**. It has a *few wavelengths only*. There are about ninety different lines in this spectrum, and only the 5 brightest ones are shown here:

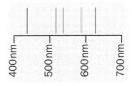

Sodium line spectrum

Why does this light appear yellow, when the spectral lines are evenly spread across the visible range?
The sodium line spectrum appears yellow because most of the lines are relatively faint. Over 98% of the energy is given out by just two spectral lines, of wavelengths 589.0 nm and 589.6 nm.
In this diagram they are too close together to resolve separately, and so they appear as the slightly thicker yellow line.

Sodium light is often referred to as *monochromatic* (= one colour) because almost all the light has the same wavelength.
Lasers (see page 183) produce pure monochromatic light.

What causes line spectra?

You always get line spectra from atoms that have been excited in some way, either by heating or by an electrical discharge.
In the atoms, the energy has been given to the electrons, which then release it as light.

Line spectra are caused by changes in the energy of the electrons. Large, complicated atoms like neon give very complex line spectra, so physicists first investigated the line spectrum of the simplest possible atom, hydrogen, which has only one electron.

This is discussed on the next page.

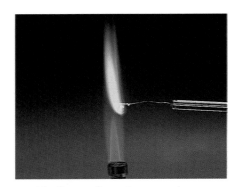

Heating sodium atoms produces the same line spectrum

▶ The hydrogen spectrum

It is not only sodium that gives a line spectrum. All elements have a line spectrum, which you can see if you pass an electric current through the element when it is vaporised.

If you look at a hydrogen discharge tube through a diffraction grating or a prism, you will see a spectrum with just 4 sharp lines. The 4 wavelengths are:

656 nm, 486 nm, 434 nm and 410 nm

Why only these four wavelengths? We need to look further.

Physicists soon found there were many more spectral lines in the invisible ultra-violet and infra-red regions of the spectrum, and found that they also are grouped in a similar series of lines.

Some lines in the hydrogen spectrum are shown in the diagram:

Can you see two different groups or **series** of lines, one series near 100 nm and the other series between 350 nm and 650 nm?

Each is named after the physicist who investigated it: the **Lyman** series in the ultraviolet near 100 nm, and the **Balmer** series between 350 nm and 650 nm.

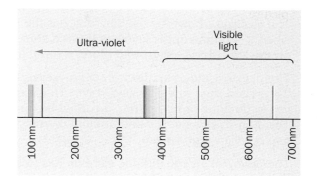

The Hydrogen spectrum

Photon energies in the hydrogen spectrum

To see what causes these series of spectral lines, we must look at the photon **energies** instead of the wavelengths.

Example 2
Calculate the photon energy of the 656 nm line in the hydrogen spectrum.

The speed of light $c = 3.00 \times 10^8$ m s^{-1}, and the Planck constant $h = 6.63 \times 10^{-34}$ J s.

From page 115: $c = f \lambda$ so: 3.00×10^8 m s$^{-1} = f \times 656 \times 10^{-9}$ m

$$\therefore f = \frac{3.00 \times 10^8 \text{ m s}^{-1}}{656 \times 10^{-9} \text{ m}} = 4.57 \times 10^{14} \text{ Hz}$$

From page 167 $E = h f$ $= 6.63 \times 10^{-34}$ J s $\times 4.57 \times 10^{14}$ Hz $= \underline{3.03 \times 10^{-19} \text{ J}}$ (3 s.f.)   This is 1.9 eV.

Repeating this calculation for other spectral lines shows that the photon energies (in eV) of the first few lines in each series are:

Lyman energies /eV: 10.2   12.1   12.8

Balmer energies /eV: 1.9   2.6

Can you spot a pattern in these numbers?

Each of the Balmer energies is the **difference** between two of the Lyman energies.
This is true of all the Balmer lines, not just the two given here.

The explanation of the spectrum of hydrogen is a story of **energy differences**. This is discussed on the next page.

▷ Energy levels and Quanta

Planck and Einstein's quantum theory of light (page 166) gives us the key to understanding the regular patterns in line spectra.

The photons in these line spectra have certain energy values only, so the electrons in those atoms can only have certain energy values. This energy level diagram shows a very simple case. It is for an atom in which there are only two possible energy levels:

The electron, shown by the blue dot, has the most potential energy when it is on the upper level, or **excited state**. When the electron is on the lower level, or **ground state**, it has the least potential energy.

The diagram shows an electron in an excited atom dropping from the excited state to the ground state. This energy jump, or **transition**, has to be done as one jump. It cannot be done in stages. This transition is the smallest amount of energy that this atom can lose, and is called a **quantum** (plural = quanta).

The potential energy that the electron has lost is given out as a photon. By $E = hf$ this energy jump corresponds to a specific frequency (or wavelength) giving a specific line in the line spectrum.

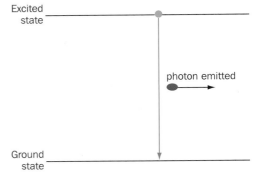

Emission of a photon

Example 3
The diagram shows an atom with 3 electron energy levels. What are the photon energies, in eV, that this atom can emit?

There are **three** energy transitions:
* the electron can drop from excited state 1 to the ground state, emitting a 10 eV photon, or
* from excited state 2 to excited state 1, emitting a 5 eV photon, or
* from excited state 2 to the ground state, emitting a photon of energy (10 eV + 5 eV) = 15 eV.

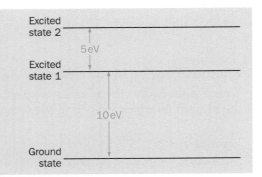

A Potential Well

In this diagram, Phiz has fallen into a steep-sided pit:

He slipped down 3 metres, and lost 2000 joules of potential energy. We often calculate potential energy from ground level, which means that his potential energy was zero on the level soil outside the pit. At the bottom of the pit Phiz's potential energy is 2000 J less than zero: it is –2000 J.

When Phiz jumps with all his might, he gains 1300 J of kinetic energy. Can he jump out of the pit?
No, because his kinetic energy is not enough to make up the potential energy he lost by falling down the pit.
His total energy is 1300 J + (–2000 J) = –700 J.
If the sum of (kinetic energy + potential energy) is negative, we say that the system is **bound**. Phiz is stuck in the pit.

This situation is described as a **potential well**.

Now think about a similar situation for an atom.
Suppose you want to ionise the atom by removing an electron.
To remove the electron completely from the attraction of the positive nucleus, you must provide enough energy for the electron to jump from the ground state to the very top of the potential well.
This is called the **ionisation energy.**

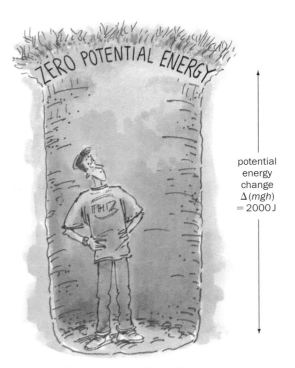

Phiz in a 'potential well'

▶ The energy levels of hydrogen

A Danish physicist called Niels Bohr found that the hydrogen spectrum could be explained by the set of energy levels shown in the diagram:

The lowest level is the ground state, and all the other levels are excited states.
The ground state is a long way below the excited states, and the excited states get closer together as you go upwards.

Look at the energy values of each level:

Just like Phiz in his pit, the electron is bound in the atom, and does not have enough energy to get out.
To get the electron out of the hydrogen atom, you have to give it extra energy.

At the bottom of his pit, Phiz had a potential energy of –2000 J. In the same way, the potential energy of all these levels is negative. Zero potential energy occurs at the very top, when the electron escapes, and leaves an ionised atom.

$E = 0$
$E = -0.85\,eV$
$E = -1.51\,eV$ ——— Second excited state

$E = -3.40\,eV$ ——— First excited state

$E = -13.61\,eV$ ——— Ground state

Energy levels of the Hydrogen atom

Example 4
Use the diagram to find the ionisation energy of hydrogen.

The ionisation energy is the energy need to raise the electron from the ground state to the highest possible energy level, when the electron will be free.
The highest possible state is always defined as zero potential energy.

Ionisation energy = energy of highest level – energy of ground state
$$= 0\ eV - (-13.61\ eV)$$
$$= \underline{13.61\ eV} \quad (4\ s.f.)$$

The hydrogen emission spectrum

The simple two-level diagram at the top of the opposite page has only one possible energy jump down from an excited state.

Example 3 has three energy levels and three possible energy jumps.

In the hydrogen atom, with all those excited states, there are many possible transitions.

Look at this diagram:
The arrows all show **down**ward energy transitions, so each would give **out** a photon. This is an **emission** line spectrum.
(We will look at an absorption spectrum on the next page.)

The transitions on the left, going down to the ground state, are all large. This is the Lyman series, giving out energetic photons, in the **ultra-violet** region of the spectrum.

The smaller transitions on the right, going down to the $E = -1.51\ eV$ excited state, give out less energetic **infra-red** photons.

Between these two sets of emissions is the Balmer series of lines, going down to the first excited state. This series includes the 4 **visible** lines in the spectrum, coloured in this diagram.

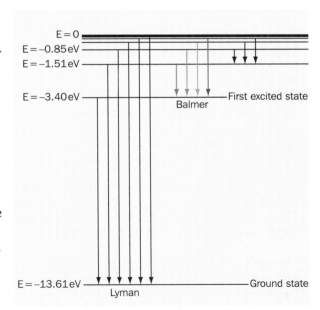

Jumps between the energy levels of the Hydrogen atom

▷ Absorption Spectra

The spectra on the previous pages are *emission* spectra, because
the electron started in an excited state and dropped **down**.
But where did the electron get this energy from in the first place?
Absorption of a photon is one way.

This diagram shows **absorption** in a simple two-level atom:

It is the exact opposite of the diagram at the top of page 180.
The electron starts in the lower state, and absorbs a photon,
which raises it to the excited state.

This photon must *exactly* match the energy jump. If it is too big or
too small, it is not absorbed.

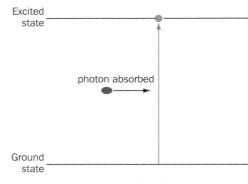

Absorption of a photon

Example 5

A hydrogen atom has its electron in the energy level at –1.51 eV.
It absorbs a photon, which promotes the electron to the –0.85 eV level.
What is the wavelength of this photon?

The electronic charge $e = 1.6 \times 10^{-19}$ C, the speed of light $c = 3.0 \times 10^8$ m s^{-1},
and the Planck constant, $h = 6.6 \times 10^{-34}$ J s.

Energy of the photon = energy jump = -0.85 eV $-$ $(-1.51$ eV$)$ = 0.66 eV

1 eV = 1.6 $\times$ 10^{-19} J (from page 165) so: 0.66 eV = $0.66 \times 1.6 \times 10^{-19}$ J $= 1.1 \times 10^{-19}$ J

$E = hf$ (from page 167) so: 1.1×10^{-19} J $= 6.6 \times 10^{-34}$ J s $\times f$ $\therefore f = \dfrac{1.1 \times 10^{-19} \text{ J}}{6.6 \times 10^{-34} \text{ J s}} = 1.6 \times 10^{14}$ Hz

$c = f\lambda$ (from page 115) so: 3.0×10^8 m s^{-1} = 1.6×10^{14} Hz $\times \lambda$

$$\therefore \lambda = \frac{3.0 \times 10^8 \text{ m s}^{-1}}{1.6 \times 10^{14} \text{ Hz}} = \underline{1.9 \times 10^{-6} \text{ m}} \quad \text{(2 s.f.) (infra-red)}$$

The Sun's spectrum

One of the first places that an absorption spectrum was observed
was in sunlight. The continuous spectrum from the Sun is covered
with vertical **dark** lines:
These were systematically measured and classified by the Bavarian
instrument maker Joseph Fraunhofer.

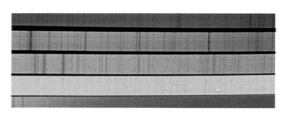

Absorption lines in the Sun's spectrum

These dark lines are due to cooler gases in the outer layers of the Sun.
As light from the hot photosphere passes out from the Sun, some light
is absorbed by these cooler atoms, promoting their electrons to excited
states. The absorbed photons must match the energy jumps exactly,
so only certain wavelengths are absorbed.

The absorbed photons are later re-emitted, but in all possible directions,
so fewer photons end up going directly outwards.
The spectrum of this light is dimmer now at these wavelengths, because
fewer photons reach us, giving the dark Fraunhofer lines.

Absorption spectra are very useful for astronomers.
The absorption lines in the spectrum of a star or galaxy give us a
'fingerprint' of the elements present. If the Doppler effect (page 156)
shifts this 'fingerprint' to a longer wavelength, we can calculate how
fast the star or galaxy is moving away from us.

*These galaxies are moving away
from us at 1200 km s^{-1}*

▷ Stimulated Emission

In his analysis of quantum theory, Albert Einstein realised that emission and absorption were not the only possible ways to cause energy jumps.

An atom that is already in an excited state can be 'persuaded' to emit a photon, by a passing photon of exactly the right energy.

There will then be two identical photons – the original one and the one created by the downward transition of the electron.

The first photon stimulated the atom into emitting the second photon, so this is called **stimulated emission**.

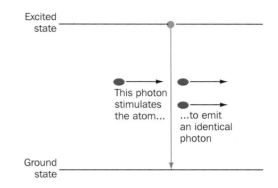

Stimulated emission of photons

When a beam of light contains identical photons like this, the light is monochromatic – its spectrum has only one wavelength.
The light is also coherent (page 149) as the phase is constant across the beam, so interference effects can be achieved much more easily.

This way of producing extremely regular, uniform radiation was first done with microwaves, but a far more famous application uses photons in or near the optical range, and is called a **laser**:

Light Amplification by Stimulated Emission of Radiation

This is such a long-winded title, that it made sense to shorten it to its initial letters – LASER.

Since their invention in 1958, lasers have become very common – they are in every CD-player and DVD-player.

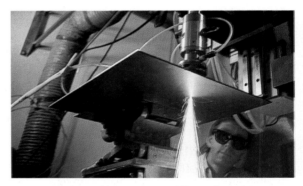

Infra-red lasers can cut through metal

Everyone knows that laser light is a narrow, parallel beam which is very intense, but their scientific usefulness is due to two facts:

- the light is **monochromatic** – one wavelength only,
- the light is **coherent** – all the waves are in step.

Laser action ('lasing') can take place in solids, liquids or gases.

What is necessary for the medium to 'lase'?
Before stimulated emission can happen, there must be more atoms with their electrons in higher excited states than in lower levels.
Under normal circumstances, the number of atoms with electrons in an excited state is always less than the number in the state below.

This means that electrons must be 'pumped' up to the excited state, often using an electric field, as in the helium-neon gas laser shown in this diagram:

To begin with, one of the excited atoms emits a photon, at random. This photon quickly stimulates another emission. The two photons then stimulate another two emissions, which rapidly becomes an avalanche of identical photons.

Mirrors at each end of the laser reflect the light, making the photons pass to and fro along the laser.
One of the two mirrors is only partially silvered, so a small percentage of the photons can continually escape.

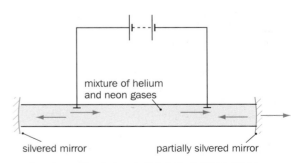

A schematic diagram of a helium-neon laser

▷ Physics at work: Fluorescence

A fluorescent lamp

Fluorescent lamps

The long fluorescent tubes in office and classroom ceilings are so familiar we hardly notice them. But how do they work? They are certainly more efficient than ordinary filament lamps.

These tubes are in fact gas discharge tubes, rather like the neon lamps used in advertising. The gas inside is mercury vapour, and it has a line spectrum, like hydrogen and sodium.

Mercury atoms are much larger than sodium or hydrogen atoms. Because the nucleus has a large positive charge, the energy levels are separated by bigger gaps. Although some of the emission lines are visible, most energy is emitted in the ultra-violet region of the spectrum, as the lowest energy jumps are large.

This is not a problem if you actually want ultra-violet light, and mercury discharge tubes are used as ultra-violet lamps.

But you don't want your workplace flooded with UV, or your health would be seriously damaged. The high-energy photons of ultra-violet light can cause conjunctivitis and even skin cancer.

The answer lies in **fluorescence**. The inside of the glass tube is coated with an opaque white material called a phosphor. The phosphor absorbs the ultra-violet radiation, and its electrons are raised to excited states, as shown in the diagram:

The electrons in the phosphor fall down from one excited state to a lower one, emitting photons each time, until they are back in the ground state. As these transitions are all smaller than the original jump, the photons emitted are not ultra-violet, but visible.

By a careful choice of phosphor materials, the mixture of photons that are emitted can blend to give the appearance of white light.

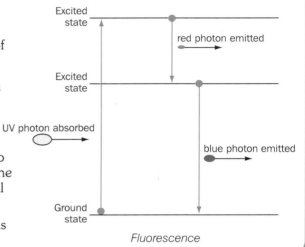
Fluorescence

Liquid scintillation counters

Liquid scintillation counting was developed to tackle the difficulty of detecting the low energies produced by β (beta) emission from radioactive isotopes such as hydrogen-3 and carbon-14.

It works by **fluorescence** of a solute (a dissolved chemical). This fluorescent chemical is excited by collision of a beta particle, not by a photon.

This is how it works. The kinetic energy of the beta particle is absorbed by an electron in a molecule of the solvent, which then jumps up to a higher energy level.

This electron does not easily drop down from this level, so the solvent molecule stays in an excited state until it collides with a dissolved molecule of the solute.
The solvent molecule passes on its energy to the solute molecule. This energy makes an electron jump up to a higher level, and then drop down immediately, emitting a photon.
This photon is detected by photoelectric effect in a photo-multiplier tube. This is a device for magnifying the effect of a single photon, so that it is easily detected.

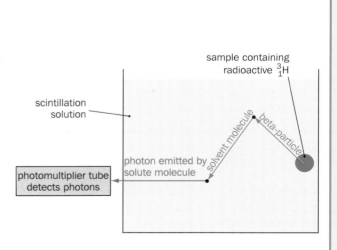

▷ Physics at work: Emission and Absorption in Chemistry

Flame tests and Fireworks

Chemists use the brightly coloured flames produced by certain reactive metals to identify their presence in unknown compounds.
In flame tests you see yellow for sodium, lilac for potassium and brick-red for calcium.

In a more attractive way, these same metals give fireworks their bright colours. But surely this is Chemistry, not Physics?

The whiz and bang of the fireworks are definitely Chemistry, but the colours given by the fireworks are most certainly Physics.

The reactive metals calcium, strontium and barium are often used in fireworks because they give distinctive colours in flames.

These particular colours are emitted because there are only a few energy transitions possible in those metals when they are ionised, so only a few types of photon are emitted.
(Atoms with a greater range of energy transitions give off a wider range of photons, and the light they emit looks white.)

In fireworks, the reactive metals are used in compounds that vaporise in the heat of the flame, releasing the ionised metal atoms.
The atoms are excited by the heat, and give out photons – just like a sodium streetlight, but far more impressive!

Electrons making energy jumps

Infra-red spectroscopy

An infra-red spectrometer used for chemical analysis

The picture shows an infra-red spectrometer. It is an instrument that is designed to obtain an infra-red spectrum of a substance.

The spectrum is obtained by first irradiating a sample with a source of infra-red radiation, usually a hot filament lamp.
The infra-red passes through the sample, which can be in solution or contained within a gel, and then on to a detector.

Molecules absorb electromagnetic energy in the infra-red region of the electromagnetic spectrum, because infra-red photons have the right energy to make molecular bonds vibrate.
The energy levels for the vibration of molecular bonds are closer together than the electron energy levels you saw earlier in this chapter.

Bonds between different atoms will absorb different infra-red photons, so absorption spectroscopy can be used to identify the different chemical bonds in a sample.

The infra-red spectrum is analysed by examining at which wavelengths these absorptions occur:

Each wavelength corresponds to a particular resonance, such as that of the chemical bond joining a carbon atom to an oxygen atom.
Each chemical compound, with its own combination of bonds, has its own infra-red spectrum, so the spectrum provides a method of identifying compounds.

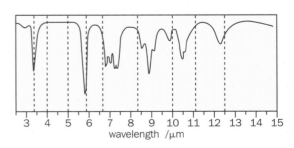

A typical infra-red absorption spectrum

Summary

The electromagnetic spectrum ranges from high-energy gamma radiation to long wavelength radio waves. Different parts of the electromagnetic spectrum are produced in different ways, but there is no clear distinction between adjacent regions.

A continuous spectrum has a complete range of wavelengths.
An emission line spectrum has only a few, exactly-defined wavelengths.
An absorption line spectrum is a continuous spectrum with a few, exactly-defined wavelengths removed.

An atom has definite electron energy levels, and transitions between these levels produce a line spectrum.
The lowest energy level is the ground state, and all the other levels are excited states.
The highest possible level occurs when the atom is ionised.
The energy level at ionisation is usually counted as 0 eV; all other levels have negative potential energies.

A photon is emitted when an electron drops from a higher level to a lower level.
The frequency can be found from $E = h f$ and the wavelength from $c = f \lambda$.

For a photon to be absorbed, it must have exactly the right energy to raise an electron from a lower level to a higher level.
Stimulated emission (laser action) occurs when a photon of the right size makes an excited atom emit an identical second photon.

▶ **Questions**

1. Can you complete these sentences?
   a) The electromagnetic spectrum ranges from high-energy .... radiation to long .... radio waves. Gamma rays come from the nucleus of .... atoms, while .... are generated by collisions of high-energy electrons.
   A well-defined part of the electromagnetic spectrum, in the wavelength range 400 nm to 700 nm is the .... part.
   The range of the spectrum with wavelengths less than 400 nm is called .... while the range with wavelengths more than 700 nm is called ....
   b) Wave effects such as diffraction and .... are most noticeable in the very long wavelength region of
   ....
   Particle effects are most noticeable for .... rays.
   c) A continuous spectrum has .... the wavelengths in a range.
   An emission .... spectrum has only a few wavelengths, while the .... spectrum for the same element is a continuous spectrum with exactly those same wavelengths missing.
   d) When an atom is excited, an electron is raised to an .... state. A line spectrum is caused by jumps between energy .... in the atom.
   e) In an emission spectrum, an electron moves from a .... level to a .... level, while in an .... spectrum the reverse happens.
   Absorption often starts with the electron in the lowest level, known as the .... state.
   f) If the atom is given enough energy for the electron to escape, it is said to be .... and the energy needed for this is called the .... energy.

2. Copy and complete this table.

   The electronic charge, $e = 1.6 \times 10^{-19}$ C, the speed of light, $c = 3.0 \times 10^8$ m s^{-1}, the Planck constant, $h = 6.6 \times 10^{-34}$ J s.

Region of the electromagnetic spectrum	wavelength	energy
	500 nm	
		50 eV
		5.0×10^{-21} J

3. The diagram shows the lowest two energy levels of an atom.

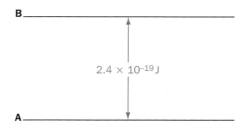

   a) Which of A and B is the ground state, and which is an excited state?
   b) The energy difference between the two states is 2.4×10^{-19} J. Use the constants from question 2 to calculate the wavelength of the photon emitted when an electron drops from level B to level A.

4. Here is the simplified energy level structure of the electrons in an atom.

0 eV ——————————————
−0.4 eV ——————————————
−0.9 eV ——————————————

−3.6 eV ——————————————

a) How many excited states are shown in this diagram?
b) Explain why the potential energy of the lowest three states is negative.
c) What is the ionisation energy of this atom (in eV)?
d) What is the largest photon energy (in eV) that can be absorbed by this atom?
e) What is the smallest photon energy (in eV) that can be absorbed by this atom?

5. Use the constants given in question 2 opposite to calculate the wavelength of the radiation given by the following energy level transitions in the diagram above, in question 4.
a) The transition from the first excited state to the ground state. Show that this is in the visible part of the spectrum.
b) The transition from the second excited state to the ground state. Show that it is in the ultra-violet part of the spectrum.
c) The transition from the second excited state to the first excited state. Show that it is in the infra-red part of the spectrum.

6. The diagram shows three energy levels of neon.

−4.03 eV ——————————————
−5.99 eV ——————————————

−21.57 eV ——————————————

A helium-neon laser emits light of wavelength 633 nm.
a) Use the constants from question 2 to show that this light emitted by a helium-neon laser has a photon energy of 1.96 eV.
b) On a copy of the diagram, use an arrow to show the electron transition in the neon atom that emits photons of this energy.

7. The *nuclear* energy levels of an atom are similar to the electron energy levels that you have met in this chapter. The diagram shows the lowest two energy levels for a heavy nucleus.

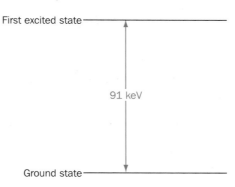

First excited state ——————————————

91 keV

Ground state ——————————————

a) Compare the diagram with those in questions 4 and 6, and explain how this diagram shows that nuclear energies are much greater than electron energies.
b) Use the constants from question 2 to calculate the wavelength of the radiation emitted in a nucleus change that takes it from the first excited state to the ground state.
c) To what part of the electromagnetic spectrum does this photon belong?

8. The diagram shows three of the electron energy levels of mercury.

Excited state 2 ——————————————
−3.7 eV

Excited state 1 ——————————————
−5.5 eV

Ground state ——————————————
−10.4 eV

a) What is the ionisation energy of mercury in eV?
b) Calculate the three possible energy transitions in eV between these energy levels.
c) Use the constants from question 2 to calculate the wavelengths of the radiation given off by the three transitions in (b), and state in which part of the electro-magnetic spectrum each is to be found.
d) Ultra-violet light emitted by a mercury-vapour lamp is absorbed by cold mercury vapour, in which most of the atoms are in the ground state. Use the energy level diagram to explain why cold mercury vapour absorbs ultra-violet but does not absorb visible light.

Further questions on page 189.

▷ Quantum Physics

Where necessary in these questions, use values for the Planck constant, and the mass and charge of an electron.

1. a) What is the *photoelectric effect*? [1]
   b) What is meant by the *threshold frequency* of the incident light? How is this quantity related to the *work function* of the metal surface? [3]
   c) Explain how the photoelectric effect provides important experimental evidence for the photon model of light. Do this by describing two experimental observations of the effect which cannot be explained using a continuous wave model but can be explained using a photon model of light. [6]

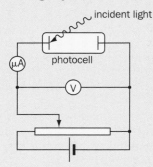

incident light

photocell

(μA)

(V)

   d) In an experiment using the circuit shown, blue light of wavelength 450 nm is incident on a potassium metal cathode. The current in the circuit falls to zero for a voltage of 0.76 V across the photocell. Find the work function of potassium and the threshold frequency of the light for this surface. [4] (OCR)

2. a) Electrons may be emitted from a surface by *thermionic emission* or by *photoelectric emission*. Distinguish between the two. [4]
   b) Write down Einstein's photoelectric equation relating the maximum kinetic energy E_{max} of the photoelectrons with the frequency f of the incident radiation and the work function ϕ for the emitting surface. [4]

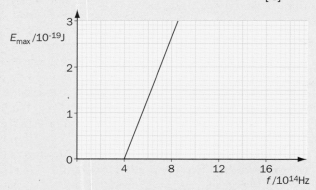

$E_{max}/10^{-19}$ J

$f/10^{14}$ Hz

   c) The graph shows how E_{max} varies with f for a particular surface. Use the graph to find the value of ϕ and the threshold wavelength of the radiation. [5]
   d) Describe and explain the effect of increasing the intensity of the incident radiation. [3] (W)

3. A monochromatic light source provides 5 W of light of wavelength 4.50×10^{-7} m.
   This light falls on a clean potassium surface and liberates 3.2×10^{11} photoelectrons per second. The photoelectrons are collected by an electrode just above the metal surface and the photoelectric current measured. Charge on electron = -1.60×10^{-19} C. Speed of light in vacuo = 3.00×10^8 m s^{-1}.
   a) Calculate the photoelectric current given by this arrangement. [1]
   b) Estimate the photoelectric current given by a similar arrangement using a source which provides 10 W of light of wavelength 4.50×10^{-7} m. [2]
   c) Explain whether or not photoelectrons would be emitted if a 20 W source operating at a wavelength of 6.00×10^{-7} m were to be used. The threshold frequency for potassium is 5.46×10^{14} Hz. [3] (AQA)

4. In order for the unaided eye to detect a distant source the rate of energy arriving at the eye from this source must be 1.0×10^{-16} W. The energy of each photon arriving at the eye is 3.6×10^{-19} J and the light emitted by the source has a wavelength of 550 nm.
   a) Calculate the number of photons arriving at the eye per second if the eye can just detect the source. [1]
   b) Give one reason why fewer photons reach the retina than are incident on the pupil of the eye. [1] (AQA)

5. Electrons are accelerated through a p.d. of 1500 V in a vacuum. They collide with a thin film of graphite.
   a) Show that the speed of the electrons before impact is 2.3×10^7 m s^{-1}. [2]
   b) Calculate the wavelength associated with the electrons in (a). [2]
   c) Explain why the electrons would be diffracted through an appreciable angle by the graphite. [2]
   d) Electron diffraction can be used to measure nuclear radii. Explain why the electrons used in such measurements would need to have much greater kinetic energies than those in the question above. [2] (AQA)

6. a) State de Broglie's relationship in words. [1]
   b) Show that the speed of electrons which have been accelerated from rest through a p.d. of 2.0 kV is equal to 2.6×10^7 m s^{-1} and calculate the wavelength associated with a beam of these electrons. [4]
   c) Suggest why electron diffraction is a useful tool for studying the arrangement of atoms in crystals, where the separation of the atoms is typically 0.3 nm. [5] (OCR)

▷ Spectra

7. a) Describe the physical appearance of
   i) a line emission spectrum,
   ii) a line absorption spectrum. [2]
   b) Describe the relationship between the two spectra named in (a) [1]
   c) The highest frequency light emitted from a mercury discharge lamp is 2.5×10^{15} Hz. In which part of the spectrum is this frequency? Calculate the ionisation energy of a mercury atom in eV. [3] (W)

8. The diagram shows some of the possible electron energy levels of a hydrogen atom.
The *ionisation energy* of hydrogen is 13.6 eV.

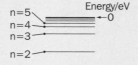

a) What is meant by ionisation energy? Mark in the energy value of the ground state of hydrogen on a copy of the diagram. [3]
b) Light from a hydrogen discharge tube consists of a *line emission spectrum*. Explain the meaning of the italicised words. [3]
c) The only emission spectra which occur in the visible region of the hydrogen spectrum are those involving transitions to level $n = 2$. The longest wavelength of these visible lines is 655 nm. Draw an arrow on your diagram to indicate this transition and calculate the energy difference (in eV) between the levels concerned. [4] (OCR)

9. The diagram shows some of the energy levels for a hydrogen atom. The level $n = 1$ is the ground state.

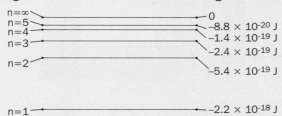

Assume $c = 3.0 \times 10^8$ m s^{-1} and $h = 6.6 \times 10^{-34}$ J s.
a) State what is meant by the *ground state*. [1]
b) With reference to the energy levels, explain how an electrical discharge through hydrogen gas gives rise to a visible line spectrum. [4]
c) Show that the shortest wavelength of em-radiation that can be emitted by a hydrogen atom is approximately 90 nm. [3] (AQA)

10. Describe evidence you have seen in a school laboratory which shows that different elements have different characteristic optical spectra. [3]

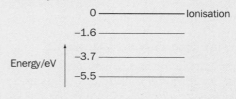

a) The diagram is a simplified energy level diagram for atomic hydrogen. A free electron with kinetic energy 12 eV collides with an atom of hydrogen and causes it to be raised to its first excited state. Calculate the kinetic energy (in eV) of the free electron after the collision. [2]
b) Find the wavelength of the photon emitted when the atom returns to its ground state. [2] (Edex)

11. The diagram shows some of the outer energy levels of the mercury atom.

```
                0 ───────────── Ionisation
              –1.6 ─────────────
              –3.7 ─────────────
Energy/eV  │
              –5.5 ─────────────


             –10.4 ─────────────
```

a) Calculate the ionisation energy in J for an electron in the –10.4 eV level. [2]
b) An electron has been excited to the –1.6 eV level. On a copy of the diagram, show all the possible ways it can return to the –10.4 eV level. [3]
c) Which change in energy levels will give rise to a yellowish line ($\lambda \sim 600$ nm) in the mercury spectrum. [4] (Edex)

12. The light from a hydrogen discharge tube contains em-radiation of wavelengths 6.6×10^{-7} m (red light) and 4.9×10^{-7} m (blue light). The light can be separated to form a line spectrum by diffraction or by refraction.
a) Explain how an electrical discharge through hydrogen gas in a discharge tube gives rise to a spectrum which consists only of certain frequencies. [3]
b) Determine the angular separation of the red and blue light of hydrogen for:
   i) the second order diffraction pattern produced by a diffraction grating which has 5.0×10^4 lines per metre; [3]
   ii) the refraction of a beam of hydrogen light passing from air to glass when the angle of incidence is 80°.
   (The refractive index from air to glass for red light is 1.65, and for blue light is 1.67.) [3] (AQA)

16 Current and Charge

Electricity is important to all of us, and our lives would be very different without it. The cartoon shows some of the ways that we use electrical energy:

We use electricity to transfer energy from one place to another. How is this energy transferred from the power station to your home?
It is carried by an electric current which flows through cables. These are supported by pylons or buried beneath the ground.

In this chapter you will learn:
- about current as a flow of electric charge,
- about potential difference and resistance,
- how to use the equations for electrical power.

Understanding current electricity

A simple circuit consists of a lamp connected to a battery. We can use a model to help us understand what is happening. Our electrical circuit works rather like the water circuit in a central heating system.

Can you see the similarities in the two circuits shown below?

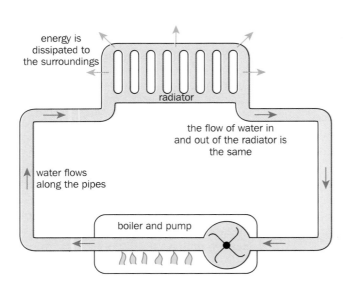

energy is dissipated to the surroundings

radiator

the flow of water in and out of the radiator is the same

water flows along the pipes

boiler and pump

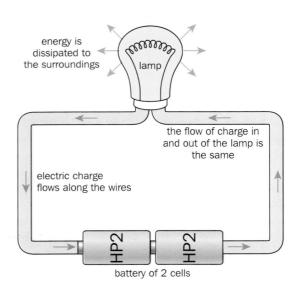

energy is dissipated to the surroundings

lamp

the flow of charge in and out of the lamp is the same

electric charge flows along the wires

HP2 HP2

battery of 2 cells

- Water flows around the complete loop of pipes.

- The boiler transfers energy to the water and the pump keeps the water circulating round.

- The radiator transfers energy from the hot water to the surroundings.

- Charge flows around the complete conducting path.

- The battery transfers energy to the charge and keeps it circulating round the circuit.

- The lamp transfers energy to the surroundings as heat and light.

What is an electric current?

Electric current is a flow of electric charges. The lamp lights because charged particles are moving through it.

Like water in the heating system, the charged particles are already in the conductors – but what are they?

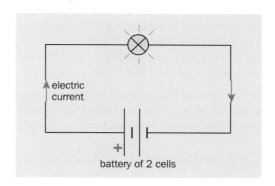

A copper wire consists of millions of copper atoms. Most of the electrons are held tightly to their atoms, but each copper atom has one or two electrons which are loosely held.
Since the electrons are negatively charged, an atom that loses an electron is left with a positive charge and is called an **ion**.

The diagram shows that the copper wire is made up of a lattice of positive ions, surrounded by *'free' electrons*:

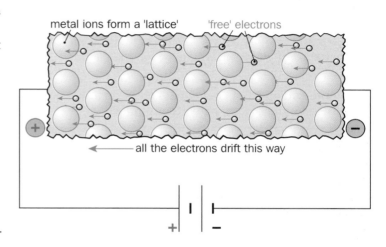

The ions can only vibrate about their fixed positions, but the electrons are free to move randomly from one ion to another through the lattice.
All metals have a structure like this.

What happens when a battery is attached to the copper wire?
The free electrons are repelled by the negative terminal and attracted to the positive one.
They still have a random movement, but in addition they all now move slowly in the same direction through the wire with a steady **drift velocity.**
We now have a flow of charge – we have electric current.

Which way do the electrons move?

At first, scientists thought that a current was made up of positive charges moving from positive to negative.

We now know that electrons really flow the opposite way, but unfortunately the convention has stuck.

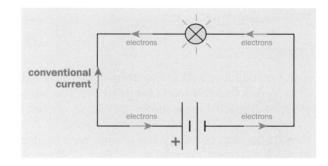

Diagrams usually show the direction of 'conventional current' going from positive to negative, but you must remember that the electrons are really flowing the opposite way.

Conductors and insulators

Why are some materials conductors and some insulators?
To answer this question we need to think about the number of free electrons per cubic metre of material: *n*

The table shows some values for *n*:

Copper is a good conductor because in just 1 mm^3 there are about 1×10^{20} or 100 million, million, million free electrons!

Can you see why an insulator cannot conduct?
In each mm^3 there is only about 1 electron free to move. Almost all of the electrons are firmly fixed to their atoms.

Semiconductors are very important in electronics.
Look at their value for *n*. Can you explain why semiconductors are neither good conductors nor good insulators?

Type of material	Number of free electrons per mm^3	n, number of free electrons per m^3
conductor	~ 1×10^{20}	~ 1×10^{29}
semiconductor	~ 1×10^{10}	~ 1×10^{19}
insulator	~ 1	~ 1×10^{9}

▷ Electric currents

Current is measured in **amperes** (A) using an ammeter.
The ammeter is placed *in* the circuit so that the electrons pass
through it. The more electrons that pass through the ammeter
in one second, the higher the current reading in amps.

Does the position of the ammeter matter in this simple circuit?
No – the number of electrons passing any point per second
is constant. The current throughout the circuit is the same.

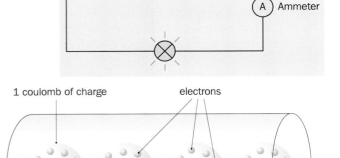

1 amp is a flow of about 6×10^{18} electrons in each second!
The electron is too small to be used as the basic unit of charge,
so instead we use a much bigger unit called the **coulomb** (C).
The charge on 1 electron is only **1.6×10^{-19} C**.

In the diagram, we have pictured one coulomb as a group of
a large number of electrons. Can you imagine the current
as coulombs of charge flowing through the circuit?

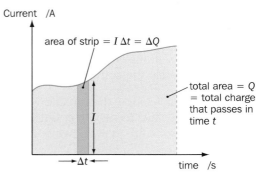

1 coulomb of charge   electrons

In fact, there are 6×10^{18} electrons in each coulomb !

The more coulombs of charge passing through the ammeter
each second, the bigger the current. In fact:

Current = number of coulombs per second

$$\text{Current } I = \frac{\text{charge } Q \text{ (coulombs)}}{\text{time } t \text{ (seconds)}} \quad \text{(amps)}$$ or $$I = \frac{Q}{t}$$ so $$Q = It$$

From this last equation you can see that:

**1 coulomb is the amount of charge that passes a point
when a current of 1 ampere flows for 1 second.**

What if the current in the circuit is changing?
If we think about a charge ΔQ passing in a small time Δt
then we can write:

$$I = \frac{\Delta Q}{\Delta t}$$ or $$\Delta Q = I \, \Delta t$$

Can you see that $I \, \Delta t$ is the **area** of the dark strip on this graph?
This means that the total charge Q that has passed after time t
must be the **total area** under the graph, shown in pale green:

Remember that current is the charge passing per second,
or more precisely, **current is the rate of flow of charge**.

Graph to show a current varying with time

Current /A

area of strip = $I \, \Delta t = \Delta Q$

total area = Q
= total charge
that passes in
time t

I

Δt time /s

Example 1
A current of 0.50 A passes through a lamp for 2.0 minutes.
a) How much charge passes through the lamp?
b) How many electrons pass through the lamp?

a) $Q = It$ (remember that t must be in seconds)
   $\therefore Q = 0.50 \text{ A} \times 120 \text{ s} = \underline{60 \text{ C}}$ (2 s.f.)

b) Each electron has a charge of 1.6×10^{-19} C,
   so 1 coulomb must contain $\dfrac{1}{1.6 \times 10^{-19}}$ electrons.
   This is 6.25×10^{18} electrons.
   So in 60 C there are $60 \times 6.25 \times 10^{18}$ electrons
            $= \underline{3.8 \times 10^{20}}$ electrons   (2 s.f.)

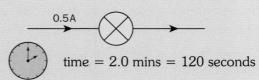

0.5A

time = 2.0 mins = 120 seconds

Hint:
Do you find part (b) difficult?
If so, think about this:
1 penny is equal to £ 0.01

So £1 must contain $\dfrac{1}{0.01} = 100$ pence

Conduction in liquids and gases.

Salt solution is an **electrolyte**. It can conduct electricity.
A solution of sugar in pure water will not conduct. Why not?
In order to conduct, the liquid must contain charged particles
that are free to move. What are these moving charges?

Electrolytes contain both positive and negative charged ions.
A positive ion is an atom or group of atoms that is short of
electrons. A negative ion is an atom with extra electrons.

How do the ions move when the electrolyte conducts?
The diagram shows some copper chromate solution after a
power supply has been connected to the electrodes.
The solution contains blue copper ions and yellow chromate ions.
At the start all the solution appeared green, but notice how
the colours have separated.
Which ions are positive and which are negative ?

Under normal circumstances, air contains very few ions
and so it does not conduct. Why is this fortunate for us?

During a lightning flash the air becomes highly ionised and
is able to conduct in a spectacular way!

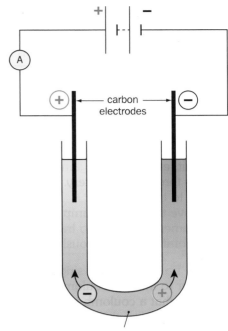

carbon electrodes

green copper chromate solution

Current and drift velocity

Is there a relationship between the current in a wire and the
drift velocity of the moving electrons?

The diagram shows part of a wire of cross-sectional area A.
The current in the wire is I.
There are n free electrons per metre³ of the wire and the
charge on each electron is e.
The electrons move with a drift velocity v.

Using the fact that current I is the charge passing per second
it can be shown that:

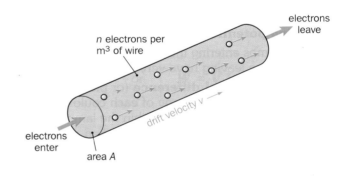

n electrons per
m³ of wire

drift velocity v

electrons
leave

electrons
enter

area A

$$I = nAve$$

Example 2
Copper contains 1×10^{29} free electrons per m³.
What is the drift velocity of electrons in a copper wire of
cross-sectional area 0.25 mm² carrying a current of 0.4 A?

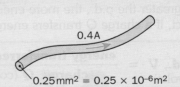

0.4A

0.25mm² = 0.25 × 10⁻⁶m²

$$I = nAve$$

$$0.4\ \text{A} = 1 \times 10^{29}\ \text{m}^{-3} \times 0.25 \times 10^{-6}\ \text{m}^2 \times v \times 1.6 \times 10^{-19}\ \text{C}$$

$$0.4\ \text{A} = 4.0 \times 10^3\ \text{C m}^{-1} \times v$$

$$\therefore\ v = \frac{0.4}{4.0 \times 10^3} = \underline{1 \times 10^{-4}\ \text{m s}^{-1}}\ \text{ or }\ \underline{0.1\ \text{mm s}^{-1}}$$

Hint:
$1\ \text{m}^2 = 1000\ \text{mm} \times 1000\ \text{mm} = 1 \times 10^6\ \text{mm}^2$

$1\ \text{mm}^2 = \dfrac{1}{1000}\ \text{m} \times \dfrac{1}{1000}\ \text{m} = 1 \times 10^{-6}\ \text{m}^2$

This drift velocity is typical for electrons flowing in metals.
Notice how small it is!

But remember, this is the drift velocity *superimposed* on the
very fast random motion of the free electrons within the metal.

What is an electric shock?

Put a voltage across the body and a current will pass through it.
This current can override the tiny electrical impulses that make
the nerves and the muscles work correctly, *and* cause burning.
The bigger the current and the longer the time it flows for,
the greater the damage, especially to the heart.
The maximum safe current through the body is only ~ 10 mA.
Why doesn't a fuse protect the body against electric shock?

Is there a maximum safe voltage for an electricity supply?
We need to know the resistance of the body.
This depends on the area of skin in contact with the supply
and whether the skin is damp or dry. A typical value is 10 kΩ.
Since $V = I R$, $V = 10 \times 10^{-3}$ A $\times 10 \times 10^{3}$ Ω = 100 V,
but even 50 V can kill you!
It is difficult to state a safe voltage, but the greater the p.d.,
the larger the current and so the greater the danger.

15 volts   *50 volts*

Car electrics

Most cars are fitted with a 12 volt lead-acid battery.
Originally, the battery was needed only for the lights and the
indicators, but modern cars have many more electrical features.

This means that the total current in the wiring can be high
and the heat produced by these large currents can be dangerous.
One solution is to use thick cables.
These carry the current more safely because they have a lower
resistance, and so the $I^2 R$ heating is smaller.

Some designers think that modern cars should be fitted with a
new standard 36 volt battery. Why would this reduce
the currents in the cables to one third of their present value?

Consider a 72 W head-lamp bulb and use the equation $P = I V$:
If $V = 12$ V, $I = $ **6.0** A   (since 6.0 A $\times$ 12 V = 72 W)
If $V = 36$ V, $I = $ **2.0** A   (since 2.0 A $\times$ 36 V = 72 W)

Of course, each component would need to have more resistance
in order to draw the correct current from the 36 V battery.

New features need more current

Electric vehicles

The only electric vehicles you are likely to see are milk floats
and fork-lift trucks. Why is this, when they produce far less
pollution on the road than petrol engine vehicles?
The problem with electric cars is giving them a large enough
store of energy. Half a tonne of lead-acid batteries can only
supply about 25 MJ of energy. A full petrol tank can store
about 600 MJ and is much lighter.

The capacity of a battery is measured in **ampere-hours** (A h).
One ampere-hour means that the battery can provide
a current of 1 amp for 1 hour, or 2 amps for $\frac{1}{2}$ hour, etc.
A typical 12 volt car battery is rated at 50 A h.

The electric car of the future will probably get its electrical
energy from a fuel-cell (using hydrogen and oxygen).
Some car makers plan to produce fuel-cell cars soon.

An electric car

▷ Physics at work: Using electricity

The strain gauge

A strain gauge is used to measure mechanical strains in
structures such as buildings, bridges and aircraft.
It consists of a very fine wire on a backing sheet. The gauge
is bonded to the structure under test, so that as the structure
deforms the wire is stretched.
From page 197, the resistance of a wire is given by $R = \dfrac{\rho\, l}{A}$

As the wire stretches it gets longer and thinner. Do you agree
that both of these changes increase the resistance of the gauge?
By measuring this change in resistance, engineers can calculate
the mechanical strain in the structure.

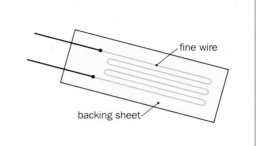

fine wire

backing sheet

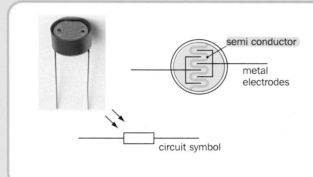

semi conductor

metal
electrodes

circuit symbol

The Light-Dependent Resistor (LDR)

We have met two semiconducting components in this chapter.
The *light-dependent resistor* is another. As its name suggests,
its resistance depends on the brightness of the light.
The energy of the light shining on the LDR, releases extra
electrons from the semiconducting material.

As the number of electrons increases, the resistance decreases:
from MΩ in dark conditions, to kΩ in bright light.

Can you think of some uses for an LDR?
How about a circuit which switches the street lights on at dusk?

Semiconductors

Modern electronics depends on semiconducting materials,
such as silicon and germanium. These pure semiconducting
materials are called *intrinsic* semiconductors.
They contain about 1×10^{19} free electrons per cubic metre,
and are poor conductors, but also poor insulators of electricity.

Semiconductors become more useful when they are *'doped'*
by adding carefully controlled numbers of impurity atoms.
These *extrinsic* semiconductors are used in components such
as diodes and transistors.
There are two types of extrinsic semiconductor:

In **n-type** semiconductors, each impurity atom donates a free
electron, which then takes part in conduction.

In **p-type** semiconductors, each impurity atom is short of one
electron. The shortage of electrons creates positive *'holes'*.
When a supply is attached the holes appear to move away
from the positive terminal and towards the negative terminal.

In fact what happens, is that an electron from one atom jumps
across to fill the hole in a neighbouring atom. In jumping it
leaves behind a hole in its own atom. As the process is
repeated the hole appears to drift through the material.

The effect is similar to that seen in a traffic queue. As one car
moves forward it leaves a gap. Each car jumps forward to fill
the space in front of it and so the gap moves quickly
backwards along the queue. The cars themselves hardly move.

diode

actual size

transistor

actual size

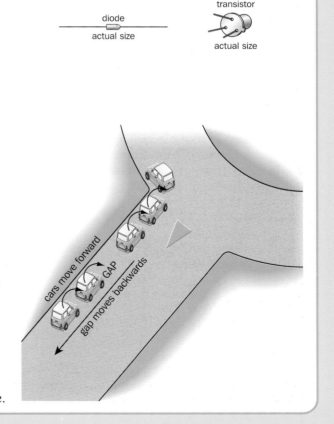

cars move forward

GAP

gap moves backwards

Summary

Electric current I is the rate of flow of charge Q. $I = \dfrac{Q}{t}$ or $I = \dfrac{\Delta Q}{\Delta t}$ and $I = nAve$
1 amp = 1 coulomb per second

Potential difference or voltage V is the energy W transferred per coulomb of charge: $V = \dfrac{W}{Q}$
1 volt = 1 joule per coulomb

The energy W transferred in a time t can be calculated using: $W = VIt$

Resistance is defined by the equation: $R = \dfrac{V}{I}$ or $V = IR$

The resistance of a sample of material depends on its temperature, $R = \dfrac{\rho l}{A}$
length l, cross-sectional area A and its resistivity ρ .

The power P of a device is the rate at which it transfers energy W, and so: $P = \dfrac{W}{t}$
Power can be calculated using: $P = IV$,   and for resistors and lamps: $P = I^2 R$ or $P = \dfrac{V^2}{R}$

▷ Questions

1. Can you complete the following sentences?
   a) In metals, current is a flow of .... As the .... move round the circuit they transfer ....
   b) The charge that flows (in ....) is equal to the current (in ....) multiplied by .... (in ....).
   c) The size of the current passing through a wire depends on the .... of the wire and the .... applied across it.
   d) Ohm's law states that the .... through a conductor is .... to the .... applied across it, providing the .... remains constant.
   e) The resistance of a wire increases as the length .... , as the temperature .... , and as the cross-sectional area ....
   f) The power (in ....) of a component is equal to the current (in ....) multiplied by the .... (in ....).

2. Use the idea of **free electrons** to explain why:
   a) Metals are good conductors of electricity.
   b) Insulators cannot conduct electricity.
   c) Semiconducting materials have higher resistivity than conducting materials.
   d) The resistance of a metal wire increases as its temperature rises.
   e) The resistance of a thermistor decreases as its temperature rises.

3. What charge flows when there is a current of:
   a) 5.0 A for 7.0 s?
   b) 0.2 A for 3.0 min?

4. What is the current when a charge of:
   a) 3.0 C passes through a lamp in 20 s?
   b) 3600 C passes a point in 3.0 minutes?
   c) 4.0 μC flows through a diode in 2.0 ms?

5. A charge of 4000 μC passes each point in a wire in 50 s. Calculate:
   a) the charge in coulombs,
   b) the current in the wire,
   c) the number of electrons per second passing each point in the wire. (electron charge $= 1.6 \times 10^{-19}$ C)

6. A cathode-ray tube produces a beam of fast moving electrons which strike a fluorescent screen. When the beam current is 150 μA, how many electrons hit the screen in 2.4 s? (electron charge $= 1.6 \times 10^{-19}$ C)

7. The current through a wire changes with time as shown in the graph. Calculate the total charge that passes through the wire.

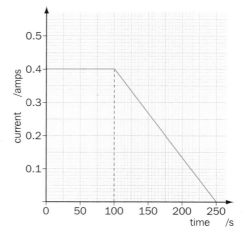

8. A copper wire has a cross-sectional area of 2.5 mm². Copper has 1.0×10^{29} free electrons per m³ and the charge on each electron is 1.6×10^{-19} C. Calculate the drift velocity of the free electrons when the wire carries a current of 5.0 A.

9. A lamp has a p.d. of 12 V across it. Calculate how much electrical energy is transferred when:
   a) a charge of 400 C passes through it,
   b) a current of 2.5 A passes through it for 30 s.

10. A 230 V electric heater takes a current of 2.0 A. Calculate the heat produced if it is switched on for 5.0 minutes.

11. Calculate the p.d. across a wire if the energy transferred is:
    a) 600 J when a charge of 50 C passes through it,
    b) 450 J when there is a steady current of 0.5 A for 20 s.

12. A 230 V kettle transfers 6.9×10^5 joules of energy in 5.0 minutes. What is the current in the kettle?

13. a) What is the p.d. across a wire of resistance 8.0 Ω when there is a current of 1.5 A through it?
    b) What is the resistance of a wire if a p.d. of 6.0 V drives a current of 0.25 A through it?
    c) A p.d. of 3.0 V is applied across a wire of resistance 15 Ω. What is the current in the wire?

14. a) The resistivity of copper is $= 1.7 \times 10^{-8}$ Ω m. Calculate the resistance of 50 m of copper cable with a cross-sectional area of 2.5×10^{-6} m^2.
    b) What is the voltage drop across this cable when it carries a current of 13 A?

15. Calculate the resistance of a constantan wire of diameter 0.5 mm and length 50 cm if its resistivity is 4.9×10^{-7} Ω m.

16. The resistivity of nichrome is 1.1×10^{-6} Ω m. Calculate the lengths of 0.4 mm diameter nichrome wire needed to make coils with resistances of
    a) 2.0 Ω and   b) 5.0 Ω.

17. The current/voltage characteristics for a metal wire at two temperatures θ_1 and θ_2 are shown below.
    a) Calculate the resistance of the wire at each temperature.
    b) Is θ_1 or θ_2 the higher temperature? Explain.

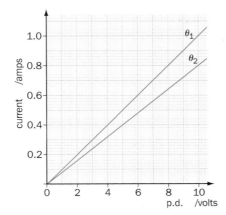

18. The current–voltage characteristics for a diode are shown below. Calculate the resistance of the diode when the p.d. across it is   a) 0.6 V   b) 0.8 V. (Remember that the current is in mA.)

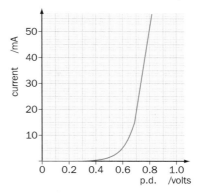

19. A 3000 W electric fire is switched on for $\frac{1}{2}$ hour. Calculate the energy transferred in a) J   b) kW h.

20. Electricity costs 8 p per kW h. How much does it cost to run a 60 W TV for 30 hours?

21. a) What is the power of a microwave oven that takes a current of 7.5 A from a 230 V supply?
    b) A small 48 W electric heater is connected to a 12 V supply. What current passes through it?

22. A coil of wire has a resistance of 10 Ω. Calculate the heat produced per second by the coil when the current in it is a) 2.0 A   b) 4.0 A. What happens to the heat output when the current is doubled?

23. What is the power loss down a copper connecting lead with a resistance of 2.5×10^{-3} Ω when it carries a current of 3.5 A?

24. A power station generates electricity at 250 MW and 400 kV. The electricity is transmitted to a distant town along cables with a resistance of 5.0 Ω.
    a) What is the current in the power lines?
    b) What is the power loss in the cables?

25. When it is hot an electric bar fire has a resistance of 50 Ω. What is its power rating on a 230 V supply?

26. The filament of a 230 V light bulb is 0.72 m long and has a radius of 6.0×10^{-2} mm. The resistivity of the filament metal is 1.2×10^{-5} Ω m.
    a) Calculate the resistance of the light bulb.
    b) Calculate its power on a 230 V supply.
    c) The filament of the bulb becomes thinner as the bulb is used. What effect will this have on
       i) the resistance of the filament?
       ii) its power output? (Hint: the p.d. across the bulb remains at 230 V.)

Further questions on page 274.

17 Electric Circuits

A string of Christmas tree lights may consist of 80 lamps, all connected to one 230 V socket.
The lamps could be connected in series, or in parallel.

In this chapter you will learn:
- how to analyse series and parallel circuits,
- about e.m.f. and internal resistance,
- how to use potential dividers.

The series circuit

Here are 2 lamps connected in **series** to a 6 V battery:

The ammeters are placed at different positions in the circuit. Why do they all show the same reading?

Remember that current is the rate of flow of charge.
All the electrons that go through one lamp must also go through the other.
No electrons are lost from the circuit, and so the number of coulombs passing any point each second must be the same.

In a series circuit, the current is the same at all points.

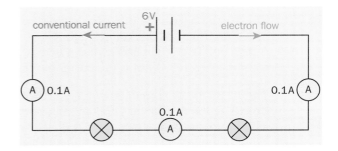

The parallel circuit

Here are 2 lamps connected in **parallel** to a 6 V battery:

You will find that the reading on the ammeter A_1 is the sum of the readings on ammeters A_2 and A_3.
Can you see that the current splits between the two branches?
As the electrons reach point Y, some pass through one lamp and some flow through the other, until they reach X, where their paths join together again.

In a parallel circuit, the current leaving and returning to the supply is the sum of the currents in the separate branches.

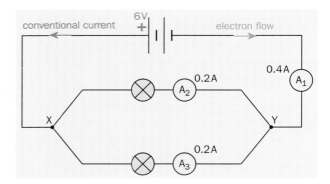

Kirchhoff's first law:

In both the circuits above, charge is 'conserved'.
In any circuit the charge cannot be created or destroyed, so when charge flows into a point it must flow out again.
This law is usually expressed in terms of current:

The sum of the currents flowing into a point equals the sum of the currents flowing out of that point.

This is Kirchhoff's first law. It is useful when you apply it to branching circuits like the parallel circuit.

Apply this law to point X.
Is the missing current I equal to 4 amps leaving the junction?

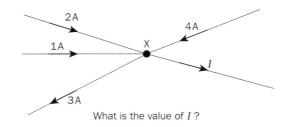

What is the value of I ?

▷ Energy transfer in a series circuit.

The two lamps in **series** have equal brightness, but each lamp is less bright than if it is connected to the battery on its own.

You can measure the potential differences in this series circuit using voltmeters connected as shown:

What do you notice about the voltmeter readings?
The total p.d. across both lamps is 6 V. This is shared between the two lamps, so that each lamp has a p.d. of 3 V across it.

In a series circuit, the total p.d. across all the lamps is the sum of the p.d.s across the separate lamps.

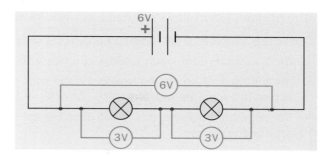

We can explain this result using our model of energy transfer. (Remember, from page 194, that p.d. is the electrical energy transferred per coulomb of charge).

Each coulomb collects 6 joules of energy from the battery. A single lamp connected to the battery would receive all 6 joules of energy. But in this circuit each coulomb transfers 3 joules at the first lamp and then 3 joules at the second lamp. The energy is shared equally because the lamps are identical.

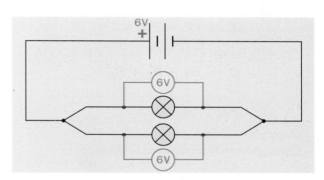

coulombs have given up some energy

▷ Energy transfer in a parallel circuit

In our **parallel** circuit each lamp is just as bright as if it were connected to the battery on its own.
Can you explain why?
You need to know the potential differences across the lamps.
Look at the voltmeter readings in this diagram:

The p.d. across each bulb is the same and is equal to 6 V.

In a parallel circuit, the p.d. across each branch is the same.

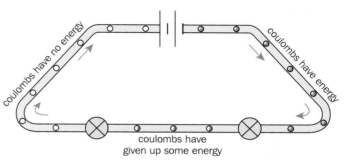

Using our model again, each coulomb of charge transports 6 joules of energy and transfers it all to *one* of the lamps.
Each lamp receives the same energy as if it were connected to the battery on its own.
Twice as many coulombs pass per second through the battery as when a single lamp is connected, and so the battery runs down more quickly.

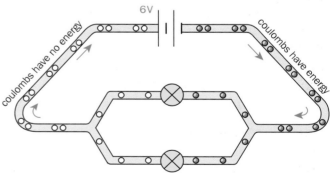

Christmas tree lamps are sometimes connected in a mixture of series and parallel circuits.

In this diagram we have 3 parallel strings of 5 lamps in series:

Can you see why the p.d. across each lamp is 46 V?

If lamp X blows what will happen to the other 14 lamps?
The 4 lamps in the same branch as X will go out, but the other 10 lamps will stay lit at the same brightness.
Can you explain why?

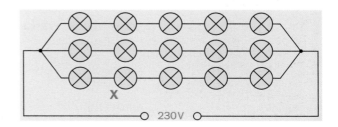

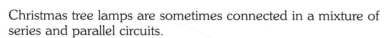

▷ Resistors in series

The diagram shows three resistors connected in **series**:

There are 3 facts that you should know for a series circuit:

- the current through each resistor in series is the same
- the total p.d. V across the resistors is the sum of the p.d.s across the separate resistors, so: $V = V_1 + V_2 + V_3$
- the combined resistance R in the circuit is the sum of the separate resistors:

$$R = R_1 + R_2 + R_3$$

We have seen the first two of these facts before (on pages 206, 207), but can we prove the third one?

Suppose we replace the 3 resistors with one resistor R that will take the same current I when the same p.d. V is placed across it. This is shown in the diagram. Let's calculate R.

We know that for the resistors in series:
$$V = V_1 + V_2 + V_3$$

But for any resistor: p.d. = current × resistance $(V = I R)$.

If we apply this to each of our resistors, and remember that the current through each resistor is the same and equal to I, we get:
$$I R = I R_1 + I R_2 + I R_3$$

If we now divide each term in the equation by I, we get:
$$R = R_1 + R_2 + R_3$$

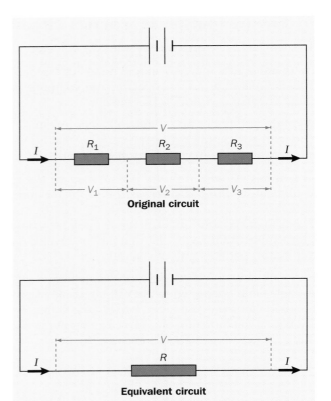

Original circuit

Equivalent circuit

Example 1
A p.d. of 3 V is applied across two resistors (4 Ω and 2 Ω) connected in series, as shown:
Calculate a) the combined resistance,
    b) the current in the circuit,
    c) the p.d. V_1 across the 4 Ω resistor,
    d) the p.d. V_2 across the 2 Ω resistor.

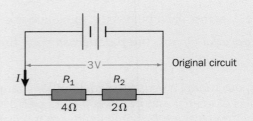

Original circuit

a) The combined resistance $R = R_1 + R_2$
$$\therefore \quad R = 4\,\Omega + 2\,\Omega \quad = \underline{6\,\Omega}$$

b) Now redraw the circuit as an equivalent circuit:
$$V = I R \qquad \text{for the combined resistance}$$
$$3\,V = I \times 6\,\Omega$$
$$\therefore \quad I = \underline{0.5\,A}$$

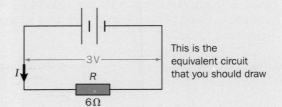

This is the equivalent circuit that you should draw

c) In the original circuit:
$$V_1 = I R_1 \qquad \text{for the 4 Ω resistor only}$$
$$V_1 = 0.5\,A \times 4\,\Omega$$
$$\therefore \quad V_1 = \underline{2\,V} \qquad \text{across the 4 Ω resistor}$$

d) Also in the original circuit:
$$V_2 = I R_2 \qquad \text{for the 2 Ω resistor only}$$
$$V_2 = 0.5\,A \times 2\,\Omega$$
$$\therefore \quad V_2 = \underline{1\,V} \qquad \text{across the 2 Ω resistor}$$

Is the p.d. greater across the bigger or the smaller resistor?
In fact, the p.d. across the 4 Ω resistor is **twice** the p.d. across the 2 Ω resistor.

▷ Resistors in parallel

We now have three resistors connected in **parallel**:

There are 3 facts that you should know for a parallel circuit:

- the p.d. across each resistor in parallel is the same
- the current in the main circuit is the sum of the currents in each of the parallel branches, so: $I = I_1 + I_2 + I_3$
- the combined resistance R is calculated from the equation:

$$\boxed{\frac{1}{R} = \frac{1}{R_1} + \frac{1}{R_2} + \frac{1}{R_3}}$$

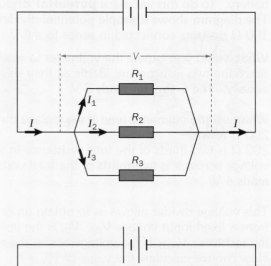

How can we prove this?

Suppose we replace the 3 resistors with one resistor R that takes the same total current I when the same p.d. V is placed across it. This is shown in the diagram. Now let's calculate R.

We know that for the resistors in parallel:
$$I = I_1 + I_2 + I_3$$

But for any resistor, current = p.d. ÷ resistance ($I = V/R$).

If we apply this to each of our resistors, and remember that the p.d. across each resistor is the same and equal to V, we get:
$$\frac{V}{R} = \frac{V}{R_1} + \frac{V}{R_2} + \frac{V}{R_3}$$

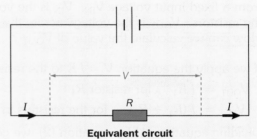

Now we divide each term by V, to get: $\dfrac{1}{R} = \dfrac{1}{R_1} + \dfrac{1}{R_2} + \dfrac{1}{R_3}$

Equivalent circuit

You will find that the total resistance R is always *less* than the smallest resistance in the parallel combination.
Check that this is true in the worked example below.

Example 2
A p.d. of 6 V is applied across two resistors (3 Ω and 6 Ω) in parallel. Calculate:
a) the combined resistance,   b) current I in the main circuit,
c) current I_1 in the 3 Ω resistor,   d) current I_2 in the 6 Ω resistor.

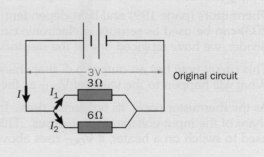

Original circuit

a) $\dfrac{1}{R} = \dfrac{1}{R_1} + \dfrac{1}{R_2}$ so: $\dfrac{1}{R} = \dfrac{1}{3} + \dfrac{1}{6} = \dfrac{2+1}{6} = \dfrac{3}{6} = \dfrac{1}{2}$

Since $\dfrac{1}{R} = \dfrac{1}{2}$ then $\dfrac{R}{1} = \dfrac{2}{1}$ so: $\underline{R = 2\,\Omega}$

b) Now redraw the circuit as an equivalent circuit:
$$\mathbf{V = I\,R}$$ for the combined resistance
$$6\,V = I \times 2\,\Omega$$
$$\therefore\ \underline{I = 3\,A}$$ in the main circuit.

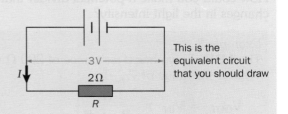

This is the equivalent circuit that you should draw

c) In the original circuit:
$$\mathbf{V = I_1\,R_1}$$ for the 3 Ω resistor only
$$6\,V = I_1 \times 3\,\Omega$$
$$\therefore\ \underline{I_1 = 2\,A}$$ in the 3 Ω resistor.

d) In the original circuit:
$$\mathbf{V = I_2\,R_2}$$ for the 6 Ω resistor only
$$6\,V = I_1 \times 6\,\Omega$$
$$\therefore\ \underline{I_1 = 1\,A}$$ in the 6 Ω resistor.

You can check your answer in the following way: does $I = I_1 + I_2$?

The current is always biggest in the parallel branch with the **least** resistance.

▷ Electromotive force

Resistors and bulbs transfer electrical energy to other forms, but which components *provide* electrical energy?
A dry cell, a dynamo and a solar cell are some examples.

Any component that supplies electrical energy is a source of **electromotive force** or **e.m.f.** It is measured in volts.
The e.m.f. of a dry cell is 1.5 V, that of a car battery is 12 V.

Cameras use small batteries

Remember our model of energy transfer from page 194.
A battery transfers chemical energy to electrical energy, so that as each coulomb moves through the battery it gains electrical potential energy.
The greater the e.m.f. of a source, the more energy is transferred per coulomb.
In fact:

The e.m.f. of a source is the electrical potential energy transferred from other forms, per coulomb of charge that passes through the source.

Compare this definition with the definition of p.d. (page 194) and make sure you know the difference between them.

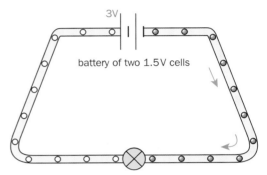

Each coulomb gains 3 J of energy as it moves through the battery of two 1.5 V cells

If a charge Q moves through a source of e.m.f. $\mathcal{E}$, then:

energy transferred, W	=	**charge, Q**	×	**e.m.f. $\mathcal{E}$**
(joules)		(coulombs)		(volts)

or $W = Q\,\mathcal{E}$

The internal resistance of a supply

In the circuit shown, the dry cell has an e.m.f. of 1.5 V:

What happens to the current in the circuit and the p.d. across the resistance box, as you reduce the value of the resistance R?

The table below shows some typical results:

Did you expect the voltmeter reading to remain at 1.5 V ?
In fact, as the current in the circuit increases, the p.d. across the resistance box *falls.*

The cell gives 1.5 joules of electrical energy to each coulomb that passes through it, but the electrical energy transferred in the resistor is less than 1.5 joules per coulomb and can vary.
The circuit seems to be losing energy – can you think where?

The cell itself has some resistance, its **internal resistance**.
Each coulomb gains energy as it travels through the cell, but some of this energy is wasted or 'lost' as the coulombs move against the resistance of the cell itself.

So, the energy delivered by each coulomb to the circuit is **less** than the energy supplied to each coulomb by the cell.

Very often the internal resistance is small and can be ignored.
Dry cells, however, have a significant internal resistance.
This is why a battery can become hot when supplying electric current. The wasted energy is dissipated as heat.

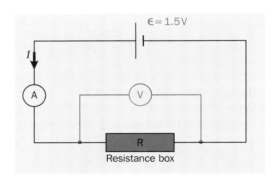

Value of R /Ω	current I /A	p.d. across R /V
100	0.015	1.5
20	0.071	1.4
5.0	0.250	1.3
2.0	0.500	1.0

▷ Kirchhoff's second law

This is a statement of the conservation of energy in a circuit.
We know that a coulomb gains electrical energy as it moves
through each e.m.f., and loses electrical energy as it moves
through each p.d.
After one loop of the circuit, the energy it has gained must
be equal to the energy it has dissipated. Therefore:

**Around any closed loop in a circuit, the sum of the emfs
is equal to the sum of the p.d.s.**

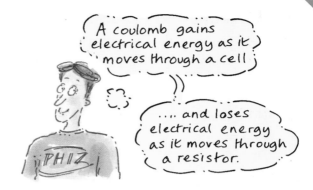

▷ The circuit equation

The diagram shows a cell of e.m.f. ϵ together with its internal
resistance r. A loop is drawn round ϵ and r to show that they
are really one component. Here, the cell is connected to a circuit
which has a total resistance R.

What does the voltmeter measure?
The voltmeter records the p.d. V across the external circuit,
but notice that V is also the p.d. across the terminals of the cell.
Can you see why V is called the **terminal p.d.**?

The diagram also shows the 'lost volts' v across the internal
resistance.

Since Kirchhoff's law tells us that energy is conserved:

energy **supplied** per coulomb from chemical energy of the cell	=	energy **delivered** per coulomb to the external circuit	+	energy **wasted** per coulomb on the internal resistance

or: e.m.f., ϵ = terminal p.d., **V** + lost volts, v or $\epsilon = V + v$

We know that the current through the resistors R and r is I.
so applying: voltage = current × resistance to each resistor:

$$\epsilon \;=\; V + I\,r \qquad \textbf{or} \qquad \epsilon \;=\; I\,R + I\,r \qquad \textbf{or} \qquad \epsilon \;=\; I\,(R + r\,)$$

Example 4
A battery of e.m.f. 6.0 V and internal resistance 1 Ω is
connected to two resistors of 4 Ω and 7 Ω in series:
Calculate   a) the total resistance in the external circuit,
　　　　　　 b) the current supplied by the battery,
　　　　　　 c) the terminal p.d of the battery.

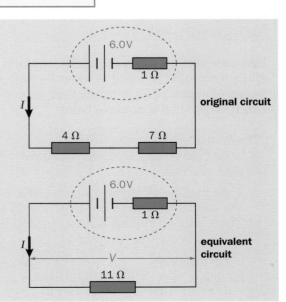

a) $R = R_1 + R_2$ ∴ $R = 4\,\Omega + 7\,\Omega$ = $\underline{11\,\Omega}$

b) Now draw the equivalent circuit:
　　　 $\epsilon = I\,(R + r)$ for the whole circuit
　 6.0 V $= I\,(11\,\Omega + 1\,\Omega)$
　 ∴ $I = \underline{0.5\,A}$

c) The p.d across the resistors in series is the terminal p.d. V:
　　　 $V = I\,R$ where R is the total series
　　　 $V = 0.5\,A \times 11\,\Omega$ resistance of 11 Ω
　 ∴ $V = \underline{5.5\,V}$

▷ Solving circuit problems

Take care when solving circuit problems using the equation $V = I \times R$.

- Be clear whether the values you put into the equation are for a single resistor, or a group of resistors, or the whole circuit.
- Learn the rules for series and parallel resistors (pages 208–9).
- Try to simplify the circuit, by drawing an equivalent circuit.
- Remember to include any internal resistance of the supply when calculating the total resistance of the circuit.
- Remember that the e.m.f. is equal to the sum of all the p.d.s, (including the 'lost volts' due to any internal resistance).

Phiz solves circuit problems

Example 5

A supply of e.m.f. 4 V and internal resistance 1 Ω is connected to two resistors as shown in the original circuit diagram.
Calculate a) the resistance of the parallel combination,
 b) the current taken from the supply,
 c) the terminal p.d. of the supply,
 d) the current through each parallel branch.

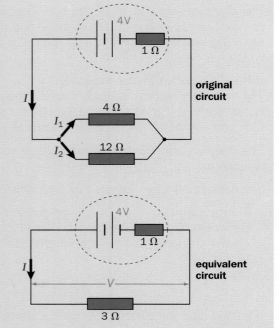

original circuit

a) Use: $\dfrac{1}{R} = \dfrac{1}{R_1} + \dfrac{1}{R_2}$ for the parallel combination

 $\therefore \dfrac{1}{R} = \dfrac{1}{4} + \dfrac{1}{12} = \dfrac{3+1}{12} = \dfrac{4}{12}$

 $\therefore R = 3\ \Omega$ where R is the total external resistance.

b) Now draw the equivalent circuit:
 Then use: $\epsilon = I\,(R + r)$ for the whole circuit
  $4\ V = I\,(3\ \Omega + 1\ \Omega)$
  $\therefore I = 1\ A$

equivalent circuit

c) The p.d. across both parallel resistors is the terminal p.d. V.
 Use: $V = I\,R$ where R is the combined parallel resistance of 3 Ω
  $V = 1\ A \times 3\ \Omega$
  $\therefore V = 3\ V$

d) Remember the p.d. across both parallel resistors is 3 V.
 Use: $V = I_1\,R$ for the 4 Ω resistor only   Use: $V = I_2\,R$ for the 12 Ω resistor only
  $3\ V = I_1 \times 4\ \Omega$ $3\ V = I_2 \times 12\ \Omega$
  $\therefore I_1 = 0.75\ A$ $\therefore I_2 = 0.25\ A$

Take care with the directions of the e.m.f.s in a circuit. When a coulomb is forced to move through an e.m.f. in the 'wrong' direction, it loses rather than gains electrical energy. This is shown in the example below.

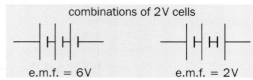

combinations of 2V cells

e.m.f. = 6V   e.m.f. = 2V

Example 6

A 12 volt car battery is recharged by passing a current through it in the reverse direction using a 14 V charger. Calculate the charging current.

- Note that the 12 V e.m.f. opposes the 14 V e.m.f., so:
 the sum of the e.m.f.s $= 14\ V + - 12\ V = 2\ V$
- There are two internal resistances, and both 'waste' electrical energy.

  $\epsilon = I\,(R + r)$
 $14\ V + - 12\ V = I\,(0 + 0.040\ \Omega + 0.50\ \Omega)$
  $2\ V = I \times 0.54\ \Omega$
  $\therefore I = 3.7\ A$ (2 s.f.)

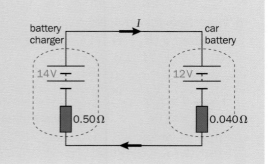

▷ Physics at work: Current, voltage, resistance

Ammeters and voltmeters

As you have seen, in order to measure the current,
an ammeter is placed **in series**, *in* the circuit.

What effect might this have on the size of the current?
The *ideal* ammeter has zero resistance, so that placing it
in the circuit does not make the current smaller.
Real ammeters do have very small resistances – around 0.01 Ω.

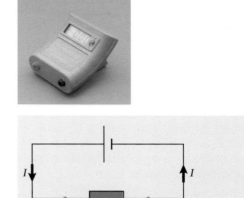

A voltmeter is connected **in parallel** with a component,
in order to measure the p.d. across it.

Why can this increase the current in the circuit?
Since the voltmeter is in parallel with the component, their
combined resistance is less than the component's resistance.
The *ideal* voltmeter has infinite resistance and takes no current.
Digital voltmeters have very high resistances, around 10 MΩ,
and so they have little effect on the circuit they are placed in.

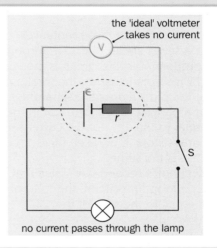

a very small current
passes through the
digital voltmeter

Can we measure e.m.f. directly?

In this diagram we have a cell that is *not* supplying currrent.
Charge does not move through the cell and so there is no
energy wasted due to the cell's internal resistance.

Remember the circuit equation: $\epsilon = V + I r$
Since $I = 0$, $\epsilon = V + 0 \times r$ so: $\epsilon = V$

This means that: ***the e.m.f. of a supply is equal to the
p.d. across its terminals when it is not supplying current.***

An 'ideal' voltmeter takes no current and so we can connect it
across a cell to measure the e.m.f. directly.
Why can a digital voltmeter be placed across a cell, to give a
reading which is very close to the e.m.f?
The voltmeter takes such a small current that the terminal p.d.
will only be slightly less than the e.m.f.

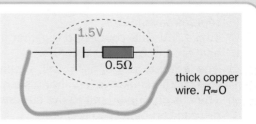

the 'ideal' voltmeter
takes no current

no current passes through the lamp

The effects of internal resistance

What is a short circuit? The 1.5 V dry cell in the diagram is
short-circuited by the low resistance copper wire connected to
its terminals. The only significant resistance in this circuit is
0.5 Ω, the internal resistance of the cell itself.

Using $\epsilon = I (R + r)$ where $R = 0$, can you show that
the current through the wire must be 3 amps?
This means that 3 A is the **maximum** possible current
that this dry cell can supply.
Some sources, such as the mains supply, have very low internal
resistances, and so they can supply high short-circuit currents.
These currents are dangerous because of the heat they produce.

A 12 V **car battery** must have a very low internal resistance,
because a starter motor needs a current of over 100 A!
What happens if a driver starts a car with the head-lamps on?
The current through the battery is so large that the 'lost volts'
are high – even though the battery's internal resistance is low.
The terminal p.d. drops to around 8 V and the head lamps go dim.

1.5V

0.5Ω

thick copper
wire. R≈0

The internal resistance
of a car battery
is almost zero

Summary

For 3 resistors in series: $R = R_1 + R_2 + R_3$

For 3 resistors in parallel: $\dfrac{1}{R} = \dfrac{1}{R_1} + \dfrac{1}{R_2} + \dfrac{1}{R_3}$

For a potential divider:

$$\dfrac{V_{OUT}}{V_{IN}} = \dfrac{R_1}{R_1 + R_2}$$

A coulomb of charge **gains** energy as it moves through each source of e.m.f., and **loses** energy as it moves through each resistor (or other component) across which there is a p.d. The unit for both e.m.f. and p.d. is the volt (V).

1 volt = 1 joule per coulomb

The e.m.f. ϵ of a supply is the electrical energy supplied per coulomb of charge:

$$\epsilon = \dfrac{W}{Q} \quad or \quad W = Q\,\epsilon$$

Any source of e.m.f. has some internal resistance r which must be included in circuit calculations (unless you are told to ignore it).

$$\epsilon = I\,(R + r)$$

▷ Questions

1. Can you complete these sentences?
   a) In a series circuit, the .... through each component in the circuit is the ....
   b) For resistors in series, the total .... is the .... of the p.d.s across the separate resistors.
   c) In a parallel circuit the .... in the main circuit is equal to the .... of the currents in the branches.
   d) For resistors in parallel, the .... across each .... is the same.
   e) Kirchhoff's second law states that around any .... loop in a circuit, the .... of the e.m.f.s is equal to the sum of the ....

2. Explain why :
   a) The combined resistance of two resistors in parallel is always less than either of the separate resistances.
   b) Two 1.5 V cells connected together in series can give an e.m.f. of 3.0 V or 0 V.
   c) The terminal p.d. of a dry cell, supplying current to a circuit, is always less than its e.m.f.
   d) There is an upper limit to the current that a dry cell can deliver to a circuit.

3. Diagrams (a) and (b) show meters that have been incorrectly connected into the circuits.
   For each circuit (i) state if the lamp is lit or not, and (ii) explain your answer.

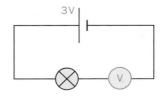
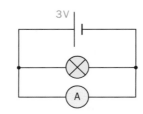

4. Calculate the combined resistance in each of the examples below:

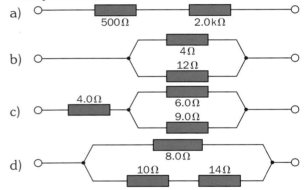

5. a) Calculate the combined resistance of two 6 Ω resistors in parallel.
   What do you notice about the result?
   b) What would be the combined resistance of two 8 Ω resistors in parallel?
   c) Predict the combined resistance of three 9 Ω resistors in parallel.
   Do the calculation to check if you are right.

6. In the circuit below the p.d across the 10 Ω resistor is 5.0 V.
   a) What is the current through the 10 Ω resistor?
   b) What is the current through the 8.0 Ω resistor?
   c) What is the p.d. across the 8.0 Ω resistor?

7. In the circuit below:
   a) What is the combined resistance?
   b) What is the p.d. across the combined resistance?
   c) What is the current in the 3 Ω resistor?
   d) What is the current in the 6 Ω resistor?

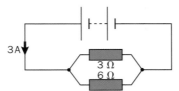

8. In the circuit below, the voltmeter reads 12 V.
   Calculate: a) the total resistance of the circuit,
               b) the current I,
               c) the p.d.s V_1 and V_2,
               d) the currents I_1 and I_2.

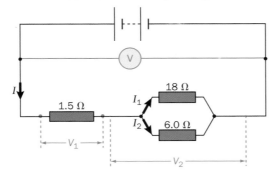

9. How much energy is transferred to 1 coulomb of charge by: a) a battery with an e.m.f. of 2.0 V?
   b) a 5.0 kV high-voltage supply?

10. How many joules of energy does a battery of e.m.f. 3.0 V supply when:
    a) a charge of 5.0 C passes through it?
    b) there is a current of 0.20 A through it for 30 seconds?

11. A battery of e.m.f. 4.0 V and an internal resistance of 1.0 Ω is connected to a 9.0 Ω resistor.
    Draw a circuit diagram and calculate the current that flows around the circuit.

12. For each of the two circuits below, calculate:
    a) the total resistance of the external circuit,
    b) the current supplied by the cell,
    c) the terminal p.d. of the cell,
    d) the energy per coulomb wasted in the cell.

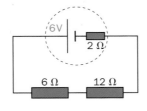

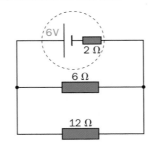

13. Three identical cells, each of e.m.f. 2.0 V and internal resistance 0.50 Ω, are connected in series to a lamp of resistance 2.5 Ω. What current flows?

14. In the circuit below the high resistance voltmeter shows a reading of 1.5 V when switch S is open. When switch S is closed the voltmeter reading falls to 1.2 V and the ammeter shows a current of 0.30 A. What is: a) the e.m.f. of the cell?
    b) the internal resistance of the cell?
    c) the resistance of the lamp?

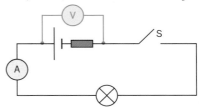

15. A battery charger is used to recharge a cell of e.m.f. 1.5 V and internal resistance 0.50 Ω. The e.m.f. of the battery charger is 6.0 V and its internal resistance is 1.0 Ω.
    Draw a circuit diagram of the arrangement and calculate the recharging current.

16. What is the value of the output voltage V_{OUT} in each of the potential dividers below.

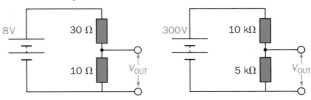

17. In the potential divider shown, what is the range of values of V_{OUT}, as the variable resistor R is adjusted over its full range from 0 Ω to 50 Ω?

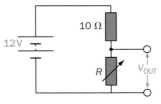

18. In the potential divider shown, the thermistor has a resistance which varies between 200 Ω at 100 °C and 5.0 kΩ at 0 °C. Calculate the value of V_{OUT} at:
    a) 100 °C   b) 0 °C

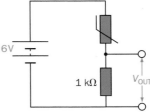

Further questions on page 274.

18 Magnetic Fields

Magnets have fascinated people for centuries. Did you know that the magnetic compass has been used for over 2000 years? The earliest compasses were probably made from lodestone, which is a naturally occurring oxide of iron.

How does a compass show direction?

If you suspend a magnet horizontally from a piece of string, it will always rotate until it points in a north–south direction. The end of the magnet that points north is called the North-seeking pole or **N-pole**. The other end is the South-seeking pole or **S-pole**.

We have come a long way since the invention of the compass! Swipe-cards, video tapes and computer discs all use magnetism to store information.

In this chapter you will learn:
- about magnetic field patterns and lines of flux,
- how to measure and calculate the strengths of magnetic fields,
- how to calculate the force on a current in a magnetic field.

▷ Magnetic fields

What happens if you bring the poles of two magnets together?

You will find that two N-poles repel, and two S-poles repel, but a N-pole and a S-pole attract.
The effect of these forces can be felt even though the magnets are not in contact with each other.
We say that a magnet has a **magnetic field** around it.
The field is a region where the magnetic force can be felt.

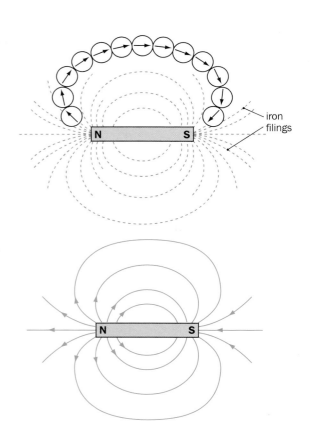

iron filings

How can we 'see the shape' of a magnetic field?
If we place iron filings or plotting compasses in the field of the magnet, they will point along curved lines called **lines of flux**, as shown in the diagram.

The lines of flux show both the *direction* and the *strength* of the magnetic field.
The direction of the line of flux at each point shows the direction of the force that a N-pole would feel, if placed at that point in the field.
This means that lines of flux always go from N-poles to S-poles.

Where is the field strongest?

The more closely packed the lines of flux, the stronger the field.
The field is strongest nearest the poles, as shown in the diagram.

More magnetic field patterns

Lines of flux can never cross: if they did it would mean that a compass would point in two directions! If two magnets are placed close to each other, the field produced is the result of the combined effect of both of the magnets:

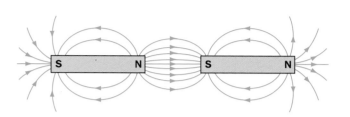

There is an attraction between the N-pole and the S-pole.
Where is the field the strongest?

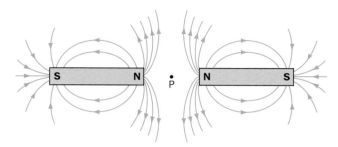

Can you see the repulsion between the two N-poles? At point P the fields from the two magnets cancel out and the resultant field strength is zero.
P is called a **neutral point**.

Magnetic flux density

The stronger the magnetic field, the more densely packed the lines of flux. In fact, we describe the strength of the magnetic field by the **magnetic flux density, B**.
This is the quantity of flux passing through unit area, at each point in the field. It is measured in **tesla** (T).

B is a vector quantity, because it has size and direction.
B is discussed in more detail on page 222.

How can we measure magnetic flux density?
A simple way is to use a **Hall probe** (see also page 229). The diagram shows a Hall probe being used to measure the flux density between the poles of a horse-shoe magnet:

The probe must be held in the field so that the lines of flux pass at right angles through its tip. The meter connected to the probe gives a direct reading of the flux density, in tesla.

The diagram shows how the flux passes through the tip of the Hall probe. Can you picture how the flux density will vary, as the probe is moved to different positions in the magnetic field?

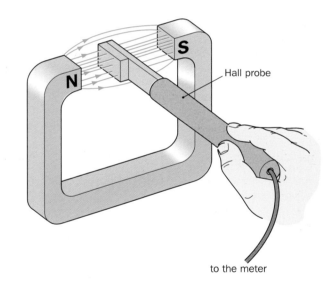

Hall probe

to the meter

The Earth's magnetic field

Why does a compass line up in a north–south direction?
The Earth acts as if there is a huge bar magnet inside it.
In the diagram, notice that the S-pole of the imaginary magnet is in the northern hemisphere so as to attract the N-pole of a compass:

Can you also see from the diagram that the lines of flux act at an **angle** to the Earth's surface, except near the equator?
This angle is called the **angle of dip**. In the UK it is about 70°.

A compass needle held horizontally is only affected by the horizontal component of the magnetic flux. What do you think will happen to a compass needle at the magnetic north pole?

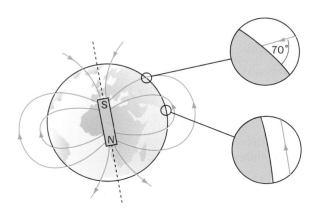

▷ The magnetic effect of a current

In 1819, Hans Christian Oersted noticed that a compass needle was deflected by an electric current in a nearby wire. In this way, he discovered the link between electricity and magnetism. An electric current is always surrounded by a magnetic field.

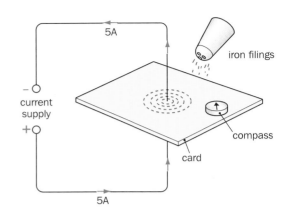

The magnetic field around a long straight wire

The diagram shows a wire carrying a current of about 5 amps. If you sprinkle some iron filings on to the horizontal card and tap it gently, the iron filings will line up along the lines of flux as shown.
Can you see that the lines of flux are circles around the wire?

You can place a small compass on the card to find the direction of the magnetic field. With the current flowing up the wire, the compass will point anti-clockwise, as shown.
What will happen if you reverse the direction of the current?

The right-hand grip rule gives a simple way to remember the **direction** of the field: imagine gripping the wire, so that your **right thumb** points in the direction of the current . . . your fingers then curl in the direction of the lines of flux:

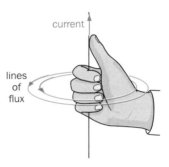

The diagrams show the magnetic field as you look down on the card:
Imagine the current direction as an arrow.
When the arrow moves away from you, into the page, you see the cross (×) of the tail of the arrow.
As the current flows towards you, you see the point of the arrow – the dot in the diagram.

Can you see that the further from the wire the circles are, the more widely separated they become?
What does this tell you?

The flux density is greatest close to the wire.
As you move away from the wire the magnetic field becomes weaker.

current into page

current out of page

The magnetic field of a flat coil

The diagram shows a flat coil carrying electric current:

Again, we can investigate the shape and direction of the magnetic field using iron filings and a compass.

Close to the wire, the lines of flux are circles.
Can you see that the lines of flux run anti-clockwise around the left side of the coil and clockwise around the right side?
What happens at the centre of the coil?

The fields due to the sides of the coil are in the same direction and they combine to give a strong magnetic field.

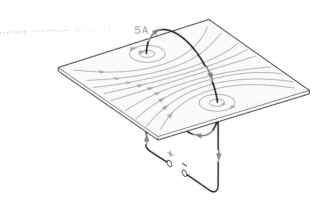

How would you expect the field to change, if the direction of the current flow around the coil was reversed?

The magnetic field of a solenoid

A **solenoid** is a long coil with a large number of turns of wire.
Look at the shape of the field, revealed by the iron filings.
Does it look familiar?

The magnetic field *outside* the solenoid has the **same shape as the field around a bar magnet.**

Inside the solenoid the lines of flux are close together, parallel and equally spaced. What does this tell you?
For most of the length of the solenoid the flux density is constant. The field is uniform and strong.

If you reverse the direction of the current flow, will the direction of the magnetic field reverse?

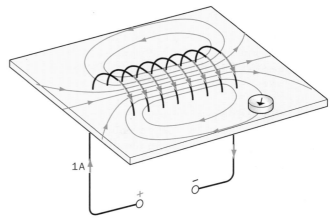

A right-hand grip rule can again be used to remember the direction of the field, **but** this time you must curl the fingers of your **right** hand in the direction of the current as shown:

Your thumb now points along the direction of the lines of flux *inside* the coil ... towards the end of the solenoid that behaves like the N-pole of the bar magnet.
This right-hand grip rule can also be used for the flat coil.

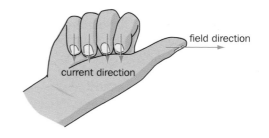

▷ Magnetic materials

We have two different ways of producing magnetic fields:
one uses permanent magnets, the other uses electric currents.
Is there a link?

Electric current is the movement of charged particles (page 190).
In 1864, James Clerk Maxwell proved that all magnetic fields are caused by the movement of charged particles.

Now think about the motion of the electrons in atoms.
As each electron spins it acts like a tiny electric current and so it produces a very tiny magnetic field.
In some atoms the magnetic effects of all the electrons cancel; in others they do not, so that each atom acts like a tiny magnet.

In **ferromagnetic** materials these tiny atomic magnets can line up with each other to produce a very strong magnetic field.
Iron, cobalt and nickel are well-known ferromagnetic elements.

Using electromagnets

Why is the magnetic field of a solenoid greatly increased when a ferromagnetic core is placed inside the coil?
The atomic magnets of the core line up along the lines of flux inside the solenoid, and so the core becomes magnetised.

What happens when the current in the solenoid is turned off?
It depends on the material.

- A **steel** core stays magnetised. The tiny atomic magnets remain lined up, even when the external field is removed.
- An **iron** core quickly demagnetises, because the atomic magnets have enough vibrational energy to turn in random directions.
  A magnet that can be switched on and off is an **electromagnet**.

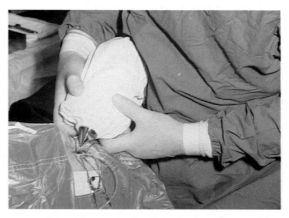

Removing a steel splinter from an eye

▷ Measuring magnetic flux density

We have seen the **shapes** of the magnetic fields around current-carrying conductors, but what do you think affects the **strength** or **magnetic flux density B** of these magnetic fields?

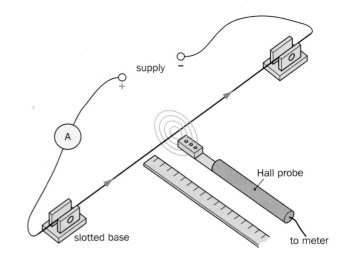

The long straight wire

You can investigate the magnetic flux density around a wire using the apparatus shown in the diagram:

Remember, that the lines of flux are circles all along the wire. How can you position the Hall probe, so that the lines of flux pass at right angles through its tip?

You can use the apparatus to answer the following questions:
1. When the probe is placed a fixed distance from the wire, how does B vary as the current in the wire is increased?
2. When the current is kept constant, how does B vary as the probe is moved away from the wire?

The graphs show some typical results. Can you see that:
* doubling the current **doubles** the flux density,
* doubling the distance from the wire **halves** the flux density.

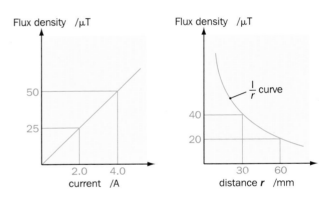

In fact:

Flux density, B (tesla) $\propto$ $\dfrac{\text{current, } I \text{ (amperes)}}{\text{distance, } r \text{ (metres)}}$ or $\quad B = k\,\dfrac{I}{r}$

k is a constant. It depends on the material round the wire.

If the wire is in a vacuum we usually write this as:

$$\textbf{Magnetic flux density, } B = \frac{\mu_o\, I}{2\pi\, r}$$

where μ_o is a constant called the **permeability of free space**.
The permeability μ of a material is a measure of its effect on the strength of the magnetic field.
For a vacuum, $\mu_o = 4\pi \times 10^{-7}$ tesla metre ampere^{-1} (T m A^{-1}).

Our wire is in air, not a vacuum, and so we should really use the permeability of air (μ_{air}) in our equation, instead of μ_o.

In fact, air and most other materials, have almost the same permeability as a vacuum.

But ferromagnetic materials have much higher permeabilities.
For example, the permeability of iron is about $8\pi \times 10^{-4}$ T m A^{-1}.

Example 1
A vertical wire carries a current of 6.0 A.
What is the flux density at (a) 20 mm and (b) 40 mm from the wire?

a) $B = \dfrac{\mu_o\, I}{2\pi\, r} = \dfrac{4\,\pi \times 10^{-7}\,\text{T m A}^{-1} \times 6.0\,\text{A}}{2\,\pi \times 20 \times 10^{-3}\,\text{m}} = \underline{6.0 \times 10^{-5}\,\text{T}}$

b) At twice the distance from the wire, the flux density is halved,

so: $B = \dfrac{6.0 \times 10^{-5}\,\text{T}}{2} = \underline{3.0 \times 10^{-5}\,\text{T}}$

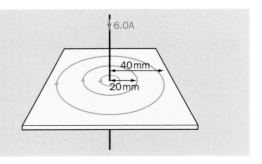

The solenoid

In the diagram, a 'slinky' is used as an adjustable solenoid:

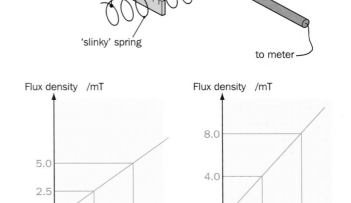

You can use this apparatus to answer the following questions:

1. Is B uniform at all points inside the solenoid?
2. How does the value of B at the centre of the solenoid vary, as the current in the solenoid is increased?
3. How does the value of B within the solenoid vary as the solenoid is stretched (so that n, the number of turns per metre, decreases)?

'slinky' spring

to meter

The graphs show some typical results. Can you see that:
- doubling the current **doubles** the flux density,
- doubling the number of turns per metre **doubles** the flux density.

In fact, B is uniform inside the solenoid, and:

Magnetic flux density, B $\propto$ turns per metre, n $\times$ current, I
    (tesla)   (amperes)

When the solenoid is in a vacuum (or in air), we can write this as an equation:

> **Magnetic flux density, $B = \mu_0 n I$**

Example 2

A solenoid is 0.40 m long and is made with 800 turns of wire.
a) What is n, the number of turns per metre?
b) What is the flux density at the centre of the solenoid when it carries a current of 2.0 A ?

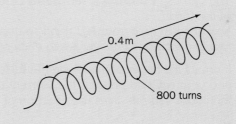

0.4 m

800 turns

a) $n = \dfrac{\text{the number of turns}}{\text{the length of the solenoid}} = \dfrac{800}{0.40 \text{ m}} = \underline{2000 \text{ m}^{-1}}$

b) $B = \mu_0 n I = 4\pi \times 10^{-7} \text{ T m A}^{-1} \times 2000 \text{ m}^{-1} \times 2.0 \text{ A} = \underline{5.0 \times 10^{-3} \text{ T}}$

Example 3

Phiz passes a current of 5.0 A down a vertical wire and uses a compass to plot the lines of flux around the wire. He obtains the pattern shown, and finds a neutral point P, 50 mm from the wire:
a)   Why has he obtained this pattern?
b)   What is the value of the horizontal component of the Earth's magnetic field?

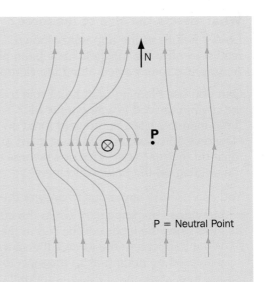

a)   This field is the **resultant** magnetic field of both the wire and the Earth in a horizontal plane.

b)   At P, the two fields must be **equal**, but in **opposite** directions.

    For the wire: $B = \dfrac{\mu_0 I}{2\pi r}$

    $\therefore$ $B = \dfrac{4\pi \times 10^{-7} \text{ T m A}^{-1} \times 5.0 \text{ A}}{2\pi \times 50 \times 10^{-3} \text{ m}} = 2.0 \times 10^{-5} \text{ T}$

So the horizontal component of the Earth's field is also $\underline{2.0 \times 10^{-5} \text{ T}}$

P = Neutral Point

▷ Magnetic force

A wire carrying a current in a magnetic field feels a force.
A simple way to demonstrate this is shown in the diagram:

The two strong magnets are attached to an iron yoke with
opposite poles facing each other. They produce a strong
almost uniform field in the space between them.

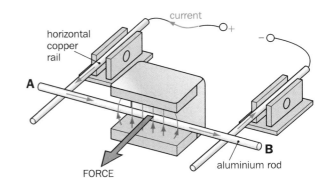

What happens when you switch the current on?
The aluminium rod AB feels a force, and moves along the
copper rails as shown.
Notice that the current, the magnetic field, and the force,
are **all at right angles** to each other.

What happens if you reverse the direction of the current flow,
or turn the magnets so that the magnetic field acts downwards?
In each case the rod moves in the opposite direction.

Why does the aluminium rod move?
The magnetic field of the permanent magnets interacts with
the magnetic field of the current in the rod.
Imagine looking from end B of the rod. The diagram shows
the combined field of the magnet and the rod:

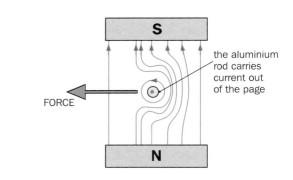

The lines of flux behave a bit like elastic bands.
Can you see that the wire tends to be catapulted to the left?

You can use **Fleming's left-hand rule** to predict the direction
of the force.
You need to hold your **left** hand so that the thumb and the first
two fingers are at right angles to each other as shown:

If your **First** finger points along the **Field** direction (from N to S),
and your se**Cond** finger is the **Current** direction (from + to −),
then your **Thumb** gives the direction of the **Thrust** (or force).

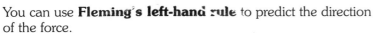
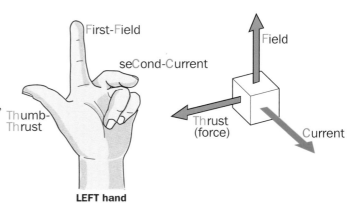

What affects the size of the force?

Look carefully at the apparatus shown. The balance is set to
read zero after the magnets have been placed on it.
A current is then passed along the clamped aluminium rod.

Can you use Fleming's left-hand rule to show that the force on
the aluminium rod is acting upwards?
If the magnets exert an upward force on the rod, then by
Newton's third law, the rod must exert an equal but opposite
force on the magnets. This downwards force will cause
the reading on the balance to increase.

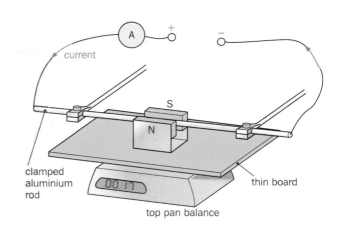

You can use the apparatus to answer the following questions:
1. How does the force vary when the current is increased?
2. How does the length of the rod in the field affect the force?
3. What happens to the force if the strength of the field is
   increased by adding extra magnets to the yoke.

Some typical results are shown on the next page.

224

The graph of force against length was obtained by placing a second and a third pair of magnets on the balance. This doubles and then triples the length of the aluminium rod in the field. Look carefully at these graphs. What do they tell us?

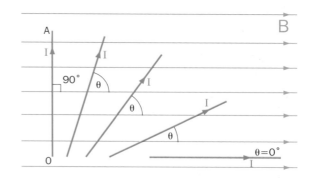

Experiments like this show us that the force F on a conductor in a magnetic field is directly proportional to:
- the magnetic flux density B
- the current I, and
- the length l of the conductor in the field.

In fact:

| **Force, F** = **flux density, B** × **current, I** × **length, l of wire** | or | $F = B I l$ |
| (newtons) (tesla) (amps) (metres) | | |

This equation applies when the current is at 90° to the field. Does changing the angle affect the size of the force?

Look at the wire OA in the diagram, at different angles:

When the angle θ is 90° the force has its maximum value. As θ is reduced the force becomes smaller. When the wire is parallel to the field, so that θ is zero, the force is also zero.

In fact, if the current makes an angle θ to the magnetic field the force is given by:

$$F = B I l \sin \theta$$

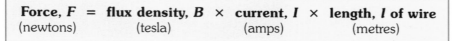

Notice that: when $\theta = 90°$, $\sin \theta = 1$, and $F = B I l$ as before.
when $\theta = 0°$, $\sin \theta = 0$, and $F = 0$, as stated above.

The **size** of the force depends on the angle that the wire makes with the magnetic field, but the **direction** of the force does not. The force is **always at 90°** to both the current and the field.

Example 4
The two wires below are in a uniform magnetic field of 0.25 T. Both wires are 0.50 m long and carry a current of 4.0 A. Calculate the size of the force on each wire.

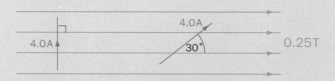

a) The wire is at 90° to the field.
   $F = B I l$
   ∴ $F = 0.25 \text{ T} \times 4.0 \text{ A} \times 0.50 \text{ m} = \underline{0.50 \text{ N}}$

b) The wire is at 30° to the field
   $F = B I l \sin \theta$
   ∴ $F = 0.25 \text{ T} \times 4.0 \text{ A} \times 0.50 \text{ m} \times \sin 30° = \underline{0.25 \text{ N}}$

In both cases the force acts at 90° to the wire – into the paper.

Magnetic flux density B and the tesla

We can rearrange the equation $F = B I l$ to give:
$$B = \frac{F}{I l}$$

What is the value of B, when $I = 1$ A and $l = 1$ m? In this case, B has the same numerical value as F.

This gives us the definition of B:
The magnetic flux density B, is the force acting per unit length, on a wire carrying unit current, which is perpendicular to the magnetic field.

The unit of B is the **tesla** (T).
Can you see that: $1 \text{ T} = 1 \text{ N A}^{-1} \text{ m}^{-1}$?

The tesla is defined in the following way:

A magnetic flux density of 1 T produces a force of 1 N on each metre of wire carrying a current of 1 A at 90° to the field.

▷ The magnetic force on a moving charge

The photograph shows the glow of the 'Northern Lights'.
Charged particles from outer space become trapped in the
Earth's magnetic field and spiral from one pole to the other.
As they enter the atmosphere, at the poles, they produce this
spectacular glow in the sky.

Aurora borealis : the 'Northern Lights'

This phenomenon occurs because a charged particle feels a force
when it moves through a magnetic field.
What factors do you think affect the size of this force?

The force F on the particle is directly proportional to:
- the magnetic flux density B,
- the charge on the particle Q, and
- the velocity v of the particle.

When the charged particle is moving at 90° to the field,
the force can be calculated from:

Force, F	=	flux density, B	×	charge, Q	×	velocity, v
(N)		(T)		(C)		(m s⁻¹)

or $$F = B\,Q\,v$$

In which direction does the force act?
The force is always at 90° to both the current and the field, and
you use **Fleming's left-hand rule** (page 224) to find its direction.

Try this for the positive particle in the first diagram:
Point your middle finger along the path of the positive particle.
Do you get the result shown?

How can you get the result for the negative particle?
(Note: the left-hand rule applies to conventional current flow.)
A negative charge moving to the right, has to be treated as a
positive charge moving to the left.
You must point your middle finger in the opposite direction
to the movement of the negative charge.

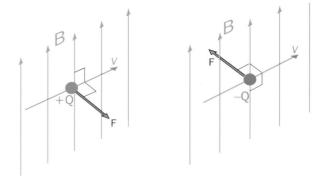

Example 5
An electron moving at 6.0×10^5 m s⁻¹ passes perpendicularly
through a magnetic field of 2.0×10^{-2} T.
The charge of the electron is 1.6×10^{-19} C.
What is the force on the electron?

$$F = B\,Q\,v$$
$$F = 2.0 \times 10^{-2}\ \text{T} \times 1.6 \times 10^{-19}\ \text{C} \times 6.0 \times 10^5\ \text{m s}^{-1}$$
$$F = 1.9 \times 10^{-15}\ \text{N} \quad (2\ \text{s.f.})$$

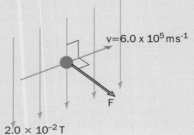

Do the equations $F = B\,I\,l$ and $F = B\,Q\,v$ agree?

Suppose a charge Q moves a distance l, in t seconds.
Current is the rate of flow of charge,
and so (from page 192):
$$I = \frac{Q}{t}$$

Substituting for I in $F = B\,I\,l$, we get $F = \dfrac{B\,Q\,l}{t}$

but $\dfrac{l}{t}$ is the velocity v of the particle, so $F = B\,Q\,v$

▷ Circular paths

The movement of charged particles in magnetic fields is very important in atomic physics. The photograph shows the path of a beam of electrons in a 'fine beam tube'. In this tube the electrons move at right angles to a horizontal magnetic field. Can you see the path of the electron beam, visible as a bright blue circle?

An electron beam in a fine beam tube

In order to move in a circle, there must be a **centripetal force** acting on each electron in the beam (see Chapter 7). What provides this force?

Look at the diagram. It shows electrons moving in a uniform magnetic field. The flux density B is **into** the paper (as shown by the × symbols). Each electron in the beam is moving with a speed v, at 90° to the field.

The field exerts a force F on the electron, where $F = B\,Q\,v$
Can you see that this force is always at 90° to the electron's velocity? Because of this, the magnetic force changes the direction, but not the speed of the electron.
The $B\,Q\,v$ force provides the centripetal force.

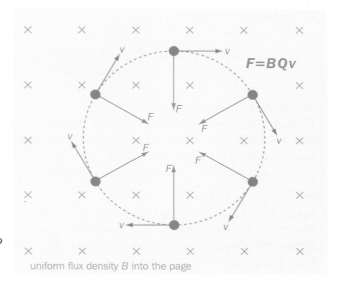

uniform flux density B into the page

The equation for centripetal force (see page 72) is:

$$F = \frac{m\,v^2}{r}$$ where m = the mass of the particle, and r = the radius of the circular path.

The centripetal force is provided by the magnetic force, and so:

$$\frac{m\,v^2}{r} = B\,Q\,v \qquad \text{or, rearranging:} \qquad r = \frac{m\,v}{B\,Q}$$

Can you see from this that the electrons move in a larger circle if their speed is increased, or the magnetic field is made weaker?

What is the time period T for the electron to make one rotation?

Since time $= \dfrac{\text{distance}}{\text{speed}}$ $T = \dfrac{\text{length of circular path}}{\text{speed of electron}}$ or $T = \dfrac{2\pi r}{v}$

but since $r = \dfrac{m\,v}{B\,Q}$ we get: $T = \dfrac{2\pi}{v} \times \dfrac{m\,v}{B\,Q}$ so: $T = \dfrac{2\,\pi\,m}{B\,Q}$

Can you see that in a magnetic field of constant flux density B, the time period T of the electron does not depend on its speed? A faster moving electron moves in a circle of larger radius, but takes exactly the **same time** to make one revolution.

Example 6
A particle of mass 9.1×10^{-31} kg, and of charge 1.6×10^{-19} C, is moving at 4.5×10^6 m s⁻¹. It enters a uniform magnetic field of flux density 0.15 mT, at 90°, as shown in the diagram:
What is the radius of its circular path?

Using: $r = \dfrac{m\,v}{B\,Q}$ (as derived above) 1 mT $= 10^{-3}$ T

$$\therefore r = \frac{9.1 \times 10^{-31} \text{ kg} \times 4.5 \times 10^6 \text{ m s}^{-1}}{0.15 \times 10^{-3} \text{ T} \times 1.6 \times 10^{-19} \text{ C}} = \underline{0.17 \text{ m}}$$

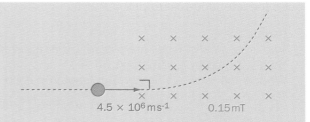

4.5×10^6 ms⁻¹   0.15 mT

You can use the left-hand rule to show that the particle must be **positively** charged

▷ Forces between currents

What happens when current is passed along two strips of foil as shown below?
The strips bend, as they attract or repel each other.

Two parallel, current-carrying wires exert equal, but opposite forces on each other.
Look carefully at these forces, and the resultant magnetic fields around the wires.

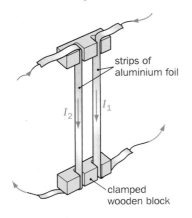

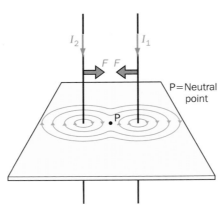

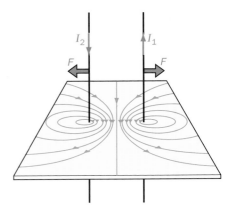

Notice that: currents flowing in the **same** direction **attract**,
currents flowing in **opposite** directions **repel**.

How do these forces arise?
The diagram shows the anti-clockwise field around wire X:
Wire Y is at 90° to this field, and so it experiences a force.
Apply Fleming's left-hand rule (page 224) to wire Y.
Do you find that the force on wire Y is to the left, as shown?

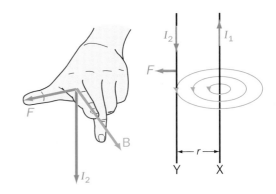

What is the size of the force?
Notice that the wires are a distance r apart.
Wire X carries a current I_1. Wire Y carries a current I_2.
What is the flux density B at wire Y, due to the current I_1 in X?
From page 222 we know that:

$$B = \frac{\mu_o I_1}{2\pi r} \qquad \text{- - - (1)}$$

What is the force F on a length l of wire Y?
From page 225 we know that:

$$F = B I_2 l \qquad \text{- - - (2)}$$

If we use equation (1) to
replace B in equation (2):

$$\boxed{F = \frac{\mu_o I_1 I_2 l}{2\pi r}} \qquad \text{- - - (3)}$$

Similarly, wire X feels a force due to the field of wire Y.
Can you show that equation (3) also gives the force on wire X?
Use the left-hand rule to prove that the force on X is to the right.

The definition of the ampere

The unit of current, the ampere, is defined
in terms of the force between two currents.

As shown in Example 7 below:
when two long wires are parallel,
and placed 1 metre apart in air,
and if the current in each wire is 1 ampere,
then the force on each metre of wire is 2×10^{-7} N.

Example 7
Two long parallel wires are placed 1.0 m apart in air as shown.
Both wires carry a current of 1.0 A.
What is the force acting per unit length on each wire?

$$F = \frac{\mu_o I_1 I_2 l}{2\pi r} \quad \text{where } l = 1.0 \text{ m and } \mu_o = 4\pi \times 10^{-7} \text{ T m A}^{-1}$$

$$F = \frac{4\pi \times 10^{-7} \text{ T m A}^{-1} \times 1.0 \text{ A} \times 1.0 \text{ A} \times 1.0 \text{ m}}{2\pi \times 1.0 \text{ m}} = \underline{2 \times 10^{-7} \text{ N}} \text{ on each metre}$$

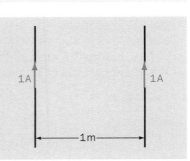

228

▷ Physics at work: Magnetic fields

The magnetic levitation train

The Maglev train in the photograph does not need wheels,
because it 'floats' above its track by **magnetic levitation**.
The diagram below shows how magnetic levitation works.

The levitation magnets are powerful electromagnets.
Can you see that they are attached to the chassis of the train?
The magnets are **attracted** upwards towards the levitation rail.
This force lifts the train 15 mm above its T-shaped track.

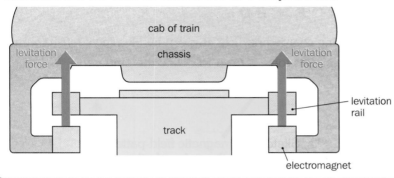

How does the train maintain its exact position
above the track? Computers control the
current in the electromagnets, and so the
strength of the levitation force can be varied.

The Hall effect

How does a Hall probe measure the strength of a magnetic field?
The diagram shows the semiconducting slice at the tip of a Hall probe.
A small current is passed through the slice as shown:
The electrons are moving with a velocity v.

When a magnetic field is applied the BQv force pushes these electrons
towards the upper edge of the slice. This becomes negatively charged.
The lower edge, which is short of electrons, becomes positively charged.

If a voltmeter is placed across the top and bottom edges of the slice
it detects a small p.d. The stronger the field, the larger the p.d.

You can calibrate the voltmeter so that it reads in tesla, instead of volts.

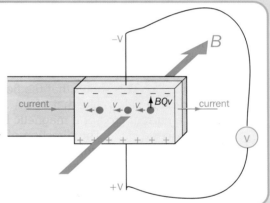

The mass spectrometer

Mass spectrometers are used to identify
the different **isotopes** (see page 331) in
a sample of material, and measure their
relative abundance.
The diagram shows the principle of how they work:

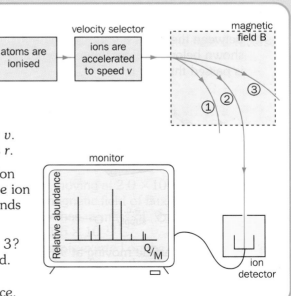

Each isotope in the sample forms ions with a different mass, but the
velocity selector ensures that all the ions at A have the same velocity v.
The magnetic field B deflects these ions into a circular path of radius r.

From page 227, r is given by: $r = \dfrac{m\,v}{B\,Q}$ where m = mass of the ion
and Q = charge on the ion

Since B and v are fixed, the radius of the path taken by an ion depends
on its value of m/Q. Only the ions following path 2 are detected.

Ions with a smaller value of m/Q take path 1. Which ions take path 3?
These ions need to have a different value of v in order to be detected.
As the accelerating voltage in the velocity selector is changed each
isotope is detected in turn. The screen shows their relative abundance.

▷ Physics at work: Using electromagnetic induction

The metal detector
How does Phiz's metal detector work?
A.c. flows through the search coil in the search head and this produces a constantly changing magnetic field around the coil.

What happens if there is a metal object in this changing field?
Eddy currents are induced in the metal object. This means that energy is transferred from the search coil to the metal object, and the current in the search coil changes. This is detected by the control box, which produces an audible signal.

How effective is the metal detector?
This depends on the size and the orientation of the metal object and how far below the ground it is buried.

Traffic lights are triggered in a similar way.
There is an induction loop in the road surface, and this creates an alternating magnetic field (like that of the search coil).
A car passing over the loop is detected, because it changes the current in the loop; just like a metal object near a metal detector.

Induction heating
A ceramic hob is a type of electric cooker. It consists of three or four flat coils embedded in a ceramic surface.
Each coil is supplied with high frequency a.c. – about 18 kHz.

What happens when a metal pan is placed over one of the coils?
Eddy currents are induced in the base and the sides of the pan.
As these currents flow through the metal pan, it becomes hot and so the food in the pan is cooked.
Can you explain why the ceramic surface stays relatively cool?

Electromagnetic brakes
Eddy current brakes are often fitted to coaches and lorries.
Two discs (called rotors) are fixed to the wheel-shaft, so that they spin as the wheels turn.
Can you see the stator, fixed in place between the rotors?
The stator is an electromagnet made up of a number of coils.

What do you notice about the way the coils are wound?
When the driver activates the brake, a current is passed through the coils so that adjacent coils produce reversed magnetic fields.
The spinning rotors cut through the magnetic flux, and so eddy currents are induced in the discs.
The eddy currents flow so as to *oppose* the change producing them; hence the braking effect on the rotors and the wheels.

Why are the brakes not effective at slow speeds?
The discs spin slowly and the rate of flux cutting is reduced.
The smaller eddy currents produce a smaller braking effect.
Contact brakes (see page 24) are still needed for the final braking at slow speed.

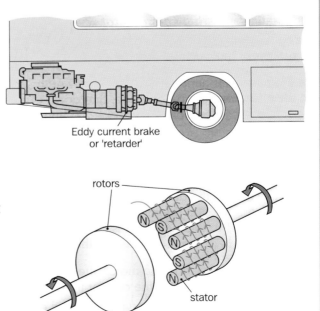

Eddy current brake or 'retarder'

rotors

stator

Summary

The magnetic flux Φ linking an area A which is at right angles to a uniform field of magnetic flux density B is: $$\Phi = B\,A$$

For a coil with N turns,
total flux linkage $= N\,B\,A$

An e.m.f. is induced when the magnetic flux linkage changes, because either the flux density changes or the area linked by the flux changes.

Faraday's law gives us the **size** of the induced e.m.f.
It states that the e.m.f. is equal to the **rate** of change of flux linkage:

$$\epsilon = N\frac{\Delta\Phi}{\Delta t}$$

Lenz's law gives us the **direction** of the induced e.m.f. It states that the e.m.f. is induced so as to try to **oppose** the change that is causing it.

▷ Questions

1. Can you complete these sentences?
   a) When the magnetic .... linking a coil changes, an e.m.f. is ....
   b) Faraday's law states that the .... of the induced .... is equal to the .... of change of .... linkage.
   c) Lenz's law states that the .... of the induced .... is always so as to .... the change causing it.
   d) When a magnet moves towards a coil, the size of the induced e.m.f. depends on the .... of the movement, the .... of the magnet , and the cross-sectional .... and number of .... on the coil.

2. Explain the following:
   a) No e.m.f. is induced when a straight wire is moved parallel to lines of magnetic flux.
   b) A brass ring set to swing in a magnetic field quickly comes to rest; a plastic ring swings for much longer.
   c) When a magnet is dropped through a plastic pipe it accelerates towards the ground; if dropped down an identical sized copper pipe it falls more slowly.

3. In the UK the vertical component of the Earth's magnetic field is 5.0×10^{-5} T. If the area of a village is 2.2×10^{6} m^2, how much flux passes through it?

4. A rectangular coil measures 5.0 cm by 8.0 cm. It is placed at 90° to a magnetic field of flux density 1.5 T. What is the flux linkage of the coil if it has 250 turns?

5. A search coil has 3400 turns and an area of 1.0 cm^2. It is placed between the poles of a magnet where the flux density is 0.40 T.
   What is the average e.m.f. induced across the coil when it is snatched out of the field in 0.20 s?

6. A search coil with 2000 turns and an area of 1.5 cm^2 is used to measure the flux density between the poles of a horseshoe magnet. The coil is pulled out of the field in 0.30 s and the induced e.m.f. is 0.50 V. What is the flux density of the magnet?

7. A wire of length 10.0 cm is moved downwards at a speed of 4.0 cm s^{-1} through a horizontal field of flux density 2.0 T. What is the e.m.f. induced in the wire?

8. An aircraft of wingspan 40 m flies horizontally at a speed of 250 m s^{-1}. An e.m.f. of 0.2 V is induced across the tips of the wings. What is the vertical component of the Earth's magnetic flux density?

9. The diagram shows a coil being turned in a horizontal magnetic field of flux density 50 mT.
   a) In the position shown, does the induced current flow in the direction ABCD or DCBA?
   b) The coil has 300 turns, area 15 cm^2 and rotates 10 times per second. What is the peak e.m.f.?

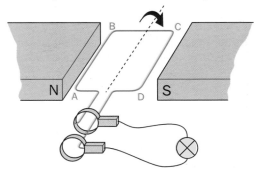

10. A search coil with 2500 turns and area 1.5 cm^2 is connected to a data logger, placed between the poles of a magnet and quickly withdrawn.
    a) Use the graph shown below to estimate the total change in flux linkage of the coil. (You can treat the graph as a triangle as shown.)
    b) Calculate the flux density of the magnet.

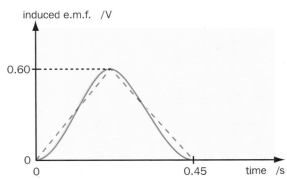

Further questions on page 278.

20 Alternating Current

Have you ever experienced a power cut?
If so, you will know how much we rely on our electricity supply.
Mains electricity has only been available for about 100 years and initially each area had its own different supply.
Now we all receive the same standardised a.c. supply, and this is delivered to our homes by the National Grid system.

In this chapter you will learn:
- the meaning of the root-mean-square (r.m.s.) value,
- how to use an oscilloscope to measure time and p.d.,
- about the transformer.

The control room in a power station

▷ What is a.c.?

The diagram shows a bicycle 'dynamo' connected to a lamp:
The dynamo is a small a.c. generator.
What will happen as you turn the generator slowly by hand?

The generator produces an **alternating** e.m.f. This causes current to flow one way and then the other way round the circuit.
The free electrons release energy as they flow to and fro through the lamp filament, but as they stop to change direction there is no current and so the lamp flashes on and off.

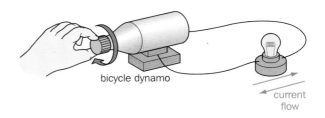

The lamp has an alternating p.d. across it. How does the current I through the bulb change, as the p.d. V varies?
We can investigate this, using the apparatus in the diagram:
The a.c. supply is a signal generator set at a low frequency.

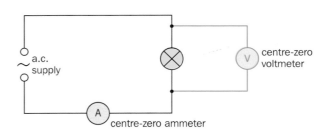

The graph shows the values of V and I plotted against time:
Can you see that the graphs for both V and I are **sine** curves?
They both vary **sinusoidally** with time.
Can you see that the p.d. and the current rise and fall **together**?
We say that V and I are **in phase**. (See also page 92.)

The **time period T** of an alternating p.d. or current is the time for one complete cycle. This is shown on the graph:

The **frequency f** of an alternating p.d. or current is the number of cycles in one second.

The **peak values V_o** and **I_o** of the alternating p.d. and current are also shown on the graph:

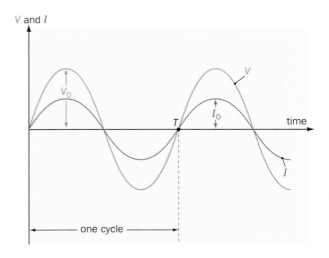

Why don't we see our lights flickering as they flash on and off?
The frequency of the mains supply is 50 Hz and so each cycle lasts for only $\frac{1}{50}$ second or 20 milliseconds.
At this frequency the filament has no time to cool down as the current through it varies, and so we see constant illumination.

▷ Root-mean-square (r.m.s.) values

How do we measure the size of an alternating p.d. (or current) when its value changes from one instant to the next?

We could use the peak value, but this occurs only for a moment. What about the average value?
This is zero over a complete cycle and so is not very helpful!

In fact, we use the **root-mean-square (r.m.s.)** value.
This is also called the **effective value**.
The r.m.s. value is chosen, because it is the value which is *equivalent to a steady direct current*.

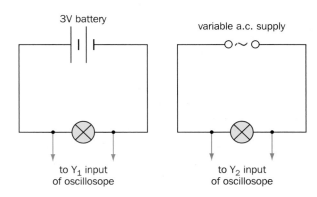

3V battery   variable a.c. supply

to Y_1 input of oscillosope   to Y_2 input of oscillosope

You can investigate this using the apparatus in the diagram:
Place two identical lamps side by side.
Connect one lamp to a battery; the other to an a.c. supply.
The p.d. across each lamp must be displayed on the screen of a double-beam oscilloscope.

Adjust the a.c. supply, so that both lamps are equally bright.
The graph shows a typical trace from the oscilloscope:
We can use it to compare the voltage across each lamp.

Since both lamps are equally bright, the d.c. and a.c. supplies are transferring energy to the bulbs at the same rate.
Therefore, the d.c. voltage is equivalent to the a.c. voltage.
The d.c. voltage equals the r.m.s. value of the a.c. voltage.
Notice that the r.m.s. value is about 70% of the peak value.

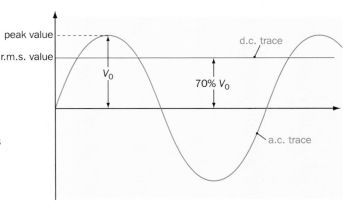

peak value

r.m.s. value

V_0

d.c. trace

70% V_0

a.c. trace

In fact:

$$\text{r.m.s. value} = \frac{\text{peak value}}{\sqrt{2}}$$ or $$\text{peak value} = \sqrt{2} \times \text{r.m.s. value}$$

These equations apply to both the current and the p.d. and so:

$$I_{rms} = \frac{I_0}{\sqrt{2}}$$ or $$V_{rms} = \frac{V_0}{\sqrt{2}}$$

Example 1
The r.m.s. value of the mains in Britain is 230 V.
What is its peak value?

$V_0 = \sqrt{2} \times 230\,V = 325\,V$ (3 s.f.)

The mains supply in Britain is 230 V, 50 Hz, but the electricity companies are allowed to vary the supply between +10% and −6% of 230V. This means that the r.m.s. value of the voltage ranges from 216 V to 253 V. Have you ever noticed this fluctuation?

Why $\sqrt{2}$?
The power dissipated in a lamp varies as the p.d. across it, and the current passing through it, alternate.
Remember (page 200) **power, P = current, I × p.d., V**

If we multiply the values of I and V at any instant, we get the power at that moment in time, as the graph shows:

The power varies between $I_0 V_0$ and zero.

$$\therefore \quad \text{average power} = \frac{I_0 \times V_0}{2} = \frac{I_0}{\sqrt{2}} \times \frac{V_0}{\sqrt{2}} = I_{rms} \times V_{rms}$$

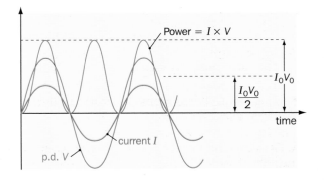

Power = $I \times V$

$I_0 V_0$

$\dfrac{I_0 V_0}{2}$

time

current I

p.d. V

▷ The cathode-ray oscilloscope (CRO)

The oscilloscope is an important measuring instrument.
It contains a cathode-ray tube as shown in the diagram:
An electron gun produces a fine beam of fast-moving electrons.
(There are more details on pages 164 and 260.)

The electrons move along the length of the tube and hit the
fluorescent screen. Can you see that a spot of light is produced?

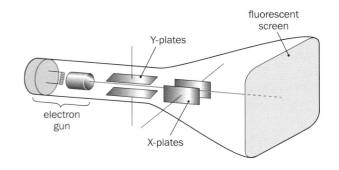

Two sets of parallel plates are used to deflect the electron beam
and vary the position of the spot on the screen.
The X-plates move the spot horizontally; the Y-plates vertically.

The diagrams show how applying a p.d. across each set of plates,
can deflect the spot to any position on the screen:

How could the spot be deflected to the upper left-hand corner?

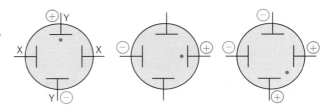

Built into the oscilloscope is a circuit called the **time-base**.
The time-base applies a p.d. across the **X**-plates, so that the spot
moves at a constant speed across the screen, from left to right,
and then jumps back very quickly to start again.

You can vary the speed of the spot. At high speeds it appears as
a line, due to your 'persistence of vision'.

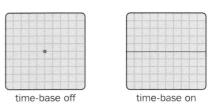

time-base off   time-base on

The controls

The picture shows a simple oscilloscope.
It has several controls:

1. The **brilliance control** changes the brightness of the spot,
   by varying the number of electrons that strike the screen
   each second.

2. The **focus control** is adjusted to give a well defined spot.

3. The voltage signal from an external circuit is connected to
   the **input terminals** as shown.
   This signal is amplified and then applied to the Y-plates.
   In which direction does the input signal move the spot?

4. The **Y-gain control** varies the amplification of the input p.d.
   What is the setting of the Y-gain control in the picture?

   5 V/cm means that the spot moves 1 cm up (or down)
   for every 5 V applied across the input terminals.

5. The **time-base control** is used to vary the speed of the spot.

   In the picture the time-base is set to 10 ms/cm.
   This means that it takes 10 milliseconds for the spot to move
   1 cm across the screen.

6. You can use the **X-shift** and **Y-shift** controls to move the spot
   in the X or Y directions, if necessary.

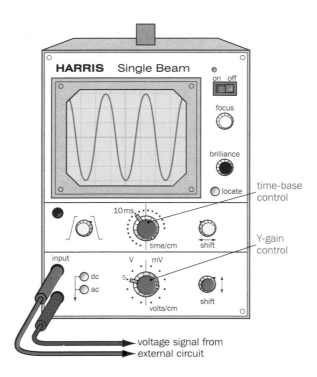

▷ Using the oscilloscope

The oscilloscope has 3 main uses:

1. Measuring d.c. and a.c. voltages

First move the spot or line to the centre of the screen.
Then connect the p.d. to be measured to the input terminals.

A **d.c. voltage** makes the spot move up (or down) as shown.
The deflection **d** in cm of the spot must be measured.
How can you convert this into volts?
Check the Y-gain setting in volts per cm. You then multiply **d** by
the Y-gain to find the d.c. voltage. eg. 2 cm × 5 V/cm = 10 V

no input
time-base off

d.c. input
time-base off

d.c. input
time-base on

An **a.c. input** makes the spot move up and down repeatedly.
If the time-base is on, it moves the spot horizontally at the same
time. You can then see the shape of the voltage waveform.

Notice that when you multiply the length **y** by the Y-gain,
you are measuring the **peak to peak voltage** of the a.c. input.
Remember, this is *twice* the value of the peak voltage V_o.

no input
time-base off

a.c. input
time-base off

a.c. input
time-base on

2. Displaying wave forms

An oscilloscope can be used to display any varying p.d., as long
as the time-base is switched on.

A microphone converts sound signals into electrical signals.
If you connect a microphone to the oscilloscope input terminals
you can see the waveforms that you make as you sing!

In hospitals, sensors are used to convert a heartbeat into an
electrical signal, which is then displayed on an oscilloscope.

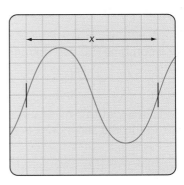

3. Measuring time and frequency

How can you measure the time period T for an alternating p.d.?
Measure the horizontal distance for one cycle of the a.c.
This is **x** cm in the diagram.
Now check the time-base setting.
This tells you that each centimetre represents a certain time.
If you multiply **x** by the time-base setting, you get the time T.

Remember (from page 70): **frequency, $f = \dfrac{1}{\text{time period, } T}$**

You can now use the time period to find the frequency of the a.c.

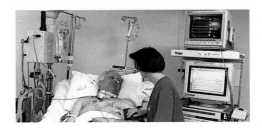

Example 2
The CRO trace shows the output from a laboratory power supply:
The time-base is set at 5 ms/cm, and the Y-gain is 2 V/cm.
Calculate: a) the r.m.s. value of the a.c. voltage,
         b) the time period T and the frequency f of the a.c.

a) Peak to peak voltage $= 9.0 \text{ cm} \times 2 \text{ V/cm} = 18.0 \text{ V}$

$\therefore \ V_o = \dfrac{18.0 \text{ V}}{2} = 9.0 \text{ V}$ and so: $V_{rms} = \dfrac{9.0 \text{ V}}{\sqrt{2}} = \underline{6.4 \text{ V}}$

b) $T = 4.0 \text{ cm} \times 5 \text{ ms/cm} = 20 \text{ ms or } \underline{0.02 \text{ s}}$

$\therefore \ f = \dfrac{1}{T} = \dfrac{1}{0.02} = \underline{50 \text{ Hz}}$

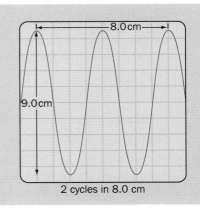
2 cycles in 8.0 cm

▷ The transformer

A transformer changes the value of an **alternating** voltage.
It consists of two coils, wound around a soft-iron core, as shown:
In this transformer, when an input p.d. of 2 V is applied to the
primary coil, the output p.d. of the secondary coil is 8V.

How does the transformer work?
An alternating current flows in the **primary** coil. This produces
an alternating magnetic field in the soft iron core. This means
that the flux linkage of the **secondary** coil is constantly changing
and so an alternating voltage is induced across it.

A transformer cannot work on d.c. Can you explain why?

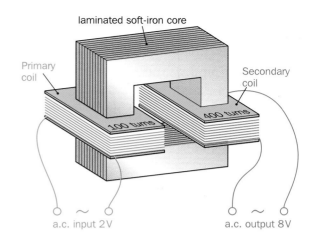
laminated soft-iron core
Primary coil
Secondary coil
400 turns
100 turns
a.c. input 2 V
a.c. output 8V

Look at the diagram to find the connection between the primary
and secondary voltages and the number of turns on each coil.
For an ideal transformer we can write:

$$\frac{\text{Secondary voltage}}{\text{Primary voltage}} = \frac{\text{Number of turns on the secondary coil}}{\text{Number of turns on the primary coil}} \quad \text{or} \quad \frac{V_S}{V_P} = \frac{N_S}{N_P}$$

A **step-up** transformer increases the a.c. voltage, because
the secondary coil has more turns than the primary coil.

In a **step-down** transformer, the voltage is reduced and
the secondary coil has fewer turns than the primary coil.

Primary 50 turns — 10V ∼ — Secondary 200 turns — ∼ 40V
Step-up (ratio 1:4)

In an ideal transformer no energy is lost and so we can write:

$$\frac{\text{Power supplied}}{\text{to primary coil}} = \frac{\text{Power delivered}}{\text{to secondary coil}} \quad \text{or} \quad \begin{array}{c} V_P \, I_P = V_S \, I_S \\ \text{(from page 200)} \end{array}$$

Primary 50 turns — 10V ∼ — Secondary 10 turns — ∼ 2 V
Step-down (ratio 5:1)

We can combine the two equations on this page to give us:

$$\frac{V_S}{V_P} = \frac{I_P}{I_S} = \frac{N_S}{N_P}$$

Can you see that this means that if the voltage is stepped **up**,
the current in the secondary is stepped **down** by the **same** ratio?

Note:
- *In the transformer equations, the voltages and currents that you use must all be peak values or all r.m.s. values. Do not mix the two.*
- *Strictly, the equations apply only to an ideal transformer, which is 100 % efficient.*

Example 3
A step-up transformer has a primary coil with 100 turns.
It transforms the mains voltage of 230 V a.c. to 11 500 V a.c.
a) How many turns must there be on the secondary coil?
b) When the current in the secondary coil is 0.10 A,
   what is the current in the primary coil?

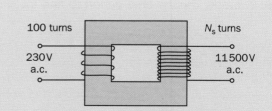
100 turns — 230V a.c. — N_s turns — 11 500V a.c.

a) $$\frac{V_S}{V_P} = \frac{N_S}{N_P}$$

$$\therefore \quad \frac{11\,500\text{ V}}{230\text{ V}} = \frac{N_S}{100} \qquad \therefore \ N_S = \frac{11\,500\text{ V}}{230\text{ V}} \times 100 = 50 \times 100 = \underline{5000\text{ turns}}$$

b) The secondary voltage is 50 times the primary voltage and so
   the secondary current must be $\frac{1}{50}$th of the primary current.
   Therefore, the primary current is: $50 \times 0.10\text{ A} = \underline{5.0\text{ A}}$

Energy losses in a transformer

In practice the efficiency of a transformer is never 100 %, although it may be as high as 99 %.

One possible cause of energy loss is reduced by the design of the transformer.
As the magnetic field alternates, **eddy currents** (see page 238) are induced in the soft-iron core. These currents could cause the core to become very hot.
To reduce this energy loss the core is made of thin sheets of iron, called laminations, separated by insulating material.
This makes it much harder for the eddy currents to flow.

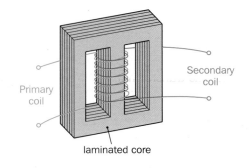
Secondary coil
Primary coil
laminated core

Circuit symbol:

Transmission of electrical energy

The National Grid transmits large amounts of electrical energy each second, from the power stations to the consumers, often over large distances.
Since power = current × voltage, we could use:
either a) a low voltage and a high current,
  or b) a high voltage and a low current.

Why does the National Grid always use method (b)?
Remember that a current always produces heat in a resistor.
If the cables have resistance R, and carry a current I,
the energy converted to heat each second is $I^2 R$ (see page 200).

This means that in method (a) the high current produces a lot of heat in the cables and little of the energy from the power station gets to the consumer.

Method (b) is used because the low current minimises the power loss.
Transformers at each end of the system step the voltage up and then down:

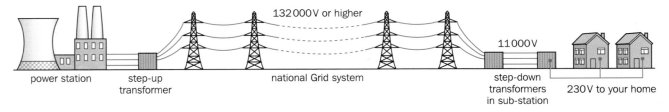

132 000 V or higher
11 000 V
power station
step-up transformer
national Grid system
step-down transformers in sub-station
230 V to your home

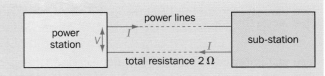

Example 4
A small power station generates 2 MW of electricity.
How much power is lost in cables of resistance 2 Ω if the electricity is transmitted at (a) 40 kV (b) 4 kV.

power lines
power station
V I
I
sub-station
total resistance 2 Ω

First, we need to calculate the current in the cables using $P = I\,V$:

In (a) $I = \dfrac{P}{V} = \dfrac{2 \times 10^6 \text{ W}}{40 \times 10^3 \text{ V}} = 50 \text{ A}$ In (b) $I = \dfrac{P}{V} = \dfrac{2 \times 10^6 \text{ W}}{4 \times 10^3 \text{ V}} = 500 \text{ A}$

Now we know the current we can calculate the $I^2 R$ heating losses in the cables:
In (a) $P = I^2 R = (50 \text{ A})^2 \times 2 \text{ Ω}$ In (b) $P = I^2 R = (500 \text{ A})^2 \times 2 \text{ Ω}$
∴ $P = 5000 \text{ W} = 5 \text{ kW}$ ∴ $P = 500\,000 \text{ W} = 500 \text{ kW}$

When the current is 10 times bigger the power loss is 100 times bigger.

Hint: Notice that V is not the p.d. across the cables – it is the p.d. across the terminals at the power station.
  As shown in the circuit diagram, when $V = 40$ kV, the p.d. across the 2 Ω resistance of the power cables is in total 100 V.

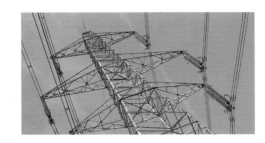

cables of total resistance 2 Ω
40 kV
neutral live
I $I = 50$ A
1 Ω 50 V
50 V 1 Ω
40 kV–100 V
sub-station
Equivalent circuit for transmission at 40 kV

▷ Rectification

Although we transmit our electrical energy as an alternating current, many electronic devices need a d.c. power supply. How is a.c. converted to d.c.?
One way is to use the semiconducting **diode** (see page 198).
Remember, the diode allows a current to flow **only one way**.

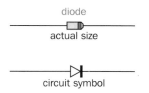

diode
actual size

circuit symbol

The diagram shows a diode connected in series with a 1000 Ω resistor and a low voltage a.c. supply:
You can use an oscilloscope (CRO) to look at the waveform. First connect the CRO across the a.c. supply (the input) and look at the a.c. waveform. Then connect the CRO across the 1000 Ω load resistor and look at the output waveform.

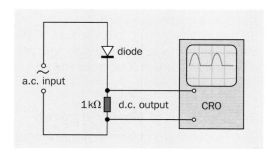

Why is only half the a.c. waveform still present?
The diode conducts for only half of the a.c. cycle – only when it is forward biased. The alternating current has been **rectified** to give an uneven direct current.

The diagram also shows a smoothed d.c. output:
This is done by placing a capacitor (see Chapter 22) in parallel with the load resistor (across the output terminals).
The capacitor stores some energy when the voltage is high, and then releases it when the voltage falls.

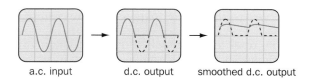

a.c. input   d.c. output   smoothed d.c. output

▷ The Light-Emitting Diode (LED)

Some special diodes called LEDs give out light when they conduct. The usual colour is red, but it is possible to get yellow, green and, more recently, blue LEDs.

LED circuit symbol

The **current–voltage characteristic** (see page 198) of a red LED is shown in the diagram:
Notice how similar it is to that of the diode, but whereas most diodes need a forward voltage of about 0.6 V to conduct, the forward voltage needed to make an LED conduct is greater. In fact, the size of the voltage varies with the colour of the LED.

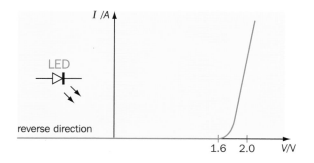

You can investigate the LED using the circuit shown:
Use the potential divider (see page 210) to slowly increase the p.d. across the LED. What p.d. is needed for the LED to light?

You will find that the red LED starts to conduct and glows dimly when the p.d. across it is 1.6 V. As you increase the p.d. the current rises and the LED glows more and more brightly. The light output of an LED depends on the p.d. applied to it.

What happens if the voltage output from an audio system, is connected across an LED?
The light output of the LED will vary in exactly the same way as the audio voltage applied across it. In this way, audio information can be transmitted as optical information.

The red LED shines brightly with a p.d. of 2.0 V across it. But if the full 6 V was applied, the LED would be damaged. An LED must always have a protective resistor in series with it to limit the current through it to a maximum of about 20 mA.

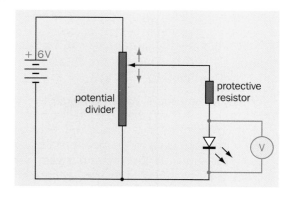

Summary

An a.c. supply causes charge to flow alternately one way and then the other way around the circuit.
A diode allows current to flow one way only and can be used to rectify a.c. to d.c.

The r.m.s. value of an alternating current or p.d. $= \dfrac{\text{peak value}}{\sqrt{2}}$ For a transformer: $\dfrac{V_S}{V_P} = \dfrac{N_S}{N_P}$

When the voltage is stepped down the current is stepped up, in almost the same ratio.
In the Grid system electricity is transmitted at high voltage and therefore low current, so less energy is lost.

▷ Questions

1. Can you complete these sentences?
   a) The peak value of a.c. is .... times its .... value.
   b) In a transformer, when the voltage is stepped up the current is .... in the same .... (providing the transformer is .... % efficient).
   c) In a cathode-ray oscilloscope the vertical deflection of the spot is proportional to the .... applied across the Y-plates. The horizontal movement of the spot is controlled by the ....

2. Explain why:
   a) The core of a transformer is laminated.
   b) A transformer will not work with direct current.
   c) In the Grid system,
      i) electricity is transmitted at high voltage,
      ii) a.c. is used rather than d.c.

3. The r.m.s. value of an alternating voltage is 12 V. What is the value of the peak voltage?

4. What is (a) the time period, (b) the frequency, (c) the peak value, and (d) the r.m.s. value of the alternating p.d. shown by the graph below?

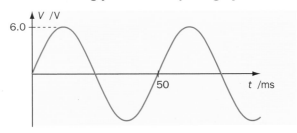

5. 3.0 MW of power is transmitted at a p.d. of 100 kV along cables of total resistance 5.0 Ω.
   a) What current flows in the cables?
   b) What is the power wasted in the cables?

6. Complete the following table of transformers:

7. A CRO screen with 1 cm squares displays this trace:

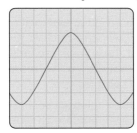

   The Y-gain is set at 0.5 V/cm and the time-base is set at 5 ms/cm. Calculate:
   a) the peak to peak voltage, (b) the r.m.s. voltage,
   c) the time period and (d) the frequency of the signal.

8. The CRO trace below shows a patient's heartbeat obtained with the time-base set at 200 ms/cm. Calculate the number of heartbeats per minute.

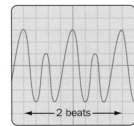

9. A transformer has a primary coil of 5000 turns. When the output p.d. is 12 V r.m.s., the input p.d. is 240 V r.m.s.
   a) How many turns are there on the secondary coil?
   b) The output from the secondary coil is connected across a 20 Ω lamp.
      i) What is the r.m.s. current in the secondary coil?
      ii) What is the r.m.s. current in the primary coil?
      (Assume the efficiency of the transformer is 100%.)

Further questions on page 281.

Primary p.d.	Secondary p.d.	Primary turns	Secondary turns	Step-up or step-down
230 V r.m.s.		500	50	
230 V r.m.s.	1150 V r.m.s.		2000	
11 000 V r.m.s.	132 000 V r.m.s.	1000		

▷ Physics at work: Energy for the 21st century

Non-renewable energy sources

98% of Britain's electrical energy is produced in a power station as shown below:

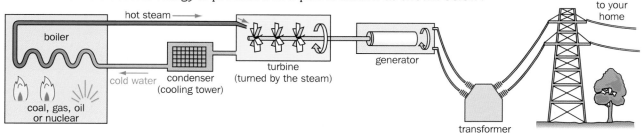

Most power stations in Britain burn fossil fuels (coal, oil and gas),
but about 20% produce electricity using nuclear fuel (see page 354).
Why are fossil fuels and nuclear fuel called **non-renewable** energy sources?
The reserves of these fuels are limited and one day they will run out.
It is estimated that the known reserves of gas, oil and nuclear fuels will
last between 40 and 60 years. Coal has longer – about 200 years.

Burning fossil fuels releases vast amounts of carbon dioxide
(a greenhouse gas), leading to global warming.
Sulphur dioxide is also released, causing acid rain.
Nuclear power produces highly radioactive waste (see page 356).

So why do we rely so heavily on non-renewables?
These power stations are able to generate electricity at all times.
Fossil fuel power stations are relatively cheap to build and their
power output is high – typically around 2000 MW
Nuclear power stations are costly to build (and to dismantle)
but the fuel is relatively cheap and the power output is high.

The effect of acid rain

Hydroelectricity and tidal power

Our reserves of non-renewable energy sources are dwindling
and concerns about their impact on the environment are rising.
We need to look at alternative ways of producing electricity.
At present Britain produces just 2% of its electricity needs
using **renewable** energy – energy sources that never run out.
But the government has set targets of 10% by the year 2010
and 25% by 2025. How will these targets be met?

Large hydroelectric power stations generate most of this 2%.
Dams are built to store rain water. The water is released
and as it falls it turns turbines which turn the generators.
This is a clean way of generating electricity for mountainous
regions such as Scotland and Wales. The capital outlay to
build the plants is high, but the fuel costs are zero.
Can we generate more electricity from hydroelectricity?
Unfortunately the best sites in Britain have already been used.

A tidal barrage built across an estuary uses the same principle,
but the water is moved behind the dam by the flow of the tide.
At low tide the water is released generating electricity.
A tidal barrage across the Severn estuary could supply about 5%
of our electricity, but the construction costs would be huge.
Hydroelectric schemes produce no pollution, but the ecology of
the area can be disrupted by changing the natural flow of water.

This dam can generate up to 1000 MW of electricity

▷ Physics at work: Renewable energy sources

Biomass

New power stations that burn renewable biomass such as wood, straw, animal waste, and specially grown crops such as willow, are already producing electricity. Many more are planned.

Doesn't this also produce the 'greenhouse gas' carbon dioxide? No, because the amount of gas released by burning is equal to the amount absorbed by the growing plants in photosynthesis.

Rotting plants and animal waste also produce methane gas. If they rot in a tank called a digestor, as shown, the gas can be piped away and used as a fuel. Methane can also be collected from land-fill sites used to tip domestic rubbish.
These plants are small, but they can make a useful contribution.

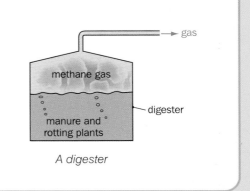

A digester

Wind and wave energy

A large aerogenerator can produce up to 7 MW of power from the kinetic energy of the wind. A typical wind farm consists of about 20 machines covering 3 or 4 square kilometres of land. At present Britain generates only about 0.25 % of its electricity using wind power. Why, when this is a clean source of energy? Firstly, the supply is unpredictable because wind speeds vary. Secondly, aerogenerators are noisy and visually intrusive.

The sea provides us with another source of energy. The kinetic energy of the waves can be captured by floats and used to generate electricity. However, 20 km of floats would produce only as much energy as a small power station. The building and maintenance costs of wind and wave energy equipment in the harsh environment of the sea are very high.

Geothermal energy

The inside of the earth is very hot due to radioactive decay. Bore-holes can be drilled down into the hot rock and cold water is forced down the holes. The water is heated by the rock and returns to the surface as steam.
This steam is then used to turn turbines to generate electricity. Geothermal plants are clean, since they produce only steam. But the installation costs are high and the power output is low.

Solar energy

The Earth receives an enormous amount of energy directly from the Sun each day, around 1.4 kW per square metre of its surface. Some homes have solar panels on the roof to provide hot water.

Solar photo-voltaic cells (PV cells) convert sunlight directly into electricity. The cells are non-polluting, silent and require little maintenance, but at present they are still expensive. Most convert only about 12 % of the energy from the sun into electrical energy, but the latest cells have an efficiency of 25 %.

Of course, less energy is produced in winter and wet weather. However many conservation groups believe that PV cells could supply 12 % of our electricity by 2025. See also page 172.

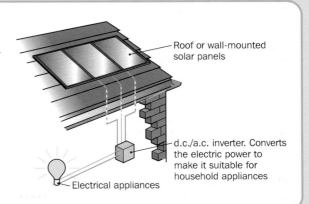

Roof or wall-mounted solar panels

d.c./a.c. inverter. Converts the electric power to make it suitable for household appliances

Electrical appliances

21 Electric Fields

Static electricity can often be a nuisance in everyday life.
Have you ever had an electric shock when getting out of a car?

Lightning is a spectacular display of static electricity.
In 1752, in a famous but highly dangerous experiment,
Benjamin Franklin flew a kite during a thunderstorm and
proved that lightning is a form of electricity.
Some people were killed as they tried to repeat Franklin's work!

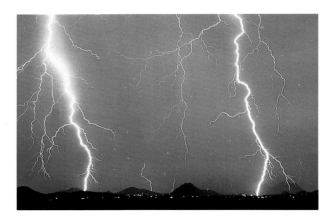

You have already studied moving charges or electric current
in Chapter 16.
In *static* electricity the electric charges are either at rest,
or only flow for a very short time.

Electrostatics has many useful applications.
These include the electrostatic spraying of paints and powders
and removing smoke particles from power station chimneys.

In this chapter you will learn:
- how to calculate the electric force between two charges,
- about electric fields,
- about electric field strength and electric potential.

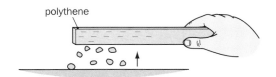

The diagrams show some simple experiments in
electrostatics, that you may have done before:

Do you remember the following facts?

- Objects are usually uncharged and so are
  electrically neutral.

- Objects can become charged by friction, when
  one material is rubbed against another material.
  This is discussed on the opposite page.

- A charged object can attract an uncharged object,
  for example, small pieces of paper.

- There are two types of electric charge.
  We call them positive and negative.

- A rubbed polythene strip gains a negative charge.
  A cellulose acetate strip gains a positive charge.

- When two charged objects are brought together,
  we find that:
  > **Like electric charges repel.**
  > **Opposite electric charges attract.**

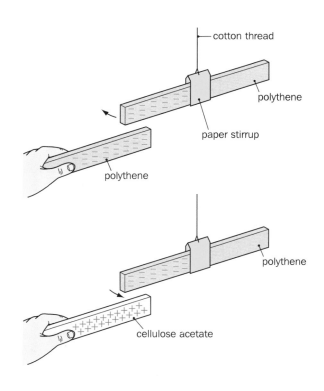

How do objects become electrically charged?

Normally, objects are uncharged because each atom has the same number of positive protons as negative electrons. Charging occurs when *electrons are transferred* from one material to another.

Friction can transfer electrons as shown in the diagram:

The polythene has gained extra electrons and so it is negatively charged. The duster is left short of electrons. What is its charge?

Polythene (like all insulating materials) has few free electrons (see Chapter 16) and so the negative charge does not flow away from the rubbed region – it is a static charge.

Can you put a metal rod in your hand and charge it by rubbing? Any charge transferred to the rod will flow along the rod and through your body to Earth, because your body and the Earth are poor insulators of electricity.
A conductor can only be charged if it is insulated from Earth.

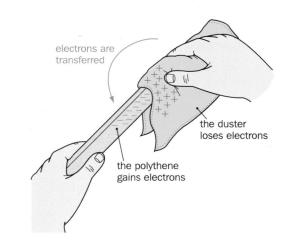

electrons are transferred

the duster loses electrons

the polythene gains electrons

Charging by electrostatic induction

A charged conductor will share its charge with an uncharged conductor that is placed in contact with it. Electrons can flow between the two conductors because they are touching.

A charged strip can also be used to *induce* a charge in an uncharged conductor *without* touching it.
The diagrams show how two conducting spheres can be oppositely charged by **induction**:

1. When a negative strip is brought close to 2 metal spheres, electrons from sphere A are repelled to sphere B.

2. The spheres are separated with the strip still held nearby.

3. Then the strip is removed. The free electrons in each sphere now spread out, so that the charge is distributed evenly over the surface of each sphere.

Why does a balloon, charged by rubbing, stick to a wall?
The negative charge on the balloon repels some of the electrons in the wall away from the surface. This leaves the wall surface positively-charged and so the balloon is attracted to the wall.

1. A   B   A and B are in contact

electrons

insulating stands

2. A   B

3. A   B

Measuring charge

One way of measuring charge is to use a **coulombmeter**:
Some of the charge on the polythene strip is transferred to the coulombmeter when the strip is scraped across its metal cap.
The coulombmeter then measures the charge placed on its cap.

Why is this coulombmeter giving a negative reading?
This confirms that the polythene strip is negatively charged.

The size of this charge is 0.032 nC or 0.032×10^{-9} coulombs. Remember, the coulomb is a very large unit (see page 192). In fact, the coulombmeter has been given 200 billion electrons from the polythene strip!

Charging a coulombmeter

▷ Forces between charges

What affects the force that charged objects exert on each other?
You can investigate this using the apparatus in the photograph:

Place a charged polythene strip on top of an insulating material
on an electronic balance and set the balance to read zero.
What happens as you bring up a second charged polythene strip?

The strip in your hand repels the strip on the balance and
this downwards force causes the balance reading to increase.

Does the force increase as the strips are brought closer together?
Does the force increase if you increase the charge on each strip?

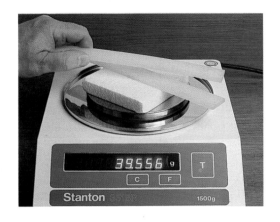

Coulomb's law

In 1785, the French physicist Charles Coulomb carried out
a series of experiments and discovered that the force F
between two charges was:

- directly proportional to each of the charges Q_1 and Q_2
- inversely proportional to the **square** of their separation r

Coulomb's law is written:

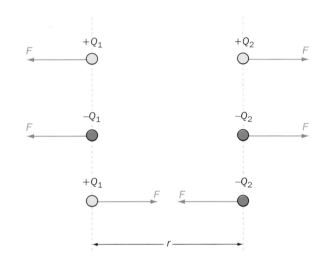

$$F \propto \frac{Q_1 Q_2}{r^2} \quad \text{or} \quad \boxed{F = \frac{k\, Q_1\, Q_2}{r^2}}$$

where: F is the force, in newtons
Q_1 and Q_2 are the charges, in coulombs
r is the distance apart, in metres
k is the constant of proportionality

Strictly, Coulomb's equation applies only to point charges, but
a sphere of charge behaves as if all its charge is concentrated at
its centre (providing it is not placed too close to another charge).

The value of the constant k

When the two charges are separated by a vacuum
the value of the constant k is 9.0×10^9 N m^2 C^{-2}.
When they are separated by air, it is effectively the same.

In fact, this is the largest value that k can have because the size of
the force is always reduced when an insulating material, other than
air, separates the two charges.

In a vacuum (or air) the value of k can be written as: $k = \dfrac{1}{4\pi\,\varepsilon_o}$

where ε_o is a constant called the **permittivity of free space**.
Its value is 8.85×10^{-12} F m^{-1} (The farad F is explained in Chapter 22.)

So $k = \dfrac{1}{4\pi\,\varepsilon_o} = \dfrac{1}{4\pi \times 8.85 \times 10^{-12} \text{ F m}^{-1}} = 9.0 \times 10^9$ N m^2 C^{-2}

Every insulating material has a permittivity ε which is greater than ε_o.

▷ Another inverse square law

Can you see that the two equations below are very similar?

Coulomb's law:

$$F = \frac{k\, Q_1\, Q_2}{r^2}$$

Newton's law of gravitation (page 78):

$$F = \frac{G\, m_1\, m_2}{r^2}$$

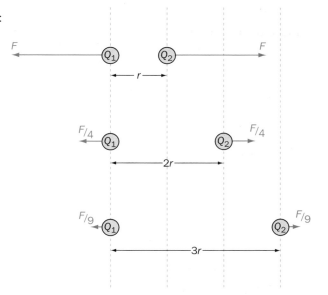

Coulomb's law is similar to Newton's law, except that for gravity the force can only attract, whereas the force between charges can attract **or** repel. The diagram shows 2 charges repelling:

Like Newton's law, Coulomb's law is an inverse square law. This means that if we double the distance between the charges, the force decreases to $(\frac{1}{2})^2$ or $\frac{1}{4}$ of its previous value.

Look at the diagram:
Why does the force drop to $F/9$ when the separation is tripled?
The force decreases to $(1/3)^2$ or $1/9$ of its previous value.

We can make other comparisons between these two laws.
Can you find the similarities and the differences in the table?

Newton's law of gravitation	Coulomb's law of charge
The force is 'felt' by objects with mass.	The force is 'felt' by objects with charge.
The force is proportional to the size of the masses.	The force is proportional to the size of the charges.
The force is inversely proportional to the square of the separation of the masses.	The force is inversely proportional to the square of the separation of the charges.
There is a gravitational field round a mass.	There is an electric field round a charge (see page 256).
There is only one type of mass.	There are two types of charge – positive and negative.
The force is always attractive.	The force can be attractive or repulsive.
The constant of proportionality is G. G always has the value 6.67×10^{-11} N m^{-2} kg^{-2}.	The constant is k, and its value depends on the material. In air $k = 1/4\pi\varepsilon_o = 9.0 \times 10^9$ N m^{-2} C^{-2}
The gravitational force is very weak, unless one of the masses is large.	The electric force is very strong, but not normally noticed as the charges cancel out.

Example 1
Two small conducting spheres are placed 0.10 m apart in air, and are given positive charges of 12 nC and 15 nC, as shown: Calculate the size of the repulsive force between them.
(The permittivity of air ε_o is 8.85×10^{-12} F m^{-1})

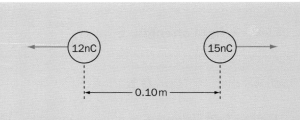

$$F = \frac{k\, Q_1\, Q_2}{r^2} \qquad \text{where } k = \frac{1}{4\pi\,\varepsilon_o}$$

$$\therefore F = \frac{Q_1\, Q_2}{4\pi\varepsilon_o\, r^2} = \frac{12 \times 10^{-9}\,\text{C} \times 15 \times 10^{-9}\,\text{C}}{4\pi \times 8.85 \times 10^{-12}\,\text{F m}^{-1} \times (0.10\,\text{m})^2} = \underline{1.6 \times 10^{-4}\,\text{N}} \quad (2\ \text{s.f.})$$

▷ Electric fields

The charged polythene strip is attracting Phiz's hair towards it.
We say that there is an **electric field** around the strip.
An electric field is a region where a charge 'feels' a force, just
as a gravitational field is a region where a mass 'feels' a force.

Is it possible to *see* the shape of an electric field?
One way is to use semolina grains sprinkled on castor oil.
Two electrodes in the oil produce the electric field, as shown.
The semolina grains line up along the electric field lines:

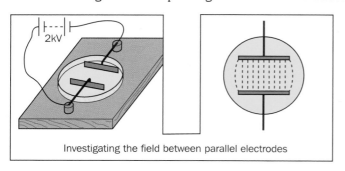

Investigating the field between parallel electrodes

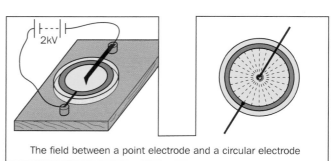

The field between a point electrode and a circular electrode

The arrows on the field lines tell us the **direction** of the field.
This is defined as the direction of the force on a **positive** charge
and so the arrows on the lines go from positive to negative.

The spacing of the lines tells us about the **strength** of the field.
The more closely packed the field lines the stronger the field.

Look at the electric field caused by the parallel electrodes.
The field lines are parallel to each other and equally spaced.
This field is **uniform**. It has the same strength at all points.

The field of the point electrode is called a **radial** field.
The diagrams show the radial field of an isolated point charge.
How can you tell that the field is strongest close to the charge?

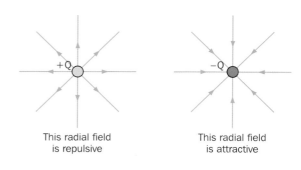

This radial field
is repulsive

This radial field
is attractive

Electric field strength *E*

On page 80 we defined gravitational field strength *g* as the
force acting per kilogram of mass.
Electric field strength *E* is defined in a similar way:

***The electric field strength at a point is the force per coulomb
exerted on a positive charge placed at that point in the field.***

The diagram shows a charge $+Q$ placed in a field of strength E:
If E is the force per coulomb (in newtons per coulomb), then:

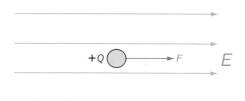

The charge $+Q$ 'feels' a force F
in the same direction as E

| **Electric field strength, E** (N C⁻¹) $= \dfrac{\textbf{Force, } \boldsymbol{F}\ \text{(N)}}{\textbf{charge, } \boldsymbol{Q}\ \text{(C)}}$ | or | $E = \dfrac{F}{Q}$ |

It follows that: $F = Q\,E$

- Electric field strength E is a vector quantity. The direction
  of the field is the direction of the force on a positive charge.

- The unit here for E is the N C⁻¹, but an alternative unit is the
  volt per metre (V m⁻¹). You will see why on the next page.

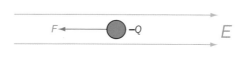

The force on the negative charge $-Q$
is in the opposite direction to E

The uniform electric field

In the diagram, there is a p.d. of about 1000 V across the parallel metal plates so that they become charged as shown:
A **uniform** electric field is produced between the plates.

You can test the electric field using a home-made **electroscope**. This consists of a strip of metal foil attached to a perspex ruler. You charge the metal foil and hold the electroscope in the field. The stronger the field, the greater the force on the charged foil, and the more it deflects from the vertical position.

How can you make the field stronger? You can:
- increase the p.d. across the plates, or
- move the plates closer together.

In fact, the field between the plates can be calculated by:

$$\text{Electric field strength, } E \ (\text{V m}^{-1}) = \frac{\text{p.d. across the plates, } V \ (\text{V})}{\text{separation of plates, } d \ (\text{m})}$$

or $E = \dfrac{V}{d}$

Note that the unit here for E is V m^{-1}. (1 V m^{-1} = 1 N C^{-1})

The radial electric field

What is the electric field strength at any point in a **radial** field?
In the diagram, a point charge $+Q$ produces the radial field and a **small** positive test charge $+q$ is placed in the field as shown:

Using Coulomb's law the force on the test charge $+q$ is given by:

$$F = \frac{k\,Q\,q}{r^2} \quad \text{where } k = \frac{1}{4\pi\varepsilon_o}$$

The electric field strength is the force per unit charge. Therefore:

$$E = \frac{F}{q} = \frac{k\,Q\,\cancel{q}}{\cancel{q}\,r^2}$$

So the field strength E a distance r away from a point charge $+Q$ is :

$$E = \frac{k\,Q}{r^2}$$

The field strength E a distance r away from a negative point charge $-Q$ is : $E = -\dfrac{k\,Q}{r^2}$
The – sign tells us the field is inwards.

Example 2

Two plates are placed 10 cm apart and connected to a 5.0 kV supply.
Calculate: a) the strength of the uniform field between the plates,
  b) the force on a +4.0 nC charge placed in the field.

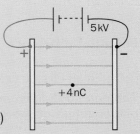

a) $E = \dfrac{V}{d}$

$E = \dfrac{5.0 \times 10^3 \ \text{V}}{0.10 \ \text{m}} = \underline{5.0 \times 10^4 \ \text{V m}^{-1}}$

b) $F = Q\,E$
$F = 4.0 \times 10^{-9} \ \text{C} \times 5.0 \times 10^4 \ \text{N C}^{-1}$
$F = \underline{2.0 \times 10^{-4} \ \text{N}}$, to the right. (2 s.f.)

Example 3

The charge on the dome of a Van de Graaff generator is 15 μC.
The dome radius is 20 cm. What is the field strength at its surface?
Remember, a sphere acts as if all its charge is at its centre.

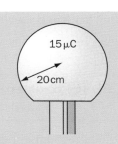

$E = \dfrac{k\,Q}{r^2}$ where $k = \dfrac{1}{4\pi\varepsilon_o}$ and ε_o is 8.85×10^{-12} F m^{-1}

$E = \dfrac{Q}{4\pi\varepsilon_o\,r^2} = \dfrac{15 \times 10^{-6} \ \text{C}}{4\pi \times 8.85 \times 10^{-12} \ \text{F m}^{-1} \times (0.20 \ \text{m})^2} = \underline{3.4 \times 10^6 \ \text{V m}^{-1}}$ (2 s.f.)

▷ Electric potential

If Phiz wants to move his charge closer to the charged sphere
he has to push against the repulsive force:
Phiz **does work** and his charge **gains** electric potential energy.

If Phiz lets go of the charge it will move away from the sphere,
losing electric potential energy, but gaining kinetic energy.

When you move a charge in an electric field its potential energy
changes. This is like moving a mass in a gravitational field.

Gravitational potential was discussed in Chapter 8.
Electric potential is a similar quantity:

The **electric potential V** at any point in an electric field is the
*potential energy that each coulomb of positive charge would
have if placed at that point in the field.*

The unit for electric potential is the joule per coulomb (J C^{-1}), or
the **volt** (V). Like gravitational potential it is a **scalar** quantity.

Earthing

In electrostatics, all the points on a conducting surface are at
the same potential. If not, electrons would flow until the
potential of all of the conductor becomes the same.

Where is the zero of electric potential?
Strictly, electric potential is defined to be zero at infinity,
just like it was for gravitational potential on page 86.
In practice, it is convenient to say that Earth is at zero potential.
Why must a conductor connected to Earth be at zero potential?

These spheres lose their charge when they are earthed:
Can you see which way the electrons flow in each case?

A conductor can retain a charge even when it is earthed!
Look at the parallel plates:
The lower plate is at zero potential (earthed), but even so it has
a negative charge which is attracted by the nearby positive plate.

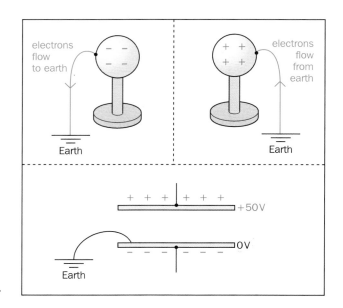

Potential difference

We often need to know the difference in potential between two
points in an electric field:

*The potential difference or p.d. is the energy transferred when
one coulomb of charge passes from one point to the other point.*

The diagram shows some values of the electric potential
at points in the electric field of a positively-charged sphere:
What is the p.d. between points A and B in the diagram?

When one coulomb moves from A to B it gains 15 J of energy.
If 2 C move from A to B then 30 J of energy are transferred. In fact:

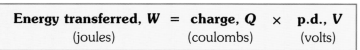

Energy transferred, **W**	=	charge, **Q**	×	p.d., **V**		or	**W = Q × V**
(joules)		(coulombs)		(volts)			

Do you recognise this equation from Chapter 16 ?
P.d. has the same meaning in static and current electricity.

Equipotential surfaces

All the points that have the **same** potential in an electric field are said to lie on an **equipotential** surface.
The diagram shows how you can investigate equipotentials:

The 2 electrodes A and B are clamped to the conducting paper. You can trace the equipotential lines using the voltmeter. It measures the p.d. between the contact needle and electrode B.

You can place the needle on electrode A and adjust the d.c. supply until the voltmeter reads 4.0 V.
Then move the needle across the paper, so that you draw a line through all the points where the voltmeter reads 3.0 V. Then draw lines for points where the potential is 2.0 V and 1.0 V.

You can draw the equipotentials in a radial field by repeating this experiment using a point electrode and circular electrode.

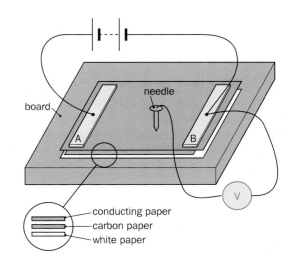

The diagrams show the results:

Look at the equipotentials between the **parallel** plates:
They are evenly spaced because the electric field is **uniform**.

In a **radial** field the equipotentials are concentric spheres:

Why are they closer together near the point charge?
Imagine moving a small positive test charge in this field.
As you get closer to the point charge the field gets stronger, the repulsive force increases and you have to do more and more work to move the test charge the same distance.

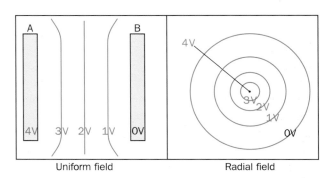

Uniform field   Radial field

When a charge moves **along** an equipotential, **no work** is done because its potential energy does not change.
This means that the equipotentials must cross electric field lines at 90°, just like in gravitational fields (see page 86).

Lightning

An electric field of about 3×10^6 V m^{-1} will ionise dry air.
This means that there must be a p.d. of around 3 million volts across each metre of air for it to conduct electricity.

Look at the equipotentials between the cloud and the church:
Can you see how the pointed spire distorts these lines?
The field is strong where the equipotentials are close together.

Why is the lightning most likely to strike the spire?
The field around the spire is strong enough to ionise the air, so that charge can flow between the cloud and the spire.

Example 4
The diagram shows the equipotentials between two plates.
How much energy is transferred when a charge of 2.0 nC
moves a) from point A to B   b) from B to C?

$\boldsymbol{W = Q\,V}$ where V is the p.d. between the points
a) $W = 2.0 \times 10^{-9}$ C $\times (3000 - 2000)$ V   b) $W = 2.0 \times 10^{-9}$ C $\times (3000 - 3000)$ V
$\quad\quad = 2.0 \times 10^{-9}$ C $\times 1000$ V $\quad\quad\quad\quad\quad = 2.0 \times 10^{-9}$ C $\times\ 0$ V
$\quad\quad = 2.0 \times 10^{-6}$ joules   (2 s.f.) $\quad\quad\quad\quad = 0$ J (on the same equipotential)

▷ Electron beams

Televisions, oscilloscopes, computer monitors and X-ray machines all produce fast-moving beams of electrons.
This Maltese Cross tube shows the principle of the **electron gun**:

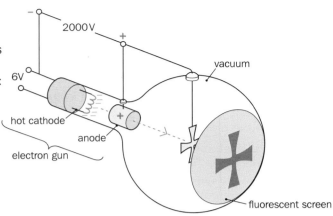

The low-voltage supply heats the cathode, so that electrons can escape from its surface. This is called **thermionic emission**. The positive anode attracts the electrons. Some pass through the anode and shoot across the tube to the fluorescent screen.

How can we calculate the speed v of the electrons in the beam? As the electrons accelerate in the field between the anode and the cathode they lose potential energy, but gain kinetic energy. For electrons of mass m and charge e, moving through a p.d. V:

gain in kinetic energy = loss in electrical potential energy

$$\tfrac{1}{2}\,m\,v^2 = e\,V$$

Why does the screen glow more brightly when you increase V?

Deflecting electron beams

The diagram shows an electron deflection tube:

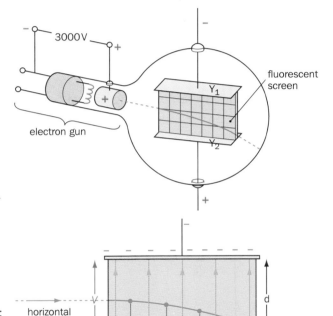

In this tube the electron beam cuts across a fluorescent screen. The screen is between two plates Y_1 and Y_2. These plates produce a vertical field and deflect the electrons:

What is the force on each electron in the vertical field? The plates are a distance d apart and have a p.d. V across them.

From page 257 we know that the electric field strength E is given by:
$$E = \frac{V}{d}$$

From page 256 we know that the force F on the electron of charge e is:
$$F = e\,E = e\,\frac{V}{d}$$

The electrons follow a curved path between the plates as shown: This is just like the path taken by a ball thrown horizontally, and acted on by the Earth's vertical gravitational field.
Just like the ball, the electrons **horizontal** velocity is unaffected by the **vertical** force due to the electric field.

horizontal velocity of electron

Example 5
In a deflection tube the p.d. between the anode and cathode is 3000 V.
2000 V is applied to the deflecting plates which are 5.0 cm apart.
(Charge on electron = 1.6×10^{-19} C; mass of electron = 9.1×10^{-31} kg)

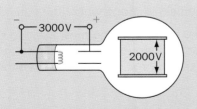

Calculate: a) the horizontal velocity acquired by the electrons,
b) the acceleration of the electrons in the vertical field of the deflecting plates.

a) Gain in kinetic energy = loss in potential energy
$$\tfrac{1}{2}\,m\,v^2 = e\,V$$
$$\tfrac{1}{2} \times 9.1 \times 10^{-31}\ \text{kg} \times v^2 = 1.6 \times 10^{-19}\ \text{C} \times 3000\ \text{V}$$
$$v^2 = \frac{1.6 \times 10^{-19}\text{C} \times 3000\ \text{V}}{\tfrac{1}{2} \times 9.1 \times 10^{-31}\ \text{kg}}$$
$$v = 3.2 \times 10^7\ \text{m s}^{-1}\quad (2\ \text{s.f.})$$

b) On each electron the vertical force, $F = e\,E = e\,\dfrac{V}{d}$

Using Newton's second law we can write:
$$a = \frac{F}{m} = \frac{e\,V}{m\,d} = \frac{1.6 \times 10^{-19}\ \text{C} \times 2000\ \text{V}}{9.1 \times 10^{-31}\ \text{kg} \times 0.050\ \text{m}}$$
$$a = 7.0 \times 10^{15}\ \text{m s}^{-2}\quad (2\ \text{s.f.})$$

▷ Physics at work: Using static electricity

Electrostatic crop spraying

Most crop pests live on the underside of leaves. Electrostatics can be used to target these 'hard to get at' places. The boom of the spray is connected to a high voltage supply. This produces positively-charged pesticide droplets, and also induces an opposite charge in the plants and in the ground.

The droplets repel each other to form an even cloud of spray, and are attracted to all parts of the oppositely charged plant. Can you see how the spray follows the electric field lines and reaches the underside of the leaves?

Bicycles and cars are painted using a similar technique.

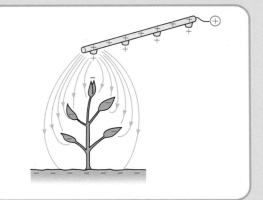

The photocopier

The diagrams show four of the stages in Xerox photocopying.

In stage **1**, a high voltage wire charges the insulating surface of the drum. The drum is now positively-charged. An intense light will allow charge to escape from this drum.

In stage **2**, intense light is flashed across the original document. The reflected light is then projected on to the drum surface. Which parts of the drum remain charged? The black parts of the original document do not reflect the light and so the corresponding regions of the drum remain charged. The drum surface now holds an image of the original.

In stage **3**, negatively-charged toner particles are attracted to the parts of the drum which are still positively-charged.

In stage **4** a sheet of paper is passed over the drum surface. There is a positively-charged transfer wire below the drum. This attracts the toner from the drum on to the paper.

Finally, the paper is passed through heated rollers, which melt the toner and fuse it to the paper to make a permanent copy.

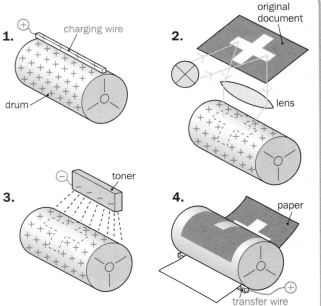

The ink-jet printer

One type of ink-jet printer is shown in the diagram: The ink gun produces 10,000 tiny droplets of ink every second. The droplets are positively-charged by the charge electrode, which surrounds the ink gun nozzle.

The ink droplets are deflected by a vertical electric field. In this printer, the p.d. across the deflector plates is constant.

The voltage of the charge electrode is computer controlled, so that each ink droplet is given a different size charge. The greater the charge on the droplet, the more it is deflected as it passes between the deflector plates. So the computer directs each droplet to a precise position.

How are the spaces between the words produced? The charge electrode does not charge all the droplets. Any uncharged droplets are not deflected. They are stopped, as shown, and the ink is returned to the gun. 'Sell-by' dates are printed on cans using this technique.

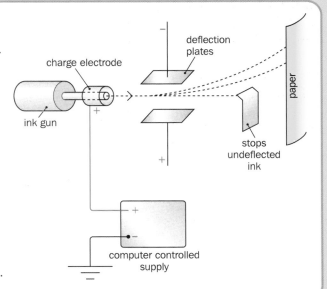

Summary

The force F between two charges is given by Coulomb's law: $\qquad F = \dfrac{k\,Q_1\,Q_2}{r^2} \qquad$ where $\quad k = \dfrac{1}{4\pi\,\varepsilon_o}$

ε_o is the permittivity of a vacuum or air.

The electric field strength E is the force acting per unit positive charge: $\qquad E = \dfrac{F}{Q}$

E is a vector quantity. It is measured in $N\,C^{-1}$ or $V\,m^{-1}$.

In a radial field: $\quad E = \dfrac{k\,Q}{r^2} \qquad$ In the uniform field between two parallel plates: $\quad E = \dfrac{V}{d}$

The electric potential V gives the potential energy per coulomb of positive charge in an electric field.
V is a scalar quantity. It is measured in volts. Energy transferred, $W = Q\,V$

The kinetic energy of an electron accelerated by an electron gun is given by: $\frac{1}{2}\,m\,v^2 = e\,V$

▷ Questions

You will need the following data:
Permittivity of free space ε_o is $8.85 \times 10^{-12}\,F\,m^{-1}$
Charge on the electron is $1.6 \times 10^{-19}\,C$
Mass of an electron is $9.1 \times 10^{-31}\,kg$

1. Can you complete these questions?
   a) The electric force between two charges depends on their .... and their ....
   b) Charge is measured in ....
      One .... is the charge on 6.25×10^{18} ....
   c) An electric field is a region in which a .... feels a .... Electric field lines can indicate the .... and the .... of a field.
   d) In a uniform field the electric field lines are .... and ....
   e) A surface joining all the points with the same potential is called an .... surface.
   f) To find the energy change when a charge moves from one point in a field to another we multiply the .... difference by the .... on the object.

2. Explain:
   a) How two insulated conductors can be oppositely charged by induction.
   b) Why no work is done when a charge moves along an equipotential surface.
   c) Why the charged conducting ball (in the diagram below) is attracted to the earthed metal plate.

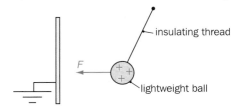

3. Describe two similarities and one difference between gravitational and electric fields.

4. The diagram below shows an electrostatic paint spray.
   a) Explain how the paint spray works
   b) Why does this technique waste little paint?

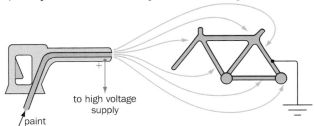

5. The two spheres A and B below are both given a charge $+Q$. The repulsive force between them is F.

   What is the size of the repulsive force when:
   a) The charge on A is doubled.
   b) The charge on both spheres is doubled.
   c) The charge on both the spheres is $+Q$, but the separation of the spheres is doubled to $2r$.

6. Calculate the electrostatic force between the proton and the electron in the hydrogen atom if the separation of the two particles is $1.0 \times 10^{-10}\,m$.

7. Two small equally charged spheres are 10 cm apart. The repulsive force between them is $3.6 \times 10^{-6}\,N$.
   a) What is the charge on each sphere?
   b) The spheres are negatively charged. How many excess electrons are there on each sphere?

8. Calculate the electric field strength at distances of (a) 2.0 cm and (b) 4.0 cm from a point charge of 16 nC. Comment on your answers.

9. The dome of a Van de Graaff generator has a radius of 15 cm. What is the charge on the dome when the electric field strength at its surface is 3.0×10^6 V m^{-1}. (Remember, the sphere acts as if the charge is concentrated at its centre.)

10. Two point charges of +4.0 nC and +2.0 nC are placed 6.0 cm apart as shown below.

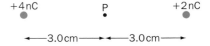

a) What is the resultant field strength at point P which is midway between the two charges?
b) What would be the field strength at P if the +2 nC charge was replaced with a –2.0 nC charge? (Hint: Find the field due to each charge and then add them together. Remember E is a vector.)

11. The diagram below shows three parallel, conducting plates each connected to a different voltage.

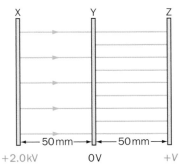

a) What is the strength of the uniform electric field between plates X and Y?
b) What is the direction of the electric field between plates Y and Z?
c) What is the strength of the uniform electric field between plates Y and Z?
d) What is the potential V of plate Z?

12. A spark can pass through dry air when the electric field strength is 3.0×10^6 V m^{-1} or greater.
a) The gap between the electrodes in the spark plug of a car is 0.80 mm. What p.d. is needed across the electrodes to produce a spark?
b) An overhead electricity cable reaches a maximum voltage of 1.86×10^5 V. How close could you get to the cable before receiving an electric shock?

13. Phiz is foolishly standing in an open field during a thunderstorm. Draw the equipotentials between the cloud and the ground and use them to explain why Phiz is in danger of being struck by lightning.

14. What is the force on a charge of 2.4 nC placed in an electric field of strength 4.0×10^3 N C^{-1}.

15. The diagram shows two metal plates A and B. Plate B is earthed; plate A is at 1200 V.

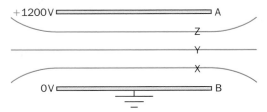

a) What is the potential of each of the equipotential lines X, Y and Z?
b) A charge of -3.2×10^{-16} C is moved from X to Y. What is its change in electrical potential energy?
c) Has the system lost or gained electrical potential energy as the charge moves from X to Y?

16. A tiny negatively-charged oil drop is held stationary in the electric field between two horizontal parallel plates, as shown below. Its mass is 4.0×10^{-15} kg.

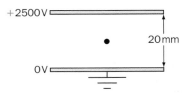

a) What are the two forces acting on the drop and in which direction do they act?
b) Use the fact that the 2 forces balance to calculate the charge on the oil drop. ($g = 10$ N kg^{-1})

17. An electron is accelerated from rest through a p.d. of 2000 V. Calculate:
a) its kinetic energy in (i) J and (ii) eV (electron volts)
b) its velocity.

18. An electron beam passes between deflecting plates. The electrons are displaced by 3.0 mm as shown:

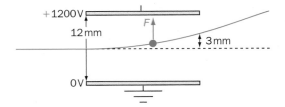

Calculate:
a) the electric field strength between the plates,
b) the deflecting force on each electron,
c) the vertical acceleration of each electron,
d) the kinetic energy gained by each electron.

Further questions on page 279.

22 Capacitors

The photograph shows some **capacitors**.
They are important in both electric and electronic circuits.
Have you seen any of them before?
You will find capacitors in radios, TV sets, and computers.
They are used to control the timing in car and burglar alarms.
The flash unit of a camera also uses a capacitor.

Although there are many different types of capacitors,
they all work in the same way.
Capacitors can store, and then release electrical energy.
The value of a capacitor is often measured in micro-farads (μF).

In this chapter you will learn:
- how capacitors work in simple circuits,
- about series and parallel combinations of capacitors,
- how the charge on a capacitor varies with time.

Can you see that all the capacitors have two leads?
The leads connect to two plates, which become charged.
The amount of energy stored by the capacitor depends on how much charge is moved on to the plates.
The conducting plates are separated by an insulating material, which is called the **dielectric**.

The plates need to have quite a large area.
How is this achieved in the capacitor shown in the diagram?
The two long strips of metal foil are separated by an insulator and then rolled up like a 'Swiss roll'.

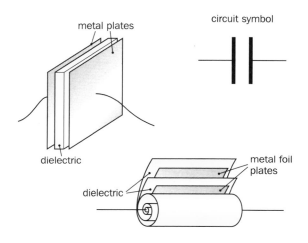

▷ Charging and discharging a capacitor

In order to charge up a capacitor we can connect it to a battery:

What happens when the switch S is closed?
Both the ammeters show equal size 'flicks', and then go back to zero. (Note: the zero is in the centre of the scale here.)
There is a surge of current (a flow of electrons) in the circuit;
but **only** while the capacitor charges up.

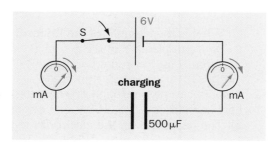

If the battery is removed, we can discharge the capacitor by connecting its leads together:

Now what happens when the switch S is closed?
Both meters again give equal flicks, and then return to zero.
Again, there is a brief current (a flow of charge) in the circuit.

What do you notice about the direction of the flicks now?
This current is in the **opposite** direction to the charging current.

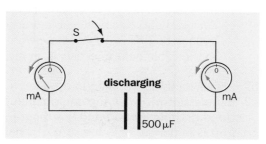

How does a capacitor charge up?

The capacitor plates are separated by an insulator. So how can charge flow?
This is explained in the diagrams below.
When the switch is closed, electrons flow from the negative terminal of
the battery on to plate B of the capacitor. At the same time, electrons
are repelled away from plate A back to the positive terminal of the battery.
This brief flow of electrons causes the 'flicks' on the ammeters.

A negative charge builds up on B as the electrons collect on it. An equal
but opposite positive charge builds up on A as the electrons move off it.
Notice that as the charge builds up, the p.d. across the plates rises.

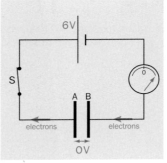

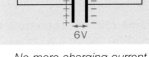

The initial charging current is high

As the charge builds up on the capacitor plates, the current falls

No more charging current. It is fully charged

Eventually, the build up of charge prevents any more charge arriving
(because like charges repel). So the movement of the electrons stops.

Now the p.d. across the capacitor is 6 V, the same as the supply voltage.
During this charging process **no** charge has crossed the insulating strip.

How does a capacitor discharge?

The charged capacitor acts rather like a very small battery. Look at the
circuit below. When the switch is closed, the electrons on plate B are
driven round the circuit to neutralise the positive charge on plate A.
The charge on both of the plates falls, as shown in the diagrams.
What happens to the p.d. across the plates as the capacitor discharges?

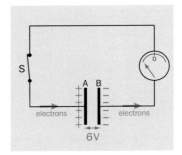

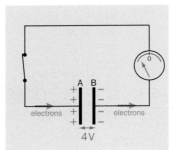

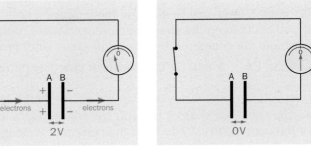

The initial discharge current is high

As the charge left on the plates falls, the current falls

No more discharge current. It is discharged

The charging and discharging processes happen very quickly.
Can we slow them down?
Remember, a resistor makes it more difficult for charge to flow.
If we place a resistor in series with the capacitor, as shown here,
the capacitor charges and discharges more slowly.

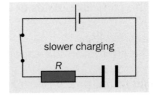

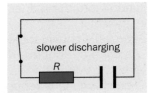

▷ Capacitance

The ability of a capacitor to 'store' charge on its plates is
called its **capacitance**. Capacitance is measured in **farads** (F).
The micro-farad (μF) is often used, where $1\,\mu F = 10^{-6}$ F.

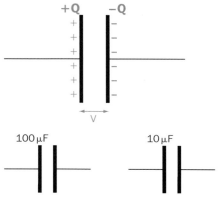

The p.d. across the plates of the capacitor in the diagram is V:
One of its plates has a charge of $+Q$; the other has a charge $-Q$.
We say that the charge 'stored' by the capacitor is Q.

The larger the capacitance, the more charge the capacitor stores
for each volt applied across its plates. In fact:

Capacitance, C $=$ $\dfrac{\text{charge, } Q \text{ (coulombs)}}{\text{p.d., } V \text{ (volts)}}$ (farads)	or	$C = \dfrac{Q}{V}$

*The 100 μF capacitor stores 10 times more
charge per volt than the 10 μF capacitor*

Can you see that capacitance is the charge stored per volt?

How can we measure the charge on the capacitor plates?

One way is to measure the current as the capacitor charges up.
On the previous page, we saw that as the capacitor charges up,
the current in the charging circuit falls.
The graph shows how the charging current varies with time:

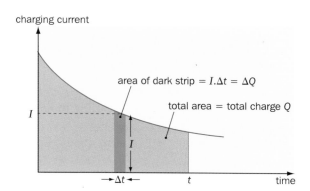

From page 192, we know that when a current I flows for a
short time Δt, the charge ΔQ that passes is given by: $\Delta Q = I\,\Delta t$
Can you see that this is the area of the dark strip on the graph?

The total charge Q that flows on to the capacitor after t seconds
is the **total area** under the graph.

Measuring capacitance

To measure the capacitance C of a capacitor we must know the
charge Q on its plates and the corresponding p.d. V across it.
We can then calculate the capacitance from the formula above.

Is there an easy way to measure the charge?
If you could keep the charging current constant, you could
calculate the charge on the capacitor plates after time t using:

$\quad Q = I\,t \quad$ where I is the **constant** charging current

Can you see how this is done in the circuit shown here?

As the capacitor charges up, you can reduce the resistance
of the variable resistor to keep the current at a steady value.
You may need a few attempts to practise the technique!

You can set the resistor at its maximum value and close switch S.
Adjust the resistor to keep the current constant at say 60 μA,
and record the p.d. across the capacitor plates every 10 seconds.

The table shows some typical results:
As the p.d. doubles, does the charge on the capacitor double?

The charge Q is proportional to the p.d. V: $\quad \mathbf{Q = C\,V}$

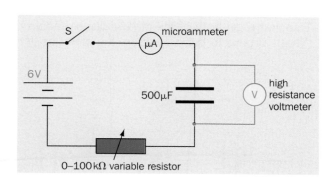

t /s	I /μA	$\therefore Q = It$ /μC	V /V	$C = \dfrac{Q}{V}$ /μF
0	60	0	0	
10	60	600	1.2	500
20	60	1200	2.4	500
30	60	1800	3.6	500
40	60	2400	4.8	500

▷ The energy of a charged capacitor

Look at the diagram shown here:
When the switch is in position A, the capacitor charges up.
What happens if you move the switch to B?
The lamp flashes briefly as the capacitor discharges.
The capacitor has released its stored electrical energy.

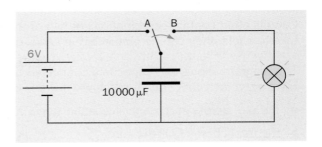

Where did this energy come from?
The energy was transferred to the capacitor by the supply.
The capacitor behaves a bit like a small rechargeable battery,
but it stores its energy in the electric field between its plates.

The p.d. across the capacitor and the size of its capacitance,
both affect the energy stored. In fact:

Energy stored, $W = \frac{1}{2} \times$ capacitance, $C \times$ p.d., V^2
(joules) (farads) (volts)^2

or $\boxed{W = \frac{1}{2} C V^2}$

How can we derive this energy equation?

The charge on a capacitor is proportional to the p.d. across it.
A graph of p.d. against charge is a straight line through (0,0).
The graph shows a capacitor charged to a p.d. V and charge Q.

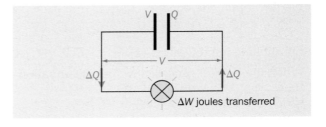

Now we allow the capacitor to discharge and release its energy.
At the start, the p.d. across the capacitor is V as shown:
A small charge ΔQ flows across this p.d. V and transfers
some energy ΔW.
Since p.d. is the energy transferred per coulomb (page 194),
the energy transferred ΔW is given by:

$$\Delta W = \Delta Q \times V$$

Can you see this is the area of the shaded strip on the graph?

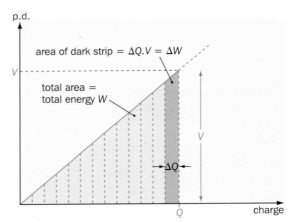

When the capacitor discharges so that V and Q fall to zero,
the **total** energy transferred = the total area of all the strips
$$= \text{the area of the triangle}$$
$$= \frac{1}{2} Q V$$

This must be the energy W originally stored in the capacitor.
Therefore:

$\boxed{W = \frac{1}{2} Q V}$ or, since $Q = C V$ $\boxed{W = \frac{1}{2} C V^2}$

Example 1
A capacitor is charged using a steady current of 20.0 μA,
from a 5.0 V supply. After 55 s it is fully charged.
Calculate a) the charge on the capacitor, b) its capacitance,
c) the energy stored in the charged capacitor.

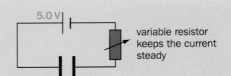

a) $Q = I t$
$= 20.0 \times 10^{-6} \text{ A} \times 55 \text{ s}$
∴ $Q = \underline{1.1 \times 10^{-3} \text{ C}}$ (2 s.f.)

b) $C = \dfrac{Q}{V} = \dfrac{1.10 \times 10^{-3} \text{ C}}{5.0 \text{ V}}$
∴ $C = \underline{220 \times 10^{-6} \text{ F}}$ (= 220 μF)

c) $W = \frac{1}{2} C V^2$
$= \frac{1}{2} \times 220 \times 10^{-6} \text{ F} \times (5.0 \text{ V})^2$
∴ $W = \underline{2.8 \times 10^{-3} \text{ J}}$ (2 s.f.)

d) How much energy is stored if the charging p.d. is doubled?
$W = \frac{1}{2} C V^2$. C is constant. V doubles, so $W = 4$ times as much $= 4 \times 2.8 \times 10^{-3} \text{ J} = \underline{1.1 \times 10^{-2} \text{ J}}$ (2 s.f.)

▷ Capacitors in parallel

Circuits often contain combinations of two or more capacitors. Like resistors, they can be connected in series or in parallel.

The diagram shows two capacitors connected **in parallel**: Here are 3 facts that you should know for this circuit:

- the p.d. across each capacitor is the same, and equal to V,

- the total charge Q is the sum of the charges on each capacitor: $$Q = Q_1 + Q_2$$

- The combined capacitance C is the **sum** of the two capacitances: $$\boxed{C = C_1 + C_2}$$

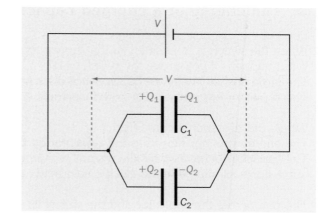

How can we prove this formula for capacitors in parallel? We wish to replace C_1 and C_2 with a single capacitor C, so that Q is the charge on C when the p.d. across it is V.

We know that: $\qquad Q = Q_1 + Q_2 \quad \ldots \ldots (1)$

We now apply the equation $Q = C\,V$ to each capacitor to get:

$$Q = C\,V \qquad Q_1 = C_1\,V \qquad Q_2 = C_2\,V$$

Substituting into equation (1): $\qquad C\cancel{V} = C_1\cancel{V} + C_2\cancel{V}$

When the V's are cancelled we get the equation shown above.

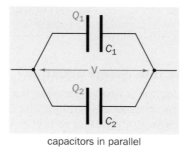

capacitors in parallel

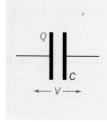

equivalent capacitor

Example 2
Calculate the charge on each capacitor in this diagram:

Using $\mathbf{Q = C\,V}$ $\qquad Q_1 = C_1\,V = 400\ \mu F \times 6.0\ V = \underline{2400\ \mu C}$

$\qquad\qquad\qquad\quad Q_2 = C_2\,V = 200\ \mu F \times 6.0\ V = \underline{1200\ \mu C}$

Notice that the 400 μF capacitor has twice as much charge as the 200 μF capacitor.

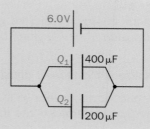

Example 3
A 20 μF capacitor is charged to 9.0 V, then disconnected from the supply, and then connected across an uncharged 10 μF capacitor.

Calculate: a) the initial charge on the 20 μF capacitor,
b) the capacitance of the parallel combination,
c) the p.d. across the parallel combination.

a) $\mathbf{Q = C\,V}$.
$\quad Q = 20 \times 10^{-6}\ F \times 9.0\ V = 180 \times 10^{-6}\ C = \underline{180\ \mu C}$

b) $\mathbf{C = C_1 + C_2}$ and leaving the values in μF
$\quad C = 20\ \mu F + 10\ \mu F = \underline{30\ \mu F}$

c) The two capacitors now share the total charge = 180 μC. Charge (as electrons) flows between the two capacitors until the p.d. across each capacitor is the same.
$$V = \frac{Q}{C} = \frac{180\ \mu C}{30\ \mu F} = \frac{180 \times 10^{-6}\ C}{30 \times 10^{-6}\ F} = \underline{6.0\ V} \quad \text{(2 s.f.)}$$

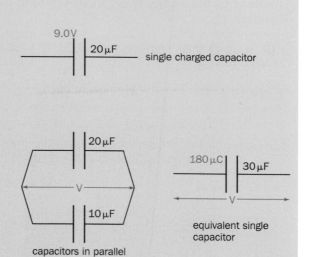

single charged capacitor

capacitors in parallel

equivalent single capacitor

▷ Capacitors in series

The diagram shows two capacitors connected **in series**.
Here are 3 facts that you should know for this circuit:

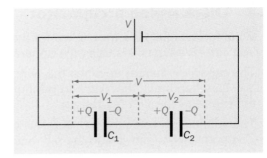

- The charge on each capacitor is the same and equal to Q, and the total charge stored by both capacitors together is Q.

- The supply p.d. V is shared between the two capacitors so that: $$V = V_1 + V_2$$

- The combined capacitance C of the series combination is given by:
$$\frac{1}{C} = \frac{1}{C_1} + \frac{1}{C_2}$$

Did you expect that the total charge stored would be $2Q$?
The cartoon shows you why this is not the case:
During the charging process, a charge Q (not $2Q$) flows between the positive and negative terminals of the supply.

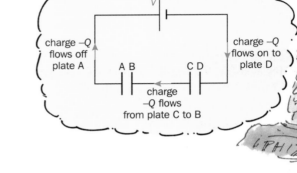

How can we prove this formula for capacitors in series?
We wish to replace C_1 and C_2 with a single capacitor C, so that Q is the charge on C when the p.d. across it is V.
We know that: $V = V_1 + V_2$ . . . . . (1)

We can apply the equation $V = Q/C$ to each capacitor, to get:

$$V = \frac{V}{C} \qquad V_1 = \frac{Q}{C_1} \qquad V_2 = \frac{Q}{C_2}$$

Substituting into equation (1): $\dfrac{\cancel{Q}}{C} = \dfrac{\cancel{Q}}{C_1} + \dfrac{\cancel{Q}}{C_2}$

When the Q's are cancelled we get the equation shown above.

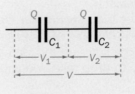 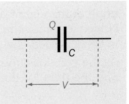

capacitors in series   equivalent capacitor

Example 4
In the circuit shown, what is   a) the combined capacitance,
b) the charge on each capacitor,   c) the p.d. across each capacitor.

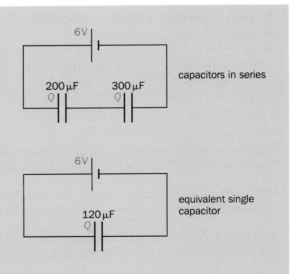

capacitors in series

a) $\dfrac{1}{C} = \dfrac{1}{C_1} + \dfrac{1}{C_2}$ and leaving the values in μF

$\dfrac{1}{C} = \dfrac{1}{200\ \mu F} + \dfrac{1}{300\ \mu F} = \dfrac{3+2}{600\ \mu F} = \dfrac{5}{600\ \mu F}$

$\therefore\ C = \dfrac{600\ \mu F}{5} = \underline{120\ \mu F}$

b) Now we can draw the equivalent circuit:

$\boldsymbol{Q = C\,V}$ for the combined capacitor
$= 120\ \mu F \times 6.0\ V$
$\therefore\ Q = \underline{720\ \mu C}$

equivalent single capacitor

c) We now know that the charge on each capacitor is 720 μC.

Using $\boldsymbol{V = \dfrac{Q}{C}}$ for the 200 μF capacitor, $V = \dfrac{720\ \mu C}{200\ \mu F} = \underline{3.6\ V}$

for the 300 μF capacitor, $V = \dfrac{720\ \mu C}{300\ \mu F} = \underline{2.4\ V}$

Notice that the **larger** capacitor in the series combination
has the **smaller** p.d. across it.

Note that the combined capacitance of capacitors in series is **smaller** than their individual capacitances.
Compare this to resistors in parallel.

▷ Discharging a capacitor

What factors affect the *time* taken for a capacitor to discharge?
You can investigate this using the apparatus shown:

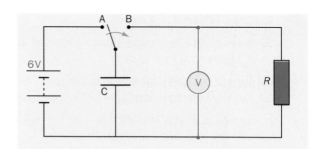

The capacitor charges up when the switch is in position A.
You can then move the switch to position B and discharge
the capacitor through the resistor.

The voltmeter records the p.d. across the capacitor.
Can you see that this is also the p.d. across the resistor?
Why will the voltmeter read 6 V at the start of the discharge?

You can record the p.d. every 10 s as the capacitor discharges.
The graph shows the results that you would get using
different values for the capacitance C and the resistor R:

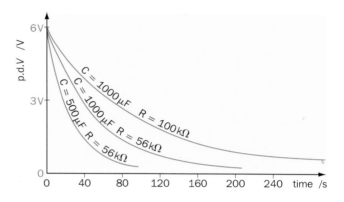

Why does the discharge take longer as C and R increase?
The larger the resistor, the more it resists the flow of charge.
The charge moves more slowly around the circuit.

The greater the capacitance the greater the charge stored.
It takes longer for the charge to flow off the capacitor plates.

Why does the p.d. fall more and more slowly with time?
Look at the circuit diagrams:
Notice that the smaller the p.d., the smaller the current.
In other words, the smaller the rate of flow of charge.
As the p.d. falls, the charge flows off the plates more slowly
and the time for the p.d. to drop takes longer and longer.

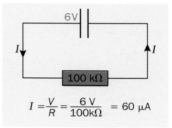 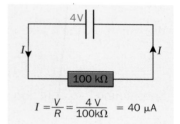

$$I = \frac{V}{R} = \frac{6\text{ V}}{100\text{k}\Omega} = 60\ \mu\text{A}$$

$$I = \frac{V}{R} = \frac{4\text{ V}}{100\text{k}\Omega} = 40\ \mu\text{A}$$

The time constant

The **time constant** τ gives us information about the time it
takes for a capacitor to discharge:

> **Time constant, τ = capacitance, C × resistance, R**
> (seconds)   (farads)   (ohms)

In fact, the time constant τ is the time it takes for the p.d. to
fall to $1/e$ of its original value V_0.

(e is one of those special mathematical numbers, rather like π.)
The value of e is 2.72 (3 s.f.) and so $1/e$ equals **0.37** (2 s.f.).

After a time CR, the p.d. V across the capacitor equals $0.37 \times V_0$.
V is now 37% (very roughly $1/3$) of its original value.

After a time $5\,CR$ the p.d. will have fallen to about 0.7% of V_0
and we can consider the capacitor to be effectively discharged.

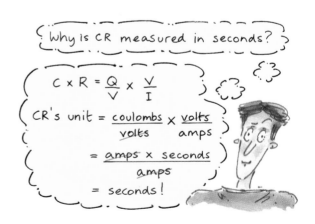

Example 5
What is the time constant for the circuit shown?

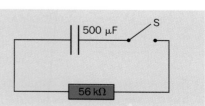

time constant, τ = capacitance, C × resistance, R
$$= 500 \times 10^{-6}\,\text{F} \times 56 \times 10^3\ \Omega$$
$$\tau = \underline{28 \text{ seconds}}$$

Exponential discharge

We've seen how the p.d. across a capacitor falls as it discharges. But how do the charge and the discharge current vary with time?

The diagram shows our discharge circuit again:
Remember, V is the p.d. across the capacitor **and** the resistor.

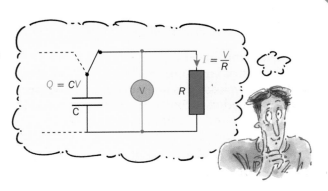

We know that:
- charge Q on a capacitor is proportional to the p.d. across it,
- current I in a resistor is proportional to the p.d. across it.

This means that both Q and I must fall in the same way as V. Look at the 3 graphs below. They all have the same shape.

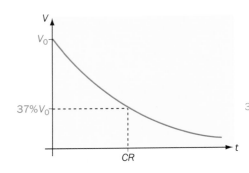 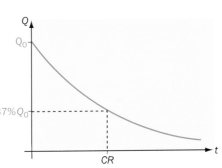 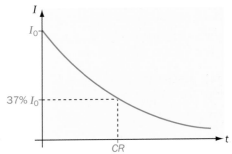

Let's look in more detail at the graph of charge against time:
After a time CR, the charge has fallen to $1/e$ (about $1/3$) of Q_0.

After a further time CR the charge has again fallen by $1/e$.
Now the charge is $1/e \times 1/e$ (roughly $1/9$) of its original value.

A further CR seconds and the charge is $1/e \times 1/e \times 1/e$ of Q_0.

The charge continues to fall by $1/e$ every CR seconds.
We say that the charge **falls exponentially** with time and:

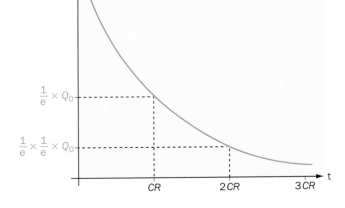

$$Q_t = Q_0\, e^{-t/CR}$$

Q_0 is the initial charge
Q_t is the charge after time t
CR is the time constant

We can write similar **exponential equations** for the p.d. V across the capacitor:

$$V_t = V_0\, e^{-t/CR}$$

and
the current I as it discharges:

$$I_t = I_0\, e^{-t/CR}$$

See also **Check Your Maths** on page 408.

Example 6
In the circuit shown, the capacitor is charged to 6.0 V.
The switch is now closed. Calculate:
a) the time constant,
b) the p.d. across the capacitor after 20 s,
c) the charge on the capacitor after 20 s.

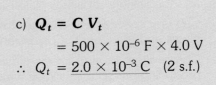

a) $\tau = C \times R$

  $= 500 \times 10^{-6}\,\text{F} \times 100 \times 10^3\,\Omega$

$\therefore\ \tau = \underline{50\,\text{s}}$ (2 s.f.)

b) $V_t = V_0\, e^{-t/CR}$

  $= 6.0 \times e^{-20\,\text{s}/50\,\text{s}}$

  $= 6.0 \times e^{-0.4}$

$\therefore\ V_t = \underline{4.0\,\text{V}}$ (2 s.f.)

c) $Q_t = C\,V_t$

  $= 500 \times 10^{-6}\,\text{F} \times 4.0\,\text{V}$

$\therefore\ Q_t = \underline{2.0 \times 10^{-3}\,\text{C}}$ (2 s.f.)

▷ Physics at work: Capacitors

Flash photography

Even a large capacitor stores only a small amount of energy,
but it can release this energy very rapidly – as in a flash gun.
The charged capacitor in the flash gun discharges and
releases around 1 joule of energy in about 1 millisecond.
So this is a **power** output of about 1 kW !

The small camera battery cannot produce this power output.
That is why it takes about 10 seconds for the battery
to recharge the capacitor between photographs.

Designing practical capacitors

How does the construction of a capacitor affect its capacitance?

The capacitance C of a parallel plate
capacitor can be calculated using:

$$C = \frac{\varepsilon \, A}{d}$$

Can you see that: increasing the area A of the plates,
decreasing the separation d of the plates,
increasing the permittivity ε of the dielectric,
all increase the capacitance of the capacitor?

In the capacitors below, how is A made large and d made small?

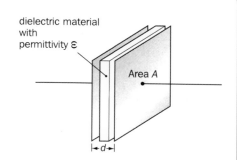

dielectric material with permittivity ε

Area A

$\leftarrow d \rightarrow$

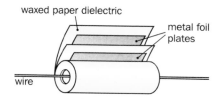

waxed paper dielectric

metal foil plates

wire

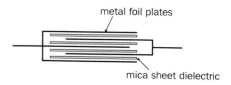

metal foil plates

mica sheet dielectric

1. A waxed paper capacitor consists
of two long strips of metal foil
separated by strips of waxed paper.
It is rolled up to form a cylinder.
Typical value 0.1 μF.

2. An electrolytic capacitor has
a similar 'Swiss roll' construction.
Its very thin dielectric is formed
chemically. The plate marked +
must never be charged negatively.
Typical value 100 μF.

3. The mica capacitor consists
of layers of metal foil separated by
thin sheets of mica.
Typical value is less than 0.01 μF,
but they have high stability –
they keep their value with age.

The 'maximum working voltage' is often written on a capacitor.
What does this mean?
If the p.d. across the plates is made too high, the electric field
between the plates will cause the dielectric to 'break down'.
Once the dielectric conducts, the capacitor cannot store charge.

Monitoring breathing patterns in babies

The sensor consists of a sealed sachet filled with a sponge.
As the baby breathes the sachet compresses and expands and
the pressure of the air in the sponge varies.
The sealed tube transfers this pressure variation to the detector
and the flexible capacitor plate moves up and down.

Can you see how this changes the separation of the capacitor
plates and therefore the capacitance of the detector?

Charge flows on and off the plates as the capacitance changes,
producing an electrical signal which is then monitored.

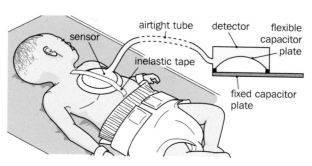

sensor

airtight tube   detector   flexible
capacitor
plate

inelastic tape

fixed capacitor
plate

Summary

A capacitor of capacitance C stores a charge Q when there is a p.d. V across it: $\qquad C = \dfrac{Q}{V}$ or $Q = CV$

Energy W is stored in the electric field between the plates of a capacitor: $\qquad W = \frac{1}{2}QV = \frac{1}{2}CV^2$

The combined capacitance C of two capacitors **in parallel** is given by: $\qquad C = C_1 + C_2$

The combined capacitance C of two capacitors **in series** is given by: $\qquad \dfrac{1}{C} = \dfrac{1}{C_1} + \dfrac{1}{C_2}$

The rate at which a capacitor discharges depends on the time constant τ: $\qquad \tau = CR$

The charge on a capacitor, its p.d. and the discharge current all fall exponentially with time. The exponential equation for charge is: $\qquad Q_t = Q_0 e^{-t/CR}$

▷ Questions

1. Can you complete these sentences?
   a) As a capacitor charges, a positive .... builds up on one plate and an equal .... charge builds up on the other plate.
   b) The charging process stops when the .... across the capacitor plates equals the p.d. of the ....
   c) If the p.d. across a capacitor is doubled, the .... that is stored is quadrupled.
   d) The p.d. is the same across each capacitor in ....
   e) The charge is the same on each capacitor in ....

2. Explain:
   a) How can there be a current in a circuit containing a capacitor, since no charge is able to pass through the insulator between the capacitor plates?
   b) Why does the current in a capacitor discharge circuit decrease with time?
   c) Why is there a maximum limit to the p.d. that can be placed across a capacitor?

3. When a capacitor is charged from a 12 V supply 6.0 μC moves on to its plates. What is its capacitance?

4. Some computer chips use a capacitor to provide energy for a short time if there is a power failure. A 100 μF capacitor is charged to 9.0 V.
   a) What is the charge on the capacitor? b) How long would it be able to supply a steady current of 50 μA?

5. A capacitor stores a charge of 60 μC when charged from a 12 V supply. How much energy does it store?

6. What is the combined capacitance of each of the examples shown below?

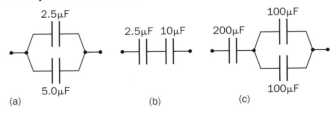

(a) 2.5 μF 5.0 μF   (b) 2.5 μF 10 μF   (c) 200 μF 100 μF 100 μF

7. Some capacitors are marked 10 μF, 25 V. How could you combine these capacitors to make:
   a) a 20 μF capacitor with a working voltage of 25 V,
   b) a 5 μF capacitor with a working voltage of 50 V,
   c) a 10 μF capacitor with a working voltage of 50 V.

8. Which stores more charge: a 2 μF capacitor charged to 20 V, or a 4 μF capacitor charged to 10 V? Which stores more energy?

9. A 5.0 μF capacitor is charged to a p.d. of 12 V and then connected across an uncharged 20 μF capacitor. Calculate: a) the initial charge on the 5 μF capacitor, b) the total capacitance of the combination, c) the p.d. across the capacitors in parallel.

10. A 6.0 V battery is used to charge a 100 μF capacitor in series with a 25 μF capacitor. Calculate:
    a) the capacitance of the combination,
    b) the charge on the capacitors,
    c) the p.d. across each capacitor.

11. A 4.0 μF capacitor is charged to 15 V and then discharged through a 0.80 MΩ resistor. What is:
    a) the initial charge on the capacitor,
    b) the time constant of the discharge circuit,
    c) the charge 5.0 s after the discharge starts.

12. A 10 000 μF capacitor is charged to 4.0 V and then discharged through a 20 kΩ resistor. Calculate: a) the initial discharge current, b) the discharge current after 100 s.

13. A timer uses a 1000 μF capacitor to switch off a security light after a pre-set time. The capacitor is charged to a p.d. of 9.0 V, and allowed to discharge through a resistor of 330 kΩ. The switch is triggered when the p.d. falls to 2.5 V. Calculate the time for which the light is on.

Further questions on page 280.

▷ Current electricity

1. An electric heater consists of three heating elements connected to a 240 V supply as in the diagram.

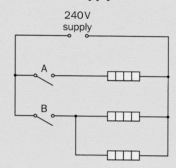

240V supply

Each heating element is rated at 240 V, 960 W.
a) Calculate the output power of the heater for the indicated positions of switches A and B. [3]

switch A	switch B	output power/W
closed	open	
closed	closed	
open	closed	

b) For one heating element at its normal operating temperature, calculate the current in, and resistance of the element. [4]
c) Calculate the total resistance of the circuit when all three heating elements are in use. [2] (OCR)

2. In the following circuits the battery has negligible internal resistance, and the lamps are identical.

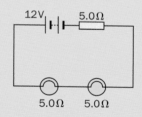
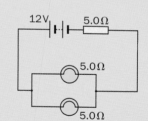

Figure 1   Figure 2

a) For the circuit shown in figure 1 calculate the current in each lamp and the power dissipated in each lamp. [2]
b) For the circuit shown in figure 2 calculate the current in each lamp. [2]
c) Explain how the brightness of the lamps in the circuit in figure 1 compares with the brightness of the lamps in the circuit in figure 2.
Explain why the battery would last longer in the circuit shown in figure 1. [3]
d) One of the lamps in the circuit in figure 2 is faulty and no longer conducts.
Describe and explain what happens to the brightness of the other lamp. [2] (AQA)

3. The graph shows the current–voltage plot for a filament lamp.

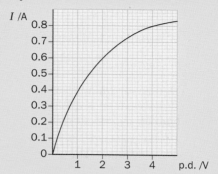

a) Explain why the graph is curved.
Use the graph to calculate the resistance of the lamp filament when connected across 4.0 V. [3]

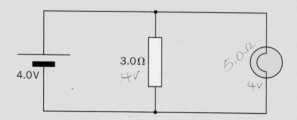

b) The lamp is connected in parallel with a 3.0 Ω resistor to a 4.0 V supply of negligible internal resistance.
Calculate the total current drawn from the supply and the power dissipated in the circuit. [3]
c) The lamp filament is made of 0.015 m of tungsten wire which has a resistivity of 3.9×10^{-7} Ω m in these conditions.
Calculate the diameter of the wire. [3] (OCR)

4. In the circuit shown each resistor has a resistance of 10 Ω; the battery has an e.m.f. of 12.0 V and is of negligible internal resistance.

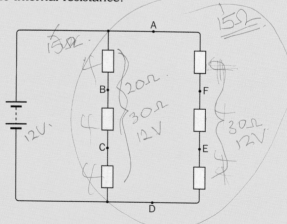

a) Calculate the power delivered by the battery.
b) Write down the p.d.'s between C and D, and between F and D, and hence calculate the p.d. between C and F. [5] (AQA)

5. The diagram shows a circuit for measuring resistance (i.e. an ohmmeter).
Before any readings are taken, the two probes are connected together and the variable resistor is adjusted so that the meter reads full scale deflection.

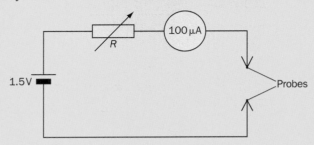

a) Calculate the resistance of R for full scale deflection. [2]
b) With R fixed at this value, what additional resistance connected between the probes would give a meter reading of
   i) one half of full scale deflection,
   ii) one quarter of full scale deflection from the 0 μA end of the scale? [2] (Edex)

6. The circuit shown is used to produce a current-voltage graph for a 12 V, 24 W lamp.

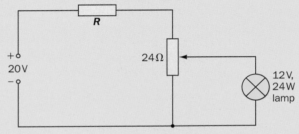

a) Show on a copy of the diagram, the correct positions for a voltmeter and an ammeter. [2]
b) Calculate the resistance of the lamp in normal operation. [3]
c) Calculate the value of R which would enable the voltage across the lamp to be varied between 0 V and 12 V. [4] (Edex)

7. The e.m.f. of the electricity supply to a remote cottage is 230 V. The resistance of the cables to the cottage may be considered as the internal resistance of the supply. When an electric cooker is used in the cottage, the measured voltage across the cooker is 210 V. The resistance of the cooker is 35 Ω.
a) Calculate
   i) the current to the cooker,
   ii) the power of the cooker,
   iii) the resistance of the cables to the cottage. [4]
b) Explain why the voltage measured at the cooker is less than the supply voltage when the cooker is in use. [2]
c) Suggest two disadvantages of this power supply. [2] (OCR)

8. A designer uses the circuit shown for the sidelights of a car. The lamps are each rated at 6 V, 12 W. The battery used is of negligible resistance.

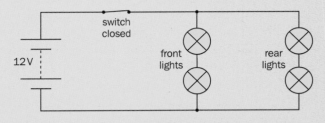

a) Calculate the current in the battery. [3]
b) A fully charged battery is able to supply a total charge of 1.2×10^5 C.
   How long could the lamps operate when connected to a fully charged battery? [2]
c) A user replaces one of the front lamps with one rated at 12 V, 24W. State and explain whether
   i) this change has any effect on the brightness of the rear sidelights,
   ii) the front sidelights will operate at their normal rated power. [4]
d) The original circuit is not normally used. In practice, four lamps, each rated at 12 V, are connected in parallel as shown below. Give one reason why this is preferred. [1] (AQA)

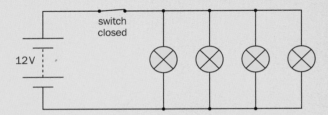

9. a) Derive a formula for the resistance of three resistors R_1, R_2 and R_3 in series. [2]

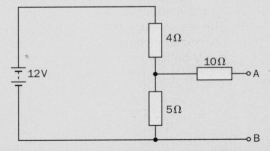

b) Calculate the p.d. between A and B in the above circuit when the 12 V battery has negligible internal resistance. [2]
c) What would the p.d. between A and B become if a 10 Ω resistor were connected between the two points? [2]
d) Calculate the current in the 10 Ω resistor connected to A and B. [2] (AQA)

Further questions on electricity

10. a) Distinguish between the e.m.f. and the terminal p.d. of a cell. [2]

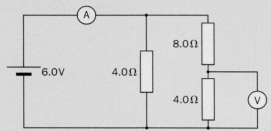

b) Find values for the ammeter and voltmeter readings in the circuit shown. Assume that the ammeter and cell have negligible resistance and the voltmeter has a very large resistance. [4]

c) In fact the cell does have an internal resistance. A student finds that the voltmeter reads 1.6 V.
  i) Show that the terminal p.d. of the cell is 4.8 V,
  ii) If the ammeter reads 1.6 A, find the value of the internal resistance of the cell. [4] (OCR)

11. The graph shows how the resistance of a thermistor varies with temperature.

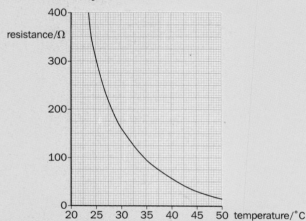

a) Determine the resistance of the thermistor at a temperature of 30 °C. [1]

b) The circuit diagram shows the thermistor connected in series with a 300 Ω resistor and a 6.0 V battery of negligible internal resistance.

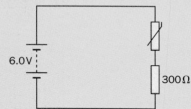

  i) Explain, without calculation, how you would expect the p.d. across the thermistor to change as its temperature is increased. [3]
  ii) Calculate the p.d. across the resistor when the temperature of the thermistor is 30 °C. [2] (AQA)

12. The circuit diagram shows a 12 V power supply connected across a potential divider R. The sliding contact P is linked to a resistance wire XY through an ammeter. A voltmeter is connected across XY.

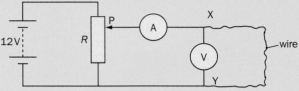

a) Explain, with reference to this circuit, the term potential divider. [2]
The circuit has been set up to measure the resistance of the wire XY.
A set of voltage and current measurements is recorded and used to draw the graph below.

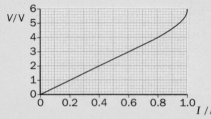

b) Explain why the curve deviates from a straight line at higher current values. [2]
Calculate the resistance of the wire for low current values. [2]
To determine the resistivity of the material of the wire, two more quantities would have to be measured. What are they? [2] (Edex)

13. An electrical component Z has the current/voltage (I/V) characteristic shown. The component is said to be forward-biassed for positive values of voltage and reverse-biassed when the voltage is negative.

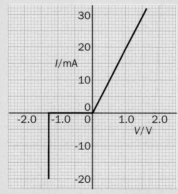

a) Determine the resistance of Z when Z is
  i) forward-biassed,
  ii) reverse-biassed with $V = -1.0$ V. [4]

b) The component Z is connected across a d.c. supply of e.m.f. 1.5 V and negligible internal resistance. Calculate the current when Z is forward-biassed and state why one would be ill-advised to connect the supply so that component Z is reverse-biassed. [3] (OCR)

276

▷ Magnetic fields

14. The diagram shows a horizontal cross-section through two long vertical wires P and Q. P carries a current into the plane of the paper. The circles on the diagram represent the magnetic field of this current. Q carries a current of 3.0 A in the opposite direction to the current in P.

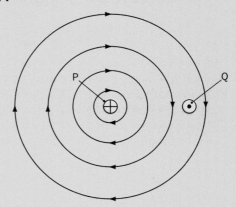

a) The magnetic flux density of the field at Q caused by the current in P is 2.0×10^{-5} T. Calculate the force experienced by unit length (1.0 m) of Q.

b) Sketch a diagram and on it draw an arrow to show the direction of this force.
Explain the rule you used to obtain the direction of the force.   [6] (OCR)

15. The long solenoid shown in the diagram has 1200 turns per m and carries a current of 2.0 A.

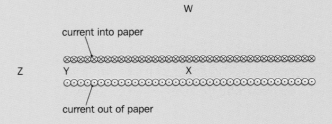

a) Draw an arrow on the diagram at X to show the direction of the field at X.

b) Describe the magnetic field inside the solenoid.

c) Arrange the letters W, X, Y and Z in the order of size of magnetic field strengths (weakest to strongest) at the points which correspond to these letters in the diagram.

d) The magnetic flux density at a point well inside and on the axis of a long solenoid is given by $B = \mu_o NI/l$, where N is the number of turns on the solenoid, l is the length of the solenoid, and μ_o and I have their usual meaning.
Show that the flux density of the magnetic field at X is 3.02×10^{-3} T.   [4] (AQA)

16. A horseshoe magnet, made from two magnets and a steel yoke, is placed on a top pan balance as shown in the upper diagram. A current is passed through a long wire which is fixed. The wire is between, and parallel to, the poles of the magnet as shown in the lower diagram.

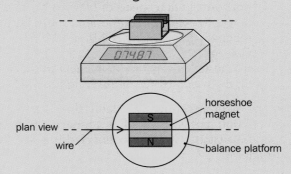

The current is varied. The following values of balance reading m and current I are recorded.

I /A	0	1.1	2.2	3.0	4.3	−1.8
m /g	74.87	75.02	75.17	75.29	75.46	74.63

a) Write down the relationship between the force F on the wire, the magnetic field B acting on length l of the wire, and the current I.   [1]

b) Explain why the force on the wire is equal in magnitude to the force on the magnet on the top pan balance.   [2]

c) Use the data to plot a graph to test the relationship between the current and the force it exerts on the magnet.   [2]

d) What happens when the current is reversed and why?   [2] (OCR)

17. PQRS is a section of a circuit, with right-angled corners at Q and R. It is mounted so that it lies in the same horizontal plane as a uniform magnetic field of flux density B, which is parallel to the sides PQ and RS. When a current, I, flows in the direction shown in the diagram, the wire QR experiences a force which acts vertically upwards.

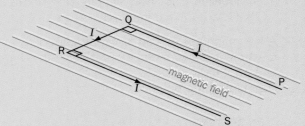

a) If the length of QR is 0.15 m and B is 0.20 T, the force on QR is 0.18 N. Calculate I.   [1]

b) Explain why the magnetic forces on sides PQ and RS need not be considered when investigating the equilibrium of PQRS.   [2] (AQA)

▷ Electromagnetic induction

18. a) Explain why you would expect an e.m.f. to be developed between the wing tips of an aircraft flying above the Earth. [1]

b) An aircraft, whose wing tips are 20 m apart, flies horizontally at a speed of 600 km h⁻¹ in a region where the vertical component of the Earth's magnetic flux density is 4.0×10^{-5} T. Calculate:
i) the area swept out by the aircraft's wings in 1 s,
ii) the e.m.f. between the wing tips. [4] (AQA)

19. The diagrams show two identical coils aligned on a common axis XX. Coil P is connected to a battery and a switch. Coil Q is connected to a sensitive meter M.

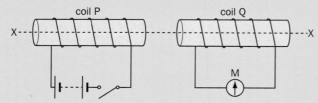

a) Before the switch is closed the reading on M is zero. On closing the switch, M records a pulse of current. The reading on M then returns to zero and remains at that value. Explain these observations by reference to Faraday's law of electromagnetic induction. [5]

b) As the switch is closed, the current in coil P creates a magnetic field B in the region between the coils. The direction of this field along the axis XX is shown in the lower diagram. The pulse of current in coil Q also produces a magnetic field along the axis XX.

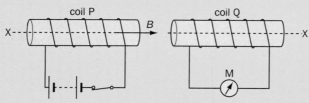

i) Sketch the diagram and draw an arrow labelled C to show the direction of this field.
ii) How is this explained by Lenz's law? [3](OCR)

20. A bar magnet is moved along the axis of, and towards, a closed metal loop. Sketch the diagram and on it indicate the direction of the induced current and the polarities of the faces of the loop.

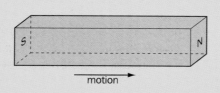

[2] (W)

21. The diagram shows a magnet being dropped through the centre of a narrow coil. The e.m.f. across the coil is monitored on an oscilloscope.

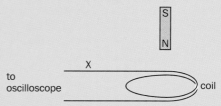

a) What is the induced polarity on the top side of the coil as the magnet falls towards the coil? Sketch the diagram and draw an arrow at position X to indicate the direction of current flow as the magnet falls towards the coil.[2]

b) The second diagram shows the variation of e.m.f. with time as the magnet falls.

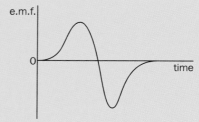

State, and explain, two ways in which the graph would change if the magnet were dropped from a greater height than that used to produce the graph in the diagram. [2] (AQA)

22. A light aluminium washer rests on the end of a solenoid as shown in the diagram. A large direct current is switched on in the solenoid.

Explain why the washer jumps up and very quickly falls back. [5] (Edex)

23. An electromagnet is used to produce a uniform magnetic field in the gap between its poles. The field outside the gap is negligible. The coil C encloses all the flux of the magnetic field. The magnetic flux density in the gap is 0.030 T and coil C has 70 turns.

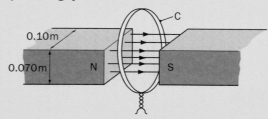

a) Calculate the flux linkage through the coil. [2]
b) The current in the electromagnet is reduced to zero at a uniform rate over a time of 2.5 s. Find the average e.m.f. induced in the coil. [2] (OCR)

▷ Electric fields

24. Define *electric field strength* at a point in space. [1]
Two point charges, $+1.6 \times 10^{-19}$ C and
-6.4×10^{-19} C, are held at a distance 8.0×10^{-10} m
apart at points A and B as shown in the diagram.

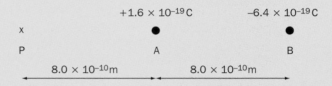

a) Find the magnitude and direction of the electric field at the midpoint between the two charges.[2]
b) Find the electric field at point P in the diagram.[2]
c) What can you say about the direction of electric field on either side of P along AB? [2] (OCR)

25. Two identical table tennis balls, A and B, each of mass 1.5 g, are attached to non-conducting threads. The balls are charged to the same positive value. When the threads are fastened to a point P the balls hang as shown in the diagram.

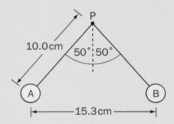

a) Draw a labelled free-body force diagram for A. [3]
b) Calculate the tension in one of the threads. [3]
c) Show that the electrostatic force between the two balls is 1.8×10^{-2} N. [1]
d) Calculate the charge on each ball. [3] (Edex)

26. Two parallel plates are set a distance of 12 mm apart in a vacuum as shown below. The top plate is at a potential of +300 V and the bottom plate is at a potential of –300 V.

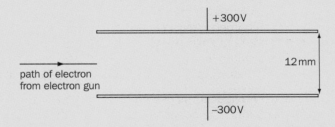

a) Sketch the diagram and on it draw lines to show the electric field lines between the plates. [3]
b) At a point midway between the plates the field is uniform. Calculate the magnitudes of
   i) the electric field strength at this point,
   ii) the force on an electron at this point. [5](OCR)

27. The electrostatic loudspeaker, shown below, has two perforated plates designed to let the sound out. A signal is applied across these plates. Between the plates is a light flexible charged diaphragm.

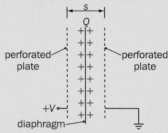

a) At one instant the p.d. V between the perforated plates is 2.2 kV. The separation s of the plates is 3.4 mm. Assuming that the presence of the charge Q has no effect on the electric field, calculate the electric field strength between the plates. [2]
b) The charge Q is 1.2×10^{-7} C. Calculate the force acting on the diaphragm. [2] (AQA)

28. The diagram shows two charged parallel conducting plates.

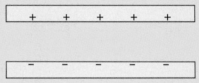

a) Copy the diagram, then add solid lines to show the electric field in the space between and just beyond the edges of the plates. [2]
b) Add to your diagram dotted lines to show three equipotentials in the same regions. [2]
c) Define electric potential at a point. Is electric potential a vector or a scalar quantity? [3] (Edex)

29. Two parallel metal plates P_1 and P_2 are placed 10 cm apart in air. P_1 is maintained at –200 kV whilst P_2 is connected to earth through a microammeter. Suspended between the plates by an insulating thread is a light plastic sphere coated with conducting paint so that it will store charge.

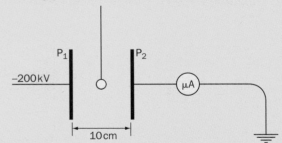

a) Calculate the electric field strength between the plates. [1]
b) Explain why the ball shuttles back and forth between the plates, contacting each plate alternately. [3] (AQA)

▷ Capacitors

30. a) Sketch a graph to show the variation with charge Q of the p.d. V across the plates of a capacitor. [2]
b) Use your graph to show that the energy E stored in a capacitor of capacitance C with a p.d. V across its plates is given by $E = \frac{1}{2}CV^2$. [2](OCR)

31. A 47 μF capacitor is used to power the flashgun of a camera. The average power output of the flashgun is 4.0 kW for the duration of flash which is 2.0 ms.
a) Show that the energy output of the flashgun per flash is 8.0 J. [2]
b) Calculate the p.d. between the terminals of the capacitor immediately before the flash. Assume that all the energy stored by the capacitor is used to provide the output power of the flashgun. [2]
c) Calculate the maximum charge stored by the capacitor. [2]
d) Calculate the average current provided by the capacitor during the flash. [1] (AQA)

32. The circuit shows a 0.47 μF capacitor which can be charged through a 3000 Ω resistor when switch S is closed.

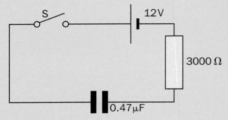

The capacitor is initially uncharged. Find:
a) the initial charging current,
b) the charging current after a long time,
c) the maximum charge stored on the capacitor,
d) the maximum energy stored on the capacitor. [5] (OCR)

33. The circuit shown is used to investigate the discharge of a capacitor. With the switch in position S_1 the capacitor is charged. The switch is then moved to S_2 and readings of current and time are taken as the capacitor discharges through the resistor. The results are plotted on the graph below.

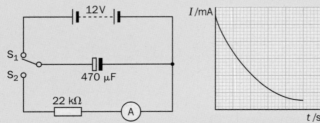

a) Calculate the maximum charge stored on the capacitor. [1]
b) Make suitable calculations to enable you to add scales to both axes of the graph. [4] (Edex)

34. An engineer required a 20 μF capacitor which operated safely using a voltage of 6.0 kV. Ten similar capacitors connected in series were found to provide a suitable arrangement when operating at their maximum safe voltage.
a) State the maximum safe working voltage of each capacitor. [1]
b) Determine the capacitance of each capacitor. [1]
c) Calculate the total energy stored by the combination of capacitors when fully charged to 6.0 kV. [2] (OCR)

35. A radio tuning circuit uses a variable capacitor with a range of 50–500 pF. A designer decides to change the range using a 500 pF capacitor.

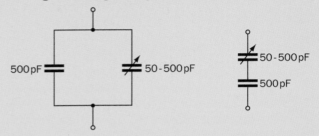

Determine the range of capacitance available when the 500 pF capacitor is connected
a) in parallel with the variable capacitor (above left)
b) in series with the variable capacitor (right-hand diagram). [4] (AQA)

36. A 100 μF capacitor is connected to a 12 V supply.

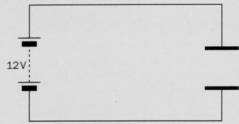

a) Calculate the charge stored. Sketch the diagram then show on it the arrangement and magnitude of the charge on the capacitor. [3]
b) This 100 μF capacitor is disconnected from the supply and is then connected across a 300 μF uncharged capacitor. What happens to the charge initially stored on the 100 μF capacitor? Calculate the new voltage across the pair of capacitors. [4] (Edex)

37. A 1.0 F capacitor is used as a battery backup in a calculator. The capacitor has been fully charged so that there is a p.d. of 6.0 V across its terminals.
a) How much energy does it store? [2]
b) It is removed from the voltage source and connected across a 1.0 kΩ resistor. Calculate:
i) the initial current in the resistor,
ii) the current when the capacitor has lost 75% of its stored energy. [6] (AQA)

▷ The CRO and a.c.

38. An alternating current varies with time in the way shown in the diagram.

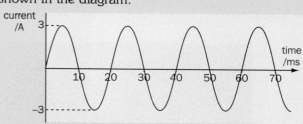

a) For this alternating current, determine
   i) the frequency,
   ii) the peak value. [2]
b) Sketch a graph which shows how the power supplied by this current to a resistor of resistance 5 Ω varies with time. Label the axes and mark on the maximum value of the power. [3] (OCR)

39. In each of the circuits below, the p.d. across the d.c. Y-input terminals of an oscilloscope is displayed on the oscilloscope screen. The Y-input voltage sensitivity is set at 1.0 V cm^{-1} and the timebase at 5.0 ms cm^{-1}. The oscilloscope is adjusted so that an input of 0 V corresponds to a horizontal straight line trace across the centre of the grid. In each case sketch the trace you would expect to see. [8] (AQA)

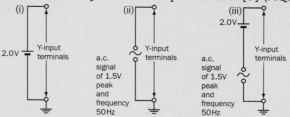

40. High voltage power lines and distribution cables may consist of four conductors. Three of these conductors supply the power and the fourth conductor is a common return conductor called the neutral. The p.d.'s between each of the three supply conductors and Earth vary as shown in graphs 1, 2 and 3 in the diagram below. The peak voltage of each supply conductor relative to Earth is 325 kV.

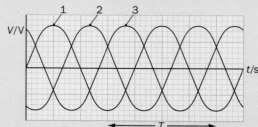

a) Estimate the maximum p.d. between any two supply conductors. Sketch the graph and show on it how you obtained this value. [2]
b) Show that the sum of the voltages in the three conductors at any instant is zero. [2] (Edex)

▷ Synoptic questions on Electricity

41. The circuit in the diagram contains an ideal diode.

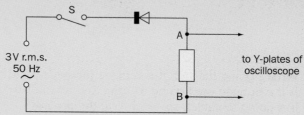

a) The power supply produces a sinusoidal alternating voltage with a peak value of 5.0 V and a frequency of 50 Hz. For this supply calculate the period. [2]
b) i) The Y-plate sensitivity and the timebase of the oscilloscope are set to 2.0 V cm^{-1} and 5.0 ms cm^{-1} respectively. The switch is now closed. Sketch a graph showing the trace displayed on the oscilloscope screen.
   ii) Draw an arrow to indicate the direction of the conventional current in the resistor when the diode is conducting. [4]
c) The trace you have sketched is rectified a.c. and not d.c. Draw on your graph the trace displayed on an oscilloscope screen when a 9.0 V d.c. supply is connected to the CRO. [4] (OCR)

42. Below is a diagram of a laboratory power supply which has an e.m.f. of 3200 V and internal resistance r. The capacitor C ensures a steady output voltage between X and Y when the switch S is in the 'on' position. The resistor R allows the capacitor to discharge when S is in the 'off' position.

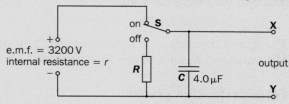

a) For safety reasons, the power supply is designed with an internal resistance r so that if X and Y are short-circuited the current does not exceed 2.0 mA. Calculate the value of r. [1]
b) For safety reasons, when the supply is switched off the capacitor must discharge from 3200 V to 50 V in 5 minutes.
   i) The time constant of the circuit is 70 s. Show that the capacitor discharges from 3200 V to 50 V in less than 5.0 minutes. [3]
   ii) Calculate the value of the resistor R. [2]
   iii) Explain briefly whether or not increasing the value of R would make the supply safer. [1]
c) Calculate the charge on the capacitor when the p.d. across it is 3200 V. Sketch a graph to show the variation of charge on the capacitor with time as it discharges through the resistor. [3] (AQA)

23 Solids under Stress

What's going through this bungee jumper's mind?
Is the bungee cord going to snap and let me fall?
Is it going to stretch so much I hit the ground?
Let's hope someone did the calculations!

In this chapter you will learn:
- how to calculate extensions when solids are stretched,
- how to find the energy stored in a stretched solid,
- how to explain what happens to the atoms.

▶ Hooke's Law

Look at the spring in this diagram:
Can you see what happens when extra weight is added?

The spring extends by equal amounts, because the stretching force
is going up in equal steps. This is called **Hooke's law**.

You can use an equation to find the force needed:

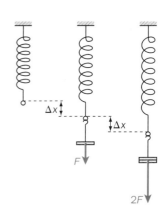

Stretching force, F	**= spring constant, k**	**× extension, Δx**
(N)	(N m^{-1})	(m)

or $\boxed{F = k\,\Delta x}$

The extension Δx ('delta-x') is sometimes written e or Δl.
You find the extension from:

Δx = stretched length – original length.

The spring constant k, is sometimes called the **stiffness**.
k is measured in units of newtons per metre (N m^{-1}).

Force–extension graphs

Look at the force–extension graph for a spring:

The line is straight up to the point X, called the **elastic limit**.
Hooke's Law holds true only for this straight-line region.
The **gradient** of this line is the spring constant, k.

For forces less than F_X, the spring behaves **elastically**. If the force is
removed, the spring goes back to its original size and shape.

For forces bigger than F_X the spring does not return to its original size.

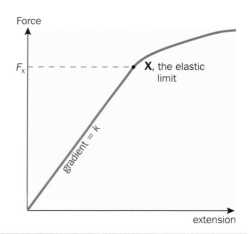

Example 1
A spring is 0.38 m long. When it is pulled by a force of 2.0 N, it stretches to 0.42 m.
What is the spring constant? Assume that the spring behaves elastically.

Extension, Δx = stretched length – original length $= 0.42\ \text{m} - 0.38\ \text{m}\ = 0.04\ \text{m}$

$$F = k \times \Delta x$$
$$\therefore\ 2.0\ \text{N} = k \times 0.04\ \text{m} \qquad \text{so}\quad k = \frac{2.0\ \text{N}}{0.04\ \text{m}} = \underline{50\ \text{N m}^{-1}}$$

▶ Elastic Potential Energy

You have to do work to stretch a spring. This energy is stored in the spring. It is called **strain** potential energy or **elastic** potential energy.

Look at this force–extension graph:
The **blue area** represents the potential energy stored in the spring as it stretches up to point A.

Since the area of this triangle $= \frac{1}{2} \times$ height $\times$ base
this gives us the equation for elastic potential energy:

Elastic Potential Energy $= \frac{1}{2} \times$ **stretching force** $\times$ **extension**
(J) (N) (m)

or: $\boxed{E_P = \frac{1}{2} F \Delta x}$ (provided the elastic limit is not exceeded)

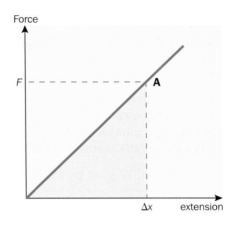

Example 2
A spring is 32 cm long. It is stretched by a force of 6.0 N until it is 54 cm long.
How much energy is stored in the stretched spring?
Hint: make sure the distance measurements are always in metres!

Extension $\Delta x = 0.54$ m $- 0.32$ m $= 0.22$ m
Elastic potential energy $= \frac{1}{2} \times F \times \Delta x \quad = \frac{1}{2} \times 6.0$ N $\times 0.22$ m $\quad = \underline{0.66 \text{ J}}$ (2 s.f.)

What if the force–extension graph is a curve?

The area under the graph always gives the energy stored, even when the graph is not a straight line.

How can you find the energy if the line is not straight?

You can draw straight-line sections closely fitting the curve, then divide the area under the curve into triangles and rectangles, and add their separate areas together:

Energy stored = area A + area B + area C

▶ Properties of materials

Materials that are hard to stretch are said to be **stiff**.
Materials that are easy to stretch are described as **flexible**.

Just like the spring on the opposite page, an **elastic** material returns to its original shape when you remove the stretching force. However if you stretch it past its elastic limit, it will be permanently deformed.

Materials that permanently deform are **plastic**.
If you deform a plastic material, it stays in its new shape.

Plastic materials are also:
- **ductile** – they can be drawn out into wires,
- **malleable** – they can be hammered into sheets.

Malleable materials, like lead, are **tough**. When you try to break lead, it deforms plastically. This makes it give way gradually, and absorb a lot of energy before it snaps.

The opposite of tough is **brittle**.
Brittle materials, like glass, do not deform plastically. They do not absorb much energy before they break. They crack or shatter suddenly.

Lead is malleable and tough

▶ Stress

Look at the diagram:

It shows 2 copper wires being stretched by the same weight.
The forces are the same, but the extensions are not.
Can you see why?

The wires have different cross-sectional **areas**.
The thinner wire stretches more.

We say that it has a greater **tensile stress**.
('Tensile' means 'under tension' or 'stretched'.)

The stress, σ, is given by this equation:

$$\text{Stress, } \sigma = \frac{\text{force, } F \text{ (N)}}{\text{cross-sectional area, } A \text{ (m}^2)} \quad \text{or} \quad \sigma = \frac{F}{A}$$

The unit of stress is newton per square metre (N m^{-2}).
Newtons per square metre (N m^{-2}) are called **pascals**.

The pascal, symbol Pa, is also the unit for pressure (see page 20).
Does this mean stress and pressure are the same thing?
No – stress occurs **inside a solid**. Pressure occurs **on a surface**.

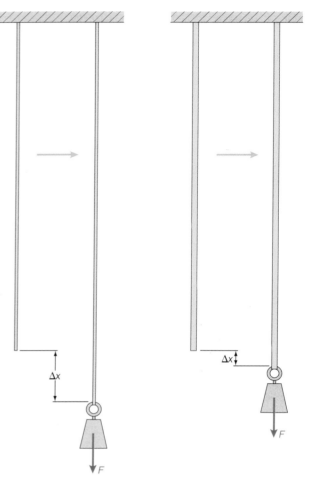

> *Example 3*
> A thin wire has a cross-sectional area of 4×10^{-8} m^2,
> and is stretched by a force of 200 N.
> What is the tensile stress in the wire?
>
> $$\sigma = \frac{F}{A} = \frac{200 \text{ N}}{4 \times 10^{-8} \text{ m}^2} = \underline{5 \times 10^9 \text{ Pa}} \quad (5 \times 10^9 \text{ N m}^{-2})$$

Strength

Look at the cartoon:
Is Phiz's rope strong enough to hold him?

It depends on:
- what the rope is made of,
- how thick the rope is – at its **thinnest** point,
- how heavy Phiz is.

The **ultimate tensile stress** is the measure of strength.
This is the tensile stress when the material breaks or yields.

> *Example 4*
> Nylon has an ultimate tensile stress of 7×10^7 Pa.
> The cross-sectional area of the nylon rope in the diagram
> is 3×10^{-5} m^2.
> Phiz weighs 600 N. Will it hold him?
>
> $$\sigma = \frac{F}{A} = \frac{600 \text{ N}}{3 \times 10^{-5} \text{ m}^2} = 2 \times 10^7 \text{ Pa}$$
>
> This is less than the ultimate tensile stress. He'll be OK.

Phiz goes rock-climbing

▶ Strain

Look at the diagram:

It shows 2 copper wires being stretched by the same weight.
This time, the wires have the **same** cross-sectional area.
The forces are the same, but the extensions are not.
The longer wire stretches twice as much, even though it has
the same tensile stress. Can you see why?

The wire on the right is twice as long to start with.
It stretches by the **same fraction** of its original length.

This fraction is called **tensile strain**.
The strain, ε, is given by this equation:

$$\text{Strain, } \varepsilon = \frac{\text{extension, } \Delta x \text{ (m)}}{\text{original length, } L \text{ (m)}} \quad \text{or} \quad \varepsilon = \frac{\Delta x}{L}$$

Strain has no units. It is just a ratio.

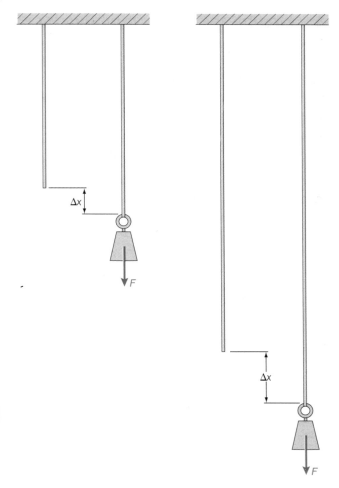

> *Example 5*
> A steel wire of length 2.3 metres stretches by 1.5 millimetres.
> What is the tensile strain?
>
> Extension, $\Delta x = 1.5$ mm $= 1.5 \times 10^{-3}$ m
>
> Strain, $\varepsilon = \dfrac{\Delta x}{L} = \dfrac{1.5 \times 10^{-3} \text{ m}}{2.3 \text{ m}} = \underline{6.5 \times 10^{-4}}$ (2 s.f.)

▶ The Young modulus

When you stretch a wire that obeys Hooke's law,
the force – extension graph is a straight line.
A graph of stress against strain is also a straight line,
because: stress $\propto$ force, and: strain $\propto$ extension.

Look at this stress–strain graph for steel:

Notice how small the strain is. A strain of only 0.01 (1%)
would exceed the elastic limit of a metal!

The **gradient** of the stress–strain graph is σ / ε.
This is called the **Young modulus of elasticity** of the material.
It is given the symbol E. (Be careful – it is not energy!)

$$\text{Young modulus, } E = \frac{\text{stress, } \sigma \text{ (Pa)}}{\text{strain, } \varepsilon \text{ (no units)}} \quad \text{or} \quad E = \frac{\sigma}{\varepsilon}$$

E is measured in pascals (Pa), the same as stress.
It is a measure of how difficult it is to change the shape of
the material. Rubber has a low value, steel has a high value.

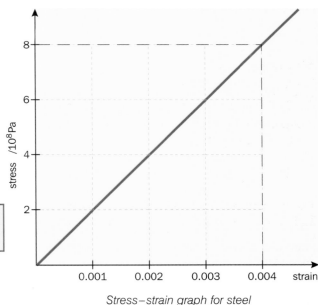

Stress – strain graph for steel

> *Example 6*
> Use the graph shown (for steel) to find the Young modulus of elasticity for steel.
>
> The Young modulus, $E = \dfrac{\text{stress, } \sigma}{\text{strain, } \varepsilon} = $ the gradient of the stress-strain graph $= \dfrac{8 \times 10^8 \text{ Pa}}{0.004} = \underline{2 \times 10^{11} \text{ Pa}}$ (1 s.f.)

▶ Finding the Young modulus for steel

Metals such as steel do not stretch easily. You need a large stress to stretch the wire. To get such a large stress, you need both a very thin wire and a heavy load.

Metals stretch elastically only for very small strains, and you need a very long wire to get measurable extensions.

Look at this picture of a long wire with a heavy load:

It is hard to measure the stress and the strain, because:

1. The large loads could pull the ceiling attachment downwards, so you would be measuring sag, not stretch.
2. The room temperature may change, making the wire expand (stretch) or contract (shrink).
3. To calculate the strain, you have to measure very small extensions, of less than 1 mm.
4. To calculate the stress, you have to measure the diameter of a very thin wire.

The diagram below shows a laboratory method for measuring the stress and strain in a long, thin steel wire:

The wire to be tested has weights added to the bottom, and a *second* wire is attached to the same support.
This *reference* wire holds the measurement scale, and a weight at the bottom keeps this reference wire taut.

This arrangement deals with the 4 difficulties. In order:

1. The scale for measuring extensions is on the reference wire. If the test wire pulls the ceiling downwards, the reference wire and the scale move with it. So the scale measures only the extension, not the sag of the support.
2. If temperature changes make the test wire expand or contract, the reference wire changes in the same way.
3. A **vernier** is used to measure the tiny extensions accurately. The vernier is a second scale on the test wire itself, which is accurate to 0.1 mm. Dividing the extension by the original length gives the strain.
4. You use a **micrometer** to measure the diameter of a thin wire. This is accurate to 0.001 mm. This gives you the cross-sectional area, and you divide the weight of each load (in N) by the area to get the stress.

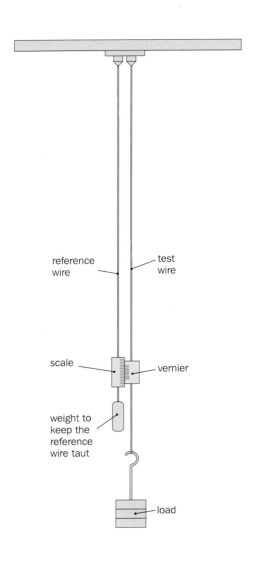

The test wire may not be uniform, so you should measure the diameter of the test wire at several places and take an average. You can then find the average cross-sectional area of the wire, using the average diameter.

You should measure the extension for several different loads.

You should also remove the loads, one at a time, to check that the length goes back to its original value. This is to check that you didn't exceed the elastic limit of the wire.

With the data provided by this experiment, you can plot a stress–strain graph to find the Young modulus of steel.

▷ Stress–strain graphs for different metals

Look at these stress–strain graphs for different mixtures of iron with carbon:

Mixtures of metals are called **alloys**.
Cast iron is a mixture of iron with about 3% carbon.
High-carbon steel contains about 0.3% carbon.
Mild steel has very little carbon – less than about 0.05%.

Notice that the graph for high-carbon steel is steeper than the graph for mild steel.
We say that high-carbon steel is **stiffer** than mild steel, or mild steel is **more flexible** than high-carbon steel.

Can you see that the graph for cast iron stops suddenly, while each of the two steel graphs curve over?
Cast iron is brittle, while most steels are tough.
The steels undergo ductile flow before they break.

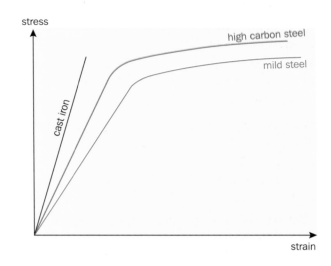

Example 7
The Young modulus of elasticity for cast iron is 2.1×10^{11} Pa.
It snaps when the strain reaches 0.0005.
What is the stress needed to break it? (Assume that it obeys Hooke's law up to its breaking point.)

The Young modulus, $E = \dfrac{\text{stress, } \sigma}{\text{strain, } \varepsilon}$

2.1×10^{11} Pa $= \dfrac{\sigma}{0.0005}$

∴ Stress, $\sigma = 2.1 \times 10^{11}$ Pa $\times$ 0.0005 $ = \underline{1.1 \times 10^8 \text{ Pa}}$

Area under stress–strain graphs

On page 283, you saw that the **area** underneath the graph of force against extension for a spring gives you the potential energy stored in the stretched spring.

What is the meaning of the area under the graph of stress against strain for a metal wire?

From pages 284–285,

$\text{Stress} = \dfrac{\text{force}}{\text{area}}$ and $\text{strain} = \dfrac{\text{extension}}{\text{length}}$

∴ the area under the graph $= $ average stress $\times$ strain

$= \dfrac{\text{average force}}{\text{area}} \times \dfrac{\text{extension}}{\text{length}}$

$= \dfrac{\text{average force} \times \text{extension}}{\text{area} \times \text{length}}$

$= \dfrac{\text{work done}}{\text{volume}}$

since energy stored = work done = force × distance moved

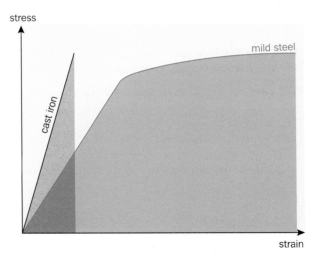

Mild steel is tougher than cast iron

So this area is the **energy stored per unit volume.**

This area is a useful measure of the **toughness** of a metal.
Tougher metals need more energy per unit volume to break them, and so the stress–strain graph up to the breaking strain has a larger area under it.

▶ Density

An old children's riddle asks: *'Which is heavier, a pound of feathers or a pound of lead?'*

People only fall for this if they confuse two different ideas:
- Mass – the amount of matter in an object.
- Density – the amount of matter in a particular volume.

A pound, like a kilogram, is a measure of **mass**.

The **density** of any substance is given by this equation:

$$\text{Density, } \rho \text{ (kg m}^{-3}) = \frac{\text{mass, } m \text{ (kg)}}{\text{volume, } V \text{ (m}^3)} \quad \text{or} \quad \rho = \frac{m}{V}$$

Heavier or denser ?

Although kg m^{-3} is the unit always used in Physics, you may meet density in other units, such as g cm^{-3} or g litre^{-1}.

Example 8

Liquid water has a density of 1000 kg m^{-3}, while ice has a density of 920 kg m^{-3}.
Calculate the volume occupied by 0.25 kg of (a) water, (b) ice.

$$\text{Density, } \rho = \frac{m}{V}$$

a) $1000 \text{ kg m}^{-3} = \dfrac{0.25 \text{ kg}}{V}$

$\therefore \quad V = \dfrac{0.25 \text{ kg}}{1000 \text{ kg m}^{-3}} = 2.5 \times 10^{-4} \text{ m}^3$

b) $920 \text{ kg m}^{-3} = \dfrac{0.25 \text{ kg}}{V}$

$\therefore \quad V = \dfrac{0.25 \text{ kg}}{920 \text{ kg m}^{-3}} = 2.7 \times 10^{-4} \text{ m}^3$

This increase in volume is what makes water pipes burst when they freeze.

▶ Crystal structure

Look at this diagram of a crystalline solid:

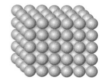

The atoms are placed in a regular arrangement, which is called a **crystalline lattice**.
The first images of crystal lattices were obtained by X-ray diffraction (page 150), but now electron microscopes (page 172) are used.

Now look at any one atom in this crystal:

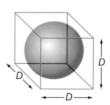

Can you see that you can divide the whole lattice into identical small cubes, each containing one atom, like this?

We can use this idea to calculate the mass of this atom:

Example 9

X-ray and electron-microscope studies show that the diameter of an iron atom is 0.23 nm.
The density of iron is 7800 kg m^{-3}.
Calculate the mass of one iron atom, assuming that the atoms in the crystal are arranged in a regular cubic lattice.

Volume of one atom's 'box' $= D^3 = (0.23 \times 10^{-9} \text{ m})^3 = 1.2 \times 10^{-29} \text{ m}^3$

$$\text{Density, } \rho = \frac{m}{V} \quad \text{so:} \quad 7800 \text{ kg m}^{-3} = \frac{m}{1.2 \times 10^{-29} \text{ m}^3}$$

$\therefore \quad$ Mass of 1 iron atom, $m = 7800 \text{ kg m}^{-3} \times 1.2 \times 10^{-29} \text{ m}^3 = 9.5 \times 10^{-26} \text{ kg}$ (2 s.f.)

▶ Faults in crystals

Look at this simplified diagram of a metal crystal. The atoms are mostly in neat rows, and it looks quite easy for them to move. For example, the left-most vertical column could move up or down along the **slip plane** between it and its neighbour.

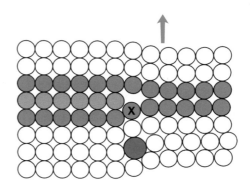

In fact, this slipping cannot happen easily, because you would have to break **all** the bonds joining the slipping atoms to their neighbours. So why is it that some metals, like copper, are ductile?

Look at the odd half-row, coloured red in the top diagram:

The right-hand end of this part-row of atoms is called an **edge dislocation**. The two neighbouring rows, coloured blue, are very distorted near the dislocation. At the end of the red part-row there is slightly more space, so the atoms there can move slightly into new positions.

The second diagram shows what happens when the crystal is put under stress, as shown by the arrow on the diagram.

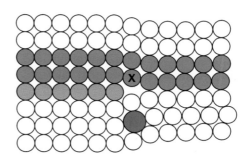

The only atom that has moved much is the one labelled 'X', but because of this the dislocation has moved down one row. In this way, the dislocation can move down to the edge of the crystal. This is how plastic flow occurs in ductile metals, and it reduces the stress in the metal.

In these diagrams, the dislocation would not be able to move much further. This is because the lattice contains a large green 'foreign' atom that will not easily move into a new position.
This metal is an **alloy**, a mixture of different metals. The foreign atoms hinder the movement of dislocations, making the alloy harder and more brittle.

Polycrystalline and amorphous materials

You may know that a diamond is a crystal, but is copper crystalline? Look at this magnified photograph of a copper surface:

Copper is polycrystalline

It shows that copper is made of many tiny **crystal grains**. Many solids, such as metals, consist of very tiny crystals, and these materials are described as *polycrystalline*.

Heating metals affects the size of the crystal grains. If you heat a metal and then cool it *rapidly* – a process called **quenching** – you get very small crystal grains. In a quenched metal, the dislocations cannot move far before they reach the **grain boundary** at the edge of the crystal grain. A dislocation cannot move out of its own crystal, and the absence of plastic flow makes the metal hard and brittle.

In the same way, if you let a hot metal cool *slowly*, large crystal grains are formed. This process is called **annealing**, and it makes the metal malleable and tough.

Glass is amorphous and brittle

Some solids, such as glass, are not crystalline at all. Their atoms are not in a lattice, but randomly placed, as in a liquid. These materials are described as **amorphous**. Glass is brittle, because it doesn't have a crystal lattice for dislocations to move in.

▶ Yielding and breaking

Ductile flow

Metals like copper are *ductile* – they can have large plastic deformations without fracturing.

If you stretch a copper rod, it gets thinner by plastic deformation before it snaps. This is shown in the photo:

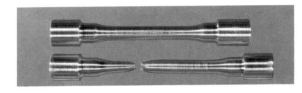
The copper rod 'necked' before it broke

It happens because atoms move, as the dislocations in the crystal structure move, to places of lower stress. The metal becomes thinner when the atoms move away from the stressed part. The stress then increases because the cross-sectional area is now less. This increases the ductile flow and so the metal 'yields' or 'gives' and gets thinner and thinner.

Once plastic deformation starts, atoms will continue to flow without any increase in stress. This stretching under a constant load is called **creep**. The thinning of the rod is called **necking**.

Brittle fracture

Brittle materials like glass cannot flow, so they do not 'neck'. The stress cannot be reduced by the movement of atoms.

The photo shows some stressed plastic viewed in polarised light:

The coloured fringes are 'contours' of lines of equal stress.
Can you see where the stress is greatest?
It is concentrated at the tip of a crack in the plastic. The stress is greater if the crack is deeper or sharper.
Tension will make the crack split open further, which increases the stress even more. The brittle solid then shatters.

Compression and tension in brittle materials

Brittle materials can crack under tension as the cracks deepen, but they are strong in compression, because this closes the cracks.

See how Phiz cuts a glass rod:

He cuts a sharp scratch into the rod where he wants it to break. Then he bends the rod with the scratch on the **outside** of the bend. The rod cracks through cleanly.

If he bends the rod with the cut on the **in**side, it would not break at the cut, because the crack is being compressed.

Work hardening

On page 289, you saw that quenching a heated metal makes the metal hard but brittle. Metals can also become harder if they are bent, stretched or hammered *repeatedly* – this is called **work hardening**.

When you stretch copper wire past its elastic limit, the metal deforms in ductile flow and starts to 'neck,' due to movement of dislocations. This plastic deformation ends when the dislocations become tangled in a 'traffic jam' and they stop each other from moving. This makes the copper wire harder and more brittle, so it suddenly snaps in brittle fracture.

You can use this work hardening to snap thick copper wire: just bend it backwards and forwards many times.
You will feel it suddenly get stiffer and then snap.

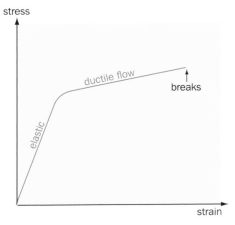
Copper snaps when dislocations cannot move

▶ Polymers

Rubber and polythene are examples of **polymers**.
Polymer molecules consist of very long chains of atoms.

The diagram shows three polymer chains, tangled together
in a random way:

In **rubber**, some chains are joined together by cross-links, shown
in black in this diagram:

When you stretch a rubber band and let it go, the cross-links pull
the chains back into shape. This is why rubber is elastic.

Rubber is a polymer

Look at this **stress–strain graph of rubber**:

Why is it such a strange shape? It has two sections:

- Why is it so easy to stretch a rubber band at the start?

  When you pull it, you are straightening the tangled chains.
  This is quite easy to do, so very large strains are possible.

- Why does the rubber band become stiffer at large strains?

  The chain molecules are now as straight as possible.
  To stretch it any more, you must stretch the atomic bonds.
  This is hard to do, and so the rubber is much stiffer.

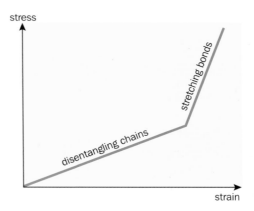

Energy losses in rubber

Look at this **force–extension graph for a rubber band**:

It shows the rubber being stretched (OAB) and then released (BCO).
The graph is a similar shape while it is being stretched and being
released, but the extensions are greater while it is being released.
The straightened chains do not move back easily into place.
The 'release' graph does go back to the origin eventually, as the
cross-links in the rubber 'remember' the original positions of the
chain molecules and pull them back into place.
This delayed-action return of rubber is called **hysteresis**.

Area OABDO shows the work that you do stretching the rubber.
Area OCBDO is the energy given out when the rubber is released.
The difference in energy (OABCO) warms up the rubber.

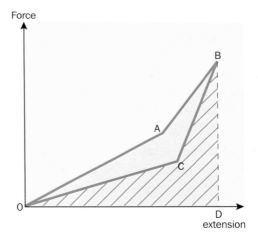

Thermoplastic and thermoset polymers

Artificial polymers, made from oil products, are popular because
they are cheap and do not corrode or rot.

Thermoplastic polymers, like polythene and perspex, have no
cross-links between molecules.
They soften and deform easily when they are warmed, which
makes them ideal for moulding into containers.

Thermoset polymers, such as the melamine used for kitchen worksurfaces and the phenolic resin used for electrical fitments, have
many cross-links between the chains, produced chemically when
the polymer is cast.
Thermosets are rigid and do not soften with heat.

Thermoplastics and thermosets are part of everyday life

▶ Tension and compression

Most of this chapter has been about materials in *tension*. However squashing also produces a change in length. This is not extension but *compression*.

Phiz is painting the ceiling. Look at his plank:

In some places, his weight is stretching the plank. This is tensile stress, and it produces tensile strain.

In some places, his weight is squashing the plank. This is compressive stress, and it produces a compressive strain.

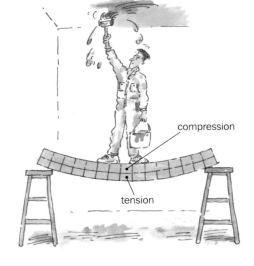

compression

tension

Can you see that his plank is compressed on the top surface where the plank is squashed up? The molecules are closer together.

Can you see that the plank is in tension on the bottom surface where the plank is stretched out? The molecules are farther apart.

If the plank is brittle, it could snap in the middle. **Brittle materials are strong in compression, but they are very weak in tension.**

Stays and struts

Structures are often supported from above by **stays**.

Look at this diagram of a shelf:

The shelf is attached to the wall at the edge marked A, but a wire stay (coloured blue) is fixed to the other edge.

This tension in this wire exerts a force on the shelf. This force can be resolved into two components (see page 14).

The horizontal component (not shown) compresses the shelf inwards. The vertical component holds up the shelf.

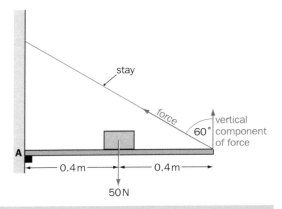

stay

force

60° vertical component of force

A

0.4 m — 0.4 m

50 N

Example 10
Calculate the tension in the wire stay in the diagram above.

The forces are in equilibrium, so there is no resultant moment about any point. (See page 26.)
Taking moments about the end A of the shelf:

Clockwise moment = anti-clockwise moment

$$50 \text{ N} \times 0.4 \text{ m} = \text{vertical component of tension} \times 0.8 \text{ m}$$

$$\therefore \text{ vertical component of tension} = \frac{50 \text{ N} \times 0.4 \text{ m}}{0.8 \text{ m}} = 25 \text{ N}$$

But this vertical component of 25 N is also $= F \times \cos 60° = F \times 0.5$ (See diagram and page 14.)

$$\therefore \text{ The tension in the wire stay, } F = \frac{25 \text{ N}}{0.5} = \underline{50 \text{ N}}$$

Instead of a stay you can use a **strut** underneath the shelf to support it, like this:

Of course, you can't use a wire – a strut has to be rigid. It is in compression.

The force in the compressed strut can be calculated in *exactly the same way* as the force in the stretched stay in Example 10.

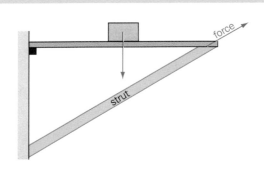

force

strut

Building with stone

Like glass, stone is a very brittle material.

Why have ancient buildings lasted so long without falling?

Stone buildings like the Parthenon in Athens are strong because the stone is kept *in compression* everywhere.
This is done because brittle materials are weak under tension. Under compression they are strong.

The 'span' distance between pillars has to be quite small to stop the concrete going into tension, like the plank under Phiz's feet on the opposite page.

The Parthenon in Athens

In the centuries after the Parthenon was built, people discovered that you can increase a span by using an **arch**.

The stones in the centre of the arch are higher than the ones nearer the edges, so they are partly supported from underneath. The resultant forces from neighbouring stones keep the stones compressed.

If you look inside an old church or cathedral, you will see clever use of arches to span the space and support the roof.

Stone buildings cannot span far without arches

Building with concrete

Concrete is as brittle as stone, but a concrete beam can be made stronger by *reinforcing* it with steel bars. The steel bars are embedded inside the concrete:

Steel is very strong under tension, and does not crack. If the reinforced concrete should begin to crumble underneath, the steel bars will become slightly extended, and carry the tensile stress. This stops the stress from building up in the concrete.

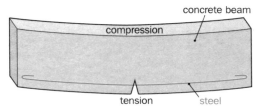
Steel reinforcement stops cracks spreading

Reinforcement can be improved by *pre-stressing* the concrete. The steel bars are put under tension before putting into the wet concrete, and they are kept stretched while the concrete is setting. Once the concrete has hardened, the tension on the steel bars is released, so they contract and pull the concrete inwards.
This means that the concrete beam is already compressed before it is used in building.

When this **pre-stressed reinforced concrete** beam is bent by a load, it does not go into tension at the bottom, like the beam in the diagram above.
Bending will reduce the compression that is built into the beam, but the bottom of the beam still stays compressed.

A pre-stressed reinforced concrete beam can be made much thinner than a simple reinforced concrete beam of the same strength.

Modern engineering projects make extensive use of pre-stressed reinforced concrete.
Just compare a modern building with an old church or cathedral – there is much less building material, and much more space inside.

Modern bridges use pre-stressed concrete

▷ Physics at Work: Composite materials

Tennis rackets

Tennis rackets have always been made of **composite materials**. Composite materials are combinations of different materials. The advantages of one material can compensate for the disadvantages of the other.

Early tennis rackets were made of wood – a natural composite which consists of stiff, brittle fibres of cellulose embedded in a tough 'background material' or 'matrix' called lignin.

Modern rackets contain strong, stiff fibres of carbon. These fibres are much stiffer than cellulose fibres, but they are brittle, and snap easily. So the fibres are embedded in a tough matrix of epoxy resin.

These new rackets are lighter, stronger and much stiffer. They also will not rot or warp like wooden ones.

Composite materials based on wood

The cellulose fibres in wood make it strong in the direction of the grain, but it snaps easily perpendicular to the grain.

Plywood, one of the oldest composites, is a 'sandwich' of several layers of thin wood. The grain in each layer is at right angles to the grain in the layer below. This gives you a thin, strong panel that can be used for a range of surfaces from advertising hoardings to boat hulls.

Chipboard is another common composite material, made from chips or fibres of wood embedded in a matrix of glue. This is cheap, and it is easily machined, because it does not have wood's tendency to split along the grain or to break at irregularities such as knots in the timber.

Chipboard is rather rough in appearance, but it can be made into an attractive and hardwearing material for kitchen worksurfaces by glueing a layer of rigid thermoset polymer on to it. These layered composites, or **laminates**, are modern developments of the layered structure of plywood.

Modern wood-based composites in use

Climbing ropes

This climber needs to have confidence in his rope. If he slips, the rope must stop him falling to his death.

Early climbers used light, strong ropes of hemp. Unfortunately, hemp has a high Young modulus, and it does not deform plastically.
This means that a hemp rope does not stretch much in a fall. The sudden stop meant that the rope injured the falling climber.

A rubber rope would have the opposite problem. It would stretch far too much, and the climber could hit the ground.

Modern climbing ropes are composites: a tough woven sheath protects the nylon core.
The nylon core stretches enough to absorb the kinetic energy of the falling climber, without the deceleration force injuring him.

294

Summary

For elastic materials, $F = k \, \Delta x$ where k is the spring constant of the material.

Energy stored in a stretched spring = area under the force–extension graph = $\frac{1}{2} F \, \Delta x$ (if graph is a straight line)

$$\text{Stress, } \sigma = \frac{\text{force, } F}{\text{cross-sectional area, } A} \qquad \text{Strain, } \varepsilon = \frac{\text{extension, } \Delta x}{\text{original length, } L} \qquad \text{Young modulus, } E = \frac{\text{stress, } \sigma}{\text{strain, } \varepsilon}$$

$$\text{Density, } \rho = \frac{\text{mass, } m}{\text{volume, } V}$$

The behaviour of solid materials can be explained in terms of their atomic structure.
Materials can be classified as crystalline (including polycrystalline), polymeric and amorphous.

▷ Questions

1. Can you complete these sentences?
   a) The extension of a spring is directly .... to the force extending it, providing that the elastic .... has not been exceeded.
   Calculating the area under the force–extension graph gives you the .... potential energy.
   b) Stress = ... ÷ .... and strain = ... ÷ ....
   For an elastic solid, if you divide stress by strain you get the .... modulus.
   c) Copper is .... under large stresses because energy is absorbed when atoms flow in a plastic way. Materials like glass are .... because atoms cannot flow plastically.
   Polymers like rubber or polythene can extend with large strains because their molecules are long ...., which can be straightened out easily.

2. A force of 5.0 N extends a spring 0.10 m.
   a) Calculate its spring constant.
   b) Calculate the elastic potential energy stored in the spring.

3. An experiment with a spring gave the following data:

Force /N	extension /m
0	0
2.0	0.10
4.0	0.21
6.0	0.29
8.0	0.41
10.0	0.50
12.0	0.64
14.0	0.81

   Plot a force–extension graph with this data.
   Use it to find: (a) the spring constant, k,
   b) the energy stored when the spring has been stretched 0.60 metres, and
   c) the elastic limit of the spring used.

4. The cross-sectional area of a rope is $1.4 \times 10^{-4} \, m^2$, and it is stretched by a 7000 N force. Calculate the tensile stress.

5. The ultimate tensile stress of aluminium is $1.0 \times 10^8 \, Pa$. What is the maximum tension that is possible in an aluminium wire of cross-sectional area $2.5 \times 10^{-7} m^2$?

6. A high-carbon steel wire, circular in cross-section, has a diameter of 0.1 mm. What is the force needed to break it? (The ultimate tensile stress of high-carbon steel is $1.0 \times 10^9 \, Pa$.)

7. A rubber cord of original length 0.2 m can be stretched until it is 1.4 m long.
   a) What is its maximum extension?
   b) Calculate its maximum strain.

8. A copper wire has a strain of 0.000 20 under a tensile stress of $2.6 \times 10^7 \, Pa$.
   Calculate the Young modulus of copper.

9. In detective films, bank robbers often make off with piles of gold bars.
   The density of gold is $19\,300 \, kg \, m^{-3}$. A bar measures $0.2 \, m \times 0.08 \, m \times 0.05 \, m$.
   What is its mass? Do you think a robber could escape with 5 gold bars?

10. The molar mass of gold is 0.197 kg (see page 318). Use this data and the density in question 9 to show that the size of a gold atom is about $2.6 \times 10^{-10} \, m$. (Avogadro constant $N_A = 6.0 \times 10^{23} \, mol^{-1}$)

11. Canoes are made from 'fibre-glass,' which is a composite material made from stiff glass fibres embedded in a tough epoxy resin.
    Why is this better than glass or resin alone?

Further questions on page 324.

24 Thermodynamics

Thermodynamics is the study of energy and its effects on a system.

This branch of Physics started with the men who built the earliest steam engines. They wanted to know how to make their engines more efficient.

This helped to develop our ideas about temperature and energy.

In this chapter you will learn about:
- internal energy, heat and work,
- absolute zero, and temperature changes,
- changes of state between solid, liquid and gas.

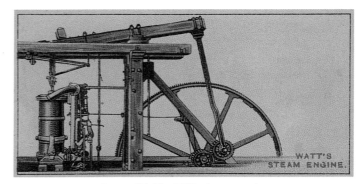

James Watt's 1785 steam engine

Heat and temperature

The words 'hot' and 'heat' can be confusing.

Look at the cartoon, of a bath of water and a burning match:

Think about these two questions:
- Which is hotter, the bath water or the burning match?
- Which needed more energy to heat it?

You can use **hot** to mean 'at a high temperature'.

The match is hotter than the bath water. It is at a higher temperature than the bath water.

But the bath water needed more energy to heat it, because there are many more molecules in it. You couldn't heat up a whole bath of water with just one match!

Some people use the name 'heat energy' to mean 'the energy in a hot object', but a more correct name is **internal energy.**

A burning match is hotter than bath water

Internal energy

Look at the diagram of a hot potato:

The molecules in the hot potato jiggle about vigorously.

They have two types of energy.
The moving molecules have **kinetic energy**, but their movement is disorganised – it changes all the time, randomly.

The **potential energy** of the molecules also changes as they get squeezed closer together and move further apart.

On average, the molecules in a hot potato have more energy than the molecules in a cold potato.

This random molecular energy is called **internal energy**.
The usual symbol for internal energy is U.
It is measured in joules (J).

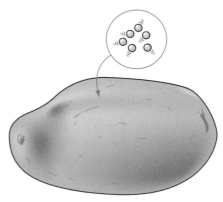

Molecular energy

Systems and Internal Energy

In thermodynamics, what is a **system**?
It is the object or group of objects that we are thinking about.
We often need to think about the transfer of energy in and out of a system.

Look at this diagram of the potato being cooked:

100 joules of energy go into the potato, and 90 joules come out again.
So there is a change in the internal energy U of the potato, because more energy went in than came out.
A change in internal energy has the symbol ΔU.
Δ (delta) means 'a change in'.

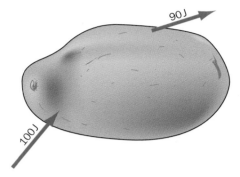

An increase in internal energy

If you put energy into a system, its internal energy increases, so ΔU is positive.
If you take energy out of a system, its internal energy drops, so ΔU is negative.

In the diagram,

Change in internal energy, ΔU = energy input – energy output

$$\Delta U = 100\ \text{J} - 90\ \text{J}$$
$$\therefore \quad \Delta U = +10\ \text{J}$$

Heating and Working

In the diagram, a cold spoon is put into hot tea:

What are the internal energy changes here?
The tea heats the spoon, so the internal energy of the spoon increases.
The spoon cools the tea, so the internal energy of the tea decreases.

Internal energy changes in a cup of tea

Heating is the name of this energy transfer process, when energy moves from a higher temperature to a lower temperature.
In this diagram, the tea is heating the spoon.

Heat is a name for the energy transferred by heating.
The symbol for the energy gained by heating is Q or ΔQ.

Now look at the diagram of Phiz pushing a crate:

The crate and the ground are at the same temperature, but the crate gets hotter as Phiz pushes it.
The internal energy of the crate goes up, due to friction with the ground.

Working is the name for a transfer of energy, usually by a force, when there is no movement of heat.
In this diagram, Phiz is working by pushing the crate against the friction force exerted by the ground.

Hard work!

Work is the name for the energy transferred by working.
The symbol for the energy gained by work is W or ΔW.

Like heat, it is measured in joules.

▶ The 1st Law of Thermodynamics

This is really just the **law of conservation of energy** (see page 64).

If you put energy into a system, its internal energy goes up. The equation is:

> **Change in internal energy, ΔU = heat transfer, ΔQ + work done, ΔW**
> (J)   (J)   (J)

or in symbols: $\boxed{\Delta U = \Delta Q + \Delta W}$

where
ΔQ = heat transferred **into** the system.
ΔW = work done **on** the system.

If ΔQ is positive, the system has **gained** energy by heating.

If ΔW is positive, the system has **gained** energy from work done on the system.

A warning:

*Some Exam Boards and textbooks write the symbol equation differently. They state that ΔW is the work done **by** the system.*

With this rule, if ΔW is positive, the internal energy has dropped. This makes ΔU negative.

The equation is now: $\Delta U = \Delta Q - \Delta W$

Common sense will always tell you what to do. Ask yourself – is the energy going in or out?

Example 1
A hot mug of tea is stirred (very vigorously) so that
5 J of work is done on the tea.
In the same time, 40 joules escape from the mug,
mostly by conduction and convection.
What is the change in internal energy?

$\Delta W = +5\,J$
It is positive, because the water has **gained** this energy in the stirring.

$\Delta Q = -40\,J$
It is negative, because the water has **lost** this energy by cooling.

$\therefore \quad \Delta U = \Delta Q + \Delta W \quad = -40\,J + 5\,J \quad = -35\,J$
The internal energy has decreased by 35 joules.

▶ The 0th Law of Thermodynamics

After naming the First Law of Thermodynamics, physicists realised that there is something more basic, which they called the zero-th law.

Look at the goldfish in their bowl:

The fish are cold-blooded, so they are at the same **temperature** as the water.
Because there is no flow of heat ΔQ, between them, we say that the water and the fish are in **thermal equilibrium**.

This is the 0th (Zero-th) Law:
If two systems are at the same temperature, there is no resultant flow of heat between them.

Thermal equilibrium

▷ The Celsius temperature scale

You are familiar with the Celsius scale of temperature.
Temperatures on this scale are given the symbol θ (theta).

In melting ice, the temperature $\theta = 0\,°\text{C}$.
This is called the **ice point**.
It is a fixed point of the Celsius scale.

The Celsius scale needs a second fixed point.
The steam from boiling water has a temperature $\theta = 100\,°\text{C}$.
This is the other fixed point of the Celsius scale.
It is called the **steam point**.

The diagrams show a typical liquid-in-glass thermometer.
How does this thermometer work?
The liquid expands as the temperature rises.

Where is $50\,°\text{C}$ on the temperature scale?
It will be halfway between the $0\,°\text{C}$ and the $100\,°\text{C}$ marks.

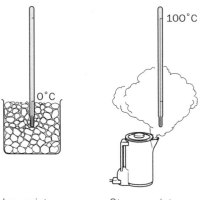

Ice point   *Steam point*

▷ Absolute zero and the Kelvin temperature scale

The Celsius scale starts at the freezing point of water.
This is not a fundamental temperature: it was chosen just for convenience.
There is a more important and fundamental temperature at **−273 °C**.
This is the **absolute zero** of temperature. See also page 316.

It is absolute because it is the lowest possible temperature, and nothing can be cooled below absolute zero.

Absolute zero is the temperature at which the internal energy of **any** system is at the lowest possible value.
You cannot cool a system that cannot lose internal energy!

260 K is not as hot as it sounds!

The **Kelvin temperature scale** starts at absolute zero,
but it has the same size units as the Celsius scale.
So $0\,°\text{C} = 273\,\text{K}$ You just add 273.

> **Temperature in kelvin, T = temperature in degrees Celsius, θ + 273**
> (K)   (°C)

or in symbols: | $T = \theta + 273$ |

- Kelvin temperatures have the symbol T,
  while Celsius temperatures have the symbol θ.
- The symbol for 'degrees kelvin' is K (*not* °K)!

Example 2
Your normal body temperature is $37\,°\text{C}$. What is this on the Kelvin scale?

$T = \theta + 273 = 37\,°\text{C} + 273 = \underline{310\,\text{K}}$

▶ Internal energy and atomic movement

Imagine you have a solid which is being heated steadily by a Bunsen burner.
Here is a graph that shows how its temperature changes:

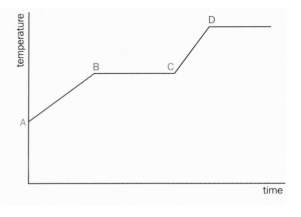

When atoms in a solid are heated, they vibrate on their inter-atomic bonds, rather like masses oscillating on springs.

Between the points marked **A** and **B**, the energy is making the temperature of the solid increase, as the atoms oscillate more vigorously. When the atoms of the solid oscillate more, their average **kinetic** energy goes up.

Can you see what happens between **B** and **C**?
The temperature stops increasing at B, even though heat is still being supplied. This is where the solid **melts** into a liquid.

As the heating continues, the system still absorbs heat, so its internal energy rises. But because the temperature is constant, the average kinetic energy of the atoms is not increasing. The extra energy is breaking bonds between atoms, and this is increasing the average **potential** energy of the atoms.

Can you see what begins to happen at the point marked **C**?
The temperature begins to increase again, because the entire solid has turned into liquid. The energy supplied is increasing the average kinetic energy of the atoms again.

This carries on until the liquid reaches its boiling point, which is the point marked **D**, and the liquid **boils** into a gas. The temperature stays constant until all the liquid has turned into gas.

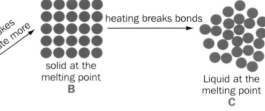

When the internal energy of a system is increased, one of two things can happen:

- it can increase in temperature,
- it can change its state (melt or boil).

The heating curve for a larger sample

The graph at the top of the page could be for a 1 kilogram sample of ice, for example.
But would you get the same graph for a 2 kilogram sample, heated at the same rate?

No – doubling the mass would double the number of atoms in the sample, and it would double the number of inter-atomic bonds.

There will be twice as many atoms to heat up to the melting point, and twice as many bonds to break as the whole sample melts.

Each section of the graph would take twice as long, as shown by the dotted line on this graph:

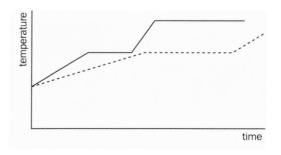

The rise in temperature and change of state both depend on the **mass** of the sample being heated.

▶ Specific Latent Heat

You saw (opposite) that energy is needed to break bonds when a substance melts or boils. This energy is sometimes called **latent heat**. The temperature is constant during this **change of state**.

To calculate the energy needed for a change of state, we use:

Heat transferred, ΔQ = **mass, m** × **specific latent heat capacity, L**	or	**$\Delta Q = mL$**
(J) (kg) (J kg^{-1})		

The specific latent heat, L is the energy needed to change the state of 1 kg of the substance (without changing the temperature).

Latent heat of *fusion* refers to the change from solid to liquid (melting).
Latent heat of *vaporisation* refers to the change from liquid to gas (boiling).

Example 3
The specific latent heat of fusion (melting) of ice is 330 000 J kg^{-1}.
What is the energy needed to melt 0.65 kg of ice?

$\Delta Q = mL$
$= 0.65 \text{ kg} \times 330\ 000 \text{ J kg}^{-1}$
$= 210\ 000 \text{ J}$ (2 s.f.)

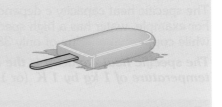

Measuring specific latent heat

Look at the diagram in Example 4 below.
The water is boiling and stays at a constant 100 °C.
Any energy delivered from the heater will turn water into steam.

If you know the power of the heater, then (from page 200) you can use: | **Energy (J) = power (W) × time (s)** |

Example 4
The power of the immersion heater in the diagram is 60 W.
In 5 minutes, the top pan balance reading falls from 282 g to 274 g.
What is the specific latent heat of vaporisation of water?

boiling water

Energy, ΔQ = power × time = 60 W × (5 × 60) s = 18 000 J
Mass of water evaporated = 282 g – 274 g = 8 g = 8 × 10^{-3} kg

$\Delta Q = mL$
$18\ 000 \text{ J} = 8 \times 10^{-3} \text{ kg} \times L$
$L = \dfrac{18\ 000 \text{ J}}{8 \times 10^{-3} \text{ kg}}$ = 2.3 × 10^6 J kg^{-1} (2 s.f.)

This diagram shows a similar method for finding the specific latent heat of fusion (melting):

You fill the funnel with ice at 0 °C, and note the mass of water produced in 5 minutes.

melting ice

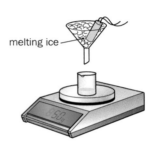

But in a warm room, some ice will melt with energy received from the room, not the heater.
To allow for this you should do the experiment *twice,* for the same length of time: once with the heater *off*, once with it *on*.

The first experiment is a control, which tells you how much ice would have melted by absorbing heat from the room.
The ice actually melted by the heater is the difference between the masses in the two experiments.

▶ Physics at Work

Marathon running

Marathon running takes people to extremes of endurance. What are the risks to the runner?

The human body is only about 20% efficient, and **most** of the energy converted in the muscle raises the internal energy of the body – you get hot!

Unfortunately, the human body cannot tolerate a large rise in temperature. You would die if your body temperature rose by $5\,^{\circ}C$!

Normally, your body keeps its temperature down to $37\,^{\circ}C$ by perspiration, because the evaporation of water reduces your internal energy and cools you.

To keep his temperature below $40\,^{\circ}C$, the runner pants as well as perspires, and the evaporation of water from his skin and in his lungs reduces his internal energy and cools him.

The runner loses so much water over the marathon than there is a real danger of becoming dehydrated, so he must drink regularly during the run.

Thermocouples

How do you measure the temperature of a lava flow? This geologist is using a **thermocouple**, which consists of two wires of **different** metals joined at two junctions. If one junction is hot and the other cold, an e.m.f. (voltage) is produced between them, which depends on the temperature difference.

This provides a good way of measuring temperature, as the hot junction can be small, and on long leads. Metals are good conductors of heat, so the thermocouple responds rapidly.

The cold junction is usually at the temperature of the surroundings, and the temperature of the hot junction may be as high as $1500\,^{\circ}C$ – in this case, the lava was at $1160\,^{\circ}C$.

Heat Pumps

Heat normally moves from a higher temperature to a lower one, but it can be made to move the opposite way – this is what a **heat pump** does.

A refrigerator is a heat pump. It works by evaporating and condensing a liquid.

You can use a heat pump to heat your house by having pipes buried in the ground outside. A liquid enters these pipes through an expansion valve. The drop in pressure makes the liquid evaporate, and the latent heat that it needs is absorbed from the ground that surrounds the pipes.

Once back inside the building, the vapour is compressed, which makes it condense into a liquid and give up its energy, so the house is heated.

If the weather is hot, you can reverse the flow of the liquid, and cool your house. This is exactly how refrigerators remove heat from the cold interior – if you put your hand round the back of a fridge, you will find out where the energy goes to.

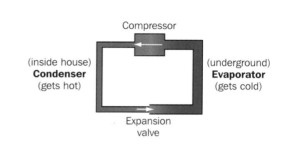

Summary

A system is the entire collection of material whose energy we are measuring.
Zero-th Law of Thermodynamics: systems are in equilibrium if they are at the same temperature.

A system has internal energy U which can be changed by transferring heat Q or by doing work W.
1st Law of Thermodynamics: $\Delta U = \Delta Q + \Delta W$ where Δ means 'a change in'.

Changing temperature: $\Delta U = mc\Delta T$ (or $\Delta Q = mc\Delta T$) where c = specific heat capacity
Changing state: $\Delta Q = mL$ where L = specific latent heat

▶ Questions

1. Can you complete these sentences?
   a) The internal .... of a system can be changed by heating or by ....
   b) On average, the molecules in a hot potato have more .... than the .... in a ...... potato.
   c) When you heat a solid, its temperature rises until it reaches its .... point and it starts to .... This is called a change of ....
   d) The energy is then used to break inter-atomic .... until it is all liquid.
   e) A similar change happens at the .... point, but it requires more .... because all the inter-atomic bonds have to be broken, to become a ....

2. A rubber band is stretched and let go many times. 50 J of work are done on the band in the stretching. While this is happening, 20 J of energy from the band heats the surroundings.
   What are (a) ΔQ, (b) ΔW, (c) ΔU for the system (the rubber band)?

3. The diagram shows a liquid-in-glass thermometer:

   The ice-point ($0\,°C$) and steam-point ($100\,°C$) have been marked.

   What is the temperature when the liquid is at the level marked X?

4. Copy and complete this table:

Temperature /°C	−78		6000
Temperature /K		20	

5. A horseshoe of mass 0.8 kg is heated from $20\,°C$ to $900\,°C$. How much does its internal energy rise? (The specific heat capacity of steel is 470 J kg^{-1} K^{-1}).

6. A kilogram of water falls 807 m (the height of the Angel Falls in Venezuela) and gains 7900 J of kinetic energy.
   Assuming that this is all converted to internal energy in the water, calculate the rise in temperature of the water.
   The specific heat capacity of water is 4200 J kg^{-1} K^{-1}.

7. A kettle contains 1.5 kg of water at $18\,°C$.
   a) How much heat energy is needed to raise the temperature of the water to $100\,°C$?
   b) Assuming no energy is lost to the room, calculate how long this will take if the power rating of the kettle is 2000 W.
   c) What else must you assume in part (b)?
   The specific heat capacity of water is 4200 J kg^{-1} K^{-1}.

8. Once the kettle of question 7 has reached $100\,°C$, the water will boil. Assume the lid has been left off, so the kettle does not switch itself off.
   a) How much energy is needed to boil away 0.5 kg of water?
   The specific latent heat of vaporisation of water, $L = 2.3 \times 10^6$ J kg^{-1}
   b) Assuming no energy is lost, calculate how long this will take if the power rating of the kettle is 2000 W.

9. The specific latent heat of fusion (melting) of ice is 330 000 J kg^{-1}.
   a) Calculate the energy needed to melt 50 grams of ice at its melting point.
   b) A glass contains 0.4 kg of lemonade at $20\,°C$, and 50 grams of ice at $0\,°C$ are put in to cool it. Show that the temperature of the lemonade drops to about $10\,°C$.
   (You can assume that the specific heat capacity of lemonade is 4200 J kg^{-1} K^{-1} and that the energy needed to melt the ice all comes from the lemonade.)

Further questions on page 327.

25 Conduction, Convection, Radiation

If the body temperature of this new-born baby drops, she could become very ill. So this special blanket is used. It greatly reduces the heat she loses to her environment.

In this chapter you will learn about:
- conduction through materials,
- convection currents,
- transfer of energy by radiation.

▷ Conduction

Look at this diagram of a pan:

How does energy get from the hot flame into the water?

The process is **thermal conduction** – conduction of heat.
Energy conducts *into* the bottom of the saucepan from the hot gases on its bottom surface.
Energy conducts *through* the metal base of the saucepan.
Energy conducts *out of* the metal base to the water inside.

Particle movement and thermal conduction

Solids are better conductors of heat than liquids, and much better than gases. Why is this?

In a hot substance, the particles – atoms or molecules – move faster than the particles in a cooler substance. They have more energy.

The more energetic particles pass on some of their energy when they jostle against slower neighbouring particles. This transfer of energy by jostling is thermal conduction.

Particles in a solid are held closely together, and pass on their energy easily, so solids are quite good conductors.

Gas particles can pass on energy only when they collide, which is not often because they travel far apart. So gases are very poor conductors. Air is a poor conductor (a good insulator).

Why are **metals** such good conductors of heat?

Solids, like stone, conduct heat quite well because the jostling atoms pass on their energy efficiently.
However, metals conduct heat much better than stone.
This is because metals contain *free electrons* (see also page 191).
These electrons can move through the solid freely. The electrons gain kinetic energy from collisions with 'hot' atoms and then pass on energy when they collide with 'cold' atoms.

This transfers energy more quickly.

It explains why all metals are good conductors of heat (and electricity).

Conduction

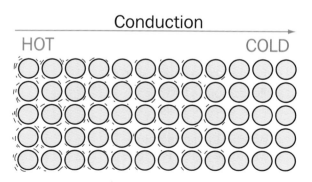

HOT   COLD

306

▶ Convection

'Heat rises' is the everyday description of convection.
Look at the photograph – you can see the hot air rising:

Air near the face is heated by conduction from the warm skin,
and then rises in convection currents.

Convection happens in all fluids – liquids **and** gases –
but what makes hot fluid rise and cold fluid fall?

Look at the photograph of the hot air balloon:

A burner fills the balloon with gas that is much hotter than the
surrounding air. The hot gas is much **less dense** than the colder
air surrounding the balloon.

Because the gases are in the Earth's gravity field, the gas in the
balloon weighs much less than the upthrust force on it (which is
due to the cold air it displaces).
This resultant upward force makes the balloon move upwards,
just like a bubble rising in water.

In exactly the same way, any hot fluid will move upwards, because
it weighs less than the upthrust it experiences from the colder fluid
around it. The colder surrounding fluid will fall.
Why do flames always move upwards?

Cavity wall insulation

The cavity in the wall of a house is full of air. This air is heated up
by conduction through the bricks from the rooms.

This hot air then rises by convection, and transfers energy to
the outside wall, or escapes from the top of the cavity into the
loft space.

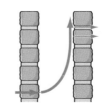

Without insulation in the cavity

One cost-effective way of reducing the heat loss in a house is to
fill the cavity in the walls with a polymer foam or mineral fibre.

Although the solid polymer is quite a good insulator, the important
part of the foam is the trapped air.
Air is a good insulator.
By filling the cavity with low-density foam or loosely-packed fibres,
the air is prevented from moving freely. This greatly reduces
convection in the cavity, reducing the loss of heat from the house.

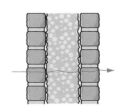

With insulation in the cavity

Example 1
If you warm a mug of coffee in a microwave oven, it can become hot at the top
while remaining cooler below, so you should stir it before drinking.
Why is this?

The microwaves in the oven heat the surface liquid more than the liquid inside
the mug, because it is more exposed. The mug absorbs some of the microwaves
entering the sides.
As the hot surface liquid is less dense, it remains at the top, and is heated more.

Convection only works when you heat the liquid at the bottom.
This is why the heating element in an electric kettle is always at the **bottom**.

▶ Heat radiation

This thermal image shows hot and cool regions of a face:

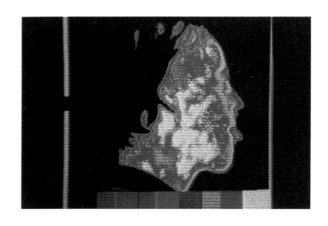

The hottest parts are white, and the coolest are black and blue. The photograph is not taken with visible light, but with **infra-red radiation**. This is also called **heat radiation**, and it is given off by all hot objects.

Look at the picture:

Can you see that the cheeks are giving out most heat, and that the man is poking out his tongue, which is hot?
And that hair reduces radiation from the back of the head?

Absorption and Emission of infra-red radiation

Infra-red radiation is part of the electromagnetic spectrum (see Chapter 15).
The radiation travels in small packets called photons (see page 166).

In infra-red radiation, the photons have energies of about the same size as the energies needed to excite atoms in matter.
When an infra-red photon strikes matter, it can be **absorbed:**

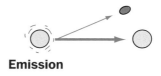

The energy of an absorbed photon is transferred into random energy in an atom of the matter – the internal energy of the matter goes up. It gets hotter.

In exactly the opposite process, an excited atom can **emit** an infra-red photon and become less excited:
So the internal energy of the matter goes down, and it gets cooler.

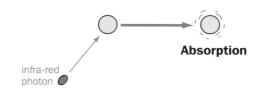

Infra-red and light radiation are similar to each other, because they are adjacent in the electromagnetic spectrum.

That is why matt black objects, which are good absorbers and emitters of visible light, are also good absorbers and emitters of infra-red radiation.

However, infra-red and visible light are not identical: many matt white paints actually absorb infra-red quite well!

Example 2
Greenhouse glass is transparent to visible light, but opaque to infra-red radiation.
How does this explain why greenhouses get hot in sunlight?

Visible light passes through the glass into the greenhouse, and some is absorbed by the soil and plants inside. They get warmer.
As the internal energy of these materials goes up, the excited atoms give off infra-red radiation.
This infra-red radiation has a longer wavelength than visible light.
It does not pass through the glass, but is reflected or absorbed by it.
The greenhouse gets warmer.

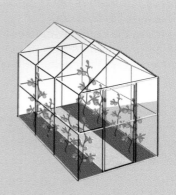

The **greenhouse effect** in our atmosphere is similar.
The 'glass' in this case consists of certain gases, particularly carbon dioxide and methane. These 'greenhouse gases' transmit both the visible light and short-wavelength infra-red radiation that we get from the Sun, but they absorb the long-wavelength infra-red given off by the warm Earth.
This is gradually making our atmosphere hotter and hotter.

▷ Black bodies

The usual meaning of 'black' is 'absorbs visible light'.
But in Physics, a **black body** is one that absorbs all the radiation
that falls on it, at **all** wavelengths. It is a perfect absorber.

A black body is also a perfect emitter or **perfect radiator**.
It emits energy in **all** regions of the electromagnetic spectrum.

One familiar 'black body' looks far from black: our Sun!

Black bodies and temperature

Every black body gives out different amounts of different
wavelengths, depending on its temperature.

The graph shows the spectrum for two black bodies:

The graph shows the energy per second given out by
each m² of surface, at different wavelengths.

The blue line is for a black body at 8000 K. This is the
temperature of the blue-white star Procyon.
The red line is for a black body at 6000 K. This is the
temperature of our Sun.

Why is the blue line so far above the red one?
The blue-white star Procyon is much hotter than our Sun,
so it gives out more energy / second from each m² of surface.

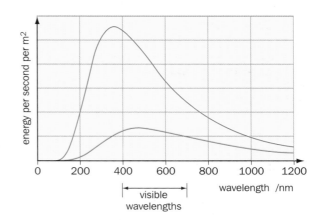

Colour and temperature

Look again at the two black body graphs.

Can you see that the peak of the blue curve, for the star Procyon,
occurs at a **shorter** wavelength than the red curve, for our Sun?

The **peak wavelength** is connected to the temperature by:

Peak wavelength, λ_{max} × Temperature, T = 0.0029
(m)   (K)   (m K)

or $\boxed{\lambda_{max} T = 0.0029 \text{ m K}}$ (Wien's law)

For our Sun, this peak wavelength is close to the middle of
the visible spectrum, while for Procyon it is near the blue end.
So the Sun looks yellow-white, while Procyon looks blue.

Example 3
The star Antares has a surface temperature of 3000 K.
Calculate the peak wavelength in its spectrum,
and explain why Antares looks red.

$\lambda_{max} T = 0.0029 \text{ m K}$ so $\lambda_{max} \times 3000 \text{ K} = 0.0029 \text{ m K}$

$\therefore \lambda_{max} = \dfrac{0.0029 \text{ m K}}{3000 \text{ K}} = 9.7 \times 10^{-7} \text{ m} = \underline{970 \text{ nm}}$

The visible spectrum is roughly between 400 nm and 700 nm.
970 nm is in the infra-red region, so the spectrum of Antares will look
very red, because it will have some red but hardly any blue wavelengths.

▶ Physics at work: Heat transfer

Satellite images

Satellite images are widely used to give us information about land formations. Unfortunately, high clouds often block off visible light, so that a satellite using visible light cannot 'see' the ground below.

However, infra-red radiation emitted by the warm ground passes through the clouds quite easily.

Once the satellite's infra-red detectors have scanned the ground, the data is displayed in an image that is easy to interpret. This satellite picture is a 'false-colour' picture:

The different intensities of infra-red are given different colours. The strongest emitter of infra-red is coloured red, and the weakest is black.

In this photograph, the red areas are mostly green vegetation, which is a good reflector of the incident infra-red from the Sun, while the cool river is black.

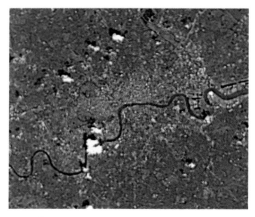

A false-colour infra-red photo of London and the river Thames

Medical thermometers

Until recently, to have your temperature measured in hospital, you would have a mercury-in-glass thermometer stuck in your mouth, and left there for about a minute.
These days, a plastic nozzle is pressed into your ear for a couple of seconds, and it's all done.

Modern thermometers detect the infra-red radiation given off by the ear-drum. This depends on the body temperature, and the instrument has been calibrated to give a reading of the body temperature directly.

Doctors and nurses find this way better because:
* the reading is very quick and easy to do,
* the digital scale is easy to read,
* the temperature of the eardrum is a better measure of the core temperature of the body than the temperature of the mouth,
* it's more hygienic.

Tornadoes

Tornadoes are huge whirlpools of air moving across the land.
They are found in parts of the world where cold air running down from high mountains meets warm, moist air moving inland from warm seas.

One such place is in the southern United States, where cold, dense air falling down from the Rocky Mountains towards the Gulf of Mexico, meets warm, moist air moving in the other direction.

These two currents meet, and the warmer air rises by convection, while the colder air sinks below it.

Due to the Earth's rotation, the rising air currents spiral around each other, rather like water spirals down the plughole of a sink. This causes the tornado.

The speed at which the air moves around the spiral can be as much as 500 km h^{-1}. Although only about a hundred metres across at the base, it contains a large amount of kinetic energy and can cause immense damage.

▶ Physics at work: Heat transfer

Heat sinks for semi-conductors

Modern electronic devices such as microprocessors are made from thin layers of the semi-conducting element silicon.
An electrical current passing through any component with resistance will heat it up, and modern 'chips' contain millions of components. These tiny circuits can be damaged if they get hot, so the device must lose heat so as not to be damaged.

The solution is to attach a **heat sink** to the device.
This uses conduction, convection and radiation to remove as much heat as possible, to keep the device cool.

Conduction

The heat sink is made of aluminium, which is a good thermal conductor. It is fastened firmly to the 'chip'.
To get a good thermal contact between the chip and its heat sink, a 'heat-sink compound' is used. This is a paste that conducts heat (but not electricity).

Convection

The surface area of the heat sink is increased greatly by shaping it into many flat layers. This allows air into contact with more metal, so conducting the heat into the air, and allowing it to convect away.
A fan is often mounted on the heat sink to increase the convection.

Radiation

The heat sink is painted matt black, which makes it emit more infra-red radiation.

Energy movement inside the Sun

Our Sun is an obvious source of infra-red as well as visible light. We can feel its warmth on our skin as well as seeing the light. This energy is generated by nuclear fusion in the core.

But how does this heat energy reach us?

Deep within the Sun, the core is surrounded by high-pressure *plasma* (ionised gas). Energy from the core escapes through this, by radiation of high-energy photons.
These photons are constantly absorbed and re-emitted, in different directions, by the densely packed plasma nuclei. Amazingly, it takes millions of years for the energy to cross this *radiative zone.*

The last part of the journey to the surface is through the *convective zone.* The particles here are no denser than the air in our atmosphere, and heat rises through it in the same way as hot air currents rise on Earth.

At the top of the convective zone, the heat is absorbed by the *photosphere.* The energy is emitted from the photosphere as electromagnetic radiation. This travels through space at the speed of light, and reaches us 8 minutes later.

The outermost layers of the sun, the chromosphere and corona, are too thin to absorb or emit much radiation, although you can see them during a total solar eclipse.

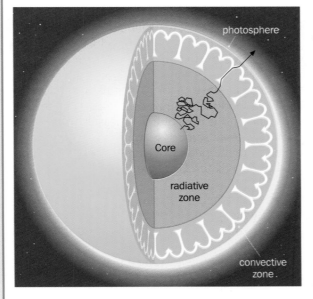

Summary

Heat flows by conduction when atoms or electrons pass on their kinetic energy through collisions.
Convection in fluids occurs when cooler denser fluid sinks under gravity, and hotter less-dense fluid rises.

Infra-red (heat) radiation is emitted by excited atoms or molecules.
Infra-red radiation is usually absorbed and emitted well by surfaces which also absorb and emit light well.
Infra-red photons are of lower energy than visible light photons.

Black bodies are perfect radiators and absorbers of electromagnetic radiation.
The shape of the spectrum emitted from a black body depends on its temperature.
The maximum of the black body spectrum occurs at a wavelength given by: $\lambda_{max} T = 0.0029$ m K

▶ Questions

1. Can you complete these sentences?
   a) When an object is at a greater .... than its surroundings, it will lose heat.

      Solids, particularly metals, transfer heat well by .... due to the easy transfer of .... energy between particles.

      Fluids expand when they are .... and contract when they are ...., and these changes in density cause .... currents.

   b) Atoms in hot materials are moving or vibrating, and they can lose energy by emitting photons of radiant energy. These photons are less energetic than visible light photons, and are found in the .... region of the electromagnetic spectrum.

   c) A perfect radiator and absorber is called a .... body and emits a range of wavelengths over the whole electromagnetic ....

      The peak wavelength produced by a black body at a higher temperature is .... than the peak wavelength of a cooler black body.

2. A metal butter dish and a plastic one are taken from the fridge. Explain why the metal dish feels colder when they are both at the same temperature.

3. Copper is a much better conductor of electricity than iron. Why does this mean that copper is also a much better conductor of heat than iron?

4. Diamond is a very good conductor of heat, but it has no free electrons.
   How is heat conducted through diamond?

5. Explain why wearing several layers of thin clothing is warmer than wearing one layer of thicker material of the same weight.

6. Fresh snow melts slowly in sunshine, but once it has become trodden on and dirty, it melts rapidly.
   Use ideas of conduction, convection and radiation to explain this.

7. As you cool water towards its freezing point, it gets denser until it reaches 4 °C. As you cool it further, the density actually gets *less* until it solidifies. Use convection to explain why, in very cold weather, garden ponds freeze from the top down, allowing fish to survive in the bottom.

8. The very first photograph in this chapter shows a baby wrapped in a thin, shiny material. Explain why this is used.

9. The stars Betelgeuse and Rigel are similar in size, but Betelgeuse appears reddish to the eye, while Rigel is blue-white. What does this tell you about the surface temperatures of the two stars?

10. The metal tungsten, which is used in the filaments of light bulbs, has a melting point of 3683 K. You can assume that the filament in a light bulb is at a temperature a bit lower than that, at 3000 K, and that the filament gives off electromagnetic radiation as a black body. Use $\lambda_{max} T = 0.0029$ m K to calculate the peak wavelength of the radiation given out by a light bulb. How does this explain why the glass of light bulbs gets so hot in use?

11. Cosmology theory suggests that the entire Universe is a black body which has cooled down from the Big Bang and is now at 2.7 K, less than 3 degrees above absolute zero. Use $\lambda_{max} T = 0.0029$ m K to calculate the peak wavelength of the radiation predicted to fill the Universe.

12. Use the wavelength calculated in question 11 to explain why the radiation filling the Universe is called Cosmic Microwave Background Radiation.

13. The hottest stars have surface temperatures of about 1×10^7 K. Use $\lambda_{max} T = 0.0029$ m K to show that these stars emit X-rays.

Further questions on page 325.

26 Gases and Kinetic Theory

A gas has a very low density, because its molecules are widely separated. But how do balloons keep their shape, when the gas molecules are so far apart? Surely the tight skin of the balloon should pull the molecules together?

In this chapter you will learn:
- about the Gas Laws and how to use them,
- about the Kinetic Theory of gases,
- about the Avogadro constant and the Boltzmann constant.

Moving molecules

Steam at atmospheric pressure is about 1000 times *less* dense than liquid water. This is because the molecules are about $10 \times$ further apart in each direction (and $10 \times 10 \times 10 = 1000$).
The molecules are so far apart that inter-molecular forces are negligible.

If the molecules are so far apart, why don't they all just fall to the bottom of their container, like liquid molecules?

The molecules in a gas are constantly moving, and their constant movement spreads them out in their container.

If you use a microscope to look at the particles of soot in smoke, you will see evidence for this movement of gas molecules:

The smoke particles look like tiny spots of light as they reflect light into the microscope. These spots of light continually jiggle about in a *random* way. What is happening?

The molecules of the air are crashing into the dust particles in an irregular manner, and these irregular collisions make the smoke particles jiggle about at random.
This random jiggling is called **Brownian motion**.

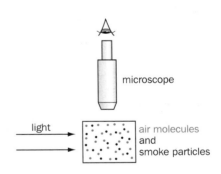

Brownian movement

Molecules and pressure

What do we mean when we talk of 'gas pressure'?

Look at the diagram of gas molecules in a container:

The molecules all move at high speed and their collisions with the walls of the container are *elastic*. The molecules do not lose energy in elastic collisions, so they travel at the same speed afterwards.

During the rebound, the molecules push on the surface.
The rebound produces a force, and the numerous molecular forces over the area of the container surface produce a pressure.

Gas pressure can be measured only by measuring this force produced by gas molecules rebounding from a surface.
All pressure sensors work by measuring this force.

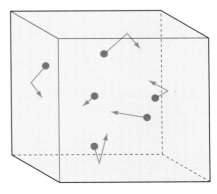

Pressure is caused by molecular collisions

▶ Boyle's law

In Chapter 23 we saw how solids stretch and compress. Robert Boyle wondered whether gases compress in the same way or not.

If you want to squash a solid, you must put it under a compressive stress. If you want to squash a gas, you must put it under pressure. When you try to squash the gas in a balloon into a smaller volume, you can feel that its pressure increases.

But what is the relationship between pressure and volume? This diagram shows the apparatus you can use to find out:

The oil traps a fixed mass of gas – air in this case – inside the glass tube. You can change the pressure and measure the volume. You need to wait a minute between readings to let the air return to room temperature, in order to keep the temperature of the gas constant during the experiment.

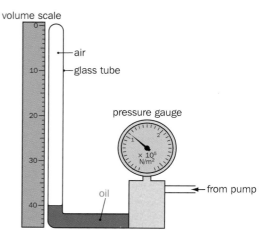

Boyle's law apparatus

The graph shows how the volume changes as the pressure changes for a sample of gas at a **constant** temperature:

Can you see that if you double the pressure from 20 kPa to 40 kPa, the volume is halved, from 4.0 m³ to 2.0 m³?
And if you halve the pressure, the volume doubles.

This is **Boyle's law**:

For a fixed mass of gas, at **constant** temperature,

> **pressure p is inversely proportional to volume V**

Inverse proportion can be written in several different ways, but here are two of the easier ones:

> **pV = constant**   or   **$p_1 V_1 = p_2 V_2$**

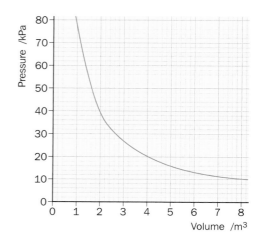

p_1 and V_1 are the pressure and volume before the change;
p_2 and V_2 are the pressure and volume after the change.

You can use either of these ways of writing inverse proportion to calculate the changes of pressure or volume, as this example shows:

Example 1
A helium balloon has a volume of 200 m³ at an atmospheric pressure of 100 kPa.
It rises into the sky, and expands until its volume is 250 m³.
What is atmospheric pressure at this height, assuming that the temperature stays constant?
(You can also assume that the balloon envelope does not exert significant extra pressure on the helium.)

Method 1
Before expanding: $p = 100$ kPa, $V = 200$ m³
$$pV = \text{constant}$$
100 kPa $\times 200$ m³ = constant
So the constant = 20 000 kPa m³

After expanding: $V = 250$ m³ and $p = ?$
$$pV = \text{constant}$$
$p \times 250$ m³ = 20 000 kPa m³
$$\therefore \ p = \frac{20\ 000 \text{ kPa m}^3}{250 \text{ m}^3} = \underline{80 \text{ kPa}} \quad (2 \text{ s.f.})$$

Method 2
Before expanding: $p_1 = 100$ kPa, $V_1 = 200$ m³
After expanding: $V_2 = 250$ m³ and $p_2 = ?$
$$p_1 V_1 = p_2 V_2$$
100 kPa $\times 200$ m³ = $p_2 \times 250$ m³
$$\therefore \ p_2 = \frac{100 \text{ kPa} \times 200 \text{ m}^3}{250 \text{ m}^3}$$
$$= \underline{80 \text{ kPa}} \quad (2 \text{ s.f.})$$

Molecules and Boyle's Law

Look at this diagram of molecules in a cylinder:

The cylinder has a movable piston, and the molecules are bouncing off it.

In the second diagram, the piston has been moved half-way along the cylinder, so that the volume has halved.
What happens to the pressure?

The density of molecules in the cylinder has now doubled, so twice as many of them will hit the piston every second.
This doubles the pressure, exactly as Boyle discovered.

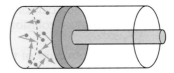

Half the volume, double the pressure

Energy changes during compression

Look at the diagrams of a gas being compressed:

The work done on the gas, ΔW, is given by the equation
$$\Delta W = \text{force} \times \text{distance} \quad \text{(from page 60)}$$

but from page 20: $\text{force} = \text{pressure} \times \text{area} \quad \ldots \ldots (1)$

and the distance the piston moves is given by
$$\text{distance} = \frac{\text{change in volume}}{\text{area}} \quad \ldots \ldots (2)$$

If you multiply equation (1) by equation (2), then area will cancel on the right-hand side, giving you:

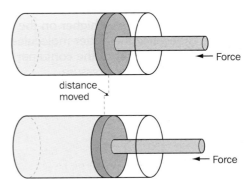

distance
moved

When you compress a gas, you do work on it

Work done, ΔW	**=**	**pressure, p**	**×**	**change in volume, ΔV**
(joules)		(pascals)		(metres^3)

or $\Delta W = p\, \Delta V$

This analysis is only correct if the force stays constant when you move the piston inwards. In practice the pressure, and the force, will change.
The equation is approximately true for **small** changes of pressure, so you can use it in those circumstances.

From the First Law of Thermodynamics (page 298), the internal energy of the gas changes if it gains heat energy or if work is done on it.
If the gas is going to stay at the same temperature, its internal energy must not change.

This means that the gas must **lose** heat when work is done on it during compression if it is to stay at a constant temperature.
That is why you need to wait between measurements in the Boyle's law experiment opposite.

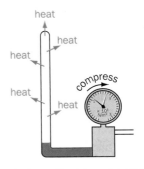

Heat escapes to keep the internal energy constant

Example 2
A cylinder contains gas at a pressure of 2.0×10^5 Pa.
A piston moves inwards, reducing the volume of the gas by 0.012 m^3.
Calculate the work done.
You can ignore the slight change in pressure during the compression.

$$\Delta W = p\, \Delta V$$
$$= 2.0 \times 10^5 \text{ Pa} \times 0.012 \text{ m}^3$$
$$= \underline{2400 \text{ J}} \quad \text{(2 s.f.)}$$

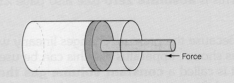

▶ The Avogadro constant and the mole

We use the **Avogadro constant** when counting atoms or molecules.
It defines a quantity of matter called a **mole**.
One mole (abbreviated to mol) contains 6.02×10^{23} particles,
so we say that:

The Avogadro constant, $N_A = 6.02 \times 10^{23}$ **particles mol^{-1}**

Its usual symbol is N_A, but sometimes the symbol L is used.

Atoms and molecules are so very tiny that a real quantity of matter
has a huge number of particles in it.
A mole of water molecules would just fill one tablespoon.
Gas molecules are more spread out, so a mole of air molecules
would fill about 5 balloons.

The mass of one mole of a substance is its **molar mass**.

There are a lot of particles in a mole

Example 4
The molar mass of oxygen is 32 grams mol^{-1}.
Find the mass of one molecule of oxygen.

One mole of oxygen molecules has a mass of 32 grams = 0.032 kg
So: one mole contains 6.02×10^{23} molecules and has a mass of 0.032 kg

∴ the mass of one molecule $= \dfrac{0.032 \text{ kg}}{6.02 \times 10^{23}} = \underline{5.3 \times 10^{-26} \text{ kg}}$ (2 s.f.)

When measuring the quantity of gas for calculations, do not use the
mass in kg. Make sure you always use the number of moles, n.

▶ The ideal gas equation

What happens if you change the pressure and the volume and
the temperature of a sample of gas?

If you increase the temperature of the gas, that would make the
volume increase. But if you increase the pressure, Boyle's law
predicts that the volume would decrease.

To predict what happens when all three variables change, you need
to use the **ideal gas equation**:

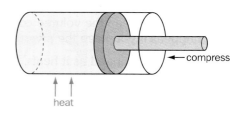

Changing pressure, volume and temperature

pressure	×	**volume**	=	n	×	**a constant, R**	×	**temperature, T**
(Pa)		(m^3)		(mol)		(J K^{-1} mol^{-1})		(K)

or $p\,V = n\,R\,T$

R, the **gas constant**, is the same for all gases = 8.31 J K^{-1} mol^{-1}. **n** is the number of moles of the gas.

Example 5
A helium gas cylinder is 0.200 m^3 in volume, and contains 50.0 mol of gas at room temperature of 293 K.
What is the pressure in the cylinder? (You can assume that helium is an ideal gas.)

$$p\,V = n\,R\,T$$

∴ $p \times 0.200 \text{ m}^3 = 50.0 \text{ mol} \times 8.31 \text{ J K}^{-1} \text{ mol}^{-1} \times 293 \text{ K} = 121\,700 \text{ J}$

∴ $p = \dfrac{121\,700 \text{ J}}{0.200 \text{ m}^3} = \underline{6.09 \times 10^5 \text{ Pa}}$ (3 s.f.)

▷ Kinetic theory

Kinetic theory is about the movement of gas molecules.

When talking about the molecules in an *ideal* gas, we assume that:

- they are perfectly elastic, so they bounce off the container and off each other without losing any kinetic energy,
- they exert forces on each other only when they collide,
- they are so tiny they take up no space at all.

Real gases do not meet these conditions, although under most conditions the collisions are perfectly elastic.
When the molecules in real gases get close, they do exert attractive forces on each other. This is why they condense.
In real gases, the molecules do take up some space and you cannot ignore their volume at high pressures.

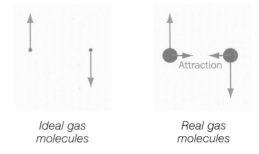

Ideal gas molecules   *Real gas molecules*

Moving molecules and gas pressure

How does kinetic theory account for pressure?
Look at these 'before-and-after' diagrams of a molecule in a box:

In the first diagram, the molecule is heading for the wall.
In the second part of the diagram, it has rebounded, and is going away.
This is because the wall has decelerated the molecule to a stop, and then accelerated it in the opposite direction to the same speed.

The wall of the box has pushed the particle to the right to produce this acceleration, and so the molecule must have pushed the wall to the left with the same force, by Newton's Third Law (page 48).

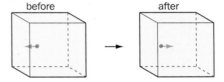

Force due to a molecular collision

Now look at the next diagram, with a *more massive* molecule:
Can you see that there is a larger force here?
The acceleration is the same, but the mass is bigger.
A bigger mass needs a larger force to accelerate it (page 47).

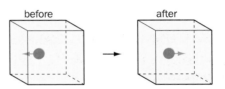

A larger molecule, so a bigger force

The third diagram has a *faster* molecule:
When this rebounds, the change in velocity is greater.
This means the molecule accelerates more when it rebounds, and so this needs a bigger force.
The faster molecule will also hit the wall more often.

There are many molecules in a container of gas, and all the tiny forces on the wall add up to give the total force.
The pressure of the gas on this wall is this total force divided by the area of the wall, and the same is true for each wall of the container.

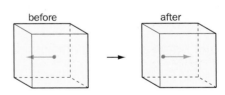

A faster molecule, so a bigger force

This shows us that the *pressure* of a gas in a given volume depends on 3 factors:

- the *mass* of the molecules,
- the speed of the molecules (this has 2 effects, see above, so the total effect depends upon the *speed squared*),
- *how many* molecules there are in the container.

On the next page these 3 factors are combined into a formula.

▶ An ideal gas – the theoretical equation

Using the 3 factors discussed on the previous page, it can be shown that:

where:

$$pV = \frac{1}{3} N m c^2$$

p is the pressure of the gas (Pa),   **V** is the volume of the gas (m³),

N is the number of molecules,   **m** is the mass of one molecule (kg),

c is an average molecular speed (m s⁻¹).

Example 6

A mole of air molecules at room temperature and a pressure of 1.0×10^5 Pa has a volume of 0.024 m³.
How fast do these air molecules move?   (The average mass of an air molecule is 4.8×10^{-26} kg.)

The Avogadro constant, $N_A = 6.0 \times 10^{23}$ molecules mol⁻¹, so $N = 6.0 \times 10^{23}$

$$p V = \frac{1}{3} N m c^2$$

$$1.0 \times 10^5 \text{ Pa} \times 0.024 \text{ m}^3 = \frac{6.0 \times 10^{23} \times 4.8 \times 10^{-26} \text{ kg} \times c^2}{3}$$

$$2400 = 0.0096 \times c^2$$

$$c^2 = \frac{2400}{0.0096} = 250\ 000$$

so the average molecular speed, $c = \sqrt{250\ 000 \text{ m}^2 \text{ s}^{-2}} = \underline{500 \text{ m s}^{-1}}$ (2 s.f.)   (1000 mph)

This is a surprisingly fast result. Can we believe it?

Yes – **sound waves** travel in air at a speed of 340 m s⁻¹,
which is of the same order of magnitude as 500 m s⁻¹.

The moving air molecules carry the sound wave, just like
the runners in a relay race carry the baton.

The baton cannot move faster than the runners, because
the time taken to hand over the baton slows it down.
In the same way, a sound wave travels a little slower than
the air molecules that carry the sound wave.

Sound travelling through air is a molecular relay race.

Mass and density

This gas equation can be rearranged to get: $p = \frac{1}{3} \frac{N m}{V} c^2$

But: $\dfrac{N m}{V} = \dfrac{\text{number of molecules} \times \text{mass of one molecule}}{\text{volume of the gas}} = \dfrac{\text{total mass of the gas}}{\text{volume of the gas}} = \textbf{density}$ of the gas, ρ

so we can re-write this ideal gas equation as: $\boxed{p = \frac{1}{3} \rho c^2}$

Example 7

At normal room temperature and pressure, the density of air is 1.2 kg m⁻³,
and the speed of the molecules is 500 m s⁻¹. What is the pressure?

$$p = \frac{1}{3} \rho c^2 = \frac{1.2 \text{ kg m}^{-3} \times (500 \text{ m s}^{-1})^2}{3} = \frac{1.2 \text{ kg m}^{-3} \times 250\ 000 \text{ m}^2 \text{ s}^{-2}}{3} = 100\ 000 \text{ Pa}   (2 \text{ s.f.})$$

This agrees with the 1.0×10^5 Pa in Example 6.

R.m.s. molecular speed

The molecules in a gas do not all travel at the same speed, just as the runners in a race do not all run equally fast.
The equation opposite refers to 'an average molecular speed.' But what average should be used?

The average value of molecular speed c that we use is not the mean, but a **root-mean-square** (r.m.s.) average. This is the square root of the average (mean) of the squares of the speeds!

This example shows you how to calculate the r.m.s. speed.

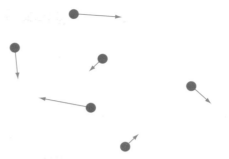

The molecules of a gas have different speeds

Example 8
Four molecules have speeds of 300, 400, 500 and 600 m s^{-1}.
Calculate (a) the mean speed (average speed), and (b) the r.m.s. speed.   Are they the same?

(a) Mean speed $= \dfrac{300 + 400 + 500 + 600}{4} = 450$ m s^{-1}.

(b) To find the r.m.s. speed, you must first find the mean of the squares of the speeds.

$$\text{Mean square speed} = \frac{300^2 + 400^2 + 500^2 + 600^2 \text{ m}^2 \text{ s}^{-2}}{4} = \frac{90\,000 + 160\,000 + 250\,000 + 360\,000 \text{ m}^2 \text{ s}^{-2}}{4}$$

$$= \frac{860\,000 \text{ m}^2 \text{ s}^{-2}}{4} = 215\,000 \text{ m}^2 \text{ s}^{-2}$$

The r.m.s. speed is the **square root** of the mean square speed, so
R.m.s. speed $= \sqrt{215\,000 \text{ m}^2 \text{ s}^{-2}} = \underline{460 \text{ m s}^{-1}}$ (2 s.f.)   The mean speed is less than the r.m.s. value.

In a real sample of gas, the difference is much bigger. In Example 6, you saw that the r.m.s. speed of air molecules at room temperature is 500 m s^{-1}. The mean speed of those molecules is much less: 390 m s^{-1}.

> *Different examination boards write the mean square speed in different ways. For example $<c^2>$ or $\overline{c^2}$*
>
> *We have just used c^2 here, to keep the equations simpler.*

▶ Kinetic energy and the Boltzmann constant, k

The theoretical equation for an ideal gas (opposite) and the ideal gas equation (page 318) both give you an equation with pV as its subject:

For one mole of gas, $pV = \dfrac{1}{3} N_A m c^2$ and $pV = RT$

You can combine these to give: $\dfrac{1}{2} m c^2 = \dfrac{3RT}{2 N_A} = \dfrac{3}{2} kT$

where k is the **Boltzmann constant**.
This is the gas constant R divided by the Avogadro constant N_A:

> Boltzmann constant, $k = \dfrac{R, \text{ the Gas constant}}{N_A, \text{ Avogadro constant}}$

But: $\dfrac{1}{2} m c^2$ is the **mean kinetic energy** of a gas molecule, so:

Mean kinetic energy of a gas molecule $= \dfrac{3}{2} \times$ the Boltzmann constant, $k \times$ temperature, T (joules) (J K^{-1}) (kelvins)	or	$E_k = \dfrac{3}{2} kT$

So the temperature of a gas is a measure of the average kinetic energy of its particles (see also page 300).

Example 9
Calculate the mean kinetic energy of a gas molecule at 288 K.
The Boltzmann constant k is 1.38×10^{-23} J K^{-1}.

Average kinetic energy $= \dfrac{3}{2} kT = 1.5 \times 1.38 \times 10^{-23}$ J K^{-1} $\times$ 288 K $= \underline{5.96 \times 10^{-21} \text{ J}}$ (3 s.f.)

▶ Physics at Work: Gases

Helium gas in the atmosphere

Why is there hardly any helium in our atmosphere, and none at all on the Moon or the planet Mercury, while the giant planets like Saturn and Jupiter have large proportions of helium?
Although it is thought that the outer planets always had more helium than the inner planets, you would expect to find helium throughout the whole Solar System.

At the higher temperatures of the inner planets, the light helium molecules move very rapidly.
The faster molecules have enough kinetic energy to escape the weaker gravitational pull of the inner planets, and so all the helium gradually leaks away.

The outer planets are much more massive and are very cold. The helium molecules are slower and cannot escape the stronger gravitational fields.

Saturn and Earth (not to scale)

Scuba diving

In normal breathing, you need about 10 to 20 litres of air every minute. Scuba (Self-Contained Underwater Breathing Apparatus) allows divers to remain under water for many minutes.
A typical Scuba gas cylinder holds 10 litres of gas at 200 times atmospheric pressure.
Boyle's law shows that at ordinary atmospheric pressure this becomes 2000 litres – enough for over an hour of diving.

As the diver goes deeper, the surrounding pressure increases. The air breathed by the diver is at that same higher pressure. At high pressures, the nitrogen dissolves in the blood, and can produce nitrogen narcosis, which is a hazard for divers. For this reason, divers often use air tanks with higher proportions of oxygen and less nitrogen than ordinary air.

Divers need a good supply of breathable gas

Hot-air balloons

Hot-air ballooning is a popular sport, but how can a heavy canopy, with basket and balloonists, be lifted by air alone?

A floating balloon, like any floating object, is the same average density as the surrounding fluid.
The hot air in the balloon is at an average temperature of 150 °C or 423 K, which is about $1\frac{1}{2}$ times the absolute temperature of the surrounding air.
At this higher temperature, the volume of every kilogram of gas will be $1\frac{1}{2}$ times bigger than the air outside, as the pressure is the same.

This means it has a lower density, and the air in a balloon can weigh about 10 000 N *less* than the same volume of cold air.

This means that the balloon can lift 10 000 N (about 1 tonne) – enough to lift the canopy, basket, burner and balloonists.

Hot air is less dense than cold air

Summary

Gas molecules are constantly moving, and exert pressure by collisions with the container walls.

For a fixed mass of gas at constant temperature, pV is constant (Boyle's Law) so: $p_1 V_1 = p_2 V_2$
For a small change in volume ΔV, at constant temperature, the work done $\Delta W = p \, \Delta V$

In all calculations with gases, the absolute (kelvin) temperature scale is used, when

$$\frac{p_1}{T_1} = \frac{p_2}{T_2} \text{ at constant volume} \qquad \frac{V_1}{T_1} = \frac{V_2}{T_2} \text{ at constant pressure} \qquad \text{so:} \qquad \frac{p_1 V_1}{T_1} = \frac{p_2 V_2}{T_2}$$

A mole of any substance contains 6.02×10^{23} particles. For n moles of an ideal gas, $pV = nRT$
The molecules in a gas have different speeds. The r.m.s. speed c is the value used in calculations.

For N ideal gas molecules, of r.m.s. speed c, each of mass m, $\quad pV = \frac{1}{3} N m c^2 \quad$ and $\quad p = \frac{1}{3} \rho c^2$
where ρ is the density of the gas.

The mean kinetic energy of a gas molecule, $\frac{1}{2} mc^2 = \frac{3}{2} kT$. $\qquad$ Boltzmann constant, $k = \dfrac{R, \text{ the Gas constant}}{N_A, \text{ Avogadro constant}}$

▶ Questions

1. Can you complete these sentences?
   a) Gases are much less dense than liquids or ....
      because in a gas the .... are widely separated.
      Brownian motion gives us evidence for the
      movement of .... The collision of gas molecules
      with the surfaces of the container causes ....
   b) If the temperature does not change, the pressure of
      the gas is .... proportional to the volume of the
      container. This is ....'s law.
   c) If the temperature also changes, you can use the
      .... gas equation $pV = nRT$ where R is the ....
      constant, and n is the number of ....
   d) To calculate the average kinetic energy of gas
      molecules, you need their .... speed.
      This kinetic energy is directly proportional to the
      temperature in ....

2. A fixed mass of gas at a constant temperature has a
   pressure of 2000 Pa and a volume of 0.02 m³.
   It is compressed until the volume is 0.005 m³.
   What is its new pressure?

3. A gas expands at a constant pressure of 1.0×10^5 Pa.
   Its volume increases from 0.1 m³ to 0.15 m³.
   How much work is done in the expansion?

4. At a temperature of 200 K, the pressure of air in a
   flask is 100 kPa. What will the pressure be at a
   temperature of 300 K? You can assume that the
   volume of the flask is constant.

5. At a temperature of 200 K, the volume of a sample of
   gas in a cylinder with a smoothly fitting piston is
   0.0024 m³. The cylinder is heated while allowing the
   gas to expand at constant pressure. Calculate the
   volume of the gas at a temperature of 300 K.

6. The molar mass of helium is 0.004 kg mol⁻¹.
   How many molecules of helium are there in 1 kg?
   (Avogadro constant $N_A = 6.0 \times 10^{23}$ mol⁻¹)

7. A room measures 4 m × 5 m × 2.5 m.
   a) Find the volume of air in the room, and calculate
      its mass. The density of air = 1.2 kg m⁻³.
   b) The average molar mass of air is 0.030 kg.
      How many moles of air are there in the room?

8. An air cylinder for a scuba diver contains 150 moles
   of air at 15 °C. The cylinder has a volume of
   0.012 m³. (The gas constant $R = 8.3$ J K⁻¹ mol⁻¹.)
   a) Calculate the pressure in the air cylinder.
   b) Calculate the volume that the gas will have when
      it is all released at atmospheric pressure of
      100 kPa and a temperature of 25 °C.

9. A tiny gas sample has 6 molecules with speeds 200,
   205, 210, 220, 230 and 245 m s⁻¹. Calculate the
   mean speed and the r.m.s. speed of the molecules.

10. A mole of hydrogen molecules, each of mass
    3.3×10^{-27} kg, are contained in a cylinder of volume
    0.05 m³. The molecules have an r.m.s. speed of
    800 m s⁻¹. Calculate the pressure of the gas.
    (Avogadro constant $N_A = 6.0 \times 10^{23}$ mol⁻¹)

11. Helium at atmospheric pressure of 100 kPa has a
    density of 0.17 kg m⁻³ at 273 K.
    a) Calculate the r.m.s. speed of the molecules.
    b) At the same temperature and pressure, the density
       of air is 1.2 kg m⁻³. What can you say about the
       speeds of sound in the two gases?

Further questions on pages 325–326.

Further questions on matter and materials

▶ Solids

1. Materials are often described as being *crystalline*, *polymeric* or *amorphous*.
Explain the meaning of the terms in italics and name one example of each type of material.   [6]   (AQA)

2. The table and graph show the properties of TWO materials A and B.

Material	Young modulus /10^{10} Pa	Ultimate tensile stress /10^8 Pa	Nature
A			
B	0.34	3.2	brittle

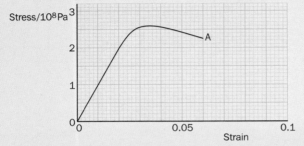

a) Use the graph to complete the table for A. [3]
b) Use the table to draw a graph showing the behaviour of material B.   [2]   (Edex)

3. a) The Young modulus is defined as the ratio of *tensile stress* to *tensile strain*. Explain what is meant by the two terms in italics.   [3]
   b) A long wire is suspended vertically and a load of 10 N is attached to its lower end. The extension of the wire is measured accurately. In order to obtain a value for the Young modulus of the wire's material two more quantities must be measured. State what these are and in each case indicate how an accurate measurement might be made. [4]
   c) Sketch a graph which shows how stress and strain are related for a ductile material.   [2]   (AQA)

4. The diagram shows the stress–strain graph for a sample of steel up to the point of fracture.

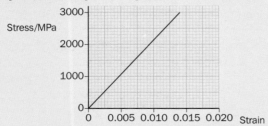

a) Use the graph to find the Young modulus of steel and the ultimate tensile strength of steel. [2]
b) A cable, consisting of 7 strands each of cross-sectional area 2.5×10^{-6} m^2 and length 12 m, is to be made from this steel. Find the force at which the cable is expected to break, the maximum extension of the cable and the elastic strain energy of the cable at maximum extension. [5]   (OCR)

5. a) Draw a diagram to illustrate a dislocation in the lattice of a single crystal free from any other defects. By referring to your diagram, explain how the motion of a dislocation can lead to the plastic deformation of such a crystal.   [5]
   The variation of load with extension for a specimen may be observed by slowly increasing the extension and recording the corresponding load. The graph illustrates the result of such a test for a steel wire.

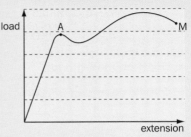

b) On a copy of the graph, draw a line showing what would have happened if the applied load had been gradually reduced to zero after reaching about 90% of the maximum value.   [2]
   c) Explain why, as the extension continues to increase, there is a reduction in load at A. Name the type of fracture occurring at point M. [3] (AQA)

6. The graph shows the results of an experiment in which stretching force is plotted against extension for a steel cylinder having an original length of 27.2 mm and an initial cross-sectional area of 1.8×10^{-5} m^2. The specimen is extended steadily to **X**, the load reduced to zero at **Y** and then reapplied. The extension is then gradually increased until the specimen breaks.

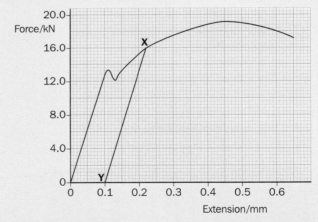

a) State Hooke's law. Sketch the graph and indicate the limit of proportionality, P.   [2]
b) Calculate the Young modulus for the specimen in the region where Hooke's law is obeyed. [2]
c) Calculate the energy stored in the specimen when the extension is 0.10 mm.   [2]
d) Explain in terms of the structure of the material why the specimen does not return to its original length when unloaded along **XY**.   [2]   (AQA)

▶ Thermal transfer

7. The diagram shows a simple solar water-heating system. Energy from the Sun falls on the solar panel. This energy is used to increase the internal energy of water flowing through a system of metal pipes in the panel. Water is pumped around the system so that a store of hot water is made available in the tank.

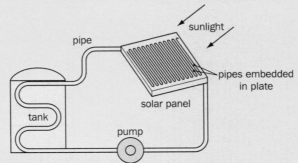

a) State what is meant by *internal energy*.   [2]
b) Describe briefly how energy is transferred by *conduction*.   [3]
c) State where the conduction mechanism is involved in the operation of the solar water-heating system.   [1]
d) Explain why water has to be pumped around the system instead of using convection.   [2] (AQA)

8. a) State how energy is transferred from the Sun to the Earth.   [1]
b) In Britain, on average, 200 W fall on each square metre of the Earth's surface during daylight hours. Estimate the total energy available from the Sun per square metre of land in Britain each year. [3]
c) Miscanthus (elephant grass) can be grown as a biofuel. It shows annual yields as high as 12 tonnes per hectare (10^4 m^2). Given that 1 tonne of miscanthus yields 1.7×10^{10} J when burnt, calculate the maximum annual energy yield per square metre of a miscanthus crop. [2]
d) Give one reason for the difference between your answers to (b) and (c).   [1] (Edex)

9. The diagram shows a simplified arrangement of an air-cooled motor-cycle engine.

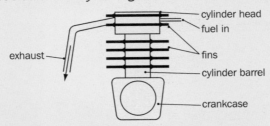

Describe the part played by *thermal conduction*, *convection* and *radiation* in cooling the engine when operating. Indicate how an engine could be designed so as to increase the efficiency of each of these processes.   [6] (AQA)

▶ Gases & Thermodynamics

10. With reference to the appropriate physical principles, explain the following in terms of the motion of the gas molecules.
a) A gas in a container exerts a pressure on the container walls.   [4]
b) The pressure increases if the temperature of a gas is increased, keeping the mass and volume constant.   [3]
c) State what is meant by the root mean square speed of the molecules of a gas. Calculate the r.m.s. speed of four molecules travelling at speeds of 400, 450, 500 and 550 m s^{-1}, respectively. [2]
d) For a constant mass of gas, explain how the r.m.s. speed of molecules changes, if at all, when the gas expands at constant temperature.   [2] (AQA)

11. a) The air pressure inside a constant volume gas thermometer is 1.010×10^5 Pa at the ice point and 1.600×10^5 Pa at the steam point. Determine the Celsius temperature when the pressure of the gas is 1.250×10^5 Pa.   [2]
b) The graph shows the variations of pressure with temperature for two constant volume gas thermometers A and B that contain the same volume of gas.

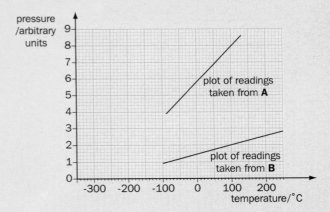

i) Show that both graphs extrapolate to the same intercept on the temperature axis and determine that temperature.   [1]
ii) A is known to contain 0.024 mol of gas. Determine the number of moles of gas in B.   [4] (AQA)

12. a) Write down the equation of state for *n* moles of an ideal gas. What is meant by an *ideal gas*? [3]
b) Calculate the mass of argon filling an electric light bulb of volume 8.2×10^{-5} m^3 if the pressure inside the light bulb is 90 kPa and the temperature of the gas is 340 K.
Standard pressure = 100 kPa
Standard temperature = 273 K
Density of argon at standard temperature and pressure = 1.56 kg m^{-3} [4] (AQA)

Further questions on matter and materials

13. 0.80 mol of an ideal gas is enclosed in a cylinder by a frictionless piston. Conditions are such that the gas expands at constant pressure (A to B); it is then compressed at constant temperature (B to C) until its volume returns to the original value. These changes are shown, with the relevant numerical data, on the graph. (Molar gas constant = 8.31 J K⁻¹ mol⁻¹)

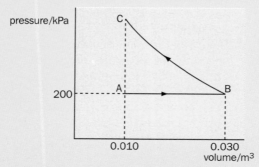

a) Show that the temperature of the gas at A is 300 K. [2]
b) Calculate the temperature of the gas at B. [2]
c) Calculate the pressure of the gas at C. [2]
d) Defining the terms used in your explanations, explain how the first law of thermodynamics applies to the changes from (A to B), and from (B to C). [5]
e) Use the graph to estimate the change in internal energy of the gas when it is returned from C to A at constant volume. Explain whether this is an increase or a decrease. [4] (AQA)

14. A 24 W filament lamp has been switched on for some time. In this situation the first law of thermodynamics, represented by the equation $\Delta U = \Delta Q + \Delta W$, may be applied to the lamp. State and explain the value of each of the terms in the equation during a period of two seconds of the lamp's operation. [6]
Typically, filament lamps have an efficiency of only a few percent. Explain what this means and how it is consistent with the law of conservation of energy. [2] (Edex)

15. a) Explain what is meant by the concept of *work*. Show that the work W done by a gas when it expands by an amount ΔV against a constant pressure p is given by $W = p\Delta V$. [5]
b) A fixed mass of oxygen at a pressure of 101 kPa occupies a volume of 1.40 m³ at 274 K and 1.54 m³ at 300 K. Calculate the work done to expand the gas against the external pressure. [2]
c) Define *internal energy* and state the *first law of thermodynamics*. State the energy conversion taking place when a gas is heated at constant volume. Explain why, when the temperature of a gas is raised, more heat energy is required when the gas is held at constant pressure than when its volume is kept constant. [7] (OCR)

16. An ideal gas is contained in a hollow cylinder, sealed at one end, with a frictionless piston at the other as in the diagram. The volume of the trapped gas is V_0 when its pressure is p_0 and its temperature T_0.

The system is used as a heat engine carrying out the following cycle of changes ABCDA. The gas is:
from A to B, compressed at constant temperature to half its initial volume V_0,
from B to C, heated at constant volume to 1.5 times its initial temperature T_0,
from C to D, expanded at constant temperature back to its initial volume
from D to A, cooled at constant volume back to its initial temperature.
a) Find the values of the pressure p of the gas at the end of each of the stages of the cycle in terms of the initial pressure p_0. Give your reasoning. [3]
b) Draw a pV diagram showing the cycle of operation of the engine. Mark the points A, B, C and D on your diagram. [3]
c) Consider the stage A to B of the cycle. Is work W done on or by the gas? Is thermal energy Q supplied to the gas or extracted from it? How are Q and W related? Explain your reasoning. [3] (OCR)

17. The diagram shows a refrigerator running in a room as a thermodynamic system which is effectively insulated from the surroundings. Within that system there are *two* subsystems: the inside of the refrigerator at a low constant temperature, and the room. The refrigerator cooling fins transfer heat from the refrigerator to the room. Work can be done on the system by means of the electrical energy supplied to the refrigerator.

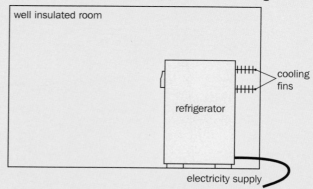

Applying the first law of thermodynamics and justifying your answers, state whether each of the quantities ΔU, Q and W is positive, negative or zero for a) the refrigerator,
b) the air in the room. [4] (AQA)

▷ Further questions on thermal physics

18. A student pours 525 g of water into a saucepan of negligible mass, heats it over a steady flame and records the temperature as it heats up.
    The temperatures are plotted as shown below.

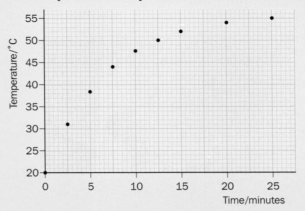

a) Calculate the heat capacity of the water and saucepan. (Specific heat capacity of water = 4200 J kg⁻¹ K⁻¹) [3]
b) Find the rate of rise of water temperature at the beginning of the heating process. [2]
c) Find the rate at which energy is supplied to the saucepan and water. [2]
d) Explain why the rate at which the temperature rises slows down progressively as the heating process continues. [2] (Edex)

19. a) A student seals 200 g of ice-cold water in a glass vacuum flask and finds that it warms up by 3.5 K in one hour. The specific heat capacity of water is 4200 J kg⁻¹ K⁻¹. Calculate the average rate of heat flow into the flask in watts. [3]
    b) To check this result over a longer period, the student fills the flask with equal amounts of ice and water, all at 0 °C, and leaves it for four hours. The specific latent heat of fusion of ice is 330 kJ kg⁻¹. How much ice would you expect to have melted at the end of four hours? [3]
    c) The student found instead that the glass flask had collapsed into small pieces. Suggest a reason for the pressure inside the glass flask to drop sufficiently for the collapse to occur. [3] (Edex)

20. a) Describe an experiment to demonstrate the Brownian motion. [4]
    b) Compare (i) the spacing, (ii) the ordering, and (iii) the motion of the molecules in ice at 0 °C and water, also at 0 °C. [6] (OCR)

21. Water is boiled in a kettle to produce steam at 100 °C
    a) Describe the motion of a typical water molecule in the steam. [1]
    b) Compare the mean kinetic energy of the water molecules in the steam with those in the boiling water. [2] (AQA)

22. 200 kJ of thermal energy is required to vaporise 1.0 kg of liquid oxygen at atmospheric pressure (100 kPa). This vaporisation is accompanied by an increase in volume of 0.23 m³.
    a) For this vaporisation, calculate
       i) the work done on the atmosphere by the expanding oxygen,
       ii) the change in internal energy of the oxygen.[4]
    b) The volume of the oxygen gas is measured as its temperature increases, the pressure remaining constant. At 100 K the volume is 0.25 m³ and at 290 K the volume is 0.79 m³. Show, by means of a calculation, whether oxygen behaves as an ideal gas over this temperature range. [3] (OCR)

23. The table shows data relating to the average power consumption for a person performing various activities.

activity	power consumption/W
sleeping	80
sitting	110
walking	300
swimming	900

a) In a 24 hour period, a hospital patient spends 15 h sleeping, 7 h sitting up in bed, 1.5 h walking around the hospital gardens, and 0.5 h swimming. Calculate
   i) the energy expended by the patient during the 24 h period,
   ii) the heat energy generated in the patient's body during the 0.5 h period in which he is swimming. The body converts energy into mechanical work with an efficiency of 30%.[5]
b) Explain the mechanisms responsible for dissipating excess heat energy from the patient when
   i) he is in the water,
   ii) he leaves the water after his swim. [3] (OCR)

24. The diagram illustrates high pressure air expelling a disc from a cylinder. The mass of the disc is 7.2 g and the maximum speed is 32 m s⁻¹.

a) Calculate the energy transferred to the disc. [3]
b) Use the kinetic theory of gases to account for the cooling of the air in the cylinder during the expulsion of the disc. [3]
c) Explain why work is done by the air on the disc but no work is done by the disc on the air. [2] (Edex)

27 Radioactivity

How many different materials can you think of?
Your list could include thousands of substances, but in fact,
they are all composed from around 100 elements.
Just as we can make words from the 26 letters of our alphabet,
the elements combine together chemically to form compounds.

So what are elements made up of?
The Greek philosopher Democritus first suggested that all matter
is made up of tiny particles, that he called atoms.
His ideas were rejected and for 2000 years scientists believed
that every substance was made up of earth, fire, air and water!

Our modern atomic theory was first put forward by John Dalton
in 1803. He imagined atoms to be tiny, indivisible particles.

In this chapter you will learn:
- about the structure of the atom,
- the properties of ionising radiations,
- the process of radioactive decay.

How big is an atom?

We can use the Avogadro constant N_A (see page 318)
to estimate the size of an atom, as in the following example.

The diagram shows some atoms arranged in a simple structure:

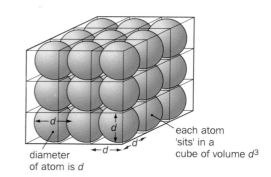

diameter of atom is d

each atom 'sits' in a cube of volume d^3

Think of chocolate oranges stacked in their boxes. The volume
of each orange is slightly less than the volume of its box.
Some crystal structures are a bit more complex than this, but
this model shows us that the volume of each atom is about d^3.

Suppose we apply this model to copper.
The molar mass of copper is 0.064 kg. This means that 0.064 kg
of copper contains N_A or 6.0×10^{23} atoms (see page 318).
We also know that the density of copper is 8900 kg m^{-3}.
We can calculate the volume (d^3) of one copper atom:

From page 288, **density** $= \dfrac{\textbf{mass}}{\textbf{volume}}$ so: $8900 \text{ kg m}^{-3} = \dfrac{0.064 \text{ kg}}{\text{volume}}$

∴ volume of 0.064 kg of copper $= \dfrac{0.064 \text{ kg}}{8900 \text{ kg m}^{-3}} = 7.2 \times 10^{-6} \text{ m}^3$

∴ volume (d^3) of 1 copper atom must be: $\dfrac{7.2 \times 10^{-6} \text{ m}^3}{6.0 \times 10^{23}} = 12 \times 10^{-30} \text{ m}^3$

∴ the diameter d of a copper atom $= \sqrt[3]{12 \times 10^{-30} \text{ m}^3} \approx \underline{2 \times 10^{-10} \text{ m}}$

We no longer picture atoms as having well-defined surfaces like a billiard ball
and so we cannot state exact diameters.
But this value agrees with the diameters measured by experimental methods
such as X-ray diffraction.

In fact most atomic diameters range from 1×10^{-10} to 5×10^{-10} m.
You could put about 10 million atoms side by side in 1 mm!

▶ Alpha particle scattering

John Dalton said that atoms were tiny indivisible spheres, but in 1897 J. J. Thomson discovered that all matter contains tiny negatively-charged particles (see page 164).
He showed that these particles are *smaller* than an atom.
He had found the first *subatomic* particle – the electron.

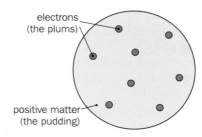

Thomson's 'plum-pudding' model

Scientists then set out to find the structure of the atom.

Thomson thought that the atom was a positive sphere of matter and the negative electrons were embedded in it as shown here:
This 'model' was called the 'plum-pudding' model of the atom.

Ernest Rutherford decided to probe the atom using fast moving alpha (α) particles. He fired the positively-charged α-particles at very thin gold foil and observed how they were scattered.

The diagram summarises his results:

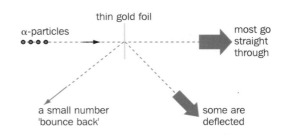

Most of the α-particles passed straight through the foil, but to his surprise a few were scattered back towards the source.
Rutherford said that this was rather like firing a gun at tissue paper and finding that some bullets bounce back towards you!

The nuclear model of the atom

Rutherford soon realised that the positive charge in the atom must be highly concentrated to repel the positive α-particles in this way.

The diagram shows a simple analogy:

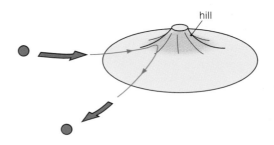

The ball is rolled towards the hill and represents the α-particle.
The steeper the 'hill' the more highly concentrated the charge.
The closer the approach of the steel ball to the hill, the greater its angle of deflection.

In 1911 Rutherford described his **nuclear model** of the atom.
He said that:

- All of an atom's positive charge and most of its mass is concentrated in a tiny core. Rutherford called this the **nucleus**.
- The electrons surround the nucleus, but they are at relatively large distances from it. The atom is mainly empty space!

Can we use this model to explain the α-particle scattering?

The concentrated positive charge produces an electric field which is very strong close to the nucleus.
The closer the path of the α-particle to the nucleus, the greater the electrostatic repulsion and the greater the deflection.

Most α-particles are hardly deflected because they are far away from the nucleus and the field is too weak to repel them much.
The electrons do not deflect the α-particles because the effect of their negative charge is spread thinly throughout the atom.

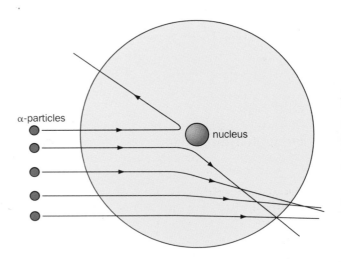

Using this model Rutherford calculated that the diameter of the gold nucleus could not be larger than 10^{-14} m.

This diagram is not to scale. With a 1 mm diameter nucleus the diameter of the atom would have to be 10 000 mm or 10 m!
The nucleus is like a pea at the centre of a football pitch.

▶ The structure of the atom

We know now that the nucleus is made up of two particles, the **proton** and the **neutron**. Protons and neutrons are both referred to as **nucleons** because they are found in the nucleus. All atoms (except for the hydrogen atom) are made up of three particles. The table shows their properties:

Since the masses of these particles are so small it is useful to measure them in a very small unit – the **atomic mass unit (u)**.

$$1\ u = 1.6605 \times 10^{-27}\ kg$$

particle	location	mass	charge
proton	in the nucleus	1.00728 u	+ e
neutron	in the nucleus	1.00867 u	0
electron	orbiting the nucleus	0.00055 u	– e

$e = 1.6 \times 10^{-19}$ coulombs

Notice that:

- the mass of the proton and the neutron are both approximately 1 u
- the electron has a much smaller mass – about $1/1800$ u
- the charge on the proton is equal and opposite to the electron charge.

The neutrons and protons make up the tiny positive nucleus. The electrons spin round the nucleus giving the effect of a thin cloud of negative charge.

The diagrams below show some examples.
Which two particles make up the simplest atom – the hydrogen atom?

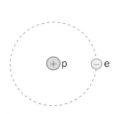

Hydrogen (H) atom

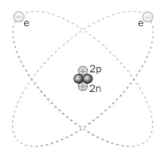

Helium (He) atom

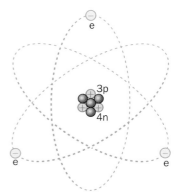

Lithium (Li) atom

What do you notice about the number of protons and electrons in each atom?
The atom is **neutral** – unless it loses an electron to become a positive **ion**.

Proton number and nucleon number

There are over 100 elements listed in the periodic table.
Some of these are not found naturally – but they can be made.

Each element has atoms with a **specific** number of protons.
For example, a lithium atom always has 3 protons.
A carbon atom always has 6 protons.
The number of protons in an atom is its **proton number Z**.
This is sometimes called the atomic number.

Another important number is the **nucleon number A**.
This is the total number of nucleons (= protons + neutrons).
It is sometimes called the mass number.
The nucleon number of lithium is 7 (= 3 protons + 4 neutrons).

The word **nuclide** is often used for a particular combination of protons and neutrons in a nucleus.
The panel shows the shorthand way of describing a nuclide:

Can you see that a Beryllium nucleus consists of 4 protons and 5 neutrons?

All nuclides can be described using this format:

Nucleon number A
                  Chemical symbol of element
Proton number Z

Eg.

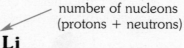

$$^{7}_{3}\text{Li}$$

number of nucleons (protons + neutrons)

number of protons

Eg. $^{9}_{4}\text{Be}$ Be = Beryllium

Isotopes

Every atom of oxygen has a proton number of 8. That is, it has 8 protons (and so 8 electrons to make it a neutral atom).

Most oxygen atoms have a nucleon number of 16. This means that these atoms also have 8 neutrons. This is $^{16}_{8}O$.

Some oxygen atoms have a nucleon number of 17. These atoms have 9 neutrons (but still 8 protons). This is $^{17}_{8}O$.

$^{16}_{8}O$ and $^{17}_{8}O$ are both oxygen atoms.
They are called **isotopes** of oxygen.

There is a third isotope of oxygen $^{18}_{8}O$.
How many neutrons are there in the nucleus of an $^{18}_{8}O$ atom?

Isotopes are atoms with the same proton number, but different nucleon numbers.

Since the isotopes of an element have the same number of electrons, they must have the same chemical properties. The atoms have different masses, however, and so their physical properties are different.

All the elements have more than one isotope. Hydrogen has three, as shown in the diagram: These are so important that each has its own name.

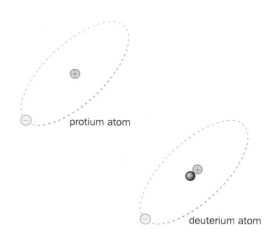

protium atom

deuterium atom

tritium atom

Isotopes of hydrogen

Nuclear diameters

The periodic table lists the elements in order of increasing proton number. Hydrogen is the first element in the table. Uranium is the last of the naturally occurring elements.

Would you expect the uranium nucleus with 238 nucleons to have the same radius as the hydrogen nucleus?

Suppose each nucleon is a sphere with a constant volume v. Then $v = \frac{4}{3}\pi r_o^3$, where r_o represents the radius of a nucleon.

The volume V of a nucleus with A nucleons will be roughly $A v$. What value does this give for the radius of the nucleus r?

Assuming that the nucleus is a sphere, then $V = \frac{4}{3}\pi r^3$

Since $V = A v$, then: $\qquad \frac{4}{3}\pi r^3 = A \times \frac{4}{3}\pi r_o^3$

Cancelling and taking the cube root:

$$r = r_o A^{1/3}$$

r_o is the radius of a nucleon and is found by experiment to be 1.2×10^{-15} m.

This equation gives nuclear radii in the range 2×10^{-15} m to 8×10^{-15} m. These values have in fact been confirmed by experiments using high-energy electrons (see page 346).

The table shows some elements.

Proton number	Element + symbol		Commonest isotope
1	Hydrogen	H	$^{1}_{1}H$
2	Helium	He	$^{4}_{2}He$
3	Lithium	Li	$^{7}_{3}Li$
4	Beryllium	Be	$^{9}_{4}Be$
5	Boron	B	$^{11}_{5}B$
6	Carbon	C	$^{12}_{6}C$
7	Nitrogen	N	$^{14}_{7}N$
8	Oxygen	O	$^{16}_{8}O$
79	Gold	Au	$^{197}_{79}Au$
92	Uranium	U	$^{238}_{92}U$

Nuclear density
The proton and the neutron have almost the same mass. Suppose each nucleon has a mass m and a volume v. The mass of a nucleus with A nucleons is therefore Am and the volume of the nucleus is about Av.

What is the density of the nucleus?

density $= \dfrac{mass}{volume}$ and so density of the nucleus is $\dfrac{Am}{Av}$

A cancels to give: nuclear density $= \dfrac{m}{v}$

This means that all nuclei have about the same density. This result is supported by experimental evidence.

Example 1
What is the radius of a lead nucleus of nucleon number 206?

$r = r_o A^{1/3}$

$r = 1.2 \times 10^{-15}$ m $\times 206^{1/3}$ *(Use the x^y button on your calculator)*

$r = 1.2 \times 10^{-15}$ m $\times 5.91 \quad = \underline{7.1 \times 10^{-15}}$ m (2 s.f.)

▶ Alpha, beta and gamma radiation

Scientists soon identified the nature of α, β and γ-rays.
You can repeat some of their experiments using sealed sources.

Remember, the count recorded on a G–M tube will be caused
by the radiation from the source **and** the background radiation.
First measure the background count and then **deduct** this value
from your other counts to find the count caused by just the source.
This is called the **corrected count-rate**.

Alpha-rays

Place an americium-241 source, which emits α-rays, close
to the window of a G–M tube as shown in the diagram:

What happens to the count rate when you place some
paper between the source and the tube?
The count rate drops to zero, so the paper must have
stopped the α-radiation.

Now remove the paper and record the count rate as you move
the α-source further away from the tube.
You will find that α-rays can only penetrate about 5 cm of air.

It is also possible to show that α-radiation can be deflected by
very strong electric and magnetic fields.

We now know that **α-radiation consists of positively-charged
particles moving at high speed.**
In fact, an α-particle consists of **2 protons and 2 neutrons**.
Do you recognise this as the **nucleus of a helium atom**?

to counter

Am-241 source
in holder

wooden supports

Beta-rays

You can investigate β-rays using a strontium-90 source.
You will find that paper does not stop these rays, but
what happens if you use different thicknesses of aluminium?

β-radiation is stopped by about 3 mm of aluminium.
The β-rays from this source can penetrate about 50 cm of air.

What happens if you place a powerful magnet between the
source and the tube as shown in the diagram?
The count rate falls, but rises again when the tube is moved.

If you use Fleming's left hand rule (page 224) you can show that
β-rays must be negatively-charged particles.
In fact **β-particles are electrons moving at very high speeds.**

Sr-90 source

N

S

no magnet

with magnet

Gamma-rays

Repeat the experiments using γ-rays from a cobalt-60 source.
You will find that γ-radiation is unaffected by a magnetic field
and is very penetrating. Although it is reduced, it is not stopped
completely even by thick pieces of lead.
γ-rays are electromagnetic waves of very short wavelength.

It is often useful to think of γ-rays as a stream of γ-ray photons
rather than waves (see Chapter 13). Remember, the shorter the
γ-wave wavelength, the higher the energy of the γ-ray photons.

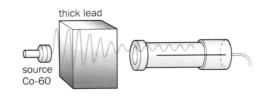

thick lead

source
Co-60

▶ How is radiation absorbed?

α-particles, β-particles and γ-ray photons are all very energetic particles.
We often measure their energy in electron-volts (eV) rather than joules.
Typically the kinetic energy of an α-particle is about 6 million eV (6 MeV).

We know that radiation ionises molecules by 'knocking' electrons off them.
As it does so, energy is transferred from the radiation to the material.
The diagrams below show what happens to an α-particle:

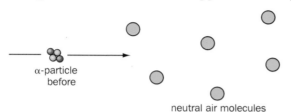

neutral air molecules

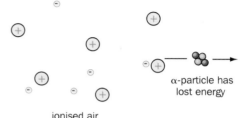

ionised air

It takes about 30 eV to produce a positive ion and a free electron – an ion pair –
from an air molecule. How many ion pairs could a 6 MeV α-particle produce?
After producing about 2×10^5 ion pairs the α-particle has given up all its energy
and has been stopped or absorbed.

Why do the 3 types of radiation have different penetrations?

Since the **α-particle** is a heavy, relatively slow-moving particle,
with a charge of +2e, it interacts strongly with matter.
It produces about 1×10^5 ion pairs per cm of its path in air.
After passing through just a few cm of air it has lost its energy.

The **β-particle** is a much lighter particle than the α-particle
and it travels much faster. Since it spends just a short time in
the vicinity of each air molecule and has a charge of only –1e,
it causes less intense ionisation than the α-particle.
The β-particle produces about 1×10^3 ion pairs per cm in air,
and so it travels about 1 m before it is absorbed.

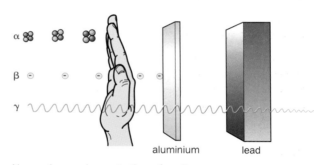

Absorption and penetration of α, β, γ rays

A **γ-ray photon** interacts weakly with matter because it is
uncharged and therefore it is difficult to stop.
A γ-ray photon often loses all its energy in one event.
However, the chance of such an event is small and on average
a γ-photon travels a long way before it is absorbed.

Here is a summary:

Property	Alpha-particle	Beta-particle	Gamma-ray
Nature:	2 protons + 2 neutrons (a helium nucleus)	an electron	an electromagnetic wave of very short wavelength
Symbol:	^4_2He or $^4_2\alpha$	$^0_{-1}\text{e}$ or $^0_{-1}\beta$	γ
Mass:	~ 4 u	~ 0.000 55 u	0
Charge:	+ 2	−1	0
Ionising ability:	very strong	strong	weak
Speed:	~ 5% the speed of light	up to 98% the speed of light	speed of light
Penetration:	stopped by paper, skin or a few cm of air	stopped by 3 mm of aluminium or about 1 m of air	reduced significantly by several cm of lead
Affected by electric and magnetic fields?	yes	yes	no

▷ Why is radiation dangerous?

α, β and γ-rays are dangerous because of their energy.
They can ionise the molecules in living cells and in this way
release energy into the cells and damage them.

Once the radiation has been stopped by 'colliding' with matter
it is no longer dangerous. Compare this to a bullet: you would
be wise to avoid a fast moving bullet from a gun, but once the
bullet has been stopped, it is no longer a threat.

The release of energy into the body cells can cause burning.
Ionisation can also disrupt the chemistry of the cells and cause
radiation sickness and hair loss.
Cells may become genetically changed by radiation. This can
lead to illnesses such as cancer and leukaemia, which may
occur years after the body was exposed to the radiation.
Damage to the genetic make-up of sex cells can also be passed
on and can cause abnormalities in the person's children.

Which type of radiation is the most dangerous? This depends on
whether the source of radiation is inside or outside the body:

- An α-source outside your body is safe. The α-particles cannot
  pass through your outer skin to get to the internal organs.
  But if you swallow an α-source or breathe in an α-emitting
  gas, that is very dangerous. It causes a lot of ionisation,
  releasing a lot of energy into the surrounding cells.
- A γ-source outside your body can be dangerous because the
  radiation is very penetrating and can affect cells deep inside.

*Workers must be protected from the radiation
emitted by highly radioactive materials*

▷ The inverse square law for gamma radiation

Place a cobalt-60 source close to the window of a G–M tube
and record the count rate. Now change the distance.
What happens to the count rate as you increase the distance
between the source and the tube?

The γ-rays spread out from the source and so fewer and fewer
rays enter the tube as it is moved away from the source.

In fact, if you double the distance between the source and the
tube the count rate falls to $\frac{1}{4}$.
At three times the distance the count rate is only $\frac{1}{9}$.

The intensity of light from a lamp changes in the same way.
Like all electromagnetic radiation, the intensity of γ-rays
obeys an **inverse square** relationship (see also page 120).

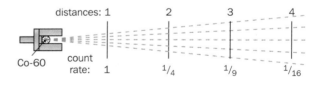

Can we explain this inverse square law? Look at the diagram:

The radiation passes through an area A at a distance r from the
source. At a distance $2r$ the radiation has spread out and now
passes through an area $4A$.
So the intensity of the radiation at $2r$ is $\frac{1}{4}$ of that at distance r.

The inverse square law applies to α and β-rays in a vacuum,
but not in air. Why?
Unlike γ-radiation, the air absorbs both α and β-radiation.

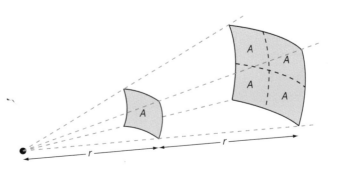

Investigating the inverse square law

You can investigate the inverse square law using the apparatus in the diagram. **Before** placing the cobalt-60 source in position you need to measure the background count-rate.

Start with the γ-ray source close to the G–M tube and measure the count-rate. Remember to subtract the background count to find the **corrected** count-rate.

Gradually increase the distance r between the source and the tube and record the corrected count-rate C at each position.

If the inverse square law is true then you should find that:

$$C \propto \frac{1}{r^2} \quad \text{or} \quad \boxed{C = \frac{k}{r^2}} \quad \text{where } k \text{ is a constant.}$$

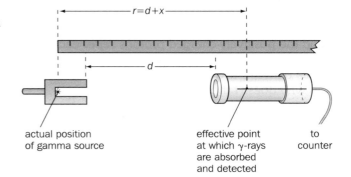

actual position of gamma source

effective point at which γ-rays are absorbed and detected

to counter

But there is a problem in measuring r. Can you see what this is?

The γ-source is in a sealed container and so you do not know its exact position. Also you do not know the exact point where the γ-rays are detected within the G–M tube.

How can we solve this problem?

You can measure the distance d from the end of the source to the tube as shown, so that $r = d + x$, where x is unknown.

What graph can you then plot to prove the law, without knowing x?

Since $C = \dfrac{k}{r^2}$ and $r = d + x$, then: $C = \dfrac{k}{(d + x)^2}$

Rearranging: $(d + x)^2 = \dfrac{k}{C}$ and so: $d + x = \dfrac{\sqrt{k}}{\sqrt{C}}$

Therefore: $d = \sqrt{k} \times \dfrac{1}{\sqrt{C}} - x$

which is like: $y = m \quad x + c$ (see page 405)

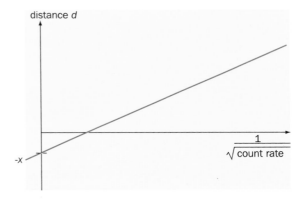

distance d

$\dfrac{1}{\sqrt{\text{count rate}}}$

$-x$

Can you see that if γ-rays do obey the inverse square law, the graph of d against $1/\sqrt{C}$ should be a straight line as shown:

Notice that this method overcomes the problem of not knowing exactly where the source is, or the effective point where the γ-rays are detected in the G–M tube.

Example 2

A G–M tube is placed 200 mm from a point source of γ-rays and registers a corrected count-rate of 60 s⁻¹.
a) What will be the corrected count-rate at 1000 mm from the source?
b) How far is the tube from the source when the count-rate is 240 s⁻¹?

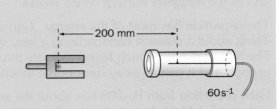

a) The separation of the source and the tube is 5 times as great, and so the count-rate must fall to $^1/_{5^2}$ or $\frac{1}{25}$ of its original value.
Therefore the new count-rate is $\frac{1}{25} \times 60$ s⁻¹ = $\underline{2.4 \text{ s}^{-1}}$

b) The count-rate has increased from 60 s⁻¹ (at 200 mm) to 240 s⁻¹.
The count-rate is now 4 times as great, so the distance must have halved.
The separation of the source and G–M tube is $\frac{1}{2} \times 200$ mm = $\underline{100 \text{ mm}}$

Nuclear stability

If you plot the neutron number N against the proton number Z, for all the known nuclides, you get the diagram shown here:

Can you see that the stable nuclides of the lighter elements have approximately equal numbers of protons and neutrons? However, as Z increases the 'stability line' curves upwards. Heavier nuclei need more and more neutrons to be stable. Can we explain why?

It is the strong nuclear force that holds the nucleons together, but this is a very short range force. The repulsive electric force between the protons is a longer range force.
So in a large nucleus all the protons repel each other, but each nucleon attracts only its nearest neighbours. More neutrons are needed to hold the nucleus together (although adding too many neutrons can also cause instability).

There is an upper limit to the size of a stable nucleus, because all the nuclides with Z higher than 83 are unstable.

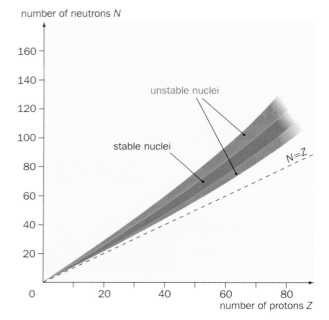

Beta⁺ decay

A radio-nuclide **above** the stability line decays by β-emission, as described on the previous page.
Because it loses a neutron and gains a proton, it moves diagonally **towards** the stability line, as shown on this graph:

But how does a radio nuclide **below** the line become more stable? There is another process called **positron-decay** or β^+ decay.

The positron is the **antiparticle** of the electron (see Chapter 29). It has the same mass as the electron, but the opposite charge. Its symbol is $^{0}_{+1}e$ or $^{0}_{+1}\beta$.

In β^+ decay, one of the protons in the unstable nucleus changes into a neutron and a positron which is emitted as a β^+-particle. The nucleus loses a proton but gains a neutron and so moves towards the stability line in the opposite direction to β^--decay.

A second particle, the neutrino ν, is emitted with the positron. (The neutrino ν and antineutrino $\bar{\nu}$ are also antiparticles.)

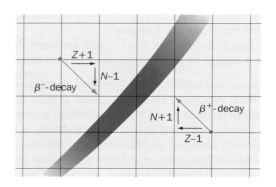

The nuclear equation is: $^{A}_{Z}X \Rightarrow {}^{A}_{Z-1}X + {}^{0}_{+1}e + {}^{0}_{0}\nu$

Notice that as always, the top and the bottom numbers balance.
Compare these two decays:

β^- decay (electron emission): $^{14}_{6}C \Rightarrow {}^{14}_{7}N + {}^{0}_{-1}e + {}^{0}_{0}\bar{\nu}$

β^+ decay (positron emission): $^{15}_{8}O \Rightarrow {}^{15}_{7}N + {}^{0}_{+1}e + {}^{0}_{0}\nu$

Decay chains

A radio-nuclide often produces an unstable daughter nuclide. The daughter will also decay, and the process will continue until finally a stable nuclide is formed.
This is called a decay chain or a decay series.
Part of one decay chain is shown below:

$^{238}_{92}U \xrightarrow{\alpha} {}^{234}_{90}Th \xrightarrow{\beta} {}^{234}_{91}Pa \xrightarrow{\beta} {}^{234}_{92}U \xrightarrow{\alpha} {}^{230}_{90}Th \xrightarrow{\alpha} {}^{226}_{88}Ra$

The stable nuclide at the very end of the chain is lead-206.

Wolfgang Pauli predicted the neutrino in 1931, but it was not discovered until 1956

▶ The random nature of radioactive decay

Suppose you have a sample of 100 identical nuclei.
All the nuclei are equally likely to decay, but you can never
predict which individual nucleus will be the next to decay.
The decay process is completely **random**.

Also, there is nothing you can do to 'persuade' one nucleus to
decay at a certain time. The decay process is **spontaneous**.

You can observe the random nature of radioactive decay by
using a G–M tube to detect the radiation from a weak source.
The counts do not occur regularly. They occur randomly.

Does this mean that we can never know the rate of decay?
No, because for any particular radio-nuclide there is a certain
probability that an individual nucleus will decay. This means
that if we start with a large number of identical nuclei we can
predict how many will decay in a certain time interval.

Which 6 numbers will be drawn at random tonight?

Radioactive decay using dice!

You can produce a good model of radioactive decay using
a large number of dice, with one face marked as shown:
Think of each of the dice as an 'atom' with an unstable nucleus,
so that the group of dice represent the identical atoms of a
particular radio-nuclide.
If you throw one of the dice and it lands with its marked face
upwards, then we say that this dice-atom has 'decayed'.

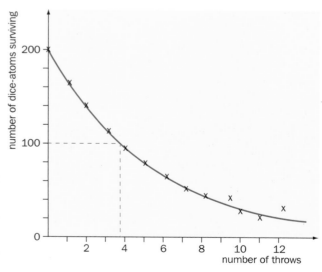

Can you predict when one individual dice-atom will decay?
No, but each dice-atom has a $\frac{1}{6}$ chance of decaying each time
it is thrown. If you throw a large number of dice-atoms at
the same time, you can predict that $\frac{1}{6}$th of them will decay.

> Number of dice-atoms = the probability × number of dice-atoms
> that decay   of decay   in the sample

Count and record the number of dice-atoms in your sample.
Throw the dice-atoms and remove those that have decayed.
Now count the number of dice-atoms that have survived.

Throw the surviving dice-atoms again and repeat the process
until only a few dice-atoms remain undecayed.

Plot a graph of the 'number of dice-atoms surviving' against
the 'number of throws'. It will look like the one drawn here:

Does it take about 3.8 throws for the number of dice-atoms to
fall from 200 to 100? And does it take another 3.8 throws
for the number of dice-atoms to halve again to 50?
The number of dice-atoms **always halves** in 3.8 throws.

The graph is an **exponential decay curve** because the number
of dice-atoms falls by the same fraction ($\frac{1}{6}$) after each throw.

Notice that the results are unreliable after about 8 throws.
When the sample is too small it becomes impossible to predict
accurately the number that will decay in each throw.

▷ The decay constant, λ

A dice-atom has a $\frac{1}{6}$ chance of decay per throw. Similarly:

The decay constant λ of a radio-nuclide is the probability that an individual nucleus will decay within a unit time.

Since λ is the chance per unit time, its unit is s^{-1}, h^{-1}, day^{-1}, etc.

If the value of λ for a particular nuclide is $0.2\ s^{-1}$, then
in one second, each nucleus has a 0.2 or $\frac{1}{5}$ chance of decay.
In a sample of 1000 nuclei, 200 will have decayed after 1 second.

The value of λ is a constant for any particular nuclide.
Can you see that the value of λ is zero for a stable nuclide?

Phiz imagines dice-atoms with different decay probabilities

Activity, A

The activity A of a source is the number of its nuclei that decay in unit time.

Since each decay produces ionising radiation, the activity of a source also
tells you the number of ionising particles that it emits in unit time.

Activity can be measured in decays per hour, per day etc., but
the SI unit of activity is the **becquerel (Bq)**.
1 Bq is an activity of 1 decay per second. $1\ Bq = 1\ s^{-1}$.

The activity of a sample must depend on the decay constant λ of the nuclide.
The greater the probability of decay, the more nuclei that decay in unit time.
Also, the activity will increase if there are more undecayed nuclei in the sample.
In fact:

Activity, A = decay constant, λ × number of undecayed nuclei, N
(s^{-1}) (s^{-1})

or $\boxed{A = \lambda N}$

Example 3
A sample of a radio-nuclide initially contains 200 000 nuclei.
Its decay constant is $0.30\ s^{-1}$. What is the initial activity?

$$A = \lambda N$$
$$\therefore\ A = 0.30\ s^{-1} \times 200\ 000\ = \underline{60\ 000\ s^{-1}}$$

You may see this equation written like this:
$$\frac{\Delta N}{\Delta t} = -\lambda N$$

ΔN is the number of nuclei that decay in time Δt,

and so $\dfrac{\Delta N}{\Delta t}$ is the activity A.

The − sign tells us that N decreases as time passes.

Measuring the decay of protactinium-234

The protactinium is in a plastic bottle. It emits β-particles,
which can pass through the wall of the bottle and are then
detected by the G–M tube.
You should record the count-rate every 10 s for several minutes.
(Remember to deduct the background count from each result.)

Does this method record the activity of the protactinium?
No, not all the β-particles emitted by the protactinium are detected
and so the count-rate is lower than the activity of the source.
If we assume that we always detect the same percentage of the
emitted radiation, the count-rate is proportional to the activity.

You will find that the count-rate falls, because as time goes by
there are fewer and fewer protactinium nuclei left to decay.

It takes 72 s for the activity to fall to half. After another 72 s
it has halved again. And after another 72 s it halves yet again.

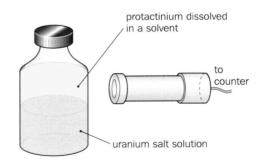

protactinium dissolved in a solvent

to counter

uranium salt solution

▶ Exponential decay

Experiments like that on the facing page show that the number of nuclei in a sample always decreases in the same way.
The graph shows this decrease:
Do you recognise the shape of the graph?
It has the same form as the one from the dice-atom experiment.
It takes a time $t_{\frac{1}{2}}$ for the number of nuclei to fall from N_0 to $N_0/2$

Can you see it takes the same time for the number of undecayed nuclei to fall from $N_0/2$ to $N_0/4$, and from $N_0/4$ to $N_0/8$?

The time $t_{\frac{1}{2}}$ is called the **half-life** of the radioactive nuclide.
It is the time taken for half the radioactive nuclei to decay.
The half-lives of different radio-nuclides vary widely, from fractions of a second up to millions of years.

This graph is an **exponential decay curve** because the number of nuclei always falls by the same fraction in the same time.
The equation for this curve is:

$$N = N_0\, e^{-\lambda t}$$

where: N = the number of nuclei at time t
N_0 = the original number of nuclei
λ = the decay constant
See also page 408.

We can also write:

$$A = A_0\, e^{-\lambda t} \quad \text{and} \quad C = C_0\, e^{-\lambda t}$$

since the activity A is proportional to the number of nuclei present ($A = \lambda N$)
and the recorded count rate C is proportional to the activity (see facing page).

The decay constant and the half-life

How does the decay constant of a nuclide affect its half-life?
The higher the probability of decay λ, the more rapidly the nuclide decays, and so the shorter its half-life. In fact:

$$t_{\frac{1}{2}} = \frac{0.693}{\lambda}$$

More details are given in the box:

- Take care with the units. If λ is in s^{-1}, t and $t_{\frac{1}{2}}$ must be in s.
- The exponential equation no longer applies when only a few nuclei remain because of the random nature of the decay.

Deriving the link between λ and $t_{\frac{1}{2}}$:

Rearranging $N = N_0\, e^{-\lambda t}$ gives: $\dfrac{N_0}{N} = e^{\lambda t}$

When $t = t_{\frac{1}{2}}$, $N = N_0/2$ so: $\dfrac{N_0}{N_0/2} = e^{\lambda t_{\frac{1}{2}}}$

Therefore: $2 = e^{\lambda t_{\frac{1}{2}}}$
taking logs to base e : $\ln 2 = \lambda\, t_{\frac{1}{2}}$

So: $t_{\frac{1}{2}} = \dfrac{\ln 2}{\lambda} = \dfrac{0.693}{\lambda}$

Example 4
A radio nuclide has a half-life of 55.0 s.
Initially a sample of the nuclide contains 5000 nuclei.
a) What is the decay constant for this nuclide?
b) How many nuclei remain undecayed after 200 s?

a) $t_{\frac{1}{2}} = \dfrac{0.693}{\lambda}$ so: $55.0 = \dfrac{0.693}{\lambda}$

$\therefore \; \lambda = \dfrac{0.693}{55.0 \text{ s}} = 1.26 \times 10^{-2}\ s^{-1}$

b) $N = N_0\, e^{-\lambda t}$
$N = 5000 \times e^{-1.26 \times 10^{-2} \times 200}$
$N = 5000 \times e^{-2.52}$
$N = \underline{400 \text{ nuclei}}$

calculator hint:
you want the value of e^x
when $x = -2.52$

▶ Physics at work: Radioactivity in medicine

Radioactive tracers

In this method a radioactive isotope is injected into the body (or is otherwise ingested) and its movement can be followed from outside the body by a suitable detector of radiation.

For example, a doctor might suspect that a patient has a blocked kidney. The patient sits with a 'gamma-camera' over each kidney as shown in the photograph:

A small amount of iodine-123 is injected into the patient. Within 5 minutes both the kidneys should extract the iodine from the blood stream. Within 20 minutes they should pass it with urine into the bladder.
Which of these kidneys do you think is blocked?

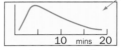

chart recorder A   chart recorder B

Why must the quantity of tracer used be as small as possible? The patient's exposure to radiation is reduced if the tracer is quickly eliminated from the body, or if it has a short half-life. (But the life span of the tracer must be matched to the biological process being studied.)

A γ-emitting tracer is the best to use because γ-rays can travel easily through matter and cause little ionisation in the body. Why are α-emitters not used as tracers? (See page 336.)

A tracer called technetium-99m is often used. It is safe, because:
- It emits only γ-rays. The γ-rays can be detected outside the body by a gamma-camera.
- It is naturally excreted and therefore removed from the body.

Gamma-ray scans of a man injected with Tc-99m
A: initially
B: after 6 hours (one half-life)

A   B

Radiotherapy

Cancer cells can be killed by the careful use of γ-rays. Cobalt-60 is often used as the source of the very energetic rays needed for the treatment. The source is sealed in a lead-lined steel container and the γ-rays emerge through a small aperture.

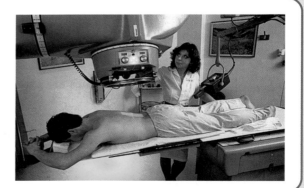

The beam of γ-rays has to be aimed carefully at the cancer cells. The source can be rotated about the patient's body so that short doses of radiation enter at several different points; but each dose is focussed on the tumour. This reduces damage to healthy cells.

The half-life of cobalt-60 is about 5 years, so its activity stays roughly constant over the few weeks of a course of treatment.

The cardiac pacemaker

Why are samples of radioactive materials always slightly warmer than their surroundings?
Remember the radiation emitted by a source has energy.
If some of the radiation is absorbed by the atoms of the source, then the energy of the radiation is transferred to the source.
We can use this heat energy to generate electricity.
A pacemaker uses the power from a radio-nuclide to produce pulses of electricity that keep the heart beating regularly.
The nuclide used is an enclosed α-emitter with a long half-life.

▶ Physics at work: Radioactive dating

The age of rocks

Radioactivity can be used to find the age of a rock. For example, uranium-238 (^{238}U) has a very long half-life of 4500 million years. It changes slowly by a decay chain into a stable nuclide, lead-206 (^{206}Pb).

After one half-life, half of it is unchanged and the other half has changed into lead. After two half-lives, $\frac{1}{4}$ of the ^{238}U is left and $\frac{3}{4}$ is lead.

By measuring how much of the ^{238}U in a rock has changed to ^{206}Pb, it is possible to calculate the age of the rock.

But what about the other nuclides in the decay chain? They can be ignored, because the half-life of ^{238}U is more than 20 000 times longer than any other half-life in its decay chain.

A rock from the Moon. Radioactive dating shows it is 4500 million years old, the same age as the Earth

Example 5
In a rock sample, the proportion of ^{238}U atoms to ^{206}Pb atoms was found to be 4 : 1. How old is the rock?

This means that, on average, for every 5 atoms of ^{238}U when the rock was formed, 1 atom has decayed and 4 atoms have not decayed yet.
That is, $^4/_5$ of the atoms are still radioactive ^{238}U.

So the activity of the ^{238}U in the rock is 80% of its initial value.

From the half-life graph for ^{238}U we find that this has taken about 1500 million years:

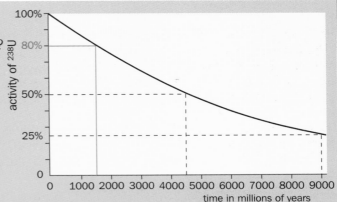

y-axis: activity of ^{238}U (100%, 80%, 50%, 25%, 0)
x-axis: time in millions of years (0, 1000, 2000, 3000, 4000, 5000, 6000, 7000, 8000, 9000)

Carbon dating

There are three naturally occurring isotopes of carbon. One, carbon-14 (^{14}C) decays with a half-life of 5700 years. ^{14}C is produced in the upper atmosphere by cosmic rays.

All living things take in ^{14}C, as well as the more usual ^{12}C, as a result of photosynthesis. When living things die, they stop taking in carbon. The ^{14}C slowly decays, and so the percentage of ^{14}C in organic matter slowly decreases with time. This can be used to date bones, wood, paper and cloth.

The Dead Sea Scrolls. ^{14}C-dating shows they are 1900 years old.

Example 6
The ratio of ^{14}C atoms to ^{12}C atoms in living material is 1.0 : 10^{12}
In an Egyptian mummy the ratio ^{14}C : ^{12}C is 0.60 : 10^{12}. How old is it?

The relative number of ^{14}C atoms in the mummy has fallen from 1.0 to 0.60

Step 1: $t_{\frac{1}{2}} = \dfrac{0.693}{\lambda}$

$\lambda = \dfrac{0.693}{5700 \text{ y}}$

$\lambda = 1.2 \times 10^{-4} \text{ y}^{-1}$

Step 2:

$$N = N_0\, e^{-\lambda t}$$
$$0.60 = 1 \times e^{-1.2 \times 10^{-4}\, t}$$
logs to base e: $\ln 0.6 = -1.2 \times 10^{-4}\, t$
$$-0.5 = -1.2 \times 10^{-4}\, t$$
$$t = 4200 \text{ y} \quad (2 \text{ s.f.})$$

Alternatively you could read the time from a decay graph as in Example 5.

Carbon dating is not exact. The count rates involved are very small and the percentage of ^{14}C in our atmosphere has not always been constant as we have assumed here. Modern methods try to allow for this variation.

The Shroud of Turin. ^{14}C dating shows that it is 600 years old.

▶ Probing the structure of matter

Rutherford's α-particle scattering experiment was important because it revealed the nuclear structure of the atom, **and** it showed that energetic **particles** could be used to probe matter.

The proton and the neutron were discovered using α-particles. The photograph shows the tracks of α-particles moving through nitrogen gas in a cloud chamber:
Can you see the forked track (circled) in the photograph?
At this point an α-particle collides with a nitrogen nucleus to form an oxygen nucleus and a proton.

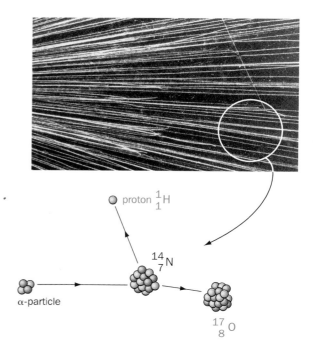

The nuclear equation is : $^{14}_{7}\text{N} + ^{4}_{2}\text{He} \Longrightarrow ^{17}_{8}\text{O} + ^{1}_{1}\text{H}$

Notice that the nucleon and the proton numbers balance. Analysis of the particle tracks shows that momentum is also conserved: the oxygen nucleus and the proton together have the same momentum as the α-particle before the collision

We can also probe the structure of matter using **waves**.
Light waves can be diffracted by the regular pattern of a diffraction grating (page 150). In the same way, X-rays can be diffracted by the regular pattern of atoms in a crystal.
The diffraction pattern reveals the arrangement of the atoms in the crystal because the wavelength of the X-rays is $\sim 10^{-10}$ m – about the same size as the spacing of the atoms in the crystal.

Remember de Broglie's equation (page 170). A **particle** can behave like a **wave**. The greater the velocity of the particle, the shorter its wavelength. Electron waves with a wavelength of 1×10^{-10} m can also be diffracted by a crystal (see page 170).

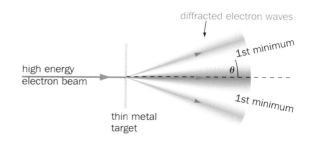

We can probe more deeply using waves of even shorter wavelength. Electrons of energy 1 GeV have a wavelength of only $\sim 10^{-15}$ m. When a thin beam of these electrons is fired at a metal target, the **nuclei** of the atoms diffract the electron waves. The angle θ of the first diffraction minimum is used to calculate the radius of the nucleus. This gives values of around 10^{-15} m.

Very high energy (10 GeV) electrons can be used to probe even deeper to reveal the structure of protons and neutrons (see page 360).

Summary

Rutherford's α-scattering experiment shows us that an atom has a small positive nucleus. It is surrounded by a cloud of negative electrons.

In radioactive decay a nucleus attempts to become more stable by emitting radiation. There are 3 types of ionising radiation, α, β and γ, each with different properties (see page 335).

Nuclear decay is a spontaneous and random process. It is predictable only with large numbers of nuclei.

$λ$ is the decay constant : the probability that a nucleus will decay in a certain time.
$t_{\frac{1}{2}}$ is the half-life : the time taken for half the nuclei in a sample to decay. $t_{\frac{1}{2}} = \dfrac{0.693}{λ}$

The radioactive decay process can be described by an exponential equation:
N is the number of undecayed nuclei, N_0 is the value of N at $t = 0$. $N = N_0 e^{-λt}$
A similar equation gives the activity A, or the count rate C, after a time t.

The structure of matter can be probed using waves or high-energy particles.

▶ Questions

1. Can you complete these sentences?
   a) Isotopes are atoms that have the same .... number, but different .... numbers.
   b) An alpha .... is ....-charged and has the same structure as a .... nucleus.
   c) Beta .... are ....-charged electrons travelling at very .... speed.
   d) .... and .... particles can be deflected by electric and .... fields, but .... rays cannot.

2. Explain why:
   a) β-particles travel further through air than α-particles.
   b) An α-source is most dangerous inside the body, and a γ-source is dangerous outside the body.
   c) The inverse square law does not apply to α and β-particles unless they are emitted in a vacuum.
   d) Large nuclei tend to be unstable.
   e) In 'Rutherford scattering' of α-particles,
      i) the metal foil must be very thin
      ii) the α-particle beam must be narrow and parallel.

3. A caesium atom has a nucleon number of 137 and a proton number of 55.
   Describe the structure of the caesium nucleus.

4. The nucleon number of a gold nucleus is 197.
   a) The value of r_o is 1.2×10^{-15} m. Calculate the radius r of the gold nucleus.
   b) Given that the volume of a sphere is $^4/_3 \pi r^3$, calculate the volume of the gold nucleus.
   c) The mass of a nucleon is 1.67×10^{-27} kg. Calculate the density of the nucleus.

5. The intensity of radiation 1 m from a γ-source is I. What is the intensity 3 m from the source?

6. The count rate recorded by a G–M tube 4.0 m from an industrial γ-radiation source is 20 s^{-1}. The maximum safe count rate is 50 s^{-1}. What is the minimum safe distance from the source?

7. An α-source emits α-particles with two different energies. Sketch the appearance of the tracks produced in a cloud chamber by this source.

8. You are given the following proton numbers: lead Pb = 82, fluorine F = 9, and iron Fe = 26, Write nuclear equations for the following decays:
   a) the emission of a β^--particle (electron) from oxygen-19 ($^{19}_{8}$O)
   b) the emission of an α-particle from polonium-212 ($^{212}_{84}$Po)
   c) the emission of a β^+-particle (positron) from cobalt-56 ($^{56}_{27}$Co)

9. Outside the nucleus a neutron is an unstable particle. It decays into a proton, an electron and an anti-neutrino with a half-life of 10.8 min. What is the probability that one such neutron will decay in the next second?

10. A radioisotope with a half-life of 5.0 days is used as a medical tracer. How many atoms of the radioisotope must be in the patient's body to give a total activity 4.0×10^5 Bq?

11. A G–M tube placed close to a radium source gives an initial average corrected count rate of 334 s^{-1}.
    a) The tube detects 10 % of the radiation. What is the initial activity of the source?
    b) Initially there were 1.5×10^9 radium nuclei in the sample. What is the decay constant for radium?
    c) What is the half-life of the radium in days?

12. The initial activity of a sample of a radio nuclide is 800 Bq. The half-life of the nuclide is 5.0 min. Draw a sketch graph to show how the activity of the sample changes over a time interval of 20 min.

13. The half-life of radium-226 is 1600 years. For an initial sample:
    a) What fraction has decayed after 4800 years?
    b) What fraction remains undecayed after 6400 y?

14. An experiment was carried out to measure the half-life of a radioactive source. The following results were obtained:

Time from start /s	0	30	60	90	120
Corrected count rate /s^{-1}	160	110	71	47	32

    a) Plot a graph of the count rate against time.
    b) Use the graph to find the half-life of the source.

15. Initially a sample of a radio nuclide contains 8000 undecayed nuclei. Its decay constant is 1.5×10^{-2} s^{-1}.
    a) How many nuclei are undecayed after 60 s?
    b) What is the activity of the radio nuclide after 60 s?

16. The half-life of bismuth-212 is 61 min. A sample of bismuth-212 has an activity of 320 Bq.
    a) Calculate the decay constant for bismuth in min^{-1}.
    b) Use this value for the decay constant to calculate the activity of the sample after 180 min.

17. Strontium-90 is a component of 'nuclear fallout' and may be absorbed into bone if ingested. It emits β-particles and its half-life is 28 years.
    a) Explain why the strontium is a serious health hazard.
    b) Calculate the time it takes for the activity of the strontium to fall to 5% of its original value.

Further questions on page 370.

28 Nuclear Energy

What do you think about nuclear power? A quarter of the electricity used in the UK now comes from nuclear power. Do you know how it works? What are the safety issues? This chapter will provide answers to your questions and let you make up your own mind about the nuclear industry.

Nuclear power stations tap into the energy stored inside an atom's nucleus. Huge amounts of energy can be released, but where does it come from and how can we get at it?

In this chapter you will learn:
- how to calculate the energy stored by an atomic nucleus,
- the difference between nuclear fission and fusion,
- how power stations control the release of nuclear energy.

A nuclear power station

▶ Missing mass

You know from the previous chapter that a helium nucleus is made up of 2 protons and 2 neutrons.
If you compare the mass of a helium nucleus with the mass of 2 protons and 2 neutrons you will notice something very odd.
The mass of the nucleus is less than the total mass of the individual particles that it contains!

This is true for all nuclei containing more than one nucleon. The missing mass is known as the **mass difference** or the **mass defect**.
As the masses involved are very small we usually measure them in atomic mass units u, where:

1 u = 1.6605 × 10⁻²⁷ kg   (see page 330)

	Mass (atomic mass units)
proton	1.00728 u
neutron	1.00867 u
helium nucleus	4.00151 u

$1\,u = 1.6605 \times 10^{-27}\ \text{kg}$

Example 1
Using the data in the table opposite, calculate the mass difference for a helium nucleus in atomic mass units, and in kilograms.

Mass of 2p + 2n = (2 × 1.00728 u) + (2 × 1.00867 u)
= 4.03190 u

But mass of helium nucleus = 4.00151 u

∴ Mass difference = 4.03190 u − 4.00151 u
= 0.03039 u
= 0.03039 × 1.6605 × 10⁻²⁷ kg
= 5.046 × 10⁻²⁹ kg

A mass of 5 × 10⁻²⁹ kg may not sound a lot in *everyday* terms. But on an atomic scale it is significant. This mass defect is about 3% of the mass of a proton, or the mass of 55 electrons!

You can see how important it is to measure nuclear masses precisely. Masses are often quoted to 6 significant figures!

▶ A famous equation

So if we split a nucleus into its individual protons and neutrons the total mass increases.
But where does this extra mass come from?
Splitting a nucleus is not easy. The nucleons are held together by very strong but short-range nuclear forces (see page 338).
Overcoming these forces requires energy.
But what happens to this energy? The energy disappears into the system and mass is created! This seems to go against our conventional conservation laws.
It was Einstein who suggested that mass and energy are **equivalent**.
He linked mass and energy in his famous equation:

$$E = m\,c^2$$

Albert Einstein

E is the energy equivalent (in joules, J) of a mass m (in kilograms, kg).
c is the velocity of light (3.00×10^8 m s^{-1}).

> ### Example 2
> Calculate the energy equivalent of the mass difference for the helium nucleus calculated in Example 1.
>
> $$\begin{aligned} E = m\,c^2 &= 5.046 \times 10^{-29}\ \text{kg} \times (3.00 \times 10^8\ \text{m s}^{-1})^2 \\ &= \underline{4.54 \times 10^{-12}\ \text{J}} \quad \text{(3 s.f.)} \end{aligned}$$

This is the energy that is needed to separate the helium nucleus into individual protons and neutrons.
In any system, **the total amount of mass and energy is conserved.**

$^{4}_{2}\text{He} + 4.54 \times 10^{-12}\ \text{J} \ \longrightarrow\ 2p + 2n$
energy

Energy equivalent of 1 u

Einstein's equation uses mass in kilograms and energy in joules.
However, in nuclear physics we are more likely to be working in atomic mass units (u) and electron-volts (eV).
Let's work out the energy equivalent (in eV) of 1 u:

Using Einstein's equation with a precise value for the velocity of light:

$$\begin{aligned} E = m\,c^2 &= 1.6605 \times 10^{-27}\ \text{kg} \times (2.9979 \times 10^8\ \text{m s}^{-1})^2 \\ &= 1.4924 \times 10^{-10}\ \text{J} \end{aligned}$$

But 1 eV = 1.6022×10^{-19} J (see box)

Dividing by 1.6022×10^{-19} J/eV, to convert to electron-volts, gives
$E = 931.5 \times 10^6$ eV, so:

$$\boxed{1\,\text{u} = 931.5\ \text{MeV}}$$

1 u $= 1.6605 \times 10^{-27}$ kg

1 eV $= 1.6022 \times 10^{-19}$ J
(see page 165)

> ### Example 3
> A carbon-12 nucleus has a mass of 11.9967 u.
> How much energy, in MeV, would be needed to split it into its 6 protons and 6 neutrons?
> ($m_p = 1.00728$ u, $m_n = 1.00867$ u)
>
> Mass of 6p + 6n $= (6 \times 1.00728\ \text{u}) + (6 \times 1.00867\ \text{u}) = 12.0957\ \text{u}$
>
> ∴ Mass difference $= 12.0957\ \text{u} - 11.9967\ \text{u} = 0.0990\ \text{u}$
>
> Energy equivalent $= 0.0990 \times 931.5\ \text{MeV} = \underline{92.2\ \text{MeV}}$ needed to separate the 12 nucleons.

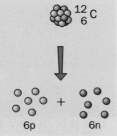

$^{12}_{6}\text{C}$

6p   6n

▶ Physics at work: Nuclear issues

Nuclear waste

The management of radioactive waste is one of the most controversial issues surrounding nuclear power. Although disposal and storage of nuclear waste is a problem, the quantities of waste produced are relatively low. Nuclear power also produces none of the atmospheric pollution caused by burning fossil fuels.

Radioactive waste falls into one of three categories:

High-level waste

A typical reactor contains 200 fuel rods. These need to be replaced *every* four years. The fuel rods are highly radioactive. Once out of the reactor, the rods continue to generate heat due to the radioactive decay of the fission products. The rods are placed in water storage pools for a year or more to cool down.

Used rods contain approximately 96% uranium isotopes and 1% plutonium. These can be separated out and reused. The remaining 3% is fission products. These have long half lives and remain hazardous for thousands of years.

This high-level waste is sealed inside glass blocks in a process called vitrification. The blocks are placed in sealed containers and then buried underground.
The technology for packaging waste safely is straightforward. What isn't certain is how long the storage can remain intact.

The Thermal Oxide Reprocessing Plant (THORP) at Sellafield recovers valuable fuel

Intermediate-level waste

Empty fuel rods, reactor components and chemical sludges used in treating nuclear fuel are classed as intermediate waste. This is 100 times less radioactive than the spent fuel. This waste is encased in cement inside stainless steel drums. The drums are then stored in concrete vaults or underground.

Low-level waste

Solid low-level waste includes protective clothing, packaging and laboratory instruments. It is only slightly radioactive. Low-level waste is compacted and placed in steel containers. The containers are then stored in concrete lined vaults.

Liquid wastes, such as cooling pond water, are cleaned and then discharged into the sea.

BNFL's low-level waste disposal site in Cumbria

Nuclear accidents

Despite stringent safety precautions accidents do still happen. Often this is due to human error.

The UK's worst nuclear accident occurred at Windscale in 1957. A fire melted fuel in the reactor core and led to the release of radioactive iodine into the atmosphere.

The world's worst nuclear disaster occurred at Chernobyl in the Ukraine in 1986. Technicians had disabled vital safety systems while testing the core! An uncontrolled chain reaction led to chemical explosions that blew a hole in the reactor.
Large amounts of radiation were released into the atmosphere and carried across Europe by the wind.
More than 30 people died in the accident and over 100 000 people were evacuated from the region. The final death toll due to radiation-related illness is not yet known.

The damaged reactor at Chernobyl

Summary

An atomic nucleus has less mass than the separate protons and neutrons it contains.
The difference is known as the mass difference or **mass defect**.

Einstein's equation $E = mc^2$ gives the energy equivalent E (in J) of a mass m (kg). c is the speed of light (m s^{-1}).

The energy equivalent of the mass difference for a nucleus is called its **binding energy**.
The greater the binding energy per nucleon, the more stable the nucleus.

Fission is the splitting up of a large nucleus into two smaller nuclei, releasing energy.
Fusion is the joining together of two light nuclei to make a heavier nucleus, releasing energy.
In both fission and fusion the binding energy per nucleon *in*creases. This means that the products are *more* stable.

$1\,u\ \ = 1.66 \times 10^{-27}\ \text{kg}$
$1\,u\ \ = 931.5\ \text{MeV}$
$1\ eV = 1.60 \times 10^{-19}\ \text{J}$

Note: For simplicity *nuclear* masses have been used in calculations throughout the chapter. If you are provided with atomic masses, you must remember to subtract the mass of the Z electrons ($m_e = 0.000\,549\,u$).

▶ Questions

You will need the following data:

proton mass $m_p = 1.007\,28\,u$
neutron mass $m_n = 1.008\,67\,u$
mass of α-particle $= 4.001\,51\,u$
velocity of light $c = 3.00 \times 10^8\ \text{m s}^{-1}$
Mass of $^{2}_{1}\text{H} = 3.3425 \times 10^{-27}\ \text{kg}$
Mass of $^{4}_{2}\text{He} = 6.6425 \times 10^{-27}\ \text{kg}$

Nuclear masses: radium-226 = 225.9771 u
radon-222 = 221.9703 u
uranium-235 = 234.9934 u
lanthanum-146 = 145.8684 u
bromine-87 = 86.9028 u
nickel-60 = 59.9153 u
zinc-63 = 62.9205 u

1. Can you complete these sentences?
   a) A nucleus has .... mass than the protons and neutrons it contains. The missing mass is known as the mass .... or mass ....
   b) The energy equivalent of the mass difference is known as the .... energy.
   c) The binding energy per .... is a useful indication of stability.
   This is the average energy needed to remove each nucleon from the ....
   d) In spontaneous nuclear decay the products weigh .... than the parent nucleus.
   The difference is released as ....
   e) In a .... reaction a large nucleus splits in two. In a .... reaction two light nuclei join together. In both reactions the binding energy per nucleon .... and the products are more stable.

2. Calculate the mass difference in u and in kilograms for the following nuclei:
   a) lithium ($^{7}_{3}\text{Li}$), nuclear mass = 7.014353 u
   b) silicon ($^{28}_{14}\text{Si}$), nuclear mass = 27.969 24 u
   c) copper ($^{63}_{29}\text{Cu}$), nuclear mass = 62.913 67 u
   d) gold ($^{197}_{79}\text{Au}$), nuclear mass = 196.923 18 u

3. For each of the nuclei in question 2, calculate:
   a) the total binding energy in eV,
   b) the binding energy per nucleon in eV.

4. The equation shows the decay of radium into radon:
   $$^{226}_{88}\text{Ra} \ \rightarrow\ ^{222}_{86}\text{Rn} + ^{4}_{2}\alpha$$
   a) Can this reaction happen naturally? Justify your answer.
   b) Calculate the energy released in eV.

5. Calculate the energy in eV released by the following reaction:
   $$^{2}_{1}\text{H} + ^{2}_{1}\text{H} \ \rightarrow\ ^{4}_{2}\text{He} + \text{energy}$$

6. A possible reaction for the fission of uranium is:
   $$^{235}_{92}\text{U} + ^{1}_{0}\text{n} \ \rightarrow\ ^{146}_{57}\text{La} + ^{87}_{35}\text{Br} + 3\,^{1}_{0}\text{n}$$
   Calculate the energy released in the reaction.

7. Calculate the minimum energy needed to make the following reaction happen:
   $$^{60}_{28}\text{Ni} + ^{4}_{2}\alpha \ \rightarrow\ ^{63}_{30}\text{Zn} + ^{1}_{0}\text{n}$$

Further questions on page 372.

357

29 Particle Physics

What is everything made of? What holds everything together? Particle physicists are continuing to search for answers to these questions. This chapter will show you some of the techniques used to study the fundamental particles of matter and what we have learnt about them so far.

In this chapter you will learn:
- what are the building blocks of all matter,
- what antimatter is and how it is created,
- about the fundamental forces that hold everything in the Universe together.

▷ Matter and antimatter

Antimatter is not just science fiction! Every particle has an equivalent antiparticle. For example: antiprotons and antineutrons. These are real particles.

Antimatter is a bit like a mirror image. A particle and its antiparticle have the same mass. They carry equal but opposite charge and they spin in opposite directions.

Some antiparticles have special names and symbols but most are represented by a bar over the particle symbol. For example, $\bar{p}$ ('p–bar') represents an antiproton.

The existence of antimatter was predicted mathematically by British physicist Paul Dirac in 1928. Dirac's equation links the complex theories of special relativity and quantum mechanics. The equation describes both negative electrons and an equivalent *positive* particle. These **anti-electrons** or **positrons** (e^+ or β^+) were discovered experimentally by Carl Anderson in 1932.

Antiprotons and antineutrons were first observed in accelerator experiments in the mid 1950's. Since then antiparticles have been observed or detected for all known particles.
Many antiparticles occur naturally. They are created by high-energy collisions of cosmic rays with the molecules in our atmosphere. Positrons are also created in β^+ decay (page 340).

Can antiparticles join together to make anti-atoms and real antimatter? In theory, yes. In 1995 at the European Laboratory for Particle Physics (CERN), atoms of antihydrogen were created by joining positrons with antiprotons:

antiproton	+	positron	⟹	antihydrogen
$\bar{p}$	+	e^+	⟹	$\bar{H}$

Only 9 anti-atoms were made in total.
These lasted less than 10^{-10} s!

mirror image

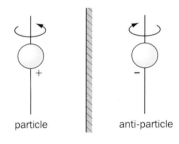

particle   anti-particle

Paul Dirac predicted the existence of antimatter in 1928

Annihilation

Why does antimatter not last long? As soon as an antiparticle meets its particle, the two destroy each other. Their mass is converted to energy. This is called **annihilation**.

For example, when an electron and a positron collide, they annihilate, producing two γ-ray photons of energy:

$$_{-1}^{0}e^- \ + \ _{+1}^{0}e^+ \ \Longrightarrow \ 2 \ _0^0\gamma$$

Why are two photons produced? One photon could conserve charge and mass/energy. But **momentum** must also be conserved, and for that to happen, 2 photons are needed.
If an electron and positron with the same speed collide head on, the total momentum before the collision is zero.
For zero momentum after the collision we must have two identical photons moving in opposite directions.

When sufficient energy is available, annihilation can produce short-lived particles. The energy is converted back into **matter**. This is how new particles are created in accelerator experiments.

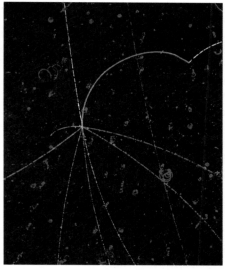

An antiproton (blue) collides with a proton in the bubble chamber liquid. The annihilation creates 4 positive (red) and 4 negative (green) particles.

Example 1

An electron and positron with negligible kinetic energy annihilate and produce two identical γ-ray photons. Calculate a) the energy released and b) the frequency of the γ-photons.

Rest mass of an electron = 9.11×10^{-31} kg $h = 6.63 \times 10^{-34}$ J s $c = 3.00 \times 10^8$ m s^{-1}

a) Using Einstein's equation (see page 349),
   $E = mc^2 = (2 \times 9.11 \times 10^{-31} \text{ kg}) \times (3.00 \times 10^8 \text{ m s}^{-1})^2 = \underline{1.64 \times 10^{-13} \text{ J}}$

b) Using Planck's equation $E = hf$ (see page 167),
   Energy of each photon $= \frac{1}{2} \times 1.64 \times 10^{-13}$ J $\therefore \ f = \dfrac{E}{h} = \dfrac{\frac{1}{2} \times 1.64 \times 10^{-13} \text{ J}}{6.63 \times 10^{-34} \text{ J s}} = \underline{1.24 \times 10^{20} \text{ Hz}}$

Pair production

Pair production is the opposite of annihilation. High-energy photons can vanish, creating particle–antiparticle pairs in their place.
For example, a γ-ray can produce an electron–positron pair:

$$_0^0\gamma \ \Longrightarrow \ _{-1}^{0}e^- \ + \ _{+1}^{0}e^+$$

A third particle such as an atomic nucleus or electron is often involved indirectly. This recoils, carrying away some of the photon energy.

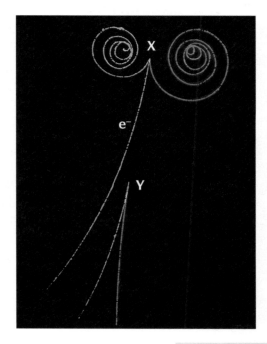

The photograph shows the creation of electron–positron pairs at X and Y in a bubble chamber (see page 333). The tracks are curved due to a magnetic field. They are shown in green (electrons) and red (positrons). Notice that the γ-ray photons leave no tracks as they are uncharged.

In event X a third particle is involved. (This is an electron ejected from the bubble chamber liquid during the interaction.)

Why are the tracks at X more curved than at Y?
In event X the ejected electron carries off some of the energy.
This leaves less energy for the electron–positron pair.
The lower the energy (and speed) of the particles produced, the more they are deflected in the magnetic field. This is why their paths curve more.

▶ Fundamental particles

So, what is everything made of? A simple answer is atoms.
But what are atoms made of? We know that an atom contains
electrons around a nucleus of protons and neutrons.
Are these *fundamental* particles, or are these too made up of
even smaller particles?
Scientists have tried to find out by studying the bits thrown out
when high-energy particles collide together.
Bubble chamber photographs such as this one show the tracks of
the particles produced. The tracks can tell us about the charge
and momentum of the particles:

- *The greater the ionisation, the thicker the tracks.*
  Slow, heavy, charged particles (eg. α-particles) leave thick tracks.
  Fast electrons leave thin irregular tracks.

- *Uncharged particles leave no tracks.* You can guess that
  they are there from the gaps between other tracks.

- *Positive and negative particles curve in opposite directions*,
  when the bubble chamber is operated in a magnetic field.
  The directions are given by Fleming's left hand rule (page 224).

- *The greater the momentum, the less curved the tracks.*
  Particles spiral inwards as they lose energy through collisions.

As a result of these collision experiments, more than 200 different
sub-atomic particles have been identified!

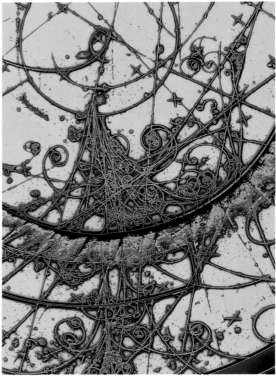

Tracks in a bubble chamber

Enter the quark

In 1963 the American physicist Murray Gell-Mann came up with
an idea that simplified things. He suggested that the properties of
all of these new particles could be explained if they were made up
of different *combinations* of *smaller* particles.
He called these smaller particles **quarks**.
Experiments soon confirmed that quarks existed.

We cannot see inside an atom with visible light as the wavelength
is too large. Seeing an object requires wavelengths that are small
compared to the size of the object.

To discover the nucleus Rutherford used α-particles (page 329).
The α-particles behaved like waves with de Broglie wavelength of
10^{-15} m (see page 170). This is much smaller than the diameter
of a nucleus (about 10^{-10} m).

The electrons that are used to probe inside protons and neutrons
need even smaller de Broglie wavelengths. Such small
wavelengths require very high-energy electrons (~10 GeV).

When the high-energy electrons are fired at protons and neutrons,
some pass almost straight through, while others are deflected
through large angles. This is called **deep inelastic scattering**:

Inelastic means that some kinetic energy is lost. This is converted
to matter as short-lived particles are produced in the collision.

This scattering can only be explained if protons and neutrons
contain charge concentrated at *three* points. These are the three
quarks that make up each proton and neutron.

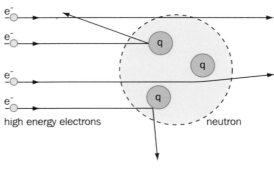

Deep inelastic scattering

360

The quark family

The original model proposed just three quarks called **up**, **down** and **strange**.

As accelerator technology developed, the higher-energy collisions allowed physicists to create heavier and heavier particles. These are made of more massive quarks.

We now know that there are **6** types or **flavours** of quark, arranged in three groups called **generations**:

Each of these also has an antiquark.

Evidence for the heaviest quark, the top quark, was only found as recently as 1994.

1st generation	increasing mass ↓	up (u) ⬆	down (d) ⬇
2nd generation		charm (c) ☘	strange (s)
3rd generation		top (t)	bottom (b)

Quarks

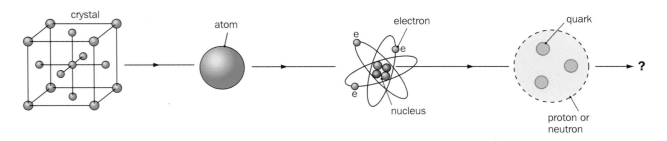

The leptons

Not everything is made of quarks. Particles can be split into two groups: **hadrons** and **leptons**.
(See also the particle family tree in the Summary on page 369.)

Hadrons are made up of quarks. These are held together by strong nuclear forces. Protons and neutrons are hadrons.

Leptons are fundamental particles. As far as we know they have **no** internal structure. They are not made up of smaller particles. Leptons do not feel strong nuclear forces.

There are **6** leptons, in three generations, to match the quarks:
Each lepton also has an antiparticle.

The muon and tau are heavier versions of the electron. They carry the same charge (1.6×10^{-19} C).
Charge is often given relative to this number.
The **relative charge** of the electron, muon and tau is −1. Neutrinos are uncharged.

Only the electron and the electron-neutrino are stable.
The other leptons rapidly decay into these.

Leptons

1st generation	increasing mass * ↓	electron e^-	electron-neutrino ν or ν_e
2nd generation		muon μ^-	muon-neutrino ν_μ
3rd generation		tau τ^-	tau-neutrino ν_τ

* neutrinos are thought to have zero rest mass

All ordinary matter is made up of first generation particles: up and down quarks, electrons and electron-neutrinos.
Second and third generation particles are routinely created in accelerators and the hot centres of stars, but they are unstable. Most decay in less than a millionth of a second.

So what is *everything* made of?
The answer appears to be leptons and quarks.

▶ Inside the hadrons

Particles that are made up of quarks are called **hadrons**.
These are split into two types:

1. **Baryons.** These contain *three quarks*.
   Protons and neutrons are baryons.
   Protons contain 2 up (u) and 1 down (d) quark.
   Neutrons contain 1 up (u) and 2 down (d) quarks.

   proton p = (u u d)   antiproton $\bar{p}$ = ($\bar{u}$ $\bar{u}$ $\bar{d}$)

   neutron n = (u d d)   antineutron $\bar{n}$ = ($\bar{u}$ $\bar{d}$ $\bar{d}$)

   The only stable baryon is the proton. All other baryons decay
   into protons. Even neutrons are unstable outside the nucleus.
   They decay with a half-life of 11 minutes:

   $$n \longrightarrow p + e^- + \bar{\nu}_e$$

2. **Mesons.** These contain *a quark and an antiquark*.
   There are no stable mesons. They rapidly decay into leptons
   and photons (energy). The only mesons that last long enough
   to leave tracks in a detector such as a bubble chamber are
   pions and kaons:

   Pions: π^0 = (u $\bar{u}$) or (d $\bar{d}$) π^+ = (u $\bar{d}$) π^- = ($\bar{u}$ d)

   Kaons: K^0 = (d $\bar{s}$) K^+ = (u $\bar{s}$) K^- = ($\bar{u}$ s)

Confused by all these new names? Have a look at the particle
family tree in the Summary on page 369. This shows all the
particles you need to know at A-level.

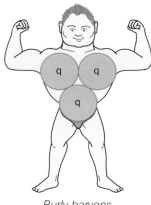

Burly baryons
(3 quarks)

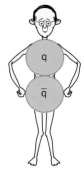

Measly mesons
(quark + anti-quark)

▶ Quark properties and conservation laws

The table shows the properties of the six quarks
and their antiquarks:

Charge
This is a property that you are familiar with.

Individual quarks have fractional charges.
They combine together to make particles
with a total relative charge of 0 or ±1.

For example (using the table),

proton (u u d)
total charge = $+\frac{2}{3}$ $+\frac{2}{3}$ $-\frac{1}{3}$ = +1

neutron (u d d)
total charge = $+\frac{2}{3}$ $-\frac{1}{3}$ $-\frac{1}{3}$ = 0

K^- ($\bar{u}$ s)
total charge = $-\frac{2}{3}$ $-\frac{1}{3}$ = −1

In any particle interaction, **total charge**
is conserved – it stays the same.

		Symbol	Relative charge*	Baryon number	Strangeness
quarks	up	u	$+\frac{2}{3}$	$+\frac{1}{3}$	0
	down	d	$-\frac{1}{3}$	$+\frac{1}{3}$	0
	charm	c	$+\frac{2}{3}$	$+\frac{1}{3}$	0
	strange	s	$-\frac{1}{3}$	$+\frac{1}{3}$	−1
	top	t	$+\frac{2}{3}$	$+\frac{1}{3}$	0
	bottom	b	$-\frac{1}{3}$	$+\frac{1}{3}$	0
antiquarks	anti-up	$\bar{u}$	$-\frac{2}{3}$	$-\frac{1}{3}$	0
	antidown	$\bar{d}$	$+\frac{1}{3}$	$-\frac{1}{3}$	0
	anticharm	$\bar{c}$	$-\frac{2}{3}$	$-\frac{1}{3}$	0
	antistrange	$\bar{s}$	$+\frac{1}{3}$	$-\frac{1}{3}$	+1
	anti-top	$\bar{t}$	$-\frac{2}{3}$	$-\frac{1}{3}$	0
	antibottom	$\bar{b}$	$+\frac{1}{3}$	$-\frac{1}{3}$	0

* relative to a charge of 1.6×10^{-19} C, the charge on an electron

Baryon number

Some particle interactions never happen even though charge and mass/energy can be conserved.
For example, protons do *not* decay into positrons:

$$p \not\rightarrow e^+ + \pi^0$$

To explain this, scientists came up with another property that must be conserved, called **baryon number**.
All quarks carry a baryon number of $+\frac{1}{3}$. For antiquarks it is $-\frac{1}{3}$.

What is the total baryon number for a proton containing 3 quarks? And for a meson containing a quark and an antiquark?

Baryon numbers for different types of particles are given in the table:

In the interaction shown above, the total baryon number is $+1$ on the left and 0 on the right. This is why the reaction cannot happen.
Baryon number is always conserved.

Particle	Baryon number
All baryons (eg. p, n)	+1
All antibaryons	−1
Mesons (eg. π, K) and leptons	0

Lepton number

In a similar way leptons are allocated a property called **lepton number**. *Lepton number is always conserved.*
This explains why leptons are always formed from non-leptons in pairs – one lepton and one antilepton.

eg.	π^+ ⟹	μ^+	+	ν_μ
lepton number:	0 →	−1	+	1

An antilepton is created with a neutrino of the *same* generation.

Particle	Lepton number
All leptons	+1
All antileptons	−1
Hadrons (baryons & mesons)	0

Strangeness

Particles that contain strange quarks are called strange particles.
Strange particles are unusually long-lived. A particle can have a strangeness number from $+3$ to -3 depending on the number of strange or antistrange quarks it contains.

Given its name it is not surprising that the conservation law is a bit odd too! Strangeness is conserved in interactions involving the strong nuclear force. In weak interactions, strangeness can be conserved or it can change by ± 1.

eg.	K^+ ⟹	μ^+	+	ν_μ
strangeness:	+1 →	0	+	0

This is allowed, as kaon decay is a weak interaction.

Example 2
Use the conservation laws to identify the unknown particles X and Y in the equations for electron (β^-) decay, and positron (β^+) decay.

β^- decay.
A neutron changes to a proton and an electron:

	n ⟹	p	+	e^-	+	X
charge:	0 →	1		−1		?
baryon no.:	1 →	1		0		?
lepton no.:	0 →	0		1		?

To balance the equation, X must have charge = 0, baryon number = 0, and lepton number −1. This is an uncharged antilepton. So X is an antineutrino ($\bar{\nu}_e$).

β^+ decay.
A proton changes to a neutron and a positron:

	p ⟹	n	+	e^+	+	Y
charge:	1 →	0		1		?
baryon no.:	1 →	1		0		?
lepton no.:	0 →	0		−1		?

To balance the equation, Y must have charge = 0, baryon number = 0, and lepton number +1. This is an uncharged lepton. So Y is a neutrino (ν_e).

Electron-neutrinos and anti-neutrinos are needed here since the decays involve first generation leptons.
Remember that a neutrino is needed in the equation to explain the energy distribution of the particles (see page 339).

▶ Fundamental forces and exchange particles

We now know what *everything* is made of.
The building blocks of matter are quarks and leptons. But what holds these together to make everything you see around you?
All the forces in the Universe and all particle interactions are the result of just **4 fundamental forces**.
Do you remember these from Chapter 2?

- **Gravitational force** (see also page 78)
  The weakest of the four forces, but it acts over an infinite distance. It pulls objects towards the Earth and holds stars and galaxies together.
- **Electromagnetic force** (see also page 254)
  This also has an infinite range. It holds atoms and molecules together. It is responsible for the chemical, mechanical and electrical properties of matter.
- **Weak nuclear force**
  Its range does not extend beyond the nucleus.
  It is responsible for β-decay and fusion reactions in stars.
- **Strong nuclear force** (see also page 338)
  This is the strongest force but it has a very short range.
  It acts only between neighbouring nucleons.
  It binds quarks and antiquarks to hold nucleons together.

We know that these forces exist. We can feel them and measure them. But what actually causes the force?
We know that two positive particles will repel but can we explain why? Particle physics provides an answer. The theory is that individual particles interact by exchanging particles called **exchange particles**.
There are different exchange particles for each type of force.
For example, the exchange particle for the electromagnetic force is the photon. So two positively-charged particles repel each other by exchanging photons.

Particle exchange can produce attractive or repulsive forces.
To get a very simple picture of how an exchange can cause this, think about the ice skaters in the diagram:

By throwing a heavy ball to each other, they are pushed further apart. The exchange produces a repulsive force.
Standing back to back and exchanging a boomerang will push them closer together, like an attractive force.

The exchange particles for each force are given in the table below.
All have now been discovered apart from the graviton.

Force	Acts on	Relative strength	Range	Exchange particle
strong nuclear	quarks	1	10^{-15} m	gluon (g)
electromagnetic	charged particles	10^{-2}	∞	photon (γ)
weak nuclear	quarks and leptons	10^{-5}	10^{-17} m	Z^0, W^+, W^- particles
gravity	everything with mass	10^{-40}	∞	graviton

▶ Feynman diagrams

The photograph shows American physicist Richard Feynman (1918–1988). He suggested a simple way of representing particle interactions in a diagram.

Feynman diagrams consist of:

- straight lines (with one free end) to represent the physical particles *before* and *after* the interaction,
- wavy lines connecting the straight lines and representing the particle exchange. Charge must be conserved at each junction.

Here are the Feynman diagrams for some common interactions.

Electromagnetic interactions

Notice the 'before' and 'after' labels:

Notice that the particle lines point in the same direction for attraction and for repulsion.
The direction of the lines is **not** significant.
They do **not** show the direction of the particles.

The photon exchanged is sometimes called a virtual photon as it is not actually observed.

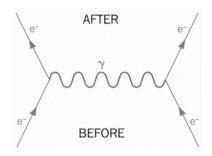

electrostatic repulsion between 2 electrons

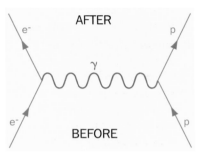

attraction between an electron and a proton

Weak interactions

Feynman diagrams can be used to show changes in quark structure.

In β⁻ decay a neutron changes into a proton. For this to happen, a down (d) quark changes to an up (u) quark emitting a W⁻ particle.
This decays into an electron and antineutrino:

The quarks can be represented by their own lines on the diagram (far right):
Notice that only the quark that changes is connected to the exchange particle line.

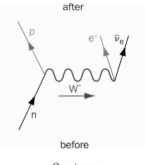

β⁻ decay

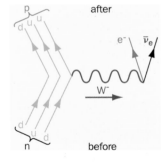

β⁻ decay showing the quarks

Strong interactions

Gluons hold the quarks together to make the hadrons (eg. protons, neutrons, pions):

Protons and neutrons are held together to make a nucleus by the exchange of pions:

The strong force results from gluon exchange between all the quarks that the protons, neutrons and pions are made of.

Gluon exchange is sometimes represented by curly rather than wavy lines.

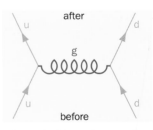

gluons hold quarks together

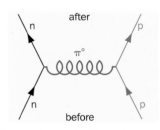

pion exchange holds protons and neutrons together to form a nucleus

▶ Particle accelerators

Particle physicists can create new particles by colliding other particles together. There are two ways of doing this:

1. Colliding beam experiments
The particles are fired towards each other and collide head on. Colliding beam experiments have the highest possible collision energy for making new particles. The main disadvantage is that only a small fraction of the particles collide when the beams meet.

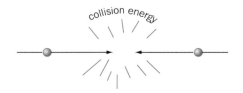

2. Fixed target experiments
Particles are fired at a fixed target. This increases the likelihood of collisions but there is less energy available for particle creation. Why is this? With only one particle moving there is less kinetic energy to begin with. Also the total momentum cannot be zero before the collision, and momentum is always conserved, so the particles that are created must be moving. This leaves less energy available to create the particles' mass.

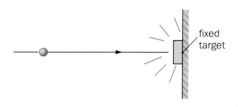

The creation of massive particles requires vast amounts of energy and so the particles need to be accelerated to high speeds. This is the job of an **accelerator**.

All accelerators are based on the same basic principles. A charged particle accelerates across a gap between two electrodes if there is a potential difference between them. From page 165:

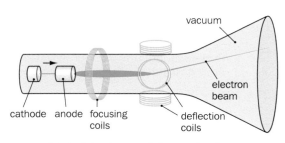

Energy transferred, E_k =	**charge, Q** ×	**p.d., V**
(joules)	(coulombs)	(volts)

A television is a particle accelerator

Did you know that most people have an accelerator in their living room? A television is a particle accelerator. It accelerates electrons towards the screen at about 20 keV. What is the p.d. needed here?
Remember that *1 eV is the energy gained by accelerating an electron through a p.d. of 1 V* (see page 165).
So for 20 keV we need a p.d. of 20 kV.

One way to get high-energy particles is to increase the size of the accelerating p.d. Van de Graaff generators, like the one in the diagram, produce a high p.d. by making a static charge build up on the dome. They can accelerate protons or small positive ions to about 10 MeV.

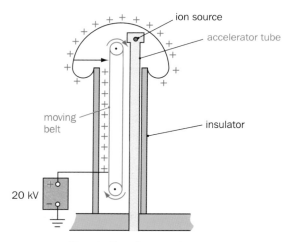

Van de Graaff generator

There is a limit to how far you can increase an accelerating p.d. before sparks start to jump between the electrodes. The three main accelerator types described on the opposite page get round this by using a relatively small p.d. again and again.

Example 3
What is the energy gained in a) eV and b) joules when a proton is accelerated through a p.d. of 2.0×10^6 V? Charge on electron, $e = -1.6 \times 10^{-19}$ C

a) 1eV = energy gained when a proton or electron is accelerated through a p.d. of 1 V (since they have equal charge)
∴ For a p.d. of 2.0×10^6 V, energy gained = 2.0×10^6 eV = 2.0 MeV (2 s.f.)

b) **Energy, E_k = charge on proton, Q × p.d., V** = $+1.6 \times 10^{-19}$ C × 2.0×10^6 V = 3.2×10^{-13} J (2 s.f.)

Linear accelerator or 'linac'

This accelerates particles in a straight line:
The cylindrical electrodes are connected to an alternating supply
so that they are alternately positive and negative. The frequency
of the p.d. is set so that as the particles emerge from each
electrode they are accelerated across the next gap.
Why do the electrodes get progressively longer? To keep in step
with the alternating p.d., the particles must take the same time to
travel through each electrode. As the particles get faster the tubes
must get longer. The accelerator may be 3 km long!
A linear accelerator can accelerate electrons to about 50 GeV.

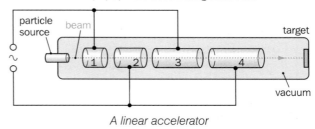

1, 2, 3, 4 are accelerating electrodes

A linear accelerator

Cyclotron

A cyclotron consists of two semicircular metal 'dees' separated by
a small gap. When a charged particle enters the cyclotron,
a perpendicular magnetic field makes it move along a circular
path at a steady speed. Each time the particle reaches the gap
between the dees, an alternating p.d. accelerates it across.

The force on a moving charged particle in a magnetic field is
given by $F = BQv$ (see page 226). Since this provides the
centripetal force ($F = mv^2/r$, see page 72), we can write:

$$\frac{mv^2}{r} = BQv \qquad \therefore \quad v = \frac{BQr}{m}$$

This shows that the velocity is proportional to the radius, so as the
particles get faster they spiral outwards. The time spent in each
dee stays the same (see the coloured box):
So the alternating p.d. must reverse every ($\pi m/BQ$) seconds.

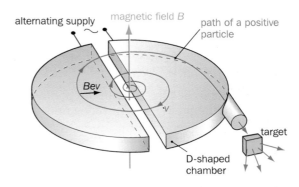

How long does a particle take to travel along
its semicircular path within each dee?

$$\text{time} = \frac{\text{distance}}{\text{speed}} = \frac{\pi r}{BQr/m} = \frac{\pi m}{BQ}$$

This is independent of the speed and radius.
See also page 227.

Did you know that as objects get faster they get **heavier**?
This is described in Einstein's theory of **special relativity**.
The effect is only really noticeable at speeds close to the speed of
light. The top speed of a particle in a cyclotron is limited by this
relativistic increase in mass. A change in mass will affect the time
taken to travel through a dee. The particle will then get out of
step with the alternating p.d.
Cyclotrons are used to accelerate heavy particles such as protons
and α-particles. These can reach energies of about 25 MeV.

Synchrotron

Synchrotrons overcome the problem of relativistic increase in mass.
Electromagnets keep the particles moving in a circle. Electrodes
accelerate the particles at various points on the loop. As the
particles gain energy, the magnetic field is increased to keep them
moving in a circle of constant radius.
Some synchrotrons have two loops which overlap to collide
particles and antiparticles head on.
Synchrotrons can accelerate protons to 1000 GeV or more.

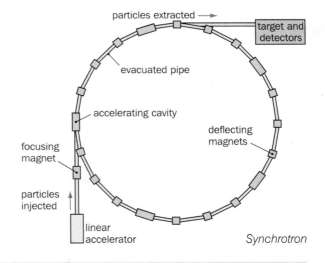

Synchrotron

Example 4
Calculate the cyclotron frequency needed to accelerate protons if the magnetic field across the chamber is 0.80 T.
($e = 1.6 \times 10^{-19}$ C, $m_p = 1.67 \times 10^{-27}$ kg)

Time in each dee $= \pi m/BQ$ (see above)

$$\therefore \text{ Frequency, } f = \frac{1}{T} = \frac{1}{2(\pi m/BQ)} = \frac{BQ}{2\pi m} = \frac{0.80 \text{ T} \times 1.6 \times 10^{-19} \text{ C}}{2 \times \pi \times 1.67 \times 10^{-27} \text{ kg}} = 1.2 \times 10^7 \text{ Hz} \text{ (12 MHz)} \text{ (2 s.f.)}$$

▶ Physics at work: Particle Physics

PET scanners

Positron Emission Tomography (PET) is a medical technique that uses the annihilation of antimatter in a patient's body to produce images of an organ's activity.

The patient is injected with a radioisotope that decays by positron emission. The positrons quickly annihilate with electrons in the body. This produces two γ-rays which fly off in opposite directions and are detected outside the body. The location of the decay can then be pinpointed.

PET is often used for brain scans:
Active areas of the brain show up clearly, as the increased blood flow leads to greater concentrations of radioisotopes.

PET images like the ones in the photograph can reveal the parts of the brain used for different activities.

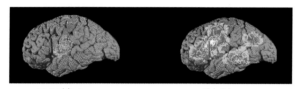

speaking   *thinking*

World Wide Web

Do you surf the net? The amount of information available is staggering. The problem is often finding what you need. The World Wide Web (www) helps to make this information more accessible by cross-referencing related web pages. You browse through connected sites by clicking on hyperlinks that take you directly to other pages.

Did you know that the World Wide Web was an offshoot of particle physics research? The Web was developed in 1989 by British scientist Tim Berners-Lee. He created a new data format called HyperText Transfer Protocol (HTTP).

This was designed to allow particle physics groups around the world to share the wide variety of data held on their different computers via the Internet. The use of embedded hyperlinks made it possible to browse the data for related information at the click of a mouse button.
Millions of people now use the World Wide Web everyday as the Internet has changed the way we work and shop.

In a cyber-café

BaBar and the missing antimatter

Why is there so little antimatter in the Universe? The Big Bang should have created equal amounts of matter and antimatter. So why didn't everything annihilate? Are there whole antimatter galaxies that we have yet to discover?
If not, where did the antimatter go?

One possibility is that matter and antimatter are not truly symmetrical. Perhaps antiparticles decay faster than particles. If antimatter decayed before it had a chance to annihilate, this could explain the excess of matter in the Universe.

BaBar is an international experiment to investigate the differences between short-lived 'B' particles and their antiparticles, 'B-bars'. It is hoped that this will help to solve the mystery of the missing antimatter.

Summary

A particle family tree:

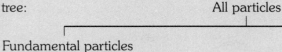

All particles

Fundamental particles (no internal structure)

Non-fundamental particles
Hadrons (made of quarks)

Leptons
(electron, muon, tau, neutrinos)

Exchange particles
(gluon, W, Z, photon)

Baryons
(contain 3 quarks)
eg. proton, neutron

Mesons
(quark + antiquark)
eg. pion, kaon

In any interaction, some properties are ***always*** conserved: charge, mass/energy, baryon number and lepton number. Strangeness is conserved in strong nuclear interactions. (Strangeness can change by 0 or ± 1 in weak interactions.)

Particle interactions can be represented by Feynman diagrams.

All particles have an antimatter equivalent with the same mass, and equal but opposite charge and spin.

▶ Questions

1. Can you complete these sentences?
   a) A particle and its antiparticle have the same ...., and equal but opposite .... and ....
   b) When a particle and its antiparticle meet they .... Their mass is converted to ....
   c) The opposite process to annihilation is called .... production.
   d) The six types or flavours of quark are ....
   e) The six leptons are ....
   f) The .... nuclear force is felt by hadrons but not by leptons.
   g) Particles that are made up of three quarks are called ....
      Particles that contain a quark and an antiquark are called ....
   h) .... and .... are examples of baryons.
      .... and .... are examples of mesons.
   i) In any interaction, the charge, the mass/energy, the .... number and the .... number are always conserved.
   j) The exchange particle for the strong nuclear force is the ....
      Z and W particles carry the .... force.
      Electromagnetic forces are carried by ....

2. What combination of quarks do the following particles contain:
   a) proton
   b) neutron
   c) π^0, π^+, π^-
   d) K^0, K^+, K^-

3. Using the data in the table on page 362, calculate the charge, baryon number and strangeness for each of the particles in question 2.

4. Each particle in question 2 has an antiparticle. Use your answer to question 2 to work out the quark combinations for these antiparticles. What do you notice about π^0 and its antiparticle?

5. What is the minimum photon energy needed to create a proton–antiproton pair?
   ($m_p = 1.67 \times 10^{-27}$ kg, $c = 3.00 \times 10^8$ m s^{-1})

6. Use the conservation laws and the data tables on pages 362–3 to work out whether the following ***weak*** interactions can happen:

   a) Muon decay: $\mu^- \xrightarrow{?} e^- + \bar{\nu}_e + \nu_\mu$

   b) Electron capture: $p + e^- \xrightarrow{?} n + \nu_e$

   c) Kaon decay: $K^+ \xrightarrow{?} \pi^+ + \pi^0$

7. Sketch Feynman diagrams showing:
   a) electron capture (see question 6b),
   b) electrostatic repulsion between two protons,
   c) strong interaction between two protons,
   d) β^+ decay.

8. Use the table of quark properties on page 362 to explain why mesons and antimesons can only have strangeness values of 0 or ± 1.

9. Protons are injected into a synchrotron with an energy of 50 MeV. The protons are accelerated by a p.d. of 6.0 kV at 12 points around the ring. Calculate:
   a) the energy gained by the protons in one lap,
   b) the number of laps needed to reach 50 GeV.

Further questions on page 373.

▶ Radioactivity

1. A source of ionising radiation contains 3.87×10^{24} radioactive atoms of a certain nuclide and has an activity of 4.05×10^{13} Bq.
   a) Calculate the decay constant and half-life of the nuclide. [4]
   b) Calculate the time taken for the activity of the source to fall to 1.26×10^{12} Bq. [2] (OCR)

2. Boron has two isotopes represented by the nuclide symbols $^{11}_{5}B$ and $^{12}_{5}B$.
   a) In what way do the nuclei Boron-11 and Boron-12 differ? [1]
   b) Calculate the number of atoms in a sample of Boron-12 of mass 6.0 kg. [2] (OCR)

3. A student carries out an experiment to determine the half-life of a radioactive isotope M. After subtracting the background count from the readings, the student plots the smooth curve shown in the diagram.

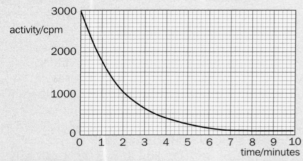

   a) From this graph he concludes that the isotope M is not pure, but contains a small proportion of another isotope C with a relatively long half-life. State a feature of the graph which supports this conclusion and estimate the activity of isotope C. [2]
   b) Determine the half-life of isotope M. Show clearly how you obtained your answer. [3] (Edex)

4. $^{235}_{92}U$ and $^{238}_{92}U$ are isotopes of uranium. The half-life of $^{235}_{92}U$ is 7.0×10^{8} y and that of $^{238}_{92}U$ is 4.5×10^{9} y.
   a) State the number of protons, neutrons and electrons in a neutral atom of each. [2]
   b) According to a popular theory, there were equal numbers of each isotope when the Earth was formed. Assuming this to be true, estimate the ratio $R = $ (number of $^{235}_{92}U$)/(number of $^{238}_{92}U$) at a time 4.5×10^{9} years after formation. [3]
   c) The present day value of R is found to be about 0.007. What does the application of this theory suggest about the age of the Earth? [2] (OCR)

5. A sample of milk is contaminated with a very small quantity of strontium-90. This isotope decays by β^{-}-emission with a half-life of approximately 28 y. Explain why it would be very difficult to use this contaminated sample of milk to obtain an accurate value for the half-life of strontium-90. [2] (Edex)

6. Radioactive sources can often be very useful, yet it is known that they are hazardous. The table lists some sources and their properties.

type of source	useful radiation	half-life
Manganese-52	γ	5.6 day
Cobalt-60	γ	5.3 year
Strontium-90	β	28 year
Thallium-210	β	1.3 minute
Radon-220	α	52 second
Americium-241	α	460 year

   a) Explain why the radiation from such sources is hazardous. [5]
   b) Radioactive sources are to be used in each of the following situations:
      i) To trace the path of an underground stream.
      ii) To kill cells in a tumour deep inside a human body, using a radiotherapy machine.
      iii) To act as a smoke detector.
      For each of these situations choose an appropriate source from the table, explain your choice and explain any safety precautions which should be taken. [10] (OCR)

7. A certain radioactive source contains several radioactive isotopes and is known to emit α, β and γ radiation. The source is to be used to produce a beam of β radiation.
   a) How would you remove α radiation from the beam without significantly removing β or γ radiation? [1]
   b) The diagram shows a proposed method of separating the remaining two types of radiation.

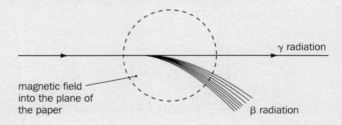

      i) Why does the magnetic field leave the γ radiation undeflected? [1]
      ii) Why does the magnetic field cause the β radiation to spread out? [3] (AQA)

8. Excavations near Welshpool, Powys, have revealed the remains of a large wooden monument two-thirds the size of Stonehenge. Archaeological finds suggest that the site is about 4000 y old. If carbon-14 dating were used to check this estimate, what activity would you expect to find for 1 g of the wood of the monument? (half-life of carbon-14 is 5700 y, activity of living wood is 19 counts min^{-1} for 1 g.) [7] (W)

9. Radiocarbon dating is possible because of the presence of radioactive carbon-14 ($^{14}_{6}C$) caused by collisions of neutrons with nitrogen-14 ($^{14}_{7}N$) in the upper atmosphere. The equation for the reaction is:

$$^{14}_{7}N + ^{1}_{0}n = ^{14}_{6}C + \quad X$$

The half-life of carbon-14 is 5700 y.

a) Identify the particle X. [2]

b) The mass of carbon-14 produced by this reaction in one year is 7.5 kg. 14 g of carbon-14 contains 6.0×10^{23} atoms. Show that the number of carbon-14 atoms produced each year is approximately 3×10^{26}. [1]

c) Calculate the decay constant of carbon-14 in y^{-1}. [2]

d) Assuming that the number of carbon-14 atoms in the Earth and its atmosphere is constant, then 3×10^{26} carbon-14 atoms must decay each year. Use this fact to calculate the number of carbon-14 atoms in the Earth and its atmosphere. [1]

e) A sample of wood containing carbon-14 from a tree which had recently been chopped down had an activity of 0.80 Bq. A sample of the same size from an ancient boat had an activity of 0.30 Bq. Sketch a graph to show how the activity of the sample, having an initial activity of 0.80 Bq, will vary with time over a period of three half-lives. Use the graph to estimate the age of the boat. [3]

f) Explain why an activity of 0.80 Bq would be difficult to measure in a school laboratory. [2] (AQA)

10. A space probe to one of the outer planets is to be powered by a radioactive source containing 2.0 kg of plutonium-238 of half-life 87 y. (1 y $\approx 3.2 \times 10^{7}$ s)

a) Calculate the approximate number of plutonium atoms initially in the source. [2]

b) Calculate the decay constant, in s^{-1}, of plutonium-238. [2]

c) Hence determine the initial activity of the source. [2]

d) Unfortunately the rocket carrying the space probe explodes on take-off and the probe's radioactive fuel is released into the Earth's atmosphere. How long will it take for the activity due to this release to fall to 10% of its initial value? [2] (Edex)

11. The activity of a sample of a radioactive isotope of iodine is 3.7×10^{4} Bq. 48 hours later the activity is found to be 3.1×10^{4} Bq.

a) Show that the decay constant is about 1.0×10^{-6} s^{-1}. [2]

b) Find the half-life of the iodine isotope. [2] (AQA)

▶ The nuclear model of the atom

12. a) Describe the principal features of the *nuclear model of the atom* suggested by Rutherford. [4]

b) When gold foil is bombarded by alpha particles it is found that most of the alpha particles pass through the foil without significant change in direction or loss of energy. A few particles are deviated from their original direction by more than 90°. Explain, in terms of the nuclear model of the atom and by considering the nature of the forces acting, why:-

i) some alpha particles are deflected through large angles,

ii) most of the alpha particles pass through the foil without any significant change in direction or significant loss in energy. [5] (AQA)

13. The 3.4 MeV (5.4×10^{-13} J) α particle shown in the diagram approaches a gold nucleus. Its trajectory is such that, at its distance of closest approach, it has lost half of its kinetic energy.

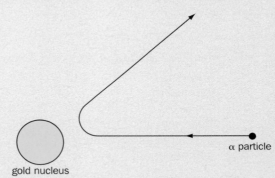

gold nucleus

α particle

a) Explain why the α particle loses kinetic energy as it approaches the gold nucleus. [2]

b) State the value of the potential energy of the α particle at the distance of closest approach. [1]

c) Sketch on a copy of the diagram, the path of another 3.4 MeV α particle for which all the kinetic energy is converted into potential energy at its position of closest approach to the nucleus. [3] (AQA)

14. When α particles are projected at a thin metal foil in an evacuated enclosure they are scattered at various angles.

a) In which direction will the maximum number of α particles coming from the foil be detected? [1]

b) Describe the angular distribution of the scattered α particles around the foil. [2]

c) What do the results suggest about the structure of the metal atoms? [2]

d) Explain why the foil used must be thin. [1]

e) Explain why the incident beam of α particles should be parallel and narrow. [2] (AQA)

▶ ## Nuclear energy

15. A neutral atom of a nuclide of tin has the following nuclear symbol $^{120}_{50}Sn$. The total mass of the atom is not equal to the mass of all its constituent protons, neutrons and electrons. State which is larger, the mass of the atom or the mass of all its constituent particles, and explain why there is this small but important difference. [3] (OCR)

16. Describe the relevance of binding energy to nuclei. In your essay you should make reference to, and where appropriate include sketches, graphs, equations and examples, illustrating the following:
a) the meaning of the term binding energy, [4]
b) the relation between mass and energy, [4]
c) the variation of binding energy per nucleon with nucleon number, [4]
d) fission and fusion reactions. [4] (OCR)

17. When a high speed α-particle strikes a stationary nitrogen nucleus, it may cause a nuclear reaction in which an oxygen nucleus and a proton are formed as shown by the following equation.

$$^{14}_{7}N + ^{4}_{2}He \longrightarrow ^{17}_{8}O + ^{1}_{1}H$$

The masses of the nuclei are given below.

Nitrogen-14	13.999 22 u
Helium-4	4.001 50 u
Oxygen-17	16.994 73 u
Hydrogen-1	1.007 28 u

Explain how mass and energy are balanced in such a nuclear equation. [7] (OCR)

18. A nuclear reaction is represented by the equation

$$^{235}_{92}U + ^{1}_{0}n \longrightarrow ^{143}_{54}Xe + ^{90}_{38}Sr + 3\,^{1}_{0}n + E$$

a) Name the physical process represented by this equation and describe what takes place in the reaction. What does E represent? [4]
b) The mass of an atom of each of the nuclides in the equation is given below.

Uranium-235	235.043 u
Xenon-143	142.908 u
Strontium-90	89.907 u
mass of neutron	1.009 u

Calculate the difference between the total mass on the left-hand side of the equation and the total mass on the right-hand side. Express this mass difference in terms of the unified atomic mass constant u and in kg. Calculate the energy equivalent to this mass difference. [6] (OCR)

19. Describe what happens to a uranium-235 nucleus when it is struck by a thermal neutron in a nuclear reactor. How is a working nuclear reactor shut down in an emergency? [5] (AQA)

20. The moderator, the control rods and the coolant are essential components of a thermal nuclear reactor which is supplying power. For each component, explain its function in the reactor, suggest one suitable material, and indicate one essential physical property the material must possess, apart from a tolerance of high temperatures. [11] (AQA)

21. When uranium-235 nuclei are fissioned by slow moving neutrons, two possible reactions are

reaction 1: $^{235}_{92}U + ^{1}_{0}n \longrightarrow ^{139}_{54}Xe + ^{95}_{38}Sr + 2\,^{1}_{0}n + E_T$

reaction 2: $^{235}_{92}U + ^{1}_{0}n \longrightarrow 2\,^{116}_{46}Pd + xc + E_T$

a) For reaction 2, identify the particle c and the number x of such particles produced in the reaction. [2]
b) The binding energy per nucleon E for the nuclides concerned is given in the table.

nuclide	$^{235}_{92}U$	$^{139}_{54}Xe$	$^{95}_{38}Sr$
E / MeV	7.52	8.33	8.62

Show that the energy released in reaction 1 is 210 MeV. [3]
c) The energy released in reaction 2 is 163 MeV. Suggest, with a reason, which one of the reactions is more likely to occur. [3] (OCR)

22. Calculate the energy released by the following reaction: $^{2}_{1}H + ^{2}_{1}H \longrightarrow ^{3}_{2}He + ^{1}_{0}n$
Mass of $^{2}_{1}H$ = 3.344×10^{-27} kg
Mass of $^{3}_{2}He$ = 5.008×10^{-27} kg
Mass of $^{1}_{0}n$ = 1.675×10^{-27} kg [3] (Edex)

23. a) Sketch a graph showing the relationship between binding energy per nucleon and nucleon (mass) number. Label the approximate positions of hydrogen, iron and uranium. [4]
b) State the difference between nuclear fission and nuclear fusion.
With reference to your graph explain why both processes release energy. [4] (Edex)

24. The fusion of deuterium nuclei can be represented by the equation $^{2}_{1}H + ^{2}_{1}H = ^{4}_{2}He$
a) Calculate the energy released by this reaction.
mass of $^{2}_{1}H$ = 2.014 19 u
mass of $^{4}_{2}He$ = 4.002 77 u
1 u is equivalent to 1.49×10^{-10} J [2]
b) 2 kg (1000 mol) of deuterium are caused to fuse and it is proposed that the energy released by fusion is used to generate electricity in a power station.
If the efficiency of the process were 52% and the electrical output of the station is to be 5.0 MW, how long would the deuterium fuel last. [5] (W)

▶ **Particle physics**

25. a) A bubble chamber is used to investigate a reaction between sub-atomic particles. Explain how visible tracks are produced. [4]

b) A charged elementary particle produced as a result of a collision in a bubble chamber has a lifetime of 2.9×10^{-10} s.
By means of a suitable calculation, determine the length of its track in the bubble chamber if the particle is travelling at $0.8 \times$ the speed of light. You may ignore the effects of relativity. [2]
(AQA)

26. a) The photograph shows tracks in a hydrogen bubble chamber. The tracks associated with one particular interaction are reproduced as a diagram alongside.
There is a magnetic field into the page.

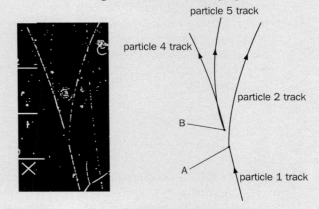

The tracks in the diagram show particle 1 decaying at A into two particles 2 and 3, with particle 3 leaving no track. What can you deduce about particle 2?
Suggest why particle 3 leaves no track. [3]

b) Particle 3 subsequently decays at B into another pair of particles, 4 and 5.
The sum of the masses of particles 4 and 5 is less than the mass of particle 3.
Explain how this can be the case. [2] (Edex)

27. This question is about hadrons.
a) Describe three characteristics of hadrons. [3]

b) Distinguish between mesons and baryons. [2]

c) Determine the charge Q, the baryon number B and strangeness S of the particles X, Y and Z produced in the following strong interaction processes:
i) $p + \pi^- \Rightarrow n + X$
ii) $p + p \Rightarrow \Delta^{++} + Y$
iii) $p + \pi^- \Rightarrow K^+ + Z$
(see page 362–363, and given that:
Δ^{++} has $Q = +2$, $B = +1$, $S = 0$, and
K^+ has $Q = +1$, $B = 0$, $S = +1$) [6] (OCR)

▶ **Further questions on nuclear physics**

28. A small proportion of the hydrogen in the air is the isotope tritium ^3_1H. This is continually being formed in the upper atmosphere by cosmic radiation so that the tritium content of air is constant.
Tritium is a beta-emitter with a half-life of 12.3 y.

a) Write down the nuclear equation that represents the decay of tritium using the symbol X for the daughter nucleus. [2]

b) Calculate the decay constant for tritium in y^{-1}. [1]

c) When wine is sealed in a bottle no new tritium forms and the activity of the tritium content of the wine gradually decreases with time. At one time the activity of the tritium in an old bottle of wine is found to be $12\frac{1}{2}\%$ of that in a new bottle. Calculate the approximate age of the old wine. [3]

d) Calculate the mass change, in kg, when a tritium nucleus is formed from its component parts, and the binding energy, in J, of a tritium nucleus.

mass of tritium nucleus	3.016 050 u
mass of proton	1.007 277 u
mass of neutron	1.008 665 u
atomic mass constant u	$1.660 566 \times 10^{-27}$ kg

[4] (AQA)

29. The diagram represents a photograph of two events, labelled X and Y, from a bubble chamber with a magnetic field directed out of the plane of the photograph.
In the events, pair production has occurred as a result of a gamma ray photon creating an electron and a positron.
In event X an electron has also been ejected from an atom. The track created by this electron is labelled 'atomic electron'. The tracks created by pair production are labelled A, B, C and D.

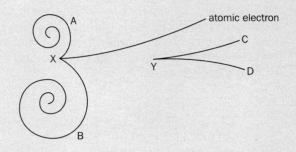

a) Which two of the tracks were produced by positrons. [2]

b) Explain why gamma ray photons do not leave visible tracks. [2]

c) Explain why the tracks created by pair production in event X are much more curved than those produced in event Y. [2] (AQA)

▷ Synoptic questions for A2

'Synoptic' questions are for A2, not AS level, and may cover a wide range of topics within one question.

1. An electric wheel chair powered by a 12 V battery has a maximum speed of 1.5 m s^{-1} on level ground. The maximum useful driving power of the motor and transmission system is 30 W. The efficiency of the system is 70%.
   a) Explain briefly why all modes of transport have a maximum speed which depends on the power output of the propulsion system. [3]
   b) For the maximum speed, calculate the power supplied by the battery, and the current in the motor circuit. [4]
   c) Air resistance is negligible at 1.5 m s^{-1}. Show that the resistance due to friction in the moving parts of the wheelchair is 20 N. [2]
   d) Ramps are often used to give wheelchair users access to buildings. One such ramp has a gradient that rises 0.12 m for every metre moved along the ramp, as shown in the diagram. The total mass of a wheelchair and a student is 110 kg.

   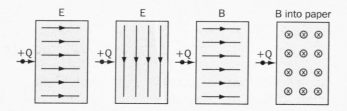

   i) Calculate the component force in the direction shown by the arrow R because of the weight of the wheelchair and student. [2]
   ii) Assuming that the resistance due to frictional forces is still 20 N, calculate the maximum speed of the wheelchair up the ramp. [2] (AQA)

2. This question is about forces on charged particles in electric and magnetic fields.
   Charged particles experience forces when moving in electric and magnetic fields. In the space below are four diagrams. Each diagram shows a charged particle entering a region in which a uniform electric or magnetic field exists.

   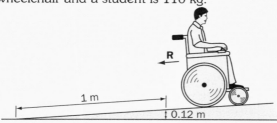

   On a copy of each diagram, draw a line to represent the continuing path of the particle in the field. Describe the effect on the velocity of the particle in each case. [8] (OCR)

3. The diagram shows the envelope of the vibrations of a stretched string that is emitting a note at its fundamental frequency.

   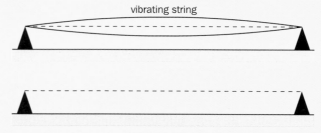

   a) On a copy of the lower diagram draw the shape of the envelope of the vibrations when the string is emitting a note at three times its fundamental frequency. [1]
   b) Explain how a stationary wave, such as that shown in the diagram, is produced. [2]
   c) A simple model of the hydrogen atom assumes that the wave associated with an electron in the atom is a stationary wave as shown below. The nodes correspond to opposite edges of the atom and the centre of the atom. The radius of the hydrogen atom is 1.0×10^{-10} m.

   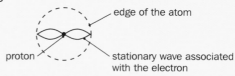

   i) State the de Broglie wavelength of the electron in the diagram. [1]
   ii) Calculate the momentum of an electron in a hydrogen atom. [2]
   iii) State and explain briefly where, using this model, the electron in a hydrogen atom is most likely to be found. [2] (AQA)

4. A partially inflated balloon containing hydrogen carries meteorological equipment up through the atmosphere. Over a short distance its speed is almost constant.

   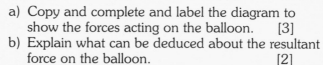

   a) Copy and complete and label the diagram to show the forces acting on the balloon. [3]
   b) Explain what can be deduced about the resultant force on the balloon. [2]
   c) Explain why the balloon would not rise if the hydrogen were replaced by an identical volume of air at the same temperature and pressure. [2]
   d) Explain what happens to
      i) the pressure,
      ii) the volume of the hydrogen as the balloon rises a significant distance through the atmosphere. [4] (Edex)

5. The diagrams show a cross-section and plan view through a moving-coil loudspeaker. A coil is situated in the magnetic field provided by a permanent magnet. The coil is fixed to the diaphragm but is otherwise free to oscillate vertically. Oscillations of the coil cause the diaphragm to vibrate.

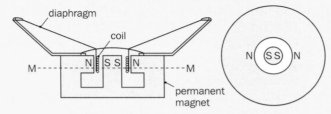

a) On a copy of the plan view, draw the magnetic field pattern between the poles of the magnet. [2]
b) The magnetic flux density at the position of the coil is 0.60 T. There are 50 turns on the coil, which has a diameter of 40 mm. Calculate the force acting on the coil when the current in it is 1.1 A. [4]
c) The effective mass of the diaphragm and coil is 12 g. Calculate the initial acceleration of the diaphragm and coil when the current in the coil is 1.1 A. [2] (AQA)

6. A hydrogen lamp is found to produce red light and blue light. The wavelengths of the light are 660 nm and 490 nm.
a) State which wavelength corresponds to red light. Explain why light of specific wavelengths is produced by the lamp. Calculate the energy change in an atom associated with the emission of a photon of red light. [5]
b) The refractive index of glass for the red light is 1.510 and for the blue light, 1.521.
Light from the hydrogen lamp is incident at an angle of 30° on the glass-air boundary, as shown.

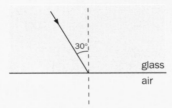

Calculate the angles of refraction for red and blue light and the angle between the red and blue refracted rays. [4]
c) The light from the hydrogen lamp is now directed normally on to a diffraction grating having 4.0×10^5 lines per metre.
Calculate the angle between the red and the blue light in the first order spectrum. [3]
d) A metal surface has a work function energy of 1.80 eV.
By reference to your answer to (a) determine whether photo-emission of electrons from this surface is possible with red light. [3] (OCR)

7. The diagram shows a simple device to release excess steam in a model steam engine boiler. A light rod is hinged at one end, A. The safety valve is a plug at point B, 10 mm from A. C is a counterweight of 0.20 N which can be moved along the rod.
When the pressure in the boiler increases above a critical value the upward force on plug B tilts the rod about A and releases steam.

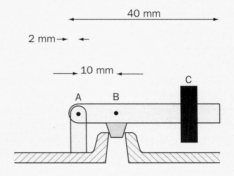

a) The force to lift the safety valve is 0.60 N. Calculate the position of the counterweight for this to happen. [2]
b) The area of the hole in the boiler is 4.0×10^{-6} m². Find the pressure difference between atmospheric pressure and boiler pressure to lift the safety valve. [2]
c) The situation is oversimplified. The uniform rod of length 40 mm has a weight of 0.10 N. Taking this into consideration, how far must the counterweight C be moved from the position calculated in (b) for the valve to open at the required pressure? [3] (OCR)

8. A large hotel and sports complex uses a heat pump to provide hot water for central heating by transferring energy from a nearby river.
The maximum thermal power output from the heat pump installation is 920 kW and, when delivering this output, the electrical power input to the system is 368 kW.

a) Determine the rate at which energy must be extracted from the river when the installation operates at maximum output. [1]
b) Explain briefly why the river is unlikely to turn to ice when the heat pump extracts energy from it. [2]
c) Estimate the annual fuel cost of running the heat pump if the heating requirement is equivalent to maximum output for 9 hours per day over 260 days each year. 1 kW h of electrical energy costs 8.0 pence. [1]
d) Calculate the annual saving in fuel costs when using the heat pump compared to an electrical heating installation of the same thermal output using heaters operating directly from the mains electricity supply. [1] (AQA)

9. a) Calculate the mean drift velocity of electrons in a copper wire, of cross-sectional area 7.9×10^{-7} m^2, when the current in the wire is 1.4 A. (The number of free electrons per m^3 in copper is 8.5×10^{28}, the charge on an electron is -1.6×10^{-19} C.) [3]

b) Metals are good thermal and electrical conductors. Briefly explain, in terms of the mechanisms of thermal and electrical conduction, why this is the case. [3] (AQA)

10. A glass U-tube is constructed from hollow tubing having a square cross-section of side 2.0 cm, as shown in the diagram.
The U-tube has vertical arms and a horizontal section between the arms. Electrodes are set in the upper and lower faces of the horizontal section. Each electrode is of length 5.0 cm and width 2.0 cm. The U-tube contains liquid sodium of density 960 kg m^{-3} and of resistivity 4.8×10^{-8} Ω m. In this question you may assume that the liquid sodium outside the electrodes has no effect on the resistance between the electrodes.

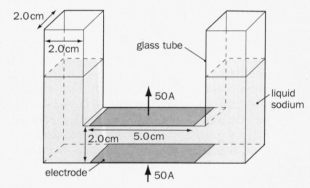

a) Calculate the resistance of the liquid sodium between the electrodes and the p.d. V between the electrodes required to maintain a current of 50 A in the liquid sodium. [4]

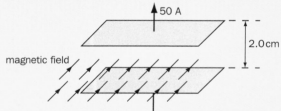

b) A uniform horizontal magnetic field of flux density 0.12 T is now applied at right angles to the horizontal section of tube in the region between the electrodes (second diagram). A force is exerted on the liquid due to the magnetic field. State and explain the direction of the force and calculate its magnitude. [4]

c) By considering the pressure difference which the force in (b) causes, determine the difference in height of the surfaces of the liquid sodium in the vertical arms of the U-tube. [4] (OCR)

11. When gas is used as a fuel, the principal steps in providing electrical power to the consumer are
a) burning the gas to boil water at high pressure,
b) using the high pressure steam to drive a turbine,
c) using the turbine to drive a generator,
d) using current to carry power to the consumer.

For each of stages (a), (c) and (d) state briefly how and why the major 'waste' of energy occurs. [6] (Edex)

12. A car has a fuel tank of rectangular cross-section. When full, the tank holds 50 l of fuel. The diagram shows the principle of a fuel gauge for this car. As the fuel level varies, the slider C moves along the potentiometer which is connected to the car battery. The gauge itself is a high resistance voltmeter but is calibrated in litres. When the tank is full, slider C is at A. When the tank is empty, C is at B.

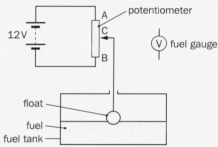

a) Copy the diagram and show clearly how the voltmeter would be connected to the rest of the circuit. [2]

b) Draw a graph to show how the output p.d. varies with the volume of fuel in the tank. [2]

c) The second diagram shows a cross-section through the fuel tank in a particular car. This tank, when full, also holds 50 l of fuel.

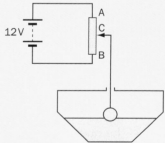

The arrangement of the voltmeter is the same as in (a). Draw a second graph to show how the output p.d. might vary with fuel volume for this tank. [3] (OCR)

13. Helium is a monatomic gas for which all the internal energy of the molecules may be considered to be translational kinetic energy.
At what temperature will the internal energy of 1.0 g of helium gas be equal to the kinetic energy of a tennis ball of mass 60 g travelling at 50 m s^{-1}? (molar mass of helium = 4×10^{-3} kg) [5] (AQA)

14. The diagram shows a positively charged oil drop held at rest between two parallel conducting plates A and B. The oil drop has a mass of 9.79×10^{-15} kg. The p.d. between the plates is 5000 V and plate B is at a potential of 0 V.

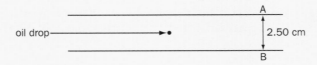

a) Is plate A positive or negative? [1]

b) Draw a labelled free-body force diagram which shows the forces acting on the oil drop. (You may ignore upthrust due to the air.) [2]

c) Calculate the electric field strength between the plates. [2]

d) Calculate the magnitude of the charge on the oil drop. How many electrons would have to be removed from a neutral oil drop for it to acquire this charge? [3] (Edex)

15. a) Explain what is meant by the concept of work. Hence derive the equation $E_p = mgh$ for the potential energy change of a mass m moved through a vertical distance h near the Earth's surface. [4]

b) Using the equation $pV = nRT$ and the kinetic theory of gases expression for the pressure exerted by a gas $p = \frac{1}{3}(Nm/V)<c^2>$, show that the internal energy of one mole of an ideal gas is $\frac{3}{2}RT$. [7]

c) In a certain waterfall, water falls through a vertical distance of 24 m as shown in the diagram:

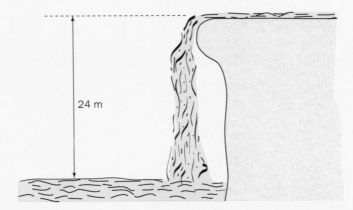

The water is brought to rest at the base of the waterfall. Calculate:

i) the change in gravitational potential energy of 18 kg of water when it descends the waterfall,

ii) the difference in temperature between the top and the bottom of the waterfall if all of the potential energy is converted into thermal energy. The specific heat capacity of water is 4.2 kJ kg^{-1} K^{-1}. [3] (OCR)

16. a) Explain what is meant by a field in physics. [2]

b) State two similarities between electric and gravitational fields. [2]

c) State two differences between electric and magnetic fields. [2]

d) A beam of electrons is accelerated from rest in an electric field of strength 8.5×10^5 N C^{-1}. Calculate the force on each electron and the acceleration of each electron. [3]

e) Draw a labelled diagram showing what would happen if this beam then entered a uniform magnetic field at right angles to the direction of the beam. Show on your diagram the direction of the magnetic field and of the force acting on the electron. [3] (Edex)

17. a) Sketch stress-strain graphs from zero stress up to breaking stress for

i) a length of rubber cord,

ii) a cast iron rod. [3]

b) The stress-strain graphs can be explained in terms of the microstructure of the materials. Explain briefly the shape of the graph you have drawn for rubber. You may draw diagrams to help you explain if you wish. [4]

c) The diagram shows a rubber cord being used to secure luggage on the roof rack of a car. The tension in the cord is the same throughout. The natural length of the rubber cord is 0.80 m and measurements show that it obeys Hooke's law for extensions as in the diagram.

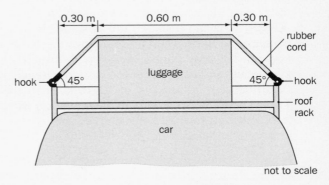

i) Calculate the extension of the rubber cord. [2]

ii) When the tension in the rubber cord is 20 N, it extends by 0.32 m. Calculate the tension in the rubber cord in the situation shown in the diagram. [2]

d) i) Calculate the energy stored in the rubber cord used to secure luggage on the roof rack. [2]

ii) A hook, of mass 0.15 kg, becomes detached from the roof rack. Neglecting the mass of the rubber cord, estimate the resulting speed of the hook. [2] (AQA)

18. Atmospheric Electricity

Lightning was probably the cause of the first fire observed by humans and today it still leads to danger and costly damage. It is now known that most lightning strokes bring negative charge to ground and that thunderstorm electric fields cause positive charges to be released from pointed objects near the ground.

Worldwide thunderstorm activity is responsible for maintaining a small negative charge on the surface of the Earth. An equal quantity of positive charge in the atmosphere leads to a typical p.d. of 300 kV between the Earth's surface and a conducting ionosphere layer at about 60 km. The resulting fair-weather electric field decreases with height because of the increasing conductivity of the air. Across the lowest metre there is a p.d. of about 100 V.

The 2000 thunderstorms estimated to be active at any one time each produce an average current of 1 A bringing negative charge to ground.
The resulting fair-weather field thus causes a leakage current of around 2000 A in the reverse direction, so that charge flows are in equilibrium.
The charge on the Earth and the fair-weather field are too small to cause us problems in everyday life. With an average current per storm of only 1 A, there is no scope for tapping into thunderstorms as an energy source.

The long-range sensing of lightning depends on detecting radio waves which lightning produces. Different frequency bands are chosen for different distances. The very high frequency (VHF) band at 30–300 MHz can only be used up to about 100 km because the Earth's curvature defines the radio horizon. Greater ranges, of several thousand kilometres, are achieved in the very low frequency (VLF) band of frequencies of 10–16 kHz. These signals bounce with little attenuation within the radio duct formed between the Earth and ionospheric layers at heights of 50–70 km.

A further system senses radio waves in the extremely low frequency (ELF) band around 1 kHz. ELF waves are diffracted in the region between the Earth's surface and the ionosphere and propagate up to several hundred kilometres. Horizontally polarised ELF waves do not propagate to any significant extent, hence this system avoids the polarisation error of conventional direction-finding systems.

a) Explain the meaning of the following terms as used in the passage:
   i) *to ground* (para. 1),
   ii) *leakage current* (para. 3),
   iii) *horizontally polarised* (para. 5).   [5]

b) i)   What is the electric field strength at the Earth's surface?
   ii) Calculate the average electric field strength between the Earth's surface and the conducting ionospheric layer.
   iii) Sketch a graph to show the variation of the Earth's fair-weather electric field with distance above the Earth's surface to a height of 60 km.
       [7]

c) The *power* associated with a lightning stroke is extremely large.
   Explain why *there is no scope for tapping into thunderstorms as an energy source* (para. 3). [3]

d) The diagram shows a lightning stroke close to the surface of the Earth.

Copy the diagram and add:
   i) rays to it to illustrate the propagation of radio waves in the VLF band, and
   ii) wavefronts to illustrate the propagation of waves in the ELF band.
   Explain the meaning of the term *radio horizon* with reference to VHF radio waves.   [7]

e) List the frequency ranges of VHF and ELF radio waves. Calculate the wavelength of
   i) a typical VHF signal,
   ii) an ELF signal.   [4]   (Edex)

19. An apparatus to demonstrate electromagnetic levitation is shown in the diagram. When there is an alternating current in the 400-turn coil, the aluminium ring rises a few centimetres above the coil.

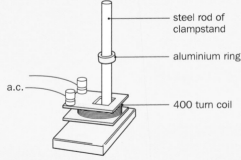

a) Explain why, when there is a varying current in the coil, there is an induced current in the aluminium ring. Suggest why the ring experiences an upward force.   [6]

b) In one experiment the power transfer to the aluminium ring is 1.6 W. The induced current is then 140 A. Calculate the resistance of the aluminium ring.   [2]

c) The dimensions of the ring are given on the diagram below. Use your value for the resistance to find the resistivity of aluminium.

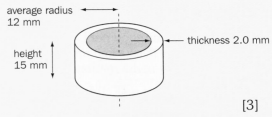

average radius 12 mm

thickness 2.0 mm

height 15 mm

[3]

d) The aluminium ring becomes hot when the alternating current is left on for a few minutes.

In order to try and measure its temperature it is removed from the steel rod and then dropped into a small plastic cup containing cold water.

State what measurements you would take and what physical properties of water and aluminium you would need to look up in order to calculate the initial temperature of the hot aluminium ring. [3] (Edex)

20. A leaf electrometer consists of an aluminium leaf which hangs at an angle θ to the vertical when a p.d. V_{XY} is applied between the metal cap X and the conducting case Y of the electrometer.

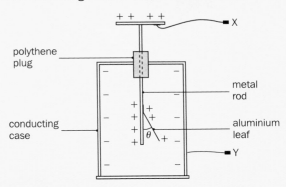

polythene plug

X

metal rod

conducting case

aluminium leaf

Y

It is calibrated by connecting different values of V_{XY} across XY, with the following results:

V_{XY} /V	100	200	300	400
θ /°	11	14	18	23

V_{XY} /V	500	600	700	800
θ /°	30	37	45	53

V_{XY} /V	900	1000	1100	1200
θ /°	62	69	74	78

a) Plot a graph of θ against V_{XY}. [4]

b) The rate of change of θ with V_{XY} is known as the sensitivity of the electrometer. Over what range of p.d.'s is the sensitivity approximately constant? Calculate the sensitivity over this range. Show all your working. [5]

c) It is suggested that, between 300 V and 700 V, the p.d. is proportional to sin θ. Draw up a suitable table of values and plot a graph to test this suggestion. Does your graph support the suggestion? [7] (Edex)

21. The mass of a retort stand and clamp is 1.6 kg and their combined centre of mass lies on the line XY. A spring of negligible mass is attached to the clamp and supports a mass of 0.9 kg as shown. The spring requires a force of 6.0 N to stretch it 100 mm.

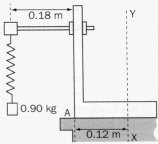

0.18 m

Y

0.90 kg A

0.12 m X

a) Calculate the extension of the spring. [2]
b) Show that this arrangement will not tip (i.e. will not rotate about point A) when the 0.9 kg mass is at rest in its equilibrium position. [2]
c) If the mass is lifted and released, it will vibrate about the equilibrium position. Explain, without calculation, why the stand will tip over if the amplitude exceeds a certain value. [3] (AQA)

22. A hot-air balloon, tethered to the ground, is ready for release. The tension in the rope connecting it to the ground is 400 N. The total weight of the balloon (including the hot air within it) is 16 500 N.

a) i) Draw a free-body force diagram of the balloon and hence calculate the upthrust force U on the balloon.
   ii) Explain how the upthrust force arises. What factors determine its magnitude during the flight of the balloon? [6]
b) Use the equation $pV = mRT/M$, where m is the total mass of air, and M is the mass of 1 mole, to find a relationship between the density ρ of the air in the balloon and its kelvin temperature T. Under what circumstances will ρ be inversely proportional to T? [3]
c) Using the data below, show that the hot air in the balloon has a temperature of 81 °C. [2]

Density of cold air outside balloon = 1.29 kg m^{-3}
Density of hot air inside balloon = 1.05 kg m^{-3}
Temperature of cold air outside balloon = 15 °C
Radius of balloon, assumed spherical = 5.5 m (Edex)

Revision skills

When you revise, you need to balance your time between:
- learning your notes,
- practising questions from past papers (for this you can use the seven Further Questions sections in this book).

This section concentrates mainly on how you can learn your notes effectively, so that you have a good knowledge and understanding of Physics when you go into the exam room.

Before you start:

- Get a copy of the syllabus from your teacher or the exam board.

- Be clear about exactly which topics you need to revise for the exam you are about to take. The website at:
  www.nelsonthornes.com/ap4u.htm
  tells you exactly which parts of this book you need for your particular exam syllabus. See also page 428.

- Work out which are your strong topics and which topics you will need to spend more time on.
  One way of doing this is to look at tests or exams that you have done in the past, to see any weaknesses.

Using a tape-recorder may help

Some helpful ideas

1. *Work out your best way of learning*
   Some people learn best from diagrams or videos, while some prefer listening (perhaps to taped notes) and making up rhymes and phrases. Others prefer to do something *active* with the information, like answering questions or making a poster on a topic. If you know which way you prefer, then this will help you to get the most out of your revision.

2. *Test yourself*
   Merely reading through notes will not make them stick.
   Get someone to test you on a section of work, or write down some questions testing your knowledge of the topic.
   One way of doing this is to tape the questions and then play them back to yourself, checking your notes if you can't answer any of the questions.

3. *Teach others*
   If you can find someone to teach a topic to (friends or family?) then this is sometimes the best way to learn. You and some friends might take it in turns to present a topic to each other.

4. *Learn formulae*
   Check which formulae are **not** going to be given to you in the exam, and learn these by heart. Most people find it best to learn the formulae which are given, as well, so that they can be quickly remembered when needed for a question.

5. *Make sure that you try to* **understand** *the work*
   It is unlikely that you will remember a lot of Physics if you do not **understand** it!

Three ways of learning:

 looking

 listening

 doing

▷ Ten revision techniques

1. ***Get an overall view of a topic first***
   Before you start revising a topic, quickly read through the whole topic so that you have a general understanding of it and of how the different bits of it connect with each other.

   A good place to start is the Summary shown at the end of each chapter.

2. ***Highlight key words*** and phrases in your notes using hi-lighter pens in different colours.

3. ***Make notes***
   Re-writing and condensing notes is a good and ***active*** way of reading and then understanding what you need to learn.

4. ***Make yourself cards*** with notes on one side and a diagram on the other. Test yourself by looking at the diagram and seeing if you can recall the notes.

5. ***Visualisation***
   When you are memorising material, always try to get a bold and bright picture in your mind, which will help you to remember.
   It helps if the picture is something that is very important to you because it is easily remembered (girl / boyfriend? football team? rock group?). Sometimes imagining something outrageous that can be connected to the fact may help.

6. ***A Poster***
   You can summarise a topic with a poster which you can put on the wall of your bedroom. Include important words and phrases in large, bold letters. If you are a ***visual*** person then include bright, colourful diagrams which illustrate the ideas.

7. ***A Mind Map***
   This is a poster that summarises a topic by showing the links between the different concepts which make it up:
   Making a Mind Map forces you to think about the links in a topic and can help your understanding of it.

8. ***Use rhymes and phrases***
   Some people are good at rhymes or raps and this can be a way of memorising work.
   Phrases such as **Roy G. Biv**, to remember the colours of the spectrum (red, orange, yellow, etc) can be useful.

9. ***Revision ROMs for a computer***
   These can be bought in many shops and often have questions for you to test yourself.
   They are an active way of revising, which may suit you.

10. ***Past Paper Questions***
    Don't forget to work through questions from past papers, to see the kind of questions that are asked.
    The seven ***Further Questions*** sections in this book contain past paper questions.

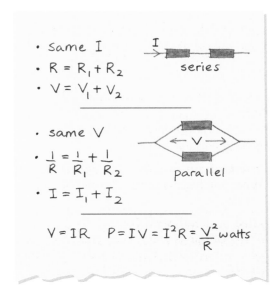

Part of a Poster on circuits

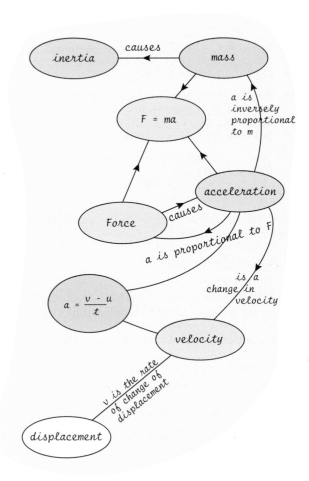

Part of a Mind Map for mechanics

▶ Organising your revision

Do you have difficulty starting revision and feel that there is so much to do that you will *never* complete it?
Do you constantly put off revising and find other things to do?

Here are some ways in which you can help yourself:

- *Think about the positive effects of starting*
  When you have finished a session you will feel good that you have made progress, and you'll feel less anxious about not getting enough work done.

- *Think about the negative effects of delaying*
  What will happen and who will be affected if you put off starting?

- *Give yourself rewards*
  Think of things with which you can reward yourself at the end of a session. eg. a cup of tea or listening to some favourite music.

- *Get help!*
  Think of ways to involve friends and family which will make revision easier and more enjoyable.

Making a Revision Timetable

Some recent research suggests that some students do better than others at Advanced Level because they:

- start their revision earlier,

- use better techniques for learning work (such as testing themselves, rather than just reading their notes),

- get help from others rather than working alone,

- have a *planned* revision timetable which includes working on their weaknesses.

You can use these ideas to help you plan an efficient Revision Timetable.

1. Start your revision a long time before your exams (at least eight weeks).
   Plan to spend quite a lot of the last two weeks before your exam on revising your weaker topics again.

2. Note down when you will cover each topic and stick to this!

3. Spend more time on your weaker topics. Try to get extra help on them from your teacher.

4. Give yourself enough time to do past paper questions.

5. Arrange in some revision periods to work with someone who can help you.

6. Do some social activities in between revision sessions, so that you don't go completely crazy!

What will you revise?

You will need to divide your time effectively so that you:

1. Learn the work which you have covered so that you have a good knowledge and understanding of it, including knowing formulae and definitions of quantities.

2. Practise past questions so that you know what to do when you get a similar question in the exam.
   This can be useful in learning work, because you will often need to read your notes to help you answer a question. You can also judge where your weaknesses are.

How long should you revise for?

Research suggests that if you start revising with no thought of when you will stop, then your learning efficiency just gets less and less.

However, if you decide on a **fixed** time, say 30 minutes, then you learn the most at the beginning of a session and **also** just before you have decided to stop, when your brain realises that it is coming to the end of a session (see first graph).

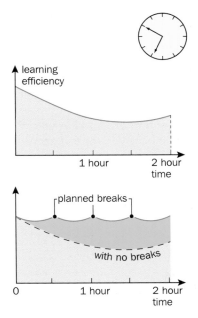

Which would be better: one 2-hour session or four 25-minute sessions with a break of 10 minutes in between them?

The four sessions would be much better, as shown by the yellow area on the second graph:
However, it is important to stick to a definite *fixed* time, using a clock, and have a break, rather than just carrying on.

This way you get through more work **and** you feel less tired!

How often should you revise?

This graph shows how much information your memory can recall at different times after you have finished a revision session:

As it shows, you very quickly forget much of what you have revised.

The next graph shows that if you briefly *review* the work again after 10 minutes, then the amount that you remember increases:

The graph stays higher!
You can do this review at the end of your 10-minute break.

So a good system of working is to:
- work against the clock for a definite time (eg. 25 minutes),
- have a 10-minute break and do something entirely different,
- review, briefly, the work you were revising in the last session,
- then begin the cycle again, by working against the clock...

If you revise this material again after a **day,** and then again after a **week,** then you remember even more of the work as shown by the last graph:

The trick is to briefly revise a topic again at regular intervals.

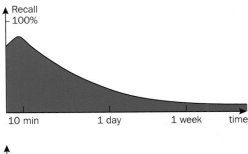

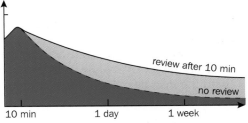

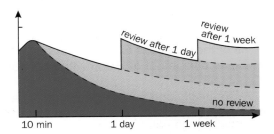

Examination Technique

Before the exam

1. Make sure that you check carefully the dates and the times of all your exams, so that you are not late!

2. Make sure that you know which type of paper (eg. multiple-choice, short answer) is on which day, and which topics are being examined on which paper.

3. Make sure that you know how many questions you have to do on each paper, how long it is and whether you will get a choice of question.
Plan how long you will spend on each question on a paper.

4. Make sure that you are familiar with the Physics formula sheet which you will be given for the exam, and that you know what all the symbols mean.

5. On the night before the exam, it may help to steady your nerves if you look briefly through your notes. But don't do too much!
Make sure that you get a good night's rest before your exam!

On the day of the exam

- Aim to arrive early at the exam and try to get into the room as early as possible. This will help you to settle your nerves and give you time to prepare.

- Don't drink alcohol before an exam, or eat too much or too little food.

- Make sure that you are properly equipped with pens and pencils (and spares in case they break), a rubber, ruler, angle measurer, calculator (check the batteries) and a watch.

During the exam

1. Don't waste time when you get the paper!
Write your name and exam number on to the front of any sheets of paper or answer booklets that you are going to use.
Read the instructions on the front page of the exam paper.

2. Read each question very carefully and underline important parts. Make sure you know exactly what you have to do.

3. If you have a choice of which questions to attempt, then read all of the questions on the paper first.
Never dive into a question without reading all of it first.

4. Write neatly and in short sentences which will be easier for the marker to understand. Try to be precise and detailed without writing too much, so that you don't waste time.

5. Do not spend too long on any question! Pace yourself carefully with a watch so that you don't run out of time.

6. If you are stuck, just leave some space so that you can go back to it later. It is easier to get 50% on all the questions than 100% on half of them.

7. Sometimes you may be stuck on one part of the question. Look to see if there are any later parts which you can do easily.

8. Check that you have done all the required questions. For example, sometimes people don't see that there is a question on the last page of the booklet!

Ten hints on answering questions

1. If the exam paper shows that a question is worth 4 marks then put down (at least) 4 points in your answer.

2. Make sure you give the right amount of detail. The question gives you clues:
   – give short answers to questions which start:
   '*State ...*' or '*List ...*' or '*Name ...*'
   – give longer answers if you are asked to '*Explain ...*' or '*Describe ...*' or asked '*Why does ...*'.

3. Use correct scientific words as much as possible.

4. Never explain something just because you know how to! You only earn marks for *exactly* what the question asks.

5. When you do calculation questions always show your working. There is often a mark for writing down the right equation. You can get your mark for this even if you don't finally get the right answer.

6. *Check* your answers! First check whether your answer is much too big or too small. Ensure also that you check *units* and significant figures, or you'll lose marks.

7. Make your diagrams clear and neat, but do not spend a long time on them trying to make them perfect.

8. If you are asked to sketch a graph, label the axes (including units) and put as many values on the graph as you can, including numbers given in the question.

9. In a multiple-choice question, narrow down your options by crossing out those answers which can't possibly be right. If you are still not sure – guess!

10. Even though you get no marks for doing working in multi-choice questions, you are more likely to get them right if you do careful calculations.

I mark   I mark
The loudspeaker works by having an alternating current in a coil. The current is in a magnetic field, so it has a force on it. The coil vibrates because the direction of the force constantly changes.
I mark   I mark

$P = \dfrac{F}{A}$ $F = 5.0\,N$ I mark for formula

I mark for formula

$A = \pi r^2$

$= \pi (0.010)^2$

$= 3.1415927 \times 10^{-4}\,m^2$

$\therefore\ P = \dfrac{5.0\,N}{3.1415927 \times 10^{-4}\,m^2}$

$P = 15915.494\,N\,m^{-2}$

$= 1.6 \times 10^4\,N\,m^{-2}$ (2 s.f.)

I mark
but only with units and to 2s.f.
(because F and r are to 2 s.f.)

Key Skills in Physics

When you study Physics you develop your knowledge and understanding of the physical world we live in. You also learn about a variety of ways in which physicists solve problems. But one of the best things about studying an A-level is that you learn how to do lots of other things which you will find useful at work or at university even if you do not become a professional physicist.

To recognise this, the government has introduced an additional qualification called the Key Skills Qualification.
To get this qualification, you need to achieve 3 units, called:

- **Communication,**
- **Application of number,**
- **Information technology (IT).**

For each of these units, you have to produce a **portfolio** of evidence (of your coursework) and pass a test (a short exam). You can pass a unit at any level from 1 to 4.
Level 3 is probably the right level for an A-level student to aim for.

'Level 3 is the right level to aim for'

The Qualification is separate from your A-level course (in fact, it is also available to people taking GNVQs, degrees, etc.) However, the idea is that you should develop these Key Skills and get your portfolio evidence (as much as possible) **within** your A-level course. But you don't have to get all the evidence from your A-levels, and certainly not all from A-level Physics.

You should aim to develop the skills where they are needed naturally, not force them in where they don't fit.
Physics is a very good subject for these 3 key skills, because you are communicating and using numbers all the time, and IT is becoming an ever more essential tool for research and analysis.

The next 3 pages give you some ideas to help you make the most of the opportunities in A-level Physics to become good at the Key Skills and to get the portfolio evidence that you need.

But remember, an important part of Key Skills is that you take the initiative yourself. So, whenever you produce a piece of work, you should ask yourself: *'Have I used any of the Key Skills, and are there any more Key Skills I could have used?'*

You should have practised your key skills better.

Your school or college will make arrangements to help you develop your Key Skills, assemble your portfolio, and prepare for the test. Find out what these arrangements are, and always ask your tutor if you are not sure what you should be doing.

Key Skills are not a soft option. But they earn you UCAS points, and employers are very keen on them. Over the next few years, more and more employers are going to be expecting people to have Key Skills qualifications. And anyway, life is much easier if you are good at communicating, using numbers and using IT.

▶ Key Skill : Communication

Communicating our ideas to other people is one of the most important things we ever do, both in **discussion** and in **writing**. Scientists sometimes have a poor reputation when it comes to communication. But we know that some scientists communicate very well. How do they do that?

Each of the Key Skills units has a leaflet explaining what is required (you should ask your tutor for your own copy).
The Level 3 Communication unit says that you should be able to:

- contribute to discussions, in twos and threes and in larger groups,

- make a presentation to an audience (a small one will do!) and find the best way to communicate your message,

- select, read and understand quite long articles and sections from books, and take out the bits you need at the time,

- write essays and reports in a way that suits what you are trying to communicate. This includes using diagrams, graphs and tables if they help you to say what you want to say.
  In Physics, they are usually an important part of a report.

'Find the best way to communicate your message'

Throughout this book you will find many opportunities to develop your communication skills.

For example you could research and then discuss in your group, the issues arising from the Energy Crisis (page 65), the current solutions to it (pages 354, 247), with their problems (page 356), and possible future solutions (pages 250, 172, 353).

Many of the 'Physics at work' pages introduce you to the latest developments, and form a suitable topic for further research.
This could be followed by a presentation to the rest of your group, or to some younger pupils.

Some examples, with the relevant page numbers, include:

Physics of Astronomy & Space
The Big Crunch (85) and the age of the Universe (158),
Doppler redshift (157), Gravity waves (122),
Satellites (82, 85, 153, 310) and Space stations (76, 84),
Radiotelescopes (147), the Hubble space telescope (84, 136),
The Sun (311) and radiation from other stars (309).

Physics of Medicine
Radioactive tracers (344) and Radiotherapy (344),
Endoscopes (132), Pacemakers (344), Thermometers (310),
Oscilloscopes (245) and Baby monitors (272),
MRI scanning (101) and PET scanning (368).

Physics of Transport
Car safety (24, 56, 240), Radar traps (158), Electric cars (202).

Physics of Sport
Tennis (53, 294), Marathons (304), Climbing (294), Diving (322),
Golf (41), Gymnastics (49), Gliding (50), Skiing (68), Stockcars (35).

Key Skills
Communication
Level 3 Summary

You must be able to:

- create opportunities for others to contribute to group discussions about complex subjects;

- make a presentation using a range of techniques to engage the audience;

- read and synthesise information from extended documents about a complex subject;

- organise information coherently, selecting a form and style of writing appropriate to complex subject matter.

Communicating is an important part of a Physics course anyway. If you can practise how to do it at Level 3, you will be well on the way to being a good communicator, in Physics or anywhere else.

▷ Key Skill : Application of number

As you know, numbers are important in Physics, and the ability to use numbers is an essential skill.
You will have many opportunities to collect evidence of this Key Skill for your portfolio.

For your Application of Number portfolio, you will need to have evidence to show that you can:

- work out what numerical data you need, for what you want to do,

- get the data from somewhere, either from your own measurements or from elsewhere (a 'secondary' source),

- carry out the right calculations, and get the right results,

- check your work and correct any mistakes,

- decide what the results are telling you,

- present the results in a way that suits the situation, using graphs and tables competently where they help to make your point.

The **Check your Maths** section (pages 400 – 409) contains a lot of help on the application of number.

There is also a useful section on **'How to tackle mathematical questions'** on page 383.

There are over 200 worked examples in this book (in the green boxes), followed by many opportunities for you to practise your number skills in:

- the questions at the end of each chapter, and

- the **Further Questions** sections which contain questions from past examination papers.

Make sure that you try hard to get correct answers to all the calculations in these questions.
If you get stuck, then:

- You will find Hints to help you (as well as the Answers to all the numerical questions), in the **Hints & Answers** section on pages 410 – 426.

- Discuss with your teacher where you went wrong before you try the question again.

- Look at some of the tips in the section on **Making Progress in Physics** (pages 380 – 389).

'Numbers are important in Physics'

Key Skills
Application of number
Level 3 Summary

You must be able to plan and carry through a substantial and complex activity that requires you to:

- plan your approach to obtaining and using information, choose appropriate methods for obtaining results you need and justify your choice;

- carry out multi-stage calculations, including use of a large data set (over 50 items) and re-arrangement of formulae;

- justify your choice of presentation methods and explain the results of your calculations.

Remember, though, that you don't necessarily have to produce all the evidence for your portfolio from your work in Physics.

You should practise the skills in Physics, but you may find that you can sometimes get the evidence more easily from another subject, such as Maths.
This is for you to decide, after talking it over with your teacher.

▷ Key Skill : Information technology (IT)

Information technology is about using computers to help you
- to do your work more quickly,
- to present your work more professionally,
- to make measurements and process the results,
- to give you access to information which would be difficult to find in books.

For your IT Key Skills portfolio at level 3, you will need evidence that shows you can:
- decide what information you want and where you are going to get it (CD-ROM? Internet? Your own experiments?),
- select the right information for what you want to do,
- input data into spreadsheets, databases, or data-loggers to do calculations, test hypotheses, find answers to questions,
- check that your results are accurate and make sense,
- present your results effectively.

Computers give you access to information

In experimental work you often find that you have a large number of measurements and have to work on them in order to find the quantity you want. The usual way to deal with these is to draw a table with suitable headings. But using a **spreadsheet** can often do the job more effectively (for example, during experiments on motion, Chapter 4). Setting up the spreadsheet can also be a good way to help you to understand how to do calculations.

You will probably not want to use a **word-processor** often because you will have to write with a pen in your Physics exams. But it is a good idea to set yourself a goal to produce a piece of word-processed work at least once per month or once a term. Discuss this with your teacher and take their advice.

When you are giving a talk for your Communication portfolio (page 391) you could use presentation software (eg. PowerPoint).

Computers are ideal for collecting data over a very short or very long period. Sensors can be used to detect or measure temperature, voltage, current, position, motion, light level, sound level, magnetic field, etc., and connected to a **data-logger** to store the information. Data-loggers are often much better than human beings because they do not forget to take readings or get called away to another lesson. And they can often produce a graph or other chart as they log the data, giving you an instant picture of what is going on. You should look for opportunities to use data-logging during your course.

Another use of computers is with **modelling** software or 'virtual lab' software, where you can explore aspects of Physics on the computer screen. Your teacher will show you examples.

Finally, don't ignore opportunities for finding information on the Internet or ROMs. They have a wealth of information and give you access to information which you would find difficult to assemble in any other way.

In other words, find ways of using IT to do your Physics more effectively.

> **Key Skills**
> **Information technology**
> Level 3 Summary
>
> You must be able to plan and carry through a substantial activity that requires you to:
>
> - plan, and use different sources and appropriate techniques to search for and select information, based on judgements of relevance and quality;
>
> - use automated routines to enter and bring together information, and create and use appropriate methods to explore, develop and exchange information;
>
> - develop the structure and content of your presentation, using others' views to guide refinements, and information from different sources.

Doing Your Practical Work

Practical work is an important aspect of AS and A-level Physics. In particular, if you find written exams difficult then doing good practical work is one of the best ways of boosting your grade.

Your practical work is similar to GCSE, where you had to do an investigation and then write it up. Remember that your write-up must be clear, neat, and you will also be assessed on your English!

Most Exam Boards will assess you on 4 skills. Different Boards may have different titles for them, but they can be summarised as:

- **P   Planning,**
- **I   Implementing,**
- **A   Analysing evidence and drawing conclusions,**
- **E   Evaluating evidence and procedures.**

These 4 skills are discussed in turn.

Each Exam Board has its own mark scheme and so you should get hold of the correct one before you start your investigation. Then you can see what exactly you need to do to score high marks.

'Practical skills are important'

▶ Planning

Your teacher may have a list of investigations which you could attempt. Try to choose one which interests you and where you will be confident about the theory behind it, without it being too easy.

Analyse the investigation and decide which variable you are going to change and which variables you will keep the same (or **control**). Explain these decisions in your plan.

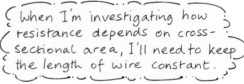

Choose the apparatus which you will be using carefully, so that your measurements will be as accurate as possible. For example, use a digital ammeter on its most sensitive setting. Think about using a data-logger (you can ask your teacher for advice on this). Make sure that your experiment is **safe** – this will be checked by your teacher.

Plan to **repeat** your readings and to make the **range** of readings as wide as possible. Repetition of readings is important to see if your results are **reliable**. If they are reliable then when you repeat the experiment you should get similar results.

You may be expected to make a prediction about the results you will get. Try to put as much detail as you can in these predictions and use as much scientific knowledge as you can. You might also predict what you think the shapes of the graphs are going to be.

You should also explain (in detail and using ideas from Physics), why you chose to use this particular method.
Doing research from textbooks or the internet when planning your practical can help you to gain marks.

▶ Implementing

For good marks in this section, you need to:
- make sure that you work safely,
- set up your apparatus correctly and skilfully,
- use data-loggers if possible, to measure quantities such as temperature, voltage, light intensity, velocity, acceleration,
- check for errors in your measuring instruments and take action if there are errors (see below on how you might do this),
- be as accurate as you can with your measurements, but then write your results to the correct degree of accuracy (see below),
- repeat your readings when necessary and check any readings which don't fit with the others (**anomalous** readings),
- show all your readings, including any averages which you calculate, in a neat table with the correct unit for each quantity,
- put all readings in a column to the same number of decimal places, so that they have the same accuracy,
- pbe flexible, and modify and adapt your plan if necessary.

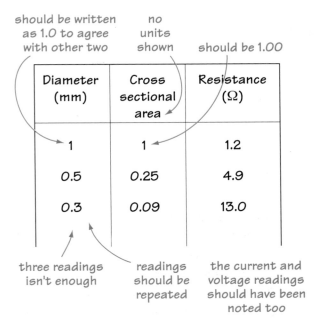

Diameter (mm)	Cross sectional area	Resistance (Ω)
1	1	1.2
0.5	0.25	4.9
0.3	0.09	13.0

should be written as 1.0 to agree with other two

no units shown

should be 1.00

three readings isn't enough

readings should be repeated

the current and voltage readings should have been noted too

Showing the accuracy of your readings

If you measured some wire as being 110 cm long, to the nearest centimetre, then how should you write this in metres?
You should write it as 1.10 m.
If you write it as 1.1 m then this suggests that you could only measure to the nearest 10 cm.
If you write it as 1.110 m then you are saying that you can measure to the nearest millimetre.

Systematic Errors

These are errors in the experimental method or equipment where readings are either always too big or always too small.

For example, if your newton-meter reads 0.2 N with no weights on it, then your measurements of force will always be 0.2 N too large. Remember to zero all your instruments before you start.

Another example is if you get **parallax** when reading scales with your eye in the wrong position, as shown in the diagram:

If you heated some water to measure its specific heat capacity (see page 302), any heat loss from the beaker would mean that your measurement of the temperature rise of the water would always be too small. This is another systematic error.

You need to design your experiment carefully to correct for errors like this heat loss (for an example of this, see page 301).

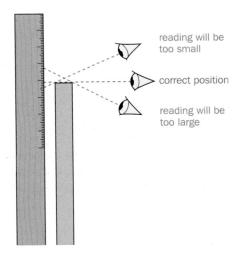

reading will be too small

correct position

reading will be too large

Parallax error

Random Errors

These are errors which sometimes mean that readings are too big, and sometimes too small.
For example, when you are timing oscillations, there is an error in your timing because of your reactions.

There are also random errors when reading ammeters or voltmeters. For example, a reading of 1.0 V means that the voltage is between 0.95 V and 1.05 V, and we are not sure if the reading is too high or too low. There is more about this on page 398, including how to estimate the size of random errors.

▷ Analysing evidence and Drawing conclusions

In order to explain this section we'll use an experiment as an example:
Imagine that you had to investigate how the period of a **pendulum**
depends on its length. Theory shows you that the relationship between
the period (T) and the length (l) is $T = 2\pi \sqrt{(l/g)}$ (see page 96).
This means that T should be proportional to $\sqrt{l}$.

You will need to explain whether your results agree with the theory
(and your prediction if you have made one).

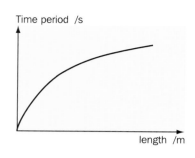

1. **Think carefully about which graph to plot.**

   For example, after measuring the time periods (T) for different lengths (l),
   if you plotted a graph of T (y–axis) against l (x–axis), you would get a
   curve. However, this curve would not show you whether T is exactly
   proportional to $\sqrt{l}$. To prove this you need to plot a graph of
   T against $\sqrt{l}$. This should be **a straight line through (0,0)**.

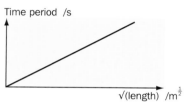

2. **Make sure you plot your graphs correctly.**

   See page 404 for advice on plotting graphs. Remember also to:

   - Use a pencil to neatly mark your points, draw your axes and
   your line of best fit, so that you can change any mistakes easily.

   - Decide what sort of best-fit line you should draw. Does theory
   suggest that your points should be in a curve or on a straight
   line? Should the graph go through (0,0)?

   - A best-fit line should have roughly the same number of offline
   points on either side of the line.

   - If some results are a long way away from your best-fit line then
   they are called **anomalous** results, and are probably due to
   errors in your readings. It is a good idea to circle these and
   label them to show that you have recognised them.
   You should ignore them when plotting your line of best fit.

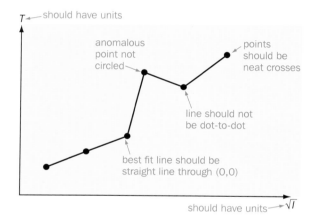

The wrong way . . .

3. **Check if the gradient of the graph agrees with theory.**

   For example, for a pendulum, $T = 2\pi \sqrt{(l/g)}$ can be written as
   $T = (2\pi / \sqrt{g}) \times \sqrt{l}$. Since $g = 9.8$ m s^{-2}, $2\pi / \sqrt{g} = 2.0$.
   So, in theory, $T = 2.0 \sqrt{l}$ and the gradient of the graph of
   T against $\sqrt{l}$ should be 2.0.

   Page 404 explains how to measure the gradient of your graph.

   - It is usually safest to give the answer to 2 sig figs (2 s.f.).
   - Remember that a gradient will have units (see page 404).
   - You can work out an error in your gradient (see page 398).
   - Sometimes you can plot your graphs quickly using spreadsheets
   or other programs which will calculate the gradient for you.
   Ask your teacher for advice on this.

. . . and the right way:

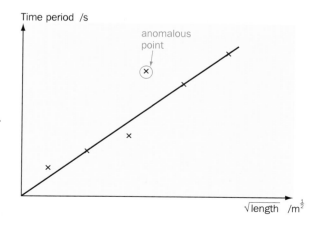

4. **Explain your results,** using your knowledge of Physics, in detail.

   - Use theory from books or the internet to explain your results.
   - When your results don't exactly agree with theory (eg. your
   gradient of T against $\sqrt{l}$ isn't 2.0 or the graph doesn't go
   through (0,0), then **say** that they don't agree! You can then go
   on to suggest **why** they don't agree. This could be due to errors
   in your measurements or the fact that the theory you have used
   only works in certain 'perfect' conditions (see the opposite page).

▷ Evaluating evidence and procedures

Accuracy and reliability

You will need to comment on the accuracy and reliability of your results, explaining which results you think are inaccurate and why.

Some things which suggest inaccuracies in your readings are:

- If your results don't agree with your predictions. (However, it could be that the theory which you used for your prediction wasn't quite right!)
- If there are some readings which don't 'fit in' with the other readings. These are anomalous results (see opposite page).
- If when you repeat readings, the readings are very different. This means that your readings are not reliable (see 'Planning').

Explaining why errors occurred

To get higher marks you will need to explain **where** the errors were and **why** you might have got some anomalous results.

Here are some sources of error (see also 'Implementing'):

- You may not have zeroed your instrument (eg. newton-meter).
- The instrument may not be reading correctly. eg. a faulty ammeter which always measures current higher than it really is.
- If you are timing, then you may not stop the watch at exactly the right moment.
- You may have read the scales incorrectly because of 'parallax'.

Also, your predictions are unlikely to be exactly right because the theory you used to make them only works in 'perfect' situations (eg. ones where there is no friction or no heat losses). In this case, don't just write comments like "my predictions were wrong because of friction" but try to explain in more detail, **why** and **how** friction, for example, affected your measurements.

For high marks, it is a good idea to estimate the **size** of the errors in your readings (see page 398). Then you can comment on which of your readings had the greatest errors in them and so affected the accuracy of your experiment the most.

Suggesting improvements

You can suggest ways in which your measurements could be made more accurate and reliable. Some ideas are:

- Repeat each reading more times.
- Take a greater number and a wider range of readings.
- Use data-loggers. Eg. for the pendulum investigation, there is a sensor and logger which will plot angle against time.
- Use more accurate instruments. Eg. an ammeter which measures to 0.001 A rather than 0.01 A.

You can also suggest ways in which the experiment might be extended. It's easy to think of other variables to investigate – for example, how mass or amplitude of a pendulum affect its period.

Try to think of something more original, to do with the variable you have already investigated. Make sure it is something which isn't too easy, but which you can explain!

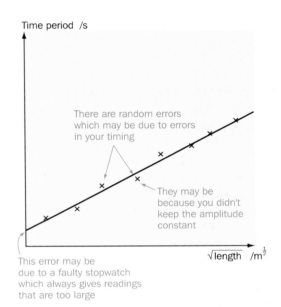

▶ Dealing with errors

When you are doing an experiment, is it ever possible to take a reading which is exact?
No reading is ever exact, even with the most accurate instrument!

This section shows you how to deal with the errors which will always occur when you are doing a practical.

How are errors written down?

In an electrical experiment, you may get a reading of 1.1 V on your voltmeter. It only measures to the nearest 0.1 V.

So you know that the voltage is about 1.1 V, not 1.0 V or 1.2 V.

This means that it lies somewhere between 1.05 V and 1.15 V. This is because if it was 1.04 V the meter would show 1.0 V, and if it was 1.16 V the meter would show 1.2 V.

The way that we show that the reading must be between 1.05 V and 1.15 V is by writing it as: 1.10 ± 0.05 V

(We use 1.10 V here because the rule is that the reading and the error should have the **same** number of decimal places.)

In this example, the **error** is $\pm$ 0.05 V

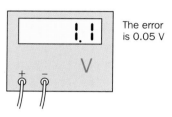

The error is 0.05 V

Often it is more important to calculate the **percentage error**.
In this example,

$$\text{Percentage error} = \frac{0.05}{1.10} \times 100 = \pm 4.5\%$$

The next diagram shows a more accurate meter:

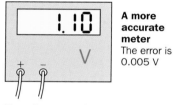

A more accurate meter
The error is 0.005 V

The voltage must be between 1.095 V and 1.105 V

Estimating an error in one reading

When you are doing practical work, you may not be able to know the errors in your readings exactly, but will have to estimate them.

For example, if you were measuring a metre length of wire, how could you estimate the error in your reading?

You need to decide how accurately you can measure the length.

- If it is to the nearest centimetre then you would write it as 100.0 cm $\pm$ 0.5 cm. This is because you know that the length would be between 99.5 cm and 100.5 cm.

- If you could measure to the nearest millimetre, what would the measurement be written as?
  It would be 100.00 cm $\pm$ 0.05 cm, because the length must be between 99.95 and 100.05 cm.

Estimating the error from many readings

Suppose you were timing 20 oscillations of a pendulum and got readings of 10.1, 9.9, 10.4, 10.9 and 10.2 sec.
Then the average is 10.3 sec to 1 decimal place.

How could you estimate the error in this time?

The lowest reading (9.9 sec) is 0.4 sec below the average, while the highest (10.9 sec) is 0.6 sec above it.
The average of these two is 0.5 sec and so the time could be written as 10.3 $\pm$ 0.5 sec.

▶ Calculating Errors

1. When adding or subtracting

When adding *or* subtracting quantities, you just **add** their errors.

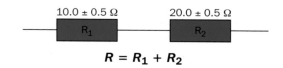

$R = R_1 + R_2$

The diagram shows 2 resistors in series. If you have to work out their total resistance, what will be the error in your calculation?

The nominal value for the total resistance $= 30.0\ \Omega$
But it could be as low as $9.5\ \Omega + 19.5\ \Omega = 29\ \Omega$,
or as high as $10.5\ \Omega + 20.5\ \Omega = 31\ \Omega$
Since we are adding the quantities, we just **add** their errors.
So: $(10.0 \pm 0.5)\ \Omega + (20.0 \pm 0.5)\ \Omega = \underline{(30.0 \pm 1.0)\ \Omega}$

2. When multiplying or dividing

When multiplying or dividing quantities you **add** their **percentage** errors to get the total percentage error.

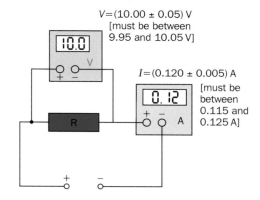

Look at the diagram:

Resistance $= V/I = 10.00\ \text{V} / 0.120\ \text{A} = 83.3\ \Omega$

To find the error in this value, we need to find the *percentage* errors in V and I:

Percentage error in $V = (0.05/10.00) \times 100 = 0.5\%$
Percentage error in $I = (0.005/0.120) \times 100 = 4.2\%$

The total percentage error in the resistance is found by adding the **percentage** errors in V and I: $0.5\% + 4.2\% = 4.7\%$

4.7% of $83.3\ \Omega = 0.047 \times 83.3 = 3.9\ \Omega$

So, we can write: Resistance $= \underline{(83.3 \pm 3.9)\ \Omega}$

3. When dealing with powers

When squaring a quantity, you multiply the percentage error by 2 to get the total percentage error.
When cubing a quantity, you multiply the percentage error by 3.
When finding a square root, you multiply by 0.5.

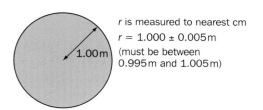

What is the area of the circle shown in the diagram?
Area of circle $= \pi r^2 = \pi \times 1.00^2 = 3.14\ \text{m}^2$

Percentage error in $r = (0.005 / 1.000) \times 100 = 0.5\%$

$\therefore$ Percentage error in $r^2 = 2 \times 0.5\% = 1.0\%$

Error in the area is 1.0% of $3.14 = 0.03\ \text{m}^2$

$\therefore$ Area $= \underline{(3.14 \pm 0.03)\ \text{m}^2}$

Errors in gradients

When you draw line of best fit through some points, it is difficult to judge exactly where the line should go.
This means that there will be an error in the value of the gradient which you calculate using this line.

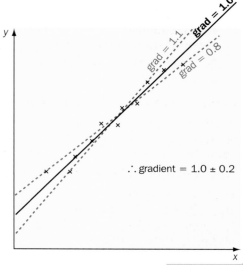

To estimate this error you can draw two other possible lines of best fit, one with a maximum possible gradient, the other with a minimum. You can work out the gradients of these two lines to give you an idea of what the error in your original gradient is.

Check Your Maths

Do you find Maths difficult?
Do you find it hard to remember?
If so, these pages can help you with some of the Maths that you need in your Physics lessons.

Symbols used in Maths

Here are some of the symbols you may meet in Physics:

$\propto$	is proportional to	$=$	is equal to
$\sim$	about the same size as	$\approx$	is approximately equal to
$>$	is greater than	$<$	is less than
$>>$	is much greater than	$<<$	is much less than
$\geq$	greater or equal to	$\pm$	plus or minus
Δx	a change in x	δx	a small change in x
$x^{\frac{1}{2}}$	the square root of x	$\sqrt{x}$	the square root of x
$\bar{x}$	mean of the values of x	Σx	sum of all the values of x
$\therefore$	therefore	$\Rightarrow$	implies that

Significant figures

There is more detailed explanation of significant figures on page 8, but here are some reminders:

- To find the number of significant figures (**s.f.**), count the number of digits starting from the first **non-zero** number on the left. Include zeros, once you have started counting. For example:

  2.7 (2 s.f.)   27.1 (3 s.f.)   271.0 (4 s.f.)

  1.200 (4 s.f.)   0.0120 (3 s.f.)   0.00012 (2 s.f.)

- In a calculation, give the answer to the **lowest** number of s.f.s of **any** of the numbers used to calculate the answer.

  eg. $56.21 \times 3.1 = 174.251$ but the answer should be written as just: 170 (2 s.f.) because 3.1 is only 2 s.f.

  A better way of writing this answer would be 1.7×10^2 (2 s.f.).

Vectors

For work on vectors please see pages 10–14.

Prefixes

For prefixes (like milli, kilo, mega, etc) see page 7.

▶ Powers

The power of a number is the small figure perched on the shoulder of the number. This is the 'index' (plural: 'indices'). It tells us how many times the number is multiplied by **itself**.

For example: $2^3 = 2 \times 2 \times 2$ and $5^4 = 5 \times 5 \times 5 \times 5$

Any number to the power 1 is itself, so $5^1 = 5$.
Any number to the power 0 is equal to 1, so $2^0 = 1$ and $7^0 = 1$.

> **Rules for powers**
>
> $y^a \times y^b = y^{a+b}$ eg. $10^2 \times 10^3 = 10^{2+3} = 10^5$
>
> $y^a / y^b = y^{a-b}$ eg. $10^3 / 10^2 = 10^{3-2} = 10^1$
>
> $(y^a)^b = y^{a \times b}$ eg. $(2^4)^3 = 2^4 \times 2^4 \times 2^4 = 2^{12}$

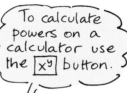

Negative powers

If a number has a negative power, like 10^{-1} , what does this mean?
This is equal to $^1/(10$ to the positive power).

For example: $10^{-1} = ^1/10^1 = ^1/10 = 0.1$
$10^{-2} = ^1/10^2 = ^1/100 = 0.01$

Standard Form

Many quantities used in Physics are very small or very large.
Eg. mass of the Earth is 6 000 000 000 000 000 000 000 000 kg.
The diameter of an atom is about 0.000 000 000 1 metres.

Can you see the problem with using such large numbers?
It is very easy to make mistakes by missing one of the noughts off!

If we use **Standard Form** it helps us to avoid this.
This is when a number is written as a number between 1 and 10 and then **multiplied by a power of 10**.

For example: $1280 = 1.28 \times 1000 = 1.28 \times 10^3$
$0.0128 = 1.28 \times 0.01 = 1.28 \times 10^{-2}$

So the mass of the Earth = 6×10^{24} kg
The diameter of an atom = 1×10^{-10} m

The index tells you how many decimal places to move. Some examples:

$2.1 \times 10^6 = 2\,100\,000$

$0.21 \times 10^7 = 2\,100\,000$

$4 \times 10^{-3} = 0.004$

$4.1 \times 10^{-4} = 0.000\,41$

Using Standard Form on a calculator

It is important to put Standard Form into your calculator correctly!

The **EXP** button on your calculator means "$\times$ 10 to the power of".

So what would you press to put 1.28×10^3 into your calculator?

You would press   then EXP then 3

Notice that there is no need to put in the $\times 10$ bit, because this is taken care of by the EXP button.

If you saw 2 ³ on your calculator, would this mean 2^3?

No, it would mean $2 \times 10^3 = 2000$.
Remember that the EXP button means: "$\times$ 10 to the power of".

Find the EXP button on your calculator

▶ Geometry and Trigonometry

Triangles

The angles of a triangle add up to 180°.   Area of a triangle $= \frac{1}{2} \times$ base $\times$ height

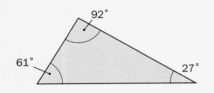

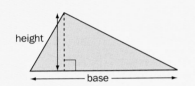

Right–angled triangles

θ ('theta') is an angle within a right–angled triangle.
The sides of the triangle are given the names
hypotenuse, **opposite** and **adjacent** as shown:

Pythagoras' theorem
This is useful when you know the lengths of 2 sides of
a right–angled triangle and you wish to find the third side.

$$a^2 = b^2 + c^2$$

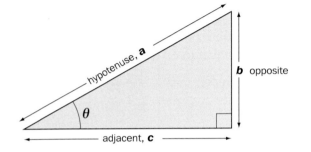

Sine, Cosine, Tangent

For a certain angle θ, the ratios b/a c/a and b/c will always
be the same whatever the size of the right–angled triangle.
These ratios are called the sine (sin), cosine (cos) and tangent (tan)
of the angle θ.

$\sin\theta = \dfrac{\text{opposite}}{\text{hypotenuse}} = \dfrac{b}{a}$	$\therefore\ b = a\sin\theta$
$\cos\theta = \dfrac{\text{adjacent}}{\text{hypotenuse}} = \dfrac{c}{a}$	$\therefore\ c = a\cos\theta$
$\tan\theta = \dfrac{\text{opposite}}{\text{adjacent}} = \dfrac{b}{c}$	$\therefore\ b = c\tan\theta$

$b = a\sin\theta$

$\Rightarrow\quad b = 5.0\ \sin 20°$

$\Rightarrow\quad b = 5.0 \times 0.342$

$\Rightarrow\quad b = 1.7\,\text{cm}\ \ (2\ \text{s.f.})$

Using a calculator with sin, cos and tan

- Check that you are working in the right units for your question (degrees or radians, see opposite).

- On some calculators you need to press the sin, cos or tan button **after** you have entered the angle.

- If you know the sin of an angle and want to know the angle itself, use the **sin^{-1}** button. See this example:
  You can use the cos^{-1} and tan^{-1} buttons in the same way.

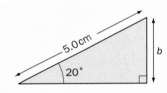

$\sin\theta = 0.75$

$\Rightarrow\quad \theta = \sin^{-1} 0.75$

$\Rightarrow\quad \theta = 49°\ \ (2\ \text{s.f.})$

More Geometry

Circumference of a circle $= 2\pi r$

Area of circle $= \pi r^2$

Surface area of sphere $= 4\pi r^2$

Volume of sphere $= \frac{4}{3}\pi r^3$

Volume of a cylinder $= \pi r^2 h$

Area of trapezium $= \frac{1}{2}(a + b)\,h$

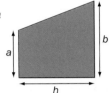

Radians

In higher level Maths it is often necessary to measure angles in units called radians (rads). *See also page 92.*
Looking at the diagram opposite:

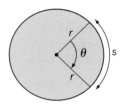

the angle θ in radians $= \dfrac{\text{arc length}}{\text{radius of circle}} = \dfrac{s}{r}$

Converting from radians to degrees

One complete revolution of a circle is 360°.
The arc length for one revolution is the whole circumference of the circle, $2\pi r$

So, the number of radians
in one complete revolution $= \dfrac{\text{arc length}}{\text{radius}} = \dfrac{2\pi r}{r} = 2\pi$ rad

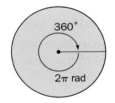

360° rad

360° is equivalent to 2π rad   1 radian = 57.3°

180° is equivalent to π rad

90° is equivalent to $\frac{\pi}{2}$ rad

Using a calculator with degrees and radians

Your calculator will work with either degrees *or* radians.

If it is working with degrees you will see **DEG** on the top of the screen.
RAD will show on the screen if you are working in radians.
You can change from one to another on most calculators by using the
MODE button. Make sure you know how to do this.

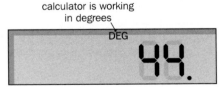

calculator is working
in degrees

DEG

Calculator screen

Small angles

It is sometimes useful to make the following approximations when an angle is *small*.

$\sin\theta \approx \tan\theta \approx \theta$ measured in radians.   Also, $\cos\theta \approx 1$

These work quite well for angles less than 10°.
The smaller the angle, the better the approximation!

▷ Plotting graphs

When you are constructing a graph after an experiment:

- Have at least 5 points to plot. If your graph curves, you may need more points to draw the curve more accurately.

- Scales must increase in equal steps. Choose scales that will make the graph as *large* as possible, without making the scale awkward for plotting points.

- Label your scales with the units being used. For example, time /s means "Time measured in seconds".

- As a general rule, the **dependent** variable (the one you are deliberately changing) goes on the x–axis. The other variable which changes as a result (the *in*dependent variable) goes on the y–axis. Time usually goes on the x–axis.

- Lines of best fit should be drawn. Sometimes they should be straight lines, sometimes curves. If you are not sure which to draw, look at the theory about your practical. Would you expect a curve or a straight line from your results? See also page 396.

- Think carefully about whether theory suggests that your graph should go through (0,0). Not all graphs should go through the origin!

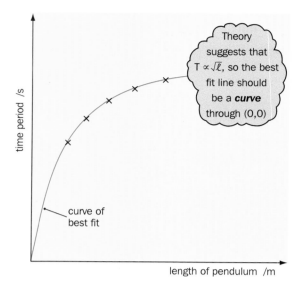

A graph showing how the period of a pendulum depends on its length

▷ The gradient of a straight line graph

The diagram shows you how to find the gradient of a line:

Δy means the change in the value of y.
Δx means the change in the value of x.

> **Gradient** $= \dfrac{\Delta y}{\Delta x}$

In the example opposite:

$$\text{Gradient} = \frac{\Delta y}{\Delta x} = \frac{30\,\text{N} - 10\,\text{N}}{0.6\,\text{m} - 0.2\,\text{m}} = \frac{20\,\text{N}}{0.4\,\text{m}} = 50\,\text{N m}^{-1}$$

A gradient will normally have units. You can find them by dividing the units of the y-axis by the units of the x-axis. Notice that the units of the gradient above are N m^{-1}.

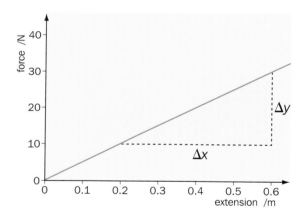

The gradient of a straight line is constant.
The gradient of a **curve** is always changing. We can measure the gradient of a curve at selected points.

To do this a **tangent** to the curve is drawn and the gradient of this tangent is measured in the same way as for a straight line:
(A tangent is a straight line which just touches the curve at one point as shown in the diagram.)

To find gradients accurately, make Δy and Δx as *large* as possible.

For the treatment of errors, see page 398.

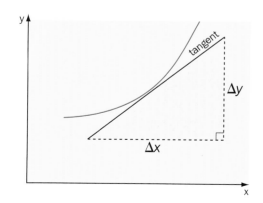

▷ The equation of a straight line graph

Look at the 4 graphs shown here and the equations
which they represent:
Notice that the number in front of the x in the equation
is the same as the **gradient** of the graph.
Notice that the number added on after the x is the same
as the place where the line cuts the y–axis (the **intercept**).

All straight line graphs have an equation of the form

$$y = mx + c$$

y and x are the quantities on the y– and x–axes.
m is the **gradient** of the graph.
c is the **intercept** of the graph on the **y**–axis.

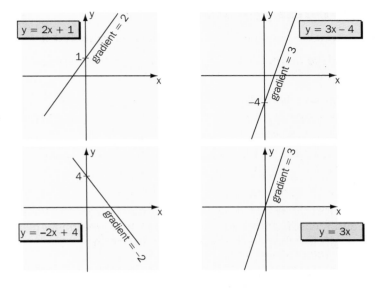

▷ Some common graph shapes

In each case, k is a constant – a number which does not change.

Inverse Proportion

$$y = \frac{k}{x}$$

as in $\quad a = \frac{F}{m} \quad$ (see page 47)

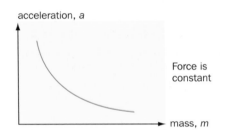

acceleration, a

Force is constant

mass, m

Inverse square relationship

$$y = \frac{k}{x^2}$$

as in $\quad E = \frac{kQ}{r^2} \quad$ (see page 257)

Notice that this has a very similar shape to the one above,
and so you need to investigate further when you get a graph
of this shape, to see which one it is.

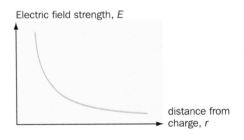

Electric field strength, E

distance from charge, r

A square relationship

$$y = kx^2$$

as in $\quad s = \frac{1}{2}at^2 \quad$ (see page 36)

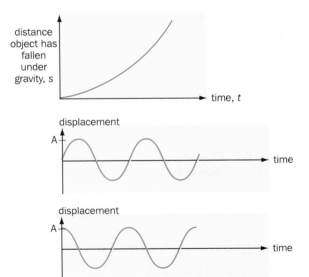

distance object has fallen under gravity, s

time, t

A sine graph

$$y = k\sin x$$ as in $\quad s = A\sin \omega t \quad$ (see page 94)

displacement

A

time

A cosine graph

$$y = k\cos x$$ as in $\quad s = A\cos \omega t \quad$ (see page 94)

displacement

A

time

For exponential graphs $y = Ae^{-kx}$ see page 408.

▶ Direct proportion

A variable y is **directly** proportional to a variable x if

$$y = kx \qquad (k \text{ is a constant number})$$

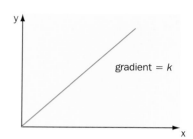

gradient = k

If this equation is true, then:

- a graph of y against x will be a straight line through $(0,0)$ with gradient k, as shown here:
- y/x will always be the same number (the constant k)
- if you double y, then x will double.

Look at the circuit shown here. If you changed the voltage and measured the current each time, then you might get results like this which show direct proportion:

Can you see that as the voltage doubles from 1 V to 2 V, then the current also doubles?
Also, when the voltage doubles from 2 V to 4 V then the current doubles again.

Notice also that voltage divided by current is always the same number, 4. This is actually the resistance of the wire. Remember that $V/I = R$ (page 196).

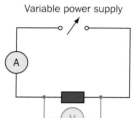

Variable power supply

Voltage (V)	Current (A)
0.00	0.00
1.00	0.25
2.00	0.50
3.00	0.75
4.00	1.00

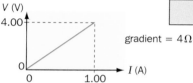

gradient = 4 Ω

▶ Inverse proportion

The two variables y and x are **inversely** proportional if

$$y = \frac{k}{x} \qquad \text{This means: } yx = k \text{ (a constant)}$$

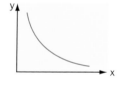

- to get a straight line through $(0,0)$, plot y against $1/x$:
- if you double y, then x will **halve**.

If you change the pressure on a gas and measure its volume (see page 314) then you could get results like the ones here, which show **inverse** proportion:

When the pressure is doubled from $1 \times 10^5 \text{ N/m}^2$ to $2 \times 10^5 \text{ N/m}^2$, the gas volume halves from 16 m³ to 8 m³. Can you see the volume halves again when the pressure is doubled again from $2 \times 10^5 \text{ N/m}^2$ to $4 \times 10^5 \text{ N/m}^2$?

What is the constant $P \times V$ equal to?
In this experiment it is always 16×10^5 N m.

Pressure (N/m²)	Volume (m³)
1×10^5	16
2×10^5	8
4×10^5	4
8×10^5	2
16×10^5	1

Inverse square relationship

$$y = \frac{k}{x^2} \qquad \text{and so} \quad yx^2 = k \text{ (a constant)}$$

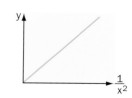

- to get a straight line through $(0,0)$, plot y against $1/x^2$:
- if you double x, then y falls to a quarter.

▶ Equations

Changing the subject of an equation

From page 36, there is an equation for acceleration, $\quad a = \dfrac{v - u}{t}$

But what if you know a, u and t, and you want to find $\boldsymbol{v}$?
You will need to change the **subject** of the equation to v.

As long as you do the **same** thing to **both** sides of an equation,
it will still balance. For example:

First multiply by t: $\qquad a \times t = \dfrac{(v - u) \times \cancel{t}}{\cancel{t}}$

then cancel: $\qquad \therefore\ a t = v - u$

Now add u: $\qquad u + a t = v - \cancel{u} + \cancel{u}$

then cancel: $\qquad \therefore\ u + a t = v$

So v is now the subject. Often it is easier to put in your numbers
before you re-arrange the equation, as shown here:

A more complex example

Change the subject of: $\qquad F = \dfrac{G m_1 m_2}{r^2}$ (page 78) to be $\boldsymbol{G}$.

First multiply by r^2 $\qquad F \times r^2 = \dfrac{G m_1 m_2}{\cancel{r^2}} \times \cancel{r^2}$

$\qquad\qquad \therefore\ F r^2 = G m_1 m_2$

Divide by m_2 $\qquad \dfrac{F r^2}{m_2} = \dfrac{G m_1 \cancel{m_2}}{\cancel{m_2}}$

$\qquad\qquad \therefore\ \dfrac{F r^2}{m_2} = G m_1$

Divide by m_1 $\qquad \dfrac{F r^2}{m_1 m_2} = \dfrac{G \cancel{m_1}}{\cancel{m_1}}$

$\qquad\qquad \therefore\ \dfrac{F r^2}{m_1 m_2} = G$

Combining equations

Sometimes you need to combine two equations.
For example, in circuit work (Chapters 16, 17) if you know that
voltage is given by $V = IR$ and power by $P = IV$,
what is the power of a resistor R with a voltage V across it?

$P = I \times V \qquad$ But: $V = I \times R$, $\quad$ so: $I = \dfrac{V}{R}$

Therefore, $P = \dfrac{V}{R} \times V$

So: $P = \dfrac{V^2}{R}$

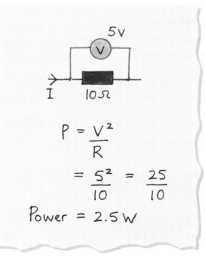

▷ Exponentials

You will come across an **exponential decay curve** in the radioactivity topic (see page 343) and also when learning about the discharge of capacitors (page 271).

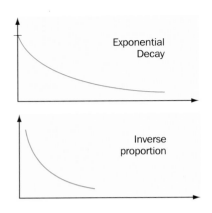

Exponential Decay

Look at the curve and compare it with the graph showing inverse proportion (page 406). How is it different?

Inverse proportion

One thing which is different is that the curve touches the y-axis, but the inverse proportion curve doesn't.
The exponential curve has some very definite features.

How can you tell if a curve is exponential?

Look at the graph:
It's a graph of the amount of radiation given off by a radioactive substance each second, called the activity of the substance.

After each 70 seconds, the activity *halves*. After 70 secs it has *halved* from 400 to 200. Then, in the next 70 seconds, it has *halved* from 200 to 100. In the next 70 seconds it halves again.

One rule for exponential curves is that they always take the same time to halve (called the **half–life**), no matter how much you have to start with. The substance above has a half–life of 70 seconds.

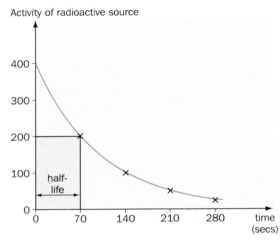

Activity of radioactive source

The exponential equation

The mathematical equation for any exponential decay is

$$y = A\,e^{-kt}$$

y is the quantity which is decaying (eg. the activity of the radioactive source).
As you can see from the graph, A is the starting value of y.
e is a special 'never–ending' number in maths (similar to π) with a value of 2.7128 to 4 decimal places.
k is a constant. It depends on how quickly the quantity decays.
t is the time that the quantity has been decaying for.

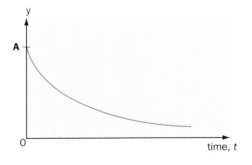

Logarithms

In order to understand exponentials better we need to know about logarithms. What is a logarithm or 'log'?

Since **100 = 10²** we say that:
the log of 100 (to the base 10) is equal to 2.

This can be written as: **log₁₀ 100 = 2**.

In the same way, since $1000 = 10^3$ then $\log_{10} 1000 = 3$.

Also, for example, $8241 = 10^{3.916}$.
So what is $\log_{10} 8241$? It is 3.916.

We can have logs to other bases. For example, $2^4 = 16$
So the log of 16 to the base 2 is 4. That is: $\log_2 16 = 4$.

Two rules for using logs (to any base)

1. $\log(a \times b) = \log a + \log b$ so: $\log(4 \times 7) = \log 4 + \log 7$

2. $\log a^b = b \log a$ so: $\log 10^3 = 3 \times \log 10$

Taking logs of both sides of a power equation

In general, if you have an equation $y = A\,x^n$

then $\log y = \log(Ax^n)$

But from rule 1 on logs above: $\log(ab) = \log a + \log b$

$\therefore$ $\log y = \log A + \log x^n$

But by rule 2: $\log a^b = b \log a$ so: $\log x^n = n \log x$

So if $y = A\,x^n$ then $\mathbf{\log y = \log A + n \log x}$ . . . . . (1)

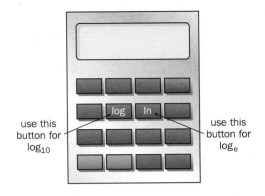

use this button for $\log_{10}$

use this button for $\log_e$

Taking logs of both sides of an exponential equation

$y = A\,e^{-kt}$ and so, from (1) $\log_e y = \log_e A + \log_e e^{-kt}$

Since $\log_{10} 10^2 = 2$ and $\log_{10} 10^3 = 3$
can you see that $\log_e e^{-kt} = -kt$?

So we get: $\mathbf{\log_e y = -kt + \log_e A}$ . . . . . (2)

This can be used to check whether a curve is exponential and to work out the constants A and k in the decay equation $y = A\,e^{-kt}$, as follows:

On many calculators you must put in the number first and then press the log/ln button.

Plotting a log graph to check whether decay is exponential

Compare equation (2) above with the equation for a straight line, $y = mx + c$ (see page 405):

$$\log_e y = -k \quad t \quad + \quad \log_e A$$
$$y = m \quad x \quad + \quad c$$

What would a graph of $\mathbf{\log_e y}$ against $\mathbf{t}$ look like?

It will be a straight line as shown, with gradient $= -k$ and an intercept on the y axis $= \log_e A$.

You will only get a straight line log-graph if the decay is exponential! This is another way of checking whether a curve is exponential.

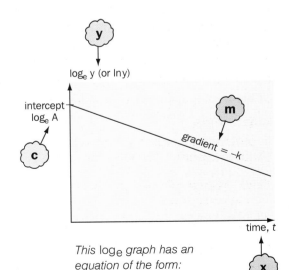

$\log_e y$ (or ln y)

intercept $\log_e A$

c

m

gradient $= -k$

time, t

This $\log_e$ graph has an equation of the form:
$$y = mx + c$$
$$\log_e y = -kt + \log_e A$$

x

The half–life equation
The constant k is useful because you can use it to work out the half-life of the decay.

It turns out that: half–life $= \dfrac{0.693}{k}$

Hints and Answers

Give me a hint...

▶ Mechanics

Chapter 1 (Basic Ideas) page 15

1. a) unit   b) base, derived
   c) size (magnitude), direction, size (magnitude)
   d) resultant   e) component
   f) component, vector, cosine

2. a) $kg\,m\,s^{-2}$, newton (N)
   b) $kg\,m^{-1}\,s^{-2}$, $N\,m^{-2}$ or pascal (Pa)

3. a) F: $kg\,m\,s^{-2}$ A: m^2 v: $m\,s^{-1}$ ρ: $kg\,m^{-3}$
   b) See Example 5.
      i) $A^2\rho v = m^4\ kg\,m^{-3}\ m\,s^{-1} = kg\,m^2\,s^{-1}$ ✘
      ii) $A\rho^2 v = m^2\ kg^2\,m^{-6}\ m\,s^{-1} = kg^2\,m^{-3}\,s^{-1}$ ✘
      iii) $A\rho v^2 = m^2\ kg\,m^{-3}\ m^2\,s^{-2} = kg\,m\,s^{-2}$ ✔

4. a) 2 GJ, b) 5.9 kg, c) 5 ms d) 345 kN e) 20 μm

5. a) 600N ⟷ 475N
   b) 125 N to the left

6. a)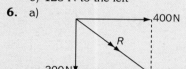
   b) $R = \sqrt{(400\,N^2 + 300\,N^2)} = 500\ N$
   $\tan\theta = 300/400$ $\therefore\ \theta = 36.9°$
   Resultant is 500 N at E 36.9° S

7.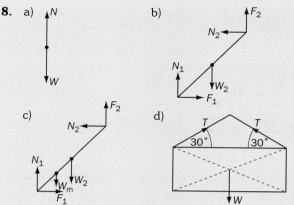
   a) $v_V = 20\cos 45° = 14\ m\,s^{-1}$
   b) $v_H = 20\cos 45° = 14\ m\,s^{-1}$

8. a) $F_H = 120\cos 25° = 109\ N$
   b) $F_V = 120\cos 65° = 50.7\ N$

Chapter 2 (Looking at Forces) page 25

1. a) mass, kilograms   b) gravity, newtons
   c) weight $= mg$ d) friction, opposite
   e) smooth, rough   f) force, area, $N\,m^{-2}$, pascals

2. See Example 1. a) 638 N, b) 150 N

3. 120 g mass on Venus weighs more (1060 N).

4. Calculate mass using $m = W \div g\ (= 1500\ kg)$ then new weight. 6450 N

5. See Example 2. Force = weight = 29.4 N
   a) Area = 70 cm² (0.007 m²). 0.42 N cm⁻² (4200 Pa)
   b) Area = 300 cm² (0.03 m²). 0.098 N cm⁻² (980 Pa)

6. a) Low pressure. Don't sink into sand.
   b) High pressure. Pierces surfaces easily.
   c) Spreads weight over large area. Reduces pressure on ice.
   d) Low pressure. Don't sink into mud.

7. a) See Example 1. 0.08 N
   b) 0.01% of 1 cm² = 1×10^{-4} cm² or 1×10^{-8} m²
   c) See Example 2. 8×10^6 Pa

8. a) b) c) d)

9. a) See Example 1. 3.4×10^6 N
   b) Lift = weight. 3.4×10^6 N
   c) See Example 3.
      (Pressure difference = $F \div A$)   7600 Pa

Chapter 3 (Turning Effects of Forces) page 31

1. a) perpendicular, force
   b) newton-metres (N m)
   c) equilibrium, clockwise, equal, anticlockwise
   d) weight
   e) size (magnitude), opposite, turning

2. a) Moment = 200 N × 0.20 m = 40 N m.
   b) A longer spanner gives more turning moment for the same force. This makes it easier to use.

3. See Example 3.
   a) $X = 9$ N   (b) $Y = 4.5$ N   (c) $Z = 5$ cm

4. a) Low centre of gravity keeps it stable.
   b) Low centre of gravity and wide base gives high stability.
   c) Large effective base area keeps him stable.
   d) Weight of wine raises overall centre of gravity.
   e) Load makes centre of gravity higher.

5. See Example 2.
   a) couple = 15 N × 0.75 m = 11 N m (2 s.f.)
   b) couple = 24 N × 0.80 m = 19 N m (2 s.f.)

6. a) Weight of ruler (1 N) acts 40 cm from pivot.
      (X × 10 cm) = (1 N × 40 cm) $\therefore\ X = 4$ N
   b) Weight of ruler (1 N) acts 35 cm from pivot.
      (1 N × 35 cm) + (5 N × Y) = (10 N × 15 cm)
      $\therefore\ Y = 23$ cm

7. a)
   b) See Example 6. Take moments about B to find
      $R_A = 110$ N (2 s.f.)
      $R_A + R_B = 250$ N $\therefore\ R_B = 140$ N (2 s.f.)

8. a)

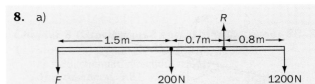

b) See Example 6. Take moments about pivot to find
$F = 370$ N (2 s.f.)

c) Total force up = total force down $\therefore R = 1770$ N

Chapter 4 (Describing Motion) pages 42–43

1. a) displacement, metres per second (m s^{-1}), velocity, metres per second squared (m s^{-2})
b) speed, direction
c) gradient, greater (faster, higher)
d) velocity, time, displacement
e) direction
f) gravity, air resistance, increases, terminal velocity
g) same, horizontal, vertical

2. a) distance = $\pi r = 3.1$ m
b) time = distance ÷ speed = 5.2 s
c) displacement = 2.0 m (diameter of circular track)
d) average velocity = displacement ÷ time = 0.39 m s^{-1} (from A to B)

3. a) acceleration = $\dfrac{\Delta v}{t} = \dfrac{12 \text{ m s}^{-1}}{4.0 \text{ s}} = 3.0$ m s^{-2}
b) time = $\dfrac{\Delta v}{a} = \dfrac{-20 \text{ m s}^{-1}}{-4 \text{ m s}^{-2}} = 5.0$ s

4. a) displacement   b) displacement

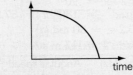

c) displacement

5. a) = (ii)   b) = (iv)   c) = (i)   d) = (iii)

6. a) acceleration = $\dfrac{\Delta v}{t} = \dfrac{14 \text{ m s}^{-1}}{5.0 \text{ s}} = 2.8$ m s^{-2}
b) deceleration = $\dfrac{\Delta v}{t} = \dfrac{14 \text{ m s}^{-1}}{10 \text{ s}} = 1.4$ m s^{-2}
c) displacement = area under graph = 35 m
d) total displacement = total area under graph = 245 m

7. a) $s = ut + \frac{1}{2}at^2 = 0 + (\frac{1}{2} \times 3.4 \times 3.0^2) = 15$ m (2 s.f.)
b) $v = u + at = 0 + (3.4 \times 3.0) = 10$ m s^{-1} (2 s.f.)
c) Time for last 85 m = distance ÷ speed = 8.3 s, so total time for race = 8.3 s + 3.0 s = 11 s (2 s.f.)

8. a) acceleration = $\dfrac{\Delta v}{t} = \dfrac{2.0 \text{ m s}^{-1}}{3.0 \text{ s}} = 0.67$ m s^{-2}
b) slows to a stop.
c) displacement = area under graph = 18 m
d) Lift accelerates downwards. It then decelerates to a stop.
e) Area DEF under graph = 6 m. So overall displacement = 18 m up + 6 m down = 12 m up

9. a) $u = 5.0$ m s^{-1} upwards
b) See Example 7. With down as positive: $s = 150$ m, $a = 10$ m s^{-2}, $u = -5.0$ m s^{-1}. Use $v^2 = u^2 + 2as$ to find $v = 55$ m s^{-1}.
Then use $v = u + at$ to find $t = 6.0$ s.

10. See Example 8.
a) Vertically, with down as positive: $s = 0.65$ m, $u = 0$, $a = 10$ m s^{-2}. Use $s = ut + \frac{1}{2}at^2$ to find $t = 0.36$ s.
b) Horizontally: $u = 2$ m s^{-1}, $t = 0.36$ s, $a = 0$. Horiz. distance = horiz. velocity × time = 0.72 m

11. See Example 8.
a) $u_{\text{HORIZ}} = 60$ m s^{-1}, $u_{\text{VERT}} = 0$ m s^{-1}
b) Vertically, with down as positive: $s = 1000$ m, $u = 0$, $a = 10$ m s^{-2}. Use $s = ut + \frac{1}{2}at^2$ to find $t = 14$ s.
c) Horizontally: $u = 60$ m s^{-1}, $t = \sqrt{200}$ s, $a = 0$. Horiz. distance = horiz. velocity × time = 850 m

12. See Example 9.

a) Vertically from A to B with up as positive: $v = 0$, $u = 26\cos45°$, $a = -10$ m s^{-2}. Use $v = u + at$ to find t. Double this for total time = 3.7 s.
b) Horizontally: $u = 26\cos45°$, $t = 3.7$ s, $a = 0$. Horiz. distance = horiz. velocity × time = 68 m
c) Vertically from A to B with up as positive: $v = 0$, $t = 1.8$ s $u = 26\cos45°$. Use $s = \frac{1}{2}(u + v)t$ to give $s = 17$ m.

Chapter 5 (Newton's Laws, Momentum) pages 58–59

1. a) force, accelerate, velocity
b) mass, velocity, kilogram metres per second (kg m s^{-1})
c) mass
d) 1 kilogram (1 kg), 1 metre per second squared (1 m s^{-2})
e) magnitude (size), directions
f) force, time, newton-seconds (N s), momentum, force-time
g) momentum, force

2. See Example 1.   a) 6000 kg m s^{-1} b) 6.0 kg m s^{-1}

3. $F = ma = 25\,000$ kg $\times 4$ m s$^{-2} = 100\,000$ N

4. a) $a = F \div m = (9000 - 1500)$N $\div 1500$ kg = 5 m s^{-2}
b) Drag increases with velocity reducing the resultant accelerating force.

5. a) $p = mv = 2.4 \times 10^{-3} \times 0.65 = 1.6 \times 10^{-3}$ kg m s^{-1}
b) $\Delta p = $ impulse $= F \times t$ $\therefore F = \Delta p \div t = 1.3$ N

6. See page 49 and Example 5.

7. i)

① Contact force of chair on man

② Gravitational pull of Earth on man (man's weight)

(We have ignored the very small gravitational attraction between the man and the chair.)

ii)

① Contact force of man on chair

④ Contact forces of ground on chair

③ Gravitational pull of Earth on chair (chair's weight)

iii)

④ Contact force of chair on ground

② ③ Gravitational pull of man and chair on Earth

19. a) 500 mm (image is 225 mm behind mirror)
b) Rays leaving the spectacle lens still diverge, so the image is virtual with $v = -250$ mm.
Converging lens of power +2 D

20. b)

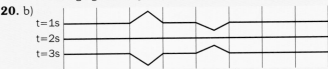

21. a) The path from T to R has changed by 0.015 m = $\lambda/2$ to give destructive interference. Signal not zero because direct and reflected beams not same amplitude.
b) Every time car moves 0.015 m signal fluctuates through one cycle. Speed = 18 m s⁻¹

22. b) See question 11.
Angle of refraction on entering fibre = (90 − c)
c) mechanical protection of the fibre,
d) $n_{\text{cladding}} < n_{\text{core}}$ but not by much

23. a) movement is parallel to wave direction
b) label C where particles are close together
c) same pattern as sketch Y but shifted $\frac{1}{4}\lambda$ to the right

24. a) at P, path difference = zero; at Q, $\lambda/2$
b) $\lambda = 0.027$ m, $f = 11$ GHz

▶ Quantum Physics

Chapter 14 (Photons and Electrons) page 173

1. a) electrons, thermionic, light (electromagnetic radiation), photoelectric
b) electron-volt (eV), 1.6×10^{-19}
c) emitted, threshold, higher (larger)
d) frequency (wavelength), photon, work
e) particle, waves

2. a) See Example 1. 1.6×10^{-18} J, 10 eV (2 s.f.)
b) 1.6×10^{-15} J, 10 keV (10^4 eV) (2 s.f.)

3. a) See Example 3. 6.6×10^{-26} J, 4.1×10^{-7} eV (2 s.f.)
b) Use $v = f\lambda$, then as (a). 2.0×10^{-24} J, 1.2×10^{-5} eV
c) 2.0×10^{-22} J, 1.2×10^{-3} eV (2 s.f.)
d) 2.0×10^{-18} J, 12 eV (2 s.f.)
e) 2.0×10^{-17} J, 120 eV (2 s.f)

4. a) See page 168.
b) See Example 4. 3.0×10^{-19} J to 3.1×10^{-19} J (1.9 eV)
c) 6.6×10^{-34} J s (2 s.f.) (It is the Planck constant.)

5. a) Compare photon energy with work function.
Yes, as 3.1 eV > 2.8 eV
b) See Example 5. 2.9×10^{-7} m (290 nm) (2 s.f.)

6. a) Kinetic energy = $\frac{1}{2}mv^2$. 1.3×10^7 m s⁻¹ (2 s.f.)
b) Momentum = mv. 1.2×10^{-23} kg m s⁻¹ (2 s.f.)
c) See Example 6. 5.5×10^{-11} m (2 s.f.)

Chapter 15 (Spectra and Energy Levels) pages 186–187

1. a) gamma, wavelength, radioactive (unstable), X-rays, visible (visible light), ultra-violet (UV), infra-red (IR)
b) interference, radio, gamma
c) all, line, absorption
d) excited, levels
e) higher, lower, absorption, ground
f) ionised, ionisation

2. See page 174 and Example 1. By rows: visible light 2.5 eV (4.0×10^{-19} J), ultra-violet 2.5×10^{-8} m (25 nm), infra-red 4.0×10^{-5} m (40 μm) (2 s.f.)

3. a) See page 180. A is the ground state, B the excited state
b) See Example 1. 8.3×10^{-7} m (830 nm) (2 s.f.)

4. a) See page 180. There are three excited states.
b) See 'A potential well' on page 180. The zero level is defined for a free electron, so an electron trapped at a lower potential energy in the potential well of an atom has negative potential energy.
c) Ionisation takes the electron from the ground state to the zero energy level. 3.6 eV
d) See pages 180 and 182. 3.6 eV
e) 0.4 eV

5. a) See page 174 for photon energies in eV.
2.7 eV is visible (wavelength of 460 nm)
b) 3.2 eV is ultra-violet (wavelength of 390 nm, < 400 nm)
c) 0.5 eV is infra-red (wavelength of 2.5 μm, > 700 nm))

6. a) See Example 1.
b) Transition must = 1.96 eV. From the − 4.03 eV level to the −5.99 eV level.

7. a) See photon energies on page 174.
91 keV photons are emitted or absorbed in transitions.
b) See Example 1. 1.4×10^{-11} m (2 s.f.)
c) See page 174. Gamma

8. a) See page 180. 10.4 eV
b) See Example 3. 1.8 eV, 4.9 eV and 6.7 eV
c) See page 174 and Example 1. 6.9×10^{-7} m (690 nm) is visible, 2.5×10^{-7} m (250 nm) is ultra-violet, 1.85×10^{-7} m (180 nm) is ultra-violet (2 s.f.)
d) Which of the transitions in part (b) involved the ground state? All transitions from the ground state require photons of ultra-violet energy.

▶ Further Questions on Quantum Physics

Quantum Physics (page 188)

1. d) Using $E = hc/\lambda$ and $E = \phi + 0.76$ eV gives $\phi = 3.2 \times 10^{-19}$ J, $f = 4.8 \times 10^{14}$ Hz

2. c) $\phi = hf$ when $E_{\text{max}} = 0$, $\phi = 2.6 \times 10^{-19}$ J, $\lambda = 750$ nm
d) more electrons released but no change in graph

3. a) 51 nA   (b) 100 nA   (c) no (600 nm > λ_{max})

4. a) 280 s⁻¹   (b) absorption, reflection off surface of eye

5. a) use $qV = \frac{1}{2}mv^2$ (b) $\lambda = h/mv = 3.2 \times 10^{-11}$ m
c) λ is smaller than the atomic spacing of graphite
d) nuclear radii $\approx 10^{-14}$ m, so $\lambda \approx 10^{-14}$ m required

6. a) use $qV = \frac{1}{2}mv^2$ $\lambda = h/mv = 2.7 \times 10^{-11}$ m
b) $\lambda < 0.3$ nm, so diffraction effects observed

Spectra (page 189)

7. c) ultraviolet, using $E = hf$, $E = 16.5 \times 10^{-19}$ J = 10.3 eV

8. a) $n = 1$ level marked –13.6 eV
c) $n = 3$ to $n = 2$ transition, 1.9 eV

9. c) Using $E = hc/\lambda$, $\lambda = 91$ nm

10. a) 1.8 eV
b) Using $E = hc/\lambda$, $\lambda = 120$ nm

11. a) 1.7×10^{-18} J,
b) 4 routes
c) 600 nm equates to 2.1 eV, −1.6 eV to −3.7 eV

12. b) i) Using $d \sin\theta = n\lambda$ for red and blue,
$\Delta\theta = 3.78° - 2.81° = 0.97°$
ii) Using $\sin i / \sin r = n$ for red and blue,
$\Delta r = 36.6° - 36.1° = 0.50°$

Chapter 16 (Current and Charge) pages 204–205

1. a) electrons (charge), electrons, energy
   b) coulombs, amperes, time, seconds
   c) resistance, p.d. (voltage)
   d) current, proportional, p.d. (voltage), temperature
   e) increases, increases, decreases
   f) watts, amperes, p.d. (voltage), volts

2. a) very large numbers of free electrons
   b) very few free electrons
   c) semiconductors have fewer ($\sim 10^{10}$ m^{-3} fewer) free electrons
   d) vibration of metal ions increases, more opposition to electron flow
   e) number of free electrons increases as temperature rises

3. Using $Q = It$, (a) $Q = 35$ C   (b) $Q = 36$ C

4. Using $Q = It$, (a) $I = 0.15$ A (b) $I = 20$ A (c) $I = 2.0$ mA

5. a) 4.0×10^{-3} C
   b) Using $Q = It$, $I = 80$ μA
   c) I is the number of coulombs per second; number of electrons s^{-1} = $I/e = 5.0 \times 10^{14}$

6. Using $Q = It$, $Q = 360$ μC; number of electrons = $Q/e = 2.3 \times 10^{15}$

7. Charge = area under graph = 70 C

8. Using $I = nAve$, $v = 1.3 \times 10^{-4}$ m s^{-1}

9. a) Using $W = QV$, $W = 4800$ J
   b) Using $W = VIt$, $W = 900$ J

10. Using $W = VIt$, $W = 1.4 \times 10^5$ J

11. a) Using $W = QV$, $V = 12$ V
    b) Using $W = VIt$, $V = 45$ V

12. Using $W = VIt$, $I = 10$ A

13. Using $V = IR$ (a) $V = 12$ V, (b) $R = 24$ Ω, (c) $I = 0.20$ A

14. a) Using $R = \rho l/A$, $R = 0.34$ Ω
    b) Using $V = IR$, $V = 4.4$ V.

15. Using $R = \rho l/A$ and $A = \pi d^2/4$, $R = 1.2$ Ω

16. Using $R = \rho l/A$ and $A = \pi d^2/4$, (a) 0.23 m (b) 0.57m

17. a) Using $R = V/I$, $R = 10$ Ω at θ_1, and $R = 13$ Ω at θ_2
    b) θ_2 is the higher temperature.

18. Using $R = V/I$,   (a) 120 Ω   (b) 16 Ω

19. Using $W = Pt$, (a) W (in J) = 3000 W $\times$ 1800 s = 5.4 MJ
    b) W (in kWh) = 3.0 kW $\times$ 0.5 h = 1.5 kWh

20. 14 p. (0.06 kW $\times$ 30 h = 1.8 kWh)

21. Using $P = VI$,   (a) $P = 1.7$ kW   (b) $I = 4.0$ A

22. Using $P = I^2R$,   (a) $P = 40$ W   (b) $P = 160$ W
    2 $\times$ current gives 4 $\times$ power.

23. Using $P = I^2R$, $P = 3.1 \times 10^{-2}$ W

24. a) Using $P = IV$, $I = 625$ A
    b) Using $P = I^2R$, $P = 2.0$ MW

25. Using $P = V^2/R$, $P = 1.1$ kW

26. a) Using $R = \rho l/A$ and $A = \pi r^2$, $R = 760$ Ω
    b) Using $P = V^2/R$, $P = 70$ W
    c) i) resistance increases (ii) power falls

Chapter 17 (Electric Circuits) pages 216–217

1. a) current, same
   b) p.d. (voltage), sum
   c) current, sum
   d) p.d. (voltage), resistor (component)
   e) closed, sum, p.d.s

2. a) Less opposition to current because more than one path for electrons to take.
   b) 3.0 V when connected in the same direction; 0 V when in opposite directions.
   c) Energy is wasted within the cell itself due to its internal resistance.

3. a) Lamp not lit, high resistance voltmeter reduces p.d. across lamp and current through it.
   b) Lamp not lit, low resistance ammeter short circuits lamp.

4. a) 2.5 kΩ   (b) 3 Ω   (c) 7.6 Ω   (d) 6 Ω

5. a) 3 Ω half of 6 Ω
   b) 4 Ω
   c) 3 Ω, one third of 9 Ω

6. a) Using $V = IR$, $I = 0.5$ A
   b) 0.5 A, current for resistors in series is the same.
   c) Using $V = IR$, $V = 4.0$ V

7. See Example 2. (a) 2 Ω   (b) 6 V   (c) 2 A   (d) 1 A

8. a) 6.0 Ω (parallel $R = 4.5$ Ω, + 1.5 Ω in series)
   b) Using $V = IR$, $I = 2.0$ A
   c) Using $V = IR$, $V_1 = 3.0$ V, $V_2 = 9.0$ V
   d) Using $V = IR$, $I_1 = 0.5$ A (9 V/18 Ω), $I_2 = 1.5$ A (9 V/6.0 Ω)

9. From definition of e.m.f. (a) 2.0 J   (b) 5000 J

10. a) Using $W = Q\epsilon$, $W = 15$ J
    b) Using $W = Q\epsilon$ and $Q = It$, $W = 18$ J

11. Using $\epsilon = I(R + r)$, $I = 0.4$ A

12. i) See Example 4. (a) 18 Ω   (b) 0.3 A   (c) 5.4 V
    d) 0.6 J C^{-1}
    ii) See Example 5. (a) 4 Ω   (b) 1 A   (c) 4 V   (d) 2 J C^{-1}

13. Using $\epsilon = I(R + r)$, $I = 1.5$ A

14. a) 1.5 V, (e.m.f. = terminal p.d. when current through cell is zero).
    b) Using $v = Ir$ and $v = 1.5$ V – 1.2 V, $r = 1.0$ Ω
    c) Using $V = IR$, $R = 4.0$ Ω

15. See Example 6.   3.0 A

16. See page 210. (i) 2 V   (ii) 100 V

17. See pages 210 and 211. 0 V to 10 V

18. See Example 3. (a) 5 V   (b) 1 V

Chapter 18 (Magnetic Fields) pages 230–231

1. a) field, stronger
   b) magnetic, current, circles (cylinders), wire
   c) parallel, spaced, uniform (constant), bar
   d) force, force, 90°, field.   e) turns, current

2. a) Direction of vertical force on wire changes with every half cycle of a.c.
   b) See page 227. Force on charged particle is always at 90° to its velocity.
   c) See page 228. Each wire experiences a repulsive force due to the field of the other wire.

3. a) See page 219.   b) See page 220.
   c) See page 228.   d) radial field, inwards from N to S

4. Currents around (b) and (a) are in same direction.

5. Using $B = \mu_0 I/2\pi r$, $B = 1.6 \times 10^{-5}$ T

6. Using $B = \mu_0 I/2\pi r$, $r = 2.0$ cm

7. Using $B = \mu_0 n I$, ($n = 1200/0.4$), $B = 9.4 \times 10^{-3}$ T

8. a) i), ii), and iv)
   b) i) perpendicular to I, towards bottom right
      ii) vertically downwards
      iv) out of page

9. Using $B = \mu_0 n I$, $n = 1.6 \times 10^4$ turns per metre

10. ii) and iv)

11. a) See example 7. Using $F = \mu_0 I_1 I_2 l / 2\pi r$,
$F = 8.0 \times 10^{-5}$ N
b) 8 mm from P;
current in P is $4 \times$ current in Q, so fields are equal at a point $4 \times$ further from P than Q.

12. Using $F = B I l \sin\theta$, (a) $F = 0.12$ N (b) $F = 0.10$ N.
c) Into the page in both cases.

13. Using $F = B I l$, (from balance $F = 2.2 \times 10^{-3} \times 10$ N),
$B = 0.11$ T

14. See page 226. (a) X positively charged, (b) Y uncharged
c) See page 227. (i) and (ii), radius of path decreases,
iii) X circles clockwise.

15. a) Using $F = BQv$, $F = 8.0 \times 10^{-14}$ N
b) Using $F = mv^2 / r$, $r = 4.6$ mm

Chapter 19 (Electromagnetic Induction) page 241

1. a) flux, induced
b) size, e.m.f., rate, flux
c) direction, e.m.f., oppose
d) speed, strength, area, turns

2. a) The wire is not 'cutting' through lines of flux.
b) See page 238, magnetic braking.
c) See page 238, magnetic braking.

3. Using $\Phi = B A$, $\Phi = 110$ Wb

4. Using $N\Phi = NBA$, $N\Phi = 1.5$ Wb

5. Using $\epsilon = N\Delta\Phi/\Delta t$, and $\Delta\Phi = B\Delta A$, $\epsilon = 0.68$ V

6. Using $\epsilon = N\Delta\Phi/\Delta t$, and $\Delta\Phi = B\Delta A$, $B = 0.50$ T

7. See Example 5. $\epsilon = 8.0$ mV

8. See Example 5. $B = 2 \times 10^{-5}$ T

9. a) Need anticlockwise couple to oppose clockwise motion; applying Fleming's left-hand rule, induced current must flow ABCD.
b) Using $\epsilon_0 = 2\pi f B A N$, $\epsilon_0 = 1.4$ V

10. a) Total change in flux linkage $N\Delta\Phi$ = area under graph,
$N\Delta\Phi = 0.12$ Wb
b) Using $N\Delta\Phi = NB\Delta A$, $B = 0.32$ T

Chapter 20 (Alternating Current) page 249

1. a) 2, r.m.s.
b) stepped down, ratio, 100%
c) p.d. (voltage), time-base

2. a) Laminations reduce induced eddy currents; reduces heating of core.
b) d.c. produces steady magnetic flux in iron core; no change in flux linkage of secondary coil, so no induced secondary voltage.
c) i) High voltage, low current, minimises power losses in cables.
ii) a.c. so that transformers can be used to step voltages up and down.

3. Using $V_0 = 2$ V r.m.s., $V_0 = 17$ V

4. See page 242. (a) 50 ms (b) 20 Hz (c) 6.0 V (d) 4.2 V

5. See Example 5. (a) Using $P = IV$, $I = 30$ A
b) Using $P = I^2 R$, $P = 4500$ W

6. Secondary p.d. = 23 V r.m.s., step down.
Primary turns = 400, step up.
Secondary turns = 12 000, step up.

7. See Example 2. (a) 3.0 V (b) 1.1 V (c) 40 ms (d) 25 Hz.

8. 75 beats per minute, (1 beat in 4×200 ms)

9. a) Using $N_S/N_P = V_S/V_P$, $N_S = 250$ turns
b) i) $I_S = 0.60$ A (ii) $V_S \times I_S = V_P \times I_P$, $I_P = 0.030$ A

Chapter 21 (Electric Fields) pages 262–263

1. a) charge, separation (distance apart)
b) coulombs, coulombs, electrons
c) charge, force, strength, direction
d) parallel, equally spaced
e) equipotential f) potential, charge

2. a) See page 253.
b) See page 259. The potential energy of the charge does not change.
c) Positive ball induces a negative charge on the earthed plate; ball and plate attract.

3. See page 255.

4. a) Spray gives positive paint droplets and induces a negative charge on bike frame; droplets attracted to bike
b) Paint droplets follow field lines to the frame.

5. Using $F = kQ_1 Q_2 / r^2$, (a) $2F$ (b) $4F$ (c) $F/4$

6. Using $F = kQ_1 Q_2 / r^2$, $F = 2.3 \times 10^{-8}$ N

7. a) Using $F = kQ_1 Q_2 / r^2$, $Q = 2.0$ nC
b) Number of electrons = charge Q /charge on electron
$= 1.3 \times 10^{10}$

8. Using $E = kQ/r^2$, a) $E = 36 \times 10^4$ N C^{-1},
b) $E = 9 \times 10^4$ N C^{-1}
The radial field is an inverse square field; when r doubles, E drops to $\frac{1}{4}$

9. See Example 3. $Q = 7.5$ μC

10. a) Using $E = kQ/r^2$ for each charge and subtracting,
$E = 2.0 \times 10^4$ N C^{-1}
b) Using $E = kQ/r^2$ for each charge and adding,
$E = 6.0 \times 10^4$ N C^{-1}

11. a) Using $E = V/d$, $E = 4.0 \times 10^4$ V m^{-1}
b) From plate Z to plate Y
c) Twice as many field lines. $E = 8.0 \times 10^4$ V m^{-1}
d) Using $E = V/d$, $V = 4.0$ kV

12. Using $E = V/d$, (a) $V = 2400$ V (b) $d = 6.2$ cm

13. See lightning, page 259.

14. Using $F = QE$, $F = 9.6 \times 10^{-6}$ N

15. a) Uniform field, so $V_X = +300$ V, $V_Y = +600$ V,
$V_Z = +900$ V
b) See Example 4. $W = -9.6 \times 10^{-14}$ J
c) Lost potential energy

16. a) weight of oil drop (mg) downwards; force due to electric field (QE) upwards.
b) Using $mg = QE$ and $E = V/d$, $Q = 3.2 \times 10^{-19}$ C

17. a) Using gain in E_K = loss in $E_P = QV$,
(i) $E_K = 3.2 \times 10^{-16}$ J (ii) $E_K = 2000$ eV

18. a) Using $E = V/d$, $E = 1.0 \times 10^5$ V m^{-1}
b) Using $F = QE$, $F = 1.6 \times 10^{-14}$ N
c) Using $a = F/m$, $a = 1.8 \times 10^{16}$ m s^{-2}
d) electron moves up through $3/12 \times 1200$ V;
gain in E_K = loss in $E_P = QV$, $= 4.8 \times 10^{-17}$ J

Chapter 22 (Capacitors) page 273

1. a) charge, negative b) p.d. (voltage), supply (battery)
c) energy d) parallel e) series

2. a) See page 265. There is current only while charging.
b) See page 270. As capacitor loses its charge, its p.d. falls and so the current falls.
c) See page 272. To avoid dielectric breakdown.

3. Using $C = Q/V$, $C = 0.50$ μF

4. a) Using $Q = CV$, $Q = 900$ μC
b) Using $Q = It$, $t = 18$ s

5. Using $W = \frac{1}{2}QV$, $W = 3.6 \times 10^{-4}$ J

6. a) Using $C = C_1 + C_2$, $C = 7.5\ \mu F$
   b) Using $1/C = 1/C_1 + 1/C_2$, $C = 2.0\ \mu F$
   c) Add capacitors in parallel, then use
      $1/C = 1/C_1 + 1/C_2$, $C = 100\ \mu F$

7. a) Two 10 μF capacitors in parallel.
   b) Two 10 μF capacitors in series.
   c) Two pairs of 10 μF in series, connected in parallel.

8. Using $Q = CV$, the capacitors store the same charge.
   Using $W = \frac{1}{2}QV$, 2 μF capacitor stores more energy.

9. See Example 3.   (a) $Q = 60\ \mu C$ (b) $C = 25\ \mu F$
   c) $V = 2.4$ V.

10. See Example 4.   (a) $C = 20\ \mu F$ (b) $Q = 120\ \mu C$
   c) $V_1 = 1.2$ V $V_2 = 4.8$ V.

11. See Example 6.   (a) Using $Q_0 = CV_0$, $Q_0 = 60\ \mu C$
   b) Using $\tau = CR$, $\tau = 3.2$ s
   c) Using $Q = Q_0\,e^{-t/CR}$, $Q = 13\ \mu C$

12. a) p.d. across resistor at $t = 0$ is 4.0 V;
      using $V_0 = I_0\,R$, $I_0 = 0.20$ mA
   b) Using $I = I_0\,e^{-t/CR}$, $I = 0.12$ mA

13. Using $V = V_0\,e^{-t/CR}$ ($V = 2.5$ V, $V_0 = 9.0$ V), $t = 420$ s

▷ **Further Questions on Electricity**

Current Electricity (pages 274–276)

1. a) 960 W,   2880 W (3×960 W),
      1920 W (2×960 W).   (all elements in parallel)
   b) Using $P = IV$ and $V = IR$, $I = 4.0$ A, $R = 60\ \Omega$
   c) 3 equal resistors in parallel, $R_T = 20\ \Omega$

2. a) Lamps and resistor in series, using $V = IR$ and
      $P = I^2R$, $I = 0.8$ A, $P = 3.2$ W
   b) Lamps in parallel and together are in series with resistor,
      $I = 0.8$ A, (total current = 1.6 A)
   c) Same current and resistance, so same brightness.
      Battery lasts longer because total current from battery is
      less in 1 (0.8 A) than in 2 (1.6 A).
   d) Remaining lamp becomes brighter as current through it
      increases (to 1.2 A).

3. a) Resistance of the filament rises as its temperature rises.
      At $V = 4.0$ V, $I = 0.8$ A and $R = 5.0\ \Omega$
   b) Current in 3 Ω resistor is 1.33 A, so total current is
      2.13 A. Using $P = IV$ gives $P = 8.5$ W
   c) Using $R = \rho l/A$ and $A = \pi d^2/4$ gives $d = 3.9 \times 10^{-5}$ m

4. a) 3 in series gives 30 Ω, two 30 Ω in parallel gives 15 Ω
      Using $P = V^2/R$, $P = 9.6$ W.
   b) Each set of 3 in series is a potential divider.
      $V_{CD} = 4$ V $V_{FD} = 8$ V $V_{CF} = 4$ V

5. a) Using $R = V/I$ $R = 15$ kΩ
   b) i) 15 kΩ (ii) 45 kΩ

6. a) Place the ammeter in series and the voltmeter in parallel
      with the lamp.   (b) Using $P = V^2/R$, $R = 6.0\ \Omega$
   c) For 12 V across 24 Ω potentiometer and lamp, slider
      must be at top of potentiometer. Current in lamp is
      2.0 A , 0.5 A in potentiometer, so current of 2.5 A in R.
      P.d. across R is 8 V with current of 2.5 A, so $R = 3.2\ \Omega$.

7. a) i) Using $V = IR$, $I = 6.0$ A
      ii) Using $P = IV$ gives $P = 1260$ W
      iii) When $I = 6.0$ A, p.d. across cables = 20 V, so 3.3 Ω
   b) The 20 V drop in voltage is the voltage across the
      supply cables to maintain a current of 6 A.
   c) The greater the current drawn by an appliance in the
      cottage, the smaller the voltage across it; energy is lost
      as heat in the cables.

8. a) Current in each lamp = 2 A giving a total current from
      the battery of 4 A.
   b) Using $I = Q/t$ gives $t = 3 \times 10^4$ s = 8.3 h
   c) i) No, they are in a separate parallel circuit.
      ii) No, from $P = V^2/R$, power decreases because
          resistance increases and voltage is the same.
   d) All four lamps are in parallel, so failure of any one lamp
      does not extinguish any other lamp.

9. b) For potential divider, $V_{AB} = (5/9) \times 12$ V $= 6.7$ V
   c) Extra resistor 'loads' the potentiometer. In the lower
      section 5 Ω is in parallel with 20 Ω, giving combined
      resistance of 4 Ω. Thus p.d. across lower section is 6 V,
      giving 3 V across AB.
   d) Using $I = V/R$ gives $I = 0.3$ A

10. b) Total $R = 3.0\ \Omega$, ammeter reads 2.0 A
      8.0 Ω and 4.0 Ω make 2:1 potential divider,
      voltmeter reads 2 V.
   c) i) terminal p.d. = p.d. across the 8.0 Ω and 4.0 Ω
          potential divider, = $3 \times$ voltmeter reading.
      ii) Using $V = E - Ir$, $r = 0.75\ \Omega$

11. a) 160 Ω
   b) i) R_{TH} drops in relation to 300 Ω, so V_{TH} drops.
      ii) Using $V_{OUT}/V_{IN} = R_1/(R_1 + R_2)$, $V_{OUT} = 3.9$ V

12. b) As the wire gets hot its resistance increases.
      Using $V = IR$, $R = 5\ \Omega$, length and diameter of wire

13. a) i) Using $V = IR$, $R = 50\ \Omega$ (ii) R very large
   b) From graph, $I = 30$ mA in forward direction; in reverse
      direction I very large, Z burns out.

Magnetic Fields (page 277)

14. a) Using $F = BIl$, $F = 6 \times 10^{-5}$ N
   b) Using Fleming's LH rule, force is to the right.

15. a) Right to left along axis of solenoid.
   b) B is uniform within solenoid remote from ends.
   c) weakest W Z Y X strongest.

16. a) $F = BIl$ (b) they form a Newton III pair of forces
   c) graph of m against I is a straight line of gradient
      0.14 g A^{-1}, or (since $g = 9.8$ N kg^{-1}) 1.4×10^{-3} N A^{-1}
   d) force is reversed and acts upwards on the magnet and
      current reading decreases.

17. a) Using $F = BIl$, $I = 6.0$ A
   b) I parallel to B so no BIl force

Electromagnetic Induction (page 278)

18. a) Aircraft is metal moving in the Earth's field.
   b) See Example 5, page 237.
      i) $\Delta A = 3.3 \times 10^3$ m^2 (ii) $\epsilon = 0.13$ V

19. a) See page 234. Note that there is an induced e.m.f. only
      when flux is changing.
   b) i) along line XX from right to left,   (ii) induced e.m.f
      drives current round Q to oppose flux change.

20. Current flows up front edge of loop, face of loop facing
   N-pole of magnet is a N-pole.

21. a) Top side is a N-pole, arrow at X points left.
   b) See page 236. Magnet moving faster, larger e.m.f. for a
      shorter time.

22. Large induced current in washer as B-field changes. By
   Lenz's law, B-field of washer repels B-field of solenoid and
   washer jumps up. No washer current when solenoid
   current is steady, washer falls back.

23. a) Using $N\Phi = NBA$, $N\Phi = 0.015$ Wb
   b) Using $\epsilon = N\Delta\Phi/\Delta t$, $\epsilon = 5.9$ mV

Electric Fields (page 279)

24. a) Using $E = Q/4\pi\varepsilon_0 r^2$, $E = 4.5 \times 10^{10}$ N C^{-1} toward B
b) zero   (c) towards P on either side of P

25. a)

b) tension, $T = 23$ mN   (c) force, $F = T\sin\theta$
d) Using $F = Q^2/4\pi\varepsilon_0 r^2$, $Q = 220$ nC

26. a) parallel vertical lines with arrows down page
b) i) $E = V/d = 50$ kV m^{-1} (ii) $F = QE = 8.0\times10^{-15}$ N

27. a) $E = V/d = 650$ kV m^{-1} (b) $F = QE = 78$ mN

28. a) See page 256. Parallel vertical lines with arrows down page, at edges of plates lines curve outwards.
b) See page 259.
c) See page 258. Electric potential is a scalar.

29. a) $E = V/d = 2.0 \times 10^6$ V m^{-1}
b) Ball is charged by contact, moves in the E-field and is earthed as it makes contact with P$_2$.

Capacitors (page 280)

30. a) straight line through the origin, $V \propto q$
b) energy stored = area under graph

31. a) energy = power $\times$ time = 8 J
b) Using $W = \frac{1}{2}CV^2$, $V = 580$ V
c) $Q = CV = 27$ mC   (d) $I = Q/t = 14$ A

32. a) Using $V = IR$, $I = 4.0$ mA   (b) zero
c) $Q = CV = 5.6$ μC   (d) $W = \frac{1}{2}CV^2 = 34$ μJ

33. a) $Q = CV = 5.6$ mC
b) See pages 270 and 271. At $t = 0$, $I = 0.55$ mA; at $t = CR = 10$ s, $I = 0.20$ mA

34. a) 600 V each in series   (b) 200 μF   (c) 360 J

35. See pages 268 and 269.
a) 550 pF to 1000 pF   (b) 45 pF to 250 pF

36. a) $Q = CV = 1.2$ mC   (+1.2 mC and –1.2 mC)
b) See Example 3, page 268. Capacitors share charge to give same p.d. across both; $V = 3$ V.

37. a) $W = \frac{1}{2}CV^2 = 18$ J.
b) i) 6.0 mA   (ii) $W = 4.5$ J; using $W = \frac{1}{2}CV^2$, V (across capacitor and resistor) $= 3.0$ V, $I = 3.0$ mA

The CRO and a.c. (page 281)

38. a) i) $f = 1/\text{period} = 50$ Hz,   (ii) 3.0 A
b) See page 243.
Max power = 45 W, min = zero, period = 10 ms

39.

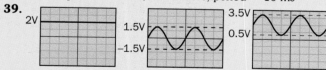

40. a) ≈ 500 kV   (b) adding ordinates at any time gives zero

41. a) period = $1/f = 20$ ms
b) i) half wave rectified waveform (see page 248), amplitude 2.5 cm, repeat every 4 cm,
ii) same direction as diode symbol
c) horizontal trace 4.5 cm above zero line

42. a) Using $V = Ir$, $r = 1.6$ MΩ
b) i) Using $V = V_0\, e^{-t/CR}$, where $CR = 70$ s, $t = 290$ s
ii) $CR = 70$ s, $R = 17.5$ MΩ   (iii) no, less safe
c) $Q_0 = CV = 13$ mC; exponential decrease; at $t = 0$, $Q = Q_0$; at $t = 70$ s, $Q = 0.37 Q_0 = 4.8$ mC

▶ Matter and Materials

Chapter 23 (Solids under Stress) page 295

1. a) proportional, limit, elastic
b) force, area, extension, length (original length), Young
c) ductile (plastic, malleable), brittle, chains

2. a) See Example 1. 50 N m^{-1} (2 s.f.)
b) See Example 2. 0.25 J   (2 s.f.)

3. a) Gradient of linear part. 20 N m^{-1} (2 s.f.)
b) Area under curve up to extension of 0.6 m, between 3.5 J and 3.6 J   (2 s.f.)
c) Where curve bends over. 10 N to 10.5 N

4. See Example 3. 5.0×10^7 Pa (N m^{-2})   (2 s.f.)

5. See Example 4. 25 N   (2 s.f.)

6. See Example 4. 7.9 N   (2 s.f.)

7. See Example 5. 1.2 m, 6.0 (600%)

8. See Example 6. 1.3×10^{11} Pa (N m^{-2})   (2 s.f.)

9. See Example 8. 15 kg   (2 s.f.), not very rapidly

10. See Example 9.

11. See *Physics at Work* on tennis rackets. Glass alone would shatter, resin alone is not stiff enough.

Chapter 24 (Thermodynamics) page 305

1. a) energy, working (work)
b) energy, molecules, cold
c) melting, melt, state   (d) bonds   (e) boiling, energy, gas

2. a) See Example 1. –20 J
b) See Example 1. +50 J
c) See Example 1. +30 J

3. What fraction of the distance between 0 °C and 100 °C is X at? 75 °C   (2 s.f.)

4. See Example 2.
By rows: 293 °C, 195 K, 6273 K (about 6000 K)

5. See Example 4. 3.3×10^5 J   (2 s.f.)

6. As Example 4, rearranging the equation.
1.9 K (1.9 °C)   (2 s.f.)

7. a) See Example 4.
5.2×10^5 J   (2 s.f.)
b) Use $P = $ energy$/t$. 260 s   (2 s.f.) (about 4 minutes) The kettle itself has no significant increase in internal energy.

8. a) See Example 7. 1.2×10^6 J   (2 s.f.)
b) Use $P = $ Energy$/t$. 580 s (about 10 minutes)   (2 s.f.)

9. a) See Example 7. 1.7×10^4 J   (2 s.f.)
b) Use answer to (a) as approximate value of energy removed from lemonade and see Example 4.
$\Delta T = 9.8$ °C, so final temperature = 10.2 °C (≈ 10 °C)

Chapter 25 (Conduction, Convection, Radiation) page 312

1. a) temperature, conduction, kinetic, hot (hotter), cold (colder), convection
b) infra-red
c) black body, spectrum, shorter (smaller, less)

2. Heat is conducted away from the warm fingers, metal conducts heat faster, so feels colder.

3. Heat conduction in metals is mainly through the movement of free electrons.
Electrons in copper are freer to move than in iron, so it is a better conductor of electricity and of heat.

4. Heat conduction in non-metals is through atomic vibrations.
   Atoms in the lattice pass on energy to their neighbours by vibration.

5. Air insulates, but also convects. Clothing insulates because of trapped air, and several layers trap air more effectively than one.

6. Trodden snow is dirty and compressed. The darker surface of trodden snow absorbs infra-red more effectively, the lack of insulating air gaps allows more effective conduction, and the warmer melted snow will sink below the cooler upper layers (see question 7 below).

7. Denser water will sink. Water at 4 °C will sink below water which is hotter or cooler, so water below 4 °C will rise to the top of the pond and freeze there, leaving the bottom water at 4 °C.

8. Besides conduction and convection, infra-red emission is a significant heat loss.
   The thin film traps insulating air, and the shiny surface is a poor emitter of infra-red.

9. Wavelength emitted depends on temperature. Shorter wavelength blue light is emitted by hotter objects.
   Rigel is hotter.

10. See Example 3 and consider the electromagnetic spectrum (page 174).
    9.7×10^{-7} m (2 s.f.), this is infra-red, which is absorbed by glass.

11. See Example 3. 0.011 m

12. Consider the electromagnetic spectrum (page 174).
    0.011 m is a microwave wavelength.

13. See Example 3 and page 174. $\lambda = 2.9 \times 10^{-10}$ m (2 s.f.) which is an X-ray wavelength.

Chapter 26 (Gases and Kinetic Theory) page 323

1. a) solids, molecules, molecules, pressure
   b) inversely, Boyle
   c) ideal, Gas, moles
   d) r.m.s. (root-mean-square), kelvins (K)

2. See Example 1. 8000 Pa (2 s.f.)

3. See Example 2. 5000 J (2 s.f.)

4. See Example 3. 150 kPa (2 s.f.)

5. Calculate exactly as for pressure in Example 4.
   0.0036 m^3 (2 s.f.)

6. Find how many moles (0.004 kg) there are in 1 kg.
   1.5×10^{26} molecules (2 s.f.)

7. a) See Example 8 in Chapter 23.
   50 m^2,   60 kg (2 s.f.)
   b) See question 6 above.
   2000 mol (2 s.f.)

8. a) See Example 5.
   3.0×10^7 Pa (2 s.f.)
   b) As part (a). 3.7 m^3 (2 s.f.)

9. See Example 8.
   218 m s^{-1} (3 s.f.),   219 m s^{-1} (3 s.f.)

10. See Example 6. 8500 Pa (2 s.f.)

11. a) See Example 7. 1300 m s^{-1} (2 s.f.)
    b) See page 320; from $p = \rho c^2/3$, a greater density ρ means a smaller r.m.s. speed c if the pressure is the same. The r.m.s. speed of helium molecules is greater than that of air molecules at the same temperature, so the speed of sound in helium is greater than that in air at the same temperature.

Solids (page 324)

1. eg. metal (crystalline), polyethene (polymer), glass (amorphous)

2. a) $E = 1.0 \times 10^{10}$ Pa,   UTS = 2.6×10^8 Pa,   ductile
   b) straight line through origin ending at 3.2×10^8 Pa, 0.094 strain

3. b) area of cross-section, original length

4. a) $E = 2.1 \times 10^{11}$ Pa,   UTS = 3.0×10^9 Pa
   b) 53 kN,   0.17 m,   energy = $\frac{1}{2}F\Delta x$ = 45 000 J

5. b) see graph in next question, Q6.
   c) cross-sectional area decreases, ductile fracture

6. a) $F = k\Delta x$, point of departure from straight line
   b) $E = Fl/A\Delta x = 2.0 \times 10^{11}$ Pa
   c) energy = $\frac{1}{2}F\Delta x$ = 0.65 J

Thermal transfer (page 325)

7. c) in solar panel from pipes to water, in tank from hotter water to pipes to cooler water
   d) hottest section is above tank not below it

8. b) for 4×10^4 s day^{-1}, energy = 3×10^9 J y^{-1} m^{-2}
   c) 2×10^7 J y^{-1} m^{-2} (d) photosynthesis efficiency 1%

9. blow air past fins, aluminium as good conductor, blacken cylinder head, etc.

Gases and Thermodynamics (pages 325–326)

10. b) faster particles, more collisions, bigger momentum change per collision   (c) 478 m s^{-1} (d) no change

11. a) assume linear scale, 41 °C
    b) i) both extrapolate to –270 °C,   (ii) 0.006 mol

12. b) find the volume at standard temperature and pressure, mass = 9.2×10^{-5} kg

13. a) use $pV = nRT$,   (b) 900 K   (c) 600 kPa
    d) A → B, ΔU positive, ΔQ positive, ΔW negative
    B → C, ΔU zero, ΔQ negative, ΔW positive
    e) Approx. the area of the 'triangle' ABC, 4 kJ, decrease

14. proportion of energy transferred into visible light

15. b) $\Delta W = p\Delta V$ = 14 kJ,   (c) use $\Delta U = \Delta Q + p\Delta V$

16. a) $2p_o$, $3p_o$, $1.5p_o$, p_o
    c) ΔW done on gas, ΔQ extracted, $\Delta W + \Delta Q = 0$

17. a) ΔW positive, ΔQ negative, ΔU zero
    b) ΔW zero, ΔQ positive, ΔU positive

Thermal Physics (page 327)

18. a) Heat capacity is the energy needed to raise the temperature of the whole system (0.525 kg of water) by 1 K,   2.2 kJ K^{-1} (b) initial gradient = 0.073 K s^{-1}
    c) 160 W   (d) energy lost to surroundings

19. a) $P = mc\Delta\theta/t$ = 0.82 W   (b) using $E = mL$, m = 36 g
    c) water vapour above ice condensed to water

20. a) eg. use a smoke cell. (b) (i) spacing slightly greater in ice,
    ii) ice more ordered, (iii) vibrational energy only in ice, translational energy in water

21. b) At 100 °C, translational KE of steam molecules = vibrational KE + PE of water molecules.

22. a) i) $\Delta W = p\Delta V$ = 23 kJ   (ii) 177 kJ
    b) ideal gas when V/T is constant: yes, nearly

23. a) i) using $E = Pt$, 10.3 MJ   (ii) 1.1 MJ
    b) i) conduction,   (ii) evaporation and convection

24. a) $E_K = \frac{1}{2}mv^2$ = 3.7 J   (b) gas molecules hitting moving disc rebound with speed reduced, hence cool down.

Nuclear Physics

Chapter 27 (Radioactivity) page 347

1. a) proton (atomic), nucleon (mass)
    b) particle, positively, helium
    c) particles, negatively, high
    d) alpha, beta, magnetic, gamma

2. a) See page 337. β less strongly ionising than α.
    b) See page 338.
    c) α and β particles are absorbed by the medium.
    d) See page 340 and 342 on nuclear stability.
    e) i) α-scattering is due to interactions with single nuclei and to avoid absorption of α-particles.
       ii) Path of incident α-particles is known and so scattering angle can be measured accurately.

3. 55 protons and 82 neutrons in nucleus.

4. a) Using $r = r_0 A^{1/3}$, $r = 7.0 \times 10^{-15}$ m
    b) 1.4×10^{-42} m³ (c) density $= m/v = 2.3 \times 10^{17}$ kg m⁻³

5. Using inverse square law pages 338 and 339, $I/9$

6. Using inverse square law pages 338 and 339, 2.5 m

7. See page 335, but with lines of two different lengths.

8. a) $^{19}_{8}O \rightarrow {}^{19}_{9}F + {}^{0}_{-1}e$
    b) $^{212}_{84}Po \rightarrow {}^{208}_{82}Pb + {}^{4}_{2}He$
    c) $^{56}_{27}Co \rightarrow {}^{56}_{26}Fe + {}^{0}_{+1}e$

9. Using $\lambda = 0.693 / t_{1/2}$ ($t_{1/2} = 10.8 \times 60$ s), $\lambda = 1.1 \times 10^{-3}$ s⁻¹

10. Using $A = \lambda N$ and $\lambda = 0.693 / t_{1/2}$ ($t_{1/2} = 5 \times 24 \times 3600$ s) $N = 2.5 \times 10^{11}$

11. a) $A_0 = 3340$ Bq
    b) $A_0 = \lambda N_0$, $\lambda = 2.2 \times 10^{-6}$ s⁻¹
    c) Using $t_{1/2} = 0.693/\lambda$, $t_{1/2} = 3.1 \times 10^5$ s $= 3.6$ days

12. Graph passes through: (0, 800), (5, 400), (10, 200), (15, 100), (20, 50).

13. a) 4800 years is $3 \times$ half-life. $1/8$ ($1/2^3$) remains and so 7/8 decayed.
    b) 6400 years is $4 \times$ half-life. $1/16$ ($1/2^4$) remains.

14. See page 345. (b) Half-life ~ 50 s

15. a) Using $N = N_0 e^{-\lambda t}$ $N = 3300$
    b) Using $A = \lambda N$ $A = 50$ Bq

16. a) Using $\lambda = 0.693/t_{1/2}$ $\lambda = 1.1 \times 10^{-2}$ min⁻¹
    b) Using $A = A_0 e^{-\lambda t}$ $A = 44$ Bq

17. a) Strontium in bones emits ionising β-particles for a long period of time.
    b) Using $A = A_0 e^{-\lambda t}$ and $\lambda = \ln 2 / t_{1/2}$ ($A = 5\%$, $A_0 = 100\%$), $t = 120$ years

Chapter 28 (Nuclear Energy) page 357

1. a) less, difference (defect)   b) binding
    c) nucleon, nucleus   d) less, energy
    e) fission, fusion, increases

2. See Example 1.
    a) 0.042 167 u 7.00×10^{-29} kg
    b) 0.254 06 u 4.22×10^{-28} kg
    c) 0.592 23 u 9.83×10^{-28} kg
    d) 1.675 00 u 2.78×10^{-27} kg

3. a) See Example 3.   b) See Example 4.
    Li : 39.28 MeV   Li : 5.61 MeV / nucleon
    Si : 236.7 MeV   Si : 8.45 MeV / nucleon
    Cu : 551.7 MeV   Cu : 8.76 MeV / nucleon
    Au : 1560 MeV   Au : 7.92 MeV / nucleon

4. a) Yes. More mass on l.h.s. than r.h.s. so reaction occurs spontaneously, releasing energy.
    b) See α-decay example on page 351.
       Mass difference of 0.005 29 u   4.93 MeV

5. Mass difference between l.h.s. and r.h.s. is 4.25×10^{-29} kg. Use $E = mc^2$ then convert from joules to eV. 23.9 MeV.

6. Mass difference between l.h.s. and r.h.s. is 0.204 86 u. Convert to MeV using 931.5 MeV per u. 190.8 MeV.

7. Mass on l.h.s. = 63.916 81 u. Mass on r.h.s. = 63.929 17 u. Extra mass/energy needed on l.h.s. is 0.012 36 u or 11.51 MeV (assuming products have zero KE)

Chapter 29 (Particle Physics) page 369

1. a) mass, charge, spin
    b) annihilate, energy   c) pair production
    d) up, down, charm, strange, top, bottom
    e) electron (e^-), electron-neutrino (ν_e), muon (μ^-) muon-neutrino (ν_μ), tau (τ^-), tau-neutrino (ν_τ)   (f) strong
    g) baryons, mesons   (h) protons, neutrons, pions, kaons
    i) baryon, lepton   (j) gluon, weak, photons

2. a) p = uud   (b) n = udd
    c) $\pi^0 = u\bar{u}$ or $d\bar{d}$, $\pi^+ = u\bar{d}$, $\pi^- = \bar{u}d$
    d) $K^0 = d\bar{s}$, $K^+ = u\bar{s}$, $K^- = \bar{u}s$

3.
	p	n	π^0	π^+	π^-	K^0	K^+	K^-
C	+1	0	0	+1	-1	0	+1	-1
B	+1	+1	0	0	0	0	0	0
S	0	0	0	0	0	+1	+1	-1

4. a) $\bar{p} = \bar{u}\bar{u}\bar{d}$ b) $\bar{n} = \bar{u}\bar{d}\bar{d}$
    c) $\bar{\pi}^0 = \bar{u}u$ or $\bar{d}d$, $\bar{\pi}^+ = \bar{u}d$, $\bar{\pi}^- = u\bar{d}$
    d) $\bar{K}^0 = \bar{d}s$, $\bar{K}^+ = \bar{u}s$, $\bar{K}^- = u\bar{s}$
    π^0 is its own antiparticle (particle and antiparticle identical)

5. Mass of p + $\bar{p}$ = $2 \times 1.67 \times 10^{-27}$ kg = 3.34×10^{-27} kg
    $E = mc^2$ $= 3.34 \times 10^{-27} \times (3.00 \times 10^8)^2$
    $= 3.01 \times 10^{-10}$ J $(= 1.88$ GeV$)$
    (Assuming created with zero kinetic energy.)

6. a)

	μ^-	$\rightarrow$	e^-	+ $\bar{\nu}_e$	+ ν_μ	
Charge:	-1		-1	0	0	✔
B:	0		0	0	0	✔
L:	+1		+1	-1	+1	✔
S:	0		0	0	0	✔

    This can happen.

    b)

	p	+ e^-	$\rightarrow$	n	+ ν_e	
Charge:	+1	-1		0	0	✔
B:	+1	0		+1	0	✔
L:	0	+1		0	+1	✔
S:	0	0		0	0	✔

    This can happen.

    c)

	K^+	$\rightarrow$	π^+	+ π^0	
Charge:	+1		+1	0	✔
B:	0		0	0	✔
L:	0		0	0	✔
S:	+1		0	0	✔

    This can happen. Strangeness can change by ± 1 in weak interactions.

7. a) Electron capture   b) Repulsion

c) Strong interaction   d) β+ decay

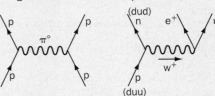

8. Only S quarks have strangeness.
Possible quark combinations in mesons & antimesons (q q̄):
strange + antistrange: $S = -1 + 1 = 0$
strange + other antiquark: $S = -1 + 0 = -1$
antistrange + other quark: $S = +1 + 0 = +1$

9. a) See Example 3.
p.d. $= 6.0 \times 10^3$ V $\times 12 = 7.2 \times 10^4$ V
∴ energy gained $= 7.2 \times 10^4$ eV
b) Need to gain 50×10^9 eV $- 50 \times 10^6$ eV
$= 49.95 \times 10^9$ eV
No. of laps $= \dfrac{49.95 \times 10^9 \text{ eV}}{7.2 \times 10^4 \text{ eV/lap}} = 6.9 \times 10^5$ laps

▶ ## Further Questions on Nuclear Physics

Radioactivity (page 370)

1. a) Using $A = \lambda N$, $\lambda = 1.05 \times 10^{-11}$ s^{-1}
$t_{1/2} = 0.693/\lambda = 6.6 \times 10^{10}$ s (about 2000 y)
b) ratio of activities $= 32:1$, 5 half lives, $= 10^4$ y.

2. a) Boron-11 has 6 neutrons, Boron-12 has 7.
b) N_A atoms in 12 g; $(600/12\times10^{-3}) \times N_A$ atoms
$= 3.0 \times 10^{26}$ atoms in 6.0 kg.

3. a) graph levels out to constant activity.
Activity of C $= 100$ cpm (counts per minute).
b) 3000 falls to 1500 cpm or 2000 falls to 1000 cpm in approx 1.3 min

4. a) $^{235}_{92}$U has 92 p, 143 n and 92 e
$^{238}_{92}$U has 92 p, 146 n and 92 e
b) $^{238}_{92}$U has halved in given time; while $^{235}_{92}$U has gone through 6.43 half-lives, a factor of 86 $(1/2^{6.43})$
Ratio is $2/86 = 0.023$.
c) Earth is older than 4.5×10^9 y.

5. Long half-life implies very low count rate for small sample of strontium-90.

6. a) Causes ionisation which kills living cells.
b) i) ^{52}Mn, short half-life, γ detected through earth,
ii) ^{60}Co, long half-life (constant dose rate), γ can penetrate to tumour,
iii) ^{241}Am, long life, α gives strong ionisation with low penetration (no shielding problems).

7. a) insert very thin absorber (eg. sheet of paper)
b) i) γ are uncharged,
ii) β have a range of energies.

8. Using $A = A_0 e^{-\lambda t}$, where $\lambda = 0.693/t_{1/2}$,
$A = 11.7$ min^{-1}.

9. a) X is a proton
b) N_A atoms in 14 g; $(7.5/14\times10^{-3}) \times N_A$ atoms
$= 3.2 \times 10^{26}$ atoms in 7.5 kg of ^{14}C.
c) Using $\lambda = 0.693/t_{1/2}$, $\lambda = 1.2 \times 10^{-4}$ y^{-1}
d) Using $A = \lambda N$, $N = 2.5 \times 10^{30}$ atoms
e) Activity falls exponentially from 0.8 to 0.1 Bq after 3×5700 years; 0.3 Bq occurs after approx 8000 y
f) activity < 1 s^{-1}, similar to background count rate

10. a) N_A atoms in 238 g; $(2.0/238\times10^{-3}) \times N_A$ atoms
$= 5.0 \times 10^{24}$ atoms in 2.0 kg plutonium-238.
b) Using $\lambda = 0.693/t_{1/2}$, $\lambda = 2.5 \times 10^{-10}$ s^{-1}
c) Using $A = \lambda N$, $A = 1.24 \times 10^{15}$ Bq.
d) Using $A = A_0 e^{-\lambda t}$, $t = 9.2 \times 10^9$ s (about 290 y)

11. a) Using $A = A_0 e^{-\lambda t}$, $\lambda = 1.0 \times 10^{-6}$ s^{-1}
b) Using $t_{1/2} = 0.693/\lambda$, $t_{1/2} = 6.9 \times 10^5$ s

12. See page 329 on Rutherford scattering experiment.

13. a) α-particle does work against repulsive force – kinetic energy transferred to potential energy.
b) 1.7 MeV $(2.7 \times 10^{-13}$ J)
c) α-particle moves directly towards centre of nucleus.

14. See page 239 on Rutherford scattering experiment.

Nuclear Energy (page 372)

15. The mass of the constituents is greater to allow for the binding energy.

16. See pages 350 – 353.

17. The mass of the reactants is 0.00129 u (1.2 MeV) less than the mass of the products. E_K for the incident α-particle must be much greater than 1.2 MeV.

18. a) Fission, a large nucleus splits into two smaller nuclei with release of energy triggered by absorption of a neutron. E represents E_K for the products (the energy liberated)
b) mass difference $= 0.21$ u $= 3.5 \times 10^{-28}$ kg, use $\Delta E = c^2 \Delta m$ to get 3.1×10^{-11} J $(= 196$ MeV)

19. See pages 352, 354–355.

20. See pages 354–355.

21. a) c is a neutron, $x = 4$
b) $(235 \times 7.52$ MeV) $- (139 \times 8.33$ MeV) $- (95 \times 8.62$ MeV)
$= 210$ MeV
c) reaction 1 more probable because liberates more energy

22. mass change $= 5.0 \times 10^{-30}$ kg $\equiv 4.5 \times 10^{-13}$ J $(E = mc^2)$

23. See pages 350, 352–353.

24. a) mass change $= 0.02561$ u, energy release $= 3.8 \times10^{-12}$ J
b) energy required s^{-1} $= 9.6$ MW which requires 2.5×10^{18} fusions s^{-1}, a burn rate of 8.4×10^{-6} mol s^{-1}. 1000 mol would last 1.2×10^8 s (~ 3.8 y)

Particle physics (page 373)

25. a) See page 333 (b) using $s = vt$, track length $= 70$ mm

26. a) particle 2 is negatively charged, particle 3 is neutral / does not ionise hydrogen atoms.
b) mass-energy is conserved. Using $\Delta E = c^2 \Delta m$, the mass lost has become E_K of particles 4 and 5.

27. a) Composed of quarks, feel strong nuclear force, have a baryon number which is always conserved.
b) meson $= q \bar{q}$, baryon $= q q q$ or $\bar{q} \bar{q} \bar{q}$
c) Conserving values for Q, B and S for each gives
i) X has $Q = 0$, $B = 0$, $S = 0$
ii) Y has $Q = 0$, $B = +1$, $S = 0$
iii) Z has $Q = -1$, $B = +1$, $S = -1$

28. a) $^3_1$H $\Rightarrow$ $^3_2$X $+$ $^0_{-1}\beta$, X is helium-3
b) $\lambda = 0.693/t_{1/2}$ $= 0.056$ yr^{-1}
c) 12.5% is 3 half lives, so age $= 36.9$ y
d) $\Delta m = 0.0086$ u $= 1.42 \times 10^{-29}$ kg
Using $E = mc^2 = 1.28 \times 10^{-12}$ J

29. a) B and D (curve opposite way to electrons)
b) Uncharged so they create little ionisation.
c) Electron takes some photon energy, so less for pair production in X. Lower-energy particles are more deflected by magnetic field.

1. a) no force to produce acceleration when max speed × resistive forces = power available
   b) power from battery = 30 W/0.70 = 43 W, I = 43 W/12 V = 3.6 A
   c) Using $P = Fv$, F = 20 N
   d) i) R = 110 g (0.12/1.0) = 130 N
      ii) total force down ramp = 150 N, $v = P/F$ = 30 W/150 N = 0.20 m s⁻¹

2. Referring to diagrams from left to right:
   1. moves parallel to E, accelerates
   2. curves downwards, horiz: const. vel. down: const. accel.
   3. moves parallel to B, no change in velocity.
   4. curves upwards in circle, constant speed.

3. a) 3 loops
   c) i) 2.0×10^{-10} m,
      ii) Using $mv = h/\lambda$ gives $mv = 3.3 \times 10^{-24}$ N s
      iii) where standing wave has largest amplitude

4. a)

   b) zero because velocity is constant
   c) no density difference, so no upthrust
   d) Pressure drops because (i) atmospheric pressure drops and there is no pressure difference across the balloon fabric; (ii) volume increases.

5. a) a radial field in gap, arrows from N to S.
   b) Using $F = BIl$, where $l = 50 \times \pi \times d$, F = 4.1 N
   c) Using $F = ma$, a = 350 m s⁻²

6. a) the red line is at 660 nm, $E = hc/\lambda = 3.0 \times 10^{-19}$ J
   b) r_{red} = 49.03°, r_{blue} = 49.51°, difference = 0.48°
   c) $\theta_{red} - \theta_{blue}$ = 4.1°
   d) $\phi = 2.9 \times 10^{-19}$ J, so just possible.

7. a) 0.60 N × 10 mm = 0.20 N × X
      X = 30 mm from pivot A
   b) $p = F/A$ = 0.60 N/4.0 × 10⁻⁶ m² = 150 kPa
   c) 0.60 × 10 mm = (0.2 N × X) + (0.10 N × 18 mm)
      X = 21 mm ∴ move counterweight 9 mm left

8. a) 550 kW
   b) river is flowing so cooled water is replaced by warmer water from upstream
   c) £69 000   (d) £103 000

9. a) Using $I = nAve$, $v = 1.3 \times 10^{-4}$ m s⁻¹

10. a) Using $R = \rho l/A$, R = 0.96 μΩ, V = 48 μV
    b) force to left – Fleming's left–hand rule,
       Using $F = BIl$, F = 0.12 N
    c) Using $P = F/A$, mass = density, ρ × volume, Ah
       pressure due to BIl force = pressure due to liquid
       $BIl/A = \rho\, Ah\, g/A$, h = 3.2 cm

11. See pages 305–306, 18–19, 247.

12. a) between B and C
    b) and (c) assume linear potentiometer.

    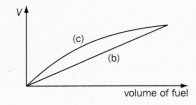

13. $E_k = 75$ J $= \frac{1}{2}N_A\, m\, c^2$ $\frac{1}{3}N_A\, m\, c^2 = pV = RT$
    T = 24 K

14. a) negative
    b) electrical force up balances weight downwards
    c) Using $E = V/d$, $E = 2.0 \times 10^5$ V m⁻¹
    d) charge = 4.8 × 10⁻¹⁹ C or 3 electronic charges

15. c) i) Using $E_p = mg\Delta h$, E_p = 4.2 kJ
       ii) Using $E = mc\Delta\theta$, $\Delta\theta$ = 0.056 °C

16. a), (b) and (c) See pages 80, 218, 255 and 256.
    d) Using $F = QE$, $F = 1.4 \times 10^{-13}$ N
       Using $F = ma$, $a = 1.5 \times 10^{17}$ m s⁻²
    e) See page 227.

17. c) i) stretched length = 1.45 m, extension = 0.65 m
       ii) tension = 41 N
    d) i) Using $E = \frac{1}{2}F\Delta x$, E = 13 J
       ii) Using $E_k = \frac{1}{2}mv^2$, v = 13 m s⁻¹

18. a) i) to the Earth's surface
       ii) current produced by the fairweather field in opposite direction to lightning
       iii) Waves (E-field) oscillating in the horizontal plane
    b) i) 100 V m⁻¹   (ii) Using $E = V/d$ = 5.0 V m⁻¹
       iii) scales marked on axes; E in V m⁻¹, h in km
            negative gradient curve, starting from (0, 100) getting less steep as h increases.
    c) ideas of storms spread out in space, and time;
       low average current (only 1 A);
       strikes last for a very short time
    d) i) straight lines reflecting off Earth/ionosphere with more than one bounce
       ii) wavefronts equally spaced and curved;
           idea of waves from above the Earth's surface meeting the surface and creating a shadow
    e) VHF at 30 – 300 MHz, ELF about 1 kHz.
       i) 1 – 10 m   (ii) about 3 × 10⁵ m

19. a) See page 238. Field produced by induced ring current opposes field produced by coil current.
    b) Using $P = I^2R$, $R = 8.2 \times 10^{-5}$ Ω
    c) Using $R = \rho l/A$, $l = 2\pi \times 12$ mm,
       A = 15 mm × 2.0 mm, gives $\rho = 3.3 \times 10^{-8}$ Ω m
    d) measure mass of ring and mass of water, rise in temperature of water and look up specific heat capacity of water and aluminium

20. a) x-axis labelled V_{XY} in V, y-axis θ in degree;
       points plotted correctly; smooth curve through points
    b) sensitivity constant when gradient of graph is constant:
       about 450 V to 850 V, about 0.077 deg V⁻¹.
    c) Produce table as below. Plot sin θ against V_{XY}, close to a straight line through origin.

V_{XY}	300	400	500	600	700
θ	18	23	30	37	45
sin θ	0.309	0.391	0.500	0.602	0.707

21. a) k = 6 N/0.1 m = 60 N m⁻¹
       $\Delta l = F/k$ = 0.90 × g/60 N m⁻¹ = 0.15 m
    b) clockwise moment = 1.6 × g × 0.12 m = 1.88 N m
       anti-cw moment = 0.90 × g × 0.18 m = 1.59 N m
       therefore no tipping.
    c) As mass vibrates, tension in spring changes.
       Maximum tension increases as amplitude increases.
       Tipping occurs when anticlockwise moment of tension exceeds clockwise moment of weight of clamp.

22. a) i) 16 900 N
       ii) displaced cold air weighs more than balloon + hot air
    b) $p (V/m) = p/\rho$ so $\rho \propto 1/T$ if p constant
    c) $\rho \propto 1/T$ so: $T_{hot}/T_{cold} = \rho_{cold}/\rho_{hot}$ (T in K).

Acknowledgements

Ace Photo Agency   94 Latin Stock, 309T Mark Stevenson;
Action Plus   20B Richard Francis, 30, 32B4, 61, Glyn Kirk;
Air Fotos   144;
AKG (London)   352;
All-Sport   6B Al Bello, 14T Gary M Prior, 23 Craig Prentis, 33 Clive Brunskill, 39 Didier Klein/Vandystadt, 52B Laurence Griffiths, 68T Gary Mortimore, 282 Craig Prentis, 294T Clive Brunskill;
Ancient Art and Architecture Collection   345B;
Autocar   73 World Copyright;
Barnaby's Picture Library   71T Bill Coward, 147T Bill Meadows, 221T, 307B Bill Meadows;
BNFL   356T, M;
Bass Brewers   132T;
Camera Press (London)   349;
CLRC   176;
Colorsport   10, 49 Dimitri Iundt;
Corbis (UK)   40;
Emilio Segré Visual Archives   158T, 340, 365;
Empics   52T Mike Egerton, 64 Tony Marshall;
Eye Ubiquitous   242 Kevin Wilton;
Fisher Scientific   215T;
Frank Spooner Pictures   199 A Morvan/Gamma, 358 Gamma/Roger Viollet;
Galaxy Picture Library   75, 136B;
Genesis Space Photo Library   80, 84T, M, B, 158M;
ICN (UK Bureau)   32B2;
IBM   164T;
Image Bank   215B C Renard;
Image Select   296 Ann Ronan Picture Library;
Images Colour Library   91 Zephyr Pictures;
Impact Photos   99L Peter Arkell;
J Allen Cash   28T;
JET   353B;
Keith Johnson   11;
Leslie Garland Picture Library   99M Andrew Lambert, 283;
Lewis Woolf Griptight   30b;
Martyn Chillmaid   6M, 8T, 13B, 21, 51, 56T, 57B, 66T, 68M, 93, 99R, 101B, 127, 136T, 141, 175B, 177, 178M, 184, 201T, B, 203, 212, 240, 253, 264, 272T, B, 290B, 291, 313, 332B, 333, 341;
Mary Evans Picture Library   332T;
MIRAS   45;
Misco   311T;
Moorfields Eye Hospital   221B;
Mothercare   90;
Museum of Historical Musical Instruments   152T;

NASA   153B, 175T;
by courtesy of the National Portrait Gallery   234, 351T;
Novosti (London)   356;
Oxford Scientific Films   46T Lee Lyon;
Pacific Tsunami Museum   122T;
Perkin Elmer   185;
Peter Gould   227, 254;
Pictor International (London)   13T, 294;
Polaroid   119B;
Powerstock ZEFA   310B, 368M;
PPARC   368T;
Rex Features   66B, 95, 97 Steve Davey, 152M Andy Chambers, 252 Warren Faidley/Int'l Stock;
Rob Ayres   232;
Robert Harding Picture Library   112, 172B, 251, 293B;
Rover Group   57T;
Royal Society   140;
RS Components   211, 272M;
Science Photolibrary   17B J. Collombet, 18B David Scharf, 46B Professor H Edgerton, 72T NASA, B Novosti Press Agency, 82 NRSC Ltd, 101M J C Revy, 122B Mount Stromlo and Siding Spring Observations, 129 David Parker, 132B BSIP/VEM, 147B David Parker, 151 NOAO, 152B David Parker, 153T David Pucros, 157T Royal Observatory Edinburgh AATB, 157B NASA, 167 Fred Burrell, 172 David Ducros, 174 Gordon Garradd, 178B Jerry Mason, 182T NOAO, B Royal Observatory Edinburgh AATB, 183 Philippe Plailly, 202B Martin Bond, 226 Pekka Parviaien, 229 Alex Bartel, 245 James King-Holmes, 289 G Muller/Sirders/GMBA, 307T Dr Ray Clarke, 308, 309, 310T CNES 1998 Distribution Spot Image, 310M Mark Clarke, 338 Patrick Blackett, 344AB Elscint, M Martin Dohrn, 345T NASA, 351B Alfred Pasieka, 359T, B, Lawrence Berkeley Laboratory, 360 CERN/P Loiez, 368LT, B;
Science and Society Picture Library   154, 34b;
Shout Pictures   156, 158B;
Sporting Pictures   35, 55L;
Stock Boston   63 Joseph Nettis;
Stockmarket   20T Richard Berenholtz, 345M;
Stone   32T David E Myers, 68B Martin Rogers, 74 Chad Slattery, 164B K MacGregor;
Telegraph Colour Library   28B Ken Reid, 37M J Cummins;
Topham Picturepoint   71B, 101T, 119T;
Toyota   202T;
Travel Ink   178T Leslie Garland;
TRIP   14B Ken Powell;
UKAEA   336, 344T, B, 348, 355;
University of Leeds   290T D Bavester;
Vasamedics   159;
Volvo Car (UK)   56M, B.

Examination Boards

We would like to thank the following Examination Boards for permission to use questions from past A-level examination papers. They are labelled in the Further Questions sections as follows:

AQA	Assessment and Qualifications Alliance	www.aqa.org.uk
Edex	Edexcel Foundation	www.edexcel.org.uk
OCR	Oxford, Cambridge and RSA Examinations	www.ocr.org.uk
W	Welsh Joint Education Committee	www.wjec.co.uk

You can find more details about syllabus coverage at: www.nelsonthornes.com/ap4u.htm

Further reading

Looking for further reading? Don't know what presents you want for Christmas or your birthday?
Try these:

- **The Cartoon Guide to Physics** by Larry Gonick & Art Huffman (HarperCollins, ISBN 006-2731009)

- **Mr Tomkins in Paperback** by George Gamow & Roger Penrose (Cambridge University Press, ISBN 0521-447712)

- **The Flying Circus of Physics** (with answers) by Jearl Walker (John Wiley, ISBN 0471-02984X)

	Examination Boards' Specifications (syllabuses) for Physics					
	Page numbers needed for each one: Blue=AS-level Red=A2-level					
	✔ = whole chapter needed, except ( ) [ ] = optional topic					
Chapter	AQA–A 5451 6451	AQA–B 5456 6456	EDEXCEL 8540 9540	OCR 3883 7883	NICCEA S1210 A1210	WJEC 54080 54090
1 Basic Ideas	✔	✔	✔	✔	✔	✔
2 Looking at Forces	✔	✔	✔	✔	✔	✔
3 Turning Effects of Forces	✔	✔	✔	✔	✔	✔
4 Describing Motion	✔	✔	✔	✔	✔	✔
5 Newton's Laws, Momentum	✔	47 ✔	✔	47-51 ✔(52-3)	44-53 ✔	47-51 ✔(52-3)
6 Work, Energy and Power	✔	62-4 ✔	✔	60-2 ✔	62-4 ✔	✔
7 Circular Motion	✔	✔	✔	✔(71)	✔	✔
8 Gravitational Forces, Fields	✔	✔	✔	✔(86-7)	✔(86-7)	✔
9 Simple Harmonic Motion	✔	90 ✔	✔	✔	✔	✔
10 Wave Motion	✔	✔ 124-5	✔	✔ [124-5]	✔	✔
11 Reflection and Refraction	✔(133-7) [✔]	✔(133-7)	–	✔(133-7) [✔]	✔(133-7)	✔(133-7)
12 Interference and Diffraction	✔(146)	✔	✔(146)	✔(146)	✔(146)	✔(146)
13 Doppler Effect	[✔]	✔	✔	[✔]	–	–
14 Photons and Electrons	✔	✔	✔	✔	✔	✔
15 Spectra and Energy Levels	✔	✔	✔	✔	✔	✔
16 Current and Charge	✔	✔	✔	✔	✔	✔
17 Electric Circuits	✔	✔	✔	✔	✔	✔
18 Magnetic Fields	218-21, 224-7	✔ (222-3)	✔(228)	218-21, 224-5 ✔	✔(228)	✔
19 Electromagnetic Induction	✔(239)	✔	✔(239)	✔	✔	✔(239)
20 Alternating Current	242-5 [248]	248, 250-1 ✔	244-7	244-7	242, 244-7	242-5
21 Electric Fields	✔(258-9)	✔	✔	✔(258-9)	✔(258-9)	✔
22 Capacitors	✔(268-9)	✔	✔	✔	✔	✔
23 Solids under Stress	✔	282-3 [✔]	[✔]	✔	✔(287-93)	✔
24 Thermodynamics	299-305 [✔]	✔	✔	✔	302-3	✔
25 Conduction, Radiation	✔	✔	[✔]	✔	–	✔(309)
26 Gases and Kinetic Theory	✔	✔	✔	✔	✔	✔
27 Radioactivity	328-31 ✔	328-39, 341-2 ✔	328-42 ✔	✔	✔	328-31 ✔
28 Nuclear Energy	✔	✔	348-50 ✔	✔	✔	✔
29 Particle Physics	✔(366-7)	358-63, 366-7	[358-65] 366-7	[✔]	✔	–

Correct at the time of printing, but see the more detailed analysis at www.nelsonthornes.com/ap4u.htm

Index